324629
8/7/3

‒ or befo‒

8

COMPUTER VISION

Computer Vision

Edited by
Michael Brady
Artificial Intelligence Laboratory, M.I.T., Cambridge, MA, U.S.A.

Contributors

H.G. Barrow
T.O. Binford
J.M. Brady
R.A. Brooks
B. Chandrasekaran
L.S. Davis
S.W. Draper
B.E. Flinchbaugh
J.P. Frisby
B.K.P. Horn

K. Ikeuchi
T. Kanade
J.E.W. Mayhew
H.K. Nishihara
A. Rosenfeld
B.G. Schunck
K.A. Stevens
J.M. Tenenbaum
A.P. Witkin
R.J. Woodham

1931 N·H 1981
P~C

North-Holland Publishing Company
Amsterdam

Reprinted from the Journal
Artificial Intelligence, Vol. 17, August 1981

PRINTED IN THE NETHERLANDS

CONTENTS

Preface — The Changing Shape of Computer Vision

Michael Brady

Artificial Intelligence Laboratory, MIT, Cambridge, MA 02139, U.S.A.

1. Introduction

This special volume of the *Artificial Intelligence* (*AI*) Journal recognises the considerable advances that have taken place in Computer Vision over the past decade. It contains fourteen papers that are representative of the best work currently in the field. Apart from being a state-of-the-art account, the issue has been designed, as far as possible, to serve two rather different aims.

First, it is intended to give AI researchers in fields other than Vision an opportunity to become familiar with recent developments in the field. The continuing growth of AI inevitably makes it difficult to keep abreast of progress in any but a narrow area. As we shall see, the increasingly technical content of Vision, and its growing concentration on visual perception, rather than on general AI ideas, make it doubly forbidding to the casual AI reader.

Second, it is intended to enable vision researchers from fields other than AI to get a clearer picture of what an AI approach to their problem might be, or might contribute. Certainly, there is increasing interest in Computer Vision among researchers in fields as disparate as psychophysics, neurophysiology, signal and image processing, optical engineering, and photogrammetry. In addition, remote sensing, visual inspection of industrial products, and other applications in the growing field of Robotics, ensure that Vision will continue to be a topic of considerable importance for many years to come.

2. As it Was in the Beginning

Even as late as 1975, Computer Vision looked rather different than it does today. A great deal of effort had been expended on the 'blocks' microworld of scenes of polyhedra. Huffman [26] and Clowes [11] had noted the advantage of making the image forming process explicit. They observed that *picture lines* and *junctions* were the images of *scene edges* and *vertices*, and they catalogued all

Artificial Intelligence **17** (1981) 1–15
North-Holland Publishing Company

those interpretations of lines and junctions that were possible, given the prior assumption of planarity and the restriction that at most three surfaces were allowed to meet at a vertex. These interpretations, taking the form of 'labellings' of lines, amounted to local constraints on the volume occupied by a vertex. The local constraints propagated along picture lines since planar edges can not change their nature between two vertices. (This is not so for curved lines, as Huffman noted. Turner [59] described one possible extension to curves of the Huffman–Clowes approach. Binford, Barrow and Tenenbaum describe rather different approaches in this volume.)

Huffman [26] further pointed out that the local vertex constraints were not sufficient to capture the important restriction that picture regions were the images of planar surfaces. Mackworth's [34] development of *Gradient Space* was expressly intended to repair this deficit. Draper's article in this volume describes the greater competence of Mackworth's program, as well as its shortcomings. Despite this, most line drawings had a remarkable number of possible interpretations. Waltz's [60] work introduced the inherently global constraint afforded by shadows cast by a single distant light source, and showed that the multiple ambiguities possible without lighting were often completely resolved to a unique interpretation with lighting. Furthermore, the process by which the unique interpretation was discovered, naturally lent itself to parallel processing of a particular sort. Each vertex had an associated processor, and they all operated in strict synchrony. At each stage, the processors changed their states depending on the state of those directly connected to them. Rosenfeld, Hummel, and Zucker [54] noted the connection between this scheme and relaxation processes in numerical analysis. Actually, several authors had suggested the use of local parallel processing for Vision rather earlier, see for example the historical remarks in Subsection 5.2 of the paper by Ikeuchi and Horn in this volume.

Waltz's scheme had a number of drawbacks. For example, as Winston [63] pointed out, the program could make no use of the direction of lines in the image. On the other hand, Mackworth's program could, since gradient lines are perpendicular to image lines (see the discussions of Gradient Space in the papers of Draper, Kanade, Woodham, and Ikeuchi and Horn in this volume.) Huffman [27] later defined *Dual Space* in which this information could be made explicit (see the articles of Draper (this volume) and Spacek [58]). Again, the Waltz labellings were extremely complex and unstructured. In essence this was because they constituted interpretations that confounded many different sources of information about lighting, surface cracks, occlusion, and edge type into a single label. Clearly these different contributions to the entire percept should be made explicit and exploited separately, as they are in the human visual system. Binford's paper in this volume reconsiders the possible interpretations of edges.

A second strand in the development of Computer Vision concerns what was referred to as 'low level' processing. It was more art than science, and largely consisted of methods for the extraction of the 'important' intensity changes in an image. In the blocks world these correspond to shadow boundaries and the edges of visible surfaces, including depth discontinuities. The approach mostly consisted of convolving images with local operators (typically 3 by 3 on a 256 by 256 image) to estimate the position, contrast, and orientation of the important intensity changes. Operators were tuned to particular applications, and fared badly outside their limited domain and in the presence of noise. Little serious analysis of actual intensity changes, including the signal to noise characteristics of real images, had been carried out. A singular exception was the work of Herskovits and Binford [16]. They suggested that there were basically three qualitatively different types of intensity changes; and that particular changes often combine features of two types. This analysis formed the basis of a line finder whose performance considerably advanced the state of the art.

Other work in 'low level' vision largely consisted of the design and construction of region finders. Region finding, essentially the dual of edge finding, aimed to isolate those regions of an image that were the images of perceptual surface patches. It was thought that such regions might be isolated by defining some descriptor with respect to which they were uniform, and distinguishable from surrounding regions. It was soon clear [2, 9] that even if such descriptors existed, they were not defined simply in terms of grey level intensity values. Some researchers proposed multi-spectral descriptors [48], while others later flatly denied that it is possible to define adequate descriptors at all [36, p. 64]. Binford's paper in this volume discusses region finding in some detail.

By the early 1970's, the consensus was that 'low level' vision was inherently incapable of producing rich useful descriptions. It was observed, by analogy to the apparent need for semantics in parsing English sentences, that downward flowing knowledge of the scene could provide additional constraint. This in turn could inform local decision making. A number of program structures were proposed to effect this interaction between top down and bottom up processing of information [4, 7, 12, 43, 55, 64]. Similar ideas were advanced about natural language understanding, and speech perception. This influenced the design of, for example, Hearsay 2 [31]. To experiment with these ideas, entire systems were constructed which mobilised knowledge at all levels of the visual system as well as information specific to some domain of application. In order to complete the construction of these systems, it was inevitable that corners were cut and many over simplified assumptions were made. By and large, the performance of these systems did not give grounds for unbridled celebration. The authors of the KRL proposal (Bobrow and Winograd [6]), for example, listed several common failings (see also [7]).

3. Is Now

Perhaps the most fundamental differences between Computer Vision as it is now and as it was a decade ago, stem from the current concentration on topics corresponding to identifiable modules in the human visual system. This volume contains papers, for example, on stereopsis, the interpretation of surface contours, the determination of surface orientation from texture, and the grouping of motion primitives. To be sure, there is still a considerable amount of work oriented toward applications, but it is also increasingly based on detailed and precise analyses of specific visual abilities. The focus of research is more narrowly defined in terms of visual abilities than in terms of a domain, and the depth of analysis is correspondingly greater. This change has produced a number of far-reaching effects in the way vision is researched. This section attempts to make them explicit.

One obvious effect has been a sharp decline in the construction of entire vision systems. Most AI vision workers have thankfully abandoned the idea that visual perception can profitably be studied in the context of a priori commitment to a particular program or machine architecture. There is, for example, no more reason to believe that 'relaxation' style processing will of itself tell us more about vision than did the excursions into heterarchy. There is no obvious reason to be encouraged by Reddy's [51] claim that the Hearsay 2 model can be adapted mutatis mutandis to vision.

What identifies a particular operation as a distinguishable module in the visual system? Normal vision confronts and exploits massive redundancy. Some of the most solid evidence for the claims of individual modules is offered by psychophysical demonstrations. Care is taken, as far as possible, to isolate a particular source of information and show that the operation in question survives. One particular instance of this is the study of patients with certain disabilities resulting from brain lesions (for example [42, 57, 61]). Many psychophysical experiments, seemingly isolating particular modules of the (human) visual system, have been reported in the literature. Notable examples include Land's demonstration of the computation of lightness [19, 30] and Julesz's [28] demonstration of stereoscopic fusion without monocular cues. In some cases there is clear evidence of a human perceptual ability, although such evidence would hardly be referred to as psychophysical. Horn's work (see the papers by Woodham, and Ikeuchi and Horn in this volume) concerns the highly developed human ability to infer shape from shading. Steven's paper concerns the human three-dimensional interpretation of surface contours. On the other hand, it is equally clear that we do not have a specific module in our visual system to recognise 'yellow Volkswagens' (see for example [62]). It is less clear whether we compute depth directly, as opposed to indirectly through integrating over surface orientations, or what use we make of directional selectivity, optical flow, or texture gradients.

Not all modules work directly on the image. Indeed, it seems that few do. Instead they operate on *representations* of the information computed, or made explicit by other processes. In the case of stereopsis, Marr and Poggio [40] argue against correlating the intensity information in the left and right views.

Instead they suggest that so called zero-crossings are matched (see [15] or Nishihara's paper in this volume). The paper by Mayhew and Frisby argues that the matching actually takes place on a different representation, called the primal sketch [35]. In any case, a great deal of attention has centered on the isolation and study of individual modules, and in each case on the development of the representations on which they operate, and on those that they produce. The first of these representations, and the one whose structure is least subject to dispute, is the image itself. Not surprisingly then, most attention has centered on those modules that operate upon the image. As we shall see, the further we progress up the processing hierarchy, the less secure the story becomes, as the exact structure of the representations becomes more subject to dispute. Again, this is not surprising. The image aside any representation is one module's co-domain and another's domain. All of them shape its eventual structure.

3.1. Modules that operate on the image

A great deal of effort has been devoted to understanding how the important intensity changes in an image can be extracted, and how the information can be best represented. Marr [35] coined the term primal sketch to describe such a representation, and he described a particular algorithm by which it might be computed. A novel feature of the work was its direct reference to neurophysiological and psychophysical findings, a commitment Marr was to continue to stress in later work. His work with Poggio led to a revision of the process of construction of the Primal Sketch. Instead they advocated the use of zero-crossings of the second derivative of the filtered image. This idea was developed in turn by Marr and Hildreth [38], who propose that an image is first filtered by four Gaussians having different bandpass characteristics. Then each filtered image is convolved with a Laplacian operator (see Nishihara's paper in this volume for more detail). One of the novel features of the Marr–Hildreth account is the size of the operators involved, the smallest being roughly 35 picture elements square. This is in stark contrast to conventional operators, which are still typically on the order of 5 by 5. Such a large operator can be in much closer agreement with a Gaussian (or any other filter for that matter) than a small operator, and its effects are therefore more predictable. Unfortunately it is no longer obvious how to compute the assertions that Marr had previously advocated for inclusion in the primal sketch (see [17, p. 75]). The whole issue of constructing the primal sketch from zero-crossings is far from being resolved. Binford's paper in this volume considers this issue, as well as the choice of an optimal filter and the use of non-oriented masks, in fair detail.

Intensity changes aside, Horn and his colleagues have studied the perception of surface shape from shading. Their work is represented in the current volume by the papers of Ikeuchi and Horn, and Woodham. In brief outline, Horn has formulated a second order differential equation which he calls the image irradiance equation which relates the orientation of the local surface normal of a visible surface, the surface reflectance characteristics, and the lighting, to the intensity value recorded at the corresponding point in the image. Horn quickly realised the need for a representation which makes such surface orientations explicit. Two parameters are needed. Horn [22] observed that gradient space provides such a parameterisation, and showed how the relationship between intensity values and surface orientations could be added to gradient space to form what he called the *reflectance map*. The papers by Ikeuchi and Horn, and Woodham give details. Gradient space is by no means the only two parameter representation of surface orientations. Ikeuchi and Horn investigate *stereographic space*, which has the additional desirable property that the constraints offered by occluding boundaries can be represented and exploited. The output of shape-from-shading is a representation that makes explicit the orientation of visible surfaces, and may make other information such as depth and surface orientation discontinuities explicit also. Horn [23] suggests the name *needle map* for the representation. Other representations have been proposed which make substantially the same information explicit. Marr [36] labels this representation the $2\frac{1}{2}D$ *Sketch*, and Barrow and Tenenbaum [4] discuss *intrinsic images*. Again the exact nature of the representation (or representations) is currently far from clear. In part this is because very little work has been devoted to modules which operate upon it.

Finally, Horn and Schunck (this volume) propose a method by which the so-called *optical flow* can be determined from a sequence of images. Several authors have investigated the information that can in principle be computed from ideal optical flow fields (see the references in Horn and Schunck's paper), but no proposals have previously been made for its computation.

3.2. Modules which operate on zero-crossings and the primal sketch

We pointed out in the previous section that there remain a vast number of unresolved issues concerning the nature of the primal sketch and its computation from zero-crossings of whatever kind of filtered image. Nevertheless, the broad outlines are clear enough for work to proceed to investigate modules which are assumed to operate upon those representations. Indeed it is necessary that it does, as it will also contribute to our understanding of the information that needs to be made explicit in the primal sketch, and hence its eventual form. One area that is not represented in this volume, but that is of considerable importance, is the investigation of the processes which impose hierarchical structure on the primal sketch (what Marr [35] called the *full primal sketch*). Riley [53] has made an initial study of such processes for static scenes. Motion is an important source of information of determining structure.

The paper by Flinchbaugh and Chandrasekaran in this volume addresses grouping on the basis of motion cues. Such grouping operations play an important role on all the representations used by the visual system, and for the most part they are poorly understood. Little if any work has been done on grouping operations on what we call the *surface orientation map*.[1]

Considerable attention has been paid to *stereopsis*. Marr and Poggio's [40] theory of human stereopsis, and its implementation and refinement by Grimson [15] is discussed at length by Mayhew and Frisby, who propose a number of further refinements.

Ever since Gibson [14] stressed the importance of texture gradients for the perception of depth and surface shape, they have been the subject of detailed psychophysical and computational investigation. Pattern recognition approaches typically consist of computing crude statistics on the image intensities. This does not work at all well since, as Horn in particular has shown, an individual intensity value is a complex encoding of the lighting, the surface reflectance characteristics, and the local surface orientation. Witkin's paper in this volume once more underscores the importance of making the image forming process explicit. His approach relies upon statistical arguments but, crucially, does not require that natural textures are uniformly distributed. Rather, it requires that their non-uniformity does not mimic projection. It relies upon deriving a probability density function which relates the orientation of a scene element via projection into an image element.

The papers of Draper, Kanade, Stevens, and Tenenbaum and Barrow address various aspects of the human ability to perceive surface shape from line drawings. The first two of these assume that the scene is composed of plane-faced objects. As such, they continue the tradition of work discussed in Section 1. Kanade's paper combines the ideas of gradient space and edge labellings. It proposes the two additional assumptions of parallelism and skewed symmetry to further constrain the orientation of a planar surface. Matching the intensity profiles across two edges provides further constraint. Crucially, the program is able to make the conservative inference that two edges have the same interpretation without knowing exactly what it is. Draper's paper discusses the limitations of gradient and dual space in supporting possible processes that interpret line drawings of polyhedra. He proposes instead symbolic reasoning about 'sidedness'. Unfortunately, such inferences are inherently long range, since they rely upon the observation that the relationship between planar regions is fixed, and therefore common to all points at which they intersect. Such reasoning is likely to be of limited usefulness when applied to images of natural or curved scenes. Tenenbaum and

---

[1]We sincerely hope that this name does not become established in the literature, as it only serves as a name for the intuitive notion which is rendered more or less precise in the three published versions referenced (namely the $2\frac{1}{2}$D sketch, needle map, or intrinsic image).

Barrow address the subject of interpreting line drawings of curved surfaces. They use junction labellings to determine whether a bounding curve depicts an extremal boundary or a depth discontinuity. Then they propose two mechanisms: one for computing the spatial layout of the bounding curves and one for interpolating local surface orientation from the boundary values. In the remaining paper on this topic, Stevens proposes a taxonomy of interpretations of surface contours. By investigating intersecting contours in an image, a local decision can be reached about the nature of the underlying three dimensional surface.

3.3. Object representations

Considerably less is known about the modules which operate upon the surface orientation map to produce object representations, and the nature of those representations is very far from clear. Some work has been done, and it is well represented in this volume. Binford [5] proposed a volumetric primitive known as *generalized cylinders*. Nevatia and Binford [46], Hollerbach [18], and later Marr and Nishihara [39] developed representational schemes based upon such volumetric primitives. Brooks (in this volume) describes the representation of complex objects such as motors and airplanes, the incorporation of constraints such as symmetry, and the specification of affixment relations by which the local coordinate frames of two objects can be inter-related. Marr and Nishihara [39] discuss the role which such representations might play in human vision (see Nishihara's paper in this volume).

3.4. Methodological comments

The previous sections have discussed some of the modules and the important representations which have begun to emerge in Computer Vision. The broad outlines are clear, even if there are many major unresolved questions in nearly every facet of the subject. We may also note some further common themes which have crystallized over the past decade.

Most of the analyses sketched above start out with a precise description of the domain and co-domain of the visual process under scrutiny. Increasingly, 'precise' means 'mathematically precise', and so Computer Vision has become steadily more technical. This is not to say that Vision was not technical before, rather it alludes to the increasing occurrence and sophistication of mathematical analyses in Vision. Many observations about the world, as well as our assumptions about it, are naturally articulated in terms of 'smoothness' of some appropriate quantity. This intuitive idea is made mathematically precise in a number of ways in real analysis, for example in conditions for differentiability. Relationships between smoothly varying quantities give rise to differential equations, such as Horn's *image irradiance equation*. We commented several times above on the value of making the image forming process explicit. This in turn leads to a concern with geometry, such as the properties of the gradient, stereographic, and dual spaces. Combining the considerations of geometry and smoothness leads naturally to multi-variate vector analysis and to differential geometry [13]. Mostly, a representation does not of itself contain sufficient information to guarantee that a module can uniquely arrive at the result computed so effortlessly by the human visual system. Additional assumptions, in the form of constraints, are required. This observation has led to a concern with constraint satisfaction and equation solving, using the techniques of numerical analysis such as Gauss–Seidel iteration and Lagrange multipliers (especially in the form of the calculus of variations). Examples of all of these approaches can be found in the papers in this volume.

For many authors, the changing style of research in Computer Vision has not been simply a matter of a narrowing of attention and a more highly developed technical content. Instead, greater significance is attached to the desire to make explicit the links between their work and corresponding theories in psychophysics and neurophysiology. From this perspective Computer Vision has as its goal the construction of computational theories of human visual perception. In large part, this approach stems from a series of papers written by David Marr and his colleagues at MIT. Marr's work stems from a background in neurophysiology, and is expressly addressed to psychophysicists and neurophysiologists. In particular, it is couched in terms they are accustomed to, and makes extensive reference to their literature, rather than that of Computer Vision. The work of the MIT group has excited considerable interest among psychologists and neurophysiologists, and is extensively referenced in the papers in this volume. A book summarising Marr's thoughts about human visual perception [37] and incorporating summaries of the contributions he and his colleagues have made across the entire range of the subject is currently in press.

There is considerably less diversity in emphasis, subject matter, and technical content than might be imagined between those researchers who see themselves constructing a computational theory of human visual perception and those for whom human visual perception is at most a matter of secondary concern. Compare, for example, the ACRONYM representation of objects based upon generalized cylinders (see the paper by Brooks in this volume) with that proposed by Marr and Nishihara [39], or the work on early processing of motion by Horn and Schunck (this volume) with Marr and Ullman [41]. Another common research theme is the need for local parallel processing which can discover global information through propagation. The paper by Davis and Rosenfeld (this volume) considers one such class of program structures, while others can be found in the papers by Horn and Schunck, Ikeuchi and Horn, Tenenbaum and Barrow, and Woodham. Such architectures naturally lend themselves to realization in hardware. Nishihara describes one such realization.

4. And Ever Shall Be?

As this introductory survey suggests, Computer Vision has progressed considerably on many fronts over the past decade. There has been a change in the
style of research as well as in its substance. However, most issues are still
poorly understood, from the exact form of representations, through the
detailed understanding of the individual modules, to topics that have so far
received little or no attention. A sampling of unresolved problems follows in
the next few paragraphs. It is by no means exhaustive.

First, the details of what we have called the surface orientation map need to
be made precise. Marr [36], Horn [23], and Barrow and Tenenbaum [4] have
suggested that it records local surface orientation, as well as depth discontinuities; but it is unclear how they are recorded. Suggestions include
Cartesian and polar formulations of the gradient, 'sequins' versus 'quills' [23],
and the separation of various kinds of information into separate 'intrinsic'
images. Nor is it obvious how accurately values are recorded. It is clear that
surface information needs to be represented at different levels of resolution: a
pebbled path may be considered approximately planar by a human who is
walking along it. Yet an ant or person on roller skates may find the same path
extremely difficult to navigate; in such cases the path is unlikely to be
considered planar. As this example indicates, the level of resolution of a
representation is determined largely by the process operating upon the
representation, and there has been little investigation of such processes to date.

It is equally clear that grouping operations need to be defined at each level
of resolution of each representation in the visual system, in order to impose
hierarchical structure upon the representation. The advantages that should
accrue from imposing such structure are likely to be precisely those which have
inspired the development of data structures generally in computer science.
Consider as an example a simple egg tray. The pattern of identical depressions
to hold the eggs is immediately obvious, even though the detailed description
of the individual egg cells is not.

A related set of problems concerns the determination of surface properties
such as its color, manufacture, and whether or not it is wet, slippery, or prickly.
Granted that we make such properties explicit, we need to determine whether
they are attached as local descriptors to representations such as the surface
orientation (say), or whether they are the content of separate representations.
It may be that there is a separate albedo map [24, 25] or it may be that albedo
information is embedded in the surface orientation map. Actually, the entire
question of the computer perception of color is still very much in its infancy,
despite its enormous literature.

Our current understanding of motion perception is crude. Horn and
Schunck's paper is a preliminary account of the computation of optical flow
from grey levels. It is less clear what information can be recovered from optical

flow. Some authors are enthusiastic about the richness of the information it can provide (Clocksin [10]), while others are more sanguine (Prazdny [50]). Marr and Ullman [41], and Richter and Ullman [52] have made a start towards determining motion from the displacement of intensity changes. Ullman [65], and Flinchbaugh and Chandrasekaran (this volume) consider the grouping of primal sketch tokens in motion. Even less is known about motion computed on the surface orientation map or on object representations. It is reasonable to suppose that the description of such object motions will need to incorporate a formulation of the object's kinematics. This has proved to be quite difficult even for simple robot arms (see for example [49]).

Perhaps the most difficult problem of all concerns the perception or planning of movements through cluttered space. Space, considered as an object, typically occupies a volume and surface whose descriptions push current representational frameworks to their limits, if not far beyond them. Some progress has been made in Robotics [32]. A further important application lies in making precise the rather vague motion of cognitive map. It is usually supposed [33] that this only refers to object representations. Actually it seems that we have quite considerable navigational processes which operate on the surface orientation map.

The current rapid pace of developments in VLSI technology has further motivated research into what were referred to above as local parallel programming architectures. It is likely that our conception of computation will change as a result of such developments. Vision will be one of the first areas to benefit from such advances. It seems that it will also be a continuing source of inspiration to VLSI designers [1, 47].

Finally, we certainly need a better understanding of the extent and use of domain specific information in visual perception. Yesterday's heterarchy and today's multi-layered relaxation systems both derive from a priori commitment to a particular mechanism. The experience of the past decade should certainly have made us wary about jumping to premature conclusions regarding which phenomena appear to inevitably implicate such downward flow. This has certainly been true of our ability to compute rich useful descriptions of the information provided in an image. It also seems reasonable to suppose that the three dimensional structure of jointed rigid objects can be recovered from a time succession of images without knowing a great deal about human physiology. This would provide an explanation for, amongst other things, the demonstrations of Johannson [29] and Muybridge [44], knowing only the basic facts of dynamics.

There is every reason to believe that there will be considerable advance on these and other issues over the next few decades, probably resulting in changes in our conception of Computing and Vision at least as large as those which have occurred over the past decade. It would be a very brave person indeed who claimed to understand other than the broadest outlines of the subject now.

5. Professor David Marr

One paper which was to be written especially for this special issue of *Artificial Intelligence* will unfortunately never appear. It would have been authored by Professor David Marr, who died toward the end of 1980 after a protracted illness. The influence of the group which he founded at MIT is evident from the preceding pages.

David's background was in neurophysiology, after completing a mathematics degree at Cambridge University. His early work proposed mathematical theories of the neocortex, archicortex, and, perhaps best known of all, the cerebellum. He was to remain deeply commited to the study of human perception and memory for the rest of his life. In 1974 he was invited to spend a little time at the Artificial Intelligence Laboratory at MIT, and stayed for six years, eventually accepting a Professorship in the Department of Psychology. He quickly appreciated that computational concepts provided a further dimension for the expression of theories of human perception, and, together with a growing group of Ph.D. students, he set out to construct what he called a computational theory of human vision. The group has been enormously creative, publishing studies across the entire breadth of human vision.

David's work was notable in many ways, but in particular notable for its style. He made extensive reference to the literatures of neurophysiology and psychology, which were his background and to which he directed his contributions. In particular, he published in the journals which would be read by his intended audience, and encouraged his students to do so too. He argued for a mathematical analysis of a perceptual problem independent of, and prior to, consideration of issues concerning the choice of an algorithm. Under the heading of 'natural computation', he championed the isolation of the constraints which the world imposes upon perception, as well as the perceiver's prior beliefs about it. Though a good deal of Marr's work was mathematical in nature, its ramifications were stated in elegant prose. A book summarising his thoughts about human visual perception [37] and incorporating summaries of the contributions he and his colleagues have made across the entire range of the subject is currently in press.

David will be missed by the wide community of scholars whose work brought them in contact with his writing. He will be missed especially by those whose lives were enriched by knowing him or working with him.

ACKNOWLEDGMENT

This paper describes research done in part at the Artificial Intelligence Laboratory of the Massachusetts Institute of Technology. Support for the Laboratory's Artificial Intelligence research is provided in part by the Advanced Research Projects Agency of the Department of Defense under Office of Naval Research contract N00014-75-C-0643. I thank Ellen Hildreth, Marilyn Matz, and Demetri Terzopoulos for their comments on a draft of this paper.

REFERENCES

1. Batali, J., forthcoming S.M. dissertation, MIT, Cambridge, MA, 1981.
2. Barrow, H.G. and Popplestone, R.J., Relational descriptions in picture processing, *Machine Intelligence* **6** (1971).
3. Barrow, H.G. and Tenenbaum, J.M., Experiments in interpretation guided semantics, Tech. Note 123, SRI International (1976).
4. Barrow, H.G. and Tenenbaum, J.M., Recovering intrinsic scene characteristics from images, in: Hanson and Riseman, Eds., *Computer Vision Systems* (Academic Press, New York, 1978).
5. Binford, T.O., Visual perception by computer, *Proc. IEEE Conf. Systems and Control* (1971).
6. Bobrow, D.G. and Winograd, T., An overview of KRL, A Knowledge Representation Language, *Cognitive Science* **1** (1977).
7. Brady, J.M., The development of a computer vision system, *Recherche Psicologica* (1979).
8. Brady, J.M. and Wielinga, B.J., Reading the writing on the wall, in: Hanson and Riseman, Eds., *Computer Vision Systems* (Academic Press, New York, 1978).
9. Brice, C.R. and Fennema, C.L., Scene analysis using regions, *Artificial Intelligence* **1** (1970) 205–226.
10. Clocksin, W.F., Perception of surface slant and edge labels from optical flow: a computational approach, *Perception* **9** (1980) 253–269.
11. Clowes, M.B., On seeing things, *Artificial Intelligence* **2** (1971) 79–116.
12. Freuder, E.C., A computer vision system for visual recognition using active knowledge, Tech. Rept. 345, MIT AI Lab. (1974).
13. Faux, I.D. and Pratt, M.J., *Computational Geometry for Design and Manufacture* (Ellis Horwood, Chichester, 1979).
14. Gibson, J.J., *The Perception of the Visual World* (Houghton–Mifflin, Boston, MA, 1950).
15. Grimson, W.E.L., Computing shape using a theory of human stereo vision, Ph.D. thesis, forthcoming book published by MIT Press, MIT, 1980.
16. Herskovits, A. and Binford, T.O., On boundary detection, AI Memo 183, MIT (1970).
17. Hildreth, E.C., Implementation of a theory of edge detection, M.S. dissertation, also Tech. Rept. 579, MIT AI Lab. (1980).
18. Hollerbach, J.M., Hierarchical shape description of objects by selection and modification of prototypes, M.S. dissertation, also Tech. Rept. 346, MIT AI Lab. (1975).
19. Horn, B.K.P., Determining lightness from an image, *Comput. Graphics and Image Processing* **3** (1974) 277–299.
20. Horn, B.K.P., The Binford–Horn line-finder, AI Memo 285, MIT (1973).
21. Horn, B.K.P., Obtaining shape from shading information, in: Winston, P.H., Ed., *The Psychology of Computer Vision* (McGraw–Hill, New York, 1975).
22. Horn, B.K.P., Understanding image intensities, *Artificial Intelligence* **8** (1977) 201–231.
23. Horn, B.K.P., Sequins and quills—Representations for surface topography, in: Bajcsy, R., Ed., *Representation of 3-Dimensional Objects* (Springer, Berlin, 1982).
24. Horn, B.K.P. and Bachman, B.L., Using synthetic images to register real images with surface models, *Comm. ACM* **21** (1978) 914–924.
25. Horn, B.K.P. and Sjoberg, R.W., Atmospheric modelling for the generation of albedo images, in: Baumann, L., Ed., *Proceedings of the Image Understanding Workshop* (Science Applications, 1980).
26. Huffman, D.A., Impossible objects as nonsense sentences, in: Meltzer, B. and Michie, D., Eds., *Machine Intelligence* **6** (Edinburgh University Press, Edinburgh, 1971).
27. Huffman, D.A., A duality concept for the analysis of polyhedral scenes, in: Elcock, E.W. and Michie, D., Eds., *Machine Intelligence* **8** (Ellis Horwood, Chichester, 1977).
28. Julesz, B., *Foundations of Cyclopean Perception* (The University of Chicago Press, Chicago, 1971).

29. Johansson, G., Visual perception of biological motion and a model for its analysis, *Perception and Psychophysics* **14** (1973) 201–211.
30. Land, E.H. and McCann, J.J., Lightness and retinex theory, *J. Optical Society of America* **61** (1971) 1–11.
31. Lesser, V.R. and Erman, L.D., A retrospective view of the Hearsay-II architecture, *Proc. Int. Jt. Conf. Artificial Intelligence* **2** (1977) 790–800.
32. Lozano-Perez, T., Spatial planning: a configuration space approach, AI Memo 605, MIT (1980).
33. Lynch, K., *The Image of the City* (MIT Press, Cambridge, MA, 1960).
34. Mackworth, A.K., Interpreting pictures of polyhedral scenes, *Artificial Intelligence* **4** (1973) 121–137.
35. Marr, D., Early processing of visual information, *Philos. Trans. Roy. Soc. London B* **275** (1976) 483–524.
36. Marr, D., Representing visual information, in: Hanson and Riseman, Eds., *Computer Vision Systems* (Academic Press, New York, 1978).
37. Marr, D., *Vision* (Freeman, San Francisco, 1981).
38. Marr, D. and Hildreth, E., Theory of edge detection, *Proc. Roy. Soc. London B* **207** (1980) 187–217.
39. Marr, D. and Nishihara, H.K., Representation and recognition of the spatial organisation of three dimensional structure, *Proc. Roy. Soc. London B* **200** (1978) 269–294.
40. Marr, D. and Poggio, T., A theory of human stereo vision, *Proc. Roy. Soc. London B* **204** (1979) 301–328.
41. Marr, D. and Ullman, S., Directional selectivity and its use in early visual processing, *Proc. Roy. Soc. London B* (1981).
42. Marshall, J.C. and Newcombe, F., Patterns of Paralexia, *J. Psycholinguistic Research* **2** (1973) 175–199.
43. Minsky, M. and Papert, S., Artificial intelligence progress report, AI Memo 252, MIT (1972).
44. Muybridge, E., *Animals in Motion* (Dover, New York, 1957).
45. Nevatia, R., Computer analysis of scenes of 3-dimensional curved objects, Stanford, 1975.
46. Nevatia, R. and Binford, T.O., Description and recognition of curved objects, *Artificial Intelligence* **8** (1977) 77–98.
47. Nudd, G.R., Fouse, S.D., Nussmeier, T.A. and Nygaard, P.A., Development of custom-designed integrated circuits for image understanding, in: Baumann, L., Ed., *Proceedings of the Image Understanding Workshop* (1979).
48. Ohlander, R., Analysis of natural scenes, Carnegie–Mellon Univ., Pittsburgh, 1975.
49. Paul, R.P., Manipulator Cartesian path control, *IEEE Trans. Systems, Man Cybernet.* **9** (1979) 702–711.
50. Prazdny, K.F., Egomotion and relative depth map from optical flow, *Biological Cybernet.* **36** (1980) 87–102.
51. Reddy, R., Pragmatic aspects of machine vision, in: Hanson and Riseman, Eds., *Computer Vision Systems* (Academic Press, New York, 1978).
52. Richter, J. and Ullman, S., A model for the spatio-temporal organization of X and Y-type ganglion cells in the primate retina, AI Memo 573, MIT (1980).
53. Riley, M., Representing image structure, MIT, Stanford, 1981.
54. Rosenfeld, A., Hummel, R.A. and Zucker, S.W., Scene labelling by relaxation operations, *IEEE Trans. Systems, Man Cybernet.* **6** (1976) 420–433.
55. Shirai, Y., A context-sensitive line finder for recognition of polyhedra, *Artificial Intelligence* **4** (1973) 95–119.
56. Stevens, K.A., Surface perception by local analysis of texture and contour, Tech. Rept. 512, MIT AI Lab. (1980).
57. Stevens, K.A., Occlusion clues and subjective contours, AI Memo 363, MIT (1976).
58. Spacek, L.A., Shape from shading and more than one view, M.S. thesis, University of Essex, UK, 1979.

59. Turner, K.J., Computer perception of curved objects using a television camera, Edinburgh, 1974 (extract appeared in *Proc. 1st. AISB Conf.*, Sussex, 1974).
60. Waltz, D., Generating semantic descriptions from drawings of scenes with shadows, in: Winston, P.H., Ed., *The Psychology of Computer Vision* (McGraw–Hill, New York, 1975).
61. Weiskrantz, L., Warrington, E.K., Sanders, M.D. and Marshall, J., Visual capacity in the hemianopic field following a restricted occipital ablation, *Brain* **97** (1974) 709–728.
62. Weisstein, N., Beyond the yellow volkswagen detector and the grandmother cell: A general strategy for the exploration of operations in human pattern recognition, in: Solso, R., Ed., *Contemporary Issues in Cognitive Psychology* (Holt, Rinehart and Winston, New York, 1973).
63. Winston, P.H., *Artificial Intelligence* (Addison Wesley, New York, 1977).
64. Winston, P.H., The MIT robot, in: Meltzer, B. and Michie, D., Eds., *Machine Intelligence* **7** (Edinburgh University Press, Edinburgh, 1972).
65. Ullman, S., The Interpretation of Visual Motion (MIT Press, Cambridge, MA, 1979).

Recovering Surface Shape and Orientation from Texture

Andrew P. Witkin

*Artificial Intelligence Center, SRI International, Menlo Park,
CA 94025, U.S.A.*

ABSTRACT

Texture provides an important source of information about the three-dimensional structure of visible surfaces, particularly for stationary monocular views. To recover 3d structure, the distorting effects of projection must be distinguished from properties of the texture on which the distortion acts. This requires that assumptions must be made about the texture, yet the unpredictability of natural textures precludes the use of highly restrictive assumptions. The recovery method reported in this paper exploits the minimal assumption that textures do not mimic projective effects. This assumption determines the strategy of attributing as much as possible of the variation observed in the image to projection. Equivalently, the interpretation is chosen for which the texture, prior to projection, is made as uniform as possible. This strategy was implemented using statistical methods, first for the restricted case of planar surfaces and then, by extension, for curved surfaces. The technique was applied successfully to natural images.

1. Introduction

A central goal for visual perception is the recovery of the three-dimensional structure of the surfaces depicted in an image. A crucial source of information about three-dimensional structure is provided by the spatial distribution of surface markings, particularly for static monocular views: projection *distorts* texture geometry in a manner that depends systematically on surface shape and orientation. To isolate and measure this projective distortion in the image is to recover the three dimensional structure of the textured surface.

This paper addresses the recovery of surface orientation from natural images of irregularly marked surfaces, first for the limited case of planar surfaces, then, by extension, for curved surfaces. The constraints imposed by projective geometry are not sufficient to determine a solution, but must be augmented by assumptions about texture geometry; otherwise the effects introduced by projection cannot be distinguished from the appearance of the original texture. However, natural textures are so unpredictable that no attempt to model their

Artificial Intelligence **17** (1981) 17–45

geometry precisely has much chance of success. It is not difficult to devise assumptions that formally determine a solution; the heart of the problem lies in the discovery of minimal assumptions that are not only formally adequate, but *true* of natural textures, or nearly enough so to lead to useful methods.

The role of texture as a basis for the recovery of surface orientation was first investigated by J.J. Gibson [1, 2, 3]. Gibson treated the case of a perspective projection of a receding plane (the ground plane). He assumed the plane to be covered with elements at uniform density, and that those elements' projections could be identified and counted. He observed that under these assumptions, the gradient of texture density specifies surface orientation, where texture density is defined as the number of elements per unit area in the image. Gibson proposed the density gradient as the primary basis for surface perception by humans. This theme has since been pursued extensively (by Purdy [4], Bajcsy [5], Haber and Hershenson [6], Rosinski [7], Bajcsy and Lieberman [8], Stevens [9] and Kender [10].) Subsequent work has largely accepted Gibson's premises and concentrated on geometric manipulations using idealized textures of known uniform properties, or on the validity of Gibson's proposal as a theory for human surface perception.[1]

Gibson's solution fails as a computational theory in two critical respects: (1) it has never been demonstrated that texture density can be meaningfully computed on natural imagery, and (2) the validity of Gibson's uniformity assumption as a model for natural textures was never addressed, beyond an informal plausibility argument. Certainly this assumption is not strictly true of natural textures, and it has never been demonstrated that the error imposed by adopting it categorically is acceptable.

An effective technique for recovering surface orientation from images of natural textured surfaces must rest on texture descriptions that can actually be computed from such images, and must avoid highly restrictive assumptions about texture geometry. Rather than assuming perfectly regular textures, the solution to be presented here emphasizes the regular nature of *projective distortion*: if one assumes that natural textures do not usually conspire to mimic projective effects, or to cancel those effects, then it is reasonable to assume that what looks like projective distortion really is, and what doesn't, is not. This strategy is expressed quantitatively by attributing as much as possible of the observed variation to projection. The surface orientation that best explains the data in this sense is a best guess for the actual orientation of the surface; the degree to which the data are explained determines the confidence assigned to the estimate. While this strategy does select the most uniform available interpretation, it does not entail an assumption that natural textures tend to be particularly uniform, but only that their non-uniformity does not mimic projection.

---

[1]Bajcsy and Lieberman [8], however, applied Fourier techniques to natural imagery in an effort to detect texture gradients.

This strategy was implemented and applied to geographic data and to natural images with good results. A simple extension of the strategy to curved surfaces, applying the planar strategy locally, is also reported.

1.1. Projective distortion

The appearance of surface markings in the image is subject to two simple geometric distortions: (1) as a surface recedes from the viewer its markings appear smaller (e.g. the convergence of railroad tracks as they approach the horizon), and (2) as a surface is inclined off the frontal plane, its markings appear compressed in the direction of inclination (e.g. the appearance of an ellipse as a tilted circle, narrowing to a line as it is viewed end-on). This paper is concerned exclusively with the second effect, called *foreshortening distortion*. Orthographic projection will therefore be assumed throughout.[2] The projective distortion on an orthographically projected planar surface is simply a one-dimensional scaling or compression in the direction of steepest decent away from the viewer (the *tilt* direction, τ) whose magnitude is the cosine of the angle between the surface and the image plane (the *slant* angle, σ).[3]

In other words, for any pattern on a planar surface, the orthographic projection of the pattern is the result of scaling the original pattern by $\cos \sigma$ in direction τ; and the original pattern may be recovered by applying the inverse transform if (σ, τ) is known. When a planar texture is viewed at an unknown orientation, neither the original texture nor (σ, τ) may be recovered just from the projective relation, because any value of (σ, τ) defines a possible surface orientation and a possible reconstruction of the unprojected texture. However, the family of all possible planar reconstructions may be generated by applying the inverse transform at all values of (σ, τ), producing a set of candidate reconstructions each associated with a particular surface orientation.

The problem of recovering surface orientation may therefore be recast as that of choosing a 'best' or most likely member from the set of possible reconstructions, or, more generally, of ordering the candidate reconstructions by some criterion of likelihood. Such an ordering cannot be induced without additional constraints in the form of assumptions about the geometry or distribution of the unprojected texture. These assumptions must simultaneously meet the formal requirement that they induce some ordering on the reconstructions, and the empirical requirement that they induce the right ordering under some reasonable criterion of reliability.

[2] In orthographic projection, points are projected to the image along lines normal to the image plane, instead of converging on a focal point. Projected size thus does not depend on distance. Orthographic projection provides a good approximation to perspective projection over small visual angles.

[3] The slant/tilt representation of surface orientation is related to the gradient space representation [11, 12] by $\sigma = \tan^{-1}(p^2 + q^2)^{1/2}$, $\tau = \tan^{-1}(q/p)$. See Fig. 1 for an illustration of the slant/tilt representation.

1.2. An image description: the projected tangent distribution

Any method for recovering surface orientation from texture must be expressed in terms of some concrete description of the image texture. The criteria for choosing such a description are clear-cut; it must be sensitive to projective distortion, and it must be computable on natural images. Since foreshortening distorts metric properties as a function of direction in the image, a description sensitive to foreshortening distortion must measure properties of the image as a function of direction. One such measure is the distribution of arc length along projected surface marking edges as a function of image tangent direction: the projected edges are broken into a collection of short 'needles', and the angle between each needle and a fixed reference direction is recorded. The distribution of tangent directions may then be represented as a histogram of these tangent angles.

It will be shown that this description transforms systematically as a function of surface orientation. The transformation will be derived quantitatevly in a later section, but its intuitive nature is demonstrated by the projection of a circle to an ellipse: arc length on a circle is uniformly distributed over tangent direction, but the distribution for an ellipse assumes maxima and minima in the directions of the major and minor axes respectively. For the projection of a circle, the direction of the minimum coincides with the tilt direction, τ, and the relative height of the peak varies with the slant, σ. That is, τ and σ correspond roughly to the 'phase' and 'amplitude' of the distribution. The particular tangent distribution obtained in the image depends on the distribution prior to projection, as well as the orientation of the textured surface. However, any tangent distribution observed in the image bears a component of systematic modulation imposed by projection.

The problems entailed in locating surface marking edges, and distinguishing them from occluding contours, shadows, and so forth, have not been entirely solved; however, it will be shown that zero-crossing contours in the convolution of the image with a $\nabla^2 G$ function [14, 15] perform well enough at least to demonstrate the feasibility of the measure.

1.3. An interpretation strategy: the most uniform reconstruction

In a previous section the recovery problem was expressed as that of ordering the set of texture reconstructions by likelihood. However, the set of planar reconstructions defined by an image texture is not an arbitrary collection of textures: all the members of that set have been generated by applying a particular kind of transformation to a single set of data. Projection 'added' a systematic component to the image data, and each reconstruction attempts to 'subtract' that component for a hypothesized surface orientation by applying the appropriate inverse transform. The image data can therefore be viewed as a mixture of this projective component with a component intrinsic to the unprojected texture, and the recovery problem as that of decomposing the mixture.

The projective component is constrained to a two parameter family of transformations, while practically nothing can be universally asserted about the textures on which the transformation acts. This distinction between the two components suggests a natural interpretation strategy: find the projective distortion that best explains the data, e.g. in the sense of accounting for the observed variation. If a large proportion of the observed variation can be so explained, then either it is actually largely due to projection, or else the unprojected texture systematically mimics projection. If one assumes that the processes that generate natural textures do not in general mimic the process of projection, then the latter possibility may be rejected. Similarly, if little of the observed variation can be explained by projection, then either the contribution of projection was in fact small, or else a large projective distortion has been systematically cancelled by the distribution of the unprojected texture. Once again, the latter possibility may be rejected if one assumes that textures don't mimic projection. In either case the interpretation that best explains the data in terms of projection is likely to be approximately correct.

This strategy may be expressed in terms of an ordering of the possible texture reconstructions by choosing the reconstruction for which the most variation has been removed by the inverse projective transform, i.e. the one which is most uniform. Crucially, adopting this strategy does not constitute an assumption that natural textures tend to be particularly uniform, only that their non-uniformity does not mimic projection. In the next section this strategy will be developed formally in statistical terms by assuming that the tangents along projected surface markings were drawn from a uniform distribution and then subjected to a projective transformation. The likelihood of the image data under this assumption is then computed as a function of (σ, τ). The result is a probability density function for surface orientation, given the image data, whose maximum is a maximum likelihood estimate for the actual orientation.

2. Planar Estimation

The development of the method begins with the derivation of a geometric model, expressing the relation among the orientation of a marked surface, the tangent to a curve on the surface, and the corresponding tangent measured in the image. Next, a statistical model expresses the expected distribution of tangents on a surface and the corresponding distribution after projection, this under a statistical uniformity assumption. Then an *estimator* is derived, expressing the probability density function for surface orientation determined by the geometric and statistical models. Then the implementation and results are described.

2.1. Geometric model

The tangent to a curve at a given point is defined as the first derivative of position on the curve with respect to arc length. The tangent is a unit vector, and may be visualized as an arrow that just grazes the curve at the specified point. The problem, as defined, is to estimate the orientation of a surface, given the tangent along an image contour, which is the projection of a curve on that surface (i.e. the edge of a surface marking). The task of the geometric model is to express the functional relationship between the quantities to be estimated and the quantities that are measured. In this section, the tangent direction at a point on an orthographically projected curve will be expressed as a function of the orientation of the plane in which the corresponding space curve lies, and of the tangent direction in that plane.

2.1.1. *Notation and terminology*

Vector quantities will be denoted in boldface (e.g. X, Y), and angles by lower case Greek letters (e.g. α, β). The components of vectors will be given in brackets (e.g. $X = [1, 0, 0]$). Projected quantities will be denoted by the same symbol as their unprojected counterparts, with a * superscript, e.g. the projection of a vector X is denoted by X^*.

The following specific symbols will be used: an image plane I; a surface S, in space, which we assume to be planar; a curve $C(s)$ on S, which, following Marr [13], we call a *contour generator*; a curve in the image, $C^*(s)$, which is the orthographic projection of $C(s)$ onto I.

The orientation of S with respect to I may be denoted by two angles σ and τ (for *slant* and *tilt* respectively) with σ the angle between I and S and τ the angle between the projection of S's normal onto I, and the x-axis in I. That is, σ says how much S is slanted, while τ says which way (see Fig. 1). The direction

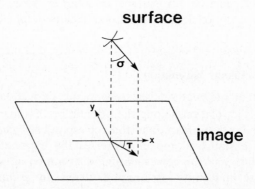

FIG. 1. Representing surface orientation by slant (σ) and tilt (τ): Slant is the angle between a normal to the surface and a normal to the image plane. Tilt is the angle between the surface normal's projection in the image plane and a fixed coordinate axis in that plane.

of a contour generator $C(s)$'s tangent at a point s will be denoted by $\beta(s)$, where β is the angle between the tangent, and a fixed coordinate axis in S.

2.1.2. The projected tangent angle

If the orientation of the surface, S, with respect to the image normal, I is given by (σ, τ), then I may be taken into S by a rotation by (σ, τ). Therefore the projection of a curve in S onto I may be obtained by placing the curve in I, rotating it by (σ, τ), and projecting it back onto I. The rotated coordinate axes of I, (x, y), can be taken as the axes for S; and the tangent angle β is measured with respect to the rotated x-axis. Then the tangent to $C(s)$ in those coordinates is $[\cos \beta, \sin \beta]$.

It will be convenient for the moment to let I's x-axis coincide with the tilt direction, so that $\tau = 0$. In that case, the equations for rotation by (σ, τ) of a point $(x, y, 0)$ into (x', y', z') reduce to

$$x' = x \cos \sigma, \qquad y' = y, \qquad z' = x \sin \sigma,$$

and the orthographic projection of (x', y', z') onto I is just (x', y'). So the tangent vector $t = [\cos \beta, \sin \beta]$ becomes after rotation and projection

$$t^* = [\cos \beta \cos \sigma, \sin \beta]$$

(which is not in general a unit vector). The projected tangent angle β^* is the angle between this vector and the x-axis, whose tangent is given by

$$\tan \beta^* = \frac{\tan \beta}{\cos \sigma}$$

so that

$$\beta^* = \tan^{-1} \frac{\tan \beta}{\cos \sigma}.$$

To reintroduce τ, suppose we now pick arbitrary coordinate axes for I, and define α^* as the angle between the x-axis in the image and the projected tangent. Since β^* is the angle between the projected tangent and the tilt direction, we have

$$\beta^* = \alpha^* - \tau \quad \text{and} \quad \alpha^* = \tan^{-1} \frac{\tan \beta}{\cos \sigma} + \tau \tag{1}$$

where α^* is the projected tangent angle, β is the angle between the unprojected tangent and the tilt direction's projection onto S, and (σ, τ) is the orientation of the curve in space. This expression relates α^*, which can be measured in the image, to (σ, τ), which we wish to recover, yielding what we sought.

2.2. Statistical model: isotropy and independence

A collection of measures of α^*, taken across the image, define a *distribution* of observed tangent directions, which might, for example, be represented as a histogram. For any hypothesized surface orientation, the geometric relation translates each value of α^* into a corresponding value of β, and so translates the observed distribution of α^* into a corresponding distribution of β; a possible distribution of β may be obtained for each value of (σ, τ). Given an expected distribution for (β, σ, τ), the likelihood of an observed distribution at any hypothesized surface orientation can be evaluated. We will express the 'uniform-as-possible' strategy by assuming that tangent direction and surface orientation are isotropic and independent.

A joint probability density function (j.p.d.f.) for a set of random variables specifies the relative likelihood of each combination of values of the variables. If β, σ, and τ are treated as random variables, and a j.p.d.f. is assumed for those variables, then (σ, τ) may be estimated statistically. To the extent that the assumed j.p.d.f. accurately describes the world this estimate will be valid in a statistical sense. We will assume that a priori all surface orientations are equally likely, all tangent directions for markings on a surface are equally likely, and surface orientation and tangent direction on the surface are independent.

The statement that all surface orientations are equally likely requires clarification: the orientation of a surface can be given by the unit normal, i.e. a 'needle' of unit length normal to the surface. The set of normals corresponding to all possible surface orientations defines a unit sphere (called the *Gaussian sphere*) which contains the points of the needles. When we say that all surface orientations are equally likely, we mean the needle is as likely to land at any one point on the sphere as any other.[4]

When surface orientation is represented by the slant and tilt angles, σ, and τ, the isotropy assumption does not translate into the assumption that all values of σ and τ are equally likely. For each value of σ, the possible values of τ define a circle on the Gaussian sphere, whose radius approaches zero as σ approaches zero, and whose radius approaches unity as σ approaches $\pi/2$. The circumference of the circle is easily shown to vary with $\sin \sigma$. Because the likelihood of landing on each point on the sphere is equal, the likelihood of landing on a curve on the sphere is proportional to the length of the curve. Since each value of σ corresponds to a circle with circumference proportional to $\sin \sigma$, the relative likelihood of σ is proportional to $\sin \sigma$. Noting that all values of τ, the tilt, and β, the tangent angle, are equally likely over the range $[0, \pi]$, we have the density function

---

[4]Since we are only concerned with visible points on opaque surfaces, we know in advance that the unit normal is confined to the hemisphere of visible directions, but this makes no difference for the derivation that follows.

$$\text{p.d.f.}(\beta, \sigma, \tau) = \frac{1}{\pi} \cdot \frac{1}{\pi} \sin \sigma = \frac{\sin \sigma}{\pi^2} \tag{2}$$

which, it is easily shown, integrates to unity over the ranges of the parameters. We now have a statistical model for the scene parameters and a geometric model relating these parameters to the image measurements. Together these measures determine a maximum likelihood estimator surface orientation, given measures on an image. This estimator will not be derived.

2.3. Estimating surface orientation

Given a geometric model which expresses the projected tangent direction α^* as a function of (β, σ, τ), and a statistical model which gives a j.p.d.f. for (β, σ, τ), we derive the maximum likelihood estimator for (σ, τ) that follows from these models.

The first step is to derive the conditional[5] p.d.f. for $(\alpha^*|\sigma, \tau)$. From this function, we obtain the joint conditional p.d.f. for $(A^*|\sigma, \tau)$ where A^* is a set of measures $A^* = \{\alpha_1^*, \alpha_2^*, \ldots, \alpha_n^*\}$. At this step we introduce the additional assumption that the projected tangent directions, α_i^*, are independently drawn from p.d.f.$(\alpha^*|\sigma, \tau)$. The implications of this assumption will be discussed in a later section. Then, using Bayes' rule, the joint conditional p.d.f. for $(\sigma, \tau|A^*)$ is obtained. A maximum likelihood estimate for (σ, τ) is the value of (σ, τ) for which that function is maximized.

2.3.1. Density function for $(\alpha^*|\sigma, \tau)$

From the previous section we have the density function

$$\text{p.d.f.}(\beta, \sigma, \tau) = \frac{\sin \sigma}{\pi^2}$$

and the geometric relation

$$\alpha^* = \tan^{-1} \frac{\tan \beta}{\cos \sigma} + \tau.$$

Thus α^* is a function of random variables with known distributions. To obtain the p.d.f. for $(\alpha^*|\sigma, \tau)$ we treat α^* as a function of β, with σ and τ as parameters. We use the relation

$$\text{p.d.f.}(\varphi(x)) = \text{p.d.f.}(x) \frac{dx}{d\varphi(x)}$$

---

[5] The *conditional probability* $(A \mid B)$ is defined as the probability of an event A, given that event B has occurred. A *conditional p.d.f.* $(\alpha \mid B)$ is the p.d.f. for a random variable α, given that event B has occurred. The conditional p.d.f. for $(\alpha^*|\sigma, \tau)$ is simply the p.d.f. for α^* given that σ and τ assume specified values.

where $\varphi(x)$ is a function of random variable x. From this relation we have

$$\text{p.d.f.}(\alpha^*(\beta)|\sigma, \tau) = \text{p.d.f.}(\beta|\sigma, \tau)\frac{\partial\beta}{\partial\alpha^*}.$$

From (1) it follows that

$$\beta = \tan^{-1}\cos\sigma\tan(\alpha^* - \tau).$$

Differentiating with respect to α^* gives

$$\frac{\partial\beta}{\partial\alpha^*} = \frac{\cos\sigma}{\cos^2(\alpha^* - \tau) + \sin^2(\alpha^* - \tau)\cos^2\sigma}$$

and p.d.f.$(\beta|\sigma, \tau)$ is simply $1/\pi$. So

$$\text{p.d.f.}(\alpha^*|\sigma, \tau) = \frac{1}{\pi}\frac{\cos\sigma}{\cos^2(\alpha^* - \tau) + \sin^2(\alpha^* - \tau)\cos^2\sigma}.$$

This density function tells us, under the assumptions of isotropy and independence for (β, σ, τ), how the image tangent direction is distributed as a function of surface orientation. This distribution is graphed at several values of σ and τ in Fig. 2.

2.3.2. *Joint density function for $(A^* = \{\alpha_1^*, \ldots, \alpha_n^*\}|\sigma, \tau)$*

Suppose we have measured the image tangent direction α^* at a series of n positions along an image contour. A basic relation in probability theory states that the joint density of n independent measures, each with density function $f(x)$ is

$$\text{p.d.f. } X = \{x_1, \ldots, x_n\} = f(x_1)f(x_2)\cdots f(x_n).$$

If we are willing to assume that a set of measures of tangent direction is independent, we have

$$\text{p.d.f.}(A^* = \{\alpha_1^*, \ldots, \alpha_n^*\}|\sigma, \tau) = \prod_{i=1}^{n}\text{p.d.f.}(\alpha_i^*|\sigma, \tau)$$

$$= \prod_{i=1}^{n}\frac{\pi^{-1}\cos\sigma}{\cos^2(\alpha_i^* - \tau) + \sin^2(\alpha_i^* - \tau)\cos^2\sigma}$$

where the symbol Π denotes an iterative product. This expression gives the relative likelihood for the set of observed image tangents at each value of (σ, τ). By Bayes' rule, the density function for (σ, τ), given A^*, is

$$\text{p.d.f.}(\sigma, \tau|A^*) = \frac{\text{p.d.f.}(\sigma, \tau)\text{p.d.f.}(A^*|\sigma, \tau)}{\displaystyle\int\int\text{p.d.f.}(\sigma, \tau)\text{p.d.f.}(A^*|\sigma\tau)\,d\sigma\,d\tau}$$

where integration is performed over the ranges of σ and τ. Dividing by the

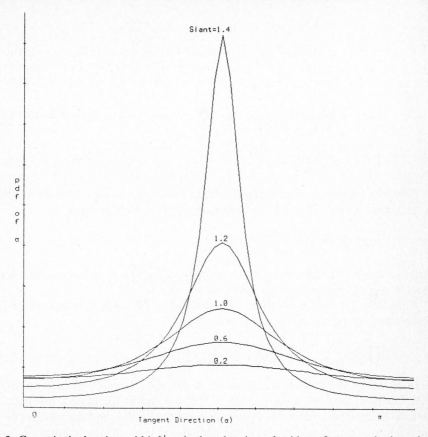

FIG. 2. Curves in the function p.d.f.$(\alpha^* | \sigma, \tau)$, plotted against α^*, with $\tau = 0$, at several values of σ.

integral simply normalizes the function to integrate to 1. The value of (σ, τ) for which this function assumes a maximum is the maximum likelihood estimate for surface orientation, and the integral of the function over a region gives the probability that the surface orientation lies inside that region.

Noting that

$$\text{p.d.f.}(\sigma, \tau) = \frac{\sin \sigma}{\pi^2}$$

the relative likelihood of $(\sigma, \tau | A^*)$ is

$$\text{p.d.f.}(\sigma, \tau)\text{p.d.f.}(A^* | \sigma, \tau) = \prod_{i=1}^{n} \frac{\pi^{-2} \sin \sigma \cos \sigma}{\cos^2(\alpha_i^* - \tau) + \sin^2(\alpha_i^* - \tau) \cos^2 \sigma}. \quad (3)$$

We normalize this relative likelihood function to obtain the density function by dividing by its integral, which can be approximated by summing values of the function taken at equal intervals of σ and τ.

2.3.3. *Summary of the model*

The geometric/statistical model from which this estimator follows constitutes a set of claims about the domain. The estimator is valid to the extent these claims are true of the domain. These, in summary, are the claims that comprise the model:

Geometric model. Each image tangent measure α^* is related to the scene parameters (β, σ, τ) by the expression

$$\alpha^* = \tan^{-1} \frac{\tan \beta}{\cos \sigma} + \tau.$$

Planarity restriction. The surface orientation (σ, τ) is constant over position.
Statistical model. The joint distribution of (β, σ, τ) is given by

$$\text{p.d.f.}(\beta, \sigma, \tau) = \frac{\sin \sigma}{\pi^2},$$

and the image measures of α^* correspond to values of β independently drawn from this distribution for some value of (σ, τ).

Estimator. Derived from these assumptions is a density function for surface orientation, given the image data, given by

$$\prod_{i=1}^{n} \frac{\pi^{-2} \sin \sigma \cos \sigma}{\cos^2(\alpha_i^* - \tau) + \sin^2(\alpha_i^* - \tau) \cos^2 \sigma},$$

normalized by its integral with respect to (σ, τ). The value of (σ, τ) at which this function assumes a maximum is the maximum likelihood estimate for surface orientation, under the assumptions of the model; and the integral of the function over a region of (σ, τ) is the probability that surface orientation lies in that region.

2.4. Implementation and results

In this section an implementation of the estimation strategy is reported and assessed. The strategy was applied to two natural domains: geographic contours, drawn from a digitized world map, and natural images, using zero-crossing contours in the $\nabla^2 G$ convolution [14, 15]. The zero-crossings of this convolution are peaks in the first derivative of the band-passed image. While these zeros are regarded by Marr and Poggio as precursors of contours, they correspond closely enough to significant events on the surface to have the desired properties for estimation. Since the strategy is limited to estimating planar orientations, images of approximately planar surfaces were chosen. The key questions addressed in assessing the performance of the strategy are: how accurately does it estimate surface orientation, and how accurately does it estimate the error of its own estimates, i.e. the confidence regions for the estimates.

2.4.1. *Computing the estimate*

The aim of the computation is to determine the density function and maximum likelihood estimate for surface orientation, given a set of tangent measures. The data are conveniently represented in grouped form, by dividing the continuum of tangent direction on the interval $(0, \pi)$ into a set of subintervals of equal length, and recording the number of measures that fall into each subinterval. Since the data are a collection of curves this amounts to recording the total arc length that falls in each orientation band.

Let $A^* = \{a_1^*, \ldots, a_n^*\}$ be the data grouped into n orientation bands, with α_i^* the midpoint of the ith band. That is, each a_i^* gives the number of data points falling in the corresponding interval. Then, for the grouped data, the relative likelihood of $(\sigma, \tau | A^*)$ becomes, from (3),

$$L(\sigma, \tau | A^*) = \exp \sum_{i=1}^{n} a_i^* \log \frac{\pi^{-2} \sin \sigma \cos \sigma}{\cos^2(\alpha_i^* - \tau) + \sin^2(\alpha_i^* - \tau) \cos^2 \sigma}. \qquad (4)$$

And, if this function is computed at m equally spaced values of σ and p equally spaced values of τ, the density function is approximated by

$$\text{p.d.f.}(\sigma, \tau | A^*) \approx \frac{L(\sigma, \tau | A^*)}{\sum_{i=1}^{m} \sum_{j=1}^{p} L(\sigma_i, \tau_j | A^*)} \qquad (5)$$

where $L(\sigma, \tau | A^*)$ is defined in (4).

The value of (σ, τ) at which this function assumes a maximum approximates the maximum likelihood estimate for surface orientation, and the sum of the function sampled at uniform intervals on a region of (σ, τ) approximates the probability that surface orientation lies inside the region. The computation was facilitated further by placing the values of $\log \text{p.d.f.}(\alpha_i^* | \sigma_j, \tau_k)$ in a lookup-table.

2.4.2. *Data and results: geographic contours*

2.4.2.1. *Data.*

The initial test of the strategy employed geographic contours drawn from a digitized world map, which obviously posed no extraction problem. Beyond this advantage, these contours provide a data base of curves which were generated by physical processes, and, when taken small enough to neglect the curvature of the earth, are planar. Moreover, by subjecting the curves to rotation/projection transforms, projections are generated whose 'real' orientation in space is known exactly. This degree of control is much more difficult to obtain using natural images.

The curves are land–water boundaries, represented in the data base as chains of points in latitude/longitude coordinates. These were converted to cartesian coordinates and projected onto the earth's tangent plane in the neighborhood

FIG. 3. Some islands drawn from the geographic data base.

of the curve, giving a frontal-plane representation. Sufficiently small curves
were selected such that the curvature of the earth was negligible. The coastlines
of islands and lakes were chosen as a class of closed curves of reasonable size.
Several of the curves are shown in Fig. 3. Projections were generated from the
frontal-plane curves by rotating them through a given (σ, τ) and orthographically projecting them to produce an image contour. These curves were converted to grouped-data form as follows: between each pair of vertices, α^* is
given by $\tan^{-1}(\Delta y/\Delta x)$, and the arc length between the vertices by $(\Delta x^2 + \Delta y^2)^{1/2}$.
The arc length was summed into the appropriate orientation cell. Seven
orientation cells were used, since it was found that finer divisions had little
effect on the estimate.

Coastlines of islands and lakes were selected from the data base on the basis
of size: chains of several hundred vertices each were chosen. The maximum
likelihood estimated and p.d.f. were computed for each curve at 36 orientations,
with orientations uniformly spaced on the Gaussian sphere.

2.4.2.2. Results.
The results for one curve at a number of orientations are shown in detail in Fig.
4. For each orientation the appearance of the curve and a contour plot of the
log p.d.f. are shown. In general, as slant increases, the accuracy of the estimate
increases and the density function falls off more steeply around the estimate.
This is to be expected: if the projective distortion is viewed as a signal, then
σ is approximately the amplitude of the signal, so increasing σ increases the
signal-to-noise ratio; that is, there is more projective distortion at larger slants.

FIG. 4. One of the geographic contours shown at various orientations, with the density function obtained at that orientation. The density function is plotted by iso-density contours, with (σ, τ) represented in polar form: σ is given by distance to the origin, τ by the angle. The radial symmetry of the plots reflects the symmetry of orthographic projection. The sharp, symmetric peaks clearly visible at higher slants are the maximum likelihood estimates for (σ, τ).

Figs. 5 and 6 summarize the results for seven curves: scatter plots are shown for estimated against actual σ and τ, as well as histograms of the observed error distributions. Clearly, for this class of shapes, the strategy makes good estimates.

Next we consider the effectiveness of the strategy at estimating its own error. A simple measure of confidence in the estimate is the maximum value of the p.d.f. Since the p.d.f. was computed at discrete points, this value may be

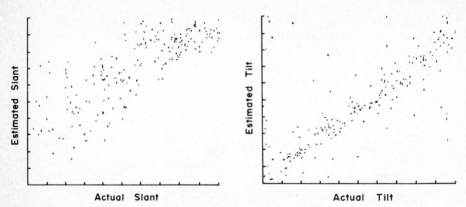

FIG. 5. Scatter plots of actual vs. estimated σ (left) and τ (right) for the geographic contours.

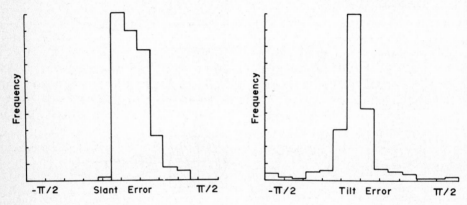

FIG. 6. Error distributions for σ (left) and τ (right). For both σ and τ the largest possible error is $\pi/2$.

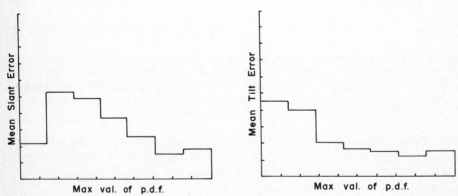

FIG. 7. Mean error of estimation as a function of the maximum value of the p.d.f. for σ (left) and τ (right). The mean error drops sharply as this value increases, showing that the reliability of the estimates can be effectively gauged.

viewed as the probability that (σ, τ) lies in a small region of fixed size around the maximum likelihood estimate. As shown in Fig. 7, the mean error of estimation drops significantly as this value increases, for both σ and τ. Thus the peak value of the p.d.f. can be used to reliably distinguish good estimates from bad ones. A more thorough gauge of confidence can be obtained by computing a confidence region, i.e. an iso-density contour within which the integral of the p.d.f. assumes a specified value.

2.4.3. *Data and results: natural images*

Extracting contours. The most substantial problem in applying the estimate to natural images is that fully adequate means of locating image contours do not yet exist. A promising basis for the location of image contours are *zero-crossing contours*, developed by Marr and Poggio, and Marr and Hildreth [14, 15]. The image is convolved with a circular $\nabla^2 G$ mask, the Laplacian of a two-dimensional Gaussian, and the zero-crossings of the convolution correspond to peaks in the magnitude of the intensity gradient in the band-passed image.

Zero-crossing contours are proposed by Marr and Poggio to be an effective description of the intensity changes in images at different spatial scales; they are regarded as precursors of perceptual contours. To provide appropriate data for the estimation strategy the shapes of zero-crossing contours must bear a regular relation to processes acting on the surface, and they appear to possess this property.

Veridical orientation. A less serious problem is that, unless a scene was photographed under carefully controlled conditions, the orientations of surfaces are not precisely known. The geographic contours provided the opportunity to systematically compare the estimates to precisely known veridical orientations. For the present purpose we can trust our own perceptions of the photographs; if the strategy and our preceptions agree, at worst they err in the same direction.

Selection of photographs. The estimation strategy under consideration is limited by the planarity restriction. By observing this restriction, pictures of approximately planar surfaces were chosen. Several kinds of contour-generating processes are represented, including surface markings and cast shadows. Also of interest are surfaces which are not planar but have an 'overall orientation', i.e. a substantial low-frequency component in the depth function. A potentially practical application of the planar strategy is the estimation of this component.

Digitization. The photographs were digitized on the Optronics Photoscanner at the MIT AI lab, an accurate, high-resolution digitizing device. The digitized images contained between three and four hundred pixels in each dimension, with intensity quantized to 256 grey levels.

Convolution. The digitized images were convolved with $\nabla^2 G$ masks, as described in [14]. The convolutions were performed on a Lisp machine at the

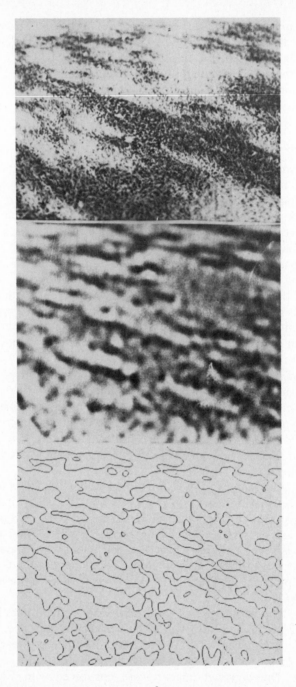

FIG. 8. A digitized image, its convolution with a $\nabla^2 G$ function, and the zeros of the convolution.

MIT AI Lab, using specialized convolution hardware. A mask with a central radius of eighteen pixels was used; the total diameter of the mask was sixty pixels. Fig. 8 shows a digitized image, its convolution with a $\nabla^2 G$ function, and the zeros of the convolution.

Extraction of tangent direction. Tangent direction was measured along the zero-crossing contours of the convolutions by first locating points on the contours and then measuring the gradient of the convolution at those points. The tangent to the contour is orthogonal to the gradient.

Grouping the data. The data were grouped by tangent direction in the form described above by sampling the contours at fixed increments of arc-length, measuring the tangent orientation, and summing into the appropriate orien-

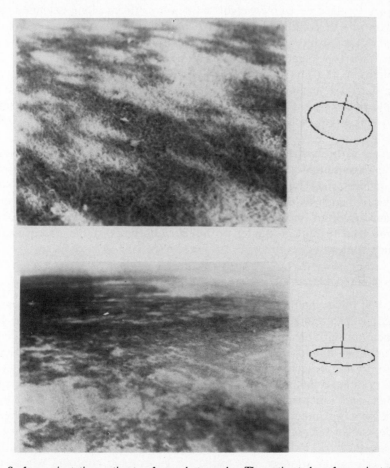

FIG. 9. Surface orientation estimates from photographs. The estimated surface orientation is indicated by an ellipse, representing the projected appearance a circle lying on the surface would have, if the maximum likelihood estimate were correct.

tation cell. From this point on, the estimate was computed as for the geographic contours.

Results. Two photographs, together with the computed density functions for
(σ, τ), are shown in Fig. 9. These should be compared with the apparent
orientations of the pictured surfaces. Most observers' perceptions of these
surfaces agree closely with the estimates.

2.5. Avoiding failures

Beyond the sampling errors incorporated in the model, the planar estimation
strategy is subject to two sources of failure, both representing serious violations
of the assumption that the tangent measures are independent. The first is a
tendency to place excessive weight on measures taken along extended smooth
contours where continuity imposes dependency among the measures. The
second is the misinterpretation of textures showing systematic projection-like
effects, such as elongated textures on striated rock.

Failures of the first kind are easily avoided by judicious sampling of the
image data. For example, counting inflections or measuring integral squared
curvature per unit arc length both give rough measures of a contour's smoothness. Using either measure to correct sampling density substantially avoids this
problem.

Failures of the second kind are more fundamental, representing a violation
of the assumption that texture geometry doesn't mimic projection.
Such failures may be avoided by recourse to parallel sources of surface
information, such as perspective and shading information. That such outside
assistance is often necessary is suggested by the observation that elongated
textures tend to appear slanted to human observers in the absence of constraining context.

2.6. Summary: planar estimation

A method for estimating the orientation of planar surfaces from contours was
derived from a model of the relevant imaging geometry and some simple
statistical assumptions about visual scenes. The geometric model related surface orientation and the tangent direction of a contour generator on the
surface, to the projected direction of the tangent in the image. The statistical
model postulated that surface orientation and tangent direction in the scene are
isotropic and independent. Together, the geometric and statistical models
determine a maximum likelihood estimator for surface orientation, given a set
of independent tangent measures in the image. This estimator was derived and
implemented.

The estimation strategy was tested on geographic contours whose orientations could be controlled exactly, and on natural images, using zero crossing
contours in the $\nabla^2 G$ convolution. The strategy was shown to give reliable
estimates as well as estimates of reliability.

3. Extension to Curved Surfaces

This section reports a simple extension of the planar technique to curved surfaces: at each image point the planar estimator is applied to a local tangent distribution computed on a circular region surrounding the point. Repeated over the image this method provides an estimate of surface orientation as a function of position. The choice of region size reflects a compromise between the estimate's spatial resolution and its accuracy: as the region size is increased, each region incorporates a larger data sample, decreasing the variance of the estimate; but variations in surface orientation within each region tend to average out, decreasing the spatial resolution of the estimate. At an appropriate region size the method provides good coarse estimates of surface shape and orientation. However, the technique in its present form is not sensitive to surface discontinuities, nor does it fully exploit surface continuity constraints [11]. Both of these issues are currently being investigated.

3.1. Implementation

The contour extraction and local estimation procedures follow exactly those described for natural images in the previous section. However, rather than computing the tangent distribution across the image, a local distribution was computed on a circular region surrounding each image point. This computation was implemented as a three-dimensional convolution in the space (x, y, α^*). The radius of the circular region was set manually.

The planar estimate was then computed on each local tangent distribution, as described in the previous section, providing an estimate of (σ, τ) as a function of position in the image. Depth maps were also computed by integrating the surface orientation map. Integrated depth maps have the undesirable tendency to propogate local errors, but are useful for display purposes.

3.2. Results

Fig. 10 shows a surface estimate for a photograph of a simple scene. The surface is represented by a collection of ellipses, as if the surface was covered by circles of constant size and uniform density. Perspective is added to the picture using a depth map obtained by integration. The global sign of the depth gradient, which is not provided by the surface estimate, was set manually. In this photograph the contours derive primarily from the pattern of shadows cast through overhanging trees. The estimated surface corresponds closely to the shape perceived in the original photograph.

Fig. 11 uses the same image to illustrate the effect of varying the radius of the summation mask. At one extreme, a single overall orientation is assigned to the entire surface. At the other, the amount of data contributing to each local estimate becomes so small that orientation varies erratically with position,

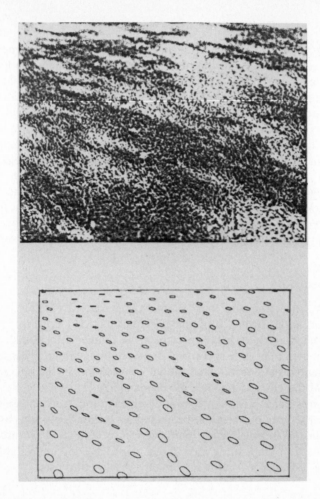

FIG. 10. A photograph and the estimated surface. Orientation is represented by ellipses, as if the surface had been covered with circles, and then projected. A perspective effect is added using a depth map obtained by integration. Note that the overall orientation coincides with that perceived in the original image, as does the increase in slant moving from foreground to background.

bearing little relation to the actual shape of the surface. Over a wide intermediate range the estimate portrays the surface reasonably well.

Figs. 12–15 show several additional images and the estimates obtained from them. Fig. 13 shows a good estimate obtained from a more complicated picture. Fig. 14 shows results for a Viking picture of the Martian surface. Slant is systematically underestimated due to the high-relief texture of the rocky surface. Such textures transform differently with projection than those in low

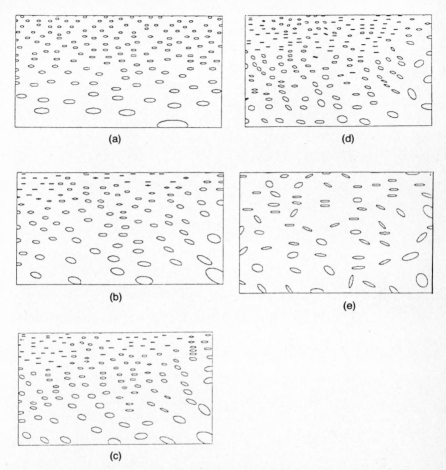

FIG. 11. The effect of the summation mask radius on the estimated surface: (a) the limiting case of a mask covering the entire image, obtaining a single overall orientation, (b) and (c) intermediate sizes that portray the surface reasonably well, and (d) and (e) show the deterioration of the estimate when the averaging radius is to small compared to the density of the data.

relief, and so must be modeled differently. Fig. 15 shows a systematically elongated texture of human hair, whose elongation, the strategy incorrectly attributes to the projection. It should be noted that such textures, seen without disambiguating context, appear incorrectly as waving surfaces to the human observer as well [9].[6]

[6]A striking example is the formation known as *landscape agate*.

FIG. 12. An additional image and the estimated surface.

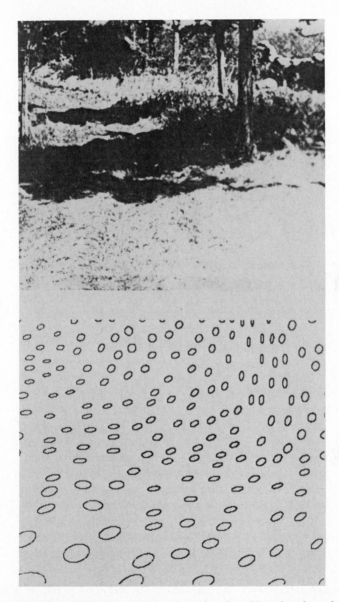

FIG. 13. A more complicated image and the estimated surface. Note that the estimate correctly distinguishes the highly slanted foreground from the more nearly frontal background. The upward pitch of the right foreground is also detected. Since the strategy doesn't know about discontinuities in depth, it is confused by the trees in the right background. Such marked local distortions might be used as evidence of a surface discontinuity.

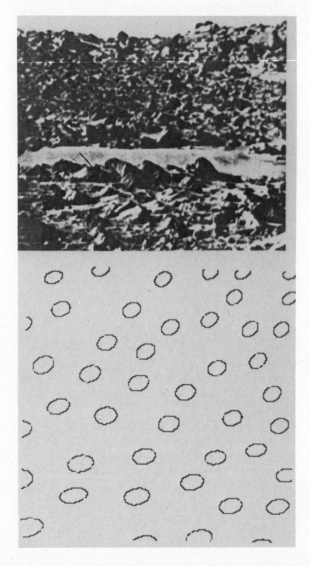

FIG. 14. A Viking picture of the Martian surface. The high-relief texture of rocks does not transform with projection in the same way as those in low relief. The strategy therefore systematically underestimates the slant of the surface. High-relief surfaces must be modeled differently.

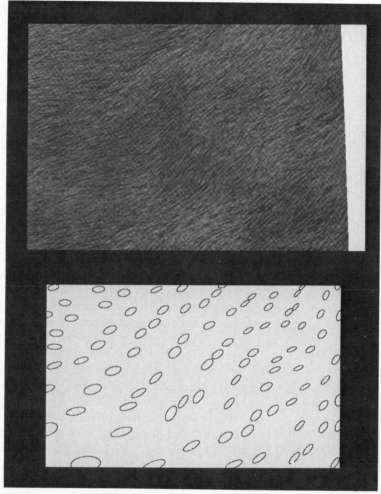

FIG. 15. A hair texture, whose systematic elongation deceives the estimation strategy. But such surfaces, viewed without disambiguating context, deceive the human observer in much the same way.

4. Discussion

The primary obstacle to using image texture to recover three-dimensional structure is that the projective distortions encoding surface orientation are confounded in the image with the properties of the original texture on which the distortion acted. Earlier treatments, beginning with those of Gibson [1–3], have sought to overcome this problem largely by recourse to restrictive assumptions of texture regularity. Such assumptions are probably too strong to apply effectively to natural textures, and in many cases they call for image measures (such as number of texture elements per unit area) that may be unrealistic for natural imagery. This paper has addressed the shape-from-texture problem for the more realistic instance of textures about which practically nothing is known a priori.

The methods reported derive from the fact that the contribution of projection to an image texture is systematic, even when the texture itself is unconstrained, and from the principle that the constituents of visual scenes and of the imaging process do not conspire to augment, cancel or mimic each others' effects on the image. The systematic texture distortions characteristic of projection should therefore be manifest in the image only to the extent that they have in fact been imposed by projection.

This strategy was realized for the limited case of planar surfaces by inverting the projective transform at each surface orientation to generate a possible texture reconstruction, then choosing the reconstruction for which the most variation had been removed—i.e. the most uniform interpretation. This most-uniform strategy does not entail an assumption that natural textures are uniform, only that their nonuniformity does not mimic projection. The strategy was expressed quantitatively by evaluating the likelihood, for each surface orientation, that the tangent directions in the reconstructed texture were drawn from a uniform distribution. This statistical method was implemented and applied successfully to geographic contours and to natural images.

The estimation strategy responds to foreshortening distortion—compression in the direction of tilt—and therefore fails for textures (such as wood grain) that are themselves systematically compressed or elongated. The incidence of these failures may be reduced by recourse to additional sources of information in the image—size gradients, shading, and so forth. While any single source may fail it is far less likely that all will fail in the same way at the same time.

A simple extension of the method to curved surfaces was also reported. The planar technique is applied locally, obtaining an estimate of surface orientation as a function of position in the image. Estimates obtained in this way from natural images were shown to provide good coarse descriptions of visible surfaces.

ACKNOWLEDGMENT

I gratefully acknowledge the support and advice of Whitman Richards, Shimon Ullman and Alex Pentland, among many others, including my thesis committee, Berthold Horn and Ruzena Bajcsy. I also thank Eric Grimson and Mike Brady for their thorough analysis of some of my derivations. The work was supported by NSF and AFOSR under MCS-7923110, by ARPA under an ONR contract NO8014-75C-0643, and by an NIH training grant number 5 T32 6MO0784.

REFERENCES

1. Gibson, J.J., *The Perception of the Visual World* (Houghton Mifflin, Boston, 1950).
2. Gibson, J.J., The perception of visual surfaces, *Amer. J. Psychology* **63** (1950) 367–384.
3. Gibson, J.J., *The Senses Considered as Perceptual Systems* (Houghton Mifflin, Boston, 1966).
4. Purdy, W.C., The hypothesis of psychophysical correspondence in space perception, *General Electric Technical Information Series*, R60ELC56 (1960).
5. Bajcsy, R., Computer identification of textured visual scenes, Memo AIM 180, Stanford University AI Lab (1972).
6. Haber, R.N. and Hershenson, M., *The Psychology of Visual Perception* (Holt, Rinehart, and Winston, New York, 1973).
7. Rosinski, R.R., On the ambiguity of visual stimulation: A reply to Eriksson, *Perception and Psychophysics* **16** (1974) 259–263.
8. Bajcsy, R. and Lieberman, L., Texture gradients as a depth cue, *Comput. Graphics and Image Processing* **5** (1976) 52–67.
9. Stevens, K., Surface perception from local analysis of texture and contour, Ph.D. Thesis, Dept. Elec. Engr. and Comp. Sci., MIT, Cambridge, MA (1979).
10. Kender, J.R., Ph.D. Thesis, Department of Computer Science, Carnegie–Mellon University, Pittsburgh, PA (1980).
11. Mackworth, A.K., Interpreting pictures of polyhedral scenes, *Artificial Intelligence* **4** (1973) 121–137.
12. Horn, B.K.P., Understanding image intensities, *Artificial Intelligence* **21**(11) (1977) 201–231.
13. Marr, D.C., Analysis of occluding contour, *Proc. Roy. Soc. London* **197** (1977) 441–475.
14. Marr, D.C. and Hildreth, E., A theory of edge detection, AI Memo 518, M.I.T., Cambridge, MA (1979).
15. Marr, D.C. and Poggio, T., A computational theory of human stereo vision, *Proc. Roy. Soc. London* **204** (1979) 301–328.

Received October 1980

The Visual Interpretation of Surface Contours

Kent A. Stevens

M.I.T. Artificial Intelligence Laboratory,
545 Technology Square, Cambridge, MA 02139, U.S.A.

ABSTRACT

This article examines the computational problems underlying the 3-D interpretation of surface contours. A surface contour is the image of a curve across a physical surface, such as the edge of a shadow cast across a surface, a gloss contour, wrinkle, seam, or pigmentation marking. Surface contours by and large are not as restricted as occluding contours and therefore pose a more difficult interpretation problem. Nonetheless, we are adept at perceiving a definite 3-D surface from even simple line drawings (e.g., graphical depictions of continuous functions of two variables). The solution of a specific surface shape comes by assuming that the physical curves are particularly restricted in their geometric relationship to the underlying surface. These geometric restrictions are examined.

1. Introduction

Of the means available to the visual system for determining the shape of a surface, stereopsis and motion predominate. Shading, when the illumination is directional, and texture gradients, when the surface is visibly textured, are also important. There are two more sources of shape information: boundary contours and surface contours. The contours that outline the boundary of a surface constrain the surface shape interior to the boundary, when the surface is smooth. Contours that lie across the surface are also useful, and they are the subject of this article.

Consider the common practice of mathematicians and engineers to graphically depict a continuous function of two variables, $z = f(x, y)$, as a surface seen from an oblique viewpoint. The technique is to project the curves that result from holding one parameter constant (for various values) while continuously varying the other parameter. An example is the sine function in Fig. 1 whose 3-D shape is readily apparent. The depiction of surfaces by contours is so familiar to us that we must pause to realize that it entails a significant problem of visual interpretation. Observe that a valid (and in fact, the correct interpretation) of Fig. 1 is that the surface is planar—it is the page of this journal on

Artificial Intelligence **17** (1981) 47–73

which the undulating curves are printed. We do not easily take that interpretation; instead we see an undulating surface in 3-D. The widespread use of
surface contours for conveying surface shapes—in mathematical texts, com-
mercial drawings, and even cartoons—shows that their visual interpretation is
definite and consistent. In short, there is a natural way of graphically conveying
the shape of a surface by depicting how certain curves would lie across it.
When drawn accordingly, we infer the intended shape.

Just as Fig. 1 has two radically different 3-D interpretations, undulating
curves on a flat sheet or curves across an undulating surface, there is also an
infinity of intermediate interpretations, at least theoretically. There are no
physical laws that force any particular surface interpretation. Therefore human
vision must incorporate particular constraints on the interpretation. This article
examines what those constraints are. (For further discussion on the role of
constraints in vision see [11, 13, 17].)

A word is needed regarding the 'restrictions' which we impose on the
physical geometry. A surface contour is the image of a physical curve Γ across
a surface Σ. This Γ may be the locus of some pigmentation change—a stripe on
a zebra, say. When seen from a particular viewpoint, the physical curve in 3-D
projects into a curve C in the 2-D image. The only evidence of surface is
indirect, in the way Γ projects to C. Therefore, inferring something about the
shape of Σ from C is possible only if the relation between Γ and Σ is
restricted. This is a crucial point: we can constrain the surface shape only if the
physical curve has some restricted relationship with the surface on which it lies.

The central problem is therefore cast as one of discovering the underlying

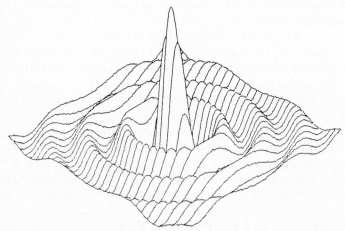

FIG. 1. It is commonplace to graphically depict a continuous function of two variables as a surface
seen from an oblique viewpoint merely by a set of curves. The 3-D surface shape is immediately
apparent.

geometric constraints. A traditional method for investigation would be to start with the basic physics of the situation, as Horn [6] successfully did with regard to shape from shading. The approach is to understand what physical laws govern the image formation process. In studying surface contours, the perspective geometry carries over from other investigations, but the problem breaks soon after into various, seemingly independent cases, according to what particular physical event causes the surface contour. Consider some possible causes of surface contours: an illumination change such as the edge of a cast shadow (tree shadow cast across fallen snow), a reflectance change such as a pigmentation marking (zebra stripe, stripe along the length of a spider plant leaf) or various sorts of surface features (circular joint between sections of a bamboo stalk, wrinkles on skin, fracture crack across a rock). Each case would be examined in order to uncover geometric restrictions on how the physical curves are produced in nature.

This approach, suggestive of the work of D'Arcy Thompson [16], seems intractable in its complexity. Certain statements may be made, e.g., that wrinkles due to compression and stripes on plants are usually close approximations to lines of curvature. But for every physical curve that has some neat geometric restriction, one may find another curve that is unrestricted, which meanders across the surface arbitrarily. Thus it would be infeasible to start with the basic physics—we would not know which physical situations to model.[1] But nonetheless, it is clear that certain assumptions about the *geometry* of the curves must be made if we are to use them to infer surface shape. So rather than study the basic physics of surface contours, we will study the basic geometric reasoning. This will give us some insight into the sorts of geometric constraints that are needed, and with that insight we may examine where those constraints arise in nature. The strategy that we will pursue is (i) to consider the various types of shape information that are plausible and useful, (ii) to determine the minimum geometric restrictions that are sufficient properties of various types of real physical curves.

We will see that there is a broad range in specificity of the 3-D shape information that might be inferred, and that the likelihood of the interpretation being correct decreases with increasing specificity. In other words, the more precisely we wish to determine the true 3-D shape, the less likely we will be successful in general. There is, therefore, a progression from weak to strong information about the shape of the surface, and associated with each type of information are restrictions that must be met in order to extract that information from the image. Rather than examine a range of possible shape descriptors, why not simply concentrate on the best that can feasibly be

[1] Stated another way, we do not know what physical interpretation we make regarding the curves in Fig. 1, if any. We might be assuming that the lines are pigmentation markings on the surface, or perhaps thin shadows cast across the surface, as if from a picket fence. Still other proposals may be made—this question probably cannot be settled by introspection.

computed from the image? The reason is that we do not yet know enough to judge what is the best, and furthermore, we do not know what specific shape information the human visual system extracts when viewing, say, Fig. 1.

While surface contours have not been studied psychophysically, the following is easily verified: we readily derive from a line drawing, such as Fig. 1, a *qualitative* appreciation for the shape of the depicted surface—e.g. where it undulates, where it is planar. We can also judge its relative orientation with some confidence, but we have little sense for its distance or scale. Reflecting on this, what can we infer from an ability to judge some 3-D property? It does not immediately follow that that property is explicitly represented. Surface orientation, however, is arguably represented explicitly by the human visual system [10, 12]. But what about the more qualitative descriptions of surface shape— are they also explicitly represented in the visual system? It is premature to say; the possibility is raised here primarily to emphasize that surface orientation is not the only possibility for local surface representation.

Furthermore, the fact that we have a definite impression of surface orientation does not necessarily mean that we compute it *directly* from the contours in the image. A 'direct' computation would derive the given output without intervening representations. The input would be the set of curves in the image, the output would be a surface orientation map. An alternative 'indirect' method would consist of two representations: the final representation would be a surface orientation map as before; the earlier representation would be a symbolic shape representation specifying, say, where the surface is planar, where it is singly curved, and where it is doubly curved. Associated with each representation would be a visual process that develops the representation. So in this case, the input to the first process would be the surface contours in the image and the output would be the qualitative shape representation. That information would then feed a subsequent process whose job it is to make the surface orientation map consistent with the symbolic shape information and other constraints such as smoothness and various boundary conditions.

In summary, there are several possible representations of local surface shape incorporated in human vision. We do not yet know whether the more qualitative representations are incorporated in human vision at this level of processing, but we should examine how they would be developed from surface contour information.

2. Describing Surface Shape

This section examines a range of shape descriptors, but in doing so it introduces a number of concepts from differential geometry.[2] So we first list the

---

[2] The reader is referred to Hilbert and Cohn-Vossen [4] for an excellent discussion of differential geometry.

descriptors, in order to avoid losing track of them in the middle of all terminology.

(i) *Planar* versus *curved*. This is the most primitive qualitative statement about local surface shape we will consider.

(ii) *Developable* (and *cylindrical*) versus *locally convex* versus *hyperbolic*. Developable surfaces are single curved and correspond to smooth twisting and foldings of a paper sheet. (A cylinder is a further restriction to an untwisted paper sheet.) The hyperbolid (saddle shaped) and locally convex surfaces, on the other hand, are doubly curved. This three-way distinction is complete and is captured by the sign (zero, positive, negative) of the local Gaussian curvature.

(iii) *Local surface orientation* (*slant-tilt*). While (i) and (ii) are qualitative and describe the surface in a manner independent of the viewpoint, the local surface orientation is quantitative and describes the local shape relative to a particular viewpoint. Slant and tilt is a useful and natural formalism for this task.

Probably the most conservative statement about surface shape is simply to distinguish whether the surface is *curved* or *planar*.[3] While this attributes special status to planarity, the distinction is probably biologically important. In lay terms, 'planar' is synonymous with 'flat', and the distinction 'flat' versus 'curved' is highly intuitive and seemingly primitive. The planar/curved distinction tells us little about the surface; nonetheless, the knowledge that certain regions are planar would be useful to a smooth surface interpolation of the sort just discussed. We will not spend time considering whether planar/curved is made explicit in human vision—it is simply a starting point for a range of shape descriptors.

A stronger statement about shape than (i) is to describe *how* the curvature of the surface varies locally. If a patch of surface is non-planar, then a path drawn across it will be a curve in space whose curvature depends on the direction of the path across the surface, in general.[4] This gives us the basis for describing the way surface curvature varies locally. It will be treated formally momentarily, first let us visualize this notion with several examples. To begin with, consider the various directions in which one could proceed away from a point on a (right circular) cylinder. In the direction parallel to the cylinder axis the path is a straight line, in the perpendicular direction the path is circular, and in intermediate directions the paths are elliptical. If the surface patch is saddle-shaped, however, some paths would arc downward while others would arc upward. Finally, on a round pebble every path would arc in the same way. More formally, by 'path' we mean a curve defined by the intersection of a plane with a patch of surface, where the plane is oriented so that it contains the

---

[3] A planar surface patch has zero normal curvature in every direction at a point. I will use 'curved' to mean 'non-planar'.

[4] If the curvature is constant in all directions the surface patch is either spherical or planar.

normal to the surface at a given point and cuts the surface in some direction. The curvature of that curve measures the *normal curvature* at a point on a surface taken in the given direction. As the examples show, normal curvature depends on the type of surface and on the direction in which the surface is cut. A fact of fundamental importance to us is that the directions of maximum and minimum normal curvature, the so-called *principal directions*, are always mutually perpendicular at any point on a smooth surface. For example, the two principal directions on a cylinder are parallel and perpendicular to the axis of the cylinder.

The curvature in either principal direction is termed *principal curvature*. It is a signed quantity, and the previous examples illustrated three combinations of the two principal curvatures. On the saddle surface the principal curvatures have opposite sign, on the pebble they have the same sign, and on the cylinder one of the principal curves vanishes to zero.[5] These possibilities correspond to a three-way distinction which seems primitive and natural, as does the distinction between planar and curved. A curved surface is either singly curved (like a curtain or a gently folded sheet of paper) or doubly curved and either saddle-shaped or convex.

It is important to note that we seek only a qualitative description of shape here, and not any quantitative measure of surface curvature. Therefore it is sufficient to only consider the sign of the two principal curvatures. It so happens that the *Gaussian curvature* is convenient in this regard. Gaussian curvature κ is the product of the two principal curvatures κ_1 and κ_2 (the curvatures measured in the two principal directions). So if the two principal curvatures have the same sign, the Gaussian curvature will be positive; the surface at that point is called *elliptic*. A surface patch consisting entirely of elliptic points is termed *locally convex*, or simply *convex*, an example being a round pebble.[6] When the two principal curvatures have opposite sign their product κ is negative—the point is called *hyperbolic* and the surface is locally saddle shaped. We will call a surface patch *hyperbolic* as well, if it consists entirely of hyperbolic points. When either (or both) principal curvatures vanish, their product, the Gaussian curvature κ, is zero. A surface patch of zero Gaussian curvature is called *developable*.

Developable surfaces, or 'singly curved' surfaces, correspond to the smooth bendings and twistings of a piece of paper that are possible without tearing. If the paper is allowed to bend but not twist, one has the special class of surfaces called *cylinders*. To give a more precise definition it will be necessary to introduce the notion of *line of curvature*, a curve which follows one of the two principal directions. A line of *greatest* curvature, for instance, follows the direction of greatest normal curvature across the surface. (Since the two

---

[5] The fourth possibility is that both curvatures vanish, i.e. the surface is planar.

[6] We will not distinguish convex from concave—that distinction can only be made relative to a viewpoint.

principal directions are perpendicular at each point on a smooth surface, the lines of greatest and least curvature form an orthogonal net across the surface.) In an extended region where κ is zero, at least one of the principal curvatures vanishes, hence at least one of the lines of curvature is a straight line. We can now define a cylinder as a surface for which the lines of least curvature are parallel straight lines. (This is illustrated in Fig. 8a.) Cylinders have several important properties that we will exploit later. Furthermore, one may locally approximate real surfaces by cylinders, so long as the principal curvatures are very different in magnitude.

Some illustrations may help. The plane in Fig. 2a and the cylinder in Fig. 2b both have zero Gaussian curvature. The convex surface in Fig. 2c has positive curvature and the saddle surface in Fig. 2d has negative curvature.

Note that much of the surface in Fig. 1 may be approximated locally by cylindrical patches. This idea of local cylinder approximations to arbitrary doubly curved surfaces is powerful, but it is successful only if the two principal curvatures are very different in magnitude.

The sign of the Gaussian curvature (whether κ is positive, negative, or zero) provides a weak but useful characterization of surface shape in the immediate vicinity of a point. An artibrary surface may have some regions of positive and some regions of negative Gaussian curvature, with necessarily intermediate points of zero curvature. The description of the visible surfaces of an object in this manner would be potentially useful for visual recognition, for the description is object-centered [12]. Another representation of shape would consist of merely noting those places of zero versus non-zero Gaussian curvature. There

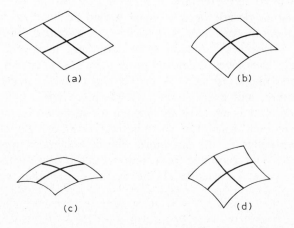

FIG. 2. Examples of surface patches of zero, positive, and negative Gaussian curvature. The planar surface in a and the cylinder in b both have zero Gaussian curvature. The surface in c is locally convex (positive curvature) and in d the surface is hyperbolic (negative curvature).

are two reasons for proposing this representation. First, an image often gives positive evidence for distinguishing patches of zero from non-zero Gaussian curvature (we will discuss some later, see also [2] regarding occluding contours [19] on shading). Second, Bruss [3] has shown that patches of negative and positive Gaussian curvature cannot be distinguished locally on the basis of the shading. Therefore an early representation of surface shape might only differentiate zero from non-zero Gaussian curvature, for that is often the most that can be stated conservatively (see 'the principal of least commitment' regarding visual processing discussed in [8]).

So far the shape descriptions are qualitative. To be quantitative about surface shape (e.g. to describe the magnitude of the Gaussian curvature, not just the sign) requires information relative to the particular viewpoint. The difficulty this would entail is equivalent to determining the relative surface orientation.

Surface orientation may be described in terms of the *slant* and *tilt* introduced in [15], which specify how much (slant) and which way (tilt) the tangent plane of the surface is inclined with respect to the image plane. Tilt is measured as an orientation in the image plane, and can be thought of as the orientation to which the surface normal would project. Slant is an angle, ranging from zero (where the surface is parallel to the image plane) to 90° (where the surface is completely foreshortened). Their relation to the more familiar Cartesian coordinates p and q of gradient space [6, 7] is:

$$\text{slant } \sigma = \tan^{-1}(p^2 + q^2)^{1/2} \quad \text{and} \quad \text{tilt } \tau = \tan^{-1}(q/p).$$

The slant-tilt form will be used in Section 3.3, where we consider the restrictions that allow us to derive surface orientation (see also [5, 14, 18]).

The various shape descriptors just given should be justified, for one might equally propose descriptors such as 'spherical', 'egg shaped', 'hour-glass', and so forth. The descriptors based on local curvature, however, have several advantages. First, each level of description is complete: every smooth patch of surface is either planar or curved, has either positive, negative, or zero Gaussian curvature, and every smooth visible point has a definable surface orientation. Second, they are local and (except for surface orientation) they are qualitative, while such descriptors as 'spherical' are more global and require quantitative knowledge of the curvature. Third, and most important, these descriptors are feasibly computed from contours in the image without requiring multiple views, prior knowledge of the surfaces, or other sources of information.

3. Geometric Restrictions

We now take each level of shape descriptor and examine what is required in order to infer that information from the surface contours in the image. It is important to keep in mind that the following discussion is only geometric with the goal of finding least restrictions. The justification or the relevance of these restrictions is a separate matter which will be examined subsequently. To give an example, we will find that restricting the physical curve to be a line of greatest curvature is useful. But when, in reality, are physical curves so restricted? In fact they often are, but for now we will merely seek geometric restrictions that are useful. And perhaps contrary to intuition, differential geometry has shown that there are few possibilities open to us.

We must assume that the surface in the vicinity of a curve (where we have no information) is 'well behaved'—that there are no invisible troughs or undulations. We rule out, for instance, the possibility the curves in Fig. 2a lie on two intersecting ridges. The property of the surface being 'well behaved' is captured by assuming the placement of the physical curves on the surface is not critical—that if displaced slightly relative to the surface they would appear qualitatively the same in the image.[7] This assumption is analogous to so-called *general position* which, as usually considered, means the viewpoint is not misleading—that the image is taken from a representative viewpoint. That assumption leads to many specific consequences: a curve that is straight in the image is straight in 3-D, lines that are collinear or parallinear or parallel in the image are collinear or parallel in 3-D, and so forth. Analogously, if the physical curves are assumed to lie in general position on the surface, we assume that a given curve of a given type is representative of those in its immediate vicinity. This also leads to a number of specific consequences, e.g., if two lines of curvature are parallel we assume that nearby lines of curvature are also parallel.[8] In practice this form of general position dovetails with the conventional form involving viewpoint (see Section 3.2.2). Superficially, general position of contour placement amounts to an expectation for surface smoothness, but more than that, it allows us to infer that any geometric property which holds along a particular curve (across a given surface) also holds in the vicinity of that curve.

3.1. Planar/curved

How can one determine whether or not a surface is curved when the only evidence is a curve C in the image, the projection of some physical curve Γ on some surface Σ? Observe that this cannot be determined simply on the basis of whether C is straight or curved—C being straight does not imply the surface is planar (or that it is cylindrical, or even that it is developable). Likewise, the mere fact that C is curved does not mean the surface is curved. The physical

---

[7] We must be careful with concepts such as 'displaced slightly' and 'qualitatively the same'. For now, these notions should seem intuitive; they are used more rigorously in Section 3.2.2.

[8] This implies that the underlying surface is cylindrical (see Section 3.2.2), a surprisingly strong consequence.

curve might be drawn on a planar surface, as are the figures on the pages of this journal.

We consider a single contour, for there are instances where that is sufficient. If we are to use the curvature of C to infer curvature of the surface Σ there are two hurdles: (i) inferring whether the physical curve Γ is curved or straight on the basis of the curvature of C, and (ii) inferring whether the surface is curved or planar from curvature of the physical curve Γ.

The first inference is straightforward, for in general we have that C is curved if and only if Γ is curved. The only exception is where C is a straight line but Γ is curved and planar and its curvature is hidden from view because the plane containing the curve is foreshortened into a line. This misleading situation is avoided by restricting the viewpoint to be in general position.

The second inference is more difficult. To use the curvature of Γ to tell us whether the surface is curved requires that we restrict the relation between the physical curve and the surface. To understand the restrictions that must be imposed, it is important to see when curvature (or lack of curvature) of Γ falsely implies curvature (or lack of curvature) of Σ. We have two cases to consider.

First suppose Γ is curved but Σ is actually planar. Then none of the curvature of Γ is normal curvature. In other words, the principal normal of Γ lies everywhere in the plane of Σ. In that special situation Γ is called *asymptotic*.[9] The other case is where Γ is straight but Σ is curved. When can this occur? (Since one cannot imbed a straight line on a surface of positive Gaussian curvature, we need only consider cases involving surfaces of either negative or zero Gaussian curvature.) There are special doubly curved surfaces (the hyperboloid of one sheet and the hyperbolic paraboloid) on which one may place a straight line. But of greater interest to us is the common occurrence of straight lines on developable surfaces (those of zero Gaussian curvature). The lines of least curvature on a developable surface are straight lines (see Figs. 2b and 8a), so this case would mislead us because the curve C would be straight despite the fact that the surface Σ is curved.

In summary, the two cases where the deduction 'C curved iff Σ curved' would fail are (i) when Γ is curved and asymptotic, and (ii) when Γ is straight and a line of least curvature. Both cases occur sufficiently often in real scenes that they must be seriously regarded. The first case arises, for instance, in water lapping on a beach, wood grain on a table top, mottle shadows on the ground, pigmentation markings on a relatively planar surface, and so forth. The second case arises in shading contours and glossy reflections on cylindrical surfaces (the 'terminator' or 'self-shadow' edge is straight and parallel to the axis of the cylinder, as is any specular reflection along the cylinder) and virtually all man-made objects have linear markings (seams, pigmentation edges, or what-

---

[9] The asymptotic case is discussed again in Section 4.1.

ever) which are rulings. The only situation which we may disregard as improbable concerns the rulings on a saddle surface as noted earlier.

The minimal restrictions necessary for distinguishing planar versus curved may be stated as follows: if Γ is curved, it cannot be asymptotic, and if straight, it cannot be a line of least curvature. We can accomplish the same thing by restricting Γ to a line of greatest curvature, but that is a much stronger restriction. Importantly, we will have independent motivation for this restriction momentarily. The geometric reasoning for distinguishing planar versus curved is summarized below. Observe that while we only need '$\Rightarrow$' for our purposes, we actually have the stronger biconditional '$\Leftrightarrow$'.

---

given a curve C, the geometric restriction
       Γ is neither a line of least curvature nor an asymptotic curve
or the stronger restriction:
       that Γ is a line of greatest curvature
plus general position (of viewpoint) allows the inference
       C curved $\Leftrightarrow \Gamma$ curved $\Leftrightarrow \Sigma$ curved.

3.2. Sign of Gaussian curvature

We now examine geometric constraints that would allow one to determine whether a patch of surface has zero, positive, or negative Gaussian curvature. In order to reason about Gaussian curvature one clearly needs more than a single curve. The two cases that we will consider are intersecting curves and parallel curves.

3.2.1. *Intersecting contours*

We start with the intersection, illustrated in Fig. 2. Note that these four cases are exhaustive: either we have that both contours are straight (Fig. 2a) or one is straight and the other curved (Fig. 2b) or they are both curved with the two senses of relative curvature in the image (Figs. 2c and 2d).

To infer the sign of the Gaussian curvature the basic problem is to determine the signs of the two principal curvatures. The only input, remember, is the intersecting pair of curves C_1 and C_2 in the image. The corresponding physical curves Γ_1 and Γ_2 must therefore have a known relationship to the lines of curvature at that point. To illustrate this difficulty, Fig. 3 shows a cylinder with two choices of intersecting curves across it. In Fig. 3a the two curves are lines of curvature, and since the surface is developable, one of the lines of curvature is a straight line. In Fig. 3b both curves lie at an angle to the principal directions, and consequently both are curved. In Figs. 3c and 3d the outlines of the surfaces are removed, showing only the two curves. Note that in Fig. 3d the

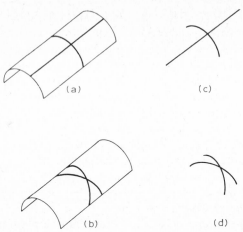

FIG. 3. The cylinder in a has two intersecting curves across it that are lines of curvature. Note that the straight line is a line of least curvature. The same cylindrical surface is shown in b, but this time the two intersecting curves do not lie in the principal directions, and therefore both are curved. In c and d the outline of the cylinder is removed, leaving only the intersecting curves in each case. The interpretation of c is the same as before, but d appears locally convex (like a sphere).

curves appear to lie on a convex surface. There is no information to indicate the special angular relation of the curves to the principal directions, and hence the relation between their curvature and the principal curvatures cannot be deduced. Given the goal of deducing the sign of the Gaussian curvature at an intersection of two curves in an image, there is apparently no feasible alternative to assuming that the corresponding physical curves are lines of curvature.

With the restriction of both physical curves to being lines of curvature, one may successfully deduce the sign of the Gaussian curvature by examining the curvature of the image curves at the intersection. In Fig. 2a the two lines are straight in the image, hence straight in 3-D, hence the surface is planar. In Fig. 2b one of the lines is straight, hence the surface has zero Gaussian curvature (it is developable, but we cannot further infer the surface is a cylinder—it may twist in space like a ribbon). In Fig. 2c the two lines have curvature of the same sign,[10] therefore the physical curves have the same sign[11] as well, and the

[10] There are many ways one may compare the sign of contour curvature in these intersection configurations. One approach is to proceed away from the intersection on two arcs, one from each curve, and compare how their normals rotate (whether they rotate clockwise or counterclockwise in the image). Note that one may attend to either of two pairs of arcs: those that bound the obtuse angle and those that bound the acute angle. If we take the arcs that define the acute angle of intersection and proceed on each away from the intersection, we will say that the curves have the same curvature if both normals rotate the same way.

[11] The sign of contour curvature in 3-D is with reference to the surface, as is customary. The two curves have the same sign of curvature if their principal normals are on the same side of the surface.

surface has positive Gaussian curvature (is locally convex). Finally, in Fig. 2d the two lines have opposite curvature and the surface has negative Gaussian curvature (is hyberbolic). The geometric reasoning is summarized below.

---

given intersecting contours C_1 and C_2, the geometric restriction
             that Γ_1 and Γ_2 are lines of curvature
plus general position (of viewpoint) allows the inference

C_1 or C_2 straight	$\Leftrightarrow \Gamma_1$ or Γ_2 straight	$\Leftrightarrow \Sigma$ developable
C_1 and C_2 have same curvature sign	$\Leftrightarrow \Gamma_1$ and Γ_2 have same curvature sign	$\Leftrightarrow \Sigma$ locally convex
C_1 and C_2 have opposite curvature sign	$\Leftrightarrow \Gamma_1$ and Γ_2 have opposite curvature sign	$\Leftrightarrow \Sigma$ hyperbolic

---

3.2.2. *Parallel contours*

Now we will examine parallel contours.[12] If two curves are parallel in the image and in general position relative to the viewer, the corresponding physical curves are also parallel in 3-D. What then can this tell us of the Gaussian curvature? Strictly speaking, the surface may have arbitrary shape[13] between the two parallel curves, so there are no inevitable consequences of parallelism. But if the surface is 'well behaved', as discussed earlier, then a strong restriction on the shape ensues. Specifically, if the placement of the physical curves on the surface is not critical (that if displaced slightly they would remain parallel), the surface is a *cylinder*. That is to say, a cylinder is the only surface in which one may embed parallel curves, in general. Note that one may find special situations that violate one or the other form of general position—either non-parallel curves on some non-cylindrical surface which look parallel from a particular viewpoint, or parallel curves on some non-cylindrical surface which are critically placed on the surface—but these are arguably improbable occurrences in nature. Hence these two forms of general position, of viewpoint and of placement of the curves on the surface, together allow one to infer the surface is a cylinder wherever the contours are parallel.

A word of caution is needed, however, regarding the practical definition of 'parallel'. For example, two lines of latitude on a globe are close to parallel, especially if they are closely spaced—and yet the surface is convex, not

---

[12] Two arbitrary curves are parallel if one may be superimposed onto the other by merely a translation.

[13] Actually, some restriction on the shape is imposed if the surface is opaque. Since the two curves are visible along their length, at no point can the intervening surface lie between the viewer and the physical curves. But this restriction is quite weak in terms of constraining the surface shape.

cylindrical. The cylinder deduction is valid only when the curves are precisely parallel. (And unfortunately, the deduction does not degrade gracefully: in the example just given even though the contours would appear roughly parallel, the surface would not be roughly cylindrical.) The geometric reasoning is summarized below.

---

given parallel contours C_1 and C_2 the geometric restrictions
        that Γ_1 and Γ_2 are in general position on the surface and are *not*
        asymptotic
plus general position (of viewpoint) allows the inference
        $C_1 \| C_2 \Leftrightarrow \Gamma_1 \| \Gamma_2 \Leftrightarrow \Sigma$ cylindrical.

3.3. Surface orientation

We have examined some geometric restrictions for determining whether a surface is planar versus curved, and for determining the sign of the Gaussian curvature. The final step is to consider surface orientation. As before, we will consider two cases where we can gain information about a patch of the surface: intersections and parallel contours.

3.3.1. *Intersecting contours*

The intersection in Fig. 4a will be the focus of our attention for the moment. The crucial measurement that we will use is the angle of intersection β measured in the image (Fig. 4b). The normal to the surface at that point is

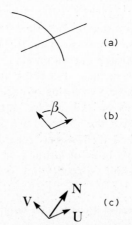

FIG. 4. The intersecting contours in a may be analyzed in terms of surface orientation given certain restrictions. The angle β shown in b is measured in the image plane. In c the three-dimensional vectors U and V lie on the surface, and N is the surface normal at their intersection.

shown in Fig. 4c. How might it be determined? We will find that the solution builds on the geometric restrictions established in the previous discussions.

Local surface orientation has two degrees of freedom, but the restriction of the physical curves to be lines of curvature reduces the degrees of freedom to one. To show this, we will derive a vector expression for the surface normal. Construct two vectors U and V that correspond to the tangents to the two physical curves at the intersection. For convenience they are constructed so as to project as unit vectors (Fig. 4c) and, without loss of generality, the x-axis is oriented with the projection of U. The angle β is measured between the projections of U and V.

$$U = \{1, 0, a\} \quad \text{and} \quad V = \{\cos \beta, \sin \beta, b\}.$$

The quantities a and b are the unknown components of U and V along the z-axis (perpendicular to the image plane). The surface normal N is the cross product:

$$N = \{-a \sin \beta, a \cos \beta - b, \sin \beta\} \tag{1}$$

and tilt τ and the slant σ are:

$$\tau = \tan^{-1} \frac{N_y}{N_x} \quad \text{and} \quad \sigma = \cos^{-1} \frac{N_z}{(N_x^2 + N_y^2 + N_z^2)^{1/2}} \tag{2}$$

where N_x, N_y, and N_z are the three components of the normal vector. Observe from (2) that the slant is the angle between the normal vector and the view vector and the tilt is the orientation to which the normal would project.

The expression for the normal in (1) carries two unknowns. This reflects the two degrees of freedom of surface orientation when no restrictions are imposed. Now, if the intersecting physical curves are lines of curvature, they are perpendicular at the intersection. Hence the dot product of U and V is zero, from which we have

$$b = - \frac{\cos \beta}{a}$$

which when substituted into (1) gives

$$N = \left\{-a \sin \beta, \cos \beta \frac{a^2 + 1}{a}, \sin \beta\right\} \tag{3}$$

and therefore the surface orientation is determined up to only one unknown, a.

Perpendicularity of the two physical curves therefore removes one degree of freedom of surface orientation. The constraint can be expressed geometrically in terms of slant and tilt, parameterized by the angle of intersection β in the image. For a given angle β to correspond to the projection of a perpendicular intersection, the intersection could only have certain orientations in 3-D

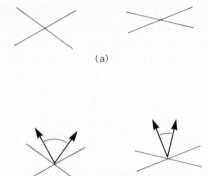

(a)

(b)

FIG. 5. A perpendicular intersection in 3-D is foreshortened in the image (a) in general. The projected angle of intersection in the image increasingly constrains the range of tilt as the angle approaches π.

relative to the viewer.[14] These limits are shown in Fig. 5. Observe that if β is near π, the foreshortening of the 3-D intersection must be large (Fig. 5a), but if β is near $\frac{1}{2}\pi$ one can say little about the surface orientation. This restriction has a simple geometric interpretation in terms of tilt, as shown in Fig. 5b. Suppose the tangents to the curves in the image plane have orientations τ_1 and τ_2 at their intersection. Then the surface tilt τ must lie within the perpendiculars to these tangents:

$$\tau_1 + \tfrac{1}{2}\pi \leq \tau \leq \tau_2 - \tfrac{1}{2}\pi.$$

Fig. 6 graphs this restriction and the corresponding restriction on slant, given β is a foreshortened right angle. For example, at $\beta = 135°$ the slant is $77.75 \pm 12.25°$, and the tilt is the bisector $\pm 22.5°$. And at $\beta = 150°$ the slant is $82.25 \pm 7.75°$, and the tilt is the bisector $\pm 15.0°$.

In conclusion, by restricting the physical curves to be lines of curvature, we can place bounds on the surface orientation at the intersection. For instance, the surface tilt at each intersection in Fig. 7a must lie within the limits shown in Fig. 7b. This restriction also places bounds on slant as a function of β.

Thus far we have only attended to the point of intersection of two surface contours, and have only utilized the angle of their intersection. Intuitively, it seems that we should be able to use the more global shape of the surface contour in order to determine surface orientation. But to do this requires substantially stronger geometric restrictions.

---

[14] We will ignore the reversals in the *direction* to which the normal would project due to depth reversals. This ambiguity is inherent in the orthographic projection and will not be considered here (see [15]).

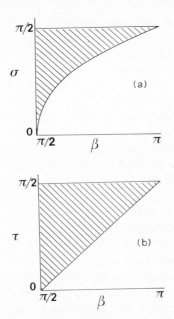

FIG. 6. The constraint on slant σ (shown in a) and on tilt τ (shown in b) is graphed as a function of the obtuse angle of intersection β, which ranges from $\frac{1}{2}\pi$ to π.

The problem of computing the surface orientation at a point along a curve on the basis of its 2-D projection is exceedingly underconstrained. It will be worthwhile discussing the problem informally for a moment. The three independent factors that enter into the problem are the viewpoint, the shape of the physical curve, and the behavior of the surface under the curve. Visualize the physical curve as a wire in 3-D and the surface along the curve as a thin ribbon that is glued to the wire. While the shape of the wire must be such that it projects to the given contour in the image, there are infinitely many bendings of the wire that would project identically. Furthermore, the wire may have

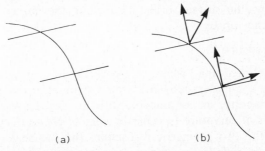

FIG. 7. The curve in a is intersected at two places. Assuming the intersections are perpendicular on the surface, the tilt at each point is constrained to lie somewhere within the bounds shown in b.

torsion, and the ribbon, which represents the strip of surface under the curve, may twist along the length of the wire arbitrarily.

Using the wire-and-ribbon analogy, let us rephrase the problem of solving surface orientation along a contour. One would start with an image of a wire (whose specific shape is not known *a priori*), and with information about how wires twist and curve in general and information about how ribbons are glued onto wires in general, determine how the particular ribbon would appear at each point along the wire from the particular viewpoint. It would amount to bending a wire appropriately then gluing the ribbon along its length in some manner, and holding the finished construction in some specific orientation in space relative to you. We discussed the bounds on slant and tilt afforded by a perpendicular intersection in 3-D. The intersection may be visualized as a line drawn across the ribbon so that it is perpendicular to the wire. Then, given an image which shows some angle β (Fig. 4b) one knows roughly how to hold the ribbon, but only at the point of intersection—the wire and ribbon would be free to bend and twist away from that point.

It is important to stress that the information about wires and ribbons must be specific enough to allow one to solve the problem, but general enough to be useful. We now will consider two geometric restrictions that together meet these criteria: that the wire lies in some plane and the ribbon is everywhere perpendicular to that plane. More formally, we restrict the physical curve Γ to be planar and geodesic. Our current goal is to show why these restrictions solve the problem; the motivation for proposing the geodesic and planar properties will be evident momentarily.

Suppose the physical curve Γ is planar, i.e., it lies in some plane Π. Then the problem of determining the 3-D shape of Γ reduces to determining the orientation of Π relative to the viewer—Γ is then simply the projection of the given image curve C back onto Π. A method for estimating the 3-D orientation of a planar curve (for example an extension of the method developed by Witkin [18]) may then be used to solve Γ. Now, given the 3-D shape of Γ, the fact that it is geodesic means the surface normal is identically the principal normal of Γ at each point. The geodesic and planar restrictions are clearly sufficient to solve the surface orientation along the curve. Now we should consider where they arise.

3.3.2. *Parallel contours*

Earlier we established that where contours in the image are parallel, the surface is locally a cylinder, subject to some assumptions of general position. This cylinder property, in conjunction with the restrictions of the physical curves to be lines of curvature (specifically lines of *greatest* curvature) will give us immediately the two geometric restrictions that we seek, because *lines of curvature across a cylinder are planar and geodesic*. The reasoning is summarized below.

for parallel contours C_1 and C_2, the geometric restrictions
> that Γ_1 and Γ_2 are in general position on surface and are *not* asymptotic

plus general position (of viewpoint) allows the inference
> $C_1\|C_2 \Leftrightarrow \Gamma_1\|\Gamma_2 \Leftrightarrow \Sigma$ cylindrical
> *and*
> Σ cylindrical and Γ line of curvature $\Rightarrow \Gamma$ planar and geodesic.

A complementary approach will now be considered, which deals geometrically with pairs of parallel contours.

The lines of least curvature, or *rulings* on a cylinder are parallel, straight lines, and are perpendicular to the lines of greatest curvature. Their projection would be parallel straight lines, but because of foreshortening they would no longer be perpendicular to the projected lines of greatest curvature (Fig. 8a). Nonetheless, a given ruling would intersect successive lines of greatest cur-

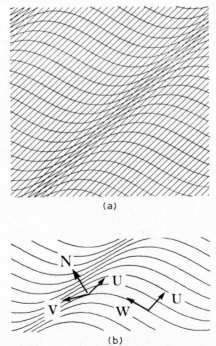

(a)

(b)

FIG. 8. In the orthographic projection of a cylinder (a) the lines of least curvature project as straight and parallel, and each intersects successive contours at a constant angle. In b the vectors at two intersections are shown. In the text it is shown how the constraint can be propagated along the curve.

vature at a constant angle. This fact allows us to reconstruct how the rulings would project in the image. We identify points on adjacent contours with parallel tangents, and connect those points with straight lines that are themselves parallel. This may be thought of as bringing points on adjacent contours into *parallel correspondence*. The line that connects corresponding points is the image of a ruling. The correspondence is unique in general. With reference to Fig. 9a, note that where the contours are straight the tangent to a point P on one contour would be parallel to various tangents on the adjacent contour, but only one choice would result in a correspondence line that is parallel to the correspondence lines elsewhere (Fig. 9b). With the rulings reconstructed in the image (as in Fig. 8a), we have at each intersection an angle β which corresponds to a foreshortened right angle, since lines of curvature are perpendicular. Thus we can place bounds on slant and tilt at each intersection, as discussed earlier. But we have another important dividend which stems from the fact that the rulings are perpendicular to the plane containing the lines of greatest curvature. To see this, consider the vector constructions in Fig. 8b.

The 3-D vector U is collinear with a given ruling, and V, with a line of greatest curvature. Being perpendicular, the surface normal N at the intersection is their cross product. We wish to define the spatial orientation of the plane Π containing Γ. Since Γ is geodesic, the two vectors V and N define that

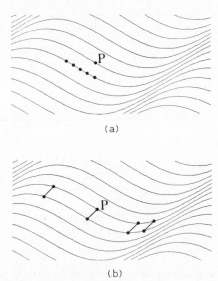

(a)

(b)

FIG. 9. Where the surface contours are straight, as in a, the tangent to a point P on one contour would be parallel to various tangents on the adjacent contour, however only one choice would result in a correspondence line that is parallel to the correspondence lines elsewhere.

plane. Furthermore, since U, V, and N are mutually orthogonal, U is the normal to the plane Π. This is important, because the orientation of the ruling immediately gives us the *tilt* of Π.

Earlier we lamented that somehow the shape of the curve in the image should help solve the surface orientation. Now we see how to do this. The planarity and geodesic restrictions allow us to propagate the surface orientation *along* a curve, from places where it is strongly constrained to places where it is not. Consider the two intersections in Fig. 8b.

$$U = \{1, 0, a\}, \quad V = \{\cos \beta_1, \sin \beta_1, b\}, \quad \text{and} \quad W = \{\cos \beta_2, \sin \beta_2, c\}.$$

where

$$c = -\frac{\cos \beta_2}{a}.$$

The normals at the two intersections are

$$N_1 = \left\{-a \sin \beta_1, \cos \beta_1 \frac{a^2 + 1}{a}, \sin \beta_1\right\} \quad \text{and}$$

$$N_2 = \left\{-a \sin \beta_2, \cos \beta_2 \frac{a^2 + 1}{a}, \sin \beta_2\right\}. \tag{4}$$

Observe that β_1 is large, and therefore the slant and tilt are strongly constrained at that point. We take the bisector of the range of tilt as a best estimate[15] of τ in order to solve for the unknown a. Since

$$\tau = \tan^{-1}\frac{N_y}{N_x} = \tan^{-1}\frac{\cos \beta_1 \dfrac{a^2 + 1}{a}}{-a \sin \beta_1}$$

we have that

$$a = \left(\frac{-1}{\tan \tau \tan \beta_1 + 1}\right)^{1/2}. \tag{5}$$

Now, for some other point where the surface orientation is not at strongly constrained, such as at the other intersection (where β_2 is smaller) we may substitute (5) and (4) to find that the normal N_2 is determined completely.

Note that the parallel correspondence process which reconstructs the rulings is local, and therefore might be applied to the images of surfaces that are not cylinders globally, such as Fig. 10 and even Fig. 1. This suggests a computation for generating local cylinder approximations to doubly-curved surfaces.

---

[15] Incidentally, for a given intersection the bisector choice results in the surface orientation with the least slant.

FIG. 10. Parallel correspondence is defined only locally, hence is applicable to surfaces that are not cylinders. If the contours are locally parallel, the surface may be approximated locally as cylindrical.

4. Discussion

4.1. The distinction between asymptotic curves and lines of curvature

Earlier when we were determining the restrictions necessary to distinguish planar from curved surfaces, the asymptotic curve emerged as a special case because its curvature is not related to surface curvature. Recall that an asymptotic curve follows the direction of zero normal curvature on the surface. It may therefore be regarded as the antithesis of a line of curvature, which follows the direction of extremal normal curvature. Asymptotic curves only exist of surfaces of negative or zero Gaussian curvature, i.e., hyperbolic and developable surfaces.

Asymptotic curves exist on hyperbolic surfaces because the principal curvatures have opposite sign and so the normal curvature must pass through zero in some direction between the two principal directions. In fact, an asymptotic curve's tangent always bisects the two principal directions; it is therefore a rather special curve across a saddle surface and will be disregarded because it is virtually non-existent in actual situations (and non-intuitive and hard to visualize as well).

Asymptotic curves also occur on developable surfaces—they correspond to rulings. But a degenerate case is when the surface is planar, for any curve across the plane is asymptotic trivially, since there is no normal curvature in any direction on a plane. It was this case that we explicitly excluded in our analysis of surface shape. Nonetheless, asymptotic curves on planar surfaces may be used to estimate the orientation of the planar patches. Witkin [18] describes a method for estimating the direction and magnitude of the *foreshortening* a planar curve has undergone in projecting into the image. From measurements of contour curvature and the distribution of tangent orientation in the image one may estimate the tilt and slant of the plane containing the corresponding 3-D curve. This approach seems useful, for instance, with mottled shadows on the ground or the spots on a dalmatian, and many other natural situations involving curves on relatively[16] planar surfaces.

I would suggest that there is a meaningful distinction to be made between the analysis of asymptotic curves described by Witkin and the analysis of lines of curvature introduced here. Fig. 11 shows an interesting case where the human visual system interprets the contours as asymptotic, i.e., as lying on a flat surface. There are probably geometric criteria which govern whether the contours are interpreted as lines of curvature or as asymptotic curves.

FIG. 11. The contours are interpreted as lying across a planar surface, i.e., as asymptotic curves.

4.2. Where do geodesics, lines of curvature, and planar curves occur in reality?

The previous discussions revealed three important geometric restrictions on physical curves: *line of curvature, geodesic,* and *planarity.* Where can we expect these restrictions to hold in actuality? A brief discussion will be given here.

The curves across the surfaces of virtually all synthetic objects are seldom arbitrary in the geometrical sense. In fact, they are almost always planar and geodesic lines of curvature. This is a consequence of the way we fabricate, label, and decorate objects. In particular, we tend to generate complicated surfaces piecewise out of developable surfaces (usually cylinders) and planes. The seam where these surfaces join is usually planar, and that plane is usually normal to the surface—hence the seam is both planar and geodesic. Moreover, for synthetic objects that are surfaces of revolution, the markings almost

---

[16] I.e. the curvature of the surface is small relative to the contour detail on the surface.

invariably follow the object's axis or are perpendicular to it. Importantly, lines on a surface of revolution that are parallel and perpendicular to the axis of rotation are lines of curvature and are planar. I am purposefully staying at a general level of discussion. The reader is invited to examine nearby objects to find specific examples. Without addressing the issue of nature versus nurture, it is clear that the fabricated objects which comprise our everyday environment have the geometric restrictions that we seek—the curves across their surfaces are almost invariably planar, geodesic, and lines of curvature.

One may also seek to find geometric restrictions on natural curves as well. Several interesting observations may be made, but the task is significantly more difficult, in general. As mentioned in the introduction, planar lines of curvature may be found in many biological forms: stripes on plant leaves, wrinkles, the joints on bamboo stalks (they are also geodesic). As also discussed earlier, it is difficult to weigh this evidence, for one may easily give counterexamples— curves that meander across the surface rather arbitrarily. The stripes on a zebra are one example.[17]

An interesting case of geometric restriction in nature is provided by the glossy reflections from surfaces that have a strong specular component in their reflectance functions. If a surface is specular, then given directional illumination and a favorable viewpoint, a specular reflection—either a point-like *highlight* or a *gloss contour*—will appear in the image. For this to occur some patch on the surface must be oriented such that the surface normal bisects the angle defined by the point light source, the given surface point, and the viewer. I will refer to this alignment as the *specularity condition*. If the surface is doubly curved, the specularity condition is met only at a point, if at all, and causes a point-like reflection in the image—a so-called highlight. Similarly, on developable surfaces a specular reflection would be point-like in general—the important exception being a cylinder. On a cylinder, the fact that the tangent plane does not twist along a ruling means that if the specularity condition is met at some point, it will also be met along the ruling passing through that point. Furthermore, the specularity condition is strong enough that if a given gloss contour C (produced by specular reflection) is straight, the surface is locally a cylinder:

$$C \text{ straight} \Leftrightarrow \Sigma \text{ cylindrical.}$$

While this is true in the case of orthographic projection with a distant viewer and distant point light source, in reality the viewer is often near the surface and the light source is neither distant nor a point source. The most important

---

[17] Incidentally, that may be one reason why they are effective in obscuring the true shape of the animal. It is well-known that one technique that nature seems to have adopted for protective coloration is to place high contrast contours across the animal which do not correspond to the underlying 3-D shape. In our terms, those contours would be non-planar, and would not be lines of curvature or geodesic.

exception concerns an extended light source, such as a bright window or a ceiling light panel. Instead of a tiny point or thin line of specular reflection, the reflection will be extended. Nevertheless, if the outline of the reflection is straight, the surface is cylindrical.

Can we infer anything about surface shape in other situations? For instance, if the gloss contour is an arc, rather than straight, what does that tell us? Generally it means the surface is doubly curved, and the curvature across the arc is much greater than the curvature along it (in other words, the surface may be approximated locally as a cylinder along the arc.)[18] To be more analytic would be quite difficult: the arc is the projection of some path along which the specularity condition is met, but if the viewer is relatively near the surface, and especially if the light source is also near by, that condition changes from point to point. Without knowledge of the viewer (and illumination) geometry, the specular reflection cannot be interpreted further. I suggest that images of specular surfaces are not feasibly analyzed by any analytic 'shape-from-shading' method. Rather, only the qualitative shape of the gloss contours are used in order provide rough information about the local Gaussian curvature, and only with the additional constraint afforded by the smooth boundaries can one feasibly compute local surface orientation. But it is clear that specular reflections can tell us not only something of the reflectance properties of the surface (that the surface is specular [1]), but also some qualitative information about the surface shape.

4.3. Summing up

This article has introduced an approach towards understanding how surface contours may be used as information about surface shape. Rather than start with the 'physics of the situation', which would be intractably difficult in its generality, we started with the basic geometric reasoning required to make 3-D shape assertions of various sorts. A range of assertions were studied: whether the surface is planar versus curved, the sign of the Gaussian curvature, and finally, the local surface orientation. Even the simple task of distinguishing planar from curved required some strong geometric restriction. The weakest restriction is that the physical curve is neither asymptotic nor a line of least curvature. A somewhat stronger restriction is that the curve is a line of greatest curvature. Next we saw that to conclude anything about the sign of Gaussian curvature, the physical curves must be lines of curvature. (Actually, the special case of parallel contours requires only that the corresponding physical curves be in general position on the surface and not be asymptotic—then parallelism implies the surface is a cylinder.) We then looked at the problem of computing

---

[18] One often resorts to physical movement relative to the surface in order to sort out the various reflections. Those reflections that stay fixed relative to the surface (or displace only slightly) correspond to places of high curvature, i.e., corners.

surface orientation and found that the perpendicularity of lines of curvature places useful constraint on the possible surface orientation at the intersection. Furthermore, it reduces the degrees of freedom of surface orientation to one. And provided that the curve is geodesic and planar (which is the case if the curves are parallel in general), we found that one may propagate the surface orientation from places where it is strongly constrained or known outright, to places where it is not. Thus parallelism emerged as very important in this analysis. It also emerged that the physical curve should be restricted to being planar, a line of curvature, and geodesic. Then we noted the strong distinction between lines of curvature and asymptotic curves. Finally we reflected momentarily on where these various restrictions occur, both in the man-made world, and in nature.

ACKNOWLEDGMENT

Primarily I must thank David Marr, who supervised the dissertation from which this article derives. Discussions with Shimon Ullman, Whitman Richards, Mike Riley, and Eric Grimson were most helpful. I also thank the two reviewers for their criticism. This article describes research done at the Artificial Intelligence Laboratory of the Massachusetts Institute of Technology. Support for the laboratory's artificial intelligence research is provided in part by the Advanced Research Projects Agency of the Department of Defense under Office of Naval Research contract N00014-75-C-0643 and in part by National Science Foundation Grant MCS77-07569.

REFERENCES

1. Beck, J., *Surface Color Perception* (Cornell University Press, Ithaca, 1972).
2. Brady, M., Finding the axis of an egg, *Proceeding Sixth International Joint Conference on Artificial Intelligence* (1979) 85–87.
3. Bruss, A., The image irradiance equation: its solution and application, Ph.D. Thesis (Electrical Engineering and Computer Science), M.I.T., forthcoming.
4. Hilbert, D. and Cohn-Vossen, S., *Geometry and the Imagination* (Chelsea, New York, 1952).
5. Hoffman, D.D., Inferring shape from motion, *Biological Cybernetics* (submitted for publication). Also available as *M.I.T. A.I. Lab. Memo* 592 (1980).
6. Horn, B.K.P., Obtaining shape from shading information, in: P.H. Winston, ed., *The Psychology of Computer Vision* (McGraw-Hill, New York, 1975).
7. Mackworth, A.K., Interpreting pictures of polyhedral scenes, *Artificial Intelligence* 4 (1973) 121–137.
8. Marr, D., Early processing of visual information, *Philos. Trans. Roy. Soc. B.* 275 (1976) 483–524.
9. Marr, D., Analysis of occluding contour, *Proc. R. Soc. Lond. B.* 197 (1977) 441–475. Also available as M.I.T. A.I. Lab. Memo 372.
10. Marr, D., Representing visual information, A.A.A.S. 143rd Annual Meeting, Symposium on: Some mathematical questions in biology, February 1977, published in *Lectures on Mathematics in the Life Sciences* 10 (1978) 10–180. Also available as M.I.T. A.I. Lab. Memo 415.
11. Marr, D., *Vision: A Computational Investigation into the Human Representation and Processing of Visual Information* (W.H. Freeman, San Francisco, in press).
12. Marr, D. and Nishihara, K., Representation and recognition of the spatial organization of three-dimensional shapes, *Philos. Trans. Roy. Soc. B* 200 (1978) 269–294.

13. Marr, D. and Poggio, T., From understanding computation to understanding neural circuitry, *Neuroscience Research Progress Bulletin* **15** (1977) 470–488. Also available as M.I.T. A.I. Lab. Memo 357.
14. Prazdny, K., Egomotion and relative depth from optical flow, *Biological Cybernetics* **36** (1980) 87–102.
15. Stevens, K.A., Surface perception by local analysis of texture and contour, M.I.T. A.I. Lab. Technical Report 512 (1980).
16. Thompson, W. D'Arcy, *On Growth and Form* (Cambridge University Press, Cambridge, 1961).
17. Ullman, S., *The Interpretation of Visual Motion* (MIT Press, Cambridge, MA, 1979).
18. Witkin, A.P., Estimating shape from texture, *Artificial Intelligence* **17** (1981) 17–45 [this volume].
19. Woodham, R.J., Reflectance map techniques for analyzing surface defects in metal castings, *M.I.T. A.I. Lab. Technical Report* 457 (1978).

Received March 1980; revised version received September 1980

Interpreting Line Drawings as Three-Dimensional Surfaces

H.G. Barrow and J.M. Tenenbaum*

Artificial Intelligence Center, SRI International, Menlo Park, CA 94025, U.S.A.

ABSTRACT

Understanding how line drawings convey tri-dimensionality is of fundamental importance in explaining surface perception when photometry is either uninformative or too complex to model analytically.

We put forward here a computational model for interpreting line drawings as three-dimensional surfaces, based on constraints on local surface orientation along extremal and discontinuity boundaries. Specific techniques are described for two key processes: recovering the three-dimensional conformation of a space curve (e.g., a surface boundary) from its two-dimensional projection in an image, and interpolating smooth surfaces from orientation constraints along extremal boundaries. The relevance of the model to a general theory of low-level vision is discussed.

1. Introduction

Recent research in computational vision has sought to understand some of the principles underlying early stages of visual processing in both man and machine. An important function of early vision appears to be the transformation of brightness information in the input image into an intermediate representation that describes the intrinsic characteristics (depth, orientation, reflectance, color, and so on) of the three-dimensional surface element at each point in the image [1–4]. Support for this idea comes from four sources: (1) The observed ability of humans to determine these characteristics, regardless of viewing conditions or familiarity with the scene. (2) The direct value of such characteristics to applications like manipulation and obstacle avoidance. (3) The utility of such a representation for facilitating higher-level processing (e.g. segmentation or object recognition) in computer vision systems. (4) Theoretical

*Both authors are now at the Artificial Intelligence Research Laboratory, Fairchild Camera and Instrument Corporation, Palo Alto, CA 94304.

Artificial Intelligence **17** (1981) 75–116

arguments that such descriptions could, in fact, be recovered by nonpurposive, noncognitive processes, at least for simple scene domains [4].

In principle, information about surfaces can be obtained from many sources: stereopsis, motion parallax, texture gradient, and shading, to name a few. Each of these cues, however, is valid only for a particular class of situations. For example, stereopsis and motion parallax require multiple images; determining surface shape from texture requires statistical regularity of the textural elements. Analytic techniques for determining shape from shading require accurate modeling of the incident illumination and surface photometry, which is difficult to do for most natural scenes.

Even in the absence of such powerful analytic cues, much valuable information about surface structure is still available. In particular, much is conveyed by brightness discontinuities, which occur wherever there are discontinuities in incident illumination (at shadow boundaries), reflectance (at surface markings), or surface orientation (at surface boundaries). The significance of surface discontinuities alone is evident from our ability to infer the three-dimensional structure of objects depicted in line drawings, such as Fig. 1.1. Boundary information is such a fundamental cue to tri-dimensionality that it is hard for humans to suppress it. The shaded parallelograms in Fig. 1.2 are two-dimensionally congruent, but appear strikingly different because their three-dimensional interpretations are so different (from [5]).

FIG. 1.1. Line drawing of a three-dimensional scene.
   Surface and boundary structure are distinctly perceived despite the ambiguity inherent in the imaging process.

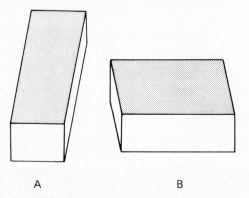

A   B

FIG. 1.2. The influence of three-dimensional interpretation (after Shepard).

Further insights into the role of boundary information are provided by some informal psychological experiments. In the first of these, performed recently at SRI, markedly different shading patterns were superimposed on given surface outlines, with negligible effect on perceived shape (Fig. 1.3). It seems that one ascribes the different brightness patterns to particular reflectance functions and illumination directions, rather than to surface shape, which seems to be determined largely by the shape of the outline. The general direction of the shading gradient, however, does seem to be an important qualitative cue. When the gradient is orthogonal to the principal curvature of the surface implied by the outline, the image is confusing (Fig. 1.3f). While a rigorous investigation of the effect of qualitative brightness events on perceived surface shape has not yet been completed, it appears that in many cases outline dominates shading as a shape cue.

The second experiment, described by Gregory [6, p. 46] (and brought to our attention by Albert Yonas of the University of Minnesota), suggests that outline may also dominate such cues as perspective and motion parallax. A three-dimensional wireframe cube viewed monocularly can be perceived to reverse in depth, in a manner similar to that of the familiar two-dimensional Necker cube figure (Fig. 1.4). In its reversed state, the figure is seen as a truncated pyramid (Fig. 1.5), with the nearer face smaller than the farther one. Perspective and the regularity of cubes might be expected to exert a bias against this interpretation, but it is remarkably robust. Moreover, if the observer or the object moves, we would expect the reversed perception to be immediately shattered by the inconsistency of motion parallax with the assumption of a rigid body. Surprisingly, this does not happen; instead, the pyramid is perceived to bend and stretch. The effect is so compelling that the reader is urged to experience it himself. These reversal phenomena are not unique to cubes: they are observed for any wireframe object, including a single wire curved in space and with practice, even for solid objects.

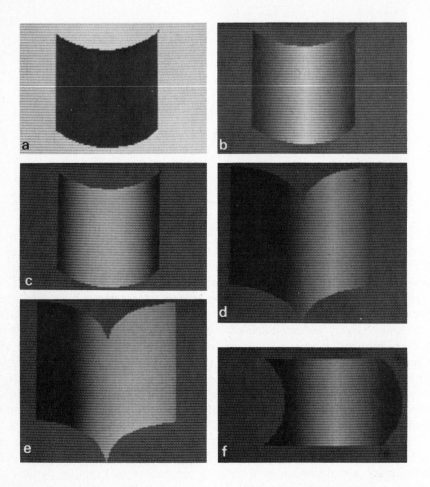

FIG. 1.3. An informal experiment demonstrating the relative importance of shading and boundary curves as determinants of surface shape.

Different one-dimensional shading gradients appear to have little effect on the perceived shape of a surface defined by a given outline. The direction of the shading gradient does seem important, however, as a qualitative cue for line sorting. Fig. (f), where the shading gradient runs orthogonal to the cylindrical curvature implied by the contour, is difficult to interpret.

(a) A cylindrical patch in silhouette.

(b) A cylindrical patch with shading falling off linearly on both sides of the highlight.

(c) A cylindrical patch with shading falling off quadratically from the highlight.

(d) A cuspate surface with shading falling off linearly.

(e) A cuspate surface with shading falling off quadratically.

(f) A cylindrical patch with inconsistent shading.

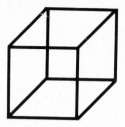

FIG. 1.4. A Necker cube.
This figure undergoes spontaneous reversals in depth.

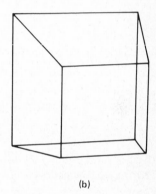

(b)

FIG. 1.5. The monocular appearance of a 'reversed' wire frame cube.
(a) Spectator using one eye.
(b) What the spectator sees when the cube reverses.

In sum, brightness discontinuities at surface boundaries, as depicted in line drawings, are often the primary source of information about surface shape available from an image. Understanding how line drawings convey tri-dimensionality is therefore of fundamental importance.

2. The Nature of the Problem

A line drawing can be viewed as the minimal representation of intensity discontinuities in a gray-level image that conveys surface structure adequately. In general, a line drawing depicts intensity discontinuities corresponding to discontinuities (and possibly inflexions) of surface orientation, range, reflectance, and illumination. In this paper we shall deal only with orientation and range boundaries.

Given a perspectively correct line drawing depicting discontinuities of smooth surfaces, our desired output consists of arrays that contain values for orientation and relative range at each point on the implied surfaces (see Fig.

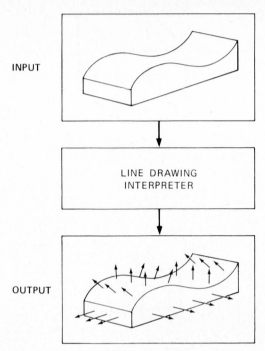

Fig. 2.1. An input/output model of line drawing interpretation.

2.1). These output arrays are analogous to our intrinsic images [4] or Marr's 2.5-D sketch [3].

The central problem in perceiving line drawings is one of ambiguity. Since each point in an image determines only a ray in space and not a unique point, a two-dimensional line in the image could, in theory, correspond to a possible projection of an infinitude of three-dimensional space curves (see Fig. 2.2). Yet people are not aware of this massive ambiguity. When they are asked to provide a three-dimensional interpretation of an ellipse, the overwhelming response is a tilted circle, not some bizarrely twisting curve (or even a discontinuous one) that has the same image. What assumptions about the scene and the imaging process are invoked to constrain this unique interpretation?

In previous work, attempts were made to resolve this ambiguity by interpreting line drawings in terms of such high-level knowledge as object models [7, 8], junction catalogs [9, 10, 11], or generalized cylinders [12]. Following this approach, the interpretation of an ellipse is commonly explained in terms of a prototypical circle. However, this cannot account for the significant observation that, for any given view of an arbitrary space curve, only two of the infinite set of possible interpretations are normally perceived—the (approximately) correct one and a single Necker inverse. There is thus reason to believe that the human visual stystem relies on constraints that are more fundamental than prototypes.

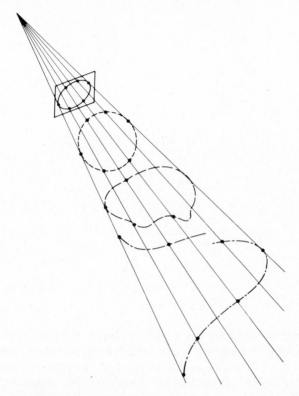

FIG. 2.2. The three-dimensional conformation of lines depicted in a line drawing is inherently ambiguous.

All the space curves in this figure project into an ellipse in the image plane, but they are not all equally likely interpretations.

3. Nature of the Solution

We observe that, although all the lines in Fig. 1.1 look fundamentally alike, two distinct types of scene events are depicted: extremal boundaries (e.g., the sides of the vase), where a surface turns smoothly away from the viewer; discontinuity boundaries (e.g., the edges of the leaves), where smooth surfaces terminate or intersect (see Fig. 3.1). Each type exerts its own specific constraints upon three-dimensional interpretation.

At an extremal boundary, the surface orientation can be inferred exactly; at every point along the boundary, orientation is normal to the line of sight and to the tangent to the curve in the image [4].

A discontinuity boundary, by contrast, does not constrain surface orientation directly. However, its local two-dimensional curvature in the image does exert a statistical constraint upon the local plane of the corresponding three-dimen-

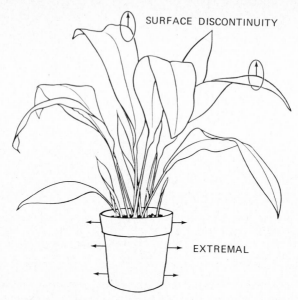

FIG. 3.1. Different edge types in a line drawing.

sional space curve, and thus upon relative depth along the curve. Moreover, the surface normal at each point along the boundary is then constrained to be orthogonal to the three-dimensional tangent in the plane of the space curve, leaving only one degree of freedom unknown; i.e., the surface normal is hinged to the tangent—free to swing about it as shown in Fig. 3.2.

The ability to infer three-dimensional surface structure from extremal and discontinuity boundaries suggests a three-step model for line drawing interpretation (see Fig. 3.3), analogous to those involved in our intrinsic-image model [4]: line sorting, three-dimensional boundary interpretation, and surface

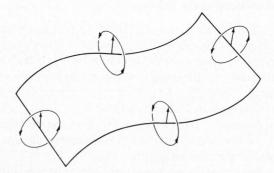

FIG. 3.2. Surface orientation is constrained to one degree of freedom along discontinuity boundaries.

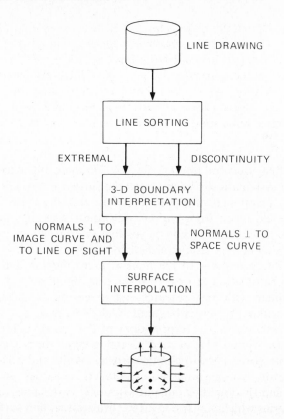

FIG. 3.3. A model for interpretation of line drawings.

interpolation. Each line is first classified according to the type of surface boundary it represents (extremal or discontinuity). Surface contours are interpreted as three-dimensional space curves, providing relative 3-D distances along each curve; local surface normals are assigned along the extremal boundaries. Finally, three-dimensional surfaces consistent with these boundary conditions are constructed by interpolation. (For an alternative model, see [13].)

4. Line Sorting

4.1. Line classification

The first step in interpreting an ideal line drawing is to classify the various lines according to the type of surface boundary they represent. Each type involves different constraints in arriving at a three-dimensional interpretation, and imposes different boundary conditions. The problem is that all lines in a line drawing look fundamentally alike. How, then, are we able to distinguish the extremal boundaries and surface contours in an image like Fig. 1.1?

The two principal bases for classifying lines are local cues provided by line junctions and global cues provided by geometric relations, such as symmetry and parallelism. A third possibility, considered less likely on combinatorial grounds, is that line classification is performed in tandem with surface interpretation to optimize some joint measure of boundary and surface smoothness.

4.1.1. *Junctions*

Junctions were first used for line labeling by Huffman [9], Clowes [14], and Waltz [10]. They systematically enumerated the surface intersections that could occur in scenes composed of trihedral solids and the corresponding line junctions that would result from various viewpoints. Catalogs were produced listing for each type of junction sets of possible interpretations of the emanating lines. Line labeling was accomplished by using the catalogs to assign all locally possible interpretations to the lines at each junction and then using a global constraint satisfaction process to resolve ambiguities.

To those familiar with this research, an extension to arbitrarily curved objects is, at first thought, overwhelming. Waltz's catalog, for example, enumerated nearly 3000 physical interpretations of the junctions in line drawings of trihedral scenes. Turner [11] needed a catalog many times larger to accommodate solids with parabolic and elliptic surfaces. Waltz and Turner, however, attempted to classify lines into numerous detailed categories, such as convex, concave, crack, and shadow. For our purposes only two classes are significant: extremal boundaries which constrain surface orientation, and surface contours, which constrain relative distance. This drastically reduces the number of junction types.

Fig. 4.1a shows a simple junction catalog recently published by Chakravarty [15] that can handle a wide variety of curved objects, including all those shown in Fig. 4.1b. These junctions exert remarkably strong local constraints upon the interpretation of lines as extremal, occluding, or intersecting edges. Junction S, for example, implies a vertex formed by an extremal edge that meets intersecting and occluding edges, as occurs where the side of a cylinder meets the visible end; junction A implies an extremal edge meeting the hidden end; junction W suggests the intersection of two surfaces bounded by discontinuity edges; T junctions play their usual role of an occlusion cue, indicating relative depth. These junctions also resolve figure-ground ambiguities in regard to which surface(s) a line bounds.[1]

One caveat about using junctions for labeling line drawings of curved objects is that determination of the junction category may depend on subtle variations in geometry that are difficult to distinguish in practice. For example, Fig. 4.2a, which depicts a slice of cake, can easily be confused with Fig. 4.2b, which

---

[1] For a derivation of some of the catalog entries from a general position assumption, see [29].

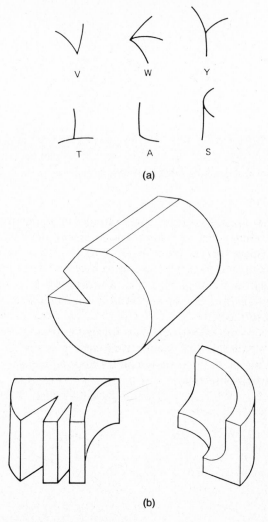

FIG. 4.1. A junction catalog for curved objects.
  (a) A simple junction catalog (after Chakravarty).
  (b) Curved objects that can be labeled using Chakravarty's catalog.

depicts the nose cone of a rocket. The crucial difference is the angle at which the curves meet the straight lines; the vertical lines can be extremal boundaries only if they are tangential to the curves.

4.1.2. Symmetry and parallelism

Global geometric relations, such as symmetry and parallelism, provide the other major clue to line interpretation. The role of these properties has recently been studied by Marr [16] and his student, Stevens [17]. As they

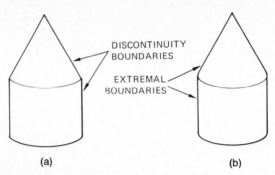

FIG. 4.2. Junction labeling depends on subtle geometric distinctions.
  (a) Slice of cake.
  (b) Rocket nose cone.

observed, lines that appear approximately parallel or symmetrical in an image can be assumed, under the general-position assumption, to correspond to similarly related space curves. Moreover, if the relation is preserved with changes in viewpoint, the lines correspond to extremal boundaries of generalized cylinders, such as those in Fig. 4.3a. Unfortunately, as Fig. 4.3b shows, symmetry and parallelism are also common characteristics of the defining contours of ruled surfaces.

Global relations do provide strong clues for figure-ground discrimination and may also play a significant role in inferring surface orientation. Achieving a better understanding of the role of symmetry and parallelism in perception is an important research objective.

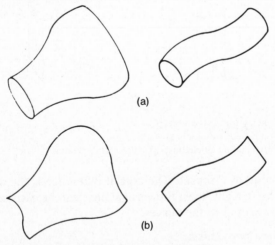

FIG. 4.3. Role of symmetry and parallelism in line classification.
  (a) As evidence of extremal boundaries of generalized cylinders (after Marr).
  (b) As evidence of occluding contours on asymptotic surfaces.

5. Three-Dimensional Line Interpretation

Once lines are classified as physical boundaries, the next step is to determine the constraints (i.e. boundary conditions) they impose on three-dimensional surfaces.

In principle, extremal boundaries are especially simple to interpret; since the surface normal is orthogonal to both the line of sight and the curve in the image, it is determined uniquely at every point. In practice, however, the normal to a noisy, quantized image curve cannot be ascertained with a high degree of accuracy. Some refinement of the estimate of surface normal, based on the results of the subsequent surface interpolation process, may thus be necessary. This problem is dealt with further in Section 6.

Surface discontinuity boundaries constrain the surface normal to one degree of freedom, but first it is necessary to recover the three-dimensional conformation of the corresponding space curve. To recover this conformation from the two-dimensional image, we invoke two domain-independent assumptions: surface smoothness and general position.

The smoothness assumption implies that the space curve bounding a surface will also be smooth. Since continuity is preserved under projection, a smooth curve in space results in a smooth curve in the image. However, because of the inherent ambiguity introduced in projection to a lower dimension, it does not necessarily follow that a smooth image curve must correspond to a smooth space curve. This inference requires the additional assumption that a scene is being viewed from a general position, so that perceived smoothness is not an accident of viewpoint. A general-viewpoint assumption is quite reasonable. In Fig. 2.2, for example, the sharply receding curve is projected into a smooth ellipse from only one viewpoint. Thus, such a curve would be a highly improbable three-dimensional interpretation of an ellipse.

The problem now is to determine which smooth space curve is most likely. Strictly speaking, a maximum-likelihood decision requires knowledge of the nature of the process that generated the space curve. For example, is it a bent wire, the edge of a curved ribbon, or the intersection of two soap films? In the absence of such knowledge, it is reasonable to assume that a given image curve is most likely to correspond to the smoothest possible projectively equivalent space curve. This conjecture appears consistent with human perception [18]: The ellipse in Fig. 2.2 is almost universally perceived as a tilted circle. In many cases, it is also justified on the ecological ground that surfaces tend to assume smooth, minimal-energy configurations.

5.1. Measures of smoothness

The smoothness of a space curve is expressed quantitatively in terms of its intrinsic characteristics, such as differential curvature (k) and torsion (t), as well as vectors giving intrinsic axes of the curve: tangent (T), principal normal (N),

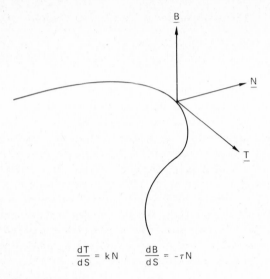

$$\frac{dT}{dS} = kN \qquad \frac{dB}{dS} = -\tau N$$

FIG. 5.1. Intrinsic characteristics of a space curve.

and binormal (B) (See Fig. 5.1). We define k as the reciprocal of the radius of the osculating circle at each point on the curve. N is the vector from the center of curvature normal to the tangent. B, the vector cross product of T and N, defines the normal to the plane of the curve. Torsion t is the spatial derivative of the binormal, and expresses the degree to which the curve twists out of a plane. (For further details, see any standard text on vector differential geometry.)

An obvious measure of the smoothness of a space curve is uniformity of curvature. Thus, one might seek the space curve corresponding to a given image curve for which the integral of k' (the spatial derivative of k) was minimal. This alone, however, is insufficient since the integral of k' could be made arbitrarily small by stretching out the space curve so that it approaches a twisting straight line (see Fig. 5.2). Nor does uniformity of curvature indicate whether a circular arc in the image should correspond to a 3-D circular arc or to part of a helix. A necessary additional constraint in both cases is that the space curve corresponding to a given image curve should be as planar as

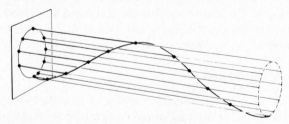

FIG. 5.2. An interpretation that increases uniformity of curvature.

possible or, more precisely, that the integral of its torsion should be minimized.

Integral (1) expresses both the smoothness and planarity of a space curve in terms of a single, locally computed differential measure $d(kB)/ds$. To interpret an image curve, it is thus necessary to find the projectively equivalent space curve that minimizes this integral:

$$\int \left(\frac{d(kB)}{ds}\right)^2 ds = \int (k'^2 + k^2 t^2)\, ds. \tag{1}$$

Intuitively, minimizing (1) corresponds to finding the three-dimensional projection of an image curve that most closely approximates a planar, circular arc for which k' and t are both everywhere zero.

5.2. Recovery techniques

A computer model of this recovery theory was implemented to test its competence. The program accepts a description of an input curve as a sequence of two-dimensional image coordinates. Each input point, in conjunction with

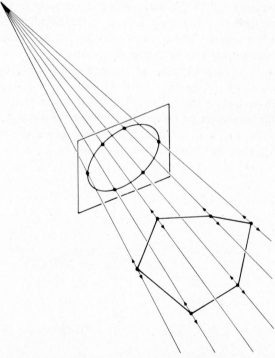

FIG. 5.3. An iterative procedure for determining the optimal space curve corresponding to a given line drawing.

Projective rays constrain the three-dimensional position associated with each image point to one degree of freedom.

an assumed center of projection, defines a ray in space along which the corresponding space curve point is constrained to lie (Fig. 5.3). The program can adjust the distance associated with each space curve point by sliding it along its ray like a bead on a wire. The 3-D coordinates of three consecutive points on the curve determine a circle in space, the normal to which gives the direction of B, and the radius of which gives $1/k$, as shown in Fig. 5.4. From these, a discrete approximation to the smoothness measure, $d(kB)/ds$, can be obtained.

An iterative optimization procedure was used to determine the configuration of points that minimized the integral in (1). The optimization proceeded by independently adjusting each space curve point to minimize $d(kB)/ds$ locally. (Note that local perturbations of z have only local effects on curvature and torsion.)

The program was tested using input coordinates synthesized from known 3-D space curves, so that results could be readily evaluated. Correct 3-D interpretations were produced for simple and closed curves, such as an ellipse, which was interpreted as a tilted circle. However, convergence was slow and somewhat dependent on the initial choice of z-values. For example, the program had difficulties converging to the 'tilted-circle' interpretation of an ellipse if it had been started with z-values either all in a plane parallel to the image plane or randomized to be highly nonplanar.

To overcome these deficiencies, we experimented with an alternative approach based on ellipse-fitting that involved more local constraints. A smooth space curve can be approximated locally by arcs of circles. Circular arcs are projected as elliptic arcs in an image. We already know that an ellipse in the image corresponds to a circle in three-dimensional space; the plane of the circle is obtained by rotating the plane of the ellipse about its major axis by an angle

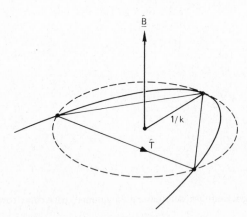

FIG. 5.4. Discrete approximation to B, T, k from 3 points.

equal to arc cos(minor axis/major axis). The relative depth at points along a surface contour can thus be established, in principle, by fitting an ellipse locally (five points suffice to fit a general conic), and then projecting the local curve fragment back onto the plane of the corresponding circular arc of the space curve. If we assume orthographic projection, a simple linear equation results, relating differential depth along the curve to differential changes in its image coordinates, as shown in (2):

$$dz = a \cdot dx + b \cdot dy. \tag{2}$$

The ellipse-fitting method yielded correct 3-D interpretations for ideal image data but, not surprisingly, broke down because of large fitting errors when small amounts of quantization noise were added. Presently under investigation are several alternative approaches that attempt to overcome these problems by exploiting global properties (e.g., segmenting the curve and fitting ellipses to large fragments) and by integrating boundary interpretation with surface interpolation.

5.3. Recovery of polyhedra

Techniques for reconstructing three-dimensional curves based on such criteria as uniformity of curvature break down when the lines involved are not smooth. An important special case concerns figures involving straight lines (polygons and polyhedra). The general-position assumption implies that a straight line in the image corresponds to a straight line in space. For a single line, since curvature is everywhere zero, inclination to the image plane is unconstrained. For figures with multiple straight lines, however, an analog to curvature is provided by the angles between the lines, thus allowing a three-dimensional conformation to be recovered.

To interpret a polygon in the image, we try to find a configuration of the vertices in space that makes the three-dimensional figure as regular as possible. Regularity might be measured in a variety of ways, such as uniformity of lengths of sides or uniformity of angles, but we prefer local features which are more likely to survive occlusion. Accordingly, we tried a few simple experiments on polygons with our 'bead-on-wire' program, using as a regularity measure the sum of the squares of the exterior angles of the projected figure. (Minimizing this measure is equivalent to minimizing the variance of the angles, since their sum is constant.) Although this version of the program was not extensively tested, it was able, for example, to interpret a trapezoid as a tilted rectangle, where that was projectively possible. An interesting subject for further research is to test the program on polygons such as those in Fig. 5.5, for which a planar interpretation seems unnatural. In such cases, regularity should be optimized by a nonplanar interpretation.

For line drawings of polyhedra, a similar approach can be adopted that

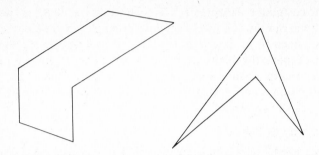

FIG. 5.5. 'Non-planar' polygons.

attempts to find the configuration of vertices that makes the three-dimensional reconstruction as regular as possible. Each vertex of the drawing has an estimated z value, which can be adjusted (by sliding the vertex along a line of sight). Adjustments are made to optimize some global measure of regularity. We have tried using the following: the sum of the squares of angles of faces (which tends to make all angles equal); the sum of the squares of two pi minus the sum of angles at a vertex (which tends to equalize an analog of Gaussian curvature at the vertices); the sum of squares of cosines of face angles (which tends to produce right angles). All these measures have been tried on simple drawings of wireframe tetrahedra, and they all produce similar results: a fairly regular tetrahedral solid.

The program optimizes a measure that is independent of viewpoint and thus tends to produce regular figures. While this result is satisfying, there is evidence that the human visual system is not so objective. If a subject views a nearly symmetrical figure, such as Fig. 5.6, resembling a view of a tetrahedron resting on a table and seen from above, he does not perceive a truly regular solid. Instead he perceives the central vertex as an approximate cubical corner; hence the height of the pyramid produced is less than that of a true tetrahedron. This phenomenon is revealing and worthy of further investigation.

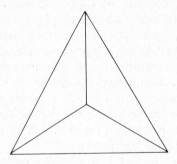

FIG. 5.6. Tetrahedron (top view).

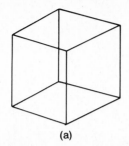 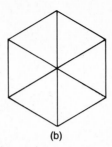

(a)   (b)

FIG. 5.7. Determining the 3-D connectivity of line drawings.
(a) X-junctions suggest a 3-D interpretation.
(b) Central junction suggests a 2-D interpretation.

In interpreting wireframe polyhedra, the vertices and their connectivity were entered into the program. A complete system for interpreting line drawings must determine this information for itself. In Fig. 5.7a, for example, the two X-shaped junctions must be interpreted as two lines passing in space, rather than as four intersecting lines. If this is done, a wireframe cube is readily reconstructed. For Fig. 5.7b, which is a possible, though unlikely, view of a wireframe cube, the central junction tends to be perceived by humans as a single vertex with six radiating lines. Given this assumption, our program will reconstruct a regular hexagonal planar figure in three dimensions, which is also the natural human interpretation.

Psychologists of the Gestalt school have long speculated that the choice of two-space or three-dimensional interpretation is made according to the simplicity and regularity of the result. We think that the mechanism is more subtle, requiring initial local decisions regarding connectivity and occlusion. For example, X-junctions commonly occur in pictures of wireframe figures and frequently indicate occlusion. A perception of three or more concurrent lines, however, is extremely unlikely to result from an accident of viewpoint, and is therefore usually indicative of a true intersection.

While the same basic 'bead-on-wire' model has been successfully applied to figures composed of either smooth curves or straight lines, the optimization criteria used in each case have been different. A complete theory of line drawing interpretation should be able to accommodate both cases; it would be indeed gratifying if a single underlying mechanism could be found.

6. Surface Interpolation

The interpretation of curves in a line drawing, as discussed in the previous section, provides constraints on surface orientation along extremal and discontinuity surface boundaries. The next stage of processing must interpolate smooth surfaces consistent with these boundary conditions.

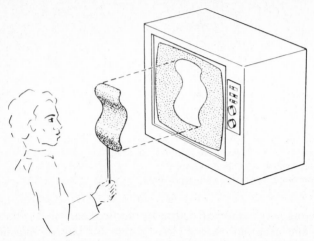

FIG. 6.1. Demonstration of human tendency to perceive a specific surface spanning a closed space curve.

When humans perceive a closed space curve, they also tend to perceive a specific surface spanning it. This phenomenon can be demonstrated very nicely by moving a closed space curve (made from a piece of wire) in front of a field of random visual noise, as provided by a TV set without a signal. The portion of the field framed by the wire appears to leave the plane of the TV screen, and forms a textured three-dimensional surface spanning the space curve like a soap film (see Fig. 6.1).[2] If the space curve undergoes a Necker reversal, so does the perceived surface.

The problem of surface interpolation is not peculiar to line drawing interpretation, but arises as well in surface reconstruction from stereo, texture, and other cues, since data are generally not available at every point in the image. We have implemented a solution for an important general case: the interpolation of quasi-uniformly curved surfaces from initial orientation values and constraints on orientation. The input is assumed to be in the form of sparse arrays, containing local estimates of surface range and orientation, in a viewer-centered coordinate frame, clustered along the curves corresponding to surface boundaries. As we have seen, local estimates are generally subject to error and may be only partially constrained, as at a discontinuity boundary where the surface normals are constrained only to be orthogonal to the boundary elements. The desired output are the filled arrays of range and surface orientation representing the most likely surfaces consistent with the input data.

For any given set of input data, an infinitude of possible surfaces can be

[2]This phenomenon was discovered in collaboration with Richard Gregory of the University of Bristol.

found to fit arbitrarily well. Which of these is indeed the best depends upon assumptions about the nature of surfaces in the world and about the image formation process. Ad hoc smoothing and interpolation schemes that are not rooted in these assumptions lead to incorrect results in simple cases. For example, given an image array containing range values for a few points on the surface of a sphere, iterative local averaging in the image will recover not a spherical surface, but a parabolic one.

6.1. Assumptions about surfaces

Our principal assumption about physical surfaces is that range and orientation are continuous over them. We further assume that each point on the surface is essentially indistinguishable from neighboring points. Thus, in the absence of evidence to the contrary, it follows that local surface characteristics must vary as smoothly as possible and that the total variation over the surface is minimal. Because range and orientation are both defined with reference to a viewer-centered coordinate system, they cannot serve directly as criteria for evaluating the intrinsic smoothness of hypothetical surfaces. The simplest appropriate measures involve the rate at which orientation changes over the surface; principal curvatures (k_1, k_2), Gaussian (total) curvature $(k_1 \cdot k_2)$, mean curvature $(k_1 + k_2)$, and variations thereof all reflect this rate of change [19]. Two reasonable definitions of surface smoothness are the uniformity of some appropriate measure of curvature (as in [4, p. 19]) and the minimality of integrated squared curvature [18]. Uniformity can be defined as minimal variance or minimal integrated magnitude of gradient.

The choice of a measure and how to employ it (e.g., whether to minimize the measure or its derivative) depends, in general, upon the nature of the process that gave rise to the surface. For example, surfaces formed by elastic membranes (e.g., soap films) are constrained to minimum-energy configurations characterized by minimal area and zero mean curvature [20]; surfaces formed by bending sheets of inelastic material (e.g., paper or sheet metal) are characterized by zero Gaussian curvature [21]; surfaces formed by machining operations (e.g., planes, cylinders, and spheres) have constant principal curvatures.

Probably none of the above mentioned curvature measures is inherently superior, particularly in view of the various close relationships that exist among them. We note, for example, that minimizing the integrated square of mean curvature is equivalent to minimizing the sum of integrated squares of principal curvatures and the integrated Gaussian curvature, G, as shown by

$$\int (k_1 + k_2)^2 \, da = \int k_1^2 \, da + \int k_2^2 \, da + 2 \int k_1 \cdot k_2 \, da$$

$$= \int k_1^2 \, da + \int k_2^2 \, da + 2 \int G \, da. \tag{3}$$

We also note that to make a curvature uniform by minimizing the variance of any measure over a surface is equivalent to minimizing the total squared curvature, provided that the integral of curvature is constant. This follows from the well-known fact that, for any function $f(x)$,

$$\text{Variance of } f = \int (f - \bar{f})^2 \, dx = \int f^2 \, dx - \left[\int f \, dx\right]^2 \Big/ \Delta x \qquad (4)$$

On any developable surface for which the Gaussian curvature G is everywhere zero, and on a surface for which the orientation is known everywhere at its boundary (e.g., the boundary is extremal), the integral of G and its integrated square are equivalent.

In itself, however, uniformity of the Gaussian curvature is not sufficiently constraining. By this criterion, any developable surface is perfectly uniform. Therefore, considerable ambiguity remains, as is evident in Fig. 6.2 where all the developable surfaces satisfy the same boundary conditions (provided by two parallel lines in the image). A secondary constraint, such as uniformity of mean curvature, is thus necessary to find the smoothest developable surface.

In the absence of specific assumptions about the nature of a surface, it is reasonable to adopt a pragmatic approach. We seek a technique that yields exact reconstructions for the special symmetrical cases of spherical and cylindrical surfaces, as well as intuitively reasonable reconstructions for other smooth surfaces. In particular, given surface orientations that are defined around a circular outline corresponding to the extremal boundary of a sphere, or along two parallel lines corresponding to the extremal boundary of a right circular cylinder, we require interpolation to yield the correct spherical or cylindrical surface with uniform (Gaussian, mean, and principal) curvature. These test cases are important because they require reconstructions that are symmetrical in three dimensions and are independent of viewpoint. Many

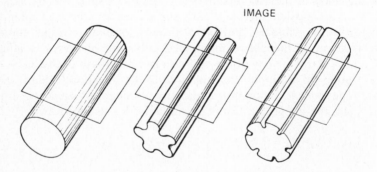

FIG. 6.2. Surfaces with zero Gaussian curvature satisfying common boundary conditions.

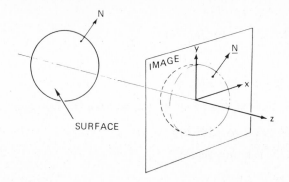

FIG. 6.3. Coordinate frame.

simple interpolation techniques fail this test, producing surfaces that are too flat or too peaked. If we get good performance on the test cases, we can expect reasonable performance in general.

6.2. A reconstruction algorithm

Although in principle correct reconstruction for our test cases can be obtained in many ways, the complexity and generality of the interpolation process depends critically upon the representation employed. For example, representing surface orientation in terms of gradient space leads to difficulties, because gradient variation is extremely nonlinear across the image of a smooth surface, becoming infinite at extremal boundaries. We shall now propose an approach that results in elegantly simple interpolation for our test cases.

6.2.1. *Coordinate frames*

Given an image plane, we shall assume a right-handed Cartesian coordinate system with x- and y-axes lying in the plane (see Fig. 6.3). We also assume orthogonal projection in the direction of the z-axis. Each image point (x, y) has an associated range, $Z(x, y)$; the corresponding scene point is thus specified by $(x, y, Z(x, y))$.

Each image point also has an associated unit vector that specifies the local surface orientation at the corresponding scene point:

$$N(x, y) = (N_x(x, y), N_y(x, y), N_z(x, y)) .$$

Since N is normal to the surface Z,

$$N_x/N_z = -\partial Z/\partial x \quad \text{and} \quad N_y/N_z = -\partial Z/\partial y . \tag{5}$$

(The derivatives $\partial Z/\partial x$ and $\partial Z/\partial y$ correspond to p and q when the surface normal is represented in gradient space form $(p, q, -1)$.)

Differentiating (5), we obtain

$$\partial(N_x/N_z)/\partial y = -\partial^2 Z/\partial y \cdot \partial x$$

and   (6)

$$\partial(N_y/N_z)/\partial x = -\partial^2 Z/\partial x \cdot \partial y.$$

For a smooth surface, the terms on the right of (6) are equal; hence

$$\partial(N_x/N_z)/\partial y = \partial(N_y/N_z)/\partial x.\tag{7}$$

Finally, since N is a unit vector,

$$N_x^2 + N_y^2 + N_z^2 = 1.\tag{8}$$

6.2.2. Semicircle

Let us begin by considering a two-dimensional version of surface reconstruction. In Fig. 6.4 we observe that the unit normal to a semicircular surface cross section is everywhere aligned with the radius. It therefore follows that triangles OPQ and PST are similar, and so

$$OP:OQ:QP = PS:PT:TS.\tag{9}$$

But the vector OP is the radius vector (x, z), and PS is the unit normal vector (N_x, N_z). Moreover, the length OP is constant (equal to R), and the length PS is also constant (equal to unity). Hence

$$N_x = x/R \quad \text{and} \quad N_z = z/R.\tag{10}$$

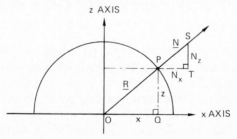

z AXIS

x AXIS

FIG. 6.4. Linear variation of N on a semicircle.

6.2.3. Sphere

Now consider a three-dimensional spherical surface, as shown in Fig. 6.5. Here too the radius and normal vectors are aligned, and so from similar figures we have

$$N_x = x/R, \quad N_y = y/R \quad \text{and} \quad N_z = z/R.\tag{11}$$

It should be noted that N_x and N_y are both linear functions of x unit length.

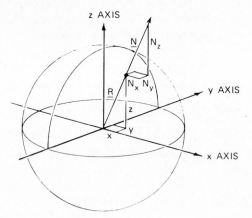

FIG. 6.5. Linear variation of N on a sphere.

6.2.4. *Cylinder*

The case of the right circular cylinder is only a little more complicated. In Fig. 6.6 observe a cylinder of radius R centered upon a line in the x–y plane, inclined at an angle A to the x axis. Let d be the distance of point $(x, y, 0)$ from the axis of the cylinder. Then

$$d = y \cdot \cos A - x \cdot \sin A \tag{12}$$

and

$$z^2 = R^2 - d^2 . \tag{13}$$

Let N_d be the component of vector N parallel to the x–y plane: it is clearly

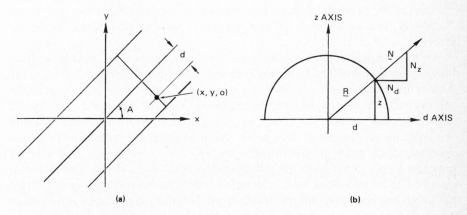

FIG. 6.6. Linear variation of N on a cylinder.

perpendicular to the axis of the cylinder. Now, since a cross section of the cylinder is analogous to our first, two-dimensional case,

$$N_d = d/R .\tag{14}$$

Taking components of N_d parallel to the x and y axes:

$$N_x = N_d \cdot \sin A \quad \text{and} \quad N_y = -N_d \cdot \cos A .\tag{15}$$

Substituting in this equation for N_d and then for d, yields

$$N_x = ((y \cos A - x \cdot \sin A) \cdot \sin A)/R$$

and   (16)

$$N_y = (-(y \cdot \cos A - x \cdot \sin A) \cdot \cos A)/R .$$

Observe that, as was true for the sphere, N_x and N_y are linear functions of x and y, and that N_z can be derived from N_x and N_y.

6.3. A computational model for surface reconstruction

Because of the global nature of the linearity of N_x and N_y for spherical and cylindrical surfaces, it is possible to interpolate the normal vector everywhere in the image from known values at any three noncollinear points. Moreover, N_x and N_y can be treated as independent variables, and yet the vector field produced is guaranteed to satisfy the integrability constraint of (7). This may be verified by substituting for N_x, N_y, and N_z from (11) or (16) (for the sphere or cylinder, respectively) and (8). Hence, the orientation field can be integrated to recover range values.

   For arbitrary surfaces, approximated locally by spherical or cylindrical patches, N_x and N_y may be regarded as linear locally, but not globally. The interpolation scheme, therefore, must also be local in nature. While in principle the integrability constraint should not be ignored, in actual practice it is weak; N_x and N_y can be interpolated independently without introducing significant errors.

   We have implemented a recovery model that exploits these notions of local linearity and separability to reconstruct arbitrary smooth surfaces. The overall system organization is a subset of the array stack architecture first proposed in [4]. In concept it consists of two primary arrays: one for range and the other for surface normal vectors. The arrays are in registration with each other and with the input image. Values at each point within an array are constrained by local processes that maintain smoothness, as well as by processes that operate between arrays to maintain the differential/integral relationship. The system is designed to be initialized with orientation values and constraints derived from the preceding boundary interpretation stage. (Partially constrained orientations along discontinuity boundaries, however, have not yet been implemented.)

6.4. The interpolation process

At each point in the orientation array we can imagine a process that is attempting to make the two observable components of the normal, N_x and N_y, each vary as linearly as possible in both x and y. The process looks at the values of N_x (or N_y) in a small patch surrounding the point, and attempts to infer the linear function, $f = ax + by + c$, that best models N_x locally. It then tries to relax the value for the point so as to reduce the supposed error.

There are numerous ways to implement such a process, and we shall describe some with which we have experimented. One of the simplest is to perform a local least-squares fit, deriving the three parameters a, b, and c. The function f is then used to estimate a corrected value for the central point. The least-squares fitting process is equivalent to taking weighted averages of the values in the patch, using three different sets of weights:

$$\sum_i x_i \cdot N_{xi}, \qquad \sum_i y_i \cdot N_{xi}, \qquad \sum_i N_{xi}. \tag{17}$$

The three parameters of f are given by three linear combinations of these three averages.

If we are careful to use a symmetrical patch with its origin at the point in question, the sets of weights and the linear combinations are particularly simple—the three sums in (17) correspond, respectively, to

$$a \cdot \sum_i x_i^2, \qquad b \cdot \sum_i y_i^2, \qquad c \cdot \sum_i 1. \tag{18}$$

Equations (17) and (18) can be readily solved for a, b, and c; but note that under the above assumptions $f(0, 0) = c$, so that computation of a and b is unnecessary for updating the central point, unless derivatives are also of interest.

An alternative approach to interpolation follows from the fact that a linear function satisfies the equation

$$\nabla^2 f = 0. \tag{19}$$

The numerical solution of this equation, subject to boundary conditions, is well known. The ∇^2 operator may be discretely approximated by the operator

$$\begin{array}{ccc} & -1 & \\ -1 & 4 & -1 \\ & -1 & \end{array}.$$

Applying this operator at a point in the image leads to an equation of the form

$$4N_{x0} - N_{x1} - N_{x2} - N_{x3} - N_{x4} = 0, \tag{20}$$

and hence, rewriting,

$$N_{x0} = (N_{x1} + N_{x2} + N_{x3} + N_{x4})/4 \ . \tag{21}$$

Equation (21) is used in a relaxation process that iteratively replaces the value of N_{x0} at each point with the average of its neighbors. Although the underlying theory is different from least-squares fitting, the two methods lead to essentially the same discrete numerical implementation.

The iterative local-averaging approach works well in the interior regions of a surface, but difficulties arise near surface boundaries where orientation is permitted to be discontinuous. Care must be taken to ensure that the patch under consideration does not fall across the boundary, otherwise estimation of the parameters will be in error. On the other hand, it is necessary to be able to estimate values right up to the boundary, which, for example, may result from occlusion by another surface.

The least-squares method is applicable to any shape of patch which we can simply truncate at the boundary. However, the linear combination used to compute each parameter depends upon the particular shape, so we must either precompute the coefficients for all possible patches (256 for a 3×3 area) or resort to inverting a 3×3 matrix to derive them for each particular patch. Neither of these alternatives is attractive, although we might consider pre-computing coefficients for the more common patch shapes, and deriving them when needed for the less common ones.

The above disadvantages can be overcome by decomposing the two-dimensional fitting process into several one-dimensional fits. We do this by considering a set of line segments passing through the central point, as shown in Fig. 6.7. Along each line we fit a function, $f = ax + c$, to the data values and thus establish a corrected value for the point. The independent estimates produced from the set of line segments can then be averaged. If the line segments are each symmetrical about the central point, then the corrected central value is here too simply the average of the values along the line. The principal advantage of the decomposition is that we can discard line segments that overlap a boundary; often at least one is left to provide a corrected value. We would prefer to use short symmetrical line segments, since they form a compact

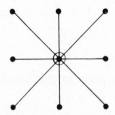

FIG. 6.7. Symmetric linear interpolation operators.

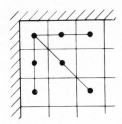

FIG. 6.8. Asymmetric linear interpolation operators.

operator, but to get into corners we also need to resort to one-sided segments (which effectively extrapolate the central value). We have implemented a scheme that uses the compact symmetric operator when it can, or, if this is not possible an asymmetric operator (see Fig. 6.8).

We have experimented with a rather different technique for coping with boundary discontinuities. It is of interest because it involves multiple inter-related arrays of information. For each component of the orientation vector we introduce two auxiliary arrays containing estimates of its gradient in the x and y directions. For surfaces of uniform curvature, such as the sphere and cylinder, these gradients will be constant over the surface. For others we assume they will be slowly varying. To reconstruct the components of the normal, we first compute its derivatives, then locally average the derivatives and, finally, reintegrate them to obtain updated orientation estimates.

Derivatives at a point are estimated by considering line segments through the point parallel to the axes. We again fit a linear function, but now we record its slope, rather than its intercept, and insert it into the appropriate gradient array. In the interior of a region we may use a symmetric line segment, while near boundaries, as before, we use a one-sided segment. The gradient arrays are smoothed by an operator that takes a weighted average over a patch which may easily be truncated at a boundary. (To form the average over an arbitrarily shaped patch all that is necessary is to compute the sum of weighted values of points within the patch and the sum of the weights, and then divide the former by the latter.) A corrected orientation value can be computed from a neigh-boring value by adding (or subtracting) the appropriate gradient. Each neigh-boring point not separated by a boundary produces such an estimate, where-upon all the estimates are averaged.

6.5. Estimation of surface range

The process of integrating orientation values to obtain estimates of range Z is very similar to that used in reintegrating orientation gradients. We again use a relaxation technique and iteratively compute estimates for Z from neighboring values and the local surface orientation. Here we need orientations expressed as $\partial Z/\partial x$ and $\partial Z/\partial y$, which are obtained from N_x and N_y by (5). At least one absolute value of Z must be furnished to serve as a constant of integration. Providing more than one initial Z value constrains the surface to pass through the specified points. However, since the inverse path from Z to N has not yet been implemented, the resulting range surface is not guaranteed to be consistent with the orientations.

6.6. Experimental results

An interactive system was implemented in MAINSAIL [22] to experiment with and to evaluate the various interpolation algorithms discussed above. This system includes facilities for generating quadric surface test cases, selecting interpolation options, and plotting error distributions.

6.6.1. *Test cases*

How well does each of the above interpolation techniques reconstruct the test surfaces? To answer this, we performed a series of experiments in which the correct values of N_x and N_y were fixed along the extremal boundaries of a sphere or cylinder, as shown in Fig. 6.9. The surface orientations reconstructed from these boundary conditions were compared with those of ideal spherical or cylindrical surfaces generated analytically.

The first set of experiments involved a sphere of radius 7, centered in a 17×17 interpolation array. We deliberately used a coarse grid to test the accuracy of the reconstruction under difficult conditions. (A coarse grid also has the experimental advantage of minimizing the number of iterations needed for convergence.) Correct values for N_x and N_y were fixed at points in the array falling just inside the circular extremal boundary of the sphere. Table 6.1 summarizes the results for this test case, in which various interpolation operators were used.

The results of the spherical test case are almost uniformly good. In all cases except gradient smoothing, the maximum absolute error is less than one percent after 100 iterations ($-1.0 < N_x, N_y < 1.0$). On any cross section through

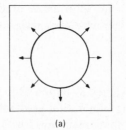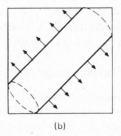

(a)   (b)

FIG. 6.9. Spherical (a) and cylindrical (b) test cases.

TABLE 6.1. Interpolation results for spherical test case

Operator	Iterations	Errors in N_x, N_y	
		Max. abs.	RMS
Uniformly weighted average over a	50	0.0165	0.0075
4-connected 3×3 patch	100	0.0004	0.0002
Uniformly weighted average over an	50	0.0007	0.0003
8-connected 3×3 patch	100	0.0000006	0.0000003
∇^2 over a 4-connected 3×3 patch	50	0.006	0.003
	100	0.00006	0.00003
8-way linear interpolation/	50	0.004	0.002
extrapolation	100	0.00002	0.00001
4-way linear interpolation/extrapolation	50	0.03	0.01
(just parallel to x and y axes)	100	0.001	0.0007
Gradient smoothing over a 4-connected	50	0.40	0.19
3×3 patch	100	0.26	0.12
	200	0.10	0.05
Gradient smoothing over an 8-connected	50	0.13	0.05
3×3 patch	100	0.03	0.01
	200	0.001	0.0005

the sphere the maximum error occurs approximately a quarter of the way in from both boundary points, the error being zero at the boundary points and also on the symmetry axis halfway between them. We conclude that 8-connected, uniformly weighted averaging and 8-way linear inter-polation/extrapolation are superior in terms of speed of convergence, with the linear operator preferred because of its advantages at boundaries and corners. These conclusions generalize to all the test cases we have studied to date. Thus, for the sake of brevity, the experimental results that follow are reported only for the 8-way linear operator.

The second set of experiments involved a cylinder of radius 6, centered in a 17×17 interpolation array. Here too correct values for N_x and N_y were fixed at points in the array falling just inside the parallel lines representing the extremal boundaries of the cylinder. With the cylinder oriented parallel to the x- or y-axis, the maximum absolute error in N_x or N_y after 50 iterations was 0.018 and the RMS average error 0.01. After 100 iterations, the absolute error dropped to 0.0004 and the RMS average to 0.0002. When the major axis of the cylinder was inclined 60 degrees to the x-axis, the errors look much larger: 0.12 absolute and 0.03 RMS after 50 iterations; 0.108 absolute and 0.03 RMS after 100 iterations; 0.09 absolute and 0.02 RMS after 300 iterations.

The erroneous orientations were concentrated solely in the upper right and lower left corners of the array, where the cylinder boundary is effectively occluded by the array edge. The slow rate of convergence is due to extrapola-tion of values from the central region, where the orientations are very accurate, into these partially occluded corners. After 1000 iterations, however, orientations are highly accurate throughout the array.

6.6.2. *Other smooth surfaces*

Since that orientations for uniformly curved surfaces can be accurately reconstructed, the obvious next question to ask is how well the algorithms perform on other surfaces for which curvature is not globally uniform. A simple but interesting case is that of a right circular cone for which curvature along a generator is zero everywhere and curvature in an orthogonal direction is inversely proportional to the distance from the apex. From Fig. 6.10 it is clear that the component of the surface normal in the direction of the cone's axis is constant. Thus it is trivially linear and will be properly reconstructed by local averaging. For any cross section of the cone in the image the normal component perpendicular to the cone's axis varies linearly between the antisymmetric values at the extremal boundaries. The rate of variation, however, is inversely proportional to the distance from the apex, which violates the assumption of global linearity. (For a cone with its apex at the origin and its axis aligned with the y-axis we have $N_x = K \cdot x/y$, where K is a constant of proportionality.) Nonetheless, the algorithm performed more than adequately on a number of conical test cases. For example, a reconstruction was performed for a 17×17 image of a cone (semiangle of 0.4 radians) with orientations initialized along extremal boundaries. After 100 iterations the errors were as follows: for N_x, 0.192 maximum absolute error and 0.073 average RMS error, and for N_y, 0.0014 maximum absolute and 0.0065 RMS error. After 400 iterations the maximum absolute errors had dropped to 0.0098 for N_x and 0.013 for N_y while the RMS errors were 0.0036 for N_x and 0.0064 for N_y. The maximum error in N_x was located at the point farthest from the boundaries (i.e. on the axis of symmetry, at the edge of the image), and N_x was underestimated. The latter was to be expected, since it was extrapolated linearly from the interior of the image; the true value, however, falls off as $1/y$.

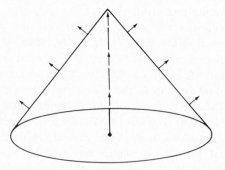

FIG. 6.10. Normals of a cone.

The results for cones should extend to generalized cylinders, which have a circular cross-section whose radius varies along a well-defined axis. Such bodies comprise a broad range of common shapes, from anatomical components (limbs, trunk) to household items, such as the vases in Fig. 6.11. Where the radius of the cross section is locally constant the surface approximates a cylinder and will be reconstructed fairly accurately; where the variation in radius is roughly linear the surface is approximately conical and, as we have seen, will be treated reasonably.

Any inaccuracies in reconstructing cones and generalized cylinders arise because the interpolation is two-dimensional. A one-dimensional algorithm, interpolating perpendicularly to the symmetry axis, would reconstruct the circular cross sections of these objects exactly. While one-dimensional interpolation is simpler, it requires the additional step of first determining the symmetry axis. A simple experiment suggests that people perform two-dimensional interpolation, despite their well-known ability to determine axes of symmetry. The two vases of Fig. 6.11 have generators of the same shape, but differing radii. For the broader vase the perceived variation of depth along the axis of symmetry is less pronounced than it would be if reconstruction were perfect. One explanation is that the reconstruction is two-dimensional, which tends to smooth the surface far from the boundaries, rather than one-dimensional, which produces accurate cross sections. There may, of course, be other explanations. It is interesting to note that, if the broad vase is interpreted as a rectangular sheet undulating in depth, rather than a solid of revolution, the perceived variation of depth along the symmetry axis becomes much more pronounced.

Another interesting case to consider is interpretation of the surface defined by an elliptical boundary. In this case, however, we immediately run into the problem of what is to be taken as the 'correct' reconstruction. When people are asked what solid surface they perceive, they usually report either an elongated or squat object, roughly corresponding to a solid of revolution about the major or minor axis, respectively. The elongated object is preferred, and one can

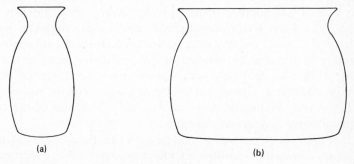

(a)   (b)

FIG. 6.11. The same generator, but different perceived surfaces.

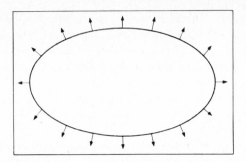

FIG. 6.12. Elliptical test case.

argue that it is more plausible on the grounds of general viewpoint (a fat, squat object looks elongated only from a narrow range of viewpoints). When presented with initial orientations for an elliptical extremal boundary (Fig. 6.12), our algorithms reconstruct an elongated object with approximately uniform curvature about the major axis. In effect, they reconstruct a generalized cylinder [16], but without explicitly invoking processes to find the axis of symmetry or matching the opposite boundaries.

In a representative experiment, initial values for N_x and N_y were fixed inside an elliptic extremal boundary (major axis 15, minor axis 5). The reconstructed orientations were then compared with the orientations of the solid of revolution, generated when the ellipse was rotated about its major axis. The resulting errors after 50 iterations were as follows: for N_x, 0.02 maximum absolute error and 0.006 average RMS error; for N_y, 0.005 maximum absolute and 0.002 RMS.

6.6.3. Occluding boundaries

We also wish to know how well the reconstruction process performs when the orientation is not known at all boundary points. In particular, when the surface of interest is occluded by another object, the occluding boundary imposes no constraints. In such cases the orientation at the boundary must be inferred from that of neighboring points, just as at any other interior point of the surface. The 8-way linear operator will handle these situations correctly, since it is careful to avoid interpolating across boundaries. We take advantage of this capability by treating the borders of the orientation array as occluding boundaries, so that we may deal with objects that extend beyond the image. For example, spherical surface orientations were correctly recovered from the partially visible boundary shown in Fig. 6.13. The case of the tilted cylinder discussed above is a second example.

Experiments with occluded boundaries raised the question of just how little boundary information suffices to effect recovery. We experimented with a limiting case in which we attempted to reconstruct surface orientation of a

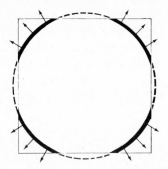
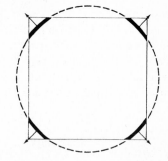

FIG. 6.13. Test case with occluding boundaries.   FIG. 6.14. Test case with sparse boundary
conditions.

sphere from only four initial boundary values at the corners of the array. This
corresponds to the image of a large sphere whose boundary circumscribes the
square array (see Fig. 6.14). The surface orientations produced from these
extremely sparse initial conditions were as accurate as when all the boundary
orientations are given, but more iterations were required. For example, when
the N_x and N_y orientations at the corners of a 17×17 square array were fixed
to the values for a sphere of radius 12, the maximum absolute error of the
reconstructed interior orientations after 400 iterations was less than 0.005.

6.6.4. *Qualitative boundary conditions*

In each of the above experiments, boundary conditions were provided by
specifying exact orientations at all unoccluded points along extremal boundaries. The values of N_x and N_y at these points were initially inserted in the
arrays and were held fixed through all iterations. In a complete visual system it
is necessary to derive these values from the shape of extremal boundaries in
the image. In principle this can be done easily since the surface normal at each
point is constrained to be orthogonal both to the tangent to the boundary and
to the line of sight. (For orthogonal projection, the normal must thus be
parallel to the image plane.) In a spatially quantized image, the accurate
determination of tangent is difficult, particularly when the object is not very
large compared with the quantization grid.

One way to overcome this problem is to introduce the notion of qualitative,
partially constraining boundary conditions. We can, for example, constrain the
surface normals along a quantized extremal boundary to be approximately
parallel to the image plane and point outward across the boundary. We then
rely on the iterative process to reconstruct exact values for the normals at
points on the boundary, treating them just like interior points. To implement
this approach we introduce a step that, with each iteration, checks the orientation at boundary points. For each boundary element adjacent to the point we
check whether the surface normal has a component directed outward across it.

If it does not, the value of N_x or N_y is modified appropriately. The value of N_z is also checked to be close to zero, and vector N is normalized to ensure that it remains a unit vector. This process was applied to the spherical, cylindrical, and elliptical test cases; after only 100 iterations it was found to yield orientation values accurate to within ten percent for both interior and boundary points. The principal limitation on accuracy appears to be the coarse quantization grid being used.

7. Discussion

7.1. Summary

We have made a start toward a computational model for interpreting line drawings as three-dimensional surfaces. In the first section we proposed a three-step model for interpretation, based on constraints on local surface orientation along extremal and discontinuity boundaries. We then described specific computational approaches for two key processes: recovering the three-dimensional conformation of a space curve (e.g., a surface boundary) from its two-dimensional projection in an image, and interpolating smooth surfaces from orientation constraints along extremal boundaries.

Some important unresolved problems remain. Our technique for interpreting a three-dimensional space curve is slow and ineffectual on noisy image curves. Furthermore, the surface interpolation technique must be extended to handle partially constrained orientations along discontinuity boundaries.

Aspects of line-drawing understanding not yet considered include the effects of context and high-level knowledge. As Fig. 7.1 illustrates, the interpretation of a surface depends strongly on the perception of adjoining surfaces. Thus, the top surface of the object in Fig. 7.1a appears to undulate in height, while the identically drawn top surface of the object in Fig. 7.1b appears to undulate in depth. Moreover, as suggested in Fig. 7.2, interpretation

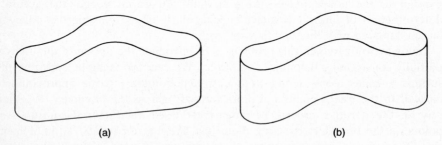

(a)   (b)

FIG. 7.1. Perception of surface shape depends upon adjoining surfaces (after Yonas).
  (a) Top surface appears to undulate in height.
  (b) Top surface appears to undulate in depth.

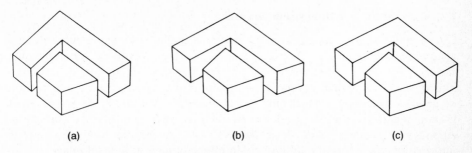

(a)   (b)   (c)

FIG. 7.2. Perception of object shape depends on context (after Shepard).

is influenced even by nearby surfaces that are not directly connected (although we suspect that this influence depends upon a connection through an implied ground plane). Higher levels of interpretation interact with surface perception, as illustrated in Boring's familiar ambiguous figure, "Mother-in-Law/Wife"; when the interpretation flips at the cognitive level, it does so at the surface level as well (Fig. 7.3). Many psychologists believe that environmental cues, such as the predominance of vertical and horizontal orientations, right angles, parallel lines (leading to vanishing points), and, of course, familiar views of familiar objects play an important role in interpreting pictures of both natural and man-made scenes [23]. A competent line drawing interpretation system must eventually take all of these factors into account.

FIG. 7.3. E.G. Boring's figure—ambiguous mother-in-law.
   She is seen sometimes as a young girl, at other times as an old woman. These are the two most probable object interpretations of this figure, which are entertained in turn.

7.2. Relevance to machine vision research

Our interest in line drawings is motivated principally by their possible role in a general theory of low-level vision, specifically their potential for explaining surface perception in regions where photometry is uninformative or too complex to model analytically. Line drawings are, however, an extreme abstraction of gray-level imagery, containing no photometric variation. As every artist knows, qualitative shading gradients can be extremely helpful—for example in emphasizing surface relief. It is thus relevant to inquire how photometric information can be used qualitatively in interpreting a gray-level image.

Photometric information is initially used to extract a line drawing from the image. The two major steps in extraction are the detection of intensity discontinuities and the discrimination of those discontinuities that correspond to significant surface discontinuities.

While it is naive to expect a perfect description of intensity discontinuities from any low-level process, David Marr's recent technique for edge detection appears to perform somewhat better than earlier approaches [24]. Marr suggests that edge events correspond to zero crossings in the second derivative of band-passed versions of an image, obtained by convolving the image with Gaussian masks of various sizes. Aside from the physiological justifications that motivated Marr, the approach has some very attractive practical consequences: edges are found without arbitrary thresholds, they are guaranteed to form closed contours; both step and gradient edges are detected over a wide range of slopes, independent of orientation; weak edges are detected in noise (because of the use of large mask sizes, the smallest of which covers nearly 1000 pixels); the convolved image can be reconstructed from just zero crossing information (which suggests that little information may be lost in a line drawing). Drawings derived from zero crossings, while still far from perfect, should be good enough to at least initialize the recovery process; erroneous fragments can be subsequently refined in the light of three-dimensional interpretations [4].

Following detection, intensity discontinuities corresponding to surface discontinuities must be distinguished from those corresponding to shadows, surface markings, and other nonstructural features. Our research on intrinsic images leads us to believe that such discrimination may be possible using local image features that do not involve analytic photometry. Illumination edges (shadows), for example, can be distinguished on the basis of their high contrast (typically greater than 30:1) and textural continuity across the edge. Reflectance edges (painted surface markings, textures) can be distinguished by equality of the ratios of intensity to the intensity gradient on both sides of the edge, as well as by the continuity of gradient direction across the edge. Gloss, highlights, and other specularities have the properties of light sources and can be distinguished by means of local tests developed by Ullman [25] and Forbus [26]. After illumination, reflectance, and specular edges are eliminated, the remaining discontinuities correspond to legitimate surface discontinuities: extremal boundaries, occlusion edges, intersection edges, creases, folds, dents, and so forth.

A natural scene often contains so much surface detail that a line drawing representing all visible edges would be of unmanageable complexity. The crucial question is how to determine which edges represent significant detail for the task in hand, and should therefore be included. This question, faced by every artist in sketching a scene, must also be dealt with by any automatic procedure for line-drawing extraction. While we have no solution to this problem, it would seem reasonable to employ a hierarchy of line drawings— progressing from a crude sketch of major surfaces to the detailed micro-structure of local surface features. The levels at which a given edge should be represented would seem to be related to the spatial frequency bands of a hierarchical edge detection scheme such as Marr's. The lowest-frequency edges would delimit the larger surfaces, and the resulting reconstruction would correspond to a first-order approximation of them. Evidence from higher-frequency bands corresponding to smaller surface detail could refine this description.

Having established a subset of edges comprising a line drawing at a manageable level of detail, photometric information can be used qualitatively for inferring the physical nature of both boundaries and surfaces.

The reasonable assumption that illumination incident on a surface is locally continuous (e.g., from some unspecified, distant point source) leads to a variety of potentially valuable clues. For example, it implies that shading gradients on Lambertian surfaces are caused predominantly by surface curvature and not by a falloff of illumination with distance, that gradient direction corresponds approximately to the direction of maximum curvature on the surface, and that inflections in gray value often correspond to inflections in surface curvature. At extremal boundaries the gradient normal to the boundary is thus likely to be very high, while at occluding contours the gradient is likely to be high along the boundary in the direction of maximum curvature (Fig. 7.4). At arbitrary points on a surface, intensity gradients and their derivatives in two orthogonal directions can provide a clue to Gaussian curvature, indicating whether the surface is locally planar, cylindrical, elliptic (e.g., spherical), or hyperbolic (inflexive) [11]. They indicate the presence of a bump or dent on an otherwise smooth surface, as well as the relative height of the anomaly.

Qualitative photometric cues are also valuable on specular surfaces. As Kent Stevens observed [17, Section 3.2.2, p. 143], a localized highlight is indicative of an elliptic surface, while a linearly extended one is indicative of a cylindrical surface. Steven's mathematical results are consistent with psychological findings by J. Beck that the presence or absence of a few highlights profoundly influence a viewer's perception of a surface as entirely shiny or matte, or as either curved or flat (see Fig. 7.5) [27]. It is almost as if the presence of

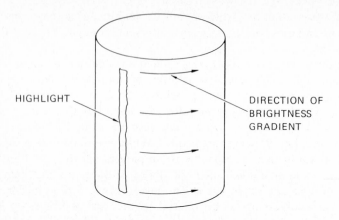

HIGHLIGHT

DIRECTION OF
BRIGHTNESS
GRADIENT

FIG. 7.4. Qualitative photometric cues to surface shape and boundary type.

FIG. 7.5. The effect of highlights on surface perception (after Beck).

Highlights, or regions of strong specular reflection, on a three-dimensional object such as a vase help to make the entire surface of the vase appear glossy (left). When the photograph is retouched to remove the highlights, the surface of the vase appears matte (right).

highlights serves as a switch for selecting a global interpretation. Here too it is significant that highlights and gloss contours can be locally distinguished from other image intensity features [25, 26].

The above observations, together with the experimental results documented in Fig. 1.3, lead us to speculate that the primary role of photometric cues in human vision may be in qualitative determination of boundary and surface types, rather than in quantitative determination of shape, as has long been advocated by Horn [1]. If this is true, an analogous case could be made for the qualitative interpretation of texture gradients.

Surface boundaries depicted in line drawings provide a good estimation of surface structure in the absence of other information. In a complete vision system information from contours must be combined with information from many other sources—such as texture gradient, stereopsis, and shading—to recover a more accurate and complete description of surface shape. Since contour, texture, and stereopsis rely on the geometry of intensity discontinuities, rather than the photometry of shading gradients, they are inherently easier to model. Moreover, since discontinuities can be classified by using only qualitative photometry, it is easier to decide that a geometric cue is applicable than to decide that a shading gradient should be attributed to surface curvature (in contrast to, say, an illumination gradient). These thoughts suggest that geometric cues may be primary in early vision, providing an estimate of surface structure that can then be refined, where possible, by exploiting photometric cues, e.g., to detect bumps and dents. Once the surface structure has been recovered, reflectance characteristics can be properly estimated by using the techniques of Land [28] and Horn [2]; strictly speaking, these are applicable only over continuous surfaces.

This view that geometric cues may be primary is not necessarily inconsistent with our previous recovery model for intrinsic images [4]; a key concept of which was the simultaneous recovery of all surface attributes. The geometric cues simply provide additional information that can be used to improve the boundary conditions that initialize the recovery process. However, the possibility of an alternative sequential recovery model that recovers surface structure from geometric cues before involving photometric characteristics is intriguing. A critical psychological experiment to determine which model most closely resembles the human visual process would be valuable.

ACKNOWLEDGMENT

This paper was begun at SRI, jointly supported by NSF, DARPA, and NASA, and was completed at Fairchild.

Albert Yonas, University of Minnesota, and Andrew Hansen, currently at SRI, participated significantly in the early development of our ideas. Discussions with Richard Gregory, University of Bristol, and Andrew Witkin, MIT (now at SRI), were also valuable.

REFERENCES

1. Horn, B.K.P., Understanding image intensities, *Artificial Intelligence* **8**(2) (1977) 201–231.
2. Horn, B.K.P., Determining lightness from an image, *Comput. Graphics and Image Processing* **3** (1974) 277–299.
3. Marr, D., Representing visual information, in: A. Hanson and E.M. Riseman, Eds., *Computer Vision Systems* (Academic Press, New York, 1978).
4. Barrow, H.G. and Tenenbaum, J.M., Recovering intrinsic scene characteristics from images, in: A. Hanson and E. Riseman, Eds., *Computer Vision Systems* (Academic Press, New York, 1978).
5. Shepard, R.N., Psychophysical complementarity, in: M. Kubovy and J.R. Pomeranz, Eds., *Perceptual Organization* (Lawrence Erlbaum Ass., Hillsdale, 1979).
6. Gregory, R., *The Intelligent Eye* (McGraw–Hill, New York, 1970).
7. Roberts, L.G., Machine perception of three-dimensional solids, in: J.T. Tippett et al., Eds., *Optical and Electro-Optical Information Processing* (M.I.T. Press, Cambridge, MA, 1965).
8. Falk, G., Interpretation of imperfect line data as a three-dimensional scene, *Artificial Intelligence* **4**(2) (1972) 101–144.
9. Huffman, D.A., Impossible objects as nonsense sentences, in: B. Meltzer and D. Michie, Eds., *Machine Intelligence* (Edinburgh University Press, Edinburgh, 1971).
10. Waltz, D.L., Generating semantic descriptions from drawings of scenes with shadows, Tech. Rept. AI-TR-271, M.I.T., Cambridge, MA (1972).
11. Turner, K.J., Computer perception of curved objects using a television camera, Ph.D. Dissertation, Edinburgh University, November 1974.
12. Marr, D. and Nishihara, H.K., Representation and recognition of the spatial organization of three-dimensional shapes, *Proc. Roy. Soc. London Ser. B* **200** (1977) 269–294.
13. Stevens, K.A., Constraints on the visual interpretation of surface contours, AI Memo 522, M.I.T., Cambridge, MA (1979).
14. Clowes, M.B., On seeing things, *Artificial Intelligence* **2**(1) (1971) 79–112.
15. Chakravarty, I., A generalized line and junction labeling scheme with applications to scene analysis, *IEEE Trans. Pattern Analysis, Machine Intelligence* **1**(2) (1979) 202–205.
16. Marr, D., Analysis of occluding contour, *Proc. Roy. Soc. London Ser. B* **197** (1977) 441–475.
17. Stevens, K.A. Surface perception from local analysis of texture and contour, Ph.D. Dissertation, M.I.T., Cambridge, MA, February 1979.
18. Witkin, A.P., The minimum curvature assumption and perceived surface orientation, *J. Optical Soc. Amer.* **68** (1978) 1450.
19. Brand, L., *Vector and Tensor Analysis* (Wiley, New York, 1953).
20. Almgren, Jr., F.J. and Taylor, J.E., The geometry of soap films and soap bubbles, *Sci. Amer.* (July 1976) 82–93.
21. Huffman, D.A., Curvature and creases: A primer on paper, *IEEE Trans. Computers* **25**(10) (1976).
22. Wilcox, C., Dageforde, M. and Jirak, G., *MAINSAIL Language Manual*, Stanford University, Stanford, 1979.
23. Haber, R.N., Perception of visual space in scenes and pictures, Paper presented at Conference on the Interrelations among the Communicative Senses, Asilomar, CA, September 1978.
24. Marr, D. and Hildreth, E., Theory of edge detection, AI Memo 518, M.I.T., Cambridge, MA (1979).
25. Ullman, S., On visual detection of light sources, *Biol. Cybernet.* **21** (1976) 205–212.
26. Forbus, K.D., Light source effects, AI Memo 422, M.I.T., Cambridge, MA (1977).
27. Beck, J., *Surface Color Perception* (Cornell University Press, Ithaca, 1974).
28. Land, E.H., The retinex theory of color vision, *Sci. Amer.* **237**(6) (1977) 108–128.
29. Binford, T.O., Inferring surfaces from images, *Artificial Intelligence* **17** (1981) 205–244 [this volume].

Revised version received October 1980

Analysing Images of Curved Surfaces

Robert J. Woodham

Forestry/Computer Science, University of British Columbia, Vancouver, B.C., Canada

ABSTRACT

A reflectance map makes the relationship between image intensity and surface orientation explicit. Trade-offs between image intensity and surface orientation emerge which cannot be resolved locally in a single view. Existing methods for determining surface orientation from a single view embody assumptions about surface curvature. The Hessian matrix is introduced to represent surface curvature. Properties of surface curvature are expressed as properties of the Hessian matrix. For several classes of surface, image analysis simplifies. This result has already been established for planar surfaces forming trihedral corners. Similar simplification is demonstrated for developable surfaces and for the subclass of surfaces known as generalized cones. These studies help to delineate shape information that can be determined from geometric measurements at object boundaries and shape information that can be determined from intensity measurements over sections of smoothly curved surface.

A novel technique called photometric stereo is discussed. The idea of stereo is to obtain multiple images in order to determine the underlying scene precisely. In photometric stereo, the viewing direction is constant. Multiple images are obtained by varying the incident illumination. It is shown that this provides sufficient information to determine surface orientation at each image point.

1. Introduction

Computer-based image analysis is the study of computational systems that interpret images; that is, they recover symbolic descriptions of a world from images of that world. The central concern is the design and implementation of effective algorithms that represent and exploit knowledge of the world and knowledge of how images are formed. This knowledge includes properties of sensors, laws of physical optics and information about possible configurations in the world.

The purpose of this paper is to demonstrate that image intensities carry a great deal of useful information about the underlying object scene and that algorithms can be developed to exploit this fact. Unfortunately, there is no simple correspondence between image irradiance, the quantity measured in an image, and properties of the underlying scene. Image irradiance results from

Artificial Intelligence **17** (1981) 117–140

the interaction of several factors, some of which are properties of the objects in view and some of which are not. The effects of those which are, shape and surface material, must be separated from each other and from the artifacts of those which are not, illumination, shadows, viewing direction and path phenomena.

To separate these factors, it is necessary to understand how images are formed. One aspect is the geometry of image projection. Of equal importance is the radiometry of image formation. Relating image irradiance to object shape requires a model of the way surfaces reflect light.

Many of the needed tools now exist. Section 2 develops an image irradiance equation to model how the physical world determines what we see. The reflectance map, originated by Horn, allows image irradiance to be written as a function of surface orientation in a viewer-centered coordinate system. The reflectance map uses the gradient space, popularized by Huffman and Mackworth, to represent surface orientation.

In computer-based image analysis, one uses the image irradiance equation to analyse what is seen. Unfortunately, the reflectance map itself is not invertible since surface orientation has two degrees of freedom and image intensity provides only one measurement. In order to determine the underlying scene, additional information must be provided.

Existing methods for determining object shape from a single view embody assumptions about surface curvature. The Hessian matrix, defined in Section 3, is introduced as a convenient viewer-centered representation of surface curvature. Assumptions about surface curvature are expressed as properties of the Hessian matrix. For several classes of surface, surface orientation can be determined locally. This result has already been established for planar surfaces forming trihedral corners. Here, the analysis is extended to include developable surfaces and the subclass of surfaces known as generalized cones. These results help to delineate shape information that can be determined from geometric measurements at object boundaries and shape information that can be determined from intensity measurements over sections of smoothly curved surface.

Another way to provide additional information is to obtain multiple images. A novel technique called photometric stereo is discussed in Section 4. Traditional stereo determines range by relating two images of an object viewed from different directions. If the correspondence between picture elements is known, then distance to the object can be calculated by triangulation. Unfortunately, it is difficult to determine this correspondence. The idea of photometric stereo is to vary the incident illumination between successive images, while holding the viewing direction constant. It is shown that this provides sufficient information to determine surface orientation at each image point. Since the imaging geometry is not changed, the correspondence between image points is fixed. The technique is photometric because it uses the radiance values recorded at a single image location, in successive views, rather than the relative positions of displaced features.

2. Developing the Image Irradiance Equation

The apparent brightness of a surface element depends on the orientation of that element relative to the viewer and the light sources. Different surface elements of a nonplanar object will reflect different amounts of light toward an observer as a consequence of their differing attitude in space. A smooth opaque object will thus give rise to a shaded image (i.e., one in which brightness varies spatially) even though the object may be illuminated evenly and covered by a surface material with uniform optical properties. Shading provides essential information about the object's shape and has been exploited in image analysis [1–7].

There are two parts to the problem: one deals with the geometry of image projection, the other with the intensity values recorded in the image. An image irradiance equation can be developed to relate the geometry and radiometry of image formation. The development given here parallels that first given by Horn [4].

2.1. Image projection

The relation between scene coordinates and image coordinates is given by the well-known perspective projection as illustrated in Fig. 1(a). If the size of the objects in view is small compared to the viewing distance, then the perspective projection can be approximated as an orthographic projection as illustrated in Fig. 1(b). In this paper, we only consider image forming systems that perform an orthographic projection. To standardize the imaging geometry, it is convenient to choose a coordinate system such that the viewing direction is aligned with the negative z-axis. Also, one can assume appropriate scaling of the image plane such that surface point (x, y, z) maps onto image point (u, v) where $u = x$ and $v = y$. With these assumptions, image coordinates (x, y) and surface coordinates (x, y) can be referred to interchangeably.

2.2. Surface reflectance

The amount of light reflected by a surface element depends on its microstructure, on its optical properties and on the distribution and state of polarization of the incident illumination. For most surfaces, the fraction of incident illumination reflected in a particular direction depends only on the surface orientation. The reflectance characteristics of such a surface can be represented as a function $\phi(i, e, g)$ of the three angles i, e and g defined in Fig. 2. These angles are called, respectively, the *incident, emergent* and *phase* angles. The reflectance function $\phi(i, e, g)$ determines the ratio of surface radiance to irradiance measured per unit surface area, per unit solid angle, in the direction of the viewer. To be precise, one would have to specify the quantities and units used to define the required ratio. Several papers do just that [4, 8, 9]. Here, it is sufficient to point out the role that surface orientation,

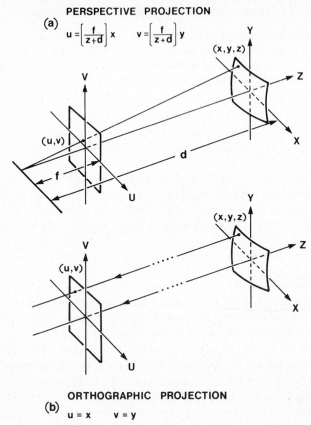

PERSPECTIVE PROJECTION

(a) $u = \left[\dfrac{f}{z+d}\right] x$ $v = \left[\dfrac{f}{z+d}\right] y$

ORTHOGRAPHIC PROJECTION

(b) $u = x$ $v = y$

FIG. 1. Characterizing image projections. Fig. 1(a) illustrates the perspective projection. For objects that are small compared to the viewing distance, image projection can be modeled by the orthographic projection illustrated in Fig. 1(b). In an orthographic projection all rays from object surface to image are parallel.

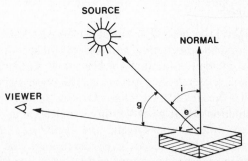

FIG. 2. Defining the angles i, e and g. The incident angle i is the angle between the incident ray and the surface normal. The emergent angle e is the angle between the emergent ray and the surface normal. The phase angle g is the angle between the incident and emergent rays.

as given by the surface normal vector, plays in the determination of the required angles i and e.

To illustrate, consider the example of perfect specular or mirror-like reflection. In specular reflection, the incident angle equals the emergent angle ($i = e$) and the incident, emergent and normal vectors lie in the same plane ($i + e = g$). Expressing this formally, one obtains a reflectance function $\phi_s(i, e, g)$ given by:

$$\phi_s(i, e, g) = \begin{cases} 1 & \text{if } i = e \text{ and } i + e = g, \\ 0 & \text{otherwise.} \end{cases} \tag{1}$$

Eq. (1) says that there is only one surface orientation correct for reflecting the light source towards the viewer. This is a simple fact familiar to any child who has used a pocket mirror to direct the sun's rays towards a desired target.

The interaction of light with surfaces of varying roughness and material composition leads to a more complex spatial distribution of reflected light. Surface reflectance characteristics can be determined empirically, derived from analytic models of surface microstructure or derived from phenomenological models of surface reflectance. The examples presented in this paper make use of two simple idealized models of surface reflectance.

The first model of surface reflectance is given by:

$$\phi_a(i, e, g) = \rho \cos(i). \tag{2}$$

This reflectance function corresponds to the phenomenological model of a perfectly diffuse (lambertian) surface which appears equally bright from all viewing directions. Here, ρ is a reflectance factor and the cosine of the incident angle accounts for the foreshortening of the surface as seen from the source.

The second reflectance function, similar to that of material in the maria of the moon and rocky planets, is given by:

$$\phi_b(i, e, g) = \frac{\rho \cos(i)}{\cos(e)}. \tag{3}$$

This reflectance function corresponds to the phenomenological model of a surface which reflects equal amounts of light in all directions. The cosine of the emergent angle accounts for the foreshortening of the surface as seen from the viewer.

2.3. Surface orientation and gradient space

There are various ways to specify the surface orientation of a plane. One can use, for example, the equation defining the plane or the direction of a vector perpendicular to the plane. If the equation of the plane is $ax + by + cz + d = 0$, then a surface normal is $[a, b, c]$.

This method is easily extended to curved surfaces by applying it to tangent planes. If the equation of a surface is given explicitly as:

$$z = f(x, y), \tag{4}$$

then a surface normal is given by the vector:

$$\left[\frac{\partial f(x, y)}{\partial x}, \frac{\partial f(x, y)}{\partial y}, -1 \right]. \tag{5}$$

If parameters p and q are defined by:

$$p = \frac{\partial f(x, y)}{\partial x} \quad \text{and} \quad q = \frac{\partial f(x, y)}{\partial y}, \tag{6}$$

then the surface normal can be written as $[p, q, -1]$. The quantity (p, q) is called the *gradient* of $f(x, y)$ and *gradient space* is the two-dimensional space of all such points (p, q).

Gradient space is a convenient viewer-centered representation of surface orientation. Some examples will give a feel for gradient space. Parallel planes map into a common point in gradient space. Planes perpendicular to the viewing direction map into the origin of gradient space. Moving away from the origin in gradient space, one can show that the distance from the origin equals the tangent of the emergent angle e between the surface normal and the viewing direction. One can also show that the angular position of a point in gradient space corresponds to the direction of steepest descent on the original surface.

Geometric arguments, based on properties of gradient space, have been used in the scene analysis of line drawings of polyhedra [10, 11]. In image analysis, gradient space is used to relate the geometry of image projection to the radiometry of image formation, as will now be shown.

2.4. The reflectance map

The surface normal vector relates surface geometry to image irradiance because it determines the angles i and e appearing in the surface reflectance function $\phi(i, e, g)$. An ideal imaging device produces image irradiance proportional to scene radiance. In an orthographic projection, the viewing direction, and hence the phase angle g, is constant for all surface elements. Thus, for a fixed light source and viewer geometry, the ratio of scene radiance to scene irradiance depends only on the surface normal vector (i.e., on gradient coordinates p and q). Further, suppose each surface element receives the same irradiance. Then, the scene radiance, and hence image intensity, depends only on gradient coordinates p and q.

A *reflectance map* $R(p, q)$ determines image intensity as a function of p and q. Using a reflectance map, an image irradiance equation can be written as:

$$I(x, y) = R(p, q) \tag{7}$$

where $I(x, y)$ is the image intensity and $R(p, q)$ is the corresponding reflectance map.

A reflectance map provides a uniform representation for specifying the surface reflectance of a surface material for a particular light source, object surface and viewer geometry. A comprehensive survey of reflectance maps, derived for a variety of surface and light source conditions, has been given by Horn [12]. Recently, a unified approach to the specification of surface reflectance map has been proposed [8]. The result is called bidirectional reflectance distribution function (BRDF). Horn and Sjoberg have provided a systematic approach for deriving the reflectance map $R(p, q)$ in terms of the BRDF and the distribution of source radiance [9].

Expressions for $\cos(i)$, $\cos(e)$ and $\cos(g)$ can be derived using normalized dot products of the surface normal vector $[p, q, -1]$, the vector $[p_s, q_s, -1]$ which points in the direction of the light source and the vector $[0, 0, -1]$ which points in the direction of the viewer. One obtains:

$$\cos(i) = \frac{1 + pp_s + qq_s}{\sqrt{1 + p^2 + q^2}\sqrt{1 + p_s^2 + q_s^2}}, \tag{8}$$

$$\cos(e) = \frac{1}{\sqrt{1 + p^2 + q^2}}, \tag{9}$$

$$\cos(g) = \frac{1}{\sqrt{1 + p_s^2 + q_s^2}}. \tag{10}$$

Eqs. (8), (9) and (10) are used to transform a surface reflectance function $\phi(i, e, g)$ into a reflectance map $R(p, q)$.

For example, the reflectance map corresponding to $\phi_a(i, e, g)$, defined in eq. (2), is given by:

$$R_a(p, q) = \frac{\rho(1 + pp_s + qq_s)}{\sqrt{1 + p^2 + q^2}\sqrt{1 + p_s^2 + q_s^2}}. \tag{11}$$

Similarly, the reflectance map corresponding to $\phi_b(i, e, g)$, defined in eq. (3), is given by:

$$R_b(p, q) = \frac{\rho(1 + pp_s + qq_s)}{\sqrt{1 + p_s^2 + q_s^2}}. \tag{12}$$

It is convenient to represent $R(p, q)$ as a series of contours of constant brightness in gradient space. Fig. 3 and Fig. 4 illustrate the two simple reflectance maps $R_a(p, q)$ and $R_b(p, q)$, defined above, for the case $p_s = 0.7$, $q_s = 0.3$ and $\rho = 1$. Reflectance maps $R_a(p, q)$ and $R_b(p, q)$ have been used to synthesize images from digital terrain models for the automatic rectification and interpretation of Landsat images [13, 14]. Fig. 5 is the image of a sphere synthesized using the reflectance map of Fig. 3.

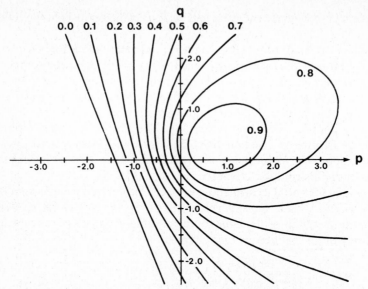

FIG. 3. The reflectance map $R_a(p, q)$ for a surface illuminated from gradient $p_s = 0.7$ and $q_s = 0.3$ (with $\rho = 1.0$). The reflectance map is plotted as a series of contours spaced 0.1 units apart.

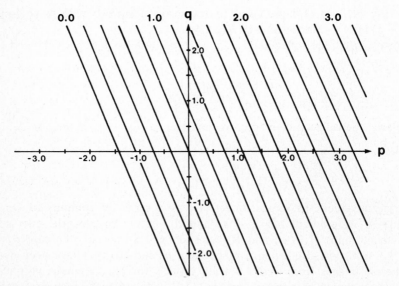

FIG. 4. The reflectance map $R_b(p, q)$ for a surface illuminated from gradient $p_s = 0.7$ and $q_s = 0.3$ (with $\rho = 1.0$). The reflectance map is plotted as a series of contours spaced 0.2 units apart.

FIG. 5. The synthesized image of a sphere generated using the reflectance map of Fig. 3.

Until recently, the calculation of surface orientation from image intensity could be attempted only by a rather tedious method involving the direct solution of eq. (7), a nonlinear first-order partial differential equation, using something like the method of characteristic strip expansion [3]. Progress has been made in the development of an iterative local method based on relaxation [5]. Attempts have been made to determine formal conditions under which a direct solution of eq. (7) might be possible [15]. All these methods, however, embody assumptions about surface curvature.

Alternatively, one can view eq. (7) as a single equation in the two unknowns p and q. In order to determine p and q from measured intensity, additional information must be provided. The remainder of this paper is concerned with providing additional information. Constraints on surface curvature are one source of additional information. Multiple images are the other.

3. Surface Curvature Constraints

Section 2 developed an image irradiance equation to show that image intensity is related to surface orientation. It will now be shown that local variations in image intensity are related to surface curvature. First, a representation for surface curvature is introduced. The image irradiance equation is then re-examined to see what can and cannot be determined from local intensity measurements. Finally, the results are applied to consider several different classes of surface: convex surfaces, planar surfaces with trihedral corners, developable surfaces and generalized cones. An example is then presented to point out that the intensity values recorded in a single view do not fully constrain the underlying scene.

3.1. Surface curvature and the Hessian matrix

One parameter is required to specify range or distance to a point on a surface. For the viewing geometry of Fig. 1(b), eq. (4) determines range explicitly as a function of x and y. Two parameters are required to specify the orientation at a point on a surface. Eq. (6) defined the gradient (p, q) which is one way to represent surface orientation. Gradient coordinates p and q are the first partial derivatives, with respect to x and y, of the surface equation $z = f(x, y)$.

Three parameters are required to specify the curvature at a point on a surface. There are several ways to express these parameters. One representation is based on the second partial derivatives, with respect to x and y, of the surface equation $z = f(x, y)$. Let H be the 2×2 matrix given by:

$$H = \begin{bmatrix} \dfrac{\partial^2 f(x, y)}{\partial x^2} & \dfrac{\partial^2 f(x, y)}{\partial x \partial y} \\ \dfrac{\partial^2 f(x, y)}{\partial y \partial x} & \dfrac{\partial^2 f(x, y)}{\partial y^2} \end{bmatrix}. \tag{13}$$

H is called the *Hessian matrix* of the function $z = f(x, y)$. Hessian matrices are used extensively in nonlinear programming [16, 17].

At first it would appear that four parameters are required to determine the Hessian matrix H. For smooth surfaces, the order of differentiation can be interchanged. That is:

$$\frac{\partial^2 f(x, y)}{\partial x \partial y} = \frac{\partial^2 f(x, y)}{\partial y \partial x}. \tag{14}$$

Thus, the Hessian matrix H is symmetric. H is a three parameter function of x and y.

The Hessian matrix can be related to other representations of surface curvature. Here, it is sufficient to show how the Hessian matrix is used in image analysis. One can write the approximate equation:

$$[\mathrm{d}p, \mathrm{d}q]' = H[\mathrm{d}x, \mathrm{d}y]' \tag{15}$$

(' denotes vector transpose) to illustrate that H determines the change in surface orientation $[\mathrm{d}p, \mathrm{d}q]$ corresponding to a small movement $[\mathrm{d}x, \mathrm{d}y]$ in the image. If two linearly independent directions $[dx_1, dy_1]$ and $[dx_2, dy_2]$ and the corresponding $[dp_1, dq_1]$ and $[dp_2, dq_2]$ are known, then H is determined by:

$$H = \begin{bmatrix} dp_1 & dp_2 \\ dq_1 & dq_2 \end{bmatrix} \begin{bmatrix} dx_1 & dx_2 \\ dy_1 & dy_2 \end{bmatrix}^{-1}. \qquad (16)$$

We can now show that image intensity determines exactly one of these two correspondences. By taking partial derivatives of the image irradiance eq. (7), with respect to x and y, two equations are obtained which can be written as the single matrix equation:

$$[I_x, I_y]' = H[R_p, R_q]' \qquad (17)$$

(subscripts denote partial differentiation). Eq. (17) has a simple geometric interpretation. Suppose a point (x, y) in the image is known to have gradient (p, q). Choose a small movement $[dx, dy]$ in the direction determined by $[R_p, R_q]$. Then, the corresponding change in surface orientation $[dp, dq]$ is in the direction $[I_x, I_y]$. More precisely, if $[dx, dy] = [R_p, R_q]\,ds$, then $[dp, dq] = [I_x, I_y]\,ds$ where ds is a differential element of path length. Note that $[R_p, R_q]$ defines a normal to the contour of constant reflectance at the current (p, q) and that $[I_x, I_y]$ defines a normal to the contour of constant intensity at the current (x, y). This observation was the basis for Horn's original method for determining shape from shading [3].

Using the information provided by image intensity, eq. (16) can be rewritten as:

$$H = \begin{bmatrix} I_x & dp \\ I_y & dq \end{bmatrix} \begin{bmatrix} R_p & dx \\ R_q & dy \end{bmatrix}^{-1}. \qquad (18)$$

But, eq. (18) still admits an infinite number of solutions. Image intensity allows us to determine the change in gradient corresponding to movement in the image in the direction $[R_p, R_q]$ but determines nothing about the change in gradient corresponding to movement in the perpendicular direction. When properties of surface curvature are known, they can provide additional constraint on the Hessian matrix H. For several classes of surface, image analysis simplifies, as will now be shown.

3.2. Convex surfaces

The convexity of a surface $z = f(x, y)$ is related to the positiveness of its Hessian matrix H. in particular, a surface $z = f(x, y)$ is convex if and only if the corresponding Hessian matrix H is positive semidefinite [16]. (An identical result holds replacing convex with concave and positive semidefinite with negative semidefinite.)

Recall that H positive semidefinite simply means that $x'Hx \geq 0$ for all vectors x. If a surface $z = f(x, y)$ is known to be convex, eqs. (15) and (17) give rise to the two inequalities:

$$dp \, dx + dq \, dy \geq 0, \tag{19}$$

$$R_p I_x + R_q I_y \geq 0. \tag{20}$$

Inequalities (19) and (20) are not sufficient to solve eq. (18) but they do provide some additional constraint. The propagation of constraint provided by these inequalities has been explored [5].

Analysis of convexity leads to the following observation. If $I(x, y)$ is the image, determined by eq. (7), of a convex surface $z = f(x, y)$ illuminated by a single distant point source with gradient (p_s, q_s), then $I(x, y)$ is also the image, determined by eq. (7), of the concave surface $z = -f(x, y)$ illuminated by a single distant point source with gradient $(-p_s, -q_s)$. This observation is the basis for a number of visual illusions. Humans have difficulty distinguishing protrusions illuminated from above from indentations illuminated from below. Shading alone does not resolve the ambiguity. Second order phenomena such as shadows, edge effects and mutual illumination must be pursued [4].

3.3. Planar surfaces with trihedral corners

Objects whose surfaces are planar form the familiar polyhedra domain. For such surfaces, the Hessian matrix is identically zero at all non-edge points (i.e., a plane has no curvature). Horn has shown, however, that when three planes meet at a point, the orientation of each plane can be determined locally [4].

Call the three planes A, B and C. Let GA, GB and GC be the corresponding gradients. Mackworth has shown that the line in gradient space joining the gradients of two planes is perpendicular to the line in the image formed by the intersection of the two planes [11]. This provides three constraints but is not enough to determine the position and scale of the triangle formed by the three gradients GA, GB and GC. Three additional constraints are provided by measurements of image intensity for the three planes. The six constraints, taken together, determine the orientations of the three planes A, B and C.

Horn's technique combines the quantitative approach to interpreting line drawings of polyhedra, developed by Mackworth, with the additional information provided by the image irradiance eq. (7). It illustrates one example of how to combine geometric measurements at object boundaries (i.e., the line drawing) with intensity measurements over sections of smooth surface in order to determine the underlying scene precisely.

3.4. Developable surfaces

Many surfaces have the property that, through every point on the surface, there passes at least one straight line lying entirely on the surface. Such a surface is called a *ruled surface*. The straight line lying entirely on the surface is called a *ruling*. If a ruled surface has the additional property that all points on a given ruling have the same tangent plane, then the surface is called a *developable surface*. Huffman charmingly refers to developable surfaces as 'paper' surfaces and has proposed that such surfaces possess a complexity that is midway between that of a general surface and that of a plane [18]. It will now be shown that, in image analysis, developable surfaces do indeed possess a complexity between that of a general surface and that of a plane.

The result to be established is that for a developable surface the Hessian matrix can be determined locally from image intensity. The mathematics follows. A surface $z = f(x, y)$ is developable if and only if the determinant of the corresponding Hessian matrix is everywhere zero [19]. Thus, for a developable surface, at least one of the eigenvalues of the corresponding Hessian matrix H must be zero. Assume that one of the two eigenvalues of H is nonzero at each point (x, y). (If both eigenvalues of H are zero, then the equation $z = f(x, y)$ locally describes a plane. Planar surfaces, while certainly developable, have been considered above and will not be dealt with further here.)

Suppose the point (x, y) is known to have gradient (p, q). Then the Hessian matrix H at (x, y) is determined by the matrix product:

$$H = \begin{bmatrix} \cos(\alpha) & -\sin(\alpha) \\ \sin(\alpha) & \cos(\alpha) \end{bmatrix} \begin{bmatrix} \lambda & 0 \\ 0 & 0 \end{bmatrix} \begin{bmatrix} \cos(\alpha) & \sin(\alpha) \\ -\sin(\alpha) & \cos(\alpha) \end{bmatrix} \tag{21}$$

where

$$\lambda = \frac{\sqrt{I_x^2 + I_y^2}}{R_p \cos(\alpha) + R_q \sin(\alpha)} \tag{22}$$

and

$$\tan(\alpha) = \frac{I_y}{I_x}. \tag{23}$$

As above, I_x and I_y denote the first partial derivatives of $I(x, y)$ with respect to x and y and R_p and R_q denote the first partial derivatives of $R(p, q)$ with respect to p and q.

Given an image point (x, y) known to have gradient (p, q), eqs. (15) and (21) can be used to iteratively trace out an arbitrary path on the surface $z = f(x, y)$. Eq. (21) determines H. For a small movement $[dx, dy]$, eq. (15) determines the change in gradient $[dp, dq]$.

The fact that H has one zero eigenvalue means that there is one direction of movement in the image which results in no change to surface orientation. This direction is orthogonal to the direction α determined by the vector $[I_x, I_y]$. The component of any movement $[dx, dy]$ perpendicular to $[I_x, I_y]$ is in the direction of a ruling on the surface and thus does not change the gradient (p, q). The component of $[dx, dy]$ in the direction $[I_x, I_y]$ causes a change in gradient $[dp, dq]$ in the direction α where the 'scale factor' for that change is given by λ.

The gradients corresponding to points on a developable surface are constrained to lie on a one-parameter curve in gradient space. This illustrates that developable surfaces possess a complexity midway between that of a plane, where surface points map into a single point in gradient space, and that of a general surface, where surface points map into a region in gradient space.

An example will demonstrate. Fig. 6 is the image of a right circular cone of base radius b and height a synthesized using the reflectance map of Fig. 3. (For the example, $a = 2b$.) The gradients of points on a right circular cone with axis parallel to the image plane lie on the one-parameter curve in gradient space given parametrically by:

$$p = \tan(t) \quad \text{and} \quad q = \frac{b}{a}\frac{1}{\cos(t)} \tag{24}$$

where $-\frac{1}{2}\pi < t < \frac{1}{2}\pi$. The parameter t has a physical interpretation. The circular

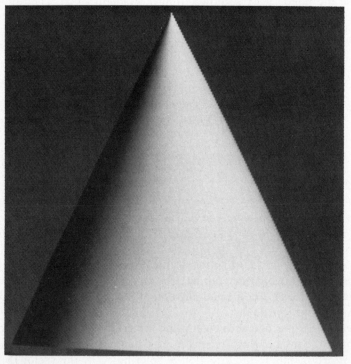

FIG. 6. The synthesized image of a right circular cone, with height equal to twice the base radius radius and axis parallel to the image plane, generated using the reflectance map of Fig. 3.

cross-section of the cone can be represented, in cylindrical coordinates, by the function $r(\theta) = k$, where θ measures angular position about the y-axis. If θ is chosen so that $\theta = 0$ points in the direction of the viewer, then the parameter t in eq. (24) is this angle θ.

Fig. 7 shows the curve in gradient space determined by eq. (24) superimposed on the reflectance map used to generate Fig. 6. There exists a 1–1 continuous mapping between any image line and the curve in gradient space determined by eq. (24). Thus, finding the gradient corresponding to any point where $I(x, y) = \alpha$ simplifies to the problem of determining reflectance map values on the curve given by eq. (24) for which $R(p, q) = \alpha$. Since all 1–1 continuous mappings are monotonic, multiple solutions can be resolved by systematically scanning each image line from left to right. The required ratio b/a is determined by the boundary contour of Fig. 6.

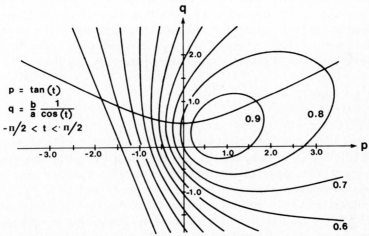

FIG. 7. The one-parameter curve in gradient space corresponding to points on the right circular cone of Fig. 6.

3.5. Generalized cones

A generalized cone is defined to be the surface swept out by moving a simple smooth cross-section $r(\theta)$ along a straight axis Λ, at the same time magnifying or contracting it in a smoothly varying way [20]. The concept of a generalized cone is similar to the generalized cylinder representation of Agin and Binford [21].

For the present work, some additional terminology is required. Let $h(\lambda)$ be the axial scaling function, where λ denotes distance along the Λ axis. The angle

ψ between the axis Λ and a plane containing a cross-section is called the eccentricity of the cone. If $\psi = \frac{1}{2}\pi$, then the cone is called a *right generalized cone*. In addition, if the cross-section is circular, then the cone is called a *right generalized cone with circular cross-section*.

The curvature of a generalized cone conveniently decouples into a component due to the axial scaling function $h(\lambda)$ and a component due to the cross-section function $r(\theta)$. For appropriate viewing conditions, this decoupling carries over to images of generalized cones. These images can be analysed as if the surface were developable, as will now be shown.

Consider a right generalized cone with circular cross-section. Without loss of generality, one can assume that the axis Λ passes through the center of the circular cross-section. For the moment, one additional assumption is needed. Assume that the axis Λ is parallel to the image plane. For convenience, let the image x-y axes be chosen so that Λ coincides with the image y-axis. Distance along the Λ-axis is then equal to distance along the y-axis so that the axial scaling function can be denoted as $h(y)$. Further, let the circular cross-section be denoted by $r(\theta) = 1$, where $\theta = 0$ points in the direction of the viewer. The gradients corresponding to points on such a generalized cone lie in the two-parameter region of gradient space given parametrically by:

$$p = \tan(\theta) \quad \text{and} \quad q = \frac{-h'(y)}{\cos(\theta)} \tag{25}$$

where $h'(y)$ denotes the derivative of $h(y)$ with respect to y and $-\frac{1}{2}\pi < \theta < \frac{1}{2}\pi$.

Fig. 6 was an example of a right generalized cone with circular cross-section. There, $h'(y) = -b/a$. In general, eq. (25) defines a two-parameter region of gradient space. The important observation, however, is that the value of $h'(y)$ can always be determined directly from the boundary contour.

Fig. 8 illustrates a more general example. Here, the axial scaling function is a sinusoid while the cross-section function remains circular. Fig. 9 superimposes a collection of the curves determined by eq. (25) on the reflectance map used to generate Fig. 8. In this case, finding the gradient corresponding to a point where $I(x, y) = \alpha$ simplifies to a two step process. First, for the particular y, determine $h'(y)$ as the rate of change of object radius with respect to y (equivalently, as $\frac{1}{2}$ the rate of change of object diameter with respect to y) at the object boundary along image line y. Second, as in the case of a developable surface, scan the curve determined by eq. (25) to find the gradient where $R(p, q) = \alpha$.

Suppose now that the axis Λ is not parallel to the image plane. Nevertheless, the image axes can still be chosen so that the projection of Λ coincides with the image y-axis. Let the angle between the Λ-axis and the image plane be ϕ (measured so that positive ϕ implies that Λ is tilted toward the viewer). The gradients corresponding to points on such a generalized cone lie in the

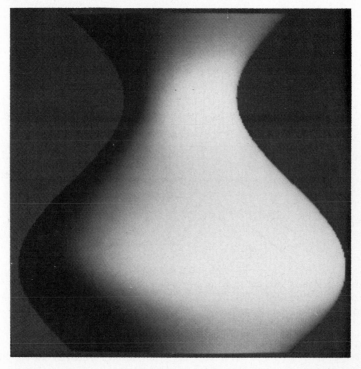

FIG. 8. The synthesized image of a right generalized cone with circular cross-section generated using the reflectance map of Fig. 3. The axis of the cone is parallel to the image plane and the axial scaling function is a sinusoid.

two-parameter region of gradient space given parametrically by:

$$p = \frac{\sin(\theta)}{\cos(\phi)\cos(\theta) - \sin(\phi)h'(y)},$$

$$q = -\tan(\phi) + \frac{-h'(y)}{\cos(\phi)[\cos(\phi)\cos(\theta) - \sin(\phi)h'(y)]}$$

(26)

where $h'(y)$ and θ are as before. The derivation of eq. (26) is not of particular interest here. It is sufficient to note the dependence of p and q on the tilt angle ϕ. If ϕ is known, one can proceed as before, with only a slight complication in the mathematical expressions required. If ϕ is unknown, two difficulties arise. First, the curve generated by eq. (26) cannot be determined. Second, the image profile corresponding to the value of y used to determine $h'(y)$ is no longer a straight line. Without knowing ϕ, the correct image profile cannot be determined. It is possible to estimate a value for ϕ as a preprocessing step but this has not proven useful in practice.

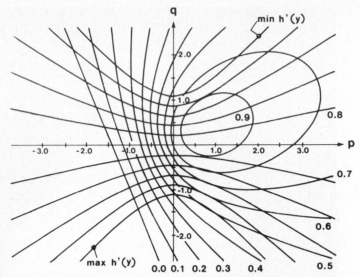

FIG. 9. The region in gradient space corresponding to points on the cone of Fig. 8 plotted as a family of curves. The region depicted lies below the curve determined by the minimum value of $h'(y)$ and above the curve determined by the maximum value of $h'(y)$.

Greater difficulties arise if the cross-section is allowed to be an arbitrary smooth convex function. Roughly speaking, it becomes impossible to decouple axis tilt, cross-section shape and axial scaling function using the intensity values and boundary information contained in a single view.

3.6. Ambiguities

The intensity values recorded in a single view do not fully constrain the underlying object scene. For the cases considered above, progress is made by combining information obtained from object boundaries with information obtained from intensity measurements. Certain ambiguities that are difficult to resolve can also be pointed out.

In Section 3.2, it was noted that convexity and concavity are difficult to resolve because a concave surface can generate an image identical to that of the corresponding convex surface, under different conditions of illumination. In Section 3.5, it was noted that it is difficult to resolve axis tilt from cross-section shape. For example, the cross-section of a circular cylinder would, in general, project to an ellipse on the image plane. If one assumes that the cross-section is circular, then parameters of tilt can be determined from the shape of the projected ellipse. But, what if the cross-section was itself elliptical? Assuming circularity would lead to errors in the estimation of tilt.

Fig. 10 illustrates another difficulty. This figure is the image of a right circular

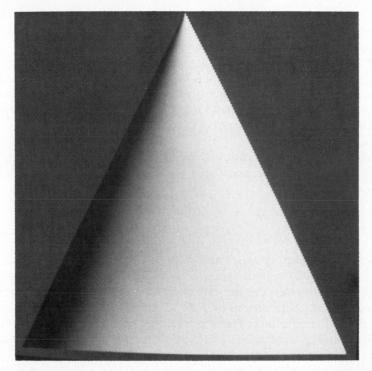

FIG. 10. The synthesized image of a right circular cone, with height equal to twice the base radius r, generated using the reflectance map $R_b(p, q)$ with $p_s = 0.7$, $q_s = 0.3$ and $\rho = 0.75$. But, this is also the synthesized image of a right cone with elliptical cross-section (semi-major axis r and semi-minor axis $\frac{2}{3}r$) generated using the reflectance map $R_b(p, q)$ with $p_s = 1.05$, $q_s = 0.45$ and $\rho = 0.906$.

cone (with base radius r) synthesized using the reflectance map function $R_b(p, q)$, for the case $p_s = 0.7$, $q_s = 0.3$ and $\rho = 0.75$. But, Fig. 10 is also the image of a right cone whose cross-section is elliptical (with semi-major axis r and semi-minor axis $\frac{2}{3}r$) synthesized using the reflectance map function $R_b(p, q)$, for the case $p_s = 1.05$, $q_s = 0.45$ and $\rho = 0.906$. Thus, cross-section shape is difficult to determine because different cross-section shapes can generate identical images under slightly different conditions of illumination and surface reflectance. Elliptical cross-sections are rare so it seems reasonable to adjust assumptions about surface reflectance and illumination before adjusting assumptions about cross-section shape.

4. Photometric Stereo

The idea of photometric stereo is to vary the direction of incident illumination between successive views, while holding the viewing direction constant. Intensity measurements from multiple images provide sufficient constraint to determine surface orientation locally. A discussion of photometric stereo has appeared elsewhere [7]. The details are summarized here.

Suppose two images $I_1(x, y)$ and $I_2(x, y)$ are obtained by varying the direction of incident illumination. Since there is no change in the imaging geometry, each picture element (x, y) in the two images corresponds to the same object point and hence to the same gradient (p, q). The effect of varying the direction of incident illumination is to change the reflectance map $R(p, q)$ that characterizes the imaging situation.

Let the reflectance maps corresponding to $I_1(x, y)$ and $I_2(x, y)$ be $R_1(p, q)$ and $R_2(p, q)$ respectively. The two views are characterized by two independent equations:

$$I_1(x, y) = R_1(p, q), \qquad (27)$$

$$I_2(x, y) = R_2(p, q). \qquad (28)$$

Two reflectance maps $R_1(p, q)$ and $R_2(p, q)$ are required. But, if the phase angle g is the same in both views (i.e., the illumination is rotated about the viewing direction), then the two reflectance maps are rotations of each other.

For reflectance characterized by $R_b(p, q)$ above, eqs. (27) and (28) are linear in p and q. If the reflectance factor ρ is known, then two views are sufficient to determine surface orientation at each image point, provided the directions of incident illumination are not collinear in azimuth.

In general, eqs. (27) and (28) are nonlinear in p and q so that more than one solution is possible. One idea would be to obtain a third image:

$$I_3(x, y) = R_3(p, q) \qquad (29)$$

to overdetermine the solution.

For reflectance characterized by $R_a(p, q)$ above, three views are sufficient to uniquely determine both the surface orientation and reflectance factor ρ at each image point, provided the three directions of incident illumination are not coplanar.

Photometric stereo is easily implemented. The stereo computation, after an initial calibration step, is purely local and may be implemented by table lookup, allowing real-time performance. Photometric stereo is a practical scheme for environments, such as industrial inspection, in which the nature and position of the incident illumination can be controlled.

The multiple images required for photometric stereo can be obtained by explicitly moving a single light source, by using multiple sources calibrated with respect to each other or by rotating the object surface and imaging hardware together to simulate the effect of moving a single light source. The equivalent of photometric stereo can also be achieved in a single view by using multiple sources which can be separated by colour.

4.1. Applications of photometric stereo

Photometric stereo can be used in two ways. First, photometric stereo is a general technique for determining surface orientation at each image point. For a given image point (x, y), the image irradiance equations can be combined to determine the corresponding gradient (p, q).

Second, photometric stereo is a general technique for determining object points that have a particular surface orientation. This use of photometric stereo corresponds to interpreting the image irradiance eq. (7) as one equation in the unknowns x and y. For a given gradient (p, q), the image irradiance equations can be combined to determine corresponding object points (x, y). This second use of photometric stereo is appropriate for the so-called industrial 'bin-of-parts' problem. The location in an image of key object points is often sufficient to determine the position and orientation of a known object on a table or conveyor belt so that the object may be grasped by an automatic manipulator.

A particularly useful special case concerns object points whose surface normal directly faces the viewer (i.e., object points with $p = 0$ and $q = 0$). Such points form a unique class of image points whose intensity value is invariant under rotation of the illumination direction about the viewing direction. Object points with surface normal directly facing the viewer can be located without explicitly determining the reflectance map $R(p, q)$. The value of $R(0, 0)$ is not changed by varying the direction of incident illumination, provided only that the phase angle g is held constant.

4.2. Accuracy considerations

Photometric stereo is most accurate for surface orientations corresponding to regions of gradient space where the density of reflectance map contours is great and where the contours to be intersected are nearly perpendicular. Several factors influence the density and direction of reflectance map contours. The reflectance properties of the surface material play a role. Figs. 3 and 4 illustrate the difference between two idealized materials viewed under identical conditions of illumination. In general, an increased specular component in the surface reflectance will increase the density of contours in one region of gradient space at the expense of other regions. Using extended light sources rather than point sources will alter the shape and distribution of reflectance map contours. Imaging systems can be configured to exploit these facts [22]. A recent thesis has extended photometric stereo to handle certain types of non-uniform surface materials [23]. This thesis also provides a quantitative evaluation of a working implementation of photometric stereo.

For a given surface material, the main determiner of accuracy is the choice of phase angle g. In photometric stereo, there is a trade-off to acknowledge. A large phase angle increases the density of reflectance map contours in illuminated portions of gradient space (i.e., regions where $R(p, q) > 0$). At the same time, a large phase angle results in more of gradient space lying in shadow (i.e., regions where $R(p, q) = 0$). A practical compromise must be arrived at for each application. One idea is to use additional light sources. Arrangements can be configured so that points of interest are illuminated by at least three independent sources and reflectance map contours can be selected to intersect which are nearly perpendicular and where error regions are small.

4.3. Comparison with traditional stereo

Photometric methods for determining surface orientation can be considered complementary to methods based on the identification of corresponding points in two images taken from different viewpoints:

(1) Traditional stereo allows the accurate determination of distances to objects. Photometric stereo is best when the surface gradient is to be found.

(2) Traditional stereo works well on rough surfaces with discontinuities in surface orientation. Photometric stereo works best on smooth surfaces with few discontinuities.

(3) Traditional stereo works well on textured surfaces with varying surface reflectance. Photometric stereo is best when applied to surfaces with uniform properties.

Photometric stereo does have some unique advantages:

(1) Since the images are obtained from the same point of view, there is no difficulty identifying corresponding points in the two images. This is the major computational task in traditional stereo.

(2) Under appropriate circumstances, the surface reflectance factor can be found because the effect of surface orientation on image intensity can be removed. Traditional stereo provides no such capability.

(3) Describing object shape in terms of surface orientation is preferable in a number of applications to description in terms of range or altitude above a reference plane.

5. Conclusions

Methods for determining shape from intensity measurements in a single view embody assumptions about surface curvature. Such assumptions may arise naturally from analysis of boundary contour. Such assumptions may also be imposed externally from constraints on object design or manufacture.

A reflectance map makes the relationship between image intensity and surface orientation explicit. The Hessian matrix makes properties of surface curvature explicit. For several classes of surface, surface orientation can be determined locally. These classes include planar surfaces with trihedral corners, developable surfaces and right generalized cones with circular cross-section. In general, however, trade-offs emerge which cannot be resolved in a single view.

Surface orientation can be determined locally using multiple images. Photometric stereo is a method which determines surface orientation from intensity measurements obtained under a fixed geometry but with varying lighting conditions.

Photometric methods for determining object shape depend on a detailed understanding of the imaging process. In addition, the imaging instrument must be of high calibre so that the gray levels produced can be dependably related to scene radiance. Fortunately, the quality of imaging devices is now high enough to make this endeavour feasible.

ACKNOWLEDGMENT

The author would like to thank Berthold K.P. Horn of the M.I.T. Artificial Intelligence Laboratory for his help and guidance. Mike Brady, Anna Bruss, Mark Lavin, Tomas Lozano-Perez, Alan Mackworth, David Marr and Patrick Winston provided useful comments and criticisms at various stages of this work. The author would also like to thank John Kender who provided a very thoughtful review of this paper.

Figs. 5, 6, 8 and 10 were photographed directly from the screen of the Comtal Vision One image processing and display system of the UBC Interdisciplinary Program in Remote Sensing. Other figures were drawn by Nedenia Holm.

This paper describes research done in part while the author was at the Artificial Intelligence Laboratory of the Massachusetts Institute of Technology. Support for the laboratory's artificial intelligence research was provided in part by the Advanced Research Projects Agency of the Department of Defence under Office of Naval Research Contract N00014-75-C-0643 and in part by the Office of Naval Research under Office of Naval Research Contract N00014-77-C-0389.

REFERENCES

1. Van Diggelen, J., A photometric investigation of the slopes and heights of the ranges and hills in the maria of the moon, *Bull. Astron. Inst. Netherlands* **11** (1951) 283–289.
2. Rindfleisch, T., Photometric method for lunar topography, *Photogrammetric Engineering* **32** (1966) 262–276.
3. Horn, B.K.P., Obtaining shape from shading information, in: P.H. Winston, ed., *The Psychology of Computer Vision* (McGraw-Hill, New York, 1975) 115–155.
4. Horn, B.K.P., Understanding image intensities, *Artificial Intelligence* **8** (1977) 201–231.
5. Woodham, R.J., A cooperative algorithm for determining surface orientation from a single view, *Proc. IJCAI-77*, Cambridge, MA (1977) 635–641.
6. Woodham, R.J., Relating properties of surface curvature to image intensity, *Proc. IJCAI-79*, Tokyo (1979) 971–977.
7. Woodham, R.J., Photometric method for determining surface orientation from multiple images, *Optical Engineering* **19** (1980) 139–144.
8. Nicodemus, F.E., Richmond, J.C. and Hisa, J.J., Geometrical considerations and nomenclature for reflectance, *NBS Monograph 160* (National Bureau of Standards, Washington, DC, 1977).
9. Horn, B.K.P. and Sjoberg, R.W., Calculating the reflectance map, *Applied Optics* **18** (1979) 1770–1779.
10. Huffman, D.A., Impossible objects as nonsense sentences, in: B. Meltzer and D. Michie, eds., *Machine Intelligence* **6** (Edinburgh University Press, Edinburgh, 1971) 295–323.
11. Mackworth, A.K., Interpreting pictures of polyhedral scenes, *Artificial Intelligence* **4** (1973) 121–137.
12. Horn, B.K.P., Hill-shading and the reflectance map, *Proc. DARPA Image Understanding Workshop*, Palo Alto, CA (1979) 79–120.

13. Horn, B.K.P. and Bachman, B.L., Using synthetic images to register real images with surface models, *Comm. ACM* **21** (1978) 914–924.
14. Woodham, R.J., Using digital terrain data to model image formation in remote sensing, *Proc. SPIE* **238** (1980) 361–369.
15. Bruss, A.R., Some properties of discontinuities in the image irradiance equation, AI-TR-517, M.I.T. Artificial Intelligence laboratory, Cambridge, MA (1979).
16. Luenberger, D.G., *Introduction to Linear and Nonlinear Programming* (Addison-Wesley, Reading, MA, 1973).
17. Mangarsarian, O.L., *Nonlinear Programming* (McGraw-Hill, New York, 1969).
18. Huffman, D.A., Curvature and creases: a primer on paper, *Proc. Conf. Computer Graphics, Pattern Recognition and Data Structures*, IEEE Publ. 75CH0981-1C (1975) 360–370.
19. Kepr, B., Differential geometry, in: K. Rectorys, ed., *Survey of Applicable Mathematics* (M.I.T. Press, Cambridge, MA, 1969) 298–373.
20. Marr, D., Analysis of occluding contour, *Proc. R. Soc. Lond. B.* **197** (1977) 441–475.
21. Agin, G.J. and Binford, T.O., Computer description of curved objects, *Proc. IJCAI-73*, Stanford, CA (1973) 629–640.
22. Ikeuchi, K. and Horn, B.K.P., An application of the photometric stereo method, *Proc. IJCAI-79*, Tokyo (1979) 413–415.
23. Silver, W.M., Determining shape and reflectance using multiple images, Ph.D. Thesis, Dept. of Electrical Engineering and Computer Science, M.I.T., Cambridge, MA (1980).

Received November 1980

Numerical Shape from Shading and Occluding Boundaries

Katsushi Ikeuchi

Electrotechnical Laboratory, Information Science Division, 1-1-4 Umezono, Sakura-mura, Niihari-gun, Ibaraki-ken 305, Japan

Berthold K.P. Horn

Massachusetts Institute of Technology, Artificial Intelligence Laboratory, 545 Technology Square, Cambridge, MA 02139, U.S.A.

ABSTRACT

An iterative method for computing shape from shading using occluding boundary information is proposed. Some applications of this method are shown.

We employ the stereographic plane to express the orientations of surface patches, rather than the more commonly used gradient space. Use of the stereographic plane makes it possible to incorporate occluding boundary information, but forces us to employ a smoothness constraint different from the one previously proposed. The new constraint follows directly from a particular definition of surface smoothness.

We solve the set of equations arising from the smoothness constraints and the image-irradiance equation iteratively, using occluding boundary information to supply boundary conditions. Good initial values are found at certain points to help reduce the number of iterations required to reach a reasonable solution. Numerical experiments show that the method is effective and robust. Finally, we analyze scanning electron microscope (SEM) pictures using this method. Other applications are also proposed.

1. Introduction

This paper explores the relationship between image brightness and object shape. Much of the work in machine vision does not explicitly exploit the information contained in the brightness values recorded in the image, using

Artificial Intelligence **17** (1981) 141–184
North-Holland Publishing Company

these values only to segment the image, based on the difference of average brightnesses in adjacent regions. A great deal of information is contained in the image brightness values, however, since it has been shown that image brightness is related to surface orientation [Horn, 1975].

The problem of computing the shape of an object from the shading in an image can be thought of as the problem of reconstructing one surface (height of the object above some reference plane) from another surface (brightness in the image plane). Information at each point of the image is used to compute the orientation of the corresponding point on the object, using the assumption that the surface is smooth. This is in contrast with other machine-vision methods which analyze surface depth based on discontinuities in surface orientation and boundary information alone.

1.1. Historical background

The photometric approach to determining surface orientation from image brightness was first formulated in the form of a non-linear first-order partial differential equation in two unknowns [Horn, 1975]. This equation can be solved using a modified characteristic strip-expansion method. This method assumes that the surface is smooth, as does the method described in this paper. We will see, however, that slightly different interpretations of the term 'smooth' are employed.

The reflectance map, introduced later [Horn, 1977], represents the relationship between surface orientation and surface brightness. The map is defined in gradient space, which appeared in the work on scene analysis of line drawings [Huffman, 1971; Mackworth, 1973; Draper, 1980]. We assume orthographic image projection and take the viewing direction as parallel to the z-axis. The shape of the object can be described by its height, z, above the xy-plane. It is convenient to use the short-hand notation p and q for the first partial derivatives of z with respect to x and y:

$$p = \partial z/\partial x \quad \text{and} \quad q = \partial z/\partial y.$$

The pq-plane is referred to as *gradient space*, since every point in it corresponds to a particular surface gradient. Distance from the origin of gradient space equals the slope of the surface, while the direction is the direction of steepest ascent.

Fixed scene illumination, surface-reflectance properties, and imaging geometry can be incorporated into an explicit model that allows image brightness to be related directly to surface orientation. Thus we can associate with each point in gradient space the brightness of a surface patch with the specified orientation. The result, usually depicted by means of iso-brightness contours, is called the *reflectance map*, and denoted $R(p, q)$. The reflectance map can be obtained experimentally using a test object or a sample mounted on a goniometer stage. It can also be determined theoretically if the surface-reflectance is known as a function of the incident, emittance, and phase angles. The reflectance map can be computed, for example, if the so-called Bidirectional Reflectance Distribution Function (BRDF) [Nicodemus et al., 1977] and the distribution of light sources is known [Horn and Sjoberg, 1979].

The reflectance map is a convenient tool, since it provides a simple representation of the constraint inherent in one image-brightness measurement. Once the brightness, $E(x, y)$, is known at a point, one can ask what the surface orientation might be there. A measurement of image brightness restricts the possible surface orientations at the corresponding point on the surface of the object. This constraint is expressed by the *image-irradiance equation* [Horn, 1977]

$$R(p, q) = E(x, y),$$

where the gradient (p, q) denotes possible orientations and $E(x, y)$ is the brightness measured at the point (x, y). In general, one measurement cannot give us both p and q. It can only fix a relationship between the two variables. Additional constraint is required for a unique solution. This usually takes the form of some assumption about the class of surfaces that may be allowed.

One effect of the introduction of the reflectance map was that it motivated research on other ways of solving the shape-from-shading problem. It also led to the development of iterative methods, similar to those used to solve second-order partial differential equations. Such methods, now called pseudo-local, relaxation, or cooperative computation methods, were suggested some time ago [Horn, 1970, p. 192], but could not be developed for this application without these new tools.

1.2. Characteristic strip expansion

The old method [Horn, 1975] can be interpreted in terms of the reflectance map, too. In the method of characteristic strip-expansion [Garabedien, 1964; Moon and Spencer, 1969; Carrier and Pearson, 1976; Courant and Hilbert, 1962; John, 1978] the partial differential equation given above is replaced by a set of five ordinary differential equations, one for each of x, y, z, p, and q:

$$dx/ds = R_p \quad \text{and} \quad dy/ds = R_q,$$

$$dz/ds = pR_p + qR_q,$$

$$dp/ds = E_x \quad \text{and} \quad dq/ds = E_y,$$

where R_p and R_q are the partial derivatives of R with respect to p and q, while E_x and E_y are the partial derivatives of E with respect to x and y [Horn, 1977; Bruss, 1979].

The parameter s varies monotonically along a particular characteristic strip.

When the characteristic strip is extended, one moves to a new point (x, y) in the image and a new point (p, q) in the reflectance map [Horn, 1977; Woodham, 1978]. The orientation of the surface is known at the end of the strip. One has to move in a particular direction, (dx, dy), in the image plane in order to be able to compute the orientation at the new point (see solid arrow in Fig. 1a). The equations above tell us that this direction is the direction of steepest ascent, (R_p, R_q), at the corresponding point in the reflectance map (see dotted arrow in Fig. 1b). At the new image point so determined, a different value of image brightness is found, corresponding to a new point in the reflectance map. This point in the reflectance map also lies in a well defined direction, (dp, dq), from the previous point in the reflectance map (see solid arrow in Fig. 1b). From the equations above we know that this direction is the direction of steepest ascent, (E_x, E_y), at the corresponding point in the image (see dotted arrow in Fig. 1a).

One important observation is that these directions will be computed incorrectly if the brightness measurements are corrupted by noise. The result is that the characteristic strips deviate more and more from their ideal paths as the computation progresses. Thus, while characteristic strip-expansion works in the absence of noise, it suffers from error accumulation in practice. One way to

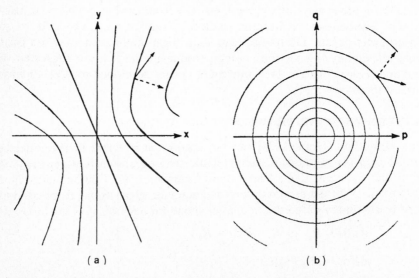

(a)   (b)

Fig. 1. Geometric interpretation of the equations arising from the application of the characteristic strip-expansion method to the image-irradiance equation. The image is shown in (a) as a set of iso-brightness contours and the reflectance map appears similarly in (b). It is known that the gradient is (p, q) on the surface of the object at the point corresponding to the image point (x, y). In order to continue the solution from this point, one must take a small step on the image in a direction determined by the gradient of the reflectance map, while the direction of the corresponding step on the reflectance map is similarly determined by the image brightness gradient.

greatly reduce this effect is to expand neighboring strips simultaneously and to adjust the solution using the assumption that the surface is smooth between strips [Horn, 1970, p. 144]. The characteristic strip-expansion method modified in this fashion can also interpolate new strips when the existing ones separate too far and delete old ones when they approach too closely.

Strips may be started near a so-called singular point (see later) and grow outwards from there. Because of the directionality of the progress of the solution, information from the ends of the characteristic strips cannot be exploited by this method. This is an important shortcoming since crucial information is obtained from occluding boundaries (see later). Normally, these would be reached at the end of the computation, with no means available to influence the (completed) solution.

There have been two new approaches based on two different ways of introducing additional constraints. In the one case, additional images are obtained from the same position with changed lighting. This will be discussed in Section 1.4. The other approach stays in the single image domain, exploiting instead suitably formulated assumptions about the nature of the surface. The work in this area employs relaxation or cooperative computation methods, which depend on the propagation of local constraints to determine global solutions [Woodham, 1977; Strat, 1979; Brooks, 1979]. These methods can often be viewed essentially as iterative algorithms for solving large sets of simultaneous equations arising from a least squares minimization. Information flow is not just along the characteristic directions, taking into account the fact that individual measurements are noisy. Instead of singular points, boundary conditions on a closed curve are used to select one of an infinite number of possible solutions.

1.3. Previous numerical methods for shape from shading

We look at these algorithms in more detail now. Woodham's [Woodham, 1977] method requires two rules which reduce the number of possible surface orientations at a particular point. Suppose that two closely spaced image points P_1 and P_2 at (x_1, y_1) and (x_2, y_2) correspond to object points on the same section of a smooth surface. Further assume that the view angle, between surface normal and the line of sight, increases and that the direction of steepest ascent, polar angle in gradient space, decreases in going from P_1 and P_2. Let C_1 and C_2 be the contours in gradient space corresponding to

$$R(p, q) = E(x_1, y_1) \quad \text{and} \quad R(p, q) = E(x_2, y_2),$$

where $R(p, q)$ is the reflectance map and $E(x_1, y_1)$ and $E(x_2, y_2)$ are the observed brightness values at the points P_1 and P_2 (see Fig. 2). Now the contour of permissible values for (p, q) at point P_1 can be restricted to those points on C_1 lying on or within the circle of maximum view-angle interpretation of P_2.

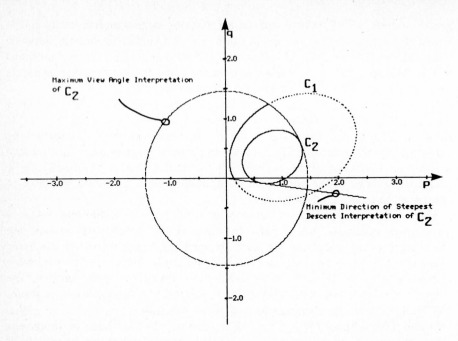

FIG. 2. The possible values of the gradients at the points P_1 and P_2 are restricted considerably if we assume that the view angle increases and the direction of steepest ascent decreases in going from P_1 to P_2.

Further, the contour of permissible values for (p, q) at point P_1 can be restricted to those points on C_1 on or above the line of the minimum direction of steepest ascent interpretation of P_2.

If a particular interpretation were applicable to the data, such an interpretation would provide a framework for ordering selected image points with respect to changes in both the view angle and the direction of steepest ascent. For example, if one can assume that the surface is elliptical or hyperbolic at a point (that is, the sign of the Gaussian curvature [Cohn-Vossen, 1952; Pogorelov, 1956; Moon and Spencer, 1969; do Carmo, 1976] is known) one can guarantee the sign of the change to the view angle or the sign of the change to the direction of steepest ascent by choosing the direction of the small step (dx, dy) from P_1 to P_2 appropriately [Woodham, 1977; Woodham, 1979]. Thus, local assumptions about surface shape provide monotonicity relations between selected image points. Thus we can start a shape-from-shading algorithm using these rules on the selected image points.

A somewhat different approach makes use of a particular way of formulating a smoothness constraint. To derive the constraint, we will assume for now that the second partial derivatives of the surface height z exist and are continuous. Then the partial derivative of z with respect to x and y is independent of the order in which the differentiations are performed:

$$\partial p / \partial y = \partial^2 z / \partial y\, \partial x = \partial^2 z / \partial x\, \partial y = \partial q / \partial x.$$

Evidently in any simply-connected region, B say,

$$\int\int \{\partial p / \partial y - \partial q / \partial x\} = 0,$$

since the integrand is zero at every point. Thus, by Green's theorem [Hildebrand, 1965], the integral of (p, q) along a closed curve (the boundary, ∂B, of the region) also equals zero:

$$\oint \{p\, \mathrm{d}x + q\, \mathrm{d}y\} = 0.$$

This is eminently sensible, since the line integral gives the difference between the height at the end of the line and its beginning, and we assumed that we remain on the same section of the surface (see Fig. 3).

If we use a numerical method based on imperfect data to compute the orientation of the surface at every point, we can expect that this integral will in fact not be exactly equal to zero. One way of imposing a smoothness constraint then is to find a solution which minimizes the errors in these loop integrals while also satisfying the image-irradiance equation as closely as possible.

This idea was pursued by Strat [Strat, 1979] as well as Brooks [Brooks, 1979]. Brooks showed that he could restrict attention to integrals around small loops in the image plane. He listed the possible orientations (quantized in a suitable way) at each point, then iteratively eliminated those conflicting with the loop integral criterion. This was accomplished using a relaxation method not unlike that developed by Waltz [Waltz, 1975] for labelling line drawings.

Strat minimized the weighted sum of the errors in integrals around small loops and the errors in the image-irradiance equations. He developed a system for iteratively solving the large, sparse set of equations arising from this minimization formulation. His method is in many ways similar to the one presented here except insofar as he used gradient space and so could not deal

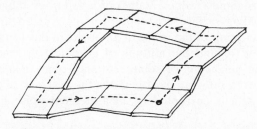

FIG. 3. Discrete version of the loop integral of (p, q). The total change in elevation as one goes around the loop should be zero if the patches belong to a differentiable, single-valued surface.

with occluding boundaries. As a result, his algorithm requires that surface orientation be given on a closed curve. This limits its applicability.

1.4. Photometric stereo methods

The other new approach uses further images to provide additional constraint. These images are taken from the same position, but with changed lighting conditions. This so-called *photometric stereo* approach [Woodham, 1977; Horn et al. 1978; Woodham, 1980] allows one to determine surface orientation locally without smoothness assumptions.

Since the images are obtained from the same position, a particular point on the object will appear at the same spot in each image. This means that one does not have the problem of identifying projections of a particular surface feature in multiple views, as happens in ordinary stereo. A different reflectance map applies to each image, however, since the lighting is different for each view. For a given point in the image we have one brightness value corresponding to each of these reflectance maps. Suppose, for example, that at a particular point, (x_0, y_0), two measurements of image brightness are available. Then we have two (non-linear) equations for p and q,

$$R_1(p, q) = E_1(x_0, y_0), \qquad R_2(p, q) = E_2(x_0, y_0),$$

where R_1 and R_2 are the reflectance maps appropriate to the two lighting situations, while E_1 and E_2 are the observed image-brightness values. The intersection of the corresponding gradient-space contours provides one with the sought after surface orientation. This is the essential idea of photometric stereo. Naturally, the above pair of nonlinear equations in two unknowns may have more than one solution, in which case additional information (such as a third image) may be needed to find the unique answer (see Fig. 4).

The graphical construction shown here can be replaced with a simple lookup-table procedure [Silver, 1980; Ikeuchi, 1981]. Quantized brightness values are used as indices into the table; the entries in the table contain the corresponding surface orientations. Detection of errors is facilitated (if more than two images are used) by blank entries which represent incompatible combinations of brightness values. Values of p and q are found for every point in the image, yielding surface orientation for the corresponding surface patches. While a description of the shape of an object in this form may be suitable for recognition and to find the attitude of an object in space, it is at times helpful to provide height above some reference plane instead. While z can obviously be found by integration of p and q, the best way to do this when it is known that the data is corrupted by measurement noise has not yet been described.

In industrial applications one has to deal with metallic parts which often exhibit specular or mirror-like reflections. In this case a distributed light source

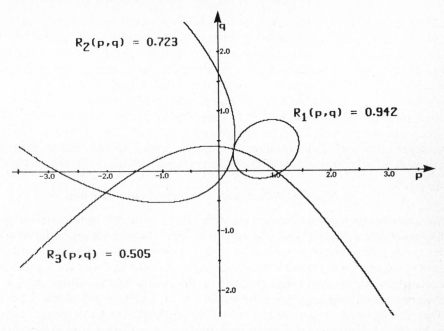

FIG. 4. Determining the surface orientation at a given image point using the photometric stereo method. Here, three measurements of image brightness are obtained using different illumination conditions. Three superimposed reflectance map contours, corresponding to the different measurements, intersect at the point sought.

with spatially varying brightness may be used [Ikeuchi, 1981]. For matte surfaces one can simply use a number of point sources [Silver, 1980]. So far experimentation has been confined to single objects, avoiding possible inaccuracies due to interflection or mutual illumination [Spacek, 1979].

1.5. Motivation of this research

The outline of the projection of an object in the image plane is called its *silhouette*. Parts of this silhouette may correspond to sharp edges on the surface, others to places where the surface curves around smoothly. The smooth parts of the surface corresponding to parts of the silhouette are referred to as occluding boundaries. The locus of (barely) visible points on the surface where the tangent plane contains the viewer is called the *occluding boundary*. Occluding boundaries supply important information about the shape of an object and one can attempt to recover the shape of the object from this information alone using rather strong assumptions [Marr, 1977]. A simple interpolation algorithm works, particularly if the surface is (locally) spherical or cylindrical [Barrow and Tenenbaum, 1981]. This can also be approached from the statistical point of view of recovering the most likely surface [Witkin, 1980].

The true surface, however, can be found only if we also pay attention to the shading information. The occluding boundary can then be used as the boundary condition for the reconstruction. There is some question about whether the problem is well posed in this form, since the partial derivatives of height become infinite on the boundary. It should be clear, though, that if a numerical method is to succeed at all, then the representation of surface orientation must allow these boundary conditions to be expressed correctly. Little is known now about the uniqueness of solutions obtained in this way. It seems likely, however, that only one solution is possible under certain rather general assumptions about the nature of the reflectance map [Bruss, 1979; Bruss, 1980].

2. The Gaussian Sphere and Reflectance Functions

We can identify surface orientations with points on a unit sphere, called the *Gaussian sphere* [Hilbert and Cohn-Vossen, 1952]. Let the viewer be far above the north pole, along the z-axis, where the z-axis is taken as the extended line from the center of the sphere to its north pole. Assume that we take a patch of the surface of an object and place it in the center of the sphere, without changing its attitude in space. The patch will face some point of the sphere. That is, a unit-surface normal erected on the patch will touch the sphere at this point. The orientation of a horizontal portion of a surface, for example, is represented by a point at the north pole, since its surface normal points directly at the viewer. Portions of the surface seen at a glancing angle by the viewer correspond to points on the equator, while surface elements turned away from the viewer are associated with points in the southern hemisphere. Thus points in the northern hemisphere are of most interest to us here.

2.1. The Gaussian sphere and apparent brightness of a surface patch

If we assume orthographic projection of the three-dimensional world, then the angle between the line of sight and the surface normal is independent of the position of the patch on the object. As far as the geometry of light reflection is concerned we need to concern ourselves only with the orientation of a surface patch as represented by a point on the Gaussian sphere. Surface patches of an object which share the same orientation are associated with the same point on the sphere, independent of their position in space (see Fig. 5).

Surface brightness depends on the surface material and the geometry of light reflection: the angles between the line of sight, the surface normal, and the incident light rays. Since each point on the Gaussian sphere expresses one particular such geometric relationship, we can associate a unique value of surface brightness with each point on its surface. Say, for example, that a surface patch perpendicular to the viewer appears with unit brightness. In that situation we assign this value to the north pole. Using this method, we can assign brightness values to all points on the Gaussian sphere. Shown in Fig. 6 is

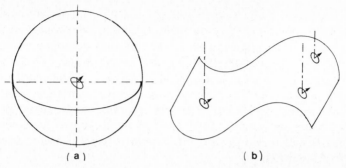

(a)   (b)

FIG. 5. Surface patches of an object (b), which share the same orientation are associated with the same point on the Gaussian sphere (a), independent of their position on the object.

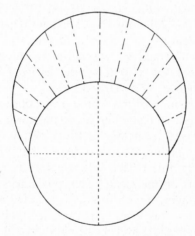

FIG. 6. Cross section through Gaussian sphere showing brightness values associated with points on the sphere. The radial distance of the curve from the surface of the sphere is proportional to the brightness. The particular reflectance function shown here happens to vary as $\sqrt{a^2 \cos^2 e + 1} + (a \cos e - 1)$, where e is the emittance angle, between the surface normal and the line of sight, and $a = 0.72$.

a cross section of the Gaussian sphere with brightness values represented by the height of a curve above the surface.

2.2. Projections of the Gaussian sphere

It may not be convenient to use this representation of the dependence of surface brightness on orientation, since the Gaussian sphere is three-dimensional. Graphic presentation of this information, for example, is difficult. It is therefore advantageous to project the Gaussian sphere onto a plane. (This is possible since we are interested only in the surface of the Gaussian sphere.)

There are, of course, many ways to perform this mapping operation. Even if we were to confine ourselves to conformal projections, we would have many to choose from, including the Mercator, Lambert, and stereographic projections used in geodesy and cartography [Thomas, 1952; Raisz, 1962]. We prefer continuous projections like these, since they map neighboring points into neighboring points. This is important because we plan to generate surface representations iteratively from boundary information. Roughly speaking, to be able to do this, we want the following to hold: a point C lying between two other points A and B is projected into a point $F(C)$ which lies approximately between $F(A)$ and $F(B)$.

It can easily be shown that,

$$n = (-p, -q, 1)/\sqrt{1 + p^2 + q^2}$$

is a unit (outward) normal to the surface [Horn, 1977; Horn, 1981]. This gives us the coordinates of the point on the Gaussian sphere corresponding to a surface patch with gradient (p, q), and immediately suggests a projection onto a plane with axes labelled p and q. Appropriately enough, the plane of projection is called gradient space in this case, as we have mentioned before [Huffman, 1971; Mackworth, 1973; Draper, 1980].

Geometrically we can think of this as the projection of the Gaussian sphere by rays from its center onto a plane tangent to the north pole (with the sense of the p and q axes reversed from that of the x and y axes). This projection, called the *gnomonic* projection, has the property that great circles are mapped into lines. (It is used for this reason in navigation to determine the shortest path between two points on the earth.) This also makes it a so-called *geodesic* projection. In our case here, the north pole is mapped into the origin, the top hemisphere is mapped into the whole pq-plane, and points on the equator end up at infinity. Points on the lower hemisphere are not projected onto the pq-plane.

Since each point in gradient space corresponds to a particular surface orientation, one can associate a unique brightness value with it. The result, as mentioned earlier, is the reflectance map [Horn, 1977]. The gnomonic projection is convenient for the following reasons: (1) the coordinates correspond to the first partial derivatives of surface height, z, (2) we can compute surface height by integrating p and q, and (3) a line integral of (p, q) along a closed loop is always zero. Unfortunately, gradient space also has a serious drawback. As we shall see, points on the equator of the Gaussian sphere correspond to surface patches on the occluding boundary. With the gradient-space projection, the equator maps to infinity. As a result, occluding boundary information cannot be expressed in gradient space.

2.3. Stereographic projection

One solution to this problem is the use of the stereographic projection [Sohon,

1941]. Hipparchus (*circa* 150 B.C.) is credited with the invention of this projection (which appears to have been employed in the astrolabe-planisphere solution of the astronomical triangle). We can think of this projection in geometric terms also as projection onto a plane tangent at the north pole. This time, however, the center of projection is the south pole, not the center of the sphere (see Fig. 7). We label the axes of the stereographic plane f and g to distinguish them from those of gradient space. It can be shown that these coordinates are related to the partial derivatives as follows:

$$f = 2p[\sqrt{1 + p^2 + q^2} - 1]/(p^2 + q^2),$$
$$g = 2q[\sqrt{1 + p^2 + q^2} - 1]/(p^2 + q^2).$$

This projection is conformal (preserves angles between lines and shapes of small figures) and maps circles on the Gaussian sphere into circles on the plane [Hilbert and Cohn-Vossen, 1952]. The whole sphere, not just the northern hemisphere, is mapped onto the plane this time. Only the south pole ends up at infinity, while the equator is mapped into a circle of radius two (see Fig. 8). We may also assign a brightness value to each point in the stereographic plane, just as we did with points in gradient space.

The two projections considered so far fall in the category of *azimuthal* projections, since latitude on the sphere simply becomes the azimuth in the plane. Another convenient projection in this class is the so-called *azimuthal equidistant* projection. Here the distance from the origin in the plane equals the distance along the surface of the sphere measured from the north pole (that is, the co-latitude). There is no obvious geometric interpretation in terms of rays emanating from a fixed center of projection. One can think of this mapping instead as one obtained by rolling the sphere on the plane, along meridians, always starting with the north pole aligned with the origin. If we call

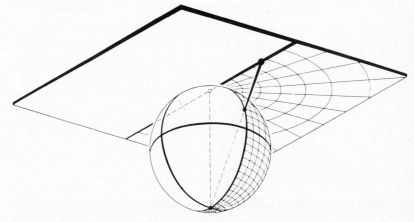

Fig. 7. The stereographic mapping projects each point on the surface of the sphere, along a ray from one pole, onto a plane tangent to the opposite pole.

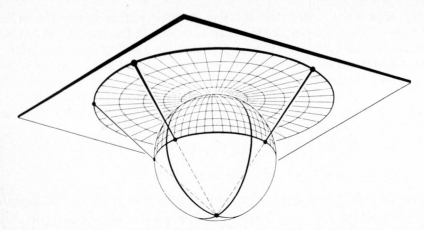

FIG. 8. The stereographic projection maps the equator onto a circle of radius two. The equator of the Gaussian sphere corresponds to points on the occluding boundary of the object.

the coordinates of the plane a and b in this case, we have

$$a = [p/\sqrt{p^2 + q^2}] \tan^{-1} \sqrt{p^2 + q^2},$$

$$b = [q/\sqrt{p^2 + q^2}] \tan^{-1} \sqrt{p^2 + q^2}.$$

As with the gnomonic projection, we project only the northern hemisphere. But, unlike the gnomonic projection, points on the equator do not end up at infinity; instead they are mapped onto a circle of radius $\pi/2$.

There are, of course, numerous other projections one might use. K. Tanaka, for example, used another azimuthal projection, the so-called *orthographic* projection in early work on hill-shading [Horn, 1981].

3. Smoothness Constraint and Boundary Conditions

In the sequel we use the stereographic projection. The form of the image-irradiance equation will be slightly different, since we use f and g instead of p and q. However, this makes no difference to the basic idea that a measurement of surface brightness restricts the possible surface orientations. We must develop a suitable smoothness constraint expressible in the coordinate system natural to the stereographic plane. We also have to determine what boundary conditions are available to constrain the solution of the image-irradiance equation. Finally, it will be helpful to find a way of determining good initial values of surface orientation for at least some of the points, in order to get the numerical solution off to a good start.

3.1. Formulation of surface smoothness constraints

If we employ the stereographic projection, we cannot use the closed loop constraint proposed by Strat [Strat, 1979] and Brooks [Brooks, 1979], because the closed loop constraint depends upon a special characteristic of the gnomonic projection. Namely, the closed loop integral can be expressed directly in terms of p and q, the coordinates of gradient space. Unfortunately, this is not true in the case of either the stereographic projection or the azimuthal equidistant projection. If a constraint expresses the property of surface smoothness, it ought to be valid regardless of the projection we happen to use. It seems reasonable to express the smoothness criterion in terms of a relationship between neighboring points.

We now turn to the definition of surface smoothness. The standard definition of a smooth function is one which has continuous first partial derivatives. This agrees with our intuitive feeling of what constitutes a smooth surface. First of all, smoothness requires that there be no depth discontinuities. That is to say, height, as a function of the image coordinates, should be continuous (height is class C^0). But we also require that surface orientation be continuous, for if a surface has a sharp edge or krinkle, the surface is not considered smooth. In other words, smoothness also requires that the first partial derivatives of height be continuous (height is class C^1).

Should one also require that the second partial derivatives of height be continuous, or equivalently, that the derivatives of orientation are continuous? The following illustration shows that this is not necessary. Imagine a planar surface attached to a portion of a cylindrical surface so that the two are tangent where they touch (see Fig. 9). Here surface orientation is constant on the planar part, but varies on the cylindrical part. Thus surface orientation is continuous, but its derivatives are not. Nevertheless, people regard this surface as smooth.

It is interesting to note at this point that the method of characteristic strip expansion can be shown to apply in general when the function sought is of class C^2. In the case of a first-order partial differential equation in two independent variables, however, it is known that the solution is unique even when the function is only class C^1 [Courant and Hilbert, 1962, p. 145]. Similarly, the derivation of the closed loop constraint shown above requires that the function be class C^2. It turns out to be sufficient, however, that the function be single-valued and (once) differentiable.

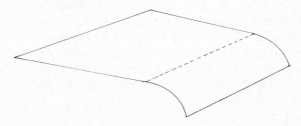

FIG. 9. A surface constructed by attaching a portion of a cylindrical surface to a plane, in such a way that they are tangent on the contact line, is considered smooth.

3.1.1. *Continuity of surface orientation*

What is the definition of continuous? A function is continuous if neighboring points map into neighboring points. If a function is vector valued, being continuous implies that each component of the function is continuous [do Carmo, 1976]. This allows us to consider each component of surface orientation separately. For example, in the stereographic plane, we can formulate two constraints which express continuity of f and g separately. We use the standard definition of continuity [do Carmo, 1976]:

A function F is continuous at (x_0, y_0) if, given any $\epsilon > 0$, there exists a δ such that when

$$(x - x_0)^2 + (y - y_0)^2 < \delta^2,$$

then,

$$|F(x, y) - F(x_0, y_0)| < \epsilon.$$

If, given a particular ϵ, we can find a single value of δ for all points in the region of interest, then the function is uniformly continuous.

In practice, we will be dealing with a discrete grid of points with values defined at the nodes of the grid. If we take the grid interval δ_0 smaller than δ, then we are guaranteed that:

$$|F(x_0 + \delta_0, y_0) - F(x_0, y_0)| < \epsilon \quad \text{and} \quad |F(x_0, y_0 + \delta_0) - F(x_0, y_0)| < \epsilon.$$

At this point we should remember that it is surface orientation which we are assuming varies continuously as a function the image coordinates. Thus equations like the one above apply to f and g.

3.1.2. *Summation of error terms*

One more check is necessary before we can use our smoothness constraint. To measure how far the computed surface departs from smoothness, we will be looking at error terms like

$$(f_{i+1,j} - f_{i,j})^2 \quad \text{and} \quad (g_{i+1,j} - g_{i,j})^2.$$

We form the sum of the squares of the differences over all adjacent pairs of nodes in the grid. When the grid interval becomes small, the number of nodes per unit area becomes large. For our purposes, the sum of all the differences squared should nevertheless remain small as we decrease the grid interval. For this to be true we actually require that the derivatives of orientation exist and are bounded. Suppose that the largest absolute value of the partial derivatives of f and g with respect to x and y is denoted by D_m. Then the square of an error term will be less than

$$[D_m \delta_0]^2.$$

Since the number of nodes per unit area equals $1/\delta_0^2$, we find that the sum of squares of the errors is less than D_m. Note that discontinuities of the derivatives of orientation, as occur on the dotted line in Fig. 9, do not constitute a problem.

3.2. Constraints from boundary information

In some areas of an image, we can determine surface orientations directly. This is true, for example, at so-called singular points and specular points. Useful initial values for the iterative solution process are found this way. More importantly, at an occluding boundary, we can determine surface orientation from the silhouette. This supplies us with the all-important boundary conditions.

3.2.1. *Occluding boundary*

At an occluding boundary we can determine the surface normal uniquely [Marr, 1977; Barrow and Tenenbaum, 1981]. The following two facts are the starting points of our discussion of the determination of the surface normals from the silhouette.

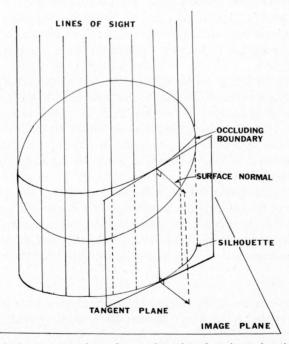

FIG. 10. The line of sight is tangent to the surface at the point where it touches the occluding boundary. The tangent plane at that point cuts the image plane in a line. This line is tangent to the silhouette in the image plane.

First: since we observe an occluding boundary there, the line connecting the surface to the viewer must be tangential to the surface patch at that point (see Fig. 10). Thus the line of sight lies in the plane tangent to the surface at the point where it grazes the surface. It is therefore perpendicular to the surface normal at that point.

Second: the line of sight is perpendicular to the image plane (Since we assumed orthographic image projection, all lines of sight are parallel to the z-axis and thus perpendicular to the image plane). It follows that the tangent plane is perpendicular to the image plane and therefore projected as a line in the image plane. This line is tangent to the silhouette in the image plane.

We see then that a normal to the silhouette in the image plane is parallel to the normal to the surface at the corresponding point on the occluding boundary. We can in this fashion obtain surface orientations for all points on the occluding boundary.

3.2.2. *Self-shadow boundary*

Consider the situation where there is a single point source. The locus of (barely) illuminated points on the surface where the tangent plane contains the light source is called the *self-shadow boundary*. On the self-shadow boundary, light rays play the role of the lines of sight in the previous discussion. Namely, the light grazes the surface there; the rays are perpendicular to the surface normal. The trouble is that now the tangent plane is not projected as a line in the image plane (see Fig. 11). Consequently we cannot determine surface orientations uniquely on a self-shadow boundary. Approximations to the correct surface orientations can be computed if we make some assumptions. This is helpful, because these can serve as initial values for the iterative algorithm. One possible assumption we might make is that the self-shadow boundary lies in a plane perpendicular to the light source. This occurs, for example, when the object is spherical, and is not a bad approximation when the object is ellipsoidal.

Let the light source lie in a direction given by the unit vector n_s. The projection of the self-shadow boundary in the image is called the *shadow edge*. Let a vector in the image plane perpendicular to the shadow edge be n_b (drawn from the lighted towards the shadowed side). The self-shadow boundary lies in a plane perpendicular to both n_b and n_s and must therefore be parallel to

$$n_s \times n_b.$$

The surface normal on the shadow boundary must be perpendicular to this line, as well as to the incident rays. It must therefore be parallel to

$$(n_s \times n_b) \times n_s = n_b - (n_b \cdot n_s)n_s.$$

The above vector vanishes when the incident rays are parallel to the image plane, indicating that in this case we cannot determine anything about the

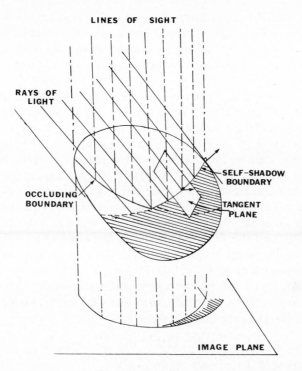

FIG. 11. The tangent planes on the self-shadow boundary do not project as lines into the image plane. The surface orientation of points on the self-shadow boundary cannot be determined uniquely.

surface normals on the shadow boundary, even with the assumption that this boundary lies in a plane perpendicular to the incident rays. Conversely, when the source is at the viewer, the surface normal is fully determined even without this assumption, since the shadow boundary then coincides with the occluding boundary.

Errors in the determination of the surface normal on the shadow boundary do not lead to errors in the final result, since they affect only the initial values. Presumably, better initial values do reduce the number of iterations required to obtain an accurate solution, however. Note that the condition that the surface normal is perpendicular to the incident rays on the self-shadow boundary is actually already implicit in the equation $R(p, q) = 0$.

3.2.3. *Specular point and singular point*

We can also determine surface orientation at so-called singular points and specular points. Assume for now that the illumination comes from a single point-source of light. Consider first a surface patch oriented so that its normal vector points directly at this light source. (It will be maximally illuminated, but not necessarily maximally luminous.) Let us call the point on the Gaussian sphere corresponding to this orientation the *source spot*, since it essentially specifies the direction towards the light source. Note, by the way, that the source spot ends up in the southern hemisphere when the object is illuminated from behind. Such a source spot will be projected into a point in the plane by the stereographic projection. This is not the case if we use the gnomonic or azimuthal-equidistant projections, since these project only the northern hemisphere.

Next, assume that we are dealing with a surface material which exhibits mirror-like or specular reflection. A surface patch on such a surface may be oriented just right to reflect rays from the light source towards the viewer. This leads to a so-called *specular point* in the image. This happens only when the incident angle, i, equals the emittance angle, e, and when the incident ray, the surface normal, and the reflected ray lie in the same plane. This orientation corresponds to the point mid-way between the source spot on the Gaussian sphere and the north pole.

If we let (p_s, q_s) be the point in gradient space which corresponds to the source spot on the Gaussian sphere, then a surface patch oriented for specular reflection has the gradient (p_m, q_m), given by:

$$p_m = p_s[\sqrt{1 + p_s^2 + q_s^2} - 1]/(p_s^2 + q_s^2),$$
$$q_m = q_s[\sqrt{1 + p_s^2 + q_s^2} - 1]/(p_s^2 + q_s^2).$$

This can be shown by noting that (p_m, q_m) must lie in the same direction in gradient space as (p_s, q_s), and that the angle between $(0, 0, 1)$ and $(-p_m, -q_m, 1)$ must be equal to the angle between $(-p_m, -q_m, 1)$ and $(-p_s, -q_s, 1)$. Similar formulae apply in the stereographic plane:

$$f_m = f_s[\sqrt{1 + f_s^2 + g_s^2} - 1]/(f_s^2 + g_s^2),$$
$$g_m = g_s[\sqrt{1 + f_s^2 + g_s^2} - 1]/(f_s^2 + g_s^2).$$

Finally, for the azimuthal equidistant projection,

$$a_m = a_s/2 \quad \text{and} \quad b_m = b_s/2.$$

For an ideal point source, an ideal specular surface (and an ideal imaging system), the specular point would be infinitely bright and infinitesimal in extent. For slightly extended sources and surfaces that are not perfectly smooth, the specular reflection is spread out somewhat, with a large, but finite maximum brightness. Surfaces with slightly undulating surface microstructure give rise to *glossy* high-lights [Horn, 1981].

For surfaces which do not exhibit specular reflection there often still is a unique surface orientation which gives rise to maximum (or minimum) brightness. A Lambertian surface, for example, is brightest when the light rays strike it perpendicularly. Suppose then that there is a particular value of brightness which corresponds uniquely to a particular surface orientation. A *singular point* is a point in the image where this value of brightness is observed. Note that specular points are special cases of singular points. Evidently, we can determine the surface orientation uniquely at a singular point.

Singular points, by the way, were used to provide starting values in an implementation of the characteristic strip-expansion method [Horn, 1975]. Note that information about the orientation of the surface at these special points is implicit in the image-irradiance equation. What we gain here are helpful initial values for the iterative method.

3.3. Minimization of errors

It helps to first consider the continuous case, ignoring for now the tesselation of the image plane into picture cells. We try to find functions $f(x, y)$ and $g(x, y)$ which make the errors in the image-irradiance equation small while also being as 'smooth' as possible. We can try to minimize

$$e = \int \int \{(f_x^2 + f_y^2) + (g_x^2 + g_y^2) + \lambda[E(x, y) - R_s(f, g)]^2\} \, dx \, dy,$$

where f_x, f_y, g_x, and g_y are the first partial derivative of f and g with respect to x and y. The errors in the image irradiance equation are weighted by the factor λ relative to the measure of departure from 'smoothness'. This factor can be made large when the reflectance map is known accurately and the brightness measurements are precise.

The minimization of an integral of the form

$$\int \int F(f, g, f_x, f_y, g_x, g_y) \, dx \, dy$$

is a problem in the calculus of variation [Courant and Hilbert, 1953; Hildebrand, 1965; Carrier and Pearson, 1976]. When the integrand depends on two functions of two independent variables as well as their first partial derivatives, then the Euler equations are,

$$F_f - \partial/\partial x(F_{f_x}) - \partial/\partial y(F_{f_y}) = 0,$$

$$F_g - \partial/\partial x(F_{g_x}) - \partial/\partial y(F_{g_y}) = 0.$$

Applying these formulae we obtain:

$$\nabla^2 f = \lambda[E(x, y) - R_s(f, g)] \, \partial R_s/\partial f,$$

$$\nabla^2 g = \lambda[E(x, y) - R_s(f, g)] \, \partial R_s/\partial g,$$

where

$$\nabla^2 = \partial^2/\partial x^2 + \partial^2/\partial y^2$$

is the Laplacian operator. These equations will provide helpful guidelines when we tackle the discrete case in the next section. It can be shown, by looking at higher order variations, that if f and g obey the above partial differential equations, then the stationary value of the sum of errors is actually a minimum.

It may also be of interest that we would have ended up with the biharmonic operator here (instead of the Laplacian) if we had tried to minimize the sum of squares of the Laplacian of f and g (instead of the sum of squares of the first partial derivatives of f and g). We will not discuss why the two functions, f and g, should be 'consistent', that is, correspond to the surface orientations of a smooth surface.

As an extension of the above analysis we may consider the minimization of

$$e' = \int\int \{(f_x^2 + f_y^2) + (g_x^2 + g_y^2)\}\, dx\, dy,$$

subject to the constraint

$$E(x, y) = R_s(f, g).$$

Introduction of the Lagrangian multiplier λ leads to the same equations as the ones considered above. Elimination of λ gives us this set of equations:

$$(\partial R_s/\partial g)\nabla^2 f = (\partial R_s/\partial f)\nabla^2 g\,,$$

$$E(x, y) = R_s(f, g).$$

We will not use the results of this constrained minimization exercise since we do expect errors in the measurements of image brightness. Instead, we will set the value of the parameter λ in inverse proportion to the root-mean-square of the noise in the image brightness measurements.

4. Proposed Algorithm and Numerical Experiments

We will construct an iterative algorithm using two kinds of constraints: one from the image-irradiance equations and the other from the smoothness condition. In addition, we depend on the occluding boundary to provide boundary conditions and a few special points to supply helpful initial values.

We will have to check whether the algorithm converges. Since we do not have a theoretical analysis of the conditions required for convergence, we resort to numerical experimentation. With exact, complete information, we expect that the algorithm will converge, and converge to the correct solution. In practice there are errors, however, due both to noise in the measurements and to discrepancies between the mathematical model and the real situation. Further, due to obscuration, for example, the information may be incomplete. Under these circumstances one would hope that the algorithm would be robust enough to converge to some solution, preferably one close to the correct one.

Consequently we have carried out numerical experiments under two different conditions: in the first case, all information given to the algorithm is exact: the reflectance map is correct, and complete boundary information is available. In the second, some of the information is erroneous: the reflectance map given may be incorrect, either because of inappropriate assumptions about the properties of the surface material or because of incorrect information about the position of the light source. We also may be lacking effective boundary conditions on part of the border, perhaps because of partial obscuration of the object by another. The algorithm would not be very useful if it did not converge, or converged to a solution very different from the correct one, when faced with these difficulties.

4.1. Proposed algorithm

We will use an iterative algorithm to determine surface orientations using the image-irradiance equations and the smoothness criterion as constraints. We can measure the departure from smoothness as follows:

$$s_{i,j} = [(f_{i+1,j} - f_{i,j})^2 + (f_{i,j+1} - f_{i,j})^2 + (g_{i+1,j} - g_{i,j})^2 + (g_{i,j+1} - g_{i,j})^2]/4.$$

The error in the image-irradiance equation, on the other hand, can be stated this way:

$$r_{i,j} = [E_{i,j} - R_s(f_{i,j}, g_{i,j})]^2,$$

where $E_{i,j}$ is the observed image brightness at the node (i, j), while R_s is the reflectance map with f, and g, the surface orientation components as arguments. We will seek a solution which minimizes the sum of the error terms over all nodes:

$$e = \sum_i \sum_j (s_{i,j} + \lambda r_{i,j}).$$

The factor λ weights the errors in the image-irradiance equation relative to the departures from surface smoothness.

We can, by the way, write a formula for the error, just like the one given above, using the components of the gradient, p and q, or the azimuthal equidistant coordinates, a and b, instead of the stereographic coordinates f and g. For that matter, we can do this directly with coordinates specified on the Gaussian sphere.

We are going to differentiate e with respect to $f_{i,j}$ and $g_{i,j}$ (note that each $f_{i,j}$ and $g_{i,j}$ occurs in four terms of the sum for e). We obtain,

$$\partial e/\partial f_{i,j} = 2(f_{i,j} - f_{i,j}^*) - 2\lambda[E_{i,j} - R_s(f_{i,j}, g_{i,j})] \, \partial R_s/\partial f,$$

$$\partial e/\partial g_{i,j} = 2(g_{i,j} - g_{i,j}^*) - 2\lambda[E_{i,j} - R_s(f_{i,j}, g_{i,j})] \, \partial R_s/\partial g,$$

where f^* and g^* are the local averages of f and g:

$$f_{i,j}^* = [f_{i+1,j} + f_{i,j+1} + f_{i-1,j} + f_{i,j-1}]/4,$$

$$g_{i,j}^* = [g_{i+1,j} + g_{i,j+1} + g_{i-1,j} + g_{i,j-1}]/4.$$

The partial derivatives of e with respect to $f_{i,j}$ and $g_{i,j}$ will all equal zero, if the set of values we have for $f_{i,j}$ and $g_{i,j}$ constitute a solution to the minimization problem. Assume that they are; then the task is to solve the resulting large, sparse set of equations [Hildebrand, 1965; Conte and de Boor, 1972; Hamming, 1972]. Iterative techniques like the Gauss–Jacobi method, the Gauss–Seidel method, or successive over-relaxation [Carrier and Pearson, 1976, p. 277; Ames, 1977, p. 103], can be used if we first rearrange the equations as follows:

$$f_{i,j} = f^*_{i,j} + \lambda [E_{i,j} - R_s(f_{i,j}, g_{i,j})] \, \partial R_s / \partial f,$$

$$g_{i,j} = g^*_{i,j} + \lambda [E_{i,j} - R_s(f_{i,j}, g_{i,j})] \, \partial R_s / \partial g.$$

We can think of these equations as suggesting an adjustment of f and g, in a direction given by the gradient of R_s, by an amount proportional to the residual error in the image-irradiance equation. (The magnitude of the adjustment is also controlled by the parameter λ.) Further, we can see that the value for the orientation at a point will be filled in from the surround when the gradient of R_s is zero, as happens at a singular point.

The basic idea now is that the difference between corresponding values of f and corresponding values of g on successive iterations will decrease as we proceed. Thus we can perhaps use the values from the nth iteration on the righthand side to compute the values for the $(n + 1)$st iteration on the lefthand side. Under certain conditions this method converges to the solution of the original set of equations. Thus we might use the rule:

$$f^{n+1}_{i,j} = f^{*n}_{i,j} + \lambda [E_{i,j} - R_s(f^n_{i,j}, g^n_{i,j})] \, \partial R_s / \partial f,$$

$$g^{n+1}_{i,j} = g^{*n}_{i,j} + \lambda [E_{i,j} - R_s(f^n_{i,j}, g^n_{i,j})] \, \partial R_s / \partial g,$$

where $f^n_{i,j}$ and $g^n_{i,j}$ are used in evaluating R_s (and the partial derivatives of R_s). To avoid a particular kind of numerical instability we resort to a slightly different set of formulae

$$f^{n+1}_{i,j} = f^{*n}_{i,j} + \lambda [E_{i,j} - R_s(f^{*n}_{i,j}, g^{*n}_{i,j})] \, \partial R_s / \partial f,$$

$$g^{n+1}_{i,j} = g^{*n}_{i,j} + \lambda [E_{i,j} - R_s(f^{*n}_{i,j}, g^{*n}_{i,j})] \, \partial R_s / \partial g,$$

where $f^{*n}_{i,j}$ and $g^{*n}_{i,j}$ are used in evaluating R_s (and the partial derivatives of R_s). The flow of information when one uses this method can be illustrated schematically as shown in Fig. 12. Note that the computations for a given iteration are local. Global consistency is achieved by the propagation of constraints over many iterations.

The numerical instability alluded to above can best be thought of in terms of a checkerboard. On each iteration the new values for the white squares are computed using the old values on the black squares and *vice versa*. Small noise components can be amplified into a checkerboard pattern in this fashion as the

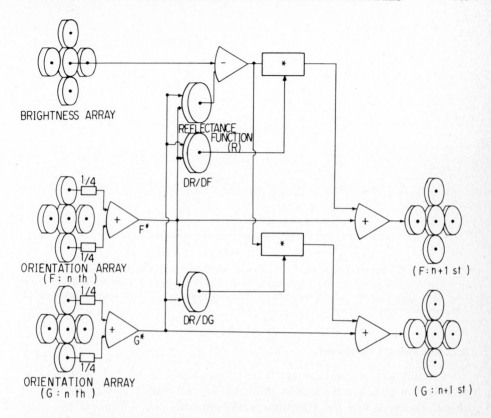

FIG. 12. This schematic diagram shows the flow of information in the iterative computation of surface orientation. It also suggests possible hardware implementations of the algorithm.

iterations progress. Say, for example, that the orientations (f, g) and (f^*, g^*) lie on opposite sides of the correct solution. Then the iterative equations above will produce an adjustment relative to (f^*, g^*) based on the error in the image-irradiance equation at (f, g), which goes in the wrong direction. (Fig. 13 illustrates how this can occur.) This undesirable process can be damped out by using the local average, rather than the value at the cell itself in evaluating R_s.

Using a better stencil for computing the local average improves stability too. A *stencil* is a pattern of weights by which neighboring values are multiplied. One may, for example, add (4/5) of the average of the four neighbors that share an edge with a particular point to (1/5) of the average of the neighbors that touch on a corner. This suggestion is based on a better discrete approximation of the Laplacian than the one we have been implicitly using here [Richtmyer and Morton, 1967; Milne 1970; Carrier and Pearson, 1976; Ames, 1977].

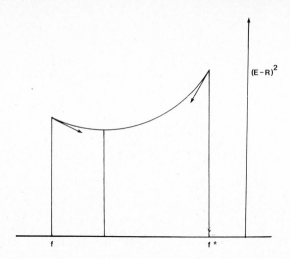

FIG. 13. This illustration shows why the simple iterative formulae may be subject to a certain kind of numerical instability. The correction to f^* (on the right) is computed from the gradient of the total error using the orientation f (on the left). The correction will have the wrong direction if the minimum lies between the two.

4.2. Numerical experiments

To start off with, we will use synthetic images based on models of objects, so that we can compare the results produced by our algorithm with the known shape. To check that the algorithm works correctly, we will give it the exact brightness distribution, complete boundary information, and the correct reflectance map. Then we will see what happens if we omit some of the boundary information, or if we estimate the light-source direction incorrectly, or assume the wrong reflectance properties. Finally, the method is applied to real images.

The shape information computed will be presented in two forms: as needle diagrams and oblique views of the surface. In a *needle diagram* we present an orthographic projection of the normals to the surface as they would be seen by the viewer [Horn, 1982]. This may be the most direct way of portraying graphically the information computed by the algorithm. The surface height above some reference plane can be estimated by integrating this surface orientation information. We can then show an oblique view of a network of lines drawn over the resulting surface by intersecting it with vertical planes parallel to the two coordinate axes. This mode of presentation is referred to as a *block-diagram* in cartography [Horn, 1981].

For several of the examples we will assume that the surface is made of a material which acts as a Lambertian reflector. A Lambertian surface is a diffuse reflector with the property that a particular surface patch looks equally bright from all viewing directions and that its brightness is proportional to the illumination falling on it. Due to foreshortening of the surface as seen from the light source, the illumination (flux per unit area) varies as the cosine of the incident angle, i (between the incident rays and the surface normal). For a Lambertian surface, then, the brightness, too, will vary as the cosine of the incident angle. For surface patches turned away from the light source, the incident angle becomes larger than 90°, and so the cosine becomes negative. Since brightness cannot be negative, we use the formula

$$\max[0, \cos i]$$

for computing brightness.

The first task is to determine the reflectance map. If we let n be a unit-surface normal and n_s a unit vector pointing in the direction of the light source, then the cosine of the incident angle is just the dot-product of these two vectors,

$$\cos i = n \cdot n_s.$$

The expression for the unit-surface normal in terms of p and q, shown earlier, allows one to express the cosine of the incident angle in terms of the first partial derivatives of the surface orientation [Horn, 1977; Horn, 1981]:

$$\cos i = \frac{(1 + p_s p + q_s q)}{[\sqrt{1 + p^2 + q^2}\sqrt{1 + p_s^2 + q_s^2}]}.$$

Using the coordinates of the stereographic plane instead:

$$\cos i = \frac{[16(f_s f + g_s g) + (4 - f^2 - g^2)(4 - f_s^2 - g_s^2)]}{[(4 + f^2 + g^2)(4 + f_s^2 + g_s^2)]}.$$

If we use the azimuthal equidistant projection we have for $\cos i$:

$$\cos \sqrt{a^2 + b^2} \cos \sqrt{a_s^2 + b_s^2} + \sin \sqrt{a^2 + b^2} \sin \sqrt{a_s^2 + b_s^2}$$

$$\times \frac{(a_s a + b_s b)}{[\sqrt{a^2 + b^2}\sqrt{a_s^2 + b_s^2}]}.$$

In several of the examples we use a sphere as a test object, or an ellipsoid obtained by anistropically scaling a sphere. To make a synthetic image we need to know the surface orientation at each point in the image. The implicit equation for a sphere with its center at the origin can be written

$$x^2 + y^2 + z^2 - R^2 = 0.$$

Computing the gradient of the lefthand side of this equation tells us that the surface normal at the point (x, y, z) is parallel to the vector (x, y, z) and that

$$\partial z/\partial x = -x/z \quad \text{and} \quad \partial z/\partial y = -y/z.$$

From these values of p and q, we can calculate f and g, or a and b. The brightness at every point in the image can then be found from

$$E(x, y) = \max[0, \cos i]$$

and the equations for $\cos i$ given above.

4.2.1. **Example 1.** *Lambertian sphere with source near the viewer*

Consider a Lambertian sphere illuminated by a single, distant light source, located near the viewer. The occluding boundary is also the self-shadow boundary in this case. The whole occluding boundary is visible to the viewer, while none of the shadowed areas is. The image-brightness data is derived analytically from a model of the surface and the known reflectance properties of a Lambertian surface. The algorithm is then applied to the synthesized image. (Fig. 14 shows a pseudo gray-level image of the object.)

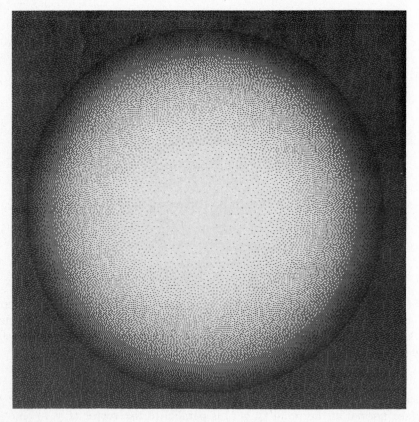

FIG. 14. Pseudo gray-level image of a Lambertian sphere illuminated by a light source near the viewer. This is the synthetic image used as input to the algorithm.

The discussion earlier showed that at an occluding boundary, the surface normal is parallel to the normal to the silhouette at the corresponding point in the image. We can therefore determine the surface orientations at the occluding boundary. This boundary information is shown in Fig. 15a in the form of a needle diagram.

The algorithm requires at least as many iterations as there are nodes across the image. This can be explained as follows: At a point near one side of a

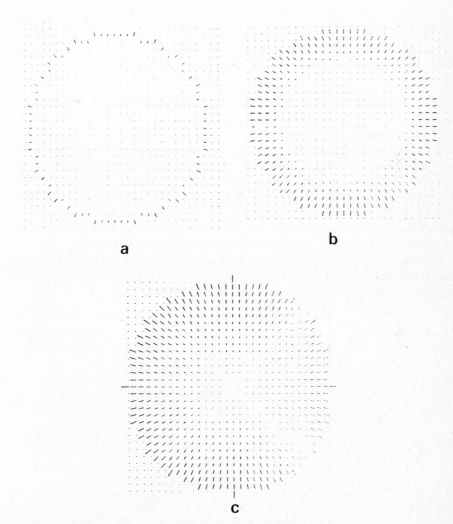

FIG. 15. Needle diagrams showing various stages of the iterative solution: (a) This is the initial orientation array, obtained from boundary information. (b) Result after 5 iterations. (c) Result after 30 iterations.

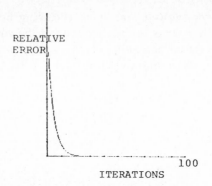

FIG. 16. This shows how the root-mean-square of error in orientation decreases with the number of iterations.

region surrounded by an occluding boundary, one needs information from the opposite side to obtain the exact orientation. At each iteration, information available at one point propagates only to its immediate neighbors. This means that it takes as many iterations as there are nodes across the object for a point near the boundary to begin to be influenced by the opposite boundary. In this case, the number of nodes across is thirty and this implies that we may need more than thirty iterations. Fig. 15b shows the results after 5 iterations, while Fig. 15c is the result after 30 iterations. Fig. 16 is the root-mean-square error (the difference between the true values of orientation and those computed by the algorithm) plotted as a function of the number of iterations.

The error gradually decreases, and after thirty iterations, the relative error is less than 0.01%. Fig. 17 is a view of the surface generated from the surface orientation data that was used to make the needle diagram.

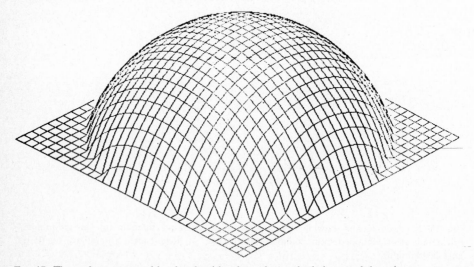

FIG. 17. The surface generated by the algorithm from the synthetic image of the sphere.

4.2.2. **Example 2.** *Effect of initial values*

We proposed the use of orientations at singular points as initial values. It may be desirable that until the boundary information propagates to a point, orientation values at that point not begin to change. At a singular point, the partial derivatives of R are always zero. This means that the constraints of the image-irradiance equations are ineffective there. The orientations at each point can be initialized to $(0.0, 0.0)$. The partial derivatives for that orientation typically are non-zero, however, with the result that the iterative equations indicate adjustments at each grid node before information from the boundary has had a chance to propagate to the node. It is not clear if the number of iterations required for a reasonable solution is affected adversely by this phenomenon.

This second example illustrates the effect of initial values. An egg-shaped object is illuminated from a direction near the extension of one of its short axes, and the viewer is looking in the direction of the long axis. We use an egg shape now to demonstrate that our algorithm works on objects other than spheres. The ratio of the length of the long axis to that of the short axis is 3 in this example. The precise position of the light source is given by $(f_s, g_s) = (0.5, 0.0)$ (the angle between the incident rays and the z-axis is 53.1°).

The surface orientations on the self-shadow boundary are given initially to simplify matters. Fig. 18 shows the resulting needle diagram and Fig. 19 the relative errors, illustrating the utility of initial values at singular points. When we use singular values as initial values, we get to a reasonable solution after fewer iterations than when all points are initialized to have the orientation $(0.0, 0.0)$. A view of the surface computed is shown in Fig. 20.

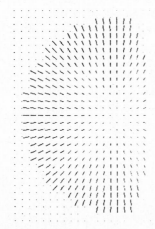

FIG. 18. The needle diagram generated for the egg-shaped object.

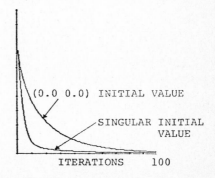

(0.0 0.0) INITIAL VALUE

SINGULAR INITIAL VALUE

ITERATIONS   100

FIG. 19. The root-mean-square error in orientation for the egg-shaped object. The error is lower after a given number of iterations when the singular point is used to provide initial values.

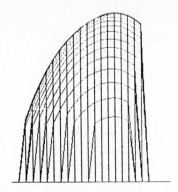

FIG. 20. The surface generated by the algorithm from the synthetic image of the egg-shaped object.

4.2.3. **Example 3.** *Negative Gaussian curvature*

The two previous examples involved surfaces whose Gaussian curvature is positive [Cohn-Vossen, 1952; Pogorelov, 1956; Moon and Spencer, 1969; do Carmo, 1976]. The third example involves a hyperbolic shape, one with negative Gaussian curvature. Unfortunately, there are no occluding boundaries on this surface. Instead, we provide the algorithm with orientations on a closed curve as boundary conditions. The light source is again near the viewer in this example. Fig. 21 is the needle diagram generated for this surface.

It takes about the same number of iterations to obtain a reasonable solution as in the first example. This result illustrates that the algorithm is not sensitive to whether a surface has negative or positive Gaussian curvature. In other

FIG. 21. The needle diagram of the solution obtained for the hyperbolic surface.

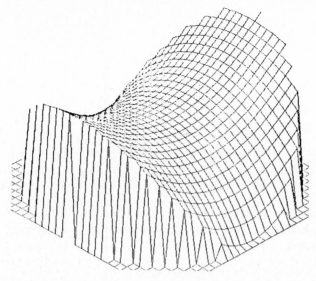

FIG. 22. The surface generated by the algorithm from the synthetic image of the hyperbolic surface.

words, we can use this algorithm without paying attention to the global characteristics of the surface, whether it be concave or convex, and whether its surface consists of hyperbolic or elliptical points [Woodham, 1977]. Fig. 22 is a view of the surface generated by the algorithm.

4.2.4. Example 4. *Effect of incomplete boundary information*

If no boundary information is available at all, then we can say very little about the shape of the surface. We would, however, like to get some estimate of the surface shape when only some of the boundary information is missing.

In the example shown here, we do not provide explicit boundary information on the self-shadow boundary. There are two motivations for considering this situation. One is that, as mentioned earlier, we cannot determine surface orientations uniquely there anyway. The other is that it sometimes happens that we cannot see all of the surface of an object, and we have to do without information on part of the boundary, leaving it unconstrained. The algorithm should try to obtain reasonable surface orientations even in situations like that (although one might expect that there may not be a unique solution to the shape-from-shading problem in this case).

We imagine that a Lambertian sphere is illuminated from the direction $(f_s, g_s) = (0.5, 0.0)$. No information is provided on the self-shadow boundary. Fig. 23 shows the relative errors in the solution obtained by the algorithm, plotted against the number of iterations.

The conclusion is that the information about orientations on the self-shadow boundary helps the algorithm arrive at a good solution after fewer steps, but is

FIG. 23. The root-mean-square error in orientation when boundary information is incomplete decreases more slowly than when it is complete. A reasonable solution is obtained in both cases.

not necessary for convergence. A closed boundary does not seem to be a necessary condition for the algorithm to arrive at a solution. If an object is partially obscured by another, it may still be possible to obtain a 'reasonable' solution, one which does not contradict any of the information provided by the image.

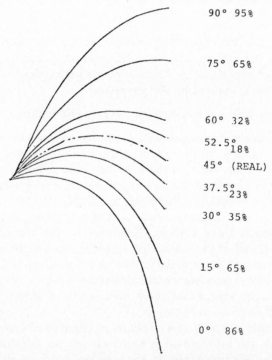

FIG. 24. The effect of inaccurate estimation of the position of the light source. The source is actually at 45°, while the program is misled into believing it is at a variety of angles, from 0° to 90°. The interrupted line shows a cross section through the correct solution.

4.2.5. **Example 5.** *Effect of error in estimating light-source position*

In practice, we may not be able to determine the light-source position precisely. In this example the light-source position is given incorrectly. It is reasonable to insist that the algorithm still work, although, of course, the solution cannot be expected to be accurate.

A synthesized image of a sphere is made with the illumination coming from a direction which makes an angle of 45° with the z-axis. Then the algorithm tries to determine surface orientations under the assumption that the light source is at some other position, ranging from 0° to 90°. As one can see from Fig. 24, an error of 7.5° in estimating the source direction causes no more than 20% error in surface height.

4.2.6. **Example 6.** *Effect of error in assumed reflectance properties*

In this experiment, the algorithm uses a reflectance map based on incorrect assumptions about the reflectance properties of the surface. Egg shapes, whose axis ratios are 5, 3, and 1 are illuminated from a light source placed near the viewer. The surface has brightness linearly dependent on the incident angle (rather than the cosine of the incident angle):

$$1 - 2i/\pi .$$

The algorithm, however, assumes that the surface is Lambertian. The output still resembles the correct result as shown by the cross sections in Fig. 25.

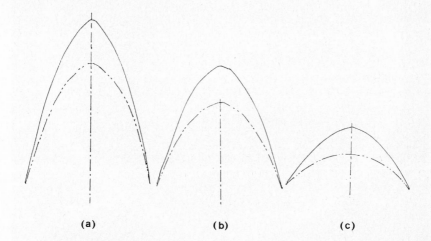

(a)   (b)   (c)

FIG. 25. Cross sections through shapes computed when the reflectance properties were different from those assumed by the program. (a) Egg shape with ratio of axes equal to 5. (b) Egg shape with ratio of axes equal to 3. (c) Egg shape with ratio of axes equal to 1. In each case the interrupted line shows a cross section through the correct solution.

4.2.7. **Example 7.** *Analysis of a SEM picture*

Here the algorithm is applied to a picture which was produced by a scanning electron microscope (SEM). Such devices are described in a book by Wells [Wells et al., 1974], and pictures made using them can be found in a number of popular books [Scharf, 1977; Grillone, 1978] and articles [Echlin, 1968]. SEM images are in many ways similar to images obtained in an optical system when the light source is symmetrically distributed about the viewer. The reflectance map is rotationally symmetric about the origin in both cases, and none of the visible areas are shadowed. One minor difference is that, in an SEM image, a surface patch oriented with its normal pointing at the viewer has minimum brightness, not maximum.

The object shown in the pseudo gray-level image that appears as Fig. 26 is a protuberance on a young leaf [Scharf, 1977, p. 96]. The reflectance map we used at first was based on the data of Laponsky [Laponsky and Whetten, 1960],

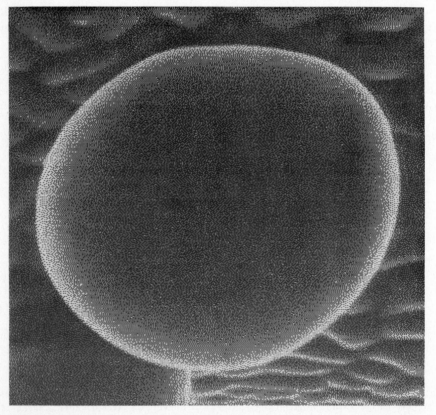

FIG. 26. A pseudo gray-level picture made from a scanning electron microscope image of a protuberance on a young leaf of *cannabis sativa indica*.

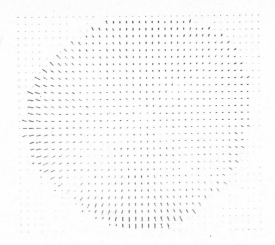

FIG. 27. The needle diagram computed for the object in the previous figure.

which suggests that secondary electron flux in a Scanning Electron Microscope varies approximately as the secant of the incident angle. Fig. 27 is the needle diagram which the algorithm computed, and views of the surface generated are shown in Fig. 28.

The computed surface appears to be a bit too flat, probably as a result of incorrect assumptions about the form of the reflectance map, as well as the fact that we did not take into account the changes in gray-level that are introduced

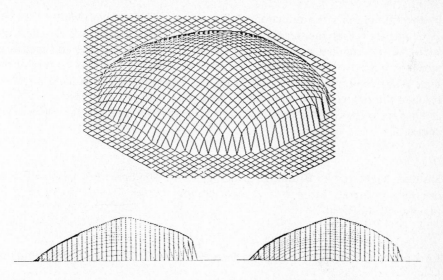

FIG. 28. Various views of the surface computed from the scanning electron microscope picture.

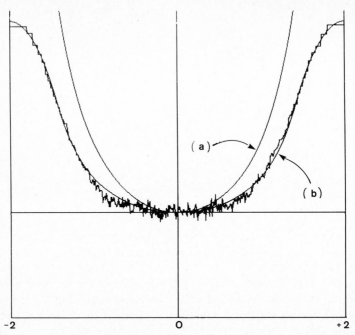

FIG. 29. Cross section through the reflectance map based on the assumption that the resin droplet is spherical. The horizontal coordinate equals $\sqrt{f^2 + g^2} = 2 \tan i/2$. Also shown for comparison are (a) the function $\sec i$ and (b) a function which equals $(1 + \sec i)/2$ for $i < 70°$ and saturates for larger incident angles.

by the lithographic reproduction of the picture. The data of Müller [Müller, 1937] suggests that the secondary electron flux grows more slowly than the secant of the incident angle, at least for amorphous metals. Careful measurements on a more or less spherical resin droplet imaged in another picture of the same plant confirmed this for our example. Shown in Fig. 29 is a cross section through the reflectance map obtained from this 'calibration object'.

An approximation for the brightness, which remains finite for all incident angles,

$$e^{\alpha(1 - \cos i)},$$

has been suggested by Bruining [Bruining, 1954]. The best fit of this function to our data occurred for $\alpha \approx 1$. A considerably better fit was provided by a function of the form

$$\sec ki$$

for $k \approx 0.8$. For incident angles less than 70°, however, the best fit was obtained from

$$(1 - s) + s \sec i$$

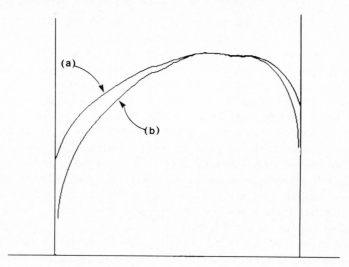

FIG. 30. Cross sections through the surfaces computed from the image of the protuberance using the two reflectance functions shown in Fig. 29.

for $s \approx \frac{1}{2}$. The only remaining discrepancy results from the fact that the observed brightness saturates at a finite value for incident angles close to 90°. An ad hoc correction for this was incorporated in our estimate, also shown in Fig. 29.

Shown in Fig. 30 are cross sections through two reconstructions. The upper one (a) corresponds to the result shown in Fig. 28, while the lower one (b) was obtained using the reflectance function $(1 + \sec i)/2$, modified to take into account the saturation of brightness for large incident angles. The shape computed using the latter reflectance function is in better accord with human judgment.

The lesson is that it is better to use a calibration object of known shape for the determination of the reflectance map than to depend on measurements obtained under somewhat different circumstances, or on a theoretically derived approximation.

5. Concluding Remarks

We proposed an algorithm for computing surface orientations from shading information using an iterative method. We then demonstrated that this algorithm does successfully compute surface orientations under a variety of conditions.

5.1. Relevance to applications in machine vision

One use of the algorithm is, of course, to compute shape from shading in a single image. This algorithm is especially effective in the analysis of scanning electron microscope pictures of smooth parts of objects.

Another application is the improvement of the results produced by the photometric stereo method. We do not need any assumptions about surface smoothness to implement the photometric stereo method. However, when there is noise in the measured brightness values, the computed orientations will be in error. This error can be drastically reduced if we do introduce the constraint of surface smoothness. If, for example, there is a dirty spot on the object, the measured brightness values will be too low. The lookup table used in the photometric stereo method may then not have a surface orientation entry for these erroneous values. In this case, surface orientation can be filled in from the neighboring points by averaging. This is the simplest use of the method. Output from a photometric stereo system [Silver, 1980] has been smoothed successfully using this method.

An even better way to proceed is to minimize the weighted sum of the errors in the image-irradiance equations and the smoothness measure. The solution is then, in effect, pulled towards each of the constraint lines of the reflectance map and towards the local average of the surface orientations. It ends up in some compromise position which minimizes the overall 'strain'. The weights, by the way, can be set according to known values of noise in the measurements. This method has in fact been used in some recent work on photometric stereo. (Compare Fig. 8.2 with Fig. 8.4 in [Ikeuchi, 1981].) In the cases shown there, the algorithm not only smoothed the output, but also extended the area in which a solution could be found.

5.2. Relevance to basic research in machine vision

The algorithm still works reasonably when the reflectance map is only a crude approximation. As can be seen from Example 5, if one is prepared to tolerate errors of up to 20%, then one can be off by as much as 7.5° in estimating where the light source is. Similarly, Example 6 shows that if this kind of error is acceptable, it does not matter whether the surface is Lambertian or one with somewhat different reflectance properties. Thus, if one is willing to accept 20% estimation errors, only six or seven reflectance maps are needed for different light-source position, multiplied by two or three to allow for different surface materials. Note that we don't really need different reflectance maps for different light-source azimuths, since the reflectance map can be rotated to accommodate changes in azimuth of the light source. The nature of the reflectance map does, however, change when the zenith angle of the light source changes.

Propagation of constraints is a powerful method for attacking vision problems. Clarification of the constraints or relationships between neighboring nodes often gives us the key to the solution of a problem. The propagation of constraints from neighboring nodes cuts down the space of possible solutions at a node [Zucker, 1976]. In vision, the number of nodes is large and the possible values lie in a continuous range. This means that the solution space is rather large. In this case, the propagation technique is more effective than the search technique. Even when the propagation technique cannot determine a unique solution, it can reduce the number of possible solutions so that subsequent search can be more effective [Waltz, 1975].

There are several examples in vision where this method has been employed effectively. An iterative method is used to invert the Laplace operator in the computation of lightness [Horn, 1974]. A *pseudo-local* operator is a global operator which can be computed by iteration of a local operator because it happens to be the inverse of a local operator [Horn, 1982]. In the computation alluded to here, the so-called G operator (pseudo-local) calculates a lightness value from those at neighboring points and the thresholded result of the so-called L operator (local) applied at the corresponding point in the image. The first stereo algorithm of Marr [Marr and Poggio, 1976] used this idea too. Here, the 'continuity rule' is an example of positive propagation, requiring that neighboring points have similar disparity values. The 'uniqueness rule' is an example of negative propagation, causing the value at a node to inhibit neighboring nodes from taking on the same value. Iterative computations similar to the ones presented in this paper also occur in the estimation of optical flow from image sequences [Horn and Schunck, 1981]. The shape from regular pattern algorithm [Ikeuchi, 1980] is another example which uses a very similar method. Needless to say, the relaxation technique [Zucker, 1976; Rosenfeld, 1978; Hummel and Zucker, 1980; Davis and Rosenfeld, 1981] is an implementation method for the propagation of constraints.

The propagation of constraint method is suggestive of parallel processing in a planar computational network. The relationship between nodes is homogeneous. Each node connects to its neighbors in the same fashion, independent of its position within the network. An essential operation in many of the algorithms mentioned here is the computation of a weighted average over the neighboring nodes. This is the kind of operation that even a simple array processor can perform easily.

ACKNOWLEDGMENT

This report describes research done at the Artificial Intelligence Laboratory of the Massachusetts Institute of Technology. Support for the Laboratory's artificial intelligence research is provided in part by the Office of Naval Research under contract N00014-77-C-0389.

Fig. 1 is from Horn's paper "Understanding Image Intensities". Figs. 2 and 4 are from R.J. Woodham's thesis, "A Machine Vision System for Understanding Surface Defects in Metal Castings". Fig. 3 is from Horn's paper "Sequins & Quills". Figs. 7 and 8 are out of D. Hilbert and S. Cohn-Vossen's book *Geometry and the Imagination* (Copyright 1952, Chelsea Publishing Company). Fig. 26 is based on a picture in David Scharf's book *Magnifications* (Copyright 1977, Schocken Books Incorporated). These figures are reproduced here by permission of the publishers. We also thank J. Jones for drawing some of the other figures.

The authors would like to extend their sincere appreciation to Professor Patrick H. Winston for encouragement. Discussions with K. Murota of the University of Tokyo, T. Kanade of Carnegie Mellon University, and A. Bruss, W. Silver, and R. Sjoberg of M.I.T. were helpful. Thanks go to M. Brady, K. Forbus, E. Grimson, E. Hildreth, K. Prendergast, C. Roberts and K. Stevens of M.I.T. for helping to proofread the manuscript. We are also grateful to the LISP-Machine Group of the Artificial Intelligence Laboratory for the construction of the LISP Machine. Without the LISP Machine, we could not have completed the experimental part of this research so rapidly.

REFERENCES

1. Ames, W.F. (1977), *Numerical Methods for Partial Differential Equations*, Academic Press, New York.
2. Barrow, H.G. and Tenenbaum, J.M. (1981), Interpreting line drawings as three-dimensional surfaces, *Artificial Intelligence* **17**, 75–116 [this volume].
3. Brooks, M.J. (1979), Surface normals from closed paths, *Proceedings of the Sixth IJCAI*, Tokyo, Japan, 98–101.
4. Bruining, H. (1954), *Physics and Application of Secondary Electron Emission*, Pergamon, New York.
5. Bruss, A.R. (1979), Some properties of discontinuities in the image irradiance equation, AI Memo 517, Artificial Intelligence Laboratory, Massachusetts Institute of Technology.
6. Bruss, A.R. (1980), The image-irradiance equation, its solution and application, Ph.D. Thesis, Department of Electrical Engineering and Computer Science, Massachusetts Institute of Technology.
7. do Carmo, M.P. (1976), *Differential Geometry of Curves and Surfaces*, Prentice-Hall, Englewood Cliffs.
8. Carrier, G.F. and Pearson, C.E. (1976), *Partial Differential Equations—Theory and Technique*, Academic Press, New York.
9. Conte, S.D. and de Boor, C. (1972), *Elementary Numerical Analysis*, McGraw-Hill, New York.
10. Courant, R. and Hilbert, D. (1953), *Methods of Mathematical Physics—Volume I*, Interscience, New York.
11. Courant, R. and Hilbert, D. (1962), *Methods of Mathematical Physics—Volume II*, Interscience, New York.
12. Davis, L.S. and Rosenfeld, A. (1981), Cooperative processes for low-level vision: a survey, *Artificial Intelligence*.
13. Draper, S.W. (1980), The use of gradient and dual space in vision, Internal Report, Department of Computer Science, Sussex University.
14. Echlin, P. (1968), Pollen, *Scientific American* **218** (4) 80–90.
15. Garabedian, P.R. (1964), *Partial Differential Equations*, Wiley, New York.
16. Grillone, L. and Gennaro, J. (1978), *Small Worlds Close Up*, Crown Publishers, New York.
17. Hamming, R.W. (1962), *Numerical Methods for Scientists and Engineers*, McGraw-Hill, New York.
18. Hilbert, D. and Cohn-Vossen, S. (1952), *Geometry and the Imagination*, Chelsea, New York.
19. Hildebrand, F.B. (1965), *Methods of Applied Mathematics*, Prentice-Hall, Englewood Cliffs.
20. Hildebrand, F.B. (1974), *Introduction to Numerical Analysis*, McGraw-Hill, New York.
21. Horn, B.K.P. (1970), Shape from shading: a method for obtaining the shape of a smooth opaque object from one view, Technical Report MAC-TR-79, Project MAC, Massachusetts Institute of Technology.
22. Horn, B.K.P. (1974), Determining lightness from an image, *Computer Graphics and Image Processing* **3**(1) 111–299.
23. Horn, B.K.P. (1975), Obtaining shape from shading information, in: Winston, P.H. (Ed.), *Psychology of Computer Vision*, McGraw-Hill, New York, 115–155.

24. Horn, B.K.P. (1977), Understanding image intensities, *Artificial Intelligence* **8** (2) 201–231.
25. Horn, B.K.P. (1981), Hill-shading and the reflectance map, *Proceedings of the IEEE* **19** (1) 14–47.
26. Horn, B.K.P. (1981), Sequins & Quills—representations for surface topography, in: Bajcsy, R. (Ed.), *Representation of 3-Dimensional Objects*, Springer, Berlin.
27. Horn, B.K.P. and Schunck, B.G. (1981), Determining optical flow, *Artificial Intelligence* **17**, 185–203 [this volume].
28. Horn, B.K.P. and Sjoberg, R.W. (1979), Calculating the reflectance map, *Applied Optics* **18** (11) 1770–1779.
29. Horn, B.K.P., Woodham, R.J. and Silver, W.M. (1978), Determining shape and reflectance using multiple images, AI Memo 490, Artificial Intelligence Laboratory, Massachusetts Institute of Technology.
30. Huffman, D.A. (1971), Impossible objects as nonsense sentences, in: Meltzer, R. and Michie, D. (Eds.), *Machine Intelligence* **6**, Edinburgh University Press, Edinburgh, 295–323.
31. Hummel, R.A. and Zucker, S.W. (1980), On the foundations of relaxation labeling processes, Report No. 80-7, Computer Vision and Graphics Laboratory, Department of Electrical Engineering, McGill University, Montreal, Quebec.
32. Ikeuchi, K. (1980), Shape from regular patterns—an example of constraint propagation in vision, *Proceedings of the Fifth IJCPR*, Miami Beach.
33. Ikeuchi, K. (1981), Determination of surface orientations of specular surfaces by using the photometric stereo method, accepted for publication by *IEEE-PAMI*.
34. John, F. (1978), *Partial Differential Equations*, Springer, New York.
35. Laponsky, A.B. and Whetten, N.R. (1960), Dependence of secondary emission from MgO single crystals on angle of incidence, *Physics Review* **120** (3) 801–806.
36. Mackworth, A.K. (1973), Interpreting pictures of polyhedral scenes, *Artificial Intelligence* **4** (2) 121–137.
37. Marr, D. (1977), Analysis of occluding contour, *Proc. Roy. Soc. London Ser. B* **197**, 441–475.
38. Marr, D. and Poggio, T. (1976), Cooperative computation of stereo disparity, *Science* **194**, 283–287.
39. Milne, W.E. (1970), *Numerical Solution of Differential Equations*, Dover, New York.
40. Moon, P. and Spencer, D.E. (1969), *Partial Differential Equations*, D.C. Heath, Lexington.
41. Müller, H.O. (1937), Die Abhängigkeit der Sekundärelektronemission einiger Metalle vom Einfallswinkel des primären Kathodenstrahls, *Zeitschrift für Physik* **104**, 475–486.
42. Nicodemus, F.E., Richmond, J.C., Hsia, J.J., Ginsberg, I.W. and Limperis, T. (1977), *Geometrical Considerations and Nomenclature for Reflectance*, NBS Monograph 160, U.S. Department of Commerce, National Bureau of Standards.
43. Pogorelov, A.V. (1956), *Differential Geometry*, Noordhoff, Groningen, The Netherlands.
44. Raisz, E. (1962), *Principles of Cartography*, McGraw-Hill, New York.
45. Richtmyer, R.D. and Morton, K.W. (1967), *Difference Methods for Initial-Value Problems*, Interscience, New York.
46. Rosenfeld, A. (1978), Iterative methods for image analysis, *Pattern Recognition* **10**, 181–187.
47. Scharf, D. (1977), *Magnifications—Photography with the Scanning Electron Microscope*, Schocken Books, New York.
48. Silver, W. (1980), Determining shape and reflectance using multiple images, S.M. Thesis, Department of Electrical Engineering and Computer Science, Massachusetts Institute of Technology.
49. Sohon, F.W. (1941), *The Stereographic Projection*, Chelsea, New York.
50. Spacek, L.A. (1979), Shape from shading and more than one view, Internal Communication, Department of Computer Science, Essex University.
51. Strat, T.M. (1979), A numerical method for shape from shading from a single image, S.M. Thesis, Department of Electrical Engineering and Computer Science, Massachusetts Institute of Technology.

52. Thomas, P.D. (1952), *Conformal Projections in Geodesy and Cartography*, Special Publication No. 251, U.S. Department of Commerce, Coast and Geodetic Survey, Washington, D.C.
53. Waltz, D. (1975), Understanding line drawings of scenes with shadows, in: Winston, P.H. (Ed.), *The Psychology of Computer Vision*, McGraw-Hill, New York, 19–91.
54. Wells, O.C., Boyde, A., Lifshin, E. and Rezanowich, A. (1974), *Scanning Electron Microscopy*, McGraw-Hill, New York.
55. Witkin, A.P. (1980), Shape from contour, Ph.D. Thesis, Department of Psychology, Massachusetts Institute of Technology.
56. Woodham, R.J. (1977), A cooperative algorithm for determining surface orientation from a single view, *Proceedings of the Fifth IJCAI*, Cambridge, MA, 635–641.
57. Woodham, R.J. (1978), Reflectance map techniques for analyzing surface defects in metal castings, Technical Report AI-TR-457, Artificial Intelligence Laboratory, Massachusetts Institute of Technology.
58. Woodham, R.J. (1979), Relating properties of surface curvature to image intensity, *Proceedings of the Sixth IJCAI*, Tokyo, Japan, 971–977.
59. Woodham, R.J. (1980), Photometric method for determining surface orientation from multiple images, *Optical Engineering* **19** (1) 139–144.
60. Zucker, S.W. (1976), Relaxation labelling and the reduction of local ambiguities, *Proceedings of the Third IJCPR*, San Diego, CA.

Received March 1980; revised version received October 1980

Determining Optical Flow

Berthold K.P. Horn and Brian G. Schunck

Artificial Intelligence Laboratory, Massachusetts Institute of Technology, Cambridge, MA 02139, U.S.A.

ABSTRACT

Optical flow cannot be computed locally, since only one independent measurement is available from the image sequence at a point, while the flow velocity has two components. A second constraint is needed. A method for finding the optical flow pattern is presented which assumes that the apparent velocity of the brightness pattern varies smoothly almost everywhere in the image. An iterative implementation is shown which successfully computes the optical flow for a number of synthetic image sequences. The algorithm is robust in that it can handle image sequences that are quantized rather coarsely in space and time. It is also insensitive to quantization of brightness levels and additive noise. Examples are included where the assumption of smoothness is violated at singular points or along lines in the image.

1. Introduction

Optical flow is the distribution of apparent velocities of movement of brightness patterns in an image. Optical flow can arise from relative motion of objects and the viewer [6, 7]. Consequently, optical flow can give important information about the spatial arrangement of the objects viewed and the rate of change of this arrangement [8]. Discontinuities in the optical flow can help in segmenting images into regions that correspond to different objects [27]. Attempts have been made to perform such segmentation using differences between successive image frames [15, 16, 17, 20, 25]. Several papers address the problem of recovering the motions of objects relative to the viewer from the optical flow [10, 18, 19, 21, 29]. Some recent papers provide a clear exposition of this enterprise [30, 31]. The mathematics can be made rather difficult, by the way, by choosing an inconvenient coordinate system. In some cases information about the shape of an object may also be recovered [3, 18, 19].

These papers begin by assuming that the optical flow has already been determined. Although some reference has been made to schemes for comput-

Artificial Intelligence **17** (1981) 185–203

ing the flow from successive views of a scene [5, 10], the specifics of a scheme for determining the flow from the image have not been described. Related work has been done in an attempt to formulate a model for the short range motion detection processes in human vision [2, 22]. The pixel recursive equations of Netravali and Robbins [28], designed for coding motion in television signals, bear some similarity to the iterative equations developed in this paper. A recent review [26] of computational techniques for the analysis of image sequences contains over 150 references.

The optical flow cannot be computed at a point in the image independently of neighboring points without introducing additional constraints, because the velocity field at each image point has two components while the change in image brightness at a point in the image plane due to motion yields only one constraint. Consider, for example, a patch of a pattern where brightness[1] varies as a function of one image coordinate but not the other. Movement of the pattern in one direction alters the brightness at a particular point, but motion in the other direction yields no change. Thus components of movement in the latter direction cannot be determined locally.

2. Relationship to Object Motion

The relationship between the optical flow in the image plane and the velocities of objects in the three dimensional world is not necessarily obvious. We perceive motion when a changing picture is projected onto a stationary screen, for example. Conversely, a moving object may give rise to a constant brightness pattern. Consider, for example, a uniform sphere which exhibits shading because its surface elements are oriented in many different directions. Yet, when it is rotated, the optical flow is zero at all points in the image, since the shading does not move with the surface. Also, specular reflections move with a velocity characteristic of the virtual image, not the surface in which light is reflected.

For convenience, we tackle a particularly simple world where the apparent velocity of brightness patterns can be directly identified with the movement of surfaces in the scene.

3. The Restricted Problem Domain

To avoid variations in brightness due to shading effects we initially assume that the surface being imaged is flat. We further assume that the incident illumination is uniform across the surface. The brightness at a point in the image is then proportional to the reflectance of the surface at the corresponding point on the object. Also, we assume at first that reflectance varies smoothly and has no

---

[1]In this paper, the term brightness means image irradiance. The brightness pattern is the distribution of irradiance in the image.

spatial discontinuities. This latter condition assures us that the image brightness is differentiable. We exclude situations where objects occlude one another, in part, because discontinuities in reflectance are found at object boundaries. In two of the experiments discussed later, some of the problems occasioned by occluding edges are exposed.

In the simple situation described, the motion of the brightness patterns in the image is determined directly by the motions of corresponding points on the surface of the object. Computing the velocities of points on the object is a matter of simple geometry once the optical flow is known.

4. Constraints

We will derive an equation that relates the change in image brightness at a point to the motion of the brightness pattern. Let the image brightness at the point (x, y) in the image plane at time t be denoted by $E(x, y, t)$. Now consider what happens when the pattern moves. The brightness of a particular point in the pattern is constant, so that

$$\frac{dE}{dt} = 0.$$

Using the chain rule for differentiation we see that,

$$\frac{\partial E}{\partial x}\frac{dx}{dt} + \frac{\partial E}{\partial y}\frac{dy}{dt} + \frac{\partial E}{\partial t} = 0.$$

(See Appendix A for a more detailed derivation.) If we let

$$u = \frac{dx}{dt} \quad \text{and} \quad v = \frac{dy}{dt},$$

then it is easy to see that we have a single linear equation in the two unknowns u and v,

$$E_x u + E_y v + E_t = 0,$$

where we have also introduced the additional abbreviations E_x, E_y, and E_t for the partial derivatives of image brightness with respect to x, y and t, respectively. The constraint on the local flow velocity expressed by this equation is illustrated in Fig. 1. Writing the equation in still another way,

$$(E_x, E_y) \cdot (u, v) = -E_t.$$

Thus the component of the movement in the direction of the brightness gradient (E_x, E_y) equals

$$-\frac{E_t}{\sqrt{E_x^2 + E_y^2}}.$$

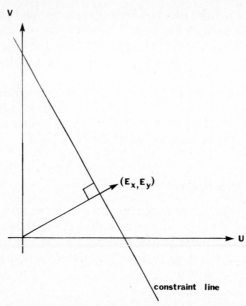

FIG. 1. The basic rate of change of image brightness equation constrains the optical flow velocity. The velocity (u, v) has to lie along a line perpendicular to the brightness gradient vector (E_x, E_y). The distance of this line from the origin equals E_t divided by the magnitude of (E_x, E_y).

We cannot, however, determine the component of the movement in the direction of the iso-brightness contours, at right angles to the brightness gradient. As a consequence, the flow velocity (u, v) cannot be computed locally without introducing additional constraints.

5. The Smoothness Constraint

If every point of the brightness pattern can move independently, there is little hope of recovering the velocities. More commonly we view opaque objects of finite size undergoing rigid motion or deformation. In this case neighboring points on the objects have similar velocities and the velocity field of the brightness patterns in the image varies smoothly almost everywhere. Discontinuities in flow can be expected where one object occludes another. An algorithm based on a smoothness constraint is likely to have difficulties with occluding edges as a result.

One way to express the additional constraint is to minimize the square of the magnitude of the gradient of the optical flow velocity:

$$\left(\frac{\partial u}{\partial x}\right)^2 + \left(\frac{\partial u}{\partial y}\right)^2 \quad \text{and} \quad \left(\frac{\partial v}{\partial x}\right)^2 + \left(\frac{\partial v}{\partial y}\right)^2.$$

Another measure of the smoothness of the optical flow field is the sum of the squares of the Laplacians of the x- and y-components of the flow. The

Laplacians of u and v are defined as

$$\nabla^2 u = \frac{\partial^2 u}{\partial x^2} + \frac{\partial^2 u}{\partial y^2} \quad \text{and} \quad \nabla^2 v = \frac{\partial^2 v}{\partial x^2} + \frac{\partial^2 v}{\partial y^2}.$$

In simple situations, both Laplacians are zero. If the viewer translates parallel to a flat object, rotates about a line perpendicular to the surface or travels orthogonally to the surface, then the second partial derivatives of both u and v vanish (assuming perspective projection in the image formation).

We will use here the square of the magnitude of the gradient as smoothness measure. Note that our approach is in contrast with that of Fennema and Thompson [5], who propose an algorithm that incorporates additional assumptions such as constant flow velocities within discrete regions of the image. Their method, based on cluster analysis, cannot deal with rotating objects, since these give rise to a continuum of flow velocities.

6. Quantization and Noise

Images may be sampled at intervals on a fixed grid of points. While tesselations other than the obvious one have certain advantages [9, 23], for convenience we will assume that the image is sampled on a square grid at regular intervals. Let the measured brightness be $E_{i,j,k}$ at the intersection of the ith row and jth column in the kth image frame. Ideally, each measurement should be an average over the area of a picture cell and over the length of the time interval. In the experiments cited here we have taken samples at discrete points in space and time instead.

In addition to being quantized in space and time, the measurements will in practice be quantized in brightness as well. Further, noise will be apparent in measurements obtained in any real system.

7. Estimating the Partial Derivatives

We must estimate the derivatives of brightness from the discrete set of image brightness measurements available. It is important that the estimates of E_x, E_y, and E_t be consistent. That is, they should all refer to the same point in the image at the same time. While there are many formulas for approximate differentiation [4, 11] we will use a set which gives us an estimate of E_x, E_y, E_t at a point in the center of a cube formed by eight measurements. The relationship in space and time between these measurements is shown in Fig. 2. Each of the estimates is the average of four first differences taken over adjacent measurements in the cube.

$$
\begin{aligned}
E_x \approx \tfrac{1}{4}\{ & E_{i,j+1,k} - E_{i,j,k} + E_{i+1,j+1,k} - E_{i+1,j,k} \\
& + E_{i,j+1,k+1} - E_{i,j,k+1} + E_{i+1,j+1,k+1} - E_{i+1,j,k+1}\}, \\
E_y \approx \tfrac{1}{4}\{ & E_{i+1,j,k} - E_{i,j,k} + E_{i+1,j+1,k} - E_{i,j+1,k} \\
& + E_{i+1,j,k+1} - E_{i,j,k+1}| + E_{i+1,j+1,k+1} - E_{i,j+1,k+1}\}, \\
E_t \approx \tfrac{1}{4}\{ & E_{i,j,k+1} - E_{i,j,k} + E_{i+1,j,k+1} - E_{i+1,j,k} \\
& + E_{i,j+1,k+1} - E_{i,j+1,k} + E_{i+1,j+1,k+1} - E_{i+1,j+1,k}\}.
\end{aligned}
$$

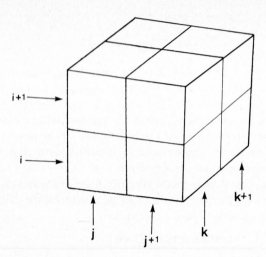

FIG. 2. The three partial derivatives of images brightness at the center of the cube are each estimated from the average of first differences along four parallel edges of the cube. Here the column index j corresponds to the x direction in the image, the row index i to the y direction, while k lies in the time direction.

Here the unit of length is the grid spacing interval in each image frame and the unit of time is the image frame sampling period. We avoid estimation formulae with larger support, since these typically are equivalent to formulae of small support applied to smoothed images [14].

8. Estimating the Laplacian of the Flow Velocities

We also need to approximate the Laplacians of u and v. One convenient approximation takes the following form

$$\nabla^2 u \approx \kappa(\bar{u}_{i,j,k} - u_{i,j,k}) \quad \text{and} \quad \nabla^2 v \approx \kappa(\bar{v}_{i,j,k} - v_{i,j,k}),$$

where the local averages $\bar{u}$ and $\bar{v}$ are defined as follows

$$\bar{u}_{i,j,k} = \tfrac{1}{6}\{u_{i-1,j,k} + u_{i,j+1,k} + u_{i+1,j,k} + u_{i,j-1,k}\}$$
$$+ \tfrac{1}{12}\{u_{i-1,j-1,k} + u_{i-1,j+1,k} + u_{i+1,j+1,k} + u_{i+1,j-1,k}\},$$

$$\bar{v}_{i,j,k} = \tfrac{1}{6}\{v_{i-1,j,k} + v_{i,j+1,k} + v_{i+1,j,k} + v_{i,j-1,k}\}$$
$$+ \tfrac{1}{12}\{v_{i-1,j-1,k} + v_{i-1,j+1,k} + v_{i+1,j+1,k} + v_{i+1,j-1,k}\}.$$

The proportionality factor κ equals 3 if the average is computed as shown and we again assume that the unit of length equals the grid spacing interval. Fig. 3 illustrates the assignment of weights to neighboring points.

FIG. 3. The Laplacian is estimated by subtracting the value at a point from a weighted average of the values at neighboring points. Shown here are suitable weights by which values can be multiplied.

9. Minimization

The problem then is to minimize the sum of the errors in the equation for the rate of change of image brightness,

$$\mathscr{E}_b = E_x u + E_y v + E_t,$$

and the measure of the departure from smoothness in the velocity flow,

$$\mathscr{E}_c^2 = \left(\frac{\partial u}{\partial x}\right)^2 + \left(\frac{\partial u}{\partial y}\right)^2 + \left(\frac{\partial v}{\partial x}\right)^2 + \left(\frac{\partial v}{\partial y}\right)^2.$$

What should be the relative weight of these two factors? In practice the image brightness measurements will be corrupted by quantization error and noise so that we cannot expect $\mathscr{E}_b$ to be identically zero. This quantity will tend to have an error magnitude that is proportional to the noise in the measurement. This fact guides us in choosing a suitable weighting factor, denoted by α^2, as will be seen later.

Let the total error to be minimized be

$$\mathscr{E}^2 = \int \int (\alpha^2 \mathscr{E}_c^2 + \mathscr{E}_b^2) \, dx \, dy.$$

The minimization is to be accomplished by finding suitable values for the optical flow velocity (u, v). Using the calculus of variation we obtain

$$E_x^2 u + E_x E_y v = \alpha^2 \nabla^2 u - E_x E_t,$$
$$E_x E_y u + E_y^2 v = \alpha^2 \nabla^2 v - E_y E_t.$$

Using the approximation to the Laplacian introduced in the previous section,

$$(\alpha^2 + E_x^2) u + E_x E_y v = (\alpha^2 \bar{u} - E_x E_t),$$
$$E_x E_y u + (\alpha^2 + E_y^2) v = (\alpha^2 \bar{v} - E_y E_t).$$

The determinant of the coefficient matrix equals $\alpha^2(\alpha^2 + E_x^2 + E_y^2)$. Solving for u and v we find that

$$(\alpha^2 + E_x^2 + E_y^2)u = +(\alpha^2 + E_y^2)\bar{u} - E_x E_y \bar{v} - E_x E_t,$$
$$(\alpha^2 + E_x^2 + E_y^2)v = -E_x E_y \bar{u} + (\alpha^2 + E_x^2)\bar{v} - E_y E_t.$$

10. Difference of Flow at a Point from Local Average

These equations can be written in the alternate form

$$(\alpha^2 + E_x^2 + E_y^2)(u - \bar{u}) = -E_x[E_x\bar{u} + E_y\bar{v} + E_t],$$
$$(\alpha^2 + E_x^2 + E_y^2)(v - \bar{v}) = -E_y[E_x\bar{u} + E_y\bar{v} + E_t].$$

This shows that the value of the flow velocity (u, v) which minimizes the error $\mathscr{E}^2$ lies in the direction towards the constraint line along a line that intersects the constraint line at right angles. This relationship is illustrated geometrically in Fig. 4. The distance from the local average is proportional to the error in the basic formula for rate of change of brightness when $\bar{u}$, $\bar{v}$ are substituted for u and v. Finally we can see that α^2 plays a significant role only for areas where the brightness gradient is small, preventing haphazard adjustments to the estimated flow velocity occasioned by noise in the estimated derivatives. This parameter should be roughly equal to the expected noise in the estimate of $E_x^2 + E_y^2$.

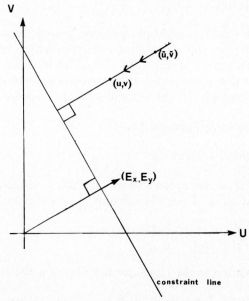

FIG. 4. The value of the flow velocity which minimizes the error lies on a line drawn from the local average of the flow velocity perpendicular to the constraint line.

11. Constrained Minimization

When we allow α^2 to tend to zero we obtain the solution to a constrained minimization problem. Applying the method of Lagrange multipliers [33, 34] to the problem of minimizing $\mathscr{E}_c^2$ while maintaining $\mathscr{E}_b = 0$ leads to

$$E_y \nabla^2 u = E_x \nabla^2 v, \qquad E_x u + E_y v + E_t = 0$$

Approximating the Laplacian by the difference of the velocity at a point and the average of its neighbors then gives us

$$(E_x^2 + E_y^2)(u - \bar{u}) = -E_x[E_x\bar{u} + E_y\bar{v} + E_t],$$
$$(E_x^2 + E_y^2)(v - \bar{v}) = -E_y[E_x\bar{u} + E_y\bar{v} + E_t].$$

Referring again to Fig. 4, we note that the point computed here lies at the intersection of the constraint line and the line at right angles through the point $(\bar{u}, \bar{v})$. We will not use these equations since we do expect errors in the estimation of the partial derivatives.

12. Iterative Solution

We now have a pair of equations for each point in the image. It would be very costly to solve these equations simultaneously by one of the standard methods, such as Gauss–Jordan elimination [11, 13]. The corresponding matrix is sparse and very large since the number of rows and columns equals twice the number of picture cells in the image. Iterative methods, such as the Gauss–Seidel method [11, 13], suggest themselves. We can compute a new set of velocity estimates (u^{n+1}, v^{n+1}) from the estimated derivatives and the average of the previous velocity estimates (u^n, v^n) by

$$u^{n+1} = \bar{u}^n - E_x[E_x\bar{u}^n + E_y\bar{v}^n + E_t]/(\alpha^2 + E_x^2 + E_y^2),$$
$$v^{n+1} = \bar{v}^n - E_y[E_x\bar{u}^n + E_y\bar{v}^n + E_t]/(\alpha^2 + E_x^2 + E_y^2).$$

(It is interesting to note that the new estimates at a particular point do not depend directly on the previous estimates at the same point.)

The natural boundary conditions for the variational problem turns out to be a zero normal derivative. At the edge of the image, some of the points needed to compute the local average of velocity lie outside the image. Here we simply copy velocities from adjacent points further in.

13. Filling In Uniform Regions

In parts of the image where the brightness gradient is zero, the velocity estimates will simply be averages of the neighboring velocity estimates. There is no local information to constrain the apparent velocity of motion of the brightness pattern in these areas. Eventually the values around such a region will propagate inwards. If the velocities on the border of the region are all equal to the same value, then points in the region will be assigned that value too, after a sufficient number of iterations. Velocity information is thus filled in from the boundary of a region of constant brightness.

If the values on the border are not all the same, it is a little more difficult to predict what will happen. In all cases, the values filled in will correspond to the solution of the Laplace equation for the given boundary condition [1, 24, 32].

The progress of this filling-in phenomena is similar to the propagation effects in the solution of the heat equation for a uniform flat plate, where the time rate of change of temperature is proportional to the Laplacian. This gives us a means of understanding the iterative method in physical terms and of estimating the number of steps required. The number of iterations should be larger than the number of picture cells across the largest region that must be filled in. If the size of such regions is not known in advance one may use the cross-section of the whole image as a conservative estimate.

14. Tightness of Constraint

When brightness in a region is a linear function of the image coordinates we can only obtain the component of optical flow in the direction of the gradient. The component at right angles is filled in from the boundary of the region as described before. In general the solution is most accurately determined in regions where the brightness gradient is not too small and varies in direction from point to point. Information which constrains both components of the optical flow velocity is then available in a relatively small neighborhood. Too violent fluctuations in brightness on the other hand are not desirable since the estimates of the derivatives will be corrupted as the result of undersampling and aliasing.

15. Choice of Iterative Scheme

As a practical matter one has a choice of how to interlace the iterations with the time steps. On the one hand, one could iterate until the solution has stabilized before advancing to the next image frame. On the other hand, given a good initial guess one may need only one iteration per time-step. A good initial guess for the optical flow velocities is usually available from the previous time-step.

The advantages of the latter approach include an ability to deal with more images per unit time and better estimates of optical flow velocities in certain regions. Areas in which the brightness gradient is small lead to uncertain, noisy estimates obtained partly by filling in from the surround. These estimates are improved by considering further images. The noise in measurements of the images will be independent and tend to cancel out. Perhaps more importantly, different parts of the pattern will drift by a given point in the image. The direction of the brightness gradient will vary with time, providing information about both components of the optical flow velocity.

A practical implementation would most likely employ one iteration per time step for these reasons. We illustrate both approaches in the experiments.

16. Experiments

The iterative scheme has been implemented and applied to image sequences corresponding to a number of simple flow patterns. The results shown here are for a relatively low resolution image of 32 by 32 picture cells. The brightness measurements were intentionally corrupted by approximately 1% noise and

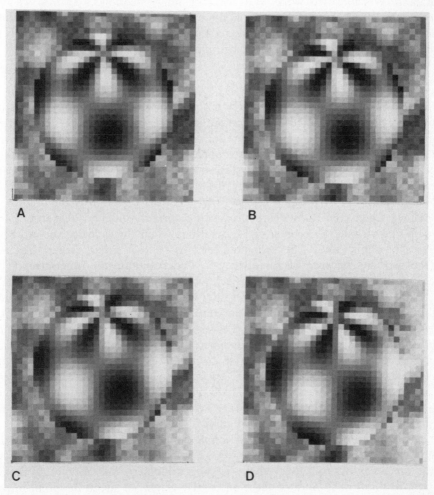

FIG. 5. Four frames out of a sequence of images of a sphere rotating about an axis inclined towards the viewer. The sphere is covered with a pattern which varies smoothly from place to place. The sphere is portrayed against a fixed, lightly textured background. Image sequences like these are processed by the optical flow algorithm.

then quantized into 256 levels to simulate a real imaging situation. The underlying surface reflectance pattern was a linear combination of spatially orthogonal sinusoids. Their wavelength was chosen to give reasonably strong brightness gradients without leading to undersampling problems. Discontinuities were avoided to ensure that the required derivatives exist everywhere.

Shown in Fig. 5, for example, are four frames of a sequence of images depicting a sphere rotating about an axis inclined towards the viewer. A smoothly varying reflectance pattern is painted on the surface of the sphere. The sphere is illuminated uniformly from all directions so that there is no shading. We chose to work with synthetic image sequences so that we can compare the results of the optical flow computation with the exact values calculated using the transformation equations relating image coordinates to coordinates on the underlying surface reflectance pattern.

17. Results

The first flow to be investigated was a simple linear translation of the entire brightness pattern. The resulting computed flow is shown as a needle diagram in Fig. 6 for 1, 4, 16, and 64 iterations. The estimated flow velocities are depicted as short lines, showing the apparent displacement during one time step. In this example a single time step was taken so that the computations are based on just two images. Initially the estimates of flow velocity are zero. Consequently the first iteration shows vectors in the direction of the brightness gradient. Later, the estimates approach the correct values in all parts of the image. Few changes occur after 32 iterations when the velocity vectors have errors of about 10%. The estimates tend to be two small, rather than too large, perhaps because of a tendency to underestimate the derivatives. The worst errors occur, as one might expect, where the brightness gradient is small.

In the second experiment one iteration was used per time step on the same linear translation image sequence. The resulting computed flow is shown in Fig. 7 for 1, 4, 16, and 64 time steps. The estimates approach the correct values more rapidly and do not have a tendency to be too small, as in the previous experiment. Few changes occur after 16 iterations when the velocity vectors have errors of about 7%. The worst errors occur, as one might expect, where the noise in recent measurements of brightness was worst. While individual estimates of velocity may not be very accurate, the average over the whole image was within 1% of the correct value.

Next, the method was applied to simple rotation and simple contraction of the brightness pattern. The results after 32 time steps are shown in Fig. 8. Note that the magnitude of the velocity is proportional to the distance from the origin of the flow in both of these cases. (By origin we mean the point in the image where the velocity is zero.)

In the examples so far the Laplacian of both flow velocity components is zero everywhere. We also studied more difficult cases where this was not the case.

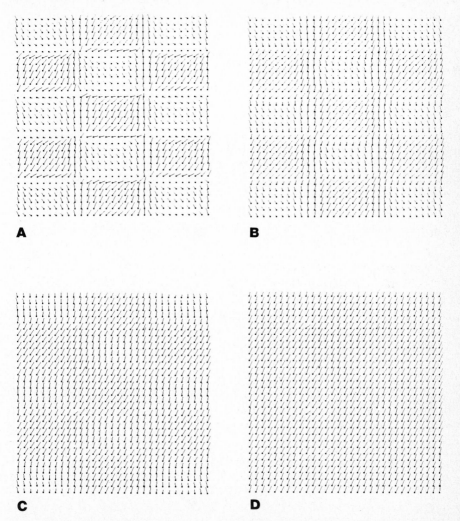

FIG. 6. Flow pattern computed for simple translation of a brightness pattern. The estimates after 1, 4, 16, and 64 iterations are shown. The velocity is 0.5 picture cells in the x direction and 1.0 picture cells in the y direction per time interval. Two images are used as input, depicting the situation at two times separated by one time interval.

In particular, if we let the magnitude of the velocity vary as the inverse of the distance from the origin we generate flow around a line vertex and two dimensional flow into a sink. The computed flow patterns are shown in Fig. 9. In these examples, the computation involved many iterations based on a single time step. The worst errors occur near the singularity at the origin of the flow pattern, where velocities are found which are much larger than one picture cell per time step.

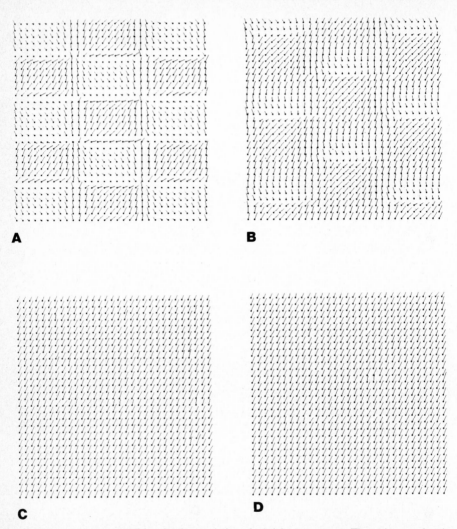

FIG. 7. Flow pattern computed for simple translation of a brightness pattern. The estimates after 1, 4, 16, and 64 time steps are shown. Here one iteration is used per time step. Convergence is more rapid and the velocities are estimated more accurately.

Finally we considered rigid body motions. Shown in Fig. 10 are the flows computed for a cylinder rotating about its axis and for a rotating sphere. In both cases the Laplacian of the flow is not zero and in fact the Laplacian for one of the velocity components becomes infinite on the occluding bound. Since the velocities themselves remain finite, resonable solutions are still obtained. The correct flow patterns are shown in Fig. 11. Comparing the computed and exact values shows that the worst errors occur on the occluding boundary. These

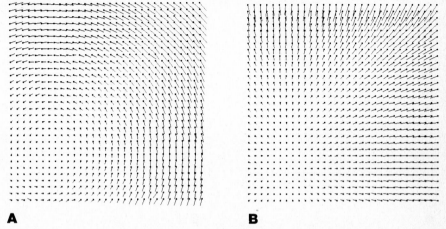

FIG. 8. Flow patterns computed for simple rotation and simple contraction of a brightness pattern. In the first case, the pattern is rotated about 2.8 degrees per time step, while it is contracted about 5% per time step in the second case. The estimates after 32 times steps are shown.

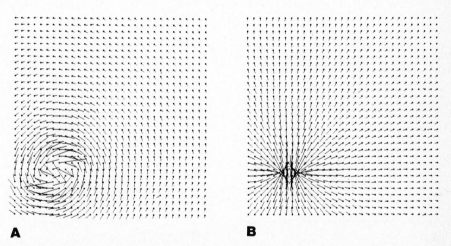

FIG. 9. Flow patterns computed for flow around a line vortex and two dimensional flow into a sink. In each case the estimates after 32 iterations are shown.

boundaries constitute a one dimensional subset of the plane and so one can expect that the relative number of points at which the estimated flow is seriously in error will decrease as the resolution of the image is made finer.

In Appendix B it is shown that there is a direct relationship between the Laplacian of the flow velocity components and the Laplacian of the surface height. This can be used to see how our smoothemess constraint will fare for different objects. For example, a rotating polyhedron will give rise to flow

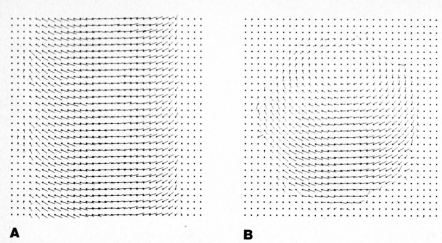

A   **B**

FIG. 10. Flow patterns computed for a cylinder rotating about its axis and for a rotating sphere. The axis of the cylinder is inclined 30 degrees towards the viewer and that of the sphere 45 degrees. Both are rotating at about 5 degrees per time step. The estimates shown are obtained after 32 time steps.

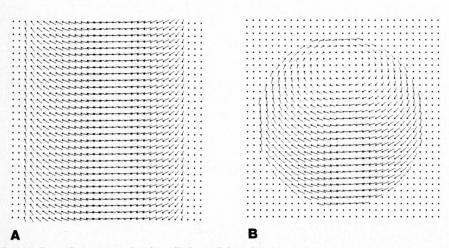

A   **B**

FIG. 11. Exact flow patterns for the cylinder and the sphere.

which has zero Laplacian except on the image lines which are the projections of the edges of the body.

18. Summary

A method has been developed for computing optical flow from a sequence of images. It is based on the observation that the flow velocity has two components and that the basic equation for the rate of change of image brightness provides only one constraint. Smoothness of the flow was introduced as a second constraint. An iterative method for solving the resulting equation was then developed. A simple implementation provided visual confirmation of convergence of the solution in the form of needle diagrams. Examples of several different types of optical flow patterns were studied. These included cases where the Laplacian of the flow was zero as well as cases where it became infinite at singular points or along bounding curves.

The computed optical flow is somewhat inaccurate since it is based on noisy, quantized measurements. Proposed methods for obtaining information about the shapes of objects using derivatives (divergence and curl) of the optical flow field may turn out to be impractical since the inaccuracies will be amplified.

ACKNOWLEDGMENT

This research was conducted at the Artificial Intelligence Laboratory of the Massachusetts Institute of Technology. Support for the laboratory's research is provided in part by the Advanced Research Projects Agency of the Department of Defense under Office of Naval Research contract number N00014-75-C0643. One of the authors (Horn) would like to thank Professor H.-H. Nagel for his hospitality. The basic equations were conceived during a visit to the University of Hamburg, stimulated by Professor Nagel's long-standing interest in motion vision. The other author (Schunck) would like to thank W.E.L. Grimson and E. Hildreth for many interesting discussions and much knowledgable criticism. W.E.L. Grimson and Katsushi Ikeuchi helped to illuminate a conceptual bug in an earlier version of this paper. We should also like to thank J. Jones for preparing the drawings.

Appendix A. Rate of Change of Image Brightness

Consider a patch of the brightness pattern that is displaced a distance δx in the x-direction and δy in the y-direction in time δt. The brightness of the patch is assumed to remain constant so that

$$E(x, y, t) = E(x + \delta x, y + \delta y, t + \delta t).$$

Expanding the right-hand side about the point (x, y, t) we get,

$$E(x, y, t) = E(x, y, t) + \delta x \frac{\partial E}{\partial x} + \delta y \frac{\partial E}{\partial y} + \delta t \frac{\partial E}{\partial t} + \epsilon.$$

Where ϵ contains second and higher order terms in δx, δy, and δt. After subtracting $E(x, y, t)$ from both sides and dividing through by δt we have

$$\frac{\delta x}{\delta t} \frac{\partial E}{\partial x} + \frac{\delta y}{\delta t} \frac{\partial E}{\partial y} + \frac{\partial E}{\partial t} + \mathcal{O}(\delta t) = 0,$$

where $\mathcal{O}(\delta t)$ is a term of order δt (we assume that δx and δy vary as δt). In the limit as $\delta t \to 0$ this becomes

$$\frac{\partial E}{\partial x}\frac{\mathrm{d}x}{\mathrm{d}t} + \frac{\partial E}{\partial y}\frac{\mathrm{d}y}{\mathrm{d}t} + \frac{\partial E}{\partial t} = 0.$$

Appendix B. Smoothness of Flow for Rigid Body Motions

Let a rigid body rotate about an axis $(\omega_x, \omega_y, \omega_z)$, where the magnitude of the vector equals the angular velocity of the motion. If this axis passes through the origin, then the velocity of a point (x, y, z) equals the cross product of $(\omega_x, \omega_y, \omega_z)$, and (x, y, z). There is a direct relationship between the image coordinates and the x and y coordinates here if we assume that the image is generated by orthographic projection. The x and y components of the velocity can be written,

$$u = \omega_y z - \omega_z y, \qquad v = \omega_z x - \omega_x z.$$

Consequently,

$$\nabla^2 u = +\omega_y \nabla^2 z, \qquad \nabla^2 v = -\omega_x \nabla^2 z.$$

This illustrates that the smoothness of the optical flow is related directly to the smoothness of the rotating body and that the Laplacian of the flow velocity will become infinite on the occluding bound, since the partial derivatives of z with respect to x and y become infinite there.

REFERENCES

1. Ames, W.F., *Numerical Methods for Partial Differential Equations* (Academic Press, New York, 1977).
2. Batali, J. and Ullman, S., Motion detection and analysis, *Proc. of the ARPA Image Understanding Workshop*, 7–8 November 1979 (Science Applications Inc., Arlington, VA 1979) pp. 69–75.
3. Clocksin, W., Determining the orientation of surfaces from optical flow, *Proc. of the Third AISB Conference*, Hamburg (1978) pp. 93–102.
4. Conte, S.D. and de Boor, C., *Elementary Numerical Analysis* (McGraw-Hill, New York, 1965, 1972).
5. Fennema, C.L. and Thompson, W.B., Velocity determination in scenes containing several moving objects, *Computer Graphics and Image Processing* **9** (4) (1979) 301–315.
6. Gibson, J.J., *The Perception of the Visual World* (Riverside Press, Cambridge, 1950).
7. Gibson, J.J., *The Senses Considered as Perceptual Systems* (Houghton-Mifflin, Boston, MA, 1966).
8. Gibson, J.J., On the analysis of change in the optic array, *Scandinavian J. Psychol.* **18** (1977) 161–163.
9. Gray, S.B., Local properties of binary images in two dimensions, *IEEE Trans. on Computers* **20** (5) (1971) 551–561.
10. Hadani, I., Ishai, G. and Gur, M., Visual stability and space perception in monocular vision: Mathematical model, *J. Optical Soc. Am.* **70** (1) (1980) 60–65.
11. Hamming, R.W., *Numerical Methods for Scientists and Engineers* (McGraw-Hill, New York, 1962).
12. Hildebrand, F.B., *Methods of Applied Mathematics* (Prentice-Hall, Englewood Cliffs, NJ, 1952, 1965).

13. Hildebrand, F.B., *Introduction to Numerical Analysis* (McGraw-Hill, New York, 1956, 1974).
14. Horn, B.K.P., (1979) Hill shading and the reflectance map, *Proc. IEEE* **69** (1) (1981) 14–47.
15. Jain, R., Martin, W.N. and Aggarwal, J.K., Segmentation through the detection of changes due to motion, *Computer Graphics and Image Processing* **11** (1) (1979) 13–34.
16. Jain, R. Militzer, D. and Nagel, H.-H., Separating non-stationary from stationary scene components in a sequence of real world TV-images, *Proc. of the 5th Int. Joint Conf. on Artificial Intelligence*, August 1977, Cambridge, MA, 612–618.
17. Jain, R. and Nagel, H.-H., On the analysis of accumulative difference pictures from image sequences of real world scenes, *IEEE Trans. on Pattern Analysis and Machine Intelligence* **1** (2) (1979) 206–214.
18. Koenderink, J.J. and van Doorn, A.J., Invariant properties of the motion parallax field due to the movement of rigid bodies relative to an observer, *Optica Acta* **22** (9) 773–791.
19. Koenderink, J.J. and van Doorn, A.J., Visual perception of rigidity of solid shape, *J. Math. Biol.* **3** (79) (1976) 79–85.
20. Limb, J.O. and Murphy, J.A., Estimating the velocity of moving images in television signals, *Computer Graphics and Image Processing* **4** (4) (1975) 311–327.
21. Longuet-Higgins, H.C. and Prazdny, K., The interpretation of moving retinal image, *Proc. of the Royal Soc.* B **208** (1980) 385–387.
22. Marr, D. and Ullman, S., Directional selectivity and its use in early visual processing, Artificial Intelligence Laboratory Memo No. 524, Massachusetts Institute of Technology (June 1979), to appear in *Proc. Roy. Soc. B.*
23. Mersereau, R.M., The processing of hexagonally sampled two-dimensional signals, *Proc. of the IEEE* **67** (6) (1979) 930–949.
24. Milne, W.E., *Numerical Solution of Differential Equations* (Dover, New York, 1953, 1979).
25. Nagel, H.-H., Analyzing sequences of TV-frames, *Proc. of the 5th Int. Joint Conf. on Artificial Intelligence*, August 1977, Cambridge, MA, 626.
26. Nagel, H.-H., Analysis techniques for image sequences, *Proc. of the 4th Int. Joint Conf. on Pattern Recognition*, 4–10 November 1978, Kyoto, Japan.
27. Nakayama, K. and Loomis, J.M., Optical velocity patterns, velocity-sensitive neurons and space perception, *Perception* **3** (1974) 63–80.
28. Netravali, A.N. and Robbins, J.D., Motion-compensated television coding: Part I, *The Bell System Tech. J.* **58** (3) (1979) 631–670.
29. Prazdny, K., Computing egomotion and surface slant from optical flow. Ph.D. Thesis, Computer Science Department, University of Essex, Colchester (1979).
30. Prazdny, K., Egomotion and relative depth map from optical flow, *Biol. Cybernet.* **36** (1980) 87–102.
31. Prazdny, K., The information in optical flows. Computer Science Department, University of Essex, Colchester (1980) mimeographed.
32. Richtmyer, R.D. and Mortin, K.W., *Difference Methods for Initial-Value Problems* (Interscience, John Wiley & Sons, New York, 1957, 1967).
33. Russell, D.L., *Calculus of Variations and Control Theory* (Academic Press, New York, 1976).
34. Yourgau, W. and Mandelstam, S., *Variational Principles in Dynamics and Quantum Theory* (Dover, New York, 1968, 1979).

Received March 1980

Inferring Surfaces from Images

Thomas O. Binford

AI Lab, Stanford University, Palo Alto, CA 94305, U.S.A.

1. Introduction

The human visual system uses sophisticated perceptual operations to achieve many goals in complex environments. By contrast, current industrial vision systems use simple algorithms to accomplish a single task in a simple, tightly constrained environment. While simple industrial vision systems find many applications, vendors find that the mass market is elusive, that they must do applications engineering for specific applications. High performance computer vision could accomplish many more applications with less risk and with less special purpose engineering. Capabilities which would provide that higher performance are effective segmentation of images into features, effective organization of image features, effective description of surfaces from image descriptions, and effective interpretation of three-dimensional structures. These same capabilities are central for other applications of computer vision in photo interpretation and cartography. Fundamental understanding of those perceptual problems is important both for understanding biological perception and for application of machine vision.

This paper discusses generating effective scene descriptions from images, that is generating descriptions of surfaces from image boundaries and generating image boundaries. I make several speculations. First, small saccades in eye motion serve the purpose of self-calibration of imperfect sensors. This approach may be useful in making good solid state cameras from bad. Second, large saccades and vergence motions are intended to test with foveal high resolution whether boundaries coincide in an image and whether their inverse images coincide in space. Coincide is used to mean intersect. Third, a strong argument is made that humans segment curves at curvature discontinuities in addition to tangent discontinuities. I introduce two perceptual principles which underlie an outline of an incomplete theory of interpretation of line drawings which appears to have psychological relevance and which may accommodate

Artificial Intelligence **17** (1981) 205–244

.ved surfaces with more than three faces at a vertex, paper surfaces, wires, shadows, surface marks, and transparency. The approach characterizes surfaces by their depth discontinuities and tangent plane discontinuities as inferred from their images. I introduce constraints corresponding to concepts of opaque and solid, and propose constraints for coincidence of edges and surfaces in space (related to position discontinuities) and assumptions for tangent discontinuities in space. These constraints lead to partial surface boundary interpretations from image boundaries. They provide boundary conditions for splines which mesh well with previous approaches for interpretation of polyhedra [27] and for surface interpolation [3].

The paper then discusses problems which a vision system must overcome in generating descriptions of image boundaries and describes solutions to these problems. I present a universal perceptual problem and argue that mechanisms for solving the problem are common among tactile and visual modes and presumably other sensory modes, and are common among different perceptual levels in visual perception. I describe the basis for directional image boundary operators similar to Hubel–Wiesel simple cells in the visual cortex. I describe the Binford–Horn line finding system of 1970 which incorporated most of these mechanisms.

2. Scene Modeling

Subsequent discussion about images relies on several scene models of increasing fidelity and the images they generate. In the cardboard cutout scene model, pieces of cardboard with different shapes and different gray values or colors are tossed one on another in a frame. They are viewed in such a way that an image contains a number of regions of constant intensity. This is the image model on which many arguments in the literature are implicity based, arguments which lead up dead-ends. Later sections point out that smooth shading is very common, and that the failure of thresholding and of image gradient operators is obvious in principle and in fact. A more accurate scene model includes illumination, varied object surface shape, reflectivity properties of pigments, and sensor response. A resulting image model includes a piecewise smooth illumination function and a piecewise smooth reflectivity function which has discontinuities at points and along curves, with delta, step, and tangent profiles. The addition of texture brings realistic complexity. Projection followed by defocussing produces a continuous image which is sampled by discrete sensors, each of which compute a weighted sum over its immediate neighborhood, on which is superimposed Gaussian noise before digitizing.

We will use the term image curves to refer to observables in the image, e.g. discontinuities of the image intensity surface. We use the term image boundaries in the same way. We refer to junctions of image curves. We reserve the term edges to refer to edges of surfaces in three-space and the term vertices to refer to their intersections. We define surfaces in three-space as segmented at discontinuities of position or of surface tangent plane. We refer to space curves and to surface boundaries. We reserve the term object to refer to physical objects in three-space and will refer to figures or areas in an image.

3. Image Formation

Image intensities can be understood by simple physics in terms of the illumination distribution, surface orientation, surface reflectivity, and sensor response. However, since we cannot characterize those elements simply, accurately, or in generality, there are strong limitations on the accuracy with which we can predict absolute image intensities and limitations on the accuracy with which we can infer object properties from image intensities. Useful analytic approximations exist for special cases. Thus, image intensities can be described qualitatively. Very useful shape calculations can be made with oversimplified assumptions about reflectivity properties [18]. It is essential to make those 'shape from shading' assumptions. In this paper we concentrate on one aspect of image description. We want to characterize surfaces from their images in ways that are not sensitive to detailed behavior of the image intensity surface. The mathematical characterization of surfaces concentrates on discontinuities. Our approach is to characterize discontinuities of surfaces and images, i.e. 'shape from shape' interpretation.

Illumination seems simple. The sun is approximately a point source at infinity, a particularly simple model. It really subtends half a degree. Of course, there are shadow surface boundaries, illumination reflected from adjacent surfaces, and diffuse illumination background from atmospheric scattering. Atmospheric scattering depends on weather conditions, like the amount of dust in the air; it is directional. The sky at sunset is red in the west and blue in the east. Illumination reflected from other surfaces is complicated and discontinuous. The face of a person lying in grass is illuminated in part by green light reflected from the grass. In a stack of blocks, strong reflections illuminate faces across adjacent concave edges. Where there is occlusion, thus shadows, illumination is discontinuous. Man-controlled lighting includes spotlights and other discontinuous illumination. Thus it is difficult to predict the intensity and spectrum of illumination. One assumption is that illumination varies smoothly throughout the scene observed. A more general assumption is that illumination discontinuities are unrelated to discontinuities in surface orientation and discontinuities in surface reflectivity, i.e. that illumination discontinuities do not coincide with discontinuities of surface properties.

Reflectivity of physical materials is a function of incident angle, exit angle, and phase angle. Even for a plane surface with a uniform pigment, incident angle and exit angle may vary over the surface. Incident angle is constant for a point source at infinity, exit angle is constant for a pinhole sensor at infinity.

There is no very satisfactory model of reflectivity vs. angles for many physical surfaces. Various physical models allow calculations which may be useful for rough estimates in special cases. Some reflectivity functions are not smooth, e.g. specular reflections, especially near glancing incidence. Also, surface pigments are not very uniform. It is useful to assume that the appearance of discontinuities is not sensitive to smooth variation of reflectivity, although intensities are sensitive.

Variation of sensor response has been essentially overlooked, especially in the treatment of biological vision systems. It seems very unlikely that biological systems have evolved sensors with absolutely uniform response over the whole retina for all intensity levels and for all time. This seems like the wrong problem to attempt to solve. It is instead plausible to make dynamic photometric self-calibration of sensors to provide local uniformity of response and to make algorithms insensitive to smooth shading. The problem is to adjust the response of each cell iteratively to make its response consistent with response of neighbors in the presence of non-uniform, perhaps discontinuous, image intensity with image motion.

Consider a simple but inadequate approach. Assume that the intensity is smooth, i.e. that the image intensity is approximately planar locally:

$$I_i = I_0 + \text{grad}(I) \cdot (r_i - r_0) ;$$

in the neighborhood of a point r_0. There are three parameters, determined by responses of a cell and two neighbors. Responses of a point and n neighbors provide $n - 2$ constraints. If the response at each cell at each instant is scaled to the best plane fit to its own response and responses of cells in its neighborhood, the iteration converges rapidly. This procedure assumes that the relative locations of cells are known, which must be true to locate position and orientation of image boundaries statically. This procedure would not explain fading of stabilized images. This form of photometric self-calibration is not adequate since it smears image boundaries. If we assume that image boundaries cross a small set of neighborhoods, then a scaling process with a long time constant would remove that objection. It would fail in texture with dense image boundaries. Still this is an attractively simple operation.

Instead, use eye motion to compare response of neighbor cells at a single image position. Eye motion may also be useful to sharpen the resolution of transverse position of image boundaries. It is enough to make a linear calibration of intensities around the local light intensity level. The signal from each cell is the integral of a weight function (e.g. box or gaussian) over the intensity surface.

Let

$$f_i(x, y) = k_i I(x, y) + c_i ;$$

where i is an index of a cell in the retina while (x, y) are angles in the image.

Also, k_i and c_i are constants separate for each cell and functions of intensity. As cell i moves over the image, x and y are functions of time. A single moving cell computes

$$\partial f_i(x, y)/\partial t = k_1 \text{ grad } I(x, y) \cdot v + k_i \partial I(x, y)/\partial t,$$

where v is the vector velocity $(\partial x/\partial t, \partial y/\partial t)$. If the image is static, the time derivative will be periodic for a repeated eye motion; the derivative vanishes for a uniform image. Thus, the time derivative of response for a single sensor is the dot product of the gradient of intensity with the velocity. Compare the gradient of intensity at a common image point $p = (x, y)$ as estimated from nearby sensors moving around the point in an arbitrary motion. Estimate the gradient of intensity at p by interpolating values of the time derivative of sensors which cross point p. If eye motion is circular, any image point is crossed by an annulus of retinal cells. The signal at a fixed image point for circular motion will be periodic; it will be non-zero as long as there are non-uniform gains for sensor cells. Thus, the difference from the mean can be fed back to make gain uniform. The constant term can be made uniform by making the differences between response of adjacent cells equal intensity differences estimated from the gradient of intensity. Thus, we match gradients and values. Note that this requires a separate representation of the image independent of the retinal image which is in motion. It might be argued that there is no need to use spatial discrimination at all, that comparison of variations between pixels is adequate, but spatial discrimination is faster than eye motion and is feasible for large receptive fields. The time constant for scaling should be long compared to times of small eye motion and long compared to transit times of image boundaries across a cell for image motions of interest. For stabilized images this calibration process would cause fading of images. That is, a constant signal in time for a moving sensor implies a uniform signal in space. Response of individual cells would be scaled to a spatially uniform signal. This conjecture was presented as an outline of an explanation of microsaccades. It does not deal with moving images, and it requires detailed analysis and comparison with experiment.

Speculation 1. Fading of stabilized images may be a result of purely in-strumental effects and not of profound perceptual operations.

This dynamic process has potential application in making uniform the response of discrete sensors in solid state cameras for which cell to cell non-uniformity is a major noise effect. The process would not need to be very dynamic. For our GE TN2500, for example, the standard deviation of nearest neighbor differences is about 6 times the standard deviation of successive frame differences for a single pixel. Similar self-normalization methods may be useful for geometric local calibration and for increasing accuracy of parallel analog image computation. These topics require theoretical analysis. We describe later a method for dynamic measurement of sensor noise. We assume that sensors are calibrated so that no image boundaries are introduced by variation of sensor response.

4. Image Description

Image interpretation involves description of object surface geometry and reflectivities of surfaces, but also description of illumination and sensor response. Interpretation takes as input a sequence of sensed images in the context of general and special knowledge. The task of interpretation is impossible without very restrictive knowledge-based assumptions, a few of which were introduced above. We seek image descriptions which are characteristic of object surfaces, characteristic of illumination, and characteristic of the sensor. The following discussion chooses image boundaries as one such image descriptor; they are stable and independent but their interpretation is not unique. An image boundary may correspond to an edge of a surface (called true edge), to a limb, i.e. an apparent edge (the limit of a visible surface, tangent to the line of sight), to a surface reflectivity discontinuity (surface mark), or an illumination discontinuity (e.g. shadow). Non-uniqueness is no more and no less a problem with image boundaries than with other image observables, which typically cannot be uniquely interpreted on a local basis. This emphasis on discontinuities of otherwise smooth functions for surface, illumination, and reflectivity has a parallel in mathematical characterization of surfaces by their discontinuities. Also, if we consider approximation of surfaces (by splines for example), segmentation with knots at discontinuities is particularly effective. We present these results as motivation for the utility of adequate image boundary finding procedures, to substantiate the value of an approach many believe discredited since 1970 or so, and to describe the intellectual history of our efforts at that time. We argue that procedures for obtaining image boundaries and interpreting line drawings are valuable modules for perception, that obtaining image boundaries is not impossible and not a waste of time, and that interpreting line drawings is not a dead-end exploited fully years ago by Huffman, Waltz, and others, with assumptions that are too restrictive to be useful. This is only one aspect of interpretation, but an important one. Methods for computing shape from shading assumes regions of uniform pigment which can be delineated by image boundaries. We show below that a few straightforward interpretations are at once more general and more powerful than earlier analyses of line drawings.

Various experiments suggest that humans do not perceive intensities of images themselves, that they do not perceive intensity gradients as image boundaries [8], and that they estimate something like surface reflectivity from image intensity discontinuities and estimated orientation of surfaces [23, 24,

25]. They pose the problem of throwing pieces of colored cardboard on a table and estimating color in the presence of unknown and non-uniform illumination. These ideas provided a major motivation in estimating surface geometry and reflectivity, i.e. characteristic properties of surfaces. Major advances originated during the period 1969–1971: the Binford–Horn boundary finder [16], shape from shading (estimation of surface orientation from shading) [14, 15], and shape from shape (estimating surface shape from image shape) [22], and later, estimation of perceived brightness [17].

5. Interpretation of Image Boundaries

If we model image intensities by the product I_*G_*R where I indicates illumination, G signifies geometric factors, and R signifies reflectivity, consider image boundaries labelled by triples I_*G_*R where I, G, R have values 1 for discontinuity and 0 for none. Then 000 is no image boundary, 001 corresponds to a reflectivity boundary (e.g. pigment change), 010 corresponds to a geometric boundary which may be a true edge (a discontinuity in surface tangent) or a limb, i.e. an apparent edge, the limit of a visible surface. A limb may have a tangent discontinuity (true edge) or the surface may be smooth, tangent to the line of sight, in which case there will be a position discontinuity of surfaces adjacent to the limb. Type 011 corresponds to a pigment boundary coincident with a geometric boundary, while type 100 corresponds to an illumination boundary (e.g. shadow).

Triples 101, 110, 111 correspond to illumination boundaries coincident with reflectivity boundaries or geometric boundaries. In absence of other evidence, we assume *general source position*, i.e., we ignore interpretations in which the source is so aligned as to cast shadow boundaries lying on geometric boundaries or pigment boundaries, or to cast shadows coincident with intersections of those surface boundaries. The same assumption is made about spotlights. For a shadow to lie on a geometric or pigment surface boundary, the surface boundary must be a projection of the limb of the remote surface which casts the shadow, and the source must be at the center of projection. These alignments are typically more constrained than those which violate the assumption of general observer position; thus it may be that the assumption of general source position is more widely valid. Of course, a shadow may cross a surface boundary. Also, a shadow is always coincident with any vertex at which the surface (limb) which casts the shadow intersects the surface on which the shadow is cast. See Fig. 1.

Locally, there are small differences between types 001, 010, and 011. Shadowed regions are darker than the unshadowed region. That helps only a factor of two, more or less. Use of that constraint requires only slight knowledge of the source. Coupled with constraints of following sections, it is a useful constraint. If the sun is the source of illumination, then the illumination

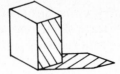

FIG. 1. Shadow coincident with vertex.

ratio between shadow and sunlight will be the ratio of diffuse to direct sunlight, which is roughly equal across shadow boundaries within an image (but not constant from image to image because of changes in diffuse illumination caused by weather variations). Otherwise, the illumination ratio between shadow and non-shadow may vary slowly over the image, which is almost as useful. However, for both sun and artificial light, reflections from other surfaces complicate matters. It might be interesting to devise experiments to quantify human use of such spatial smoothness of contrast in perception of shadows. The width of transition of shadow image boundaries will be the product $w = w_s \cdot \text{dist} / c_s$, where w_s is the angular width of the source viewed from the limb which casts the shadow (half degree for sun), dist is the distance of the shadow boundary from the edge which casts the shadow, and c_s is the cosine of the angle between the surface normal and the source. The width as viewed from the observer will be $w' = w_* c_o$, where c_o is the cosine of the angle between the surface normal and the line of sight to the observer. See Fig. 2. For an aircraft wing 7 meters above the ground, source divergence of 1/120 radians, and $c_o = c_s = 1$, the apparent shadow width is 6 cm. This is probably not usable for aerial photographs and probably usable for ground level photos. But defocussing also blurs boundaries. Shadow blurring is proportional to distance; thus disambiguating shadows and defocussing requires a three-space interpretation.

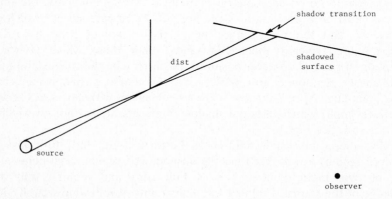

FIG. 2. Apparent width of shadows.

There are more global conditions. Where shadow boundaries cross geometric boundaries, the shadow image boundary will have position and tangent discontinuities corresponding to position and tangent discontinuities across the surface boundary. See Figs. 3(a) and 3(b). Where shadows cross reflectivity boundaries without geometric boundaries, there are no breaks in the shadow; the junction is an X. Conversely, if there is a position or tangent discontinuity in a shadow image, there is a position or tangent discontinuity in the surface on which it lies. Except where evidence indicates otherwise, if there is no discontinuity in the shadow image, assume no discontinuity in the surface. We generalize these interpretations in a later section.

If reflectivities across a surface boundary are r_1 and r_2, and the illumination ratio across a shadow boundary is r, then the ratio of image intensities across the image boundary on one side of the shadow is r_1/r_2, while on the other side of the shadow image the ratio is the same, $(r_*r_1)/(r_*r_2) = r_1/r_2$. See Figs. 3(b) and 3(c). This is a useful approximation, but not strictly accurate. In many cases, because the dynamic range of film or digitizer is limited, the computer cannot 'see' into shadows, as in an example below. A part of the available information is lost but there remains enough for successful interpretation.

In the sense of search among all possible interpretations [40], given an interpretation of an image boundary, certain constraints follow. We believe that interpretation is very different, largely a local process in which local image features have direct surface interpretations with little ambiguity, and we believe that global consistency involves small search spaces. In what follows, we introduce results to support this contention.

Consider reflectivity surface boundaries and true edges. If we assume in

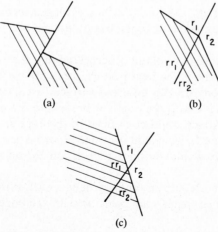

(a) (b)

(c)

Fig. 3. Shadows crossing boundaries.

addition that reflectivity may differ across the boundary but is constant on either side along the boundary, then there is a boundary condition on illumination along the boundary which can be included in an interpolation solution for shape from shading. That boundary condition can compensate for non-constant illumination. Consider true edges and apparent edges, or limbs, type 010. At limbs the surface is normal to the line of sight, thus there is a boundary condition on surface orientation. If the reflectivity is completely known or a simple model is assumed for reflectivity, there is a boundary condition on illumination. The boundary condition on surface orientation has long been recognized. It was incorporated into interpolation solutions for determining surface shape from image shape (shape from shape) [3]. The image model and surface model on which we have based these arguments is natural in terms of splines for illumination, splines for object surfaces, and for sensor response functions. Boundary conditions apply naturally to constrain the splines.

By arguments above, it is not usually necessary to characterize spatial properties of the sensor in real time, but if humans are shown a black and white section of a color film, they know that the sensor is monochromatic. Or if shown a photo taken with a fisheye lens, we are aware of the geometric distortion. We also apparently estimate sensor noise in the photo and determine which are non-noise structures, without being aware of doing so. In our research we have shown that it is possible to estimate sensor noise for usual images.

The following is a definition of a constraint for solid objects which does not exclude non-solids.

Solid Assumption S1. In absence of other evidence, assume that any edge lies on two surfaces, else:

Lamina Assumption S2. In absence of other evidence, assume that any edge lies on one surface, else assume an edge lies on no surface.

The first assumption favors volume interpretations, the second assumption makes lamina interpretations the next best choice, while wires come in last.

For each edge E, there are two adjacent surfaces, each of which may be in front of the edge, coincide with the edge, or be behind the edge. If we assume opacity, then neither surface could be in front of the edge E, because if surface S_2 were nearer than edge E, we would see edge E_2 of surface S_2, even if it were aligned with E. Thus we would consider edge E_2 on S_2 and not edge E.

Opacity Assumption. In absence of other evidence, each surface which appears adjacent to an edge in an image may coincide with the edge or be behind the edge.

An edge lies on the nearer of two surfaces. This assumption implies that the first choice is opaque surfaces, and that transparent surfaces are introduced only when necessary. If both surfaces are behind the curve, it is a wire.

Our basic approach to interpretation is the principle of prediction. A purpose of perception is prediction. For example, in hunting moths, bats intercept the moth's trajectory. Moths aren't especially cooperative; they take evasive action. In this case, the moth monitors the bat's sonar. The bat still must use his simplified prediction of the moth's trajectory, since that is the only prediction he has. Often he will miss, but sometimes he wins. Without that prediction, probability of success is small. Using prediction that is sometimes accurate is often a great advantage.

Prediction Principle. Perception uses the most general model for which there is evidence, for which predictions can be made.

This simple idea underlies many perceptual operations, making specific the idea of simplicity.

6. Coincidence Assumptions

If two space curves do not intersect, they may still appear to cross from many viewpoints, for a large family of curves for many positions of the curves. In a scene model with isolated curves tossed randomly in space, end points are distinguishable points. In that model it is unlikely that the image of the end point of one curve will fall on the image of another curve, and it would be reasonable to assume that if a curve terminates on another they are images of a point and a curve which are coincident in space. In the cardboard cutout scene model and in more general models, we cannot always distinguish images of end points from images of interior points of curves, because of obscuration. The assumption just stated is useless in these scene models.

Coincidence Assumption. In absence of other evidence, assume that if features coincide in an image, their inverse images coincide in space if sufficiently constrained.

Given assumptions of random distributions of source and observer positions together with assumptions about space curves on surfaces, probabilities could be estimated. Our proposed approach is different. We don't think any but the most local, qualitative assumptions about those distributions, such as those used here, are useful. Instead, we do not introduce such unusual interpretations unless they are apparent elsewhere in the image. This agrees with the intuition that we are unaware of unusual interpretations of line drawings.

The constraint must be as restrictive as a curve in an image, equivalently a surface in space. That is, in the case above for the cardboard cutout scene model, the stem of a T is equivalent to a half-infinite line. If we move either line independently of the other, there will be an apparent intersection over an area in the image, equivalently a volume in space. There is a dual interpretation. In absence of other evidence, ignore interpretations requiring tightly constrained alignments of observer or light source with pairs of surface boundaries in space. Tightly constrained means that source or observer lie on a surface in space or are more tightly constrained. Alignments of surfaces and edges are quite common. They are largely accomodated in the assumptions which follow. The Coincidence Assumption is a special case of a general perceptual principle for hunters: 'if anything moves, shoot it'. The Coincidence Assumption of space curves at vertices is weaker than the connect assumption of surfaces at edges [27].

We will make the assumption precise in terms of several cases. The case of T junctions of curves was just considered. See Fig. 4(a).

Assumption C1. In absence of evidence to the contrary, the stem of a T is not nearer than the top, i.e. is coincident in space or further away.

If the stem were nearer than the top of the T, then the stem would be visible if it extended beyond the top. In that case they must be coincident, since the stem terminates at the top, a coincidence of a point with a curve. Under Assumption S1 and Opacity Assumption, assume that the inverse image of the top of a T junction lies on a surface which is nearer than or coincident with the stem of the T. This is valid for shadows in which case the surface is coincident with the stem of the T and the stem is a surface mark, not an edge, since the surface is smooth there. It is not valid for a degenerate view of a block (Fig. 4(b)) for which the assumption of general observer position is violated. The observer must be coplanar with the plane in space determined by the two tangents.

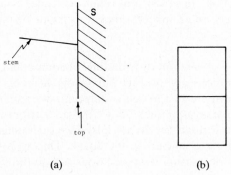

(a)   (b)

FIG. 4. (a) T interpretation; (b) exception.

A sufficiently tight constraint is that a distinguishable point lie on a curve. An observable junction between two curves, i.e. a measurable discontinuity in tangent vector is such a distinguished point.

Assumption C2. In absence of other evidence, assume that an image curve which appears to coincide with a junction of two curves is the image of a space curve coincident with two other space curves.

These are junctions of three or more curves. If a distinguished point on a curve in an image, a junction, is coincident with an image curve, either they are images of curves coincident in space, or the observer and inverse image of the junction are coplanar with the tangent of the curve in space. In the cardboard cutout scene model, if we toss surfaces randomly on the image, an image curve coincident with a junction will occur with small probability. The definition does not include T junctions because there is no distinguished point on the top of the T coincident with the stem, equivalently there are only two curves.

Any junction of two space curves can give rise to an L vertex. Even if we allow isolated lines, for images of two lines to coincide in an image, the observer must be colinear with their terminations.

Assumption C3. In absence of other evidence, assume that curves of an L junction are images of space curves which coincide.

In geometric terms, this is the coincidence of a point with a point. Equivalently the observer constraint is colinearity with endpoints.

Consider Figs. 5(a) and 5(b). If a true edge E of a solid is truncated by a visible surface S, the result is a vertex whose image is an arrow junction or Y junction, which are already included in Assumption C2. Now, consider Fig. 5(c). If limb 1 of surface S_1 which is not an edge (an apparent edge) intersects a visible surface S, the image of the limb is tangent to the image e of the boundary edge E of the visible surface. The following argument makes that

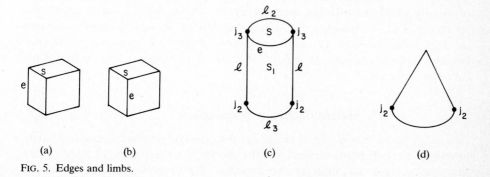

(a)   (b)   (c)   (d)

FIG. 5. Edges and limbs.

clear: Surface S_1 is tangent to the line of sight at the inverse image of limb 1, by definition. Consider the triple of vectors, the surface normal, the line of sight, and limb 1. The surface normal is orthogonal to the other two, which are not colinear. Edge E is in both surfaces, S and S_1. Since it is in S_1, it has no component normal to S_1. Where edge E intersects limb 1, the surface normal is orthogonal to the line of sight. Edge E can be specified by a component along the line of sight (invisible) and a component along the limb. Call the inverse image of 1 by the name L. If two image curves are tangent, the vector difference of their inverse images must be invisible, and therefore along the line of sight at the point of tangency.

Assumption C4. In absence of other evidence, assume that two tangent image curves are images of the intersection in space of a limb and a surface, visible or invisible. The surface they bound, S_1 is tangent to the line of sight, and there is a depth discontinuity across L with S_1 the nearer surface. L lies on S_1. By the Solid Assumption, at a three junction, unless there is evidence to the contrary, assume a surface S between edges E_2 and E, intersecting S_1 at E.

The junctions may have three curves or two. See junctions j_2 and j_3 in Fig. 5(c). These are powerful constraints which do not have an equivalent for true edges. Three-junctions are more observable.

Fig. 5(d) defines a strong condition on segmentation. The junctions labeled j_2 involve curves which are tangent. The curves have a difference in curvature at those junctions.

Speculation 2. We maintain from this observation that natural segmentation of image curves implies segmentation at curvature discontinuities, in addition to tangent discontinuities.

Thus, splines based on circles are inadequate because they cannot preserve continuity of curvature [39]. We have studied Cornu spirals, linear in arc length, as a basis for splines as solution to the problem of isotropic splines with continuity of tangent vector and curvature. Cubic splines satisfy continuity constraints but not isotropy. Salamin in our laboratory has obtained results on more general minimal curvature solutions. Brady [6] discusses a minimal curvature approach and in private discussion referred to general minimal curvature solutions.

7. Surface Continuity Assumptions

Above we noted that if a shadow crosses a true edge, a break should be visible, otherwise a constraint is implied, i.e. the source, the tangent to the edge casting the shadow, and the observer are coplanar. Observability can be quantified well as a function of angle of discontinuity, length of curves, and point scattering error. Thus the break is visible except for surfaces with a small angle break in tangent or those in which the source and observer are nearly aligned as above. The measurement of angles can be quite accurate.

That condition can be partially inverted. If there is a break in apparent tangent vector of an image curve, by Assumption C3 it is the image of coincident space curves. They must have a tangent discontinuity.

Assumption T1. If a curve has no observable break, assume it is the image of a smooth space curve, and that any surface on which it lies is smooth.

Otherwise, the observer is coplanar with the two tangents. Of course, wires give rise to images with junctions in which the wire image continues without a break. However, there is other evidence, as hinted above. The curve crossed by the image of a wire would be assumed to be a surface mark, but if it were indeed an edge or limb of a surface, that would be apparent at either of its terminations if visible. If visible, their images would be a junction of an appropriate type. If neither is visible, there may be other evidence, but if there is not adequate information, there is no way of knowing.

8. Surface Interpretations

These assumptions do not depend on planar faces; they appear to accomodate more than three faces at any vertex, paper, wires, shadows, surface markings, and transparency. We do not have a complete theory here but there is enough to show real promise. We think that these assumptions are the right level, i.e. that they are canonical in the sense that they reflect valid geometric conclusions to be drawn from the data. We believe that these assumptions have psychological validity. The assumption of coincidence appears in the Penrose triangle illusion, Fig. 6. The figure appears impossible when viewed from one direction from which points which are really separate in space appear to be coincident.

I have used the phrase, in absence of other evidence. Fig. 7(a) shows evidence for a wire. Other evidence for isolated curves including surface

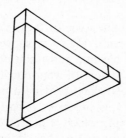

FIG. 6. Penrose triangle.

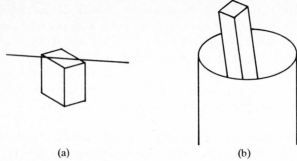

FIG. 7. Evidence to contrary: (a) wire; (b) not a solid.

markings and wires are I-junctions, i.e. termination of an isolated line. Fig. 7(b) shows occlusion evidence that the cylinder is not solid, i.e. that there is only a single surface intersecting the interior edge at the limb. In the Fig. 7(a) the image of the wire crosses images of the edges of the cube. The edges are unperturbed. They might be surface markings (surface is smooth there), but where they intersect other edges, the surface is not smooth. In Fig. 7(b) the block is inside the surface of the top of the vessel. It is behind the lip of the vessel.

Wires were mentioned several times as a class name for thin obscurations above a visible surface. Previous statements define wires, they do not describe image constraints. Wires seen in aerial photographs are quite thin and have special properties, similar to very fine lines on surfaces. The two differ in that lines follow the surface and wires go their own way, i.e. the apparent intersections of their images with other curves are very different. Images of both fine surface marks and wires appear locally distinct from images of shadows, edges, limbs, etc. The image of the surface behind the wire continues unaffected on either side of the wire or surface mark. Any surface markings and texture which extend on either side provide strong cues included in previous analysis of curves. This motivates description of other properties, shading and texture relations not included in single curves. Images of wires and fine lines appear in intensity profiles as thin peaks at the limit of sensor resolution. Detection of image boundaries with step and peak profiles is discussed in a later section.

Lowe and Binford [26] exploit some of these assumptions in interpreting an aerial photograph of an aircraft, Fig. 8(a) shows image curves extracted by hand from the output of the Nevatia and Babu line finder [34]. This is a cheat which represents our best judgment of what our line finders will produce soon. Fig. 8(b) shows occlusion cues which provide a partial ordering of surfaces in depth, based on occlusion. This produces a partial ordering of surfaces, the fuselage is nearer than the wing which is nearer than the engine pod which is nearer than the shadow which is nearer than (coincident with) the painted line.

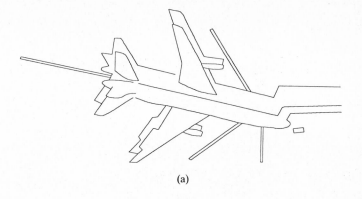

(a)

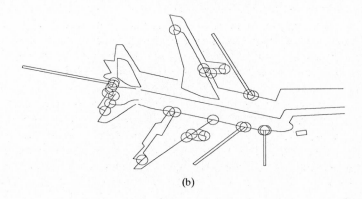

(b)

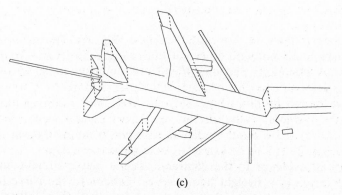

(c)

FIG. 8. (a) Curve data for aircraft; (b) occluded edges; (c) matched shadow features; (d), (e) aircraft seen from several views.

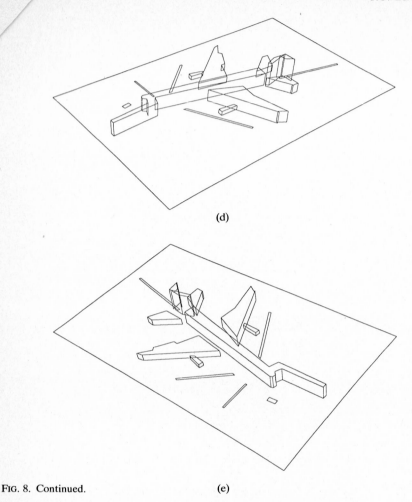

(d)

(e)

FIG. 8. Continued.

The tail is nearer than the horizontal stabilizer Fig. 8(c) shows junctions of shadow images coincident with other junctions along a projection from the sun (Coincidence Assumption). Shadows provide a form of stereo, an 'unstructured light' way to determine heights of edges which cast shadows from triangulation with the known sun position. Figs. 8(d) and 8(e) show resulting three-space models of the surfaces of the aircraft seen from several views. The entire process was calculated without human intervention from the data in Fig. 8(a). There is much more still to be extracted from these curve data.

In absence of evidence to the contrary, assume that a straight line in an image is the image of a straight line in space. Otherwise, the curve is planar and the observer is coplanar with the plane of the curve. If an image curve is not a straight line, both surfaces cannot be coincident and planar. That is well

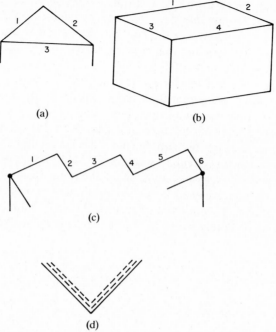

FIG. 9. Planar interpretations.

known. In the absence of evidence to the contrary, if a surface is consistent with a planar one, assume that it is planar. Consider Fig. 9(a). Edges 1, 2 and 3 are coplanar because 1 and 2 are coincident, thus coplanar, while 3 is coincident with 1 and 2, thus its endpoints are in the plane. Any quartet chain of coincident edges such as Fig. 9(b) are coplanar. Edges 1 and 2 are coincident, thus coplanar, while 3 and 4 are coincident and form another plane. If they were non-coplanar, there would be a straight line between the junctions of 1, 3 and 2, 4 along the intersection of the two planes. In Fig. 9(c) any chain of edges (1, 2, 3, 4, 5, 6) connected by L junctions is co-planar. That is, edges 1 and 2 define a plane. If 3 was not coplanar, there would be a crease (i.e. edge) in the surface on which they rest. Consider a surface with intersecting straight lines, as shown in Fig. 9(d). If the surface is curved and smooth, its contours near the edges will be approximately parallel to the inverse images of the lines, as shown in Fig. 9(d). The surface has a singularity only on the boundary. In absence of evidence to the contrary, assume that such surfaces are ruled locally. Three such straight lines are a special case of Fig. 9(c), i.e. coplanar. These assumptions suggest that it is possible to incorporate current theory for planar surfaces where applicable, as splines compatible with analysis of curved surfaces in the sense of interpolation of surfaces from their boundaries [3].

In absence of evidence to the contrary, if two image curves are projectively consistent with parallel, assume they are images of curves which are parallel in space. In absence of evidence to the contrary, if a straight line is projectively consistent with vertical, assume that it is the image of a vertical line in space.

The connected components of Fig. 10(a) are shown exploded in Fig. 10(b). Only a partial analysis can be done with what has been presented here. The assumptions enable us to say that the cup has parallel limbs and parallel edges, that surface 13 is coincident with both limbs and both edges. Both limbs are vertical. Surfaces 14 and 15 are not coincident with 13, i.e. the cup is open because surface 16 is inside the cup. Surface 13 has an elliptic boundary and it might be inferred that it is circular. Surfaces 13, 14, 15 are in front of 0, 11, and 7, but behind 9 and 12. Region 8 could be a flat cutout. Because of its junctions involving limbs, it is interpreted as a cone with curved cross section (elliptical thus possibly circular). It is in front of surfaces 9 and 7. More assumptions are necessary to deal effectively with the objects with planar surfaces.

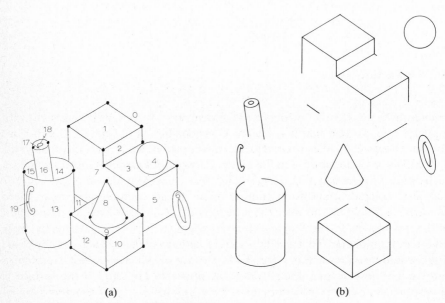

(a)   (b)

FIG. 10. (a) Scene from Turner; (b) exploded view of components.

9. Boundary Estimation

All of the preceding would be manipulation of empty symbols if we could not describe image boundaries effectively or point to some hope of doing so. For years, to do something impressive in vision, wise counsel was to avoid real data, and stick to processing symbolic input. There are several important points to make about obtaining image boundaries. It does make a crucial difference which segmentation operations are used. All are not the same. Nature has enough variety to find out a kluge and make us pay for it. It is often heard that if we just combine all operators with high level knowledge in a grand system, we will win. It is certainly true that if we leave out high level knowledge, we degrade performance, but 'signal to symbol' operations which are not accurate to the limits of the data will just as surely degrade performance. I maintain that these signal to symbol operations limit performance now, that these operations are 1% of their potential, if that.

If we don't take estimation theory seriously at each stage, we give away factors of 3 or more at each stage. There are several stages (typically 4) leading to final image descriptions, thus several factors of 3 in the error volume around measurements, e.g. angles or positions of junctions. Accurate estimation of dimensions and angles is important in interpretation. A factor of three degraded sensitivity to intensity steps means that three times as many boundaries are missed; factors of three in positional accuracy and angular accuracy mean that extrapolation to junctions will be a factor of 9 less accurate, and that a factor of three more junctions will be unobservable (i.e. will appear as T junctions rather than Y or arrow junctions). Some junctions which are separate will appear to coincide.

Speculation 3. The fundamental purpose of saccades, large eye motions, is to examine coincidence at junctions with foveal high resolution; this includes convergence control for stereo. There are two points there: the first is that eye movement is not profound; the second that coincidence is important.

Directional operators are important. I describe ways to implement them, one from Binford–Horn in 1970, and a more elegant method. I also conjecture that boundary operators are found in all sizes in powers of two from single cell to very coarse, that any non-random boundaries are observed in all sizes, from single points to large, and that they are only discarded as meaningless when no structure is found by any perceptual organization in the repertoire.

We set up one objective: determining boundaries of image regions. This is only one aspect of image description, but an important one. It ignores shading and ignores image organization operations for description of texture boundaries. We maintain that it is a precursor to texture. Yes, we are saying that we think it essential to determine boundaries of every noticeable spot in the image, small or large, and look for texture structural relations before discarding or keeping. We appeal to a complexity argument that the only effective way to describe the image is in a segmented, local spline-like way, and that boundaries define the discontinuities of such a spline. Of course, characterization of the smooth behavior of the spline is important, but earlier arguments indicate that the discontinuities are most stable, hence most characteristic of underlying surfaces.

A popular segmentation operation is thresholding. In the cardboard cutout model, a scene is composed of regions of constant intensity of color. We argued that smooth shading is very common and that an image with regions of constant intensity is an unrealistic model even for carefully prepared images. Even with extensive engineering it is difficult to set up these conditions because of non-uniform illumination and non-uniform sensor response. Even for the cardboard cutout model other techniques are preferable because they better distinguish adjacent regions with small contrast and estimate region boundaries to higher accuracy, as shown below. What this means practically is that in a case in which a vision system using thresholding might require 512×512 camera resolution, techniques described here would require 256×256 camera resolution or less. These techniques require less special case engineering, and are more robust and more predictable. In order to determine thresholds, histogramming is sometimes used [35]. If there are many levels and if the levels are not known in advance, histogramming is inadequate because peaks overlap. Using local histograms is a step in the right direction, but it still throws away local spatial information which is valuable for discrimination. It is a significant degradation of performance to discard spatial information. Thresholding is uninteresting.

Regions and region boundaries are dual. That is, a non-region point is a boundary point. Region-based techniques are boundary-based techniques with exceptionally simple local operators for determining boundary elements and simple linking of boundary elements. Thus we include region-oriented techniques in our discussion of boundary-based techniques.

The following are a list of problems and their solutions which provided the motivation for the design of the Binford–Horn line finder [16]. Developments have been made since then, but the problems and the majority of this analysis date to 1970.

10. Problem One

A key point of image segmentation is that smooth gradients are very common. A major problem is to find boundaries in the presence of these large, smooth gradients. Most boundary operators do not address this problem, but deal with the problem of a step function boundary between two regions of constant intensity [20, 21, 34]. Most operators are essentially gradient operators, i.e. the major component to their signal is the gradient. However, the gradient is sensitive to smooth shading. This is only one of the major failings of gradient operators and thresholding. Operators sensitive to the gradient are unacceptable a priori in realistic cases. The essential problem is that they produce continuous areas of spurious boundaries wherever there are large gradients; for example on the fuselage of an aircraft or near a concave edge of two blocks where there is large illumination reflected across the edge. Raising gradient threshold above the minimum determined by random noise to avoid any smooth gradients degrades performance unacceptably (a factor of 10); it is unpredictable. Furthermore, it is unnecessary. Thinning is also ineffective. If spurious image boundaries are reported over half the width of the fuselage, thinning will at best move the boundary in one fourth of the fuselage width, a degradation of a factor of 50 in spatial resolution.

11. Problem Two

An important perceptual operation is to localize intensity boundaries in transverse position and orientation as accurately as data permit. Intensity values are measured at discrete pixels representing a weighted integral of intensity values over a neighborhood. Intensity boundaries are extended two-dimensional step functions, roughly speaking, or delta functions defined along a curve in the continuous plane. We infer continuous distributions from discrete sampled data integrated over pixels. Finding spots or lines in an image can be phrased as looking for significant local peaks of the contrast function (difference from the surround). Finding step boundaries can be phrased as finding significant local maxima of the contrast gradient.

Consider a related problem. Suppose we have touch sensors embedded in an elastic medium. Deformation of the medium causes signals in nearby sensors. The coarse spacing of touch sensors and simultaneous excitation of multiple sensors could lead to very poor localization. The problem is quite general across sensory modes, to find the maximum of the contrast, or the maximum contrast gradient, for coarsely sampled data. The problem is also general across levels of perception. At higher levels of perception, we have the same problem of inferring continuous estimates based on coarsely sampled data. For example, in finding dotted lines among textures, we use sums of boundary values in elongated neighborhoods at sampled positions and angles. Detection and localization of significant peaks and steps in the presence of smooth shading and noise is the universal problem throughout perception.

Ratliff [37] points out that lateral inhibition is a general perceptual phenomenon across sensory modes. We maintain that the function of lateral inhibition is to compensate for smooth shading, to measure the local contrast. That is one part of a universal perceptual operation. By lateral inhibition we mean subtracting the local weighted average from each value. See Figs. 11(a) and 11(b). This transformation will map a linear function to zero, i.e. the laterally inhibited signal for a smooth shading is zero. See Figs. 11(c) and 11(d). Many forms of weighted average will give similar but not identical results. We will later discuss details of the lateral inhibition function.

We pointed out the universal problem of localization of peaks and steps.

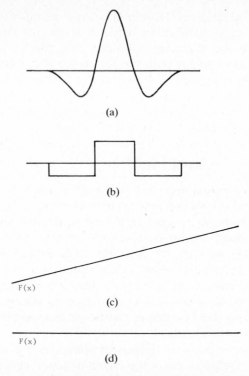

FIG. 11. (a) Laplacian of Gaussian (from Hildreth); (b) difference of boxes; (c) ramp intensity, (d) lateral inhibition signal from (c).

Consider one dimensional signals for now. At a delta or peak, the laterally inhibited signal has a maximum. A maximum is terrible for localization because the function is flat there, and the maximum shifts with fluctuations from noise. Discrete sampling introduces another problem. For that same reason, maxima are fine for detection because the function changes little over adjacent samples. Because intensity values are averages over a pixel, it can be shown easily that the maximum cannot be located more accurately by linear interpolation of intensities than the nearest integer pixel value. However, at the maximum the gradient is zero. The gradient of the signal after lateral inhibition is zero at the maximum; its position can be estimated accurately by interpolation (the error is proportional to the noise divided by the gradient). Thus zero crossings of the gradient of lateral inhibition achieve localization of transverse position of peaks, which addresses problem two. It is also easy to see that the accuracy of estimation of boundary position is better for pixels which average over a small area than for point sampling. At a step boundary the gradient has a sharp maximum. Again, the maximum of the gradient cannot be located more accurately than the nearest integer pixel. The lateral inhibition signal has a zero crossing at the maximum which can be used to estimate the boundary accurately.

Thus, zero crossings of the lateral inhibition signal or its gradient provide a partial solution to a universal perceptual problem, localization of steps or peaks. However, there are zero crossings of the lateral inhibition signal everywhere the signal has zero mean, i.e. over regions of constant intensity or smooth shading. That is, a zero signal has very dense zero crossings caused by random fluctuations over almost the whole image. In fact, the only areas of an image without dense zero crossings are near image boundaries with reasonable contrast. There are many zero crossings, only a few of them are significant. We identify two operations, detection and localization. In that sense detection is primary.

Fig. 12(a) shows a step function. Fig. 12(b) shows its lateral inhibition signal using difference of boxes with width w. Fig. 12(c) shows the first difference of sums of the lateral inhibition signal over a support w. Fig. 12(d) shows sums of the lateral inhibition signal over support w. The equivalent functions would be smoother for the Laplacian of a Gaussian [29]. At a step, the gradient of the lateral inhibition signal is a maximum. If it is large enough compared to sensor noise, the step can be detected. Anywhere the gradient of the lateral inhibition signal is large, zero crossing of the lateral inhibition signal is an accurate

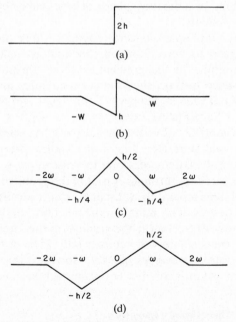

FIG. 12. (a) Step function; (b) lateral inhibition; (c) first difference of sums of lateral inhibition signal; (d) sum of lateral inhibition signal.

interpolation estimate of the step. Estimation of edge position from zero crossings corresponds to placing the step at the location with weighted average intensity midway between intensities on the two sides of the step.

An interesting way of combining detection and localization is this: for features to be interesting, we must be able to localize them accurately in the image. If they shift greatly with random fluctuations of camera noise, steps will not characterize position of underlying surface boundaries, limbs, shadows, etc. The expectation of the error of localization is proportional to intensity noise divided by the contrast. Essentially, all our discussions below are naturally expressed in units of contrast divided by noise. Detection measures how accurately boundaries can be localized.

We now look in detail at the accuracy of localization of position for thresholding and for zero crossing of the lateral inhibition signal. If signal to noise is great enough, positional accuracy is interval bounded, that is, the rms error is one pixel divided by sqrt(12). By comparison, if we interpolate the lateral inhibition signal to estimate the zero crossing, $x = f_1/(f_1 - f_2)$, where f_1, f_2 are the lateral inhibition signals at pixels x_1 and x_2. Then $dx = df_1 * \mathrm{sqrt}(2/3)/|f_1 - f_2|$ where dx is the rms position error, and df is the rms variation of f_1 and f_2. Thus dx is approximately the noise divided by the gradient for a pair of points (i.e. contrast). Localization is improved by this interpolation; the effect is important for contrast greater than about 3 times the rms noise. An analogy is estimating phase of sine waves by quadrature from cosine and sine components.

There is a problem with spurious zero crossings where the lateral inhibition signal for a step goes to zero. Random fluctuations cause zero crossings, somewhere the amplitude of the gradient is above threshold for steps with large contrast. We have distinguished between satellites and central steps by thresholding the ratio of even to odd parts of the signal. Let R be the sum on the right of point x, $R = \mathrm{Sum}(f'(x + i))$ over $0 \le i \le \omega$, while L is the sum on the left of point x, $L = \mathrm{Sum}(f'(x - 1 - i))$ over $0 \le i \le \omega$. At satellites the even part $(R + L)$ equals the odd part $(R - L)$; at the central step the even part is approximately zero. Calculations of signal to noise show that there is a small probability of letting satellites through. A root of the problem is that we consider satellites and central steps separately, without making a consistent interpretation. One way to do so is to iteratively inhibit in the neighborhood of each satellite or step. The true step will subtract away the gradient at the satellite entirely on the first iteration while the satellite will subtract only 25% of the gradient at the central step. The iteration converges quickly. However, this is just a particular deconvolution; there are probably better deconvolution operations.

12. Directional Operators

Thus far, we have considered one dimensional position localization. We want now to consider directional operators in two dimensions and the problem of localizing in direction and position. Consider lateral inhibition followed by convolution at each position with operators which are elongated in each of a fixed set of directions, e.g. every 15 degrees. The convolution signal will be large over a range of positions and angles near an image boundary. It is essential to make an estimate of the transverse position and angle of the true edge. Longitudinal position is not well determined since we assume that the intensity varies slowly along the edge. One technique for localization is to thin values which are above threshold, to pick a 'central' value. Another is to choose local maxima over pixel positions and angle. At junctions there are several such local maxima corresponding to boundaries which join.

At a position selected in one of these ad hoc ways, it is possible to interpolate for the position and angle of step boundaries by determining the least squares line which minimizes the square of the lateral inhibition signal along the line, within the neighborhood of the operator. That is, the boundary follows zero crossings of the lateral inhibition signal. Locally, the boundary can be approximated by a straight line. Because the lateral inhibition signal is dominated locally by its gradient, the solution which minimizes the square of the lateral inhibition signal is equivalent to a line with least squares variation of zero crossing position. That is, position is linearly related to value of the lateral inhibition signal.

Adjacent directional operators lead to similar but slightly different solutions. There is a more direct and cleaner procedure. The boundary position and orientation is that which maximizes the gradient of the lateral inhibition signal. As pointed out before, the maximum cannot be determined very accurately. However, the gradient of that signal is zero at the maximum. Thus the boundary is that line which maximizes the gradient of lateral inhibition signal, thus the line for which its partial derivatives with respect to angle and position are zero. Consider convolutions at various directions as a set of stacked planes, one plane for each angle. Then determining the best estimate for a boundary involves finding the cell in which the derivatives vanish, then interpolating within the cell. The solution is degenerated along the tangent to the boundary. Binford–Horn used a different procedure [16].

We postulate that these two operations of finding peaks and steps are accomplished by two sorts of universal directional operators following lateral inhibition; one with the form of a directional derivative and the other with the form of a second directional derivative. For peaks detection is accomplished with the second derivative and localization by zero crossing of the first derivative. For steps direction is accomplished by the first derivative and localization by the second derivative. It seems reasonable that the lateral geniculate nucleus performs lateral inhibition while the simple cells of the visual cortex [19] calculate its first and second directional derivatives. We conjecture that they are not bar and step masks, but that their purpose is estimating those two components for localization and detection.

Hildreth [13] states that the boundary mask should not be directional. The first difficulty is smearing of zero-crossing contours of termination of boundaries in the direction of a directional mask. The solution is to treat termination properly, as in a following section. The second problem is that spurious zero crossings appear at ninety degrees to the direction of the boundary, where the signal is zero. From previous discussion, there are many zero crossings for zero signal. The problem here is that the selection process is inadequate. There will be multiple zero crossings at any boundary for masks oriented near the direction of the boundary. Which should be chosen? The procedure above describes a clean interpolation. The third objection to directional masks is that they complicate the edge detection process. This relates again to the selection process.

13. Problem Three

It is important to determine accurately the termination of boundaries. We could require that the contrast across the edge be constant or vary linearly over small sections of the boundary, then segment where the squared error is sufficiently large. That systematically extends beyond the end of the boundary. Instead, we have found a mechanism which is clean and simple. The solution uses the mechanisms that we have already introduced. We are looking for a step in the contrast across an edge. We saw above that to find a significant step we can detect it with the gradient of the lateral inhibition signal and localize it where its derivative is zero. The other significant information is the termination of other boundaries at the junction. A complication is that the area around junctions becomes crowded. That is partially dealt with by using small, directional operators for extrapolation into junctions. The general problem is that of finding junctions, which we do not choose to deal with in this paper. One approach is to treat it in the domain of extracted curves, and to find the best extrapolation to intersection without looking back at the gray scale image in the vicinity of their intersection [4]. Several improvements in detail can be made there. Another is to use the point spread functions of sensors in a junction estimation procedure, much as was done for curves in the previous section. That appears feasible. The estimate for termination described above provides improved estimates for starting points for a junction estimation procedure.

14. Problem Four

We wish to determine boundaries with small contrast, i.e. with maximum sensitivity, as sensitively as the data allows. That is important because in typical images, boundary finding programs miss many boundaries that humans find easily. These are not problems of higher level knowledge; in a few cases we have tested informally that people see these boundaries when the rest of the image was masked, i.e. without context. In [12] we introduced a measure for sensitivity of boundary finders: the sensitivity is the threshold required to achieve a given level of false positives, e.g. 1% threshold is the 50% level for false negatives. We also gave simple procedures for calculating thresholds from first principles in terms of sensor noise. That is, thresholds can be calculated a priori from camera noise which is trivial to estimate; there is no need for ad hoc tweaking of parameters.

We have since made a program to estimate camera noise from images. An image typically has large regions of relatively smooth intensities. This procedure assumes that there are large regions over which intensity differences are small from cell to cell. Some nearest neighbor differences will fall across image boundaries. If they are relatively few, then the distribution of nearest neighbor differences will have a peak around zero with a width corresponding to sensor noise. If we used the rms estimate of sensor error, it would be seriously biased by large differences expected across boundaries. The rms error is an effective estimator of noise for a single Gaussian population, but this problem has a Gaussian sensor noise population with an unknown distribution of large nearest neighbor differences. The multi-population problem is universal in perception. We determine the width around zero which contains 67% of the points, corresponding to one standard deviation for a Gaussian. This is the rms error of the difference of two values, which is sqrt(2) times the rms error of a single value. Any clipped values are removed, since they distort the distribution; their nearest neighbor differences are primarily zero. It is possible to transform intensity values according to sensor noise characteristics, for example for a linear or log noise characteristic.

Marr and Hildreth [28] deal with sensor noise by choosing sufficiently large operators so that zero crossings are spaced at reasonable intervals. That amounts to low pass filtering of the signal, thus zero crossings have lower frequency. They also use an unspecified threshold on the gradient of lateral inhibition at zero crossings. However, even very small operators can be used since it is possible to calculate thresholds for all sizes from first principles. This is an example of extracting more information from the signal by care in estimation. The alternative is loss of resolution and considerable degradation in presence of texture, as discussed in the next section.

These comments don't address the problem of improving sensitivity. The Binford–Horn boundary finder dealt with this issue carefully. There are two issues, random sensor noise and systematic signals, which are not perceptually interesting. It is our principle to include as noise only random sensor noise. Texture and surface marks are signal. We only know that they are uninteresting for our purposes when we have failed to find any structure with any of our organizational operators. For example, a single dot in a field of dots is not interesting. A remarkably small number of them widely separated along a smooth curve can be distinguished, e.g. cloud chamber pictures from long ago. If dots are discarded based on area or any local predicate, that structure could not be found. We do not mean to say that we have effective organizational operators for texture, however. Such marks often have high contrast, and their distributions are unpredictable. Camera noise is relatively predictable. To raise thresholds in order to discriminate against surface marks limits sensitivity greatly. We choose thresholds according to the physical minimum imposed by sensor noise.

Sensitivity is improved in predictable measure by averaging over larger support. However, the larger the support, the more likely that texture elements will be included. A rule of thumb is that the sensitivity is limited by the smallest support over which thresholding is performed. Most discussion of boundary finding has dealt with finding boundaries between uniform regions. Herskovits [12] provided for small amounts of surface markings by thresholding. Surface markings were thus weighted by their number not their contrast, which diminished their effect considerably. The Binford–Horn boundary finder provided a better way, described later. Boundaries are extended; at a point, an extended boundary cannot be distinguished from sensor noise fluctuations or from point surface marks. Thus boundary operators should be extended and directional.

We rely on the *principle of structural specificity*. We want to distinguish signal by thresholding some measure. To do so, we maximize the probability of signal falling above threshold, and minimize the probability of random noise fluctuations above threshold. The probability of random noise fluctuations depends on the number of combinations equivalent under the measure. Thus, the more specific the operator is to the signal, the better the match (an extended boundary), the fewer geometric combinations of noise, the lower the threshold can be. Any technique which uses spatial relations is more powerful than one which does not. Histogram techniques (which ignore spatial relations) distinguish less sharply than techniques which use spatial information (although histogram techniques may be a simpler starting place).

We have implicitly assumed that boundary finding is a local to global process. This is based on complexity considerations. Over a small support, curves may be locally straight. Although there may be some boundaries which are locally straight over large support, curves may be quite complex and the assumption of a single structure is unlikely to be valid. In order to reduce complexity of large neighborhoods to that of small ones, smaller structures must be removed. We argue below that linear space-invariant filtering does not accomplish that. Splines of local values provide a reasonable level of complexity. All functions on gray levels on a large retina is an impossibly large space.

A detection process only increases the probability of local boundary elements relative to random fluctuations. In a situation with limited resources for measurement, sequential detection provides an optimal solution. In this case the limited resource is the number of combinations of local boundary element candidates which can be tested. The Binford–Horn boundary finder used sequential detection in this form: at each row, boundary candidates were evaluated to see whether they were above a threshold for random noise chains of that length.

It is attractive to do away with thresholds altogether. I know of no effective way of doing so. Marr [29] makes a conjecture of an extension of a theorem of Logan; a bandwidth-limited function can be reproduced from zero crossings of filters with one octave bandwidth. The number of zero crossings is very large for high frequencies, and most are random fluctuations which have no perceptual value. It was pointed out above that positional accuracy is very poor for zero crossings with small contrast. Thus those zero crossings do not relate well to surface features.

It seems reasonable to extend the support on which thresholding is based. We conjecture that one way to do this is to calculate appropriate coefficients on a small support w for various directions, then cascade these in pairs, then pairs of pairs, etc. If cascading is done for all possible paths in the plane, the computation is infeasible. If paths are restricted to circular arcs, then tangent pairs of circular arcs, the set of paths seems sufficiently restricted, as small as the set of all positions for all angles for all curvatures.

15. Problem Five

Boundaries have a range of widths. As pointed out above, only a part of an image is in focus at one time. Even though parts of the image are defocussed, there is still much important perceptual information there. Shadow boundaries may have fuzzy transitions. This is perhaps the origin of our ability to understand x-ray photos. In order to focus automatically, it is useful to measure the width of transitions at curves and junctions.

Also image figures come in a range of sizes. One consequence of the previous section is that detectability of image boundaries depends on the contrast in units of the sensor noise, Detectability also depends on the length and curvature of the boundary. A long, straight boundary is more detectable than a short straight line. A long, smooth boundary is more detectable than a long, twisted boundary. These considerations are based on the set of data available (more data, more detectable) and on the number of background combinations (the more irregular the curve, the more random combinations).

To locate sharp edges, small lateral inhibition operators suffice. For defocussed boundaries, large lateral inhibition operators are necessary. A range of lateral inhibition operators with size ranging from excitation diameter of 1, 2, 4, ... , up to the order of the image size is postulated, based on the response of lateral inhibition operators to boundaries as a function of transition width. To locate low contrast edges, large operators are necessary.

Significant boundaries are those with sufficient contrast relative to noise and which have sharp transitions at some scale of coarseness. If we recall the variation of detectability, long regular boundaries are more detectable than short ones. Thus large lateral inhibition operators are useful for large image figures. However, texture must be accounted for. Consider finding a boundary with small contrast between R_1 and R_2. See Fig. 13. On the brighter side R_1 is a dense texture of high contrast black dots. I conjecture that humans find the intensity boundary with only slight interference from the black dots. I conjecture that we evaluate the boundary as though we had cut out the dots and based the judgment on background which remains. The intent of the example, which can be tested psychophysically and may have been tested already, is that there are enough sharp, high contrast dots to tip the balance, so that a linear, position invariant operator would have the wrong sign for contrast at the boundary, and that the dots can be localized. Marr [29] has postulated that humans have frequency filters which are linear operators. My conjecture is that the mechanism is completely inadequate, that linear filters do not discriminate against small image elements sufficiently to explain human perception, nor are they adequate for machine perception. I believe that the problem of combining outputs of boundary finding operators of different scale is an open question which is difficult. I conjecture that the process goes from fine to coarse, that is fine image elements are detected and their effects minimized by non-linear operations so that they do not affect larger operators. In contrast, the usual model is coarse-to-fine. My candidate for the non-linear operator is that used in sequential detection in the Binford–Horn boundary finder for minimizing the effects of texture, i.e. weighting by Gaussian residuals.

Marr [28] argues that the optimal functional form for lateral inhibition is the Laplacian of a Gaussian, approximated by a difference of Gaussians. We agree that the lateral inhibition function should be smooth, but there are several different arguments which lead to that conclusion. Briefly, their argument is that boundaries come in a range of transition widths, therefore a range of frequencies. To distinguish different transition widths, the function should be narrow in frequency space. On the other hand, the function should be local in

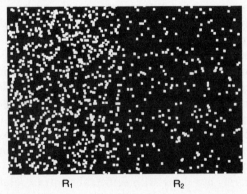

R₁   R₂

FIG. 13. Region R_1 brighter than R_2.

the spatial domain. The function that minimizes the product $dx * df$ is the Gaussian, where dx is the spatial interval and df the frequency interval. We disagree with the argument that boundaries are characterized by frequency. Of course, any linear system can be characterized by a frequency analysis. The issue is whether the frequency representation is more compact than the spatial representation. The larger is dx, the smaller df. Delta functions have all frequencies. Even much defocussed boundaries are small compared to the full image. Boundaries are not often related, i.e. periodic. Some textures are periodic, others are not periodic even though they may have repeated, unrelated elements. What arguments do we have when we ignore frequency behavior entirely? In communications, frequency behavior is important because signals are frequency signals. In vision, all observables are spatial and any recourse to frequency domain should be carefully supported analytically. If image signals were periodic, this would be a consideration.

Maximizing signal to noise for boundary detection leads to similar smooth functions. The basic rule for least squares solution which maximizes signal to noise is to weight each term by the square of its signal to noise. The effect of lateral inhibition by a difference of boxes is a linear decrease of signal away from the boundary. The effect of spatial integration in sampling of pixels is a linear decrease of signal across the boundary. The maximal signal to noise estimate for lateral inhibition with the difference of boxes produces cubic smoothing across the boundary and away from the boundary. It may be that smooth weighting is important because boundary detection is accomplished by iterative deconvolution. Signal to noise considerations for the deconvolution kernel would lead to a smooth kernel. In summary, we consider the functional form of lateral inhibition an open question.

16. Problem Six

The linking of local boundary elements is an important and poorly understood problem. This is one phase of local organization of image elements. In the case of region segments, the criteria for defining elements of a region have typically been thresholds selected from histogramming [11, 35]. Regions have been path-connected components based on four-neighbor or eight-neighbor relations as in the TOPOLOGIST [4]. This is an especially simple algorithm. Industrial vision systems are built using this contour following. However, intensity is not a generally useful basis for thresholding. Color components have been used, and while useful, they are still very weak. Thresholding has the advantage that contours are closed, thus path-connected components can be simply defined. If we use other techniques described above for detecting image boundaries which may have breaks, they will be closed, but a single break will change the topology drastically. Growing and shrinking can be used to patch up gaps in boundaries. Growing is a non-directional operation which does not take account of boundary directions, thus it gives away valuable information for distinguishing extended boundaries from noise.

The Hough transform [9] does take into account directionality, but it has the major weakness of not using proximity. That is, points which are far apart are linked in the Hough transform. That raises the background of spurious links greatly. Also, the parameterization of the Hough transform is in terms of angle and perpendicular distance from origin. The error in perpendicular distance is proportional to longitudinal distance from the origin. That is, clustering is non-uniform; clusters are blurred, thus they allow more erroneous links than necessary. I have used a local Hough-like transform based on partial projection in a number of directions (see [32]). That is, at each angle rotate the coordinate system and compress (partially projected) along the transformed y-axis, and place boundary elements in elements of an x, y, theta array. This is equivalent to forming elongated neighborhoods in a distorted coordinate system, such that if boundary elements align and are adjacent, they fall into the same bin. Square bins in the transformed space are equivalent to long, narrow bins in the original space. The number of angles is easily determined from the elongation of the bins. The computational cost is low, only $n_p \cdot n_t$, where n_p is the number of points and n_t is the number of angles. The same technique could be used for amplitudes of boundary operators without thresholding. The problem is to find peaks in x, y, theta where local maxima of points align. The following has not been implemented yet, but appears promising. This is another problem of peak finding in which we detect using the difference from the local average and localize by interpolation of directional derivatives to zero.

There are a number of techniques which involve local search, using minimal spanning trees [36] or dynamic programming [30]. In general, restricting associations to direction and proximity limits search greatly. Techniques which do not use these geometric constraints are needlessly expensive. A precondition for using the constraints is appropriate spatial representation preserving proximity. We have used multi-entry coding in the plane, a way of preserving proximity in the plane, as a way of directly implementing neighbor relations in Binford–Horn and later work.

Zero crossings are closed, thus they sound attractive for simple linking along the zero crossing. We have designed and are implementing such a boundary traversal algorithm to implement a simple vision system. However, boundary following of zero crossings is not necessarily very useful for sophisticated vision. Although zero crossings are closed, only a part of the boundary may be actual signal. Consider an intensity surface which is like a wedge lying flat, a ramp shown in Fig. 14. At the high end and along part of the sides of the ramp, the signal may be large, but the signal goes to zero at the low end of the ramp. Thus at the low end of the ramp, the zero crossing wanders about driven by random fluctuations. This example seems contrived, but in fact it occurs very frequently that closed zero crossings are valid boundaries only along a fraction

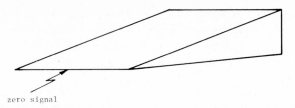

zero signal

FIG. 14. Zero crossing without significance.

of their length. For simple linking, zero crossings are not bad because even for moderate signals we have calculated that they don't wander far from the true boundary, i.e. the expected transverse point scattering error is given above. Greater accuracy is possible by using directional operators and directional continuity, as described above.

17. Binford–Horn

This section describes the Binford–Horn system, with its analytical design and objectives as they were understood in 1970. Line finding and curve linking did not work very well then. Many vision experts thought that poor performance reflected inherent limitations 'boundary finding is impossible'; they were concerned with higher level knowledge used to make up for these deficiencies, or with Warnock-like strategies (now called pyramid structures) to reduce computation by dealing first with very coarse images and then refining descriptions. We believed that effective edge-based description of images was possible and necessary for high performance vision systems at the cost of considerable computation. We aimed to combine careful signal estimation analysis with a hypothesis-and-test paradigm, equivalent to sequential detection in signal processing. We aimed for high performance while cutting some corners to achieve computation time of several minutes on a PDP-6.

Binford–Horn faced these problems: (1) Boundary finders missed low contrast edges. (2) They gave masses of spurious boundaries in the presence of shading. (3) They gave poor estimates of locations and angles of boundaries. (4) They were largely unable to find texture boundaries; texture interfered with finding intensity boundaries on otherwise uniform surfaces. (5) They had poor resolution for thin features and at junctions. (6) They required extensive computation. (7) They were not effective with diffuse boundaries found in x-rays and out of focus parts of an image.

The Binford–Horn boundary finder dealt with (1), (2), (3) and (5) and to a lesser extent with (4) and (6), Binford–Horn had the following underlying model:

(1) It incorporated directional operators spaced about seven degrees apart with extended support. Thresholds were set by analytic calculation of signal to noise for operators. There were no empirical parameters.

(2) Lateral inhibition removes smooth gradients. Humans do not sense boundaries in regions with smooth gradients [8]. In typical images, intensities vary significantly over regions which humans perceive without boundaries, where perhaps we perceive shading. Most edge operators were primarily sensitive to the gradient; clearly the gradient is the wrong function. The biological solution is called lateral inhibition; the function is something like a Laplacian, roughly subtracting the local average at each point. Edges were detected in Binford–Horn by thresholding the directional first difference of the laterally inhibited signal. It was only after we had finished that we realized what function lateral inhibition accomplished in natural vision, and that we understood that what we had done was equivalent to lateral inhibition. Also, only later did we realize that the function is very close to the third derivative used in [12].

(3) The TOPOLOGIST, predecessor to Binford–Horn, and other systems localized boundaries by finding the maximum of the gradient function or by thinning bands of points with gradient above threshold. The gradient is flat at maximum, it is a poor function for localization. Binford–Horn localized boundaries from zero crossings of the directional sum of the laterally inhibited signal. That is, it detected boundaries by the odd part of the laterally inhibited signal and localized boundaries by zero crossings of the even part of the laterally inhibited signal.

(4) Consider a boundary between two regions with slightly different shades of gray. Add a texture of small spots to one region or both. The contrast of the spots can overwhelm the small intensity difference between the regions, making detection of the intensity difference impossible for linear operators. [12] used thresholding to weight boundary points by their number, not their contrast. Binford–Horn weighted boundary points in linking curves with a sequential detection process using a non-linear function: one minus the Gaussian residual, i.e., one minus the probability of a fluctuation as great or greater than that observed, under the assumption of zero signal with Gaussian noise. The function is approximately linear near zero and approximately one (thresholding) at large signal. That non-linear weighting made significant contribution to improved performance.

(5) There are two scales involved, first, the scale of blurring of edges, i.e. the width of transitions, and second, the separation between features. There is a relation between contrast of a feature and minimum size for detection. Binford–Horn did nothing about finding features of various scales. We were concerned with high resolution for finding narrow features. We believed that edge operators of several scales were necessary to deal with defocussing, however, time allowed implementing only one scale. We had not resolved the fundamental problem of combining results of operators of various sizes, a problem which has not yet been resolved in a fundamental way. There was also resistance to increased computation, although the computation cost for all resolutions was only a little more than that for the highest resolution.

(6) We aimed for an intermediate level of computation. The TOPOLOGIST found regions with large areas, while we intended to find medium long but thin regions, and were willing to miss short, thin ones. We aimed for moderate efficiency by line sampling, sampling densely normal to edges and coarsely along edges. That is, we sampled densely along horizontal and vertical lines with coarse spacing between lines as in Fig. 15.

FIG. 15. Line sampling.

The linking process affected sensitivity; if linking were effective in discriminating against local noise, thresholds could be lowered. The linking procedure was a form of parallel line following. Scanning proceeded line by line for triples of horizontal lines, then column by column for triples of vertical lines. Within a triple of lines, find candidates as described above. If it can be linked to existing candidate chains from the previous triple, then link. If not, start a new candidate chain. Each boundary segment is characterized by direction and contrast. The intent of hypothesis and test or sequential decision process was to improve the likelihood of keeping any boundaries with low contrast if they once survived thresholding, to maintain a high likelihood of bridging gaps for which boundary contrast was significant but below threshold, to keep small the likelihood of bridging true gaps in boundaries, and to decrease the likelihood of accepting boundary candidates caused by noise fluctuations. Consider a single step thresholding operation. There will remain an unavoidable number of false positives from random fluctuations, many of which could be eliminated by a small additional effort of making new measurements. Given any desired level of acceptance of false positives, sequential detection requires the fewest measurements. Candidate chains active through the previous line were kept in a line array. Each new candidate was linked to existing chains by requiring slowly varying contrast (10%) and slowly changing direction (one angle interval, about seven degrees). Those values were chosen by calculating variations caused by random fluctuations. They serve to impose limits on the curvature and change of contrast of boundaries. Each chain which was not extended by a new candidate was extended by locally maximizing the contrast consistent with the direction and contrast of the boundary chain. At each raster triple, the decision was made whether to keep or discard boundary chains. If no new candidate was found, the contrast, summed with the non-linear measure, was compared with a contrast threshold corresponding to the 1% level for random chains with zero signal and Gaussian noise. Also a test was made to terminate boundaries which were to be kept. The contrast near the end of the boundary was compared to the average along the portion of the boundary just preceding. When the boundary was terminated, the endpoint was chosen to be the last point above the local average preceding termination. A better termination condition was described earlier in this paper.

Binford–Horn maximized signal with respect to angle at each point. We saw above that this is only a partial solution; its consequence is that near boundaries, points off the boundary may have above-threshold signal in the direction of the boundary. This was solved by requiring local maxima at both ends of the boundary segment.

Binford–Horn contained a number of simplifications for expedience. Lateral inhibition was implemented as the difference of boxes followed by the local sum of values. The composed function has linear variation between the zeros of the difference of boxes. See Fig. 12(c). This function can be computed by updating, i.e. by adding to the head and subtracting from the tail of rows and columns. Updating requires only a few operations per step. A smoother lateral inhibition function that was considered was exponential updating, which is equally simple computationally. To save memory, lateral inhibition was done only within individual rows. That was a strong limitation near corners. In a sense the choice was unnecessary; by current standards, the memory require-ments would have been modest. The system was implemented in assembly code. That made it simpler and faster to implement; faster, but inaccessible to others. Scanning in raster mode along horizontals and then verticals meant that boundaries were linked independently in horizontal and vertical, with overlaps. That raised problems of multiple instances of boundaries near the diagonals. A greater problem was the very local character of linking. This was conceptually inadequate at junctions where multiple boundaries require extension of boundaries based on evaluation of more than a single boundary.

ACKNOWLEDGMENT

Support for this research has been provided by the Image Understanding Program, DARPA, under contract MDA903-80-C-0102, and by the National Science Foundation under grant DAR-78-15914. I would like especially to thank Mike Brady for repeated encouragement and valuable discussions. Without him this paper would never have been written. I am indebted to David Lowe for suggestions of clarification.

REFERENCES

1. Agin, G.J., Representation and description of curved objects, Memo AIM-173, AI Lab, Stanford Univ. (1972).
2. Barrow, H.G. and Tenenbaum, J.M., Recovering intrinsic scene characteristics from images, in: A. Hansen and E. Riseman, Eds., *Computer Visual Systems* (Academic Press, New York, 1978).
3. Barrow, H.G. and Tenenbaum, J.M., Interpreting line drawings as three-dimensional surfaces, *Proc. AAAI*, Stanford, 1980.
4. Binford, T.O., The TOPOLOGIST, Internal Report MIT-AI, 1970.
5. Binford, T.O., Visual perception by computer, Invited talk IEEE Systems and Control Conference, Miami, 1971.
6. Brady, M., Grimson, W.E.L. and Langridge, D.J., Shape encoding and subjective contours, *Proc. AAAI* (1980).
7. Clowes, M.B., On seeing things, *Artificial Intelligence* **2**(1) (1971) 79–115.
8. Cornsweet, T.N., *Visual Perception* (Academic Press, New York, 1970).
9. Duda, R.O. and Hart, P.E., A generalized Hough transformation for detecting lines in pictures, SRI AI Group Tech. Note 36 (1971).
10. Duda, R.O. and Hart, P.E., *Pattern Classification and Scene Analysis* (Wiley, New York, 1973).
11. Fennema, C.L. and Brice, C.L., Scene analysis of pictures using regions, *Artificial Intelligence* **1**(3, 4) (1970) 205–226.
12. Herskovits, A. and Binford, T.O., On boundary detection, MIT AI Memo 182 (1970).
13. Hildreth, E.C., Implementation of a theory of edge detection, MIT-AI-TR-579 (1980).
14. Horn, B.K.P., Shape from shading: a method for obtaining the shape of a smooth opaque object from one view, MIT Tech. Rept. TR-79 (1970).
15. Horn, B.K.P., Obtaining shape from shading information, in: P.H. Winston, Ed., *The Psychology of Computer Vision* (McGraw-Hill, New York, 1975).
16. Horn, B.K.P., The Binford–Horn edge finder, MIT AI Memo 285 (1972) (revised December 1973).
17. Horn, B.K.P., Determining lightness from an image, *Comput. Graphics Image Process.* **3** (1974).
18. Horn, B.K.P., Understanding image intensities, *Artificial Intelligence* **8** (1977) 201–231.
19. Hubel, D.H., The visual cortex of the brain, *Sci. Amer.* **209** (1963) 54–77.
20. Hueckel, M., An operator which locates edges in digitized pictures, AI Memo No. 105, Stanford Univ., Stanford (1969).
21. Hueckel, M., A local visual operator which recognizes edges and lines, *J. Assoc. Comput. Mach.* **20** (1973) 634–647.
22. Huffman, D.A., Impossible objects as nonsense sentences, *Machine Intelligence* **6** (1971) 295–324.
23. Land, E.H., Experiments in color vision, *Am. Sci.* **52** (1964).
24. Land, E.H., The retinex theory of color vision, *Sci. Amer.* **237**(6) (1977) 108–129.
25. Lettvin, J., The colors of colored things, RLE Quarterly Report, MIT (1969).

26. Lowe, D. and Binford, T.O., to be submitted *Proc. Image Understanding Workshop*, April 1981.
27. Mackworth, A.K., Interpreting pictures of polyhedral scenes, *Artificial Intelligence* **4**(2) (1973) 121–139.
28. Marr, D. and Hildreth, E., Theory of edge detection, MIT AI Memo 518 (1979).
29. Marr, D., Poggio, T. and Ullman, S., Bandpass channels, zero crossings, and early visual information processing, *J. Opt. Soc. Amer.* **69**(6) (1979) 914–916.
30. Montanari, U., On the optimal detection of curves in noisy pictures, Memo AIM-115, AI Lab, Stanford University (1970).
31. Nevatia, R., Structured descriptions of complex curved objects for recognition and visual memory, Memo AIM-250, AI Lab, Stanford Univ. (1974).
32. Nevatia, R., Object boundary determination in a textured environment, *Comput. Graphics Image Process.* (1976).
33. Nevatia, R. and Binford, T.O., Description and recognition of curved objects, *Artificial Intelligence* **8** (1977) 77–98.
34. Nevatia, R. and Babu, K.R., Linear feature extraction, *Proc. ARPA Image Understanding Workshop*, Pittsburgh (1978) 73–78.
35. Ohlander, R.B., Analysis of natural scenes, Tech. Rept. Dept. of Computer Science, Carnegie–Mellon Univ. (1975).
36. Ramer, E.U., The transformation of photographic images into stroke array, IBM Research RJ-1451 (Sept. 1974).
37. Ratliff, F., *Mach Bands* (Holden–Day, San Francisco, 1965).
38. Turner, K., Computer perception of curved objects using a television camera, Ph.D. Thesis, Univ. of Edinburgh, 1974.
39. Ullman, S., Filling in the gaps: The shape of subjective contours and a model for their generation, MIT AI Memo 367 (1976).
40. Waltz, D., Generating semantic descriptions from drawings of scenes with shadows, MIT Tech. Rept. AI-TR-271 (1972).
41. Waltz, D., Understanding line drawings of scenes with shadows, in: P.H. Winston, Ed., *The Psychology of Computer Perception* (McGraw-Hill, New York, 1975).

Received January 1981

Cooperating Processes for Low-level Vision: A Survey

Larry S. Davis

Department of Computer Sciences, University of Texas, Austin, TX 78712, U.S.A.

Azriel Rosenfeld

Computer Science Center, University of Maryland, College Park, MD 20742, U.S.A.

ABSTRACT

Cooperating local parallel processes can be used as aids in assigning numerical or symbolic labels to image or scene parts. Various approaches to using such processes in low-level vision are reviewed, and their advantages are discussed. Methods of designing and controlling such processes are also considered.

1. Introduction

The early stages of computer vision involve assigning symbolic and numerical labels to image parts. For example, pixels can be assigned symbolic land-use category labels based on their spectral signatures, or numerical stereo or motion disparity labels based on local comparisons between pairs of pictures.

The enormous amount of data comprising an image demands that such labelling processes be very fast. Sequential labelling processes, while they can make full use of context, cannot be speeded up in general. Moreover, the labellings which they compute are often sensitive to the order in which the parts are considered. A more promising approach—one that is also motivated by studies of biological visual systems—is to make the processes highly *parallel*. This requires that each picture part be analyzed and labelled independently of the others. When we do this, however, many errors are made, because contextual information is not adequately used.

A solution to this problem is to assess the labelling possibilities for every part independently and then compare each part's assessments to those of other,

Artificial Intelligence **17** (1981) 245–263

related parts, in order to detect and correct potential inconsistencies. Since both the assessment and the comparison can be done independently for every part, each stage of the process is parallel. On the other hand, context is now being used at the comparison stage, when related parts are able to communicate and 'cooperate'. To keep the computational cost low, the comparisons should be *local*; they should involve only parts that are directly related (e.g., neighboring pixels). This localness can be compensated for by *iterating* the comparison process, in order to allow information to propagate.

These considerations lead naturally to the design of a 'cooperative' approach to labelling picture parts which allows context to be used in the labelling process while still permitting fast parallel implementation and low computational cost. Such processes are called 'relaxation' processes, because of their resemblance to certain iterative processes used in numerical analysis. Very generally, a relaxation process is organized as follows:

(a) A list of possible labels is independently selected for each part, based on its intrinsic characteristics. A measure of confidence can also be associated with each possible label.[1]

(b) The possibilities (and confidences) for each part are compared with those for related parts, based on a model for the relationships between the possible labels of picture parts. Labels are deleted or confidences are adjusted to reduce inconsistencies.

(c) Step (b) can be iterated as many times as required.

This approach is very general: We have not specified how to formulate label relationship models, choose possibilities, estimate confidences, or adjust them; nor have we discussed when the process should be iterated, and if so, how many times. The next three sections of this paper discuss these issues, and survey applications of such processes to problems in low-level computer vision.

2. Cooperation/Competition

A relaxation process is a computational mechanism which allows a set of 'myopic' local processes associated with picture parts to interact with one another in order to achieve a globally consistent interpretation of a picture. This interaction involves the updating of each picture part's self-assessment which is represented as a discrete or fuzzy *labelling*. A discrete labelling simply associates a set of possible labels, or names, with each picture part, while a fuzzy labelling additionally associates a likelihood with each label.

Labels are usually specified extensionally by actually listing the appropriate labels for each picture part. The list is a subset of some given, finite universe of labels. For some applications the natural label set is infinite. For example, the

---

[1] It is tacitly assumed that the correct label of each part is on the initial list of labels for that part.

label for a picture part might represent the range, or distance, from the sensor to some specific point in the picture part such as its centroid. In such cases, a labelling may need to be specified intensionally; for example, an interval of numbers may be used to specify the range—i.e., we assume that the true range is between a nearest distance r_1 and a farthest distance r_2. All the applications we will consider in this paper use only finite universes of labels.

2.1. Neighborhood models

A relaxation process is determined by specifying a model for the neighborhood of a picture part and a model for the interaction between labellings of neighboring picture parts.

The neighborhood model for a relaxation process specifies which pairs of picture parts directly communicate with one another in the relaxation process, and determines the topology of the graph on which the relaxation process operates. This graph has individual picture parts as nodes. Its arcs connect those pairs of parts that communicate with one another. The neighborhood model is usually designed to establish connections only between 'nearby' parts to satisfy the locality constraint.

A neighborhood model is specified by a set of neighbor relations $r = \{r_1, r_2, \ldots, r_n\}$. Each r_i is a binary relation defined over the appropriate set of picture parts. For example, if the picture parts are pixels, then the neighborhood model might specify that a pixel is connected to every pixel in its 3×3 neighborhood. In this case, there are still several possibilities for the relations contained in the set r. For example, r might be the set {directly above, directly below, etc.} which would distinguish between pairs of points that are horizontally adjacent, vertically adjacent, etc., or it could be the singleton relation 'in the 3×3 neighborhood'. In the latter case, the connections between pairs of pixels would not be recoverable from the graph on which the relaxation process will operate. The choice of r will, in general, be determined by the isotropy of the universe of labels. For example, if we are designing a relaxation process for edge reinforcement, then the relative positions of pixels are crucial since edges generally 'line up', while if we are designing a relaxation process to enhance an image's grey levels, then the positional information may not be required.

When the picture parts are regions rather than pixels, then connections might be formed between adjacent regions only. In some situations, it might be necessary to distinguish between regions that are above, below, inside, surrounding, etc.

The neighborhood model determines which pairs of picture parts directly communicate through the relaxation process. The next section discusses the various ways in which they may communicate.

2.2. Interaction models

The interaction model defines how a picture part changes its labelling based on the labellings of its neighbors. An interaction model is composed of two parts:

(1) a *knowledge representation* for the relationships between labels, and

(2) a mechanism, or procedure, for applying the knowledge in (1) to change, or update, labellings.

For discrete labellings the simplest knowledge representation is a set of the pairs of labels that can simultaneously be associated with pairs of neighboring picture parts. It can be represented by a binary relation R defined over the universe of labels D. Intuitively, $(d,d') \in R$ if a pair of neighbors can simultaneously be labelled with d and d'. In general, there is a binary relation associated with each neighbor relation.

The most obvious updating mechanism is a label discarding process, which looks at pairs of picture parts at a time. A label, d, can be deleted from the labelling of a picture part if, for some neighboring picture part, that neighbor does not contain a label, d', in its labelling with $(d,d') \in R$. This is, essentially, Waltz's filtering algorithm [1]. Rosenfeld et al. [2] show that label discarding can, in principle, be applied in parallel at every picture part and that by iterating the process of discarding labels a unique, maximally consistent labelling is computed. The process can be generalized in a variety of ways—e.g., the knowledge representation might be in terms of n-ary relations (for example, a 3-ary relation is required to specify that a picture part is between two others). The label discarding process now considers a picture part and n-1 of its neighbors at a time, rather than one neighbor at a time. There are many other possibilities based on computing lower-order projections of n-ary relations. See Haralick et al. [3] and Haralick and Shapiro [4] for a detailed discussion.

The binary relation knowledge representation can be generalized to fuzzy labellings by specifying a real-valued compatibility function, C, whose domain is $D \times D$. As before, in general, a compatibility function is defined for each picture relation in the set r. A variety of applications have used compatibility functions whose range is $(-1, 1)$. Intuitively, if $C(d,d') = -1$, then d and d' are maximally incompatible, and the strong presence of d' at one picture part (i.e., d' has a high likelihood at that part) should depress the likelihood of d at a neighboring picture part. If $C(d,d') = 1$, then d and d' are maximally compatible, and the strong presence of d' at a picture part should increase the likelihood of d at a neighboring picture part. Finally, if $C(d,d') = 0$, then the presence of d' at a picture part should have no effect on the likelihood of d at a neighboring part. Intermediate values of C should have intermediate effects.

As an example, suppose we are designing a relaxation process to enhance the results of a local line detection algorithm. Then the set of labels may be horizontal (h), vertical (v), left-diagonal (dl), and right-diagonal (dr), and the set r might contain the relations vertically-adjacent (V), horizontally-adjacent (H), left-diagonally-adjacent (L) and right-diagonally-adjacent (R). If, in the class of images being considered, linear features are thin and have few corners (i.e., the curvature is ordinarily low), then we would expect, e.g., that $C_V(v,v)$ would be high, while $C_V(v,h)$ would be low, since an h vertically adjacent to a v would form a right angle. $C_H(v,v)$, on the other hand, would be low, since the linear features are thin.

Several mechanisms have been suggested for applying this knowledge representation to updating labellings. For example, Rosenfeld et al. [2] suggested the formula:

$$p_i'(d) = p_i(d)(1 + Q_i(d))/N$$

where

$$Q_i(d) = \sum_j m_{ij} \sum_{d'} C(d,d')p_j(d')$$

and N is a normalizing factor which guarantees that $\Sigma\, p_i(d) = 1$. The m_{ij} values can be used to give higher weight to some neighbors at part i than others. $Q_i(d)$ measures the overall support of the neighborhood of part i for label d; it takes on values in the range $[-1, 1]$ and can be interpreted similarly to C. The above operation is applied in parallel at every part and for every label. The p' values then replace the p values, and the operation can be iterated.

Variations on the above theme are possible and lead to better results in some applications. For example, one can apply a 'max–min' rule where

$$Q_i(d) = \min_j\{\max_{d'}\{C(d,d')p_j(d')\}\}$$

which reduces to the discrete algorithm described above when C and p are constrained to take on only the values 0 or 1.

There are several disadvantages to the relational knowledge representation for the interactions between labels. First, it is a single-level representation scheme. The solution to many image understanding problems requires that images be described at several levels of abstraction. Attempting to compile all interactions between conceptually higher-level pictorial entities down to interactions between only the lowest level pictorial features is almost always cumbersome and inefficient, and is sometimes impossible. Section 2.3 discusses hierarchical relaxation systems.

A second important shortcoming of the relational framework is that the algebraic combination of evidence treats all of the interactions between labels uniformly, which is often not desirable. Furthermore, there are classes of intuitively plausible constraints that can only be represented very inefficiently in a relational framework. For example, the very simple constraint

A picture part can be a d_1 only if all adjacent picture parts can be d_2's

requires an n-ary relation to represent it, where n is the maximum degree of any node in the graph on which the relaxation procedures operates.

Such problems can be overcome by adopting a more powerful representation for label interactions than relations. For example, constraints between labels can be represented using logic statements [5]. This allows a much wider class of constraints to be efficiently represented and applied to the analysis of a picture. The natural mechanism for applying the constraints is, then, a general inference procedure. Such a scheme has not yet been applied to any image understanding problem; its application to linear feature detection is currently under investigation.

2.3. Hierarchy

Very often, a natural and economical solution to an image analysis problem requires that pictorial entities be described at several levels of detail. For example, to recognize an image segment as the top view of an airplane based on the shape of its boundary might require recognizing airplane pieces as engines, wings, tail sections, etc., and then grouping them into larger pieces of airplanes, and finally into a complete airplane shape. Or, as a second, more complex, example, reading a word in cursive script involves segmenting the word into primitive parts such as strokes, grouping the strokes into large letter pieces, those pieces into letters and finally the letters into a word.

As discussed above a single level relaxation system is specified by a neighborhood model and a label interaction model. To design a hierarchical relaxation system having k levels, one needs to not only define a neighborhood model and an interaction model at each level, but also a *construction* model (which, given the labelling of pieces at level m, can construct the pieces and their labellings at level $m + 1$), and an across-level neighborhood model. This last model is ordinarily based simply on constituency—i.e., a level $m + 1$ piece is linked to each of the level m pieces from which it was formed [6].

An important design criterion for such processes is that the construction models and the interaction models be *consistent*. Intuitively, the consistency constraint means that the relations between level m labels implied by the construction models for all higher levels do not contradict the explicit relations between level m labels mentioned in the level m interaction model. A simple example should help clarify this point.

Suppose that we are constructing a hierarchical relaxation system for reading cursive script, and that for the particular corpus of words that we wish to read, there are no words in which the letter 'h' precedes the letter 'u'. Now, suppose that at the large letter piece level, an h ends with a piece p_1 and a u begins with a piece p_2, and that no other letter contains either a p_1 or a p_2. Then clearly, the compatibility of p_1 and p_2 at the large letter piece level should be as low as possible. If it were not, then the construction model taking letters into words would be inconsistent with the interaction model for large letter pieces.

One possible approach to guaranteeing such consistency is to specify only the construction models, and then *compile* the interaction models from the construction models. This not only guarantees that the interaction models are consistent with the construction models, but also avoids the tedious task of specifying all the constraints contained in the interaction models.

For example, in reading cursive script from a known corpus, the letter cooccurrence probabilities can be compiled directly from the corpus, and these can be used as an interaction model at the letter level. Then, given a decomposition of letters into large letter pieces a similar process can produce cooccurrence probabilities for large letter pieces, etc. This was done by Hayes [7] in his handwriting analysis system.

As a second example, in [8] Davis and Henderson describe a hierarchical shape analysis system. Shapes are modeled by hierarchical relational networks which describe the arrangement and geometrical properties of shape pieces at several levels of detail. The representation is designed in such a way that local constraints about the appearance of the shape can be automatically compiled from the representation. Thus the representation serves as a set of construction models, and the compiled constraints are used as interaction models.

Although the compilation of interaction models from construction models is a powerful idea in the design of hierarchical relaxation systems, it does not address the issue of how one determines whether or not additional constraints, not derivable from the construction model, can be consistently added to the interaction models. This situation might arise when analysis of one part of an image yields information that can be used to guide the analysis of other parts, or if prior knowledge is available that is not ordinarily available. The following simple example illustrates the problem. Suppose that we are attempting to recognize airplanes, and that prior information is available about the angle that the wings of planes will make with the fuselage. How can we determine that this extra information is consistent with the existing airplane model? (If it is not, no shapes will be recognized as airplanes!) How does the relaxation process even make use of this information, assuming that it is consistent with its interaction models? For currently existing systems, there is no effective means for checking the consistency of externally specified information with current knowledge, or for uniformly applying such information to enhance the relaxation process. This points out another advantage of the logic representation mentioned in Section 2.2. If construction models are specified as statements in logic, then interaction models can still be compiled from the construction models. Furthermore, the consistency of added information with current knowledge can be determined, and the general inferencing capabilities associated with logic would enable such a system to make use of any additional information as well.

3. Applications

A wide variety of labelling processes can be used at various stages of computer vision. Many of these processes operate at the pixel level—i.e., the parts to be labelled are individual pixels, and the interaction is between neighboring pixels. In general, image segmentation can be regarded as pixel labelling, with the labels defining a partition of the image into subsets. Thus relaxation methods are applicable to most of the standard image segmentation techniques, including pixel classification based on gray level or color (thresholding, multispectral classification), as well as detection of local features (peaks or spots, ridges or curves, edges, corners, or matches to arbitrary templates). Many examples of such methods are given in Sections 3.1 and 3.2.

Relaxation methods can also be applied to situations involving several images (e.g., disparity measurement in motion or stereo), or several sets of labels simultaneously applied to a single image (e.g., 'intrinsic image' labels); see Section 3.3. They can also be used to label picture parts that are larger than single pixels, i.e., windows or regions, and to detect specified local configurations of such parts, as briefly discussed in Section 3.4.

3.1. Pixel classification based on gray level or color

Suppose that a scene is composed of a few objects or regions each of which is homogeneous in color. The colors of the pixels in an image of that scene should then display clustering behavior: There should be clusters in the scatter plot of color values, corresponding to the color characteristics of the regions. Under these circumstances, a natural way to segment the image is to classify the pixels as belonging to these clusters. In fact, this is the standard method of segmenting multispectral terrain images into terrain types or land use classes, based on clustering the spectral signatures of the pixels. It is also widely used to segment black-and-white images into light and dark regions by thresholding the gray levels so as to separate peaks on the histogram. Analogous methods can be used for arrays of other types of values, e.g., range data.

Conventionally, the pixels are classified independently. In order to use a cooperative approach, possible class memberships must be determined, or class membership confidences estimated, for each pixel, and the results compared with those for neighboring pixels. To define an appropriate interaction model, some assumptions must be made about the kinds of neighbors that we expect a pixel to have. Since the scene consists of a few homogeneous regions, most pixels will be in the interior of a region. The neighbors of those pixels should all be alike. Some pixels, of course, will be on interregion boundaries; in this case some of the neighbors of the pixel will belong to the same region as the pixel itself, but others will belong to a different region. Neighborhoods at which three or more regions meet will be rare, and will be ignored here.

The situation just described is characteristic of a large class of cooperative pixel labelling problems: the neighbors of a pixel belong, with rare exceptions, to at most two classes, one of which is the class containing the pixel itself. Several types of interaction models can be used in such situations:

(1) The neighborhood used can consist, for each pixel, of those neighbors that most resemble the pixel. If the neighbors cluster into two classes, this is straightforward; if not, one can use a fixed number of 'best' neighbors, on the assumption that these neighbors are the ones most likely to belong to the same region as the pixel. For the chosen neighbors, the interaction model is then quite simple: like reinforces like [9].

Alternatively, we can examine a set of one-sided neighborhoods of the pixel, and choose the one in which the gray level or color is most homogeneous. This one is presumably contained within a single region, so that we can safely use a like-reinforces-like scheme on it [10, 11].

(2) If we do not want to commit ourselves to choosing a fixed set of neighbors, we can assign weights to the neighbors, or define link strengths between the pixels and the neighbors, such that neighbors similar to the pixel get high weights (or link strengths). In the interaction model, the reinforcement contributions are then proportional to the weights. For example, the m_{ij} factors in eq. (2) can be chosen so as to give some neighbors more weight than others. If the reinforcement process is iterated, the weights can themselves be adjusted at each iteration, based on revised estimates of neighbor similarity—e.g., the m_{ij} might change from one iteration to the next [12–14].

(3) Finally, we can simply use the same neighborhood for every pixel, and let like reinforce like. For pixels in the interior of a region, this behaves as desired; but on the border of a region, the pixel labels are likely to remain ambiguous, since they are being influenced by neighbors that belong to two regions. In fact, sharp corners on the borders will be smoothed out, since a pixel at such a corner will have most of its neighbors in another region, so that the reinforcement process will make it confident that it too belongs to that region [15, 16].

It should be pointed out that, rather than reinforce label confidences, we can adjust the pixel gray level or color values themselves; in other words, we can use the methods just described to smooth an image without blurring the edges between regions. Fig. 1 illustrates one of the methods.

The preceding discussion assumed that each region is 'flat', i.e., has relatively constant gray level or color. This is a reasonable assumption about some classes of scenes (e.g., characters on a printed page, chromosomes against a uniform background), but is not correct for others. More generally, the image can be modeled as piecewise linear and the relaxation process can examine a set of one-sided neighborhoods of the pixel, and choose the one that best fits a plane. Within the chosen neighborhood, the reinforcements should depend on closeness of fit to the hypothesized plane, rather than on similarity [17].

A similar approach applies, in principle, if we want to classify pixels based on the values of local properties measured over their neighborhoods, assuming

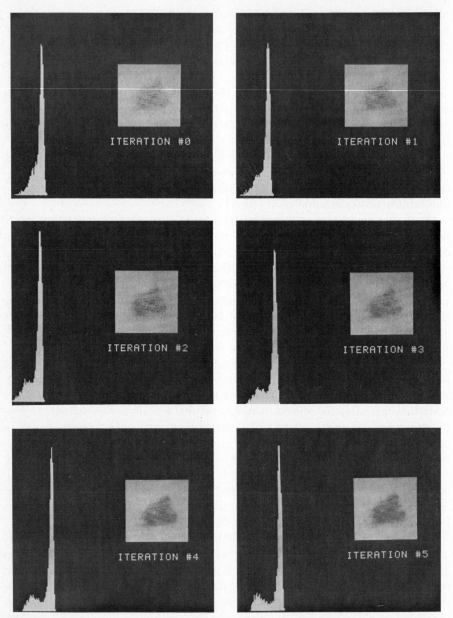

FIG. 1. Cooperative pixel classification based on gray level. (Lowest gray level: 13; highest gray level: 49.)

#0: Original (infrared image of a tank) and its histogram. The gray levels in this image were mapped into 'light' and 'dark' probabilities proportional to their distances from the ends of the grayscale.

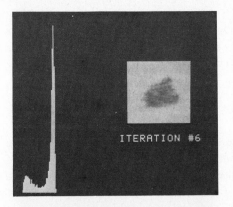

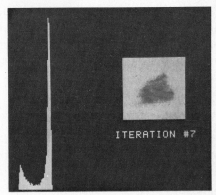

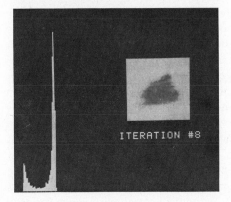

FIG. 1. Continued.

#1–#8: Eight iterations of a relaxation process (like reinforcing like) applied to the initial probabilities, with the resulting probabilities displayed as gray levels using the inverse mapping. As the histograms show, the probabilities are tending toward (0, 1) and (1, 0), resulting in good discrimination between the tank and the background.

Iteration #	Mean pixel value	Scale (pixels/dot)
0	40.20	7
1	40	7
2	40.19	6
3	40.01	7
4	39.92	7
5	39.80	7
6	39.36	8
7	39.58	8
8	39.52	10

that the image consists of regions that are homogeneously textured. Here, however, larger neighborhoods should be used, since local properties tend to be more variable than single-pixel properties. Of course, when we use large neighborhoods, the problems encountered at region borders become more severe.

3.2. Local feature detection

If the labelling task involves local feature detection or template matching, we must use neighborhood and interaction models appropriate to the type of feature or pattern being detected. In the following paragraphs we discuss the detection of spots (i.e., peaks), streaks (ridges, curves), edges, and corners, as well as matches to an arbitrary template.

To detect peaks, i.e., local maxima, the neighborhood must be large enough to contain a peak. The peak label at a pixel is then positively reinforced by the presence of lower values at its neighbors, and negatively reinforced by higher values, where the amounts of reinforcement depend on the differences in value. In other words, small reinforces large, while large competes with large. Detection of pits (local minima) is exactly analogous. The same approach can be used to detect peaks on waveforms, histograms, or scatter plots [18, 19].

To detect ridges or ravines, i.e., high-valued lines or streaks on a low-valued background or vice versa, as in linear feature detection, we use a neighborhood somewhat larger than the streak width. The reinforcement model should now depend on the orientation of the streak; high values should reinforce one another along the streak, while low values should reinforce high values across the streak. To implement this, we initially estimate a streak confidence for each orientation, or more simply, estimate a single streak confidence and an associated streak direction. For neighbors in the direction along the streak, high values reinforce one another, provided the orientations are consistent; for neighbors in the direction across the streak, low values reinforce high ones, as in the case of peak detection [20, 21]. This approach is illustrated in Fig. 2.

Detecting edges is similar to detecting streaks, since an edge is a streak-like locus of high rates of change. Note that in this case directions must be measured modulo 360° rather than modulo 180°; in other words, for a given direction, we must take into account the sign of the rate of change, so that high edge values reinforce one another only if their dark sides and light sides match, and they compete otherwise. If desired, we can associate edge values with the 'cracks' between adjacent pairs of pixels, rather than with the pixels themselves; this is more appropriate if the edges are sharp [22, 23].

For both edges and streaks, our model implicitly assumes that they are straight or smoothly curved; if they have sharp corners or angles, dissimilar directions will be present in a single neighborhood, and these will compete with one another. To detect corners, we must allow a pixel to interact with pairs of

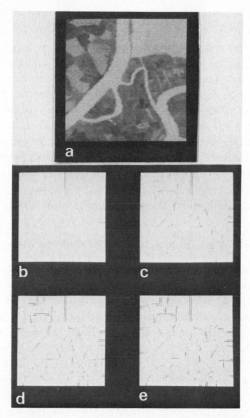

FIG. 2. Cooperative detection of smooth edges. (a): Portion of a LANDSAT image. (b): Result of applying an edge detector to (a), and scaling the results to yield a 'no edge' probability, and edge probabilities in each of 8 directions, at each point. For display purposes, if the highest probability is 'no edge', the point is displayed as white; otherwise, the highest edge probability is displayed as a gray level (1 = black). (c)–(e): Results of three iterations of a relaxation process (see text) applied to the initial probabilities, with the new probabilities displayed in the same way.

its neighbors, rather than with each neighbor separately; we can then reinforce the 'cornerity' value of the pixel if there exist pairs of neighboring edge or streak values that have sharply different directions. [Alternatively, we can detect corners in the gray level (or color) domain based on the presence of suitable combinations of high and low levels at neighbors, e.g., a high value on one side and low values on several other sides; but this requires us to work with k-tuples of neighbors for $k > 2$.] At the same time, low cornerity values at the neighbors of a pixel should reinforce a high value at the pixel, just as in the case of peak detection. Analogous methods can be used to detect corners on ideal borders or curves represented by chain codes; here again, cornerity is reinforced by the presence of neighboring slopes that differ sharply, and by low neighbor cornerity [24].

In general, we can employ a cooperative approach to detect matches of a given template with the image by considering the template as composed of pieces; detecting matches with the pieces by some conventional method; and reinforcing a match to a given piece based on the occurrence of matches to the other pieces in approximately the correct relative positions. This approach is preferable to straightforward matching of the entire template for two reasons: it has lower computational cost, and it is less sensitive to geometrical distortion. Note that in this reinforcement process, if there are matches to a given piece in several neighboring positions, we can use the best one, but we should not sum their influences, since only one of them can be correct; thus a reinforcement rule using the max, rather than the sum, is more appropriate here [25, 26].

3.3. Processes involving multiple properties or multiple images

A more complex class of cooperating processes can be used to assign two or more interrelated sets of labels to the pixels in an image. As an example, consider the gray level and edge labelling processes discussed in Sections 3.1 and 3.2. These two sets of labels are not independent; for example, the gray levels on the light side of an edge are more likely to belong to a light than to a dark class, and vice versa. Thus we can design a compound cooperating process in which both sets of labels interact; such processes should yield better results than if we use either of the individual processes alone [27, 28].

The gray level at a given pixel of an image is the resultant of several 'intrinsic' properties at the corresponding point of the scene, including illumination, reflectivity, and surface slope. It is impossible to separate the effects of these factors by examining the pixels individually; but one can attempt to separate them using a cooperative process, based on assumptions about how the factors vary from point to point. For example, let us assume that the scene is composed of regions over which the intrinsic properties are constant. It may then be possible to determine which property is changing at a given edge, by analyzing the gray level variations at the edge. If this can be done, we can try to estimate the property values cooperatively, by hypothesing initial values and letting like reinforce like except across edges [29].

Finally, we consider cooperating processes that involve more than one image. Given two images of the same scene, taken at different times or from different positions, it will not be possible in general to register the images globally, since parts of the scene may have moved, or their projections on the image may have shifted by different amounts because they are at different distances from the sensor. However, we can try to match pieces of one image with pieces of the other to determine a piecewise correspondence; from the variations in this correspondence we can then estimate the motion or distance information. The accuracy of these estimates can be enhanced using a cooperative approach, if we assume that the scene is made up of parts each having a uniform motion or distance; the approach is analogous to that used in Section 3.1 (see [30, 31]).

3.4. Region-level processes

Cooperating processes can also be used to assign labels to windows or regions of an image, or to detect configurations of regions that match given models. Such processes are briefly discussed in the following paragraphs.

As a simple example, suppose that we have broken up an image into windows, and want to classify the textures in the windows. If we use small windows, the classifications become unreliable; but if we use large ones, border effects become a major factor, since it is hard to classify windows that overlap two or more differently textured windows. One solution is to use small windows, and adjust the classifications (or the feature values) cooperatively, based on those of neighboring windows, in such a way that windows belonging to different regions (most likely) do not influence one another; this is analogous to the cooperative approach to pixel classification described in Section 3.1 (see [32]).

More generally, suppose that we have segmented an image into regions, and want to classify the regions, based on their geometrical or textural properties. If we know what pairs of classifications are possible for neighboring pairs of regions in given relative positions, we can use this knowledge to cooperatively adjust the label possibilities or confidences. For example: (1) In labelling the edges in a blocks-world scene as convex, concave, or occluding, we can use the constraints imposed when the edges meet at junction [1]. (2) In assigning regions in an indoor scene to classes such as 'door', 'doorknob', 'wall', and 'light switch', the light switch label is reinforced, and the doorknob label weakened, by the wall label on a surrounding region, and vice versa for the door label on a surrounding region [33].

Matching a configuration of regions to a given model is analogous to matching a piece of an image to a template. We can represent the regions, their properties, and their relationships by a 'scene graph' in which the nodes and arcs are labelled by property or relation names (and values). The model can be similarly represented by a labelled graph, and we can then attempt to find occurrences of the model graph as a subgraph of the scene graph. Just as in the template case, this can be done cooperatively by finding scene graph nodes that match model graph nodes, and reinforcing matches for which the proper neighboring nodes are present [34, 35].

4. Issues

Relaxation processes have proved very useful for deriving relatively unambiguous labellings of image or scene parts at a variety of levels. The design and control of such processes, however, are not as yet well understood. Given a labelling task, how do we choose appropriate neighborhood and interaction models? (In other words, how do we represent our knowledge about the given problem domain in the form of an iterative local process?) Given such a process, how many times should it be iterated, and how should its performance be evaluated? In this section we briefly review some of the approaches that have been proposed to these problems of knowledge representation and control in relaxation processes.

4.1. Knowledge representation

As mentioned in Section 2.2, for discrete relaxation processes the interaction model is defined by a set of compatible label pairs; but for fuzzy labellings, the compatibility relation must be quantitative. It can be defined, for example, by specifying a 'compatibility coefficient' for each pair of labels on each pair of neighboring parts. These coefficients can be defined in a problem-specific manner; for example, the compatibility between two given edge or line directions at a pair of neighboring pixels could be taken as inversely proportional to the bending energy required to bend a spline so that it changes direction in the given way.

Another possibility is to define compatibilities on probabilistic grounds. Consider the probability ratio $r(d,d') \equiv p(d,d')/p(d)p(d')$, where the numerator is the joint probability of the pair of labels (d,d') on the given pair of neighboring objects, and the terms in the denominator are the prior probabilities of the two labels. Intuitively, if d and d' are compatible, $p(d,d')$ should be greater than $p(d)p(d')$; if d and d' are independent, they should be equal; and if d and d' are incompatible, $p(d,d')$ should be less than $p(d)p(d')$. Thus we have $r(d,d') > 1$, $= 1$, and < 1 iff d and d' are compatible, independent, or incompatible, respectively. If we want compatibilities that lie in the range $[-1, 1]$, we can use $\log r$ rather than r; this is positive, zero, or negative according to whether d and d' are compatible, independent, or incompatible. (The log does not automatically lie in the range $[-1, 1]$; if we want it to, it must be truncated and rescaled.) Note that $\log r$ is the *mutual information* of the pair of labels d, d'. The probabilities can be estimated by counting occurrences of d and d', and joint occurrences of both. The use of mutual information to define compatibilities is suggested in [36]. If we drop the restriction that the compatibilities lie in the range $[-1, 1]$, we can use r itself, rather than $\log r$, as a compatibility function. In fact, in a Bayesian approach to relaxation developed by Peleg, the compatibility coefficients turn out to be the r's (see [37]).

4.2. Control

A second critical question concerns the control of relaxation processes: when should the iteration be stopped? How can its progress be evaluated?

For a discrete relaxation process, termination criteria are straightforward to formulate and justify. For example, when binary (or higher-order) relations are used as a knowledge representation, then the process terminates when no further labels can be discarded from any picture part. At this point, each label at each picture part (if any remain) has a consistent label at every neighboring picture part. Or, if logic statements are used as a knowledge representation, then the process terminates when no new inferences can be formed. In both cases, the destination of the process is a consistent labelling, the notion of consistency is well-defined and it is straightforward to prove that the relaxation process has as its 'fixed point' a consistent labelling.

For a probabilistic relaxation process, the situation is more complicated. One possible approach is that the relaxation process should be iterated until the probability densities for each picture part converge. There are, however, both practical and theoretical disadvantages to this approach:

(a) In practice, relaxation processes often converge to results which are quite poor, even though the first several iterations lead to significant improvements.

(b) There are very few theoretical results concerning convergence, and these simply characterize sufficient conditions for convergence, rather than necessary conditions [38]. Moreover, the limit points have not be characterized as solutions to a well-defined problem, except in some specific cases [39].

Various criteria have been proposed for evaluating the performance of relaxation processes [40], but none of them seem to be satisfactory. Convergence (i.e., decrease in rate of change) is not an acceptable criterion, since the limit point may not be a desirable labelling. Unambiguity (e.g., low entropy) is also not acceptable, since there are many unambiguous labelings, most of which are highly inconsistent with the given initial labelling. Combinations of these criteria might be used [41], but these are also subject to similar objections [42]. A more promising approach uses a composite criterion for evaluating a labelling based on its consistency with both the initial labelling and the model (i.e., the compatibilities) [43]. This area is still the subject of active research.

5. Concluding Remarks

Relaxation processes have potential speed advantages because they can be implemented in parallel (hardware permitting). They have been successfully applied to a wide variety of labelling problems by a growing number of investigators; our survey makes no claim to completeness. In spite of these successes, little is as yet known about the design and control of these processes. However, a number of promising approaches to their theoretical formulation are being pursued, and it is hoped that a deeper understanding of their nature will soon be achieved.

ACKNOWLEDGMENT

The support of the National Science Foundation under Grants MCS-76-23763 to the University of
Maryland, and ENG-79-04037 to the University of Texas, is gratefully acknowledged, as is the help of
Eleanor Waters in preparing this paper. The authors also wish to thank Shmuel Peleg and Michael O.
Shneier for helpful discussions and comments.

REFERENCES

 1. Waltz, D., Understanding line drawings of scenes with shadows, in: Winston, P.H. (Ed.), *The Psychology of Computer Vision* (McGraw-Hill, New York, 1975) 19–91.
 2. Rosenfeld, A., Hummel, R. and Zucker, S.W., Scene labelling by relaxation operations, *IEEE Trans. Systems, Man, Cybernetics* **6** (1976) 420–433.
 3. Haralick, R.M., Davis, L.S., Milgram, D.L. and Rosenfeld, A., Reduction operators for constraint satisfaction, *Information Sci.* **14** (1978) 199–219.
 4. Haralick, R.M. and Shapiro, L.G., The consistent labelling problem: Part I, *IEEE Trans. Pattern Analysis Machine Intelligence* **1** (1979) 173–183, Part II, ibid. **2** (1980) 193–203.
 5. Davis, L.S., A logic model for constraint propagation, Tech. Rept. TR-137, Computer Sciences Dept., Univ. of Texas (1980).
 6. Davis, L.S. and Rosenfeld, A., Hierarchical relaxation for waveform parsing, in: Hanson, A. and Riseman, E. (Eds.), *Computer Vision Systems* (Academic Press, New York, 1978) 101–109.
 7. Hayes, K.C. Jr., Reading handwritten words using hierarchical relaxation, TR-783, Computer Science Center, University of Maryland, College Park, MD (July 1979) Abridged version to appear in *Computer Graphics Image Processing*.
 8. Davis, L.S. and Henderson, T.C., Hierarchical constraint processes for shape analysis, TR-115, Computer Sciences Dept., University of Texas, Austin, TX (November 1979).
 9. Davis, L.S. and Rosenfeld, A., Noise cleaning by iterated local averaging, *IEEE Trans. Systems, Man, Cybernetics* **8** (1978) 705–710.
10. Tomita, F. and Tsuji, S., Extraction of multiple regions by smoothing in selected neighborhoods, *IEEE Trans. Systems, Man, Cybernetics* **7** (1977) 107–109.
11. Nagao, M. and Matsuyama, T., Edge preserving smoothing, *Computer Graphics Image Processing* **9** (1979) 394–407.
12. Lev, A., Zucker, S.W. and Rosenfeld, A., Iterative enhancement of noisy images, *IEEE Trans. Systems, Man, Cybernetics* **7** (1977) 435–442.
13. Scher, A., Velasco, F.R.D. and Rosenfeld, A., Some new image smoothing techniques, *IEEE Trans. Systems, Man, Cybernetics* **10** (1980) 153–158.
14. Eklundh, J.O. and Rosenfeld, A., Image smoothing based on neighbor linking, *IEEE Trans. Pattern Analysis Machine Intelligence* **3** (1981) in press.
15. Eklundh, J.O., Yamamoto, H. and Rosenfeld, A., A relaxation method in multispectral pixel classification, *IEEE Trans. Pattern Analysis Machine Intelligence* **2** (1980) 72–75.
16. Rosenfeld, A. and Smith, R.C., Thresholding using relaxation, *IEEE Trans. Pattern Analysis Machine Intelligence* **3** (1981) in press.
17. Haralick, R.M. and Watson, L., A facet model for image data, *Proc. IEEE Conf. Pattern Recognition Image Processing* (August 1979) 489–497.
18. Davis, L.S. and Rosenfeld, A., Iterative histogram modification, *IEEE Trans. Systems, Man, Cybernetics* **8** (1978) 300–302.
19. Peleg, S., Iterative histogram modification, 2, *IEEE Trans. Systems, Man, Cybernetics* **8** (1978) 555–556.
20. Eberlein, R., An iterative gradient edge detection algorithm, *Computer Graphics Image Processing* **5** (1976) 245–253.

21. Zucker, S.W., Hummel, R.A. and Rosenfeld, A., An application of relaxation labeling to line and curve enhancement, *IEEE Trans. Computers* **26** (1977) 394–403, 922–929.
22. Schachter, B.J., Lev, A., Zucker, S.W. and Rosenfeld, A., An application of relaxation methods to edge reinforcement, *IEEE Trans. Systems, Man, Cybernetics* **7** (1977) 813–816.
23. Hanson, A.R. and Riseman, E.M., Segmentation of natural scenes, in: Hanson, A. and Riseman, E. (Eds.), *Computer Vision Systems* (Academic Press, New York, 1978) 129–163.
24. Davis, L.S. and Rosenfeld, A., Curve segmentation by relaxation labelling, *IEEE Trans. Computers* **26** (1977) 1053–1057.
25. Davis, L.S. and Rosenfeld, A., An application of relaxation labelling to spring-loaded template matching, *Proc. 3rd Int. Joint Conf. on Pattern Recognition* (November 1976) 591–597.
26. Ranade, S. and Rosenfeld, A., Point pattern matching by relaxation, *Pattern Recognition* **12** (1980) 269–275.
27. Zucker, S.W. and Hummel, R.A., Toward a low-level description of dot clusters: Labelling edge, interior, and noise points, *Computer Graphics Image Processing* **9** (1979) 213–233.
28. Danker, A. and Rosenfeld, A., Blob extraction by relaxation, *IEEE Trans. Pattern Analysis Machine Intelligence* **3** (1981) in press.
29. Barrow, H.G. and Tenenbaum, J.M., Recovering intrinsic scene characteristics from images, in: Hanson, A. and Riseman, E. (Eds.), *Computer Vision Systems* (Academic Press, New York, 1978) 3–26.
30. Marr, D. and Poggio, T., Cooperative computation of stereo disparity, *Science* **194** (1976) 283–287.
31. Barnard, S.T. and Thompson, W.B., Disparity analysis of images, *IEEE Trans. Pattern Analysis Machine Intelligence* **2** (1980) 333–346.
32. Hong, T.H., Wu, A.Y. and Rosenfeld, A., Feature value smoothing as an aid in texture analysis, *IEEE Trans. Systems, Man, Cybernetics* **10** (1980).
33. Barrow, H.G. and Tenenbaum, J.M., MSYS: A system for reasoning about scenes, TN-121, Artificial Intelligence Center, SRI, Inc., Menlo Park, CA (April 1976).
34. Kitchen, L. and Rosenfeld, A., Discrete relaxation for matching relational structures, *IEEE Trans. Systems, Man, Cybernetics* **9** (1979) 869–874.
35. Kitchen, L., Relaxation applied to matching quantitative relational structures, *IEEE Trans. Systems, Man, Cybernetics* **10** (1980) 96–101.
36. Peleg, S. and Rosenfeld, A., Determining compatibility coefficients for curve enhancement relaxation processes, *IEEE Trans. Systems, Man, Cybernetics* **8** (1978) 548–555.
37. Peleg, S., A new probabilistic relaxation scheme, *IEEE Trans. Pattern Analysis Machine Intelligence* **2** (1980) 362–369.
38. Zucker, S.W., Leclerc, Y.G. and Mohammed, J.L., Continuous relaxation and local maxima section—conditions for equivalence, *Proc. 6th Int. Joint Conf. on Artificial Intelligence* (August 1979) 1014–1016.
39. Ullman, S., Relaxation and constrained optimization by local processes, *Computer Graphics Image Processing* **10** (1979) 115–125.
40. Fekete, G., Eklundh, J.O. and Rosenfeld, A., Relaxation: evaluation and applications, *IEEE Trans. Pattern Analysis Machine Intelligence* **3** (1981) in press.
41. Faugeras, O. and Berthod, M., Scene labelling: an optimization approach, *Proc. IEEE Conf. Pattern Recognition Image Processing* (August 1979) 318–326.
42. Peleg, S. and Rosenfeld, A., A note on the evaluation of probabilistic labellings, TR-805, Computer Science Center, University of Maryland, College Park, MD (August 1979).
43. Peleg, S., Monitoring relaxation algorithms using labelling evaluation, TR-842, Computer Science Center, University of Maryland, College Park, MD (December 1979).

Received October 1980

Intensity, Visible-Surface, and Volumetric Representations*,**

H.K. Nishihara
M.I.T. Artificial Intelligence Laboratory,
545 Technology Square, Cambridge, MA 02139, U.S.A.

ABSTRACT

One approach to studying human vision is to treat it as a computation that produces descriptions of the external world from retinal images, asking what can be said about this process based on an investigation of the information processing problems that it solves [11]. This paper examines the structure of the problem at a level of abstraction Marr and Poggio [16] call the computational theory. The type of information the vision process must make explicit at various stages is treated and used as a base for decomposing the process into subparts that can be studied independently. Examples are taken from ongoing research at M.I.T.

1. Background

It is a straightforward observation that the study of human vision ought to lead eventually to an understanding of how it works, but progress toward this goal has been slowed by the complexity of our visual systems and the inaccessibility of their physical structure. Research under such circumstances is easily confounded if we do not separate the physical details of mechanisms that solve a problem, types of solutions to the problem, and the problem itself. The study of flight provides an analogy. The physics of aerodynamics—which makes precise, factors such as lift and drag and the relationship between them imposed by an airfoil—constitutes a clear framework for describing the problem of flight and helps us to understand how the structure of a bird's body is a

---

* This is an edited version of a paper presented at the 'Workshop on the Representation of Three-Dimensional Objects', sponsored by the National Science Foundation, May 1979 at the University of Pennsylvania.

** This report describes research done at the Artificial Intelligence Laboratory of the Massachusetts Institute of Technology. Support for the laboratory's artificial intelligence research is provided in part by the Advanced Research Projects Agency of the Department of Defense under Office of Naval Research contract N00014-75-C-0643 and in part by National Science Foundation Grant MCS77-07569.

Artificial Intelligence 17 (1981) 265–284

solution to it. This abstraction allows research to focus on just those issues relevant to the problem—separating the physics of flight from the myriad of details one finds in the structure of a bird.

Marr and Poggio [16] introduced three levels of abstraction[1] at which the information processing problems of vision can be examined:

(1) the *computational theory*—formulation of a problem in terms of what you start with and what you want to produce. This includes the rationale of why this should be possible along with clarification of any further assumptions necessary to make it possible. A simple example is addition. The computational theory of addition is concerned with what it means to add two numbers which is expressed concisely by the axioms and theorems of arithmetic.

(2) *algorithm*—an abstract solution to a problem defined at the computational theory level. Usually an algorithm specifies how an input representation is to be manipulated to produce a desired output representation. In principle, there can be many distinct algorithms for the same problem which differ in the type of representations they employ, the kind of manipulations they use, and therefore in the kind of mechanisms they are best suited for. For example, the usual algorithm for adding Arabic numerals[2]—a place notation representation—is based on a column by column manipulation which is well suited for pencil and scratch pad as well as digital mechanisms. Analog addition algorithms, on the other hand, might use voltage magnitudes to represent numbers and do addition by placing those voltages in series.

(3) *mechanism*—a physical entity which implements a particular algorithm. For example, a pocket calculator contains a mechanism which implements a binary column addition algorithm where the binary number representations appear as voltages on wires and the operations on those representations occur in transistor elements.

Different research methodologies may place greater emphasis at one or another of these levels of abstraction but it is important not to confuse them. Our ability to understand a complex biological information processing system is closely tied to how well we understand the abstract problem it solves and what is required to solve that problem.

Information processing problems, when viewed at the computational theory and algorithm levels, involve the manipulation of symbolic representations to produce other symbolic representations. This means that in order to develop computational theories and algorithms for them, we must understand what these abstract representations are and how they differ. This paper presents some observations about vision and how its study can be subdivided from a

---

[1] Marr and Poggio actually presented four levels—the fourth being the *component* level—however, this last distinction is less important for this discussion and is taken to be part of the mechanism level.

[2] Note that we are not dealing with numbers but with the manipulation of symbols which represent numbers.

TABLE 1. The number 12 described in several representations which make different attributes of the number explicit

Description	Representation type
a. ************	analog
b. 1100	binary place notation
c, $2^2 \cdot 3$	prime factorization
d. *twelve*	symbolic name

consideration of the types of information involved. The central idea is the use of data representations as a conceptual device for making explicit the kind of information important to the solution of a problem as well as for defining computational problems, and we will begin with a discussion of it.

We will use the term *representation* to indicate a particular way of specifying information about a given subject. A *description* in a representation will be an instance of its use, as '12' is a description in the Arabic number representation. The same subject can be described in many different representations. Table 1 illustrates this for numbers; in each example a number is specified by making explicit an attribute sufficient for determining it uniquely. For analog representations, this attribute is the number's magnitude as indicated through a direct correspondence with some primitive quantity like the asterisks in Table 1.[3] Analog representations are most useful where absolute magnitudes are readily available or required, such as inputs from transducers or direct motor control; however, they tend to be limited in the range or the resolution of the numbers they can handle.

The place notation system decomposes a number into a sum of exponential components such as powers of 2 or 10. This gives compact descriptions for large numbers while still allowing the basic arithmetic operations such as addition and multiplication to be handled by relatively simple algorithms. An increased amount of interpretation is required, however, to relate these to actual magnitudes. A number representation can also be based on attributes other than magnitude. For example in some applications a representation based on a number's prime factors can be more useful to the solution of a problem, such as finding the greatest common divisor of two numbers, even though this type of description obscures magnitude. A symbolic name like *twelve* is the most concise description of a number in that it has no primitive parts such as the asterisks of the analog representation or the digits of a binary

---

[3] In a mechanism an analog representation might be implemented by a voltage, or a neuron's firing rate.

representation which encode information about the number in their structure. Symbols like *twelve*, π, or 9 for numbers and *cube*, *sphere*, or *torus* for three-dimensional shapes are primitive entities. They are useful in situations where the presence of a particular entity is important but the specific representation of its attributes is not. The symbols 0 and 1 are used in this manner in the binary representation.

A first pass at formulating a precise statement of an information processing problem in vision is to ask what information is available as input and what is the desired output? Answers to these questions can be thought of as specifications for representations.[4] Our interest and the purpose of this paper is to think about the study of vision in terms of subproblems delineated by input and output representations. In these terms one might say that the problem of vision is to produce information about the external world, such as descriptions of physical objects, from the intensity information available in images. This serves as a base for more substantive questions about the kinds of intensity representations available as input and the kinds of output representations produced by vision. The optical imaging process constrains the input information available while the form of the output is restricted by the purposes of vision as well as the limitations of image analysis.

2. Intensity Representations

The input we begin with is the images projected on the retinas of the two eyes. Representations that describe these images will be called *intensity representations*. A straightforward example is a representation that specifies the local brightness at evenly spaced intervals over the image as illustrated in Fig. 1(a). Since the same type of information is specified at each of many locations, it is convenient to discuss this representation in terms of its *primitive elements*—the elemental pieces of information out of which a description in the representation is constructed. In Fig. 1(a), the primitive elements are specifications of the monochromatic intensity (*via* a magnitude representation) at each of many evenly spaced locations over the image. Variations on this example can be invented by changing the primitive elements. Instead of absolute brightness, information about the way intensity changes could be represented. Illustrations 1(b) and 1(c) show a way of doing this that is based on the locations of maxima in the intensity gradient at a given scale of resolution in the image [13]. Likewise there are alternative ways of specifying the location of the primitive elements. In the above example location is indicated implicitly by position in the description; it could also be specified directly in any of a number of coordinate systems.

---

[4] Of course a clear definition of a valid information processing problem for some aspect of vision is itself a major research objective that one achieves only gradually through investigations of what is possible.

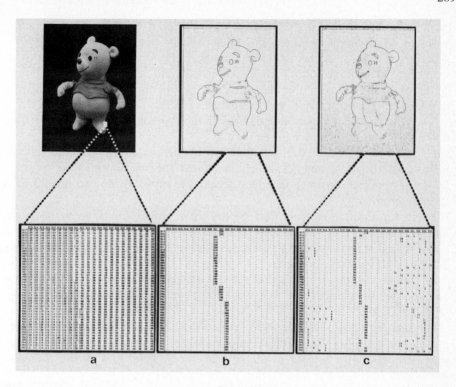

FIG. 1. One common representation for monochromatic images records the average intensity over small patches or pixels at evenly spaced intervals over the image as illustrated in (a). We call this a local intensity representation because details at the smallest scale are made explicit while larger scale properties such as the location and size of a dark region in the image is only implicit in the structure of many pixels. The array of numbers shown in the inset are the actual pixel values in the small white rectangle indicated on the photo. Notice that the left side of this patch covers part of the bear's leg while the right side is over the darker background. Thus the numbers shown in the inset are larger on the left side with a rapid transition to smaller values near the middle. Illustrations (b) and (c) show descriptions in a representation that makes information at different scales explicit. The contours shown are locations where the rate of change in intensity was a maximum in the image after smoothing by a large Gaussian for (b) and a smaller one for (c). Mathematically, these contours are zero-crossings in the Laplacian of a Gaussian convolved image. The insets show the gradient of the Laplacian along these zero-crossing contours—which indicates the sharpness of these peaks in intensity change. Each of these images has 1008 by 776 elements. (a) was obtained by scanning a 35 mm negative on an Optronics digitizer. (b) and (c) were obtained from (a) using a digital convolver, designed by N. Larson, which operates at a rate of 1 million pixels per second. The construction of this device is part of an ongoing project at M.I.T. to develop a stereo matcher that operates in real time.

An intensity representation is not limited to local intensity primitives either; the spatial Fourier transform, for example, makes a different set of image properties explicit, which has made it useful in several image processing areas such as the enhancement of blurred or noisy images or the measurement of certain limited types of regularity. A Fourier transform representation, however, completely obscures the image's local spatial geometry which is necessary for most forms of image analysis. For example, the analysis of shading to determine local surface orientation has to be based on intensity gradients over the image. Similarly the solution of the stereo correspondence problem requires a description which makes explicit

(1) the types of intensity fluctuations that are likely to be caused by fixed features on the surface being viewed, and

(2) the two-dimensional visual field coordinate locations of those fluctuations, specified in a manner which facilitates the measurement of position disparities once the correspondences between features in the two images have been determined [17].

Some representations are thus better than others for a given task; the following criteria [14][5] are useful for comparing them:

(1) *Accessibility*—can the desired description be computed from an image, and can it be done economically?

(2) *Scope and uniqueness*—what class of images is the representation designed for and do members of that class have well-defined descriptions in the representation?

(3) *Stability and sensitivity*—do differences between descriptions in the representation reflect the relative importance of differences between the images described with respect to the task at hand? That is, does the representation make explicit the information that really matters.

Local intensity representations like the examples mentioned earlier satisfy the first two criteria since they can be computed easily from an image and are sufficiently general, but descriptions in these representations are large and unwieldy and for most image analysis applications they do not satisfy the third criterion adequately. Marr [11] considered the requirements of image analysis and showed that an image could be described usefully in terms of a small but expressive vocabulary of types of intensity change. The representation based on these principles, called the *primal sketch*, indicates the way intensities change and the local geometry of those changes. It provides an image description of reduced size while still satisfying the scope and uniqueness, and accessibility criteria. Marr and Hildreth [13] have since refined the mathematics underlying the computation of the primal sketch from an image, showing that the information required is explicit in the zero-crossing contours in the Laplacian of the image after it has been smoothed by convolution with a Gaussian. The Gaussian convolution filters out small-scale variations in the image while preserving the geometric structure of variations at a larger scale. The Laplacian is a non-oriented second derivative operator so zero crossings in

---

[5] These criteria were originally developed for judging the suitability of various shape representations and are restated here for intensity representations.

the Laplacian of the smoothed image correspond to locations where the rate of intensity change is a maximum at the scale of resolution fixed by the Gaussian's space constant. Without this Gaussian filtering, zeros in the Laplacian would coincide with only the smallest scale variations present in the image. Figs. 1(b) and (c) show these zero-crossing contours for two different space constants. It is interesting to note that the Laplacian of a Gaussian convolved image is equivalent to convolving the image with the Laplacian of that Gaussian. The Laplacian of a Gaussian in turn is closely approximated by taking the difference of two Gaussians having different space constants and normalized to have the same volume.

3. Visible-Surface Representations

Perhaps the most fundamental decomposition of the vision problem follows from the observation that an image is caused by the 'visible' portions of viewed objects—that is, those aspects of an object that affect its image. These portions tend to be surfaces, hence we refer to information about them as visible-surface information. Representations of this kind of information will be called *visible-surface representations*. Any other information about the objects viewed must necessarily be deduced from the visible-surface information obtainable from the image. This observation allows us to divide our problem into two parts, *image analysis*—the direct analysis of intensity representations to obtain visible-surface representations and *visible-surface analysis*—which concerns the more application-specific questions concerned with the use of the derived visible-surface information (see Fig. 2).

While an image can be analyzed to produce visible-surface information, it is not clear that this information is sufficient to determine those surfaces without additional information from sources such as experience. Much of the early work in computer vision was in fact based on the hypothesis that information from image analysis alone was not sufficient and much effort went into the question of how to use 'higher level knowledge' effectively in guiding the

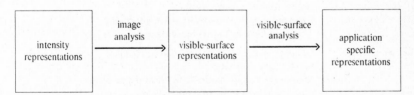

FIG. 2. The direct analysis of an image can only produce information about those properties of the external world that affected the image. Excluding properties of the illuminant and the imaging system itself, these effects are due to properties of the physical surfaces of the objects viewed. Representations of this information will be referred to as visible-surface representations. Any other information about the objects viewed must be deduced from this basic visible-surface information. This allows us to separate image analysis from what we will call visible-surface analysis as shown here.

analysis of an image (see for example Freuder [5]). Marr [11] suggested that this approach was premature and advocated a more careful study of the kind of information carried by images. This view has over the years led to the decomposition of Fig. 2 and we have learned from both psychophysical and computational studies that rather complete visible-surface information can be obtained by several independent image analysis techniques. Julesz [9, 10] showed that random dot stereograms could be fused to obtain surface depth information despite the absence of information about the surfaces encoded prior to fusion. Marr and Poggio [15, 16] and Grimson and Marr [6] have demonstrated the independence of stereo analysis from a computational standpoint. Horn [8] has shown that the shading in an image can be used independently to constrain local orientation over visible-surfaces and Ullman [20] has shown that this is also the case for the structure from motion problem.

Image analysis. The effects a visible-surface has on its image can be factored into those related to variations in depth over the surface, those related to variations in surface orientation, and those related to variations in the material composition of the surface. Table 2 lists the principal means by which these effects can be used.

Binocular stereo and structure from motion are methods for measuring and analyzing disparities between images from different perspectives to recover surface depth. In the first case these are obtained from separate vantage points—the left and right eyes—and in the second through the rotation in

TABLE 2. Sources of visible-surface information

Source type	Examples
Depth effects	*binocular stereo*—disparities due to angular displacements of the vantage point *structure from motion*—disparities due to angular displacement of the subject *accommodation*—divergence of optical wave fronts from the visible-surface *isotropic texture compression*—divergence of the visual field at the visible-surface
Orientation effects	*shading*—intensity gradients due to changes in surface orientation *anisotropic texture compression*—texture gradients due to changes in surface orientation
Material effects	*color*—changes in spectral reflectivity function due to changes in surface composition *texture*—discontinuities in the pattern or statistics of local intensity fluctuations due to changes in surface composition

depth of the viewed surfaces. It is also possible to measure depth in a static monocular image through the distance selectivity of focusing[6] [7]. One can also, in principle, make use of size compression due to perspective. The use of size as a depth cue can occur at several stages in the vision process, the ones of interest to us here are those that can be carried out at the image analysis level independent of higher level knowledge. This includes two cases in particular, size scaling due to motion toward or away from the viewer and variations in the isotropic compression of a regular texture pattern over the visual field. In both these cases, relative depth information or information about motion in depth can be obtained prior to any knowledge of what one is looking at.

Surface orientation affects an image in two principle ways, (1) via anisotropic compression of a surface's image due to the orthographic projection and (2) the formation of intensity gradients due to the surface reflectivity function. Horn [8] showed that orientation information could be computed from intensity gradients over a smooth surface if the reflectivity function and illumination over it are known. The brightness of a small patch of surface in an image is a function of the type of light source, the reflectivity function of the surface material, and the orientation of the surface relative to the viewer. If it can be determined that surface orientation is the only parameter that varies significantly over a region of the viewed surface, then intensity gradients over the image will be primarily due to variations in surface orientation. Texture gradients due to variations in surface orientation can also be used to obtain orientation information provided that the texture is uniform over the surface.

A third type of information obtainable from images concerns a visible-surface's material properties. Information about surface material can be divided into two classes, that concerned with the details of a surface's spectral reflectivity function, and that dealing with the structure or pattern of variations in the reflectivity function over a surface. Surface texture—that is, regularities in the local geometry of variations in surface reflectivity—and regularities in the motion of reflectance variations over an area (optical flow) are two examples of this latter case. In addition to providing information about local composition, this material information delimits the likely locations of surface discontinuities as well as indicating where the surface is likely to be continuous in depth.

Assumptions. By themselves, the physical effects discussed above are not sufficient to determine surface properties unambiguously. The analysis of images to obtain surface information must also rely on assumptions about the optical imaging process and about the general nature of the physical surfaces viewed. The difficulty one often has in seeing the flat surface of a good

---

[6] The curvature (divergence) at the eye of light wavefronts emanated from the viewed surfaces differs according to distance from the viewer and optical focusing has a differential effect on those wavefronts.

photograph, or the white surface of a projection screen under the illumination of a color slide are familiar reminders of this dependence on assumptions. That we can see so well is evidence that the assumptions we use are for the most part reliable.

To solve the stereo matching problem, Marr and Poggio [16] have shown that it is necessary to assume *uniqueness*—that the image locations to be matched in the left and right images correspond to unique visible-surface locations, and *continuity*—that neighboring image locations almost always correspond to neighboring surface points. For the structure from motion problem, Ullman [20] has shown that the key assumption is *rigidity*—that when a unique interpretation for the motion of a sufficiently large set of image points as a rigid body exists, it is correct. In both cases, the assumptions are based on geometry and the properties of physical surfaces; so while there can be exceptions, they generally hold.

Another class of potentially useful assumptions arise from the various kinds of homogeneity that are common in images of physical surfaces particularly in texture analysis and shading analysis. For example, orthographic and perspective projections cause only a few types of linear compression distortion, so an image of a regular texture pattern over a lumpy surface may be distinguishable from an image of a surface where the texture varies randomly. Similarly size and orientation distributions in a natural texture are not likely to shift together over a surface in the way a perspective projection would affect them. So a rule similar to Ullman's rigidity assumption may prove effective for identifying homogeneous texture patterns: if there is a unique interpretation of texture variations in an image as a homogeneous texture over an undulating surface, then assume that it is the correct interpretation. The homogeneity of optical reflectivity, illumination, or of linear surface motion or flow over a surface are other candidates for this type of analysis.

Modules and the $2\frac{1}{2}$-Dimensional Sketch. Several distinct computational problems such as stereo, structure from motion, shading, and texture analysis have been formulated based on considerations of image effects due to visible-surfaces (see Fig. 3). The development of computational theories and algorithms for several of these modules has already been carried quite far, particularly the work on stereo matching. Fig. 3 also illustrates the role of the primal sketch as an attempt to clarify the common information requirements of the various image analysis modules. It may be that each module requires a distinct primal sketch specialized for its purposes, but our work so far does not suggest this. A similar question can be raised for the visible-surface information passed to subsequent stages of the visual process. We coined the term $2\frac{1}{2}$-D sketch for the computational problem of combining visible-surface information from different sources such as stereo and shading while maintaining consistency between various surface geometry parameters such as local orientation and depth. Part of the problem of the $2\frac{1}{2}$-D sketch is to determine the type of

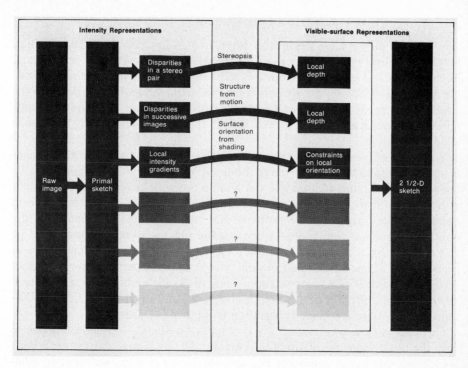

FIG. 3. Several image analysis techniques for which computational theories and algorithms exist are illustrated here as arrows from the intensity category to the visible-surface category [8, 15, 17, 20]. The placement of the primal sketch [11] and the $2\frac{1}{2}$-D sketch [14] in this diagram indicates their intended roles in the problem of clarifying the form for the available information that is best suited for subsequent analysis.

surface information best suited for use by subsequent processes in vision within the constraints of what is available from image analysis. At present we think this representation should make relative surface depth and possibly orientation information explicit along with information about the locations of discontinuities in depth and surface orientation. We expect this view to evolve as we learn more about the kind of surface information available and the specific requirements of visible-surface analysis for tasks such as shape recognition.

While a visible surface description is what one can get from an image, it is often not precisely what is needed from subsequent visual processes. One question in particular is: what does the visible-surface tell us about the shape (partially) defined by that surface? Up until this point the objective was to produce from the input intensity information whatever visible-surface information one could obtain reliably. We are now interested in using that information for a particular purpose and must address the requirements of that application.

4. Volumetric Representations

The application we have been most interested in has been shape recognition
[14]. Many kinds of visually derived information can play a role in recognition,
like the color and texture of an orange or the rapid jittering motion that excites a
cat. But in this discussion we are only concerned with *shape* which we define as the
geometry of an object's physical surface. Thus two statues cast from the same
mold will have the same shape even though different materials may have been
used.

The study of even this more narrowly defined problem of recognizing shapes
is easily confounded by the large body of non-visual information such as
contextual constraints that people can and do use with facility to augment their
performance at recognizing shapes. Our response to this difficulty has been to
define a limited aspect of the problem that can be treated adequately on the
one hand while not simplifying or denying the rich use of other knowledge. To
this end, we have concentrated on determining the kind of information about
shape that is at once available from the $2\frac{1}{2}$-D sketch and pertinent to the task of
recognizing shapes. This amounts to a study of (1) the kinds of shape representation possible, (2) criteria for comparing them, and (3) the kind of representation appropriate for shape recognition in light of the criteria.

Our task is closely related to the problem of designing a practical device to
help the blind make use of visual information. Let us assume that accurate $2\frac{1}{2}$-D
sketch information is available. For the blind person then, we want to communicate that information to him providing as much support as can be done
reliably to help him with shape recognition tasks. Since the rate at which
geometric information can be transmitted to a blind person is limited,[7] we are
forced to think harder about the type of information the user needs. By
abstracting only this critical information from the $2\frac{1}{2}$-D sketch we can reduce
the amount of information that has to be transmitted.

If this hypothetical device was being used by a blind pedestrian, he would
want it to help locate hazards and landmarks along the way. He would care
about the where, how big, and direction of motion of discernible pieces of
matter around him. If he was interested in the shape of one of those entities, he
would also be interested in information about the spatial arrangement of its
volume.

Types of representation. There are many different aspects of an object's shape
that could serve as the basis of its representation and any one aspect could be
represented in many different ways. Although a completely general
classification of shape representations would be difficult to formulate, it is

---

[7] For example by means of a tablet covered with an array of small needles that vibrate
individually according say to the nearness of the surface at the corresponding part of the visual
field. The blind user of such a device might detect locations of bumps in the visible-surface in front
of him by passing his hand over the tablet feeling for areas of increased vibration.

possible to examine the basic design choices in terms of our criteria for comparing representations in the context of shape recognition. Our three criteria, to review briefly, are (1) accessibility, (2) scope and uniqueness, and (3) stability and sensitivity. In this context accessibility is the requirement that the representation be derivable (both in principle and in an efficient manner) from the $2\frac{1}{2}$-D sketch. Scope and uniqueness is the requirement that a well-defined description exists for each shape in the class of shapes we are interested. Stability and sensitivity is the requirement that the information made explicit is what is needed for recognition. Similar shapes should have similar descriptions while very different ones should have descriptions that differ in some basic way. At the same time, even subtle differences should be expressible. These opposing conditions can be satisfied only if the representation identifies and decouples the stable properties of a shape—those that are more general and less varying—from those that capture finer distinctions.

A shape representation records, in one way or another, the spatial organization of the interior or 'bulk' of an object. To do this, three-dimensional geometric relations must be specified. For example, since left and right hands are reflections of each other in space, any representation sufficient for distinguishing them must in some manner specify the relative 3-D arrangement of the fingers and the thumb. This enables us to characterize a shape representation in terms of (1) the coordinate system used, (2) the type of primitive elements whose arrangement in space is specified, and (3) the kind of organization imposed on the information in the description.

The coordinate system used by a representation can be *viewer-centered* or *object-centered*. In a viewer-centered representation locations are indicated relative to the viewer (left, above, below, etc), whereas in an object-centered representation they are indicated relative to the object described (dorsal, ventral, etc).[8] In terms of accessibility, a viewer-centered representation is preferable to an object-centered one since it is in the same type of coordinate system as the $2\frac{1}{2}$-D sketch and does not require the identification of the object's coordinate system. However, viewer-centered descriptions depend as much on the orientation of a shape as they do on the shape itself. Consider for example, the number of distinct appearances of a person's hand even if the fingers are held fixed. There are 24 orientations in space separated by 90 degree increments (directions and rotations about those directions). With an angular separation of 30 degrees there are some 500 different orientations and at 10 degrees the number is about 15,000. When symmetries exist in a shape, the number of distinct appearances is diminished—a sphere for example has only one—but for most cases there are still very many. As a result a viewer-centered approach to shape recognition gains accessibility in exchange for an enormous

---

[8] Coordinate systems based on external reference points other than the object described will be considered to be viewer-centered here.

set of possible descriptions even when the class of shapes to be recognized is small. The obvious remedy, if this set is too large, is to reduce the effects of vantage point on the computed shape descriptions. Ideally one wants a canonical description for each shape and this requires specifying spatial relations in an object-centered coordinate frame which can be identified consistently from the $2\frac{1}{2}$-D sketch. The scope of such a representation will be limited to the class of shapes for which unique coordinate systems are defined and accessible.

With respect to the blind aid example, our observation is that it would be much easier for the blind user to interpret the information provided by the device if it always presented him with the same pattern when pointed at the same shape irrespective of the orientation of that shape. This can only be done, however, if a reliable means can be found for identifying a canonical coordinate system for a shape from the information in a $2\frac{1}{2}$-D sketch of it.

A representation's primitive elements—the shape properties or features whose three-dimensional arrangement make a description—can be *local*[9] or *volumetric*. The $2\frac{1}{2}$-D sketch is an example of a local surface-based representation for the visible portion of an object's surface. Its primitive elements correspond to small surface patches whose positions or orientations in space are specified in the description. This type of primitive is well-suited for the $2\frac{1}{2}$-D sketch which deals with the local surface information obtainable from image analysis. It is also appropriate for applications where local information is required, for example, for controlling a milling machine. In the case of shape recognition, however, a complete surface description is not accessible since only about half of the surface is visible. Furthermore, a description in terms of many surface elements does not measure up well to the stability and sensitivity criterion. Such a description tends to be large and cumbersome in the sense that it is sensitive to the many small-scale properties of the shape's surface at the expense of its larger features. For example, in the case of the blind aid, it would take the user a while to discern the attitude in space of an arm specified by hundreds of vibrating needles—each indicating the relative nearness of a small patch of surface—if he had to feel them one by one. It is of course possible to design the tablet to facilitate the detection and characterization of groups of local primitives with increased nearness. One way would be to actually model the viewed surface using small scales in place of the vibrating

---

[9] We used the terms *surface-based* and *volumetric* in our 1978 paper but this choice has caused some confusion. The distinction we intended to make was between primitives for localized shape characteristics which almost always have to do with its surface and primitives for more global shape characteristics which have more to do with the rough distribution of its volume. The former choice necessarily leads to shape descriptions incorporating many primitive specifications while the latter allows shape descriptions built out of only a few primitive specifications. It will usually be the case that the use of local primitive elements allows much more precise shape descriptions, while making it harder to ascertain more volumetric properties such as overall size or orientation.

pins, that raise or lower according to the local depth. By passing ones hand over such a tablet it would be possible to quickly locate bumps and assess their size and orientation. This is so, however, only because the representation defined by the tablet in conjunction with the particular access method used actually makes this large scale information explicit!

The primitive elements of a volumetric representation are based on more global geometric properties of a shape's volume such as center of mass, overall size or volume, and major axis of elongation or symmetry if one exists. This type of information tends to be redundant in a local surface description and so may still be accessible even if the surface description is incomplete, as is the case with the $2\frac{1}{2}$-D sketch. Of course a shape description that specified only the position, size, and orientation of the whole shape would be of little use for recognition, but if the shape can be decomposed into components; volumetric primitives for each of those components can be specified. Fig. 4 shows several pipe-cleaner figures as an example of this type of description. The ease with which one recognizes the animal shapes depicted is surprising considering the paucity of information available from the photo. Only the position, size, orientation, and perhaps curvature of the major parts of each shape is recoverable from these figures.

The concept of using volumetric primitives for representing shape has evolved over a period of time. Blum [3, 4] developed a 'symmetric axis' representation for classifying two-dimensional shapes. Symmetric axis descriptions were defined as the set of centers of maximal spheres contained within the shape. A chain of these maximal spheres indicates an orientation in space. Binford [2], Agin [1], and Nevatia [18] developed the 'generalized cylinder'[10] representation as an efficient means for describing a shape's surface in terms of its variation along the length of continuous axes. They have developed various algorithms incorporating a laser range finder for deriving stick figure descriptions based on generalized cylinders and have used them to study the problem of shape recognition.

The scale or resolution of information carried by a representation's volumetric primitives has an important effect on the representation's stability and sensitivity characteristics. For example, the sensitivity of the symmetric axis representation is inversely proportional to size. That is, smaller features of a shape tend to override larger ones in a description (see [1]). The emphasis of the work on deriving generalized cylinder representations has been to reduce the range of influence of small surface perturbations while identifying general-

---

[10] In the generalized cylinder representation a shape's surface is described in terms of cross-sections along an axis through it. There is a large class of shapes that have simple descriptions in this representation. For example, consider the class of shapes having a constant cross-section along at least one axis, such as a cylinder. This class can be further generalized by allowing the cross-section to scale in size along the axis so that shapes like cones and many bottles may be included.

FIG. 4. These pipe-cleaner figures provide information about only the size, orientation, position, and possibly the rough curvature of a small number of components of each shape depicted. The ease with which we can recognize the animal shapes depicted does not tell us the form of our internal shape representations, but it does tell us that the limited information made explicit here plays an important role in that representation.

ized cylinder axes at the highest level of resolution possible. The description of an arm, for example, would take the form of a branching tree structure with an upper-arm element linked to a fore-arm element which in turn is linked to hand and finger elements (or chains of elements for finger segments if they can be separated). Thus these representations are most sensitive to details at the finest resolution at which the respective primitive elements can be derived properly. Information about coarser details such as the orientation or size of the overall shape can only be obtained from an analysis of all the primitive elements of the description.

This brings us to the third design issue concerning the organization of the information in a shape description. In the simplest case, the representation is homogeneous and all primitive elements are at the same level of detail. That is, the shape is segmented so that each primitive element corresponds to a distinct part of the shape as is the case for the symmetric axis and generalized cylinder representations. It is also possible to represent a shape at several levels of detail simultaneously, maintaining information about the general orientation and structure of the shape at the coarsest level while also making information about the structure of smaller components explicit at finer levels of detail. It is also desirable to represent only the spatial relations between volumetric elements that are in close proximity to one another relative to their size [19]. For example, the spatial arrangement of the fingers of one hand is a more stable shape characteristic than the relative arrangement of the fingers of the left and right hands together. Thus a shape can be described with a number of modules each providing information about the spatial arrangement of a small number of primitive elements close in size and proximity. This makes it possible to separate the more stable properties of a shape found at coarser resolutions from the finer details which are important for sensitivity.

This modular organization could be imposed on the information supplied by our blind aid by equipping it with a zoom lens[11] and by designing it so that it was sensitive to bumps in the $2\frac{1}{2}$-D sketch over only a narrow range of sizes. This range would be chosen so that a viewed shape filling the whole field of view would have its major components detected as bumps. The blind user could then quickly locate objects around him by adjusting the zoom lens so that the field of view is very large. He could then point the device at one of these objects and narrow down the field of view so that its major details could be examined. By further narrowing the field of view, he could examine the volumetric structure of a smaller component of that shape.

The 3-D model representation. In summary, the three design criteria favor a shape representation that is object-centered, volumetric, and modular as dis-

---

[11] The same effect can be obtained without a zoom lens by using a logarithmic mapping that provides high resolution in the center of the visual field and decreasing resolution toward the periphery (see [19]).

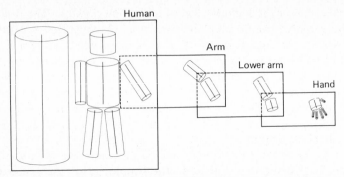

FIG. 5. This diagram illustrates the organization of shape information in a 3-D model description. Each box corresponds to a 3-D model, with its model axis—specifying the location, size, and orientation of the whole shape—on the left side of the box and the arrangement of its component parts shown on the right side. In addition some components have 3-D models associated with them and this is indicated by the way the boxes overlap. The relative arrangement of each model's components, however, is shown improperly since position should be given in an object-centered system rather than the viewer-centered projection used here. A more correct illustration of the same 3-D model is shown in Table 3 which specifies the spatial arrangement of the component volumetric primitives in an object-centered coordinate system defined by the volumetric primitive that contains it.

cussed above. A limited representation whose scope includes shapes having well-defined volumetric axes, which we have called the 3-D model representation, follows directly from these design choices. The coordinate system, primitive elements, and modularity of this representation can all be defined in terms of the shape's volumetric primitives over a broad range of scales. This design follows from the observation that a canonical primitive element specifying location, orientation, and size defines a coordinate system (up to rotation about its axis) which is stable for the volume it encompasses. The primitive's volume also provides a base for modularizing shape descriptions. We relate all smaller volumetric elements contained within this volume and not within the volume of any intermediate primitive. Fig. 5 and Table 3 depict a 3-D model description for a human shape. A single large volumetric primitive specifies the location, orientation, and size of the whole shape. It also defines as the coordinate system for specifying the locations of the other primitive elements immediately within its scope such as the major limbs and torso. These components, in turn, each defines a coordinate system for recording the arrangement of its components as is shown for one of the arms. Each of the modules—outlined by rectangular boxes in the figure—is a self-contained unit of shape information and could stand alone as a shape description. We call these modules 3-D *models* and the collection of them shown in Fig. 5 constitutes a 3-D model description for a shape. We are presently studying the problem of deriving 3-D model descriptions from the $2\frac{1}{2}$-D sketch. Since the 3-D model representation is based on volumetric primitive specifications, the problem can

TABLE 3. Object-centered specifications in one possible coordinate system are shown for several of the 3-D models illustrated in Fig. 5. Each line specifies a single part's position, size, and orientation relative to the containing volumetric primitive

3-D Model	Part	Position[a]			Size[b]		Orientation[c]	
		p	r	θ	length	thickness	ϕ	ρ
Human	head	0.1	0	0	0.2	0.8	0	0
	torso	0.4	0	0	0.5	0.5	0	0
	arm	0.4	0.2	90	0.5	0.2	0	0
	arm	0.4	0.2	−90	0.5	0.2	40	−90
	leg	0.7	0.2	90	0.75	0.2	0	0
	leg	0.7	0.2	−90	0.75	0.2	0	0
Arm	upper arm	0.25	0	0	0.5	0.4	0	0
	lower arm	0.75	0	0	0.5	0.3	10	0
Lower arm	fore arm	0.5	0	0	0.7	0.4	0	0
	hand	0.9	0	0	0.3	0.7	0	0

[a] Position is specified here in a cylindrical coordinate system $(p\,r\,\theta)$ defined by the position and orientation of the containing shape. p is the position along the length of the containing shape from 0 to 1. r is the distance away from the axis of the containing shape relative to its thickness. θ is the angle around the axis with 90 degrees to the object's left and −90 to the right.

[b] The part's size is given as a length relative to the containing shape and a width relative to its own length.

[c] Orientation is specified in a spherical coordinate system $(\phi\,\rho)$ where ϕ is the angle of inclination away from the orientation of the containing shape's axis. ρ is the angle about the axis, again with 90 degrees to the shape's left.

be stated more specifically as that of recovering volumetric shape information from the data available in the 2½-D sketch.

5. Discussion

The purpose of this paper was to examine the vision problem within the framework set forth by Marr [11] and Marr and Poggio [16] giving special attention to the types of information involved. These information types were used to subdivide the problem into image analysis and visible-surface analysis components. This subdivision occurs at the computational theory level, meaning that it is a property of the vision problem. This is not to say that a mechanism that *implements* a solution to the vision problem has to be organized strictly along these lines. Rather, the importance of this observation lies in the assistance it gives us in studying and organizing what we know about the problem and possible solutions (algorithms) to it.

ACKNOWLEDGMENT

D. Marr provided much of the insight that led to this paper. A. Sloman and C. Lu provided helpful comments.

REFERENCES

1. Agin, G.J., Representation and description of curved objects, Stanford Artificial Intelligence Project, Memo AIM-173, Stanford University (1972).
2. Binford, T.O., Visual perception by computer, presented to the IEEE Conference on Systems and Control, Miami, December 1971.
3. Blum, H., A transformation for extracting new descriptors of shape, in: Dunn, W., Ed., *Models for the Perception of Speech and Visual Form* (M.I.T. Press, Cambridge, MA, 1967).
4. Blum, H., Biological shape and visual science (Part I), *J. Theoret. Biol.* **38** (1973) 205–287.
5. Freuder, E.C., Computer system for visual recognition using active knowledge, M.I.T. AI Lab. Technical Report AI-TR-345 (1976).
6. Grimson, W.E.L. and Marr, D., A computer implementation of a theory for human stereo vision, Proceedings: Image Understanding Workshop, sponsored by Information Processing Techniques Office, Defense Advanced Research Projects Agency, April 1979. Also Grimson, W.E.L., A computer implementation of a theory for human stereo vision, *Proc. R. Soc. London*, submitted.
7. Horn, B.K.P., Focusing, M.I.T. Artificial Intelligence Laboratory Memo 160 (1968).
8. Horn, B.K.P., Obtaining shape from shading information, in: Winston, P.H., Ed., *The Psychology of Computer Vision* (McGraw-Hill, New York, 1975) 115–155.
9. Julesz, B., Binocular depth perception of computer-generated patterns, *Bell System Tech. J.* **39** (1960) 1125–1162.
10. Julesz, B., *Foundations of Cyclopean Perception* (University of Chicago Press, Chicago, 1971).
11. Marr, D., Early processing of visual information, *Philos. Trans. R. Soc. London* **B262** (1976) 483–524.
12. Marr, D., *Vision: A Computational Investigation into the Human Representation and Processing of Visual Information* (W.H. Freeman & Co., San Francisco, CA, in press).
13. Marr, D. and Hildreth, E., Theory of edge detection, *Proc. R. Soc. London* **B207** (1980) 187–217. Available also as M.I.T. AI Lab Memo 518.
14. Marr, D. and Nishihara, H.K., Representation and recognition of the spatial organization of three-dimensional shapes, *Proc. R. Soc. London* **B200**, 269–294.
15. Marr, D. and Poggio, T., Cooperative computation of stereo disparity, *Science* **194** (1976) 283–287.
16. Marr, D. and Poggio, T., From understanding computation to understanding neural circuitry, in: Poppel, E. et al., Eds., *Neuronal Mechanisms in Visual Perception. Neurosciences Research Program Bulletin* **15** (1977) 470–488.
17. Marr, D. and Poggio, T., A computational theory of human stereo vision, *Proc. R. Soc. London* **B204** (1979) 301–328. Also available as M.I.T. AI Lab Memo 451.
18. Nevatia, R., Structured descriptions of complex curved objects for recognition and visual memory, Stanford Artificial Intelligence Project, Memo AIM-250, Stanford University (1974).
19. Nishihara, H.K., Representation of the spatial organization of three-dimensional shapes for visual recognition, Ph.D. Thesis, Dept. of Mathematics, M.I.T. (1978).
20. Ullman, S., The interpretation of visual motion, Ph.D. Thesis, Dept. of Electrical Engineering and Computer Science, M.I.T. (M.I.T. Press, Cambridge, MA, 1979).

Received October 1980

Symbolic Reasoning Among 3-D Models and 2-D Images

Rodney A. Brooks

AI Laboratory, Stanford University, Palo Alto,
CA 94305, U.S.A.

ABSTRACT

We describe model-based vision systems in terms of four components: models, prediction of image features, description of image features, and interpretation which relates image features to models. We describe details of modelling, prediction and interpretation in an implemented model-based vision system. Both generic object classes and specific objects are represented by volume models which are independent of viewpoint. We model complex real world object classes. Variations of size, structure and spatial relations within object classes can be modelled. New spatial reasoning techniques are described which are useful both for prediction within a vision system, and for planning within a manipulation system. We introduce new approaches to prediction and interpretation based on the propagation of symbolic constraints. Predictions are two pronged. First, prediction graphs provide a coarse filter for hypothesizing matches of objects to image feature. Second, they contain instructions on how to use measurements of image features to deduce three dimensional information about tentative object interpretations. Interpretation proceeds by merging local hypothesized matches, subject to consistent derived implications about the size, structure and spatial configuration of the hypothesized objects. Prediction, description and interpretation proceed concurrently from coarse object subpart and class interpretations of images, to fine distinctions among object subclasses and more precise three dimensional quantification of objects. We distinguish our implementations from the fundamental geometric operations required by our general image understanding scheme. We suggest directions for future research for improved algorithms and representations.

1. Introduction

We present both a general philosophy of model-based vision and a specific implementation of many of those ideas in the ACRONYM model-based vision system. An earlier version of ACRONYM was described in [18]. Here we describe a new version of ACRONYM which is almost a completely new implementation. It includes new methods for modelling generic classes of objects, new techniques for geometric reasoning, and a method for using noisy measurements from images to gain three dimensional understandings about objects.

ACRONYM is a domain independent model-based vision system. The user describes to ACRONYM classes of three dimensional objects, and their relation-

Artificial Intelligence **17** (1981) 285–348

ships in the world. The system tries to interpret images by locating instances of modelled objects. The same models may be used for other purposes, such as planning manipulator assemblies.

1.1. Model-based vision

Much of the current work in computer vision is based on trying to extract maximal information from an image using no knowledge about the objects being viewed. Often the techniques are based on physical considerations concerning the image producing process (e.g. [7, 26, 51]). Others, principally David Marr's research group at MIT, have found in physiological evidence suggestions for algorithms which might be implemented on conventional computers to extract information from images. They call this information two and a half dimensional information as it includes identification of surfaces and their local orientation, but not three dimensional location. The idea is that higher level processes will make use of these rich descriptions to interpret the image (see [32, 33, 23] for instance).

Once such descriptions of local surface characteristics have been extracted the problem still remains of meaningfully interpreting those descriptions as instances of objects in the field of view of the imaging device. This is essentially the problem we are approaching in this paper.

We must find some mapping between the descriptive elements and objects. If we are to identify objects, we must have some a priori representation for those objects. We need to find correspondences between components of the image description and the object representations. In general the representation we have for objects might not be in terms of the same primitives as provided by low level image description processes (see Section 2). Thus there may need to be more than one mapping carried out.

One approach is to map the image description into a new description sharing the primitives used in the object models, then to match the descriptions to the models. This approach may either be impossible, due to unresolvable ambiguities, or extremely difficult due to lack of sufficient information in the image descriptions.

The approach we have taken is to map from a priori object class descriptions to descriptions in terms of the same primitives as produced by the image description processes. This can be viewed as prediction of image features. Matching is done between image and object at that level. The matches are not conservative, and in the interest of not rejecting correct matches some incorrect matches may also be accepted. Then a mapping from image description terms to object model primitive terms is made, making use both of the information gained at the image description level match and the information included in the image description prediction. Incorrect matches are found to be inconsistent with the detailed models at this stage. Eventually a three dimensional interpretation of the image is obtained in terms of the a priori models.

Thus our approach to image understanding relies on four components: object models, prediction from models, interpretation of image descriptions in terms of models, and descriptions of images. In this paper we deal with only the first three.

We have not made use of the rich descriptions available from some of the recent work mentioned above, as that is still somewhat of a moving target. Rather we chose a fairly simple and primitive system which we had available, and have used the inaccurate and crude descriptions which it produces. We feel that the system can only improve as better low level descriptive systems are used instead. Our implementation in fact goes further downwards on the predictive side than described in this paper. This is necessary because of the more primitive descriptive system used.

1.2. An overview of ACRONYM

The user gives ACRONYM models of objects and their spatial relationships, as well as classes of models and their subclass relationships. There is a choice of input techniques.[1] A text-based description language has proved to be more useful for describing classes of objects and their spatial relations. MODITOR (a model editor) implemented originally by Harald Westphal and Amy Plikerd, and revised and significantly expanded by Soroka [44] provides a GEOMED—like [8] interactive interface, via keyboard and graphics display. This tends to be more convenient for modelling specific objects. The two input systems produce the same internal representation. Volumetric models and spatial relations are represented in the *object graph*. Volume elements form the nodes while spatial relations and subpart relations form the arcs. Object class relations are represented in the *restriction graph*. Nodes are sets of constraints on volumetric models. Directed arcs represent subclass inclusion. A graphics module provides feedback to the user during the modelling process, via a raster display. It generates images of objects being modelled under the modelled camera conditions. The diagrams in this paper were made by the graphics module.

Geometric reasoning techniques are used to predict features which will be invariantly observable. This requires analysis of the ranges of variations in the size, structure, and spatial relations in the object model classes. Notice that we are not predicting the complete appearance of objects from all possible

---

[1]We have not yet tried to incorporate model acquisition from images. Techniques of segmentation and description were developed by Nevatia and Binford [39] to build tree structured generalized cone models of objects detected using a laser range finder. Wiston [50] has shown how to infer object classes over variations in both size and structure from examples and non-examples of objects. Together these techniques seem to provide a strong basis for future work on teaching object class descriptions to ACRONYM, by showing it examples whose component parts it would first instantiate to specializations of a library of qualitatively different generalized cone models, including both single cones and joined cones.

viewpoints, but rather we are predicting features which will enable us to identify instances of objects, and also determine their orientation and position. Sometimes case analysis is necessary to subdivide ranges of variations in order to establish observable features. The result is the *prediction graph*. The nodes of the graph are predictions of image features, and the arcs specify relations which must hold between them in the image. Predictions are two pronged. First, they provide a coarse filter for hypothesizing object to image feature matches. Second, they contain instructions on how to use measurements of an image feature to deduce three dimensional information about the object to which it has been hypothetically matched. The predictor is implemented as a set of production rules.

In our current implementation we use the results of images processed with the line finder of Nevatia and Babu [38]. This provides on the order of 1000 edge elements, segmented as linear pieces, ranging between approximately 3 and 100 pixels in length in a 512 by 512 image. Prediction nodes provide goal-direction to an edge linking algorithm [17] which produces descriptions of shape elements found. Typically there are 5 to 50 elements from a search of the whole image. The descriptive process is reinvoked many times during the interpretation of an image. At first the multiple invocations search for different image features to determine a coarse image interpretation. Later invocations search small areas of the image for particular features, both for detailed object class identification and to gain detailed three dimensional information about the objects. We plan to later include other low level descriptive processes, such as the stereo work underway within the Stanford vision group [5].

Invocations of the descriptive processes provide candidate image features for matching to predicted features. Matching does not proceed by comparing image feature measurements with predictions for those measurements. Rather the measurements are used to put constraints on parameters of the three dimensional models, of which the objects in the world are hypothesized to be instances. Only if the constraints are consistent with what is already known of the model in three dimensions, then these local matches are retained for later interpretation. A local match can thus constrain camera parameters, object size and structure, or perhaps only relations between camera parameters and object size. This, for instance, automatically handles problems of scaling. Local matches are combined to form more global interpretations, but all constraints implied by local matches must be mutually consistent. Combining local matches may produce additional constraints which also must be consistent. Additional iterations of prediction, description, and interpretation occur as finer and finer details of objects are identified. Once a member of an object class has been identified, it is easy to check whether it is possible that the object is also a member of a subclass. It is merely a matter of checking whether the constraints introduced by the interpretation are consistent with constraints describing the subclass.

The ACRONYM system has been used for a number of tasks other than image understanding. D. Michael Overmeyer implemented a set of rules in the rule language used for the predictor and interpreter, useful for planning manipulator tasks. The system, GRASP [10], was given ACRONYM models of simple objects, from which it automatically deduced positions and orientations which could be grasped by a manipulator arm, and which would provide a firm stable grip on the object. Soroka [44] has built SIMULATOR on top of ACRONYM. SIMULATOR is a system for off-line debugging of manipulator programs. It uses the ACRONYM modelling system to model manipulator arms and their environmant. The graphics system is used to provide stereo pair of images of the scenes, so that the user perceives a three dimensional model. Currently the system can be driven by the output of AL [22], which is normally used to drive manipulator arms directly. Instead SIMULATOR drives models of manipulators in real time, by specializing the spatial relations between manipulator links. Work is underway to extend SIMULATOR to interface to other manipulator languages.

1.3. Outline of the paper

The bulk of this paper is divided into four major sections. Sections 2–4 describe major subsystems necessary for a general purpose model-based vision system. Section 5 shows how these modules can work together to carry out image interpretation. Each section surveys related work in the field, describes the computational problems involved, and explains the particular approach taken to solve these problems in the implementation of ACRONYM.

Section 2 deals with geometric modelling. Geometric modelling is often associated with modelling specific objects. We extend the demands on geometric modelling to include generic object classes and partially specified spatial relationships between instances of object classes. We further describe how to maintain complex internal relationships between parameters of object class instances.

The deductive power for implementations of our paradigm for model-based vision is provided by a constraint manipulation system. Section 3 describes the formal requirements for the constraint manipulation system and our constraint manipulation system implemented for ACRONYM. It is demonstrated bounding nonlinear functions over nonlinearly defined subsets of the Euclidean space.

An understanding of geometry is required to make full use of volumetric models, and make inferences from their modelled spatial relations, no matter how incompletely specified. Section 4 describes methods for handling complex geometric relationships. It also provides methods for making deductions from the relationships between objects and the camera. Explicit rules are given which implement these methods.

Section 5 shows how generic models, constraint manipulation and geometric reasoning can be used to make predictions from models (as distinct from making predictions of the appearance of instances of the models) and using those predictions to interpret images. Further it is shown how to make use of noisy image measurements to gain a three dimensional understanding of the objects which generated the image. Prediction and interpretation are implemented as a set of production rules in ACRONYM.

2. Model Representation

The world is described to ACRONYM as volume elements and their spatial relationships, and as classes of objects and their subclass relationships.

A single simple mechanism is used within the geometric models to represent variations in size, structure, and spatial relationships. Sets of constraints on such variations specify classes of three dimensional objects. Adding constraints specializes classes to subclasses and eventually to specific instances.

The model representation scheme used in a vision system must be able to represent the classes of objects which the system is required to recognize. When the representation is in world terms rather than image terms, it is necessary that observables be computable from the representation.

Previous model-based vision systems have not made a distinction between models of objects in world terms and models of objects in terms of directly observable image features. The models themselves have been descriptions of observable two dimensional image features and relations among them. MSYS [6] models objects as usually homogeneous image regions. ISIS [21] includes brightness, hue and saturation of image regions in its object models which are constrained to meet viewpoint-dependent spatial relations. Ohta et al. [40] also model objects as image regions, but they include shape descriptions in two dimensions. Again viewpoint–dependent spatial relations are used.

For the general vision problem where exact contexts are unknown, and often even approximate orientations are unknown with viewpoint-dependent image models there must be multiple models or descriptions of a given object or object class. Instead, viewpoint-independent models should be given to the system. The resolution of the problem of multiple appearances from multiple viewpoints then becomes the responsibility of the vision system itself. For a model to be completely viewpoint-independent yet still provide shape information, it must embody the three dimensional structure of the object being modelled. Volume descriptions are useful for other applications too. Planning how to manipulate objects, while avoiding collisions requires volume descriptions (e.g. [31, 44]). Objects can be recognized from range data, given volume descriptions (e.g. [39, 47]). For individual applications additional information might be included; e.g. surface properties for image understanding and density of subparts for manipulation planning. Volume descriptions provide a common representational basis for various distinct but possibly interacting processes, each of which need models of the world.

Consider the situation where the vision system is one component of a much larger system which deals with models or representations of objects which will appear in the images to be examined. For example in a highly automated production system we might wish to use the CAD (computer aided design) model of some industrial part as the only description necessary for a vision system. It would be able to recognize, locate and orient instances of the part when they later appear on a conveyor belt leading to a coordinated vision and manipulation assembly station, with no description further than the CAD model. It should not be necessary to have a human in the control path, whose task is to understand the CAD model and then to translate it into a description of observable features for the vision system. CAD systems for industrial parts deal in models which are viewpoint independent and which embody a three dimensional description of the volume occupied by the part (e.g. both the PADL system [45] and that of Braid [16] meet these requirements; see also the survey [4]). The representation scheme should also facilitate automatic computation of observable features from models. Lieberman's system [28] provides for automatic computation of silhouettes of objects as they will appear in binary images. In general, more comprehensive descriptions of observable features provide for robust vision in situations which are not completely controlled.

ACRONYM is by no means the first model-based vision system to use volumetric models. Baumgart [8] and Lieberman [28] both used polyhedral representations of objects. Nevatia and Binford [39] used generalized cones. However ACRONYM goes beyond these systems. It has the capability to represent generic classes of objects as well as individual specific objects, and situations which are only partially specified and constrained, as well as specific situations.

We do not claim that ACRONYM's class mechanism is adequate for all image interpretation tasks. In fact some of the examples below may seem to have been carried out successfully in spite of the representation mechanism. Other vision and modelling systems, however, do not have even that capability.

The following description of our model representation centers around the types of things which must be represented about objects, for a variety of image interpretation tasks. We first describe a volumetric representation for objects. A method for describing variations in such models by describing allowed variations in place holders for object parameters is given. This method allows representation of variations in size, structure and position, and orientation of objects. A class mechanism, based on specialization of variations, is built orthogonally to the volumetric representations.

2.1. Volumetric representation

Generalized cones have been used by many people both as the output

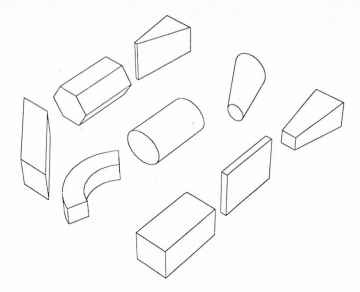

FIG. 2.1. A selection of generalized cones used by ACRONYM as primitive volume elements.

language for descriptive processes working from range data [2, 39, 43] and for modelling systems for vision [25, 32, 34, 37].

Generalized cones [9] provide a compact, viewpoint-independent representation of volume elements. A generalized cone is defined by a planar cross section, a space curve spine, and a sweeping rule. It represents the volume swept out by the cross section as it is translated along the spine, held at some constant angle to the spine, and transformed according to the sweeping rule. Each generalized cone has its own local coordinate system. We use a right handed system such that the initial end of the spine is at the origin, the initial cross section lies in the y-z plane, and the x component of the directional tangent to the spine at the origin is positive. Thus for cones where the cross section is normal to a straight spine the latter lies in the positive x-axis.

Fig. 2.1 gives examples of generalized cones used as the primitive volume elements in ACRONYM's representation. They include straight and circular spines, circles and simple polygons for cross sections and sweeping rules which can be constant, linear contractions or more generally, contractions linear in two orthogonal directions. Cross sections may be held at any constant angle to noncircular spines.

The internal representation of all ACRONYM data structures is frame-like in that each data object is an instance of a *unit*. Units have a set of associated *slots* whose *fillers* define their values [14]. Fig. 2.2 shows the unit representation of a generalized cone representing the body of a particular electric motor. Its cross section, spine and sweeping rule units are also shown. It is a simple right

```
Node: ELECTRIC_MOTOR_CONE
    CLASS:                SIMPLE_CONE
    SPINE:                Z0014
    SWEEPING_RULE:        CONSTANT_SWEEPING_RULE
    CROSS_SECTION:        Z0013

        Node: Z0014
            CLASS:        SPINE
            TYPE:         STRAIGHT
            LENGTH:       8.0

        Node: CONSTANT_SWEEPING_RULE
            CLASS:        SWEEPING_RULE
            TYPE:         CONSTANT

        Node: Z0013
            CLASS:        CROSS_SECTION
            TYPE:         CIRCLE
            RADIUS:       2.5
```

FIG. 2.2. A generalized cone model of a specific electric motor body.

circular cylinder of length 8.0 and radius 2.5 (our system currently does not enforce any particular units of measurement).

ACRONYM's volumetric representation is built around units of *class object* (a unit's class is given by its *class slot*; this corresponds roughly to the *self* slot of KRL units [14]). Objects are the nodes of the *object graph*. The arcs are units of class *subpart* and class *affixment*. Objects have slots for optional *cone-descriptor* (which is filled with a pointer to a unit, representing a generalized cone), *subparts* and *affixments* which are filled with a list of pointers to instances of the appropriate classes of units, and a few more which we will not discuss here. Subpart and affixment arcs are directional; pointing from the object whose unit references them, to the object referenced in their *object* slot.

The object graph has two natural subgraphs defined by the two classes of directional arcs. Connected components of the subpart subgraph are required to be trees. It is intended that each such tree be arranged in a coarse to fine hierarchy. Cutting the tree off at different depths gives models with different levels of detail. For example the subpart tree for the electric motors illustrated in Fig. 2.4 has a root-node whose cone descriptor is the large cylindrical body of the motor. At the next lower level of the tree are the smaller flanges and spindle. The coarse to fine representation has obvious utility in image under-standing tasks. Unless ACRONYM has already hypothesized an interpretation of some images features as an instance of an object with its own generalized cone descriptor, it does not search for subparts of the object in the image.

Currently the user inputs the subpart trees directly; there is no enforcement of coarse to fine levels of representation. It is certainly within the capabilities of ACRONYM's geometric reasoning system (see Section 4) to detect when the condition is violated. It is eminently reasonable that in such cases the system should build its own internal coarse to fine structure, while maintaining the user's hierarchical decomposition for future interaction. We have not diverted resources to implement such a capability. There may be minor problems with such a scheme in light of the discussion of modality in Section 2.2.3 below.

Every object has its own local coordinate system. If an object has a cone descriptor, then the generalized cone shares the same coordinate system as the object. Affixment arcs relate coordinate systems of objects. An affixment includes a product of symbolic coordinate transforms, which transform the coordinate system of the object pointed at by the affixment to the coordinate system of the original object.

We represent coordinate transforms as a pair (internally a unit with two slots) written (r, v) where r is a rotation and v is a translation vector. A rotation is a pair (again a unit with two slots) written $\langle a, m \rangle$ representing a rotation of scalar magnitude m about unit axis vector a. A vector is a triple (x, y, z). In this paper we will use infix $*$ for composition both of rotations and of coordinate transforms, meaning that the left argument is applied following the right. Similary we will use infix $\otimes$ for application of a left argument which is either a rotation or a coordinate transform to a vector as the right argument.

Our affixments do not carry any connotation of attachment. For instance affixments do not distinguish between the case of the coordinate transform relating an electric motor sitting on a table, and the coordinate transform relating a permanently attached flange to the motor body. The attachment notion (whether rigid or articulated) is implied by the subpart relation. There are valid objections to such an assumption. A model of an operational airfield should include the fact that aircraft must be present. The only way to represent such a fact in ACRONYM (see again the discussion modality in Section 2.2.3) is to make *aircraft* a subpart of *airfield*, and clearly in that case any assertion of permanent attachment is false. We will probably encounter problems, especially in planning manipulator tasks from this aspect of the representation.

Both subpart and affixment arcs are represented by units. Subpart units have a *quantity* slot which specifies how many instances of a subpart an object has. For example the left-most electric motor in Fig. 2.4 has four identical flanges. The subpart relation for all four was represented as a single subpart arc between an electric motor and a flange node in the object graph. Affixment arcs similarly have a *quantity* slot. In the case of a quantity greater than one, the expression for the coordinate transform includes a free variable which is iterated over the specified range to produce the distinct coordinate transforms. That process produced the spatial relations of the numerous flanges to the electric motor bodies in Fig. 2.4.

Objects are placed in a world by affixing them to a world coordinate system. A camera position and orientation is described by affixing a *camera* unit to a world coordinate system. A camera views the world along the negative z-axis of its coordinate system, with the y-axis pointing in the direction of the top of the image plane, and the x-axis to the right. A *camera* unit also has a *focal-ratio* slot, which is filled with a number. If r is focal ratio of a camera, and an object of length l is parallel to the image plane of the camera at distance d from the center of the camera, then the image of the object will measure rl/d in image plane coordinates.

2.2. Quantification and constraints

The previous section described how we represent specific objects. On top of that representation scheme we have built a mechanism for representing classes of objects. We use the term *class* rather than *set* because we use a *criterial* or *intensional* augmentation of the volumetric representation. A class is the *extension* of a description of allowed variations in values of numeric slots of a volumetric model.

In KRL-type systems [14], it is usual to describe allowed variations of a slot filler by attaching a description directly to the slot. We have chosen a different approach. Any numeric slot can be filled with an algebraic expression ranging over numeric constants, declared constant symbols, and free variables. We refer to the latter as *quantifiers*. The simplest case is when the expression is a simple numeric constant, which is exactly that described in the previous section. Declared constant symbols are purely for user convenience. Classes of objects are specified by supplying a set of *constraints* (inequalities on algebraic expressions) which define the set of values which can be taken by quantifiers. We describe the benefits of such an approach below. Clearly this approach could be extended to allow variations in non-numeric slots. The language of expressions for slot fillers and constraints would need to be extended to include nonnumeric operators and comparators. Any such extensions would require a more comprehensive constraint manipulation system than the one we describe in Section 3.

The PADL system [45] seems to be the only other geometric modelling system which allows detailed geometric models with quantifiable variations. Variations are limited to numeric tolerances on nominal values. The system uses a mixture of attaching descriptions of variations to slots, and attaching them to named variables. Slots can be filled by expressions, but each term has a tolerance associated with it, which propagate from the expression to the slot. A default tolerance is given to numbers and variables for which no explicit tolerance is given.

The current restriction of allowing variations in numeric valued slots of ACRONYM's representations still allows large generic classes of objects to be easily and naturally defined. In our work on aerial images we have made extensive use of models of the generic classes of *airports* and *wide-bodied passenger jet aircraft* (see [19] for details). Variations of numeric valued slots allows three distinct types of variations within a class of models; variations in size, limited variations in structure, and variations in spatial relationships. We examine each of these in more detail.

2.2.1. *Variations in size*

Fig. 2.3 shows the unit representation of a generalized cone which is the body of a generic electric motor. Compare it to the cone for the specific electric motor of Fig. 2.2. The only difference is that the spine length and cross section radius slots are now filled with the quantifiers MOTOR-LENGTH and MOTOR-RADIUS respectively, rather than 8.0 and 2.5.

Suppose we want to represent a class of small electric motors that might be built on a particular assembly line. (Abraham et al. [1] describe a manufacturing situation where approximately 450 different styles of motors are manufactured with an average batch size of 600 and a number of style changes each day. The example models in this paper are loosely based on examples in that report. All dimensions are in inches.) Then we could restrict the length and radius of the motor independently, using the constraints

$$6.0 \leqslant \text{MOTOR-LENGTH} \leqslant 9.0,$$

$$2.0 \leqslant \text{MOTOR-RADIUS} \leqslant 3.0.$$

Suppose, also, that the length of a motor is roughly inversely proportional to its radius; i.e. over the class of motors which are to be modelled it is true that the longer motors are of narrower diameter. Then this fact could be expressed by a constraint of the form:

$$17.0 \leqslant \text{MOTOR-LENGTH} \times \text{MOTOR-RADIUS} \leqslant 21.0.$$

If there was an exact relationship between motor length and radius (unlikely in this case), then an equality could be employed in the constraint.

Notice that the last constraint relates the fillers of two distinct slots from two distinct units. Such a relation would be harder (or at least more clumsy) to

```
Node: GENERIC_ELECTRIC_MOTOR_CONE
     CLASS:                 SIMPLE_CONE
     SPINE:                 Z0014
     SWEEPING_RULE:         CONSTANT_SWEEPING_RULE
     CROSS_SECTION:         Z0013

          Node: Z0014
               CLASS:        SPINE
               TYPE:         STRAIGHT
               LENGTH:       MOTOR_LENGTH

          Node: CONSTANT_SWEEPING_RULE
               CLASS:        SWEEPING_RULE
               TYPE:         CONSTANT

          Node: Z0013
               CLASS:        CROSS_SECTION
               TYPE:         CIRCLE
               RADIUS:       MOTOR_RADIUS
```

FIG. 2.3. A generalized cone model of a generic electric motor body.

specify if descriptions of allowed variations were attached directly to slots of units. In this case the description attached to at least one slot would have to explicitly refer to the other slot. If the system is to make use of new tighter constraints on either the length or radius to further constrain the other (we will see this happen during image interpretation in Section 5), then the description attached to the two slots would have to refer to each other. If a relation exists between more than two slots, the situation becomes worse (such relations commonly arise during the image interpretation process). By placing the restrictions directly on quantifiers no such duplication of information is necessary.

Another benefit of attaching descriptions of allowed variations to quantifiers rather than to slots is that it becomes very easy to express many symmetries and other exact geometric relationships. For instance to specify that the wings of an aircraft are the same length it suffices to fill the length slots of the spines of the two wings with the same expression; e.g. just a single quantifier WING-LENGTH. Similarly to express the fact that a chair has four legs of the same length their spine length slots could all be filled with the quantifier LEG-LENGTH. Compare this to the representation of this fact used by Shapiro et al. [41].

The PADL system [45] allows the user to supply tolerances for object models, as described above. Grossman [24] has approached tolerancing by generating a large number of instances of models, using a random number generator to produce varying dimensions of objects within prescribed bounds and distributions. The ACRONYM system of constraining quantifiers allows tolerancing of objects in a simple manner. For instance suppose we wanted to represent a particular type of electric motor in Fig. 2.4 with length 8.0 ± 0.01 inches. Then we could simply use the constraint

$$8.0 - 0.01 \leqslant \text{MOTOR-LENGTH} \leqslant 8.0 + 0.01.$$

Alternatively we might fill the spine length slot with the expression

$$8.0 + \text{LENGTH-ERROR}$$

and use the constraint

$$-0.01 \leqslant \text{LENGTH-ERROR} \leqslant 0.01.$$

FIG. 2.4. Three specializations of the generic class of small electric motors.

Notice however that ACRONYM models need not be restricted to use only such simple plus–minus tolerances as are models in the PADL system. Tolerances can be specified using arbitrary algebraic expressions.

2.2.2. *Variations in structure*

The fact that ACRONYM's subpart and affixment arcs are units with *quantity* slots allows a limited form of structural variation to be included in model classes. Filling the *quantity* slot of a subpart arc with 1 or 0 can be used to indicate the presence or absence of a subpart. The slot can alternately be filled with a quantifier, constrained to be 1 or 0, to model the possibility that the subpart may or may not be present. Similarly a variable number of identical subparts of an object can be indicated; e.g. the number of flanges on the electric motors in Fig. 2.4 or the number of engines on an aircraft wing.

Fig. 2.4 shows the generic model of an electric motor under three different sets of constraints which each fully determine values for the quantifiers BASE-QUANTITY and FLANGE-QUANTITY which fill the obvious *quantity* slots.

Given such a mechanism for representing structural variations, we must consider what class of structure varying models we can describe. Suppose we wish to specify that an electric motor has either a *base* or *flanges* but not both. Furthermore if there are *flanges*, then there are between 3 and 6 of them. This could be expressed with the following constraint.

$$((3 \leqslant \text{FLANGE-QUANTITY} \leqslant 6) \wedge (0 = \text{BASE-QUANTITY}))$$

$$\vee \ ((0 = \text{FLANGE-QUANTITY}) \wedge (1 = \text{BASE-QUANTITY})).$$

Such a constraint is beyond the currently implemented capabilities of ACRONYM. Constraints must be algebraic inequalities, with an implicit conjunction over sets of such constraints. The explicit inclusion of logical disjunction requires a more comprehensive reasoning system for prediction and interpretation than our current system (see Section 5).

Since our algebraic constraints can be nonlinear it is possible to represent many disjunctions without overtaxing our theorem prover. In fact the above constraint is equivalent to the following set of linear constraints:

$$
\begin{aligned}
0 &\leqslant & \text{BASE-QUANTITY} & \leqslant 1, \\
0 &\leqslant & \text{FLANGE-QUANTITY} & \leqslant 6, \\
& & \text{FLANGE-QUANTITY} + 6 \times \text{BASE-QUANTITY} &\leqslant 6, \\
& & 3 \leqslant \text{FLANGE-QUANTITY} + 3 \times \text{BASE-QUANTITY}. &
\end{aligned}
$$

Such a set of constraints is clearly not intuitive—unlike the previous constraint. For vision tasks it is probably not necessary. In our work with ACRONYM we have been content to underconstrain classes of objects. For example our generic model of electric motors uses only the first two constraints.

In an ideal situation the modelling language should provide easy and natural means for the user to specify objects and classes in as much detail as is wished. The system should then sift out just enough detail of constraint for its own purposes. We have not tackled these problems.

2.2.3. *Variations in spatial relationships*

An affixment specifies the spatial relationship between two objects by providing a product of coordinate transforms which relate the local coordinate systems of the objects. Each coordinate transform consists of a rotation and a translation vector. The slots in the units representing these can naturally be filled with quantifiers or even expressions on quantifiers. Thus variable spatial relationships can be represented.

Suppose that members of the class of electric motors with bases are going to be placed at a work station, upright but with arbitrary orientation about the vertical, and at a constrained but inexact position. The coordinate system of the motor has its x-axis running along the center of the spindle, and its z-axis vertical. The work station coordinates have a vertical Z-axis also. The position and orientation of the motor relative to the work station could then be represented by the transform

$$((\hat{z}, \text{ORI}), (\text{X-POS, Y-POS, BASE-THICKNESS} + \text{MOTOR-}$$
$$\text{RADIUS}))$$

where $\hat{z}$ as usual denotes a unit vector in the z direction. Typically X-POS and Y-POS might be constrained by

$$0 \leqslant \text{X-POS} \leqslant 24,$$
$$18 \leqslant \text{Y-POS} \leqslant 42,$$

and ORI would be left free. The geometric reasoning system described in Section 3 manipulates such underconstrained transforms.

There is an inadequacy in such specifications of spatial relations. It is possible to represent that aircraft can be found on runaways or on taxiways, for instance, by affixing the generic model of an aircraft to both, using similar coordinate transforms to those described above. It is not possible however to specify that the one and only motor cover which will appear in an image will be located on either the left or right parts feeder. The only way within ACRONYM's representational mechanism to allow for such a possibility is to express some connected area between both parts feeders where it might be found. Such inexactness might lead to much greater searches in locating the motor cover in an image, given that the feeders have already been located. Again, the reasoning systems described in the rest of this paper need major additions to handle a more concise specification language. Furthermore the current interpretation algorithm treats affixments as defining a necessary condition on where objects are located. A more flexible scheme would allow the user to give

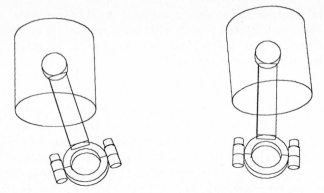

FIG. 2.5. Variable affixments are used to model articulated objects such as this piston assembly.

advice to look first in one location for a particular object and then in another higher cost location if that fails.

Variable affixments can also be used to model articulated objects. Fig. 2.5 shows two views of a piston model with different values assigned to a quantifier filling the rotation magnitude slot of the coordinate transform between the piston and the con-rod. Constraints on the quantifier express the range of travel of the con-rod.

The representation of articulated objects may be important if manipulator arms are present in images, and it is desired to visually calibrate or servo them. Soroka's [44] simulator is based on these representations.

Variable camera geometry can also be represented by filling the slots of the transforms affixing the camera to world coordinates with quantifiers. Section 4 gives two examples of variable camera geometries. If the characteristics of the imaging camera are not known exactly, the *focal-ratio* slot can be filled with a quantifier rather than a number. Any image interpretation will provide information which can be used to constrain this quantifier (see Section 5 for an example of how this comes about).

2.3. Restriction nodes and specialization

From the forgoing discussion it should be clear that given a volumetric model which includes quantifiers in various of its slots, different sets of constraints on those quantifiers define different classes of models. We organize sets of constraints using units of class *restriction* as nodes in a directed graph called the *restriction graph*.

A *restriction* unit has a *constraint* slot filled by a set of algebraic constraints on quantifiers. The constraints used earlier in this section are typical examples, although they are reduced to a normal form described in Section 3.3.1. A set of constraints on n quantifiers defines a subset of n-dimensional Euclidean space. It is the set of substitutions for the quantifiers which satisfy the given set of constraints. That set may be empty. We call this set the satisfying set of the restriction node. Set inclusion on the satisfying sets provides a natural partial order on restriction nodes, defining a distributive lattice on them. The lattice meet operation (∧) is used during image interpretation (see Section 5). Arcs of the restriction graph must be directed from a less restrictive node (a larger satisfying set) to a more restrictive node (a smaller satisfying set). Restriction-nodes keep track of the arc relations in which they participate via *suprema* and *infima* slots which are filled with lists of sources and destinations of incoming and outgoing arcs respectively. It is permissible that comparable restriction nodes do not have an explicit arc indicating that fact. In fact the restriction graph is just that part of the restriction lattice which has been computed.

A restriction graph always includes a *base-restriction* node, which has an empty set of constraints, and is thus the least restrictive node in the graph. Every other node in the graph must be an explicitly indicated infimum of another restriction node.

The user specifies part of the restriction graph to the system. Other parts are added by ACRONYM while carrying out image understanding tasks. By contrast the object graph is completely specified by the user, perhaps from a CAD data-base, and remains static during image interpretation. Eventually we plan to build from examples, using techniques of Nevatia and Binford [39].

Restriction nodes have *type* and *specialization-of* slots. In nodes specified by the user the *type* slot is filled with the atom *model-specialization* and the *specialization-of* slot with an object node from the object graph.

A restriction node specified by the user represents an object class; those objects which have the volumetric structure modelled by the object in the *specialization-of* slot subject to the constraints associated with the restriction node.

Thus the arcs of the subgraph defined by the user specify object class specialization. The arcs added later by ACRONYM also indicate specialization, but of a slightly different nature. They can specialize a model for case analysis during prediction (see Section 5.1), or they can indicate specialization implied for a particular instance of the model by a hypothesized match with an image feature or features (see Section 5.2).

Fig. 2.6 is a typical example of the portion of the restriction graph which the user might specify. The constraints associated with the node *generic-electric-motor* would be those described in the previous sections. The *motor-with-base* node includes the additional constraints

$$\text{BASE-QUANTITY} \quad = 1,$$
$$\text{FLANGE-QUANTITY} = 0,$$

while the *motor-with-flanges* node has

$$\text{BASE-QUANTITY} \quad \quad = 0,$$
$$3 \leqslant \text{FLANGE-QUANTITY} \leqslant 6.$$

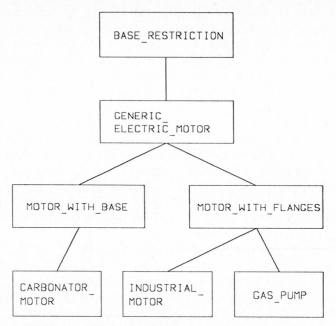

FIG. 2.6. Part of the restriction graph: a model class hierarchy defined by the user.

Of course additional constraints on quantifiers determining size, and perhaps there relationships to say the structure determining quantifier FLANGE-QUANTITY might be included at these restriction nodes.

Additional constraints specialize the subclasses of electric motors further to particular functional classes (these classes are taken from [1]), namely *industrial-motor*, *carbonator-motor* and *gas-pump*. Further constraints on these three classes were added to restrict each quantifier to specific values in order to produce Fig. 2.4, which shows instances of the three classes of motor in left to right order.

The specialization mechanism we have described here relies on complete sharing of the volumetric description amongst all its specializations. There are never multiple copies of fragments of the volume model. The specialization information is in a domain orthogonal to the underlying representation. It is therefore compact. More importantly, during image interpretation we will see that when an instance of a superclass has been identified it is rather easy to check whether it happens to also be an instance of a more specialized class. Instead of it being necessary to recompute image to model correspondences for the specialized model, we simply take the meet of the specialization restriction node with a restriction node produced in the original interpretation. If the resultant restriction node has a non-empty satisfying set, then the perceived object is also a instance of the subclass. Section 5 describes this in more detail.

3. Constraint Manipulation

In this paper we propose a number of refined or new techniques to be used in understanding what in a three dimensional world produces a given image. These include volumetric representation of generic classes of three dimensional objects, concise representation of generic spatial relationships, geometric reasoning about uncertain situations, generic prediction of appearance of objects, and use of information from matches of predicted and discovered, from goal-directed search, image features to gain three dimensional knowledge of what is in the world. In ACRONYM we tie all these pieces together by using systems of symbolic constraints. We do not solve such systems, but rather propagate their implications both downward during prediction and upward during interpretation. In our current implementation those constraints are algebraic inequalities over a set of variables (quantifiers). Our methods propagate these nonlinear constraints and handles them algebraically, rather than restoring to numerical approximations and tradition numerical methods for solution.

In this section we describe some implementation-independent requirements for a 'constraint manipulation system' (a CMS) in an ACRONYM-like system, and then the particular system which we have implemented and use.

Systems of algebraic constraints have arisen in a number of domains of artificial intelligence research.

Bobrow [13] used algebraic problems stated in English as a domain for an early natural language understanding system. The proof of understanding was to find a correct solution to the algebraic constraints implied by the English sentences. The domain was restricted to those sentences which could be represented as single linear equations and for which constraint problems could always be solved by simple linear algebra.

Fikes [20] developed a heuristic problem-solving program, where problems were described to the system in a nondeterministic programming language. The constraints were a mixture of algebraic relations and set inclusion statements over finite sets of integers. Fikes could thus solve constraint systems by backtracking, although he included a number of heuristic constraint propagation techniques to prune the search space.

A common source of algebraic constraint systems is in systems for computer aided design of electronic circuits. Stallman and Sussman [46] and de Kleer and Sussman [27] describe systems for analysis and synthesis of circuits respectively. In each case, systems of constraints are solved by using domain knowledge to order the examination of constraints, and propagate maximal information from one to the next. An algebraic simplifier is able to reduce these guided constraints to simple sets of (perhaps nonlinear) constraints which can be solved by well-known numeric methods. The original constraints usually form too large a system to be solved in this way.

Borning [15] describes an interactive environment for building simulations of things such as electrical circuits, constrained plane geometrical objects, and simple civil engineering models. Algebraic constraints are used to specify the relations to be maintained in the simulation. Borning uses the constraint propagation technique described above, along with the dual method of propagating degrees of freedom among variables. When all else fails he uses a relaxation technique which first approximates the constraints with linear equations, then uses least-mean-squares fit to guide the relaxation.

We have two main requirements for our CMS. First, we want to decide (partially, see below) whether a set of constraints is satisfiable. This is a weaker requirement than asking that the CMS provide a solution for a set of constraints when one exists, such as is done by the previously described systems. We are not interested in an actual solution (there may be many), but rather in its existence. Second, we use the CMS to estimate bounds on algebraic expressions on quantifiers over the satisfying set of values for the quantifiers. This is quite different from the tasks required of other CMS's.

3.1. Requirements for a CMS

In Section 2.3 we noted that a set of constraints on n quantifiers defines a subset of n-dimensional Euclidean space corresponding to all possible sets of substitutions for the quantifiers such that all the constraints are simultaneously satisfied. Given a set S of constraints we will write the satisfying set as C_S. We will also interchangeably use sets of constraints and restriction nodes, as in general instances of each are associated with unique instances of the other.

The algorithms presented in the remainder of this paper use the constraint manipulation system in three ways. In decreasing order of importance it would be ideal if the CMS could:

(I1) Given S decide whether or not C_S is empty.

(I2) Given satisfiable S and an expression E over quantifiers constrained by S compute the supremum and infimum of values achieved by E over the set of substitutions C_S.

(I3) Given constraint sets S and R calculate a constraint set T such that $C_T = C_S \cap C_R$; i.e. in the lattice defined in section 2.3, $T = S \wedge R$.

If the constraints were always linear in the quantifiers, then it would not be hard to construct a CMS to behave as required, based on the simplex method. See Section 3.3 for further details. (Clearly (I3) can be simply achieved by letting $T = S \cup R$.)

However, the algorithms to be described use the CMS as a pruning tool, in searches for invariant predictions and for interpretations. Imperfect pruning does not necessarily lead to failure of the algorithms. It may lead to an increase in the portion of the search space which must be examined. If the pruning is very poor, the algorithms may fail to find predictions and interpretations for lack of storage space and time.

We revise the above requirements to those actually required by the prediction and interpretation algorithms, independent of the heuristic power which is required for efficient operation of those algorithms.

(A1) Given S, partially decide whether or not C_S is empty; i.e. if C_S is non-empty, return "don't know", and if C_S is empty return either "empty" or "don't know". Conversely this can be stated as if the CMS can prove that S is unsatisfiable, it should indicate so, otherwise indicate that it may be satisfiable.

(A2) Given satisfiable S and an expression E over quantifiers constrained by S, compute an upper bound on the supremum and a lower bound on the infimum of values achieved by E over the set of substitutions C_S; i.e. compute l and u (numbers, or $\pm\infty$) such that

$$l \leq \inf_{C_S} E \leq \sup_{C_S} E \leq u.$$

(A3) Given constraint sets S and R calculate a constraint set T such that

$$(C_S \cap C_R) \subseteq C_T \subseteq (C_S \cup C_R).$$

Note that for T derived from S and R as in (A3), if C_T is empty, then so is $C_S \cap C_R$ (which is equal to $C_{S \cup R}$). At first sight it may seem strange that a straightforward requirement such as (I3) be relaxed to that of (A3). First, since the prediction and interpretation algorithms can operate under (A3), it is only a search efficiency consideration in deciding to settle for the weaker requirement. Second, it may be that the CMS works better on sets of constraints in some particular form. It may not be the case that if S and R have that form, then necessarily so will $T = S \cup R$.

While not strictly necessary it is also desirable that the CMS be monotonic, where we define monotonicity as follows. If T is a constraint set derived from S and R as in (A3), and in particular if $T \supseteq S$, then:

(M1) If the CMS decides S is unsatisfiable, then it also decides that T is unsatisfiable.

(M2) For an expression E, if l_S and u_S are the bounds on E over S calculated as in (A2), l_T and u_T the bounds over T similarly calculated, and both C_S and C_T are non-empty, then

$$l_S \leq l_T \leq u_T \leq u_S.$$

In Section 3.3 we describe the CMS which we have implemented to meet these requirements. It is capable of doing so for a wide class of nonlinear constraints, and it is monotonic.

3.2. Algebraic simplification

We digress briefly to discuss some issues involved in algebraic simplification and the idea of reducing all algebraic expressions to a canonical symbolic form. Any algebraic constraint manipulation system needs a simplifier to make use of the results of formal manipulations of expressions.

De Kleer and Sussman [27] describe their experience with an algebraic simplification system which mapped all algebraically equivalent expressions into a canonical form as the ratio of two relatively prime multivariate polynomials. Each variable has a global priority used to determine the main variables of the polynomials and other orderings recursively. They point out that the canonical form is sometimes not compact, and the size can vary greatly if the variables are globally reordered. More importantly, they discovered the algebraic manipulator spent most of its time and space calculating greatest common divisors (GCD's) of polynomials. When their circuit synthesis system failed due to lack of storage, it was always because of intermediate requirements of a single GCD calculation, whose solution was actually quite small. They point out that their system is forced into doing much more complex manipulations that would ever be attempted by a human engineer.

The solution to this problem is to have a system which uses a simplifier which can handle more complex cases than a single canonical form. Furthermore, the system should be at least mildly intelligent in what it requests of the simplifier. Lastly, it would be advantageous if the higher level system were robust in the following sense. Suppose the simplifier returns a complex expression which is really equal to 0 (since we are not insisting on a canonical form, the simplifier may not have discovered this). Suppose further that the higher level system eventually has to abandon that expression because it is greater than some complexity bound. A robust system's outward behavior would not necessarily be affected by such failure, as it would possibly find some other approach to take. The algorithms to be described in Section 5 for prediction and interpretation have some of this flavor.

3.2.1. ACRONYM's algebraic simplifier

Our particular algebraic simplifier treats the symbols ∞ and $-\infty$ in the same way as numbers, and we will include them when we refer to numeric expressions. The simplifier propagates them through operators such as $+$, $\times$, max, min, etc., where such propagations are well defined.

The simplifier has special knowledge about how to handle $+$, $-$, $\times$, $/$, max and min (other functions such as sin and cos are treated purely syntactically and no trigonomeric identities are used). The CMS we use makes heavy use of expressions involving max and min. The expressions representable cannot even be tested for equality syntactically. For instance the expression $A \max(B, C)$ is equal to max (AB, AC) if the expression A is positive, but equal to min (AB, AC) if A is negative. Thus a syntactic canonical form is not possible. We have not tried to develop a semantic canonical form, but instead have increased the interaction between the simplifier and the constraint manipulation system which uses it. Of course, inclusion of sin and cos makes the problem of simplification to a canonical form even more difficult.

The exact details of the standard form produced by the simplifier are not important. For the purpose of following the explanation of the constraint manipulation system given in Section 3.3, it is sufficient to note that all instances of '−' are removed (multiplication by −1 is used where necessary), and quotients always have a numerator of 1. In general, multiplication is distributed over addition, and addition is distributed over max and min as are multiplication and division, where possible.

The correctness of distributing division over max and min depends on the original arguments to those functions (unlike the multiplication case which depends only on properties of the term being distributed, as in the example above). For instance the simplification

$$\frac{1}{\min(A, B)} = \max\left(\frac{1}{A}, \frac{1}{B}\right)$$

cannot be made when A and B are of different signs. If their signs cannot be determined in advance therefore, the simplification should not be made. When invoked by the CMS, however, our simplifier will not return an expression having the form of the left of the above equation; doing so can lead to non-monotonicity of the system as described in point (M2) of Section 3.1. Instead it returns expressions which may not be equal to the supplied expression. For instance, given the expression on the left above, the simplifier is guaranteed to return an expression smaller or equal. Since such an expression can only arise as a lower bound on some quantity (see Section 3.3.2), this 'simplification' results in at worst a weaker bound. For instance, given the expression

$$\frac{1}{\min(A, B, C, D)},$$

the simplifier interacts with the CMS to try to determine the sign of the expressions A, B, C and D using a method described in Section 3.3.1. Suppose it determines that A and C are strictly negative, D is strictly positive, and the CMS cannot determine the sign of expression B. Then the simplifier will return the possibly smaller expression

$$\max\left(\frac{1}{A}, \frac{1}{C}\right).$$

If the original expression had been

$$\frac{1}{\max(A, B, C, D)},$$

then given the same information about the signs of subexpressions, the simplifier would return the possibly larger expression

$$\frac{1}{D}.$$

Since such an expression could only arise as an upper bound, the result is merely a weaker bound.

Finally we note that every term in a simplified expression is invariant when simplified by the simplifier.

3.3. A particular CMS

The general requirements we have stated for a CMS can be satisfied by the well-known linear programming simplex method in the case that all the constraints are linear. Finding whether a set of constraints is satisfiable is the first step of simplex—determining whether there is a feasible solution. Finding a bound on an expression is referred to as maximizing, or minimizing, a linear objective function. By the nature of the simplex method, it seems unlikely that it can be extended to nonlinear cases. We have already seen an example of a nonlinear constraint arising in model definition in Section 2.2.1. Nonlinear constraints are also regularly generated in image interpretation as will be seen in Section 5.

The CMS we have implemented is based on another method which solves linear programming problems. This is the 'SUP–INF' method, developed originally by Bledsoe [11, 12] and later improved by Shostak [42]. They developed it as part of a method for determining the validity of universally quantified logical formulas on linear integer expressions. These formulas often arise in program verification systems.

We have taken the linear method described by Shostak and extended it in a fairly natural way to handle certain nonlinear cases. We have integrated a method of bounding difficult satisfying sets by n-space rectangloids, when straightforward extensions to the method fail or are not applicable. This additional method was the major part of an earlier attempt of ours to build a CMS. By itself it weakly meets the requirements of the previous section, and may be adequate for some interpretation tasks, where fine distinctions need not be drawn and where structural considerations (see Section 5) remove most ambiguities.

3.3.1. *A normal form for constraints*

Algebraic constraints are supplied to the CMS in a variety of forms. A set of given constraints are incorporated into a consistent normal form; an implicit conjunction over a set of inequalities using the relation ' $\leq$ ' where at least one side is a single variable and the other side consists of numbers, variables and the operators +, / with numerator 1, ×, sin and cos. Furthermore every such constraint derivable from the supplied constraint is merged into the constraint set. Much of the work is done directly by the algebraic simplifier.

Constraint sets are actually attached to restriction nodes in our implementation. Constraints in the normal form are grouped into subsets, determined by the variable which appears alone on one side of the inequality. Constraints with single variables on both sides appear twice, once in each subset—for example $a \leq b$ is associated both with variable a and variable b.

A new constraint is split into one or more inequalities. Constraints involving an equality are split into two inequalities: $A = B$ becomes $A \leq B$ and $A \geq B$. Thus for instance the constraint $x = y$ eventually becomes four inequalities: $y \leq x$ and $x \leq y$ which are associated with x, and $x \leq y$ and $y \leq x$ which are associated with y. A constraint such as $A \in [B, C]$ where A, B and C are expressions, can similarly be broken into two inequalities. The operators max and min are removed, and equivalent constraints derived where possible (if not possible, then the constraint is discarded, and if externally generated, the user is warned; there should never be such constraints generated internally). Thus for instance $\max(A, B) \leq \min(C, D)$ becomes the four constraints $A \leq C$, $A \leq D$, $B \leq C$ and $B \leq D$.

Next the constraints are 'solved' for each variable which occurs in them; i.e. each variable is isolated on one side of the inequality. Since inequalities are involved, the signs of variables and expressions are important for these solutions. Sometimes the signs cannot be determined but often they can be deduced simply from explicit numeric bounds on variables given in earlier constraints (see the discussion of *parity* below). Finally inequalities using ' $\geq$ ' are converted to use ' $\leq$ '.

For example, given prior constraints of $y \leq -1$ and $x \geq 0$, the addition of constraint $x/y \leq \min(-100, 200 - z)$ generates the following set of constraints:

$$
\begin{aligned}
0 &\leq x, & x &\leq \infty, \\
-100y &\leq x, \\
200y - yz &\leq x, \\
-\infty &\leq y, & y &\leq -1, \\
-x/100 &\leq y, \\
\frac{1}{200/x - z/x} &\leq y, \\
-\infty &\leq z, & z &\leq \infty, \\
& & z &\leq 200 - x/y.
\end{aligned}
$$

Constraint sets generated by the CMS always contain single numeric upper and lower bounds on each variable—defaulted to ∞ or $-\infty$ if nothing more definite is known. If a new numeric bound is added for some variable, it is compared to the current bound (since they are both numeric or ∞, or $-\infty$ they are comparable), and the tighter bound is used.

Constraint sets are accessed by two pairs of functions. Given a set of constraints S and a variable v, $\text{HIVAL}_S(v)$ and $\text{LOVAL}_S(v)$ return the numeric upper and lower bounds respectively that are represented explicitly in S. For instance, given the example set E of constraints above, $\text{HIVAL}_E(x)$ return ∞ and $\text{LOVAL}_E(x)$ returns 0. (The CMS using SUP defined below, is able to determine that 100 is the largest value x can have and still satisfy all the constraints in E.)

More generally, the constraint sets are accessed via the functions UPPER and LOWER which return the symbolic upper and lower bounds on a variable, represented explicitly in the constraint set. $UPPER_S(v)$ constructs an expression which applies min to the set of upper bounds on x appearing explicitly in S. The algebraic simplifier SIMP is applied and the simplified expression returned. Similarly $LOWER_S(v)$ returns the symbolic max of the explicit lower bounds. Thus, for instance $LOWER_E(x)$ returns $\max(0, -100y, 200y - yz)$, while $UPPER_E(z)$ constructs $\min(\infty, 200 - x/y)$ which gets simplified to $200 - x/y$. These definitions of UPPER and LOWER closely follow those used by Bledsoe [11] and Shostak [42]. They did not use HIVAL and LOVAL.

We digress briefly to explain an important use of HIVAL and LOVAL. They are used by the algebraic simplifier to try to determine whether an expression is always nonnegative (we will loosely refer to this as positive) or always negative. We call this information the *parity* of an expression. If $LOVAL_S(v)$ and $HIVAL_S(v)$ have the same sign for a variable v, then v has a parity determined by the sign. If the lower and upper numeric bounds on v have different signs, then we say v has unknown parity. A few simple rules are used to try to determine the parity of more complex expressions. For instance the sum or product of two terms with the same known parity shares that parity. The inverse of a term with known parity has that same parity. More complex rules are possible—we have not used them.

We return now to producing a normal form for constraint sets. As symbolic bounds are added, an attempt is made to compare them to existing bounds. This is done by symbolically subtracting the new bound from each of the old, simplifying the resulting expressions and applying the parity determining function. Whenever a parity for the difference can be found, the bounds are comparable over the ranges of variables given by HIVAL and LOVAL, and the stronger bound can be determined from that parity.

These techniques can be used to meet requirement (A3) of Section 3.1. In fact they also meet the ideal requirement (I3), but they do more than merely form the union of constraint sets. Instead an equivalent set of constraints is produced which allows for efficient operation of the bounding algorithms described in the next section.

3.3.2. *Bounding algorithms*

In this section we describe algorithms used to estimate upper and lower bounds on expressions over satisfying sets of constraint sets. They satisfy the requirements of (A2) of Section 3.1. They are monotonic also. Our partial decision procedure is based on these algorithms (see Section 3.3.3).

The major algorithms SUP, SUPP and SUPPP are described in Figs. 3.1, 3.2 and 3.3 respectively. There are three similarly defined algorithms INF, INFF

Algorithm $\text{SUP}_S(J, H)$

IF	ACTION	RETURN
1. J is a number		J
2. J is a variable		
2.1 $J \in H$		J
2.2 $\text{SUP}_S(J, H)$ is already on the stack		$\text{HIVAL}_S(J)$
2.3 $J \not\in H$	Let $A \leftarrow \text{UPPER}_S(J)$ $B \leftarrow \text{SUP}_S(A, H \bigcup \{J\})$	$\text{SUPP}_S(J, \text{SIMP}(B), H)$
3. $J = \text{"}rA\text{"}$ where r is a number		
3.1 $r < 0$	Let $B \leftarrow \text{INF}_S(A, H)$	$\text{"}rB\text{"}$
3.2 $r \geq 0$	Let $B \leftarrow \text{SUP}_S(A, H)$	$\text{"}rB\text{"}$
4. $J = \text{"}rv + A\text{"}$ where r is a number, v a variable	Let $B \leftarrow \text{SUP}_S(A, H \bigcup \{v\})$	
4.1 v occurs in B	Let $C \leftarrow \text{SIMP}(\text{"}rv + B\text{"})$	$\text{SUP}_S(C, H)$
4.2 v does not occur in B	Let $C \leftarrow \text{SUP}_S(\text{"}rv\text{"}, H)$	$\text{"}C + B\text{"}$
5. $J = \text{"}\min(A, B)\text{"}$	Let $C \leftarrow \text{SUP}_S(A, H)$ $D \leftarrow \text{SUP}_S(B, H)$	$\text{"}\min(C, D)\text{"}$
6. $J = \text{"}A + B\text{"}$	Let $C \leftarrow \text{SUP}_S(A, H)$ $D \leftarrow \text{SUP}_S(B, H)$	$\text{"}C + D\text{"}$
7. $J = \text{"}\sin(A)\text{"}$		$\text{TRIG}_S(A, \text{'}\sin, \text{'SUP})$
8. $J = \text{"}\cos(A)\text{"}$		$\text{TRIG}_S(A, \text{'}\cos, \text{'SUP})$
9. $J = \text{"}1/A\text{"}$		
9.1 A has known parity	Let $B \leftarrow \text{INF}_S(A, H)$	$\text{"}1/B\text{"}$
9.2 A has unknown parity	Let $b \leftarrow \text{INF}_S(A, \emptyset)$ $c \leftarrow \text{SUP}_S(A, \emptyset)$	
9.2.1 $b > c$		$-\infty$
9.2.2 $bc > 0$		$\text{"}1/b\text{"}$
9.2.3 $bc \leq 0$		∞
10. $J = \text{"}v^n A\text{"}$ where v is a variable with known parity, not occurring in A, also of known parity		
10.1 A, J same parity	Let $B \leftarrow \text{SUP}_S(A, H \bigcup \{v\})$	
10.2 A, J opp. parity	Let $B \leftarrow \text{INF}_S(A, H \bigcup \{v\})$	
10.n.1 v occurs in B	Let $C \leftarrow \text{SIMP}(\text{"}v^n B\text{"})$	$\text{SUP}_S(C, H)$
10.n.2 v, J same parity	Let $C \leftarrow \text{SUP}_S(v, H)$	$\text{"}C^n B\text{"}$
10.n.3 v, J opp. parity	Let $C \leftarrow \text{INF}_S(v, H)$	$\text{"}C^n B\text{"}$

FIG. 3.1 (Continued overleaf).

Algorithm SUP cont.

I_F	A_CTION	R_ETURN
11. $J = $ "AB" where A and B have known parity		
11.1 A, J same parity	Let $C \leftarrow \text{SUP}_S(A, H)$	
11.2 A, J opp. parity	Let $C \leftarrow \text{INF}_S(A, H)$	
11.n.1 B, J same parity	Let $D \leftarrow \text{SUP}_S(B, H)$	"CD"
11.n.2 B, J opp. parity	Let $D \leftarrow \text{INF}_S(B, H)$	"CD"
12. $J = $ "AB" where A has known parity, B has unknown	Let $c \leftarrow \text{INF}_S(B, \emptyset)$ $d \leftarrow \text{SUP}_S(B, \emptyset)$	
12.1 $0 \leq c$	Let $E \leftarrow \text{SUP}_S(A, H)$	
12.1.1 A positive		"dE"
12.1.2 A negative		"cE"
12.2 $d < 0$	Let $E \leftarrow \text{INF}_S(A, H)$	
12.2.1 A positive		"dE"
12.2.2 A negative		"cE"
12.3 $0 \leq d$		
12.3.1 A positive	Let $E \leftarrow \text{SUP}_S(A, H)$	"dE"
12.3.2 A negative	Let $E \leftarrow \text{INF}_S(A, H)$	"cE"
13. $J = $ "AB" where A and B have unknown parity	Let $c \leftarrow \text{INF}_S(A, \emptyset)$ $d \leftarrow \text{SUP}_S(A, \emptyset)$ $e \leftarrow \text{INF}_S(B, \emptyset)$ $f \leftarrow \text{SUP}_S(B, \emptyset)$	
13.1 $c > d$		$-\infty$
13.2 $e > f$		$-\infty$
13.3		$\max(ce, cf, de, df)$
14.		$\text{SUPPP}_S(J, H)$

INF is defined exactly symmetrically to SUP above, with the following textual substitutions: SUP → INF, INF → SUP, SUPP → INFF, HIVAL → LOVAL, UPPER → LOWER, min → max, max → min, $\infty \to -\infty$ and $-\infty \to \infty$, except in the *action* columns of 12.1, 12.2 and 12.3, SUP and INF are not changed, while the inequalities in those *if* columns are reversed.

F_IG. 3.1. Definition of algorithm SUP and lexical changes needed to define algorithm INF.

and INFFF whose definitions can be derived from the others by simple textual substitutions. The necessary substitutions for each algorithm are described in the captions of the appropriate figures.

The double quote marks around expressions in the figures mean that the values of variables within their range should be substituted into the expression, but no evaluation should occur. Thus, for instance, if the value of variable A is

Algorithm $\text{SUPP}_S(x, Y, H)$

IF	ACTION	RETURN
1. x does not occur in Y		Y
2. $x = Y$		∞
3. $Y = \text{``min}(A, B)\text{''}$	Let $C \leftarrow \text{SUPP}_S(x, A, H)$ $D \leftarrow \text{SUPP}_S(x, B, H)$	$\text{``min}(C, D)\text{''}$
4. $Y = \text{``}bx + C\text{''}$ where b is a number, x does **not** occur in C		
4.1 $b > 1$		∞
4.2 $b < 1$		$\text{``}C/(1 -- b)\text{''}$
4.3 $b = 1$		
4.3.1 C has unknown parity		∞
4.3.2 $C < 0$		$-\infty$
4.3.3 $C \geq 0$		∞
5.		$\text{SUPPP}_S(Y, H)$

INFF is defined exactly symmetrically to SUPP above, with the following textual substitutions: SUPP $\rightarrow$ INFF, SUPPP $\rightarrow$ INFFF, min $\rightarrow$ max, $\infty \rightarrow -\infty$ and $-\infty \rightarrow \infty$. Also the inequalities in 4.3.2 and 4.3.3 are reversed.

FIG. 3.2. Definition of algorithm SUPP and lexical changes needed to define algorithm INFF.

symbol x, and that of B is the symbolic expression $y + 3 - x$, then the value of "$A + B$" is $x + y + 3 - x$. In general in the definitions of the algorithms the lower case variables have single numbers or symbols as their values while upper case letters may also have complete expressions as their values. The function SIMP refers to the algebraic simplifier described in Section 3.2.1 above. More liberal use of SIMP does not affect the correctness of the algorithms, it merely decreases efficiency. The function TRIG is described in detail below.

Each algorithm is described as a table of condition-action-return triples. This follows the notation used by Bledsoe [11] to describe the first version of these procedures. Our original implementation of these algorithms was in the production rule system that is used for prediction and interpretation within ACRONYM. Each step in the decision table was represented as a production rule. However, the algorithms are highly recursive, and the overhead of 'procedure' invocation for production rules made the algorithms very slow. We rewrote the algorithms directly in MACLISP, gaining significant speedups. However, even in the LISP environment, using different options for the code for procedure,

Algorithm SUPPP$_S(Y, H)$

IF	ACTION	RETURN
1. Y is a number		Y
2. Y is a variable		
2.1 $Y \in H$		Y
2.2 $Y \notin H$		HIVAL$_S(Y)$
3. $Y = "A + B"$	Let $C \leftarrow$ SUPPP$_S(A, H)$	
	$D \leftarrow$ SUPPP$_S(B, H)$	$"C + D"$
4. $Y = "\min(A, B)"$	Let $C \leftarrow$ SUPPP$_S(A, H)$	
	$D \leftarrow$ SUPPP$_S(B, H)$	$"\min(C, D)"$
5. $Y = "1/A"$ where A has		
known parity	Let $B \leftarrow$ INFFF$_S(A, H)$	$"1/B"$
6. $Y = "AB"$ where A and B have		
known parity		
6.1 Y, A same parity	Let $C \leftarrow$ SUPPP$_S(A, H)$	
6.2 Y, A opp. parity	Let $C \leftarrow$ INFFF$_S(A, H)$	
6.n.1 Y, B same parity	Let $D \leftarrow$ SUPPP$_S(B, H)$	$"CD"$
6.n.2 Y, B opp. parity	Let $D \leftarrow$ INFFF$_S(B, H)$	$"CD"$
7.		∞

INFFF is defined exactly symmetrically to SUPPP above, with the following textual substitutions: SUPPP $\rightarrow$ INFFF, INFFF $\rightarrow$ SUPPP, HIVAL $\rightarrow$ LOVAL, min $\rightarrow$ max and $\infty \rightarrow -\infty$.

FIG. 3.3. Definition of algorithm SUPPP and lexical changes needed to define algorithm INFFF.

invocation can change the running time of the algorithms by a factor of four. This gives some indication of just how recursion-intensive these algorithms are.

Algorithms SUP, INF, SUPP and INFF are extensions to algorithms of the same names given by Shostak [42]. Algorithms SUPPP and INFFF are new (as is algorithm TRIG). The first five steps of our SUP and INF, minus step 2.2, comprise Shostak's SUP and INF. Our additional steps (6–13) handle non-linearities. Our algorithms SUPP and INFF are identical to those of Shostak, with the addition of a final step which invokes SUPPP or INFFF in the respective cases. For a set of linear constraints and a linear expression to bound, our algorithms behave identically to those of Shostak.

Given a set of constraints S and an expression E, SUP$_S(E, \emptyset)$ produces an upper bound on the values achieved by E over the satisfying set of S, and INF$_S(E, \emptyset)$ a lower bound.

The following descriptions give an intuitive feel for what each of algorithms SUP, SUPP and SUPPP compute. Dual statements hold for INF, INFF and INFFF, respectively. S is always a set of constraints and H a set of variables (i.e. quantifiers) which occur in S.

$SUP_S(J, H)$: were J is a simplified (by SIMP) expression in variables constrained by S, returns an expression E in variables in H. In particular if $H = \emptyset$, the SUP returns a number. In general, if numerical values are assigned to variables in H and E evaluated for those assignments, then its value is an upper bound on the value achievable by expression J over the assignments in the satisfying set of S which have the same assignments as fixed for the variables in H.

$SUPP_S(x, Y, H)$: where x is a variable, x is not in H, and Y is a simplified expression in variables in $H \cup \{x\}$, returns an upper bound for x, which is an expression in variables in H and is computed by 'solving' $x \leq Y$, e.g. solving $x \leq 9 - 2x$ yields an upper bound of 3 for x.

$SUPPP_S(Y, H)$: where Y is a simplified expression, returns an upper bound on Y, as does SUP, but in general the bounds are weaker than those of SUP. Essentially SUP uses SUPPP when it hasn't got specific methods to handle Y.

Algorithm TRIG is called from both SUP and INF. It is invoked with three arguments, the first an expression, the second the symbol 'sin' or 'cos' and the third is the symbol SUP or INF. Implicitly it has a fourth argument S which is the constraint set. It takes lower and upper bounds on A using $INF_S(A, \emptyset)$ and $SUP_S(A, \emptyset)$ and then finds the indicated bound on the indicated trigonometric function over that interval.

Consider the example of Fig. 3.4. The given constraints are $a \geq 2$, $b \geq 1$ and $ab \leq 4$. These are normalized by the procedure described in Section 3.3.1. Then a trace of $SUP_S(a, \emptyset)$ is shown. It eventually returns 4 as an upper bound for a over the satisfying set C_S of constraint set S. In fact 4 is the maximum value which a can achieve on C_S.

Fig. 3.5 demonstrates finding an upper bound for a^2b, by invoking $SUP_S(a^2b, \emptyset)$ which returns 16. Again 16 is also the maximum value which can be achieved by a^2b over the satisfying set of S. In general, SUP will not return the maximum value for an expression, merely an upper bound. Shostak [42] gives an example of a linear constraint set and a linear expression to bound where it fails to return the maximum.

Bledsoe [11] and Shostak [42] proved a number of properties of the algorithms SUP and INF for sets of linear constraints and linear expressions to be bound. The properties of interest to us are:

(P1) The algorithms terminate.

(P2) The algorithms return upper and lower bounds on expressions.

(P3) When the expression is a variable and the auxiliary set (H in our notation) is empty, the algorithms return a maximum and minimum (including $\pm\infty$ when appropriate).

We can extend the proofs of (P1) and (P2) (due to Bledsoe [11]) to our extended algorithms.

First note that algorithms SUPPP and INFFF terminate, since all recursive calls reduce the number of symbols in their first argument and they exit simply

Given constraints $a \geq 2$, $b \geq 1$ and $ab \leq 4$ the normalization procedure produces as set S the constraints:

$$2 \leq a \qquad\qquad\qquad a \leq 4 \times 1/b$$
$$1 \leq b \qquad\qquad\qquad b \leq 4 \times 1/a$$

$\text{SUP}_S(a, \emptyset) =$
$\qquad \text{SUPP}_S(a, \text{SIMP}(\text{SUP}_S(\text{UPPER}_S(a), \{a\})), \emptyset)$ Step 2.3
$\qquad = \text{SUPP}_S(a, \text{SIMP}(\text{SUP}_S(\min(4, 4 \times 1/b), \{a\})), \emptyset)$
$\qquad = \text{SUPP}_S(a, \text{SIMP}(\min(\text{SUP}_S(4, \{a\}), \text{SUP}_S(4 \times 1/b, \{a\}))), \emptyset)$ Step 5
$\qquad\qquad \text{SUP}_S(4, \{a\}) = 4$ Step 1
$\qquad\qquad \text{SUP}_S(4 \times 1/b, \{a\}) =$
$\qquad\qquad\qquad 4 \times \text{SUP}_S(1/b, \{a\})$ Step 3.2
$\qquad\qquad\qquad = 4 \times 1/\text{INF}_S(b, \{a\})$ Step 9.1
$\qquad\qquad\qquad = 4 \times 1/\text{INFF}_S(b, \text{SIMP}(\text{INF}_S(\text{LOWER}_S(b), \{a, b\})), \{a\})$ Step 2.3
$\qquad\qquad\qquad = 4 \times 1/\text{INFF}_S(b, \text{SIMP}(\text{INF}_S(1, \{a, b\})), \{a\})$
$\qquad\qquad\qquad = 4 \times 1/\text{INFF}_S(b, 1, \{a\})$ Step 1
$\qquad\qquad\qquad = 4 \times 1/1$ Step 1 of INFF
$\qquad = \text{SUPP}_S(a, \text{SIMP}(\min(4, 4 \times 1/1), \emptyset)$
$\qquad = \text{SUPP}_S(a, 4, \emptyset)$
$\qquad = 4$ Step 1 of SUPP

Fɪɢ. 3.4. Example of algorithm SUP bounding a variable over the satisfying set of a set of constraints.

when the argument is a single symbol—via steps 1 or 2. By induction they return upper and lower bounds on their first argument. Essentially the algorithms evaluate their first argument at a vertex of a rectangloid which bounds the satisfying set of S. The rectangloid is determined by the numeric upper and lower bounds in the constraint set (as determined by HIVAL, LOVAL). If a term can't be shown to achieve its extreme value at a vertex of the projection of the rectangloid into the subspace of the variables of the term, then a most pessimistic estimate is used for its value, namely $\pm\infty$.

Algorithms SUPP and INFF are identical to those of [42], except that they can take more complex arguments, in which case they invoke SUPPP and INFFF respectively. So from Bledsoe's proof and argument above, they too terminate and provide appropriate bounds. Note that the overall performance of the constraint manipulation system may be improved by including extra techniques in SUPP and INFF to solve some nonlinear inequalities, rather than passing the bounding expressions to SUPPP and INFFF in those cases.

The proof that SUP and INF terminate follows that of Bledsoe [11], and all but steps 9.2, 12 and 13 can be so covered (step 14 is covered by the arguments above for SUPPP and INFFF). The problem with these steps is that they reset the auxiliary set to be empty, so there is the danger of infinite recursion, where

$$\text{SUP}_S(a^2 b, \emptyset) =$$

Let $B = \text{SUP}_S(b, \{a\})$ Step 10.1

$= \text{SUPP}_S(b, \text{SIMP}(\text{SUP}_S(\text{UPPER}_S(b), \{b, a\})), \{a\})$ Step 2.3

$= \text{SUPP}_S(b, \text{SIMP}(\text{SUP}_S(\min(2, 4 \times 1/a), \{b, a\})), \{a\})$

$= \text{SUPP}_S(b, \text{SIMP}(\min(\text{SUP}_S(2, \{b, a\}),$

$\quad\quad\quad\quad\quad\quad \text{SUP}_S(4 \times 1/a, \{b, a\}))), \{a\})$ Step 5

$\quad\quad \text{SUP}_S(2, \{b, a\}) = 2$ Step 1

$\quad\quad \text{SUP}_S(4 \times 1/a, \{b, a\}) =$

$\quad\quad\quad 4 \times \text{SUP}_S(1/a, \{b, a\})$ Step 3.2

$\quad\quad\quad = 4 \times 1/\text{INF}_S(a, \{b, a\})$ Step 9.1

$\quad\quad\quad = 4 \times 1/a$ Step 2.1

$= \text{SUPP}_S(b, \text{SIMP}(\min(2, 4 \times 1/a)), \{a\})$

$= \text{SUPP}_S(b, \min(2, 4 \times 1/a), \{a\})$

$= \min(2, 4 \times 1/a)$ Step 1 of SUPP

$= \text{SUP}_S(\text{SIMP}(a^2 \min(2, 4 \times 1/a)), \emptyset)$ Step 10.n.1

$= \text{SUP}_S(\min(2a^2, 4a), \emptyset)$

$= \min(\text{SUP}_S(2a^2, \emptyset), \text{SUP}_S(4a, \emptyset))$ Step 5

$\quad \text{SUP}_S(2a^2, \emptyset) =$

$\quad\quad 2 \times \text{SUP}_S(a^2, \emptyset)$ Step 3.2

$\quad\quad\quad\quad \text{Let } B = \text{SUP}_S(1, \{a\})$ Step 10.1

$\quad\quad\quad\quad = 1$ Step 1

$\quad\quad = 2 \times (\text{SUP}_S(a, \emptyset))^2$ Step 10.n.2

$\quad\quad = 2 \times 4^2$ as in fig. 3.4

$\quad \text{SUP}_S(4a, \emptyset) =$

$\quad\quad 4 \times \text{SUP}_S(a, \emptyset)$ Step 3.2

$\quad\quad = 4 \times 4$ as in fig. 3.4

$= \min(2 \times 4^2, 4 \times 4)$

$= 16$

FIG. 3.5. Example of algorithm SUP bounding a nonlinear expression subject to a set of nonlinear constraints.

an identical call is made further down the computation tree. But all of these steps make recursive calls with first arguments containing fewer symbols. The only place the number of symbols can grow is step 2.3, and there the first argument is a single variable. Since there are only a finite number of pairs consisting of a variable and a subset of the variables, any infinite recursion must include an infinite recursion on some form $\text{SUP}_S(v, H)$, and similarly for INF. But step 2.2 explicitly checks for duplication of such calls on the execution stack, so step 2.3 will not be reached (not that we can't only check for duplications of calls of the form $\text{SUP}_S(v, \emptyset)$, because steps 4 and 10, besides step 2.3, can also increase the size of set H). That SUP and INF bound their first argument is a straightforward extension of the proof of Bledsoe [11].

Finally, we note that many of the recursive calls to SUP and INF are of the form $\text{SUP}_S(v, \emptyset)$ for some variable v. Each such evaluation generates a large computation tree. Therefore we have modified the algorithms to check for this case explicitly. The first time such a call is made for a given set S, the result is compared to the numeric bound on the variable v amongst the constraints in S

(as indexed with function HIVAL—recall the normal form for constraint sets). If the calculated bound is better, then S is changed to reflect this. Subsequent invocations of $SUP_S(v, \emptyset)$ on an unchanged S simply use HIVAL to retrieve the previously calculated result. This is similar to the notion of a memo function as described by Michie [36].

3.3.3. A partial decision procedure

We are now in a position to describe the partial decision procedure used by our CMS. It is completely analogous to that used by Bledsoe and Shostak.

If for each variable (quantifier) x, constrained by a constraint set S, it is true that

$$INF_S(``x", \emptyset) \leqslant SUP_S(``x", \emptyset),$$

then S is said to be *possibly satisfiable*, otherwise it is *definitely unsatisfiable*.

As an example suppose we change the constraint $b \geqslant 1$ to $b \geqslant 3$ in the example of Fig. 3.4. Then the bounds derived for a and b using INF and SUP are

$$2 \leqslant a \leqslant 1.333,$$
$$3 \leqslant b \leqslant 2.$$

So the decision procedure concludes that the constraints are definitely not satisfiable. Note also that for these constraints INF produces a larger lower bound for a^2b than the upper bound produced by SUP.

The soundness of the partial decision procedure follows directly from the fact that for a satisfiable set S, SUP and INF return upper and lower bounds on expressions over that set (for soundness it is not necessary that they return least upper bounds and greatest lower bounds).

However, a partial decision procedure that always returned the same result, namely that the constraint set is *possibly satisfiable* is also sound. A partial decision procedure is only interesting if it sometimes detects unsatisfiable sets of constraints. The more often it successfully detects such sets, the more interesting it is.

We do not have a good characterization of what classes of inconsistent constraints our CMS can detect. In practice we have not encountered any cases where it has failed to detect an inconsistency. We hypothesize that for sets of linear constraints our CMS is in fact a full decision procedure. We further hypothesize that for sets of constraints free of sin and cos, and where every term has known parity, our CMS is also a full decision procedure. It is possible to construct inconsistent constraints which the CMC cannot decide are unsatisfiable.

Finally it should be pointed out that the decision procedure can be augmented by checking that the intervals estimated for a quantitifier which is known to be an integer—e.g. it represents the number of some type of subparts—can be checked to see whether they include an integer. If not, the set S can be rejected as unsatisfiable.

3.3.4. *Approximating complex expressions*

After implementing the CMS described in the previous section, we realize that the functions involved had some useful applications which we had not anticipated.

Since the partial decision procedure is at least exponential in the number of symbols in the constraint set it is desirable to keep the constraint set simple when possible. Informally at least, it also seems that inclusion of expressions involving cos, sin or simply expressions of indeterminate parity is expensive, as analysis of bounds on these expressions using SUP and INF involve 'resetting' of the argument H to the empty set $\emptyset$, making the invocation tree even deeper. Thus while Taylor [48] was interested in linearizing expressions so they could be handled with the simplex method, we are interested in approximating expressions with simpler expressions, with fewer symbols and perhaps free of non-monotonic subexpressions.

The algorithms SUP and INF prove to be extremely useful for precisely this task. By invoking them with a non-empty set H of variables, expressions in just those variables in H are returned, which are respectively upper and lower bounds on the given expression over the satisfying set of the constraint set. More formally, given an expression E, a set of variables H, and a set of constraints S, then $\mathrm{INF}_S(E, H)$ and $\mathrm{SUP}_S(E, H)$ are expressions involving only variables in H, and

$$\mathrm{INF}_S(E, H) \leqslant E \leqslant \mathrm{SUP}_S(E, H)$$

is true identically over the satisfying set of S.

We give a brief, and at this point largely unmotivated, example. The following expression arises from the example used throughout in Section 4 on geometric reasoning:

$$\begin{aligned}
E = {} & 83.5 \cos(-\mathrm{PAN}) \sin(\mathrm{TILT}) + \mathrm{SH\text{-}Y} \sin(\mathrm{TILT}) \sin(-\mathrm{PAN}) \\
& - 21.875 \cos(\mathrm{TILT}) - 30 \sin(\mathrm{TILT}) \sin(-\mathrm{PAN}) \\
& - \mathrm{SH\text{-}X} \cos(-\mathrm{PAN}) \sin(\mathrm{TILT}) - \cos(\mathrm{SH\text{-}ORI} - \mathrm{PAN}) \sin(\mathrm{TILT}).
\end{aligned}$$

Given a constraint set S derived from the following given constraints:

$$\begin{aligned}
\pi/12 \leqslant {} & \mathrm{TILT} \leqslant \pi/6, \\
-\pi/12 \leqslant {} & \mathrm{PAN} \leqslant \pi/12, \\
-\infty \leqslant {} & \mathrm{SH\text{-}ORI} \leqslant \infty,
\end{aligned}$$

then $\mathrm{INF}_S(E, \{\mathrm{SH\text{-}X}, \mathrm{SH\text{-}Y}\})$ produces a lower bound of

$$-4.637 - 0.5\,\mathrm{SH\text{-}X} - 0.129\,\mathrm{SH\text{-}Y},$$

and $\mathrm{SUP}_S(E, \{\mathrm{SH\text{-}X}, \mathrm{SH\text{-}Y}\})$ gives

$$27.188 - 0.25\,\mathrm{SH\text{-}X} + 0.129\,\mathrm{SH\text{-}Y}$$

as an upper bound. The only alterations we have made to the expressions actually used and generated by the system for this example, is to reintroduce the '−' sign, reorder the terms in the sums and around the numeric constants, all to increase readability.

4. Geometric Reasoning

Geometric reasoning is making deductions about spatial relationships of objects in three dimensions, given some description of their positions, orientations and shapes. There are many straightforward, and some not straightforward, ways to calculate properties of spatial relationships numerically when situations are completely specified. Given the generic classes of objects which we model in ACRONYM and generic positions and orientations which our representation admits, purely numerical techniques are obviously inadequate. A number of other workers have faced similar problems in the area of planning manipulation tasks. We briefly compare a few of their solutions to these problems below. They can be characterized as applying analytic algebraic tools to geometry. That is the general approach that we take. We deal with more general situations, however, There are other approaches to these problems; most rely on simplifying the descriptive terms to coarse predicates. Deductive results must necessarily be similarly unrefined in nature.

Ambler and Popplestone [3] assume they are given a description of a goal state of spatial relationships between a set of objects, such as 'against' and 'fits', and describe a system for determining the relative positions and orientations of objects which satisfy these relations. The method assumes that there are at least two distinct expressions for relative positions and orientations derivable from the constraints. These are equated to give a geometric equation. They then use a simplifier for geometric expressions which can handle a subset of that of our system described below in Section 4.1. Finally they use special purpose techniques to solve the small class of simplified equations that can be produced from the problem which can be handled by the system. The solution may retain degrees of freedom.

Lozano-Pérez [30] attacks a similar problem, but with more restrictions on the relationships specifiable. He is therefore able to use simpler methods to solve cases where there are no variations allowed in parameters. He describes a method for extending these to cases where parameters can vary over an interval by propagating those intervals through the constraints. He relies on strong restrictions on the allowed class of geometric situations for this to work.

Taylor [48] tackles a problem similar to ours. He has positions and locations of objects represented as parameterized coordinate transforms, and looks for bounds on the position coordinates of objects, given constraints on the parameters. An incomplete set of rules is used to simplify transform expressions as much as possible, based on the constraints. Then, if only one rotational degree of freedom remains, the transform is expanded into explicit coordinate expressions which are linearized by assuming small errors. The simplex method is used to estimate bounds on these expressions.

McDermott [35] describes a representational scheme for meteric relations between fairly unstructured objects in a planar map. Coordinates and orientations within and between frames of reference are represented by ranges. A multi-dimensional indexing scheme (based on k-d trees) is used to answer questions involving near neighbors of objects which satisfy additional constraints. The system has mostly been used for planning paths past incompletely specified obstacles. The ACRONYM constraint manipulation system and the ACRONYM geometric simplifier described below are together able to make stronger deductions than those described by McDermott.

In the ACRONYM context we have spatial relationships among objects themselves and a camera frame, which are not specified at all directly. Typically it is necessary to combine more than ten coordinate transforms, involving four or more variables (quantifiers) to determine relative positions and orientations of coordinate frames. We have two primary requirements for our geometric reasoning system.

(i) Given an expression in many variables for a position and orientation of an object relative to the camera frame, and given a set of constraints on those variables (encapsulated in a restriction node), we wish to determine what image features that object will generate quasi-invariantly over the modelled range of variations.

(ii) Discover further constraints which can be used to split the range of variations into cases in which further quasi-invariant features can be predicted.

We use the term *image feature* to mean those parts of an image which are observable by descriptive processes. We expand on that definition in Section 5.1.

As a by-product of achieving the above objectives we also gain ways of using measurements of image features to deduce three dimensional information. We also believe that the techniques we are developing for geometric reasoning will be useful in planning manipulation tasks, based on an ACRONYM-style representation of generic spatial relationships.

Throughout this section we will use as examples the two situations shown in Fig. 4.1. These two views, with different camera geometries, are of the same electric screwdriver sitting in its holder (it is one of the tools used by the manipulator arms in our coordinated robotics experimental work station). The position is represented by the quantifier SH-X inches in the x direction of table (world) coordinates and SH-Y inches in the y direction. Its orientation is a rotation about the vertical z-axis in world coordinates of magnitude SH-ORI. The following constraints apply to the position quantifiers.

$$0 \leqslant \text{SH-X} \leqslant 24,$$

$$18 \leqslant \text{SH-Y} \leqslant 42.$$

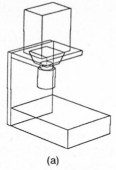
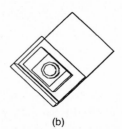

(a)   (b)

FIG. 4.1. Two views of the electric screw-driver in its holder. The left (a) is from a camera a little above the table, with variable pan and tilt. The right (b) is from a camera directly above the table, with variable pitch and roll.

The orientation SH-ORI is unconstrained.

In Fig. 4.1a the camera is at world coordinates (83.5, 30, 25), with variable pan and tilt represented by the quantifiers PAN and TILT. The following constraints apply.

$$\pi/12 \leqslant \text{TILT} \leqslant \pi/6,$$
$$-\pi/12 \leqslant \text{PAN} \leqslant \pi/12.$$

Setting TILT and PAN to zero corresponds to the camera looking along a ray parallel to, but opposite in directioon to, the world x-axis. The camera is a couple of feet above the table, tilted slightly downwards, looking at the screwdriver and its holder about five to seven feet away.

Fig. 4.1 gives a view from an overhead camera at world coordinates (24, 30, HEIGHT), where HEIGHT is a constrained quantifier (the uncertainty in the height of the camera may make this example seem a little contrived; it is meant to be illustrative in nature). The camera image plane is rotated about the y and x axes, with magnitudes represented by the quantifiers PITCH and ROLL respectively. The following constraints apply:

$$-\pi/12 \leqslant \text{PITCH} \leqslant \pi/12,$$
$$-\pi/12 \leqslant \text{ROLL} \leqslant \pi/12,$$
$$60 \leqslant \text{HEIGHT} \leqslant 84.$$

In Section 4.1 we show how to simplify large products of coordinate transforms using some identities which allow rotations to be transposed within a rotation product expression. Simplification of the coordinate transforms relating objects to each other, and the camera allows us to decide whether objects are in the field of view and what objects might be expected to occlude others. The simplified expressions are in a form which allows for prediction of invariant and quasi-invariant features. In particular we show how they can be used in the prediction of the projected two dimensional image shape objects.

4.1. Geometric simplification

The *geometric simplifier* takes a symbolic product of coordinate transforms and produces a single coordinate transform, which is a pair of expressions for a rotation and a translation, by using the following identity (recall the notation from Section 2.1).

$$(R_1, T_1) * (R_2, T_2) = (R_1 * R_2, R_1 \otimes T_2 + T_1). \qquad (4.1)$$

The rotation expression obtained is thus a product of rotations. Using distributivity of rotations over translations, the translation expression becomes a sum of terms, each of which is a product of rotations applied to a vector.

The expressions in the coordinate transform are simplified to standard *forms*. Equivalent expressions will not necessarily be reduced to the same standard expression. The non-canonical nature of the reduction methods is not due only to the fact that the algebraic simplifier they use does not produce a canonical form. It is inherent in the methods themselves. Similar arguments to those of de Kleer and Sussman [27] apply to this case also. If the mechanisms which use the simplified geometric expressions are intelligent about their use, and are robust in the face of occasional failure to identify a product of rotations as the identity, for instance, then the utility of a natural standard form, which is not necessarily canonical, far outweighs the benefits of having a canonical form which may be clumsy in expression, and may be time and space consuming to compute.

The geometric simplification mechanisms used by ACRONYM are useful because of certain inherent properties of cultural artifacts. We state some such properties here, but provide no empirical evidence for them. Suppose the objects in a human-built setting have been described by generalized cones in a 'natural' way. By that we mean that for a given generalized cone the spine (the x-axis of its coordinate system) lies along an axis of generalized translational invariance [9], and that if the cross section has an axis of generalized symmetry, then that corresponds to one of the other coordinate axes of the cone's coordinate system. Then given two mechanically coupled cones (whether attached or merely coincident in some way) frequently their coordinate systems will have a pair of parallel axes (e.g. the x-axis of one may be parallel to the z-axis of the other). Furthermore it will often be the case that there are two (and hence three) pairs of parallel axes.

One approach to geometric simplification is to turn all rotation expressions into three by three matrices involving sine and cosine terms, multiply them out and then use an algebraic simplifier. (Similar approaches use homogeneous coordinates; the same arguments apply.) We do not follow that course for two reasons. First, it means that the algebraic simplifier must search for trigonometric simplifications that are obscure in the expanded form, but obvious in the unexpanded geometric notation, both due to the abundance of the spatial relations described in the previous paragraph and due to the simple algebraic relation in axis–magnitude representation between a rotation and its inverse. Second, as we show in Section 4.2, we are able to make better use of expressions describing spatial relations as combinations of simple geometric transforms than we could make use of a single rotation and translation expression, where the axis and magnitude of the rotation are both complex trigonometric forms.

4.1.1. *Products of rotations*

Rotations of three space form a group under composition. The group is associative so it is permissible to simplify a symbolic product of rotations by collapsing adjacent ones with algebraically equal axis expressions (recall that we represent rotations as magnitudes about an axis) by adding their magnitudes. The group is not commutative, however. It is not possible to merely collect all rotations with common axis expressions. There is a slightly weaker condition on the elements of the group which allows partial use of this idea. Let a_1 and a_2 be vectors, and m_1 and m_2 be scalars. Then the following two identities are true (the proof is simple but tedious and omitted here).

$$\langle a_1, m_1 \rangle * \langle a_2, m_2 \rangle = \langle a_2, m_2 \rangle * \langle (\langle a_2, -m_2 \rangle \otimes a_1), m_1 \rangle,$$
$$\langle a_1, m_1 \rangle * \langle a_2, m_2 \rangle = \langle (\langle a_1, m_1 \rangle \otimes a_2), m_2 \rangle * \langle a_1, m_1 \rangle.$$

The geometric reasoning system of Ambler and Popplestone [3] collapses adjacent rotations sharing common axis expressions, and uses the special case of the above identities where $a_1 = \hat{x}$, $a_2 = \hat{y}$ and $m_2 = \pi$ to simplify geometric expressions.

We use a more general special case here (and the general case in parts of the system—see Section 5) to 'shift' rotations to the left and right in the product expression. However, as a rotation is shifted it leaves rotations with complex axis expressions in its wake. There is a subgroup of rotations for which these axis expresssions are no more complex than the originals. This is the group of 24 rotations which permute the positive and negative x-, y- and z-axes among themselves. When they are used with the above identities, the new axis expression is a permutation of the original axis components, perhaps with some sign changes.

Notice that these rotations are precisely the ones which relate two coordinate systems with two (or three) parallel pairs of axes; they are very common in models of human-made objects. We are particularly interested in a generating subset of this rotational subgroup. It consists of the identity rotation i, and rotations about the three coordinate axes whose magnitudes are multiples of $\pi/2$. We write them x_1, x_2, x_3, y_1, y_2, y_3, z_1, z_2 and z_3. The subscript indicates the magnitude of the rotation as a multiple of $\pi/2$. We call these ten rotations *elementary*. The fifteen other axis preserving rotations cannot be expressed as rotations about a coordinate axis, but they can be expressed as a product of at most 2 elementary rotations. Furthermore they can be pictured intuitively by someone modelling an object; so they tend to be the most common way in which users describe orientations to ACRONYM.

Since in general $\langle -a, m \rangle = \langle a, -m \rangle$, elementary rotations are closed under inverses (negation of the magnitude) and under the identities given above. For instance

$$x_3 * y_1 = y_1 * z_3, \qquad x_3 * y_1 = z_3 * x_3.$$

We call a rotation *principal* if its axis is in the direction of one of the coordinate axes. These were the other type of rotation that we mentioned above as commonly occurring in models of human-made objects. Elementary rotations map $\hat{x}$, $\hat{y}$ and $\hat{z}$ among themselves and their negations, so using the two identities we see that moving an elementary rotation past a principal rotation, either to the left or the right, leaves another principal rotation in its wake. For example

$$\langle \hat{x}, m \rangle * y_1 = y_1 * \langle \hat{z}, m \rangle, \qquad y_1 * \langle \hat{x}, m \rangle = \langle \hat{x}, -m \rangle * y_1.$$

We simplify products of rotations which include elementary rotations by transposing, using the identities above and multiplying out adjacent elementary and adjacent principal rotations which share the same axis. Consider the following five simplification rules.

(SR1) Compose adjacent elementary or adjacent principal rotations sharing the same axis of rotation, and remove all instances of the identity rotation.

(SR2) Move instances of z_1, z_2 and z_3 to the left of the expression and apply (SR1).

(SR3) While there is an x-axis elementary rotation in the expression which is not right-most, choose the left-most such, move it one place to the right, and apply (SR2).

(SR4) While there is a y-axis elementary rotation in the expression which is not right-most or immediately to the left of an x-axis elementary rotation, move it to the right one place and apply (SR1).

(SR5) Make substitutions at the right of the expression using the following identities and apply (SR2):

$$y_1 * x_1 = z_3 * y_1, \quad y_1 * x_2 = z_2 * y_1, \quad y_1 * x_3 = z_1 * y_1,$$
$$y_2 * x_1 = z_2 * x_3, \quad y_2 * x_2 = i, \qquad\quad y_2 * x_3 = z_2 * x_1,$$
$$y_3 * x_1 = z_1 * y_3, \quad y_3 * x_2 = z_2 * y_3, \quad y_3 * x_3 = z_3 * y_3.$$

If these are applied to a symbolic product of rotations, then, after applying each of the five rules in order, the expression contain at most two elementary rotations. Any such elementary rotation will either be left-most and one of z_1, z_2 or z_3, or it will be right-most and one of x_1, x_2, x_3, y_1 or y_3.

To show that the five rules do indeed produce such a standard form is straightforward. The only potential difficulty is in showing the termination of

(SR3), since at each step the application of (SR2) may produce an x-axis elementary rotation left of that which was previously left-most. Observe however that if z_e and x_e are elementary z-axis and x-axis rotations, respectively, and $w * z_e = z_e * x_e$, then w must be an elementary y-axis rotation. Using this, termination follows from showing that the number of elementary rotations in the expression, apart from a left-most z-axis elementary rotation, is reduced by one at each phase of (SR3).

The following expression is the 'raw' product of rotations expressing the orientation of the screwdriver *tool* (the only cylinder in the left hand illustration of Fig. 4.1) relative to the camera. It was obtained by inverting the rotation expression for the camera relative to world coordinates and composing that with the expression for the orientation of the *tool* in world coordinates, found by tracing down the affixment tree.

$$\langle \hat{x}, \text{TILT} \rangle * \langle \hat{y}, -\text{PAN} \rangle * z_3 * y_3 * i * \langle \hat{z}, \text{SH-ORI} \rangle$$
$$* i * y_3 * y_1 * y_1 * i * i * i * i. \tag{4.2}$$

When we apply the five rules (SR1)–(SR5) we obtain the much simpler expression

$$z_3 * \langle \hat{y}, \text{TILT} \rangle * \langle \hat{x}, \text{PAN} - \text{SH-ORI} \rangle. \tag{4.3}$$

(In this case (SR3) had no effect.)

The appearance of a given object may be invariant with respect to certain changes in relative orientation of object and camera. The standard form for the rotation expressions was chosen to make it easy to further simplify the expression by making use of such invariants. Section 4.3.2 gives an example of this. The standard form for rotation expressions also happens to be very convenient for the simplification of the translational component of a coordinate transform.

4.1.2. *Simplification of translation expressions*

Simplification of translation expressions is quite straightforward and relies on the rules given below. Rule (SR6) is applicable to a product of rotations in the standard form described in the previous section. Rules (SR7)–(SR11) are applicable to a sum of terms, each of which is a product of rotations applied to a vector.

(SR6) Shift elementary z-axis rotations to the right end of products of rotations.

(SR7) For each term in the sum, apply rule (SR6) to the rotation product, then apply the elementary rotations at the right to the vector by permuting its components and changing their signs appropriately.

(SR8) Remove terms in the sum where the vector is zero.

(SR9) Collect terms with symbolically identical rotation expressions by symbolically summing the components of the vectors to which they are applied, then apply rule (SR8)

(SR10) In each term remove a right-most rotation from the rotation product if its axis vector is collinear with the vector to which the product is being applied.

(SR11) While there is a term whose right-most rotation has an axis which is neither collinear with, nor normal to, the vector to which the product is applied, split the vector into collinear and normal component vectors, replace the single term with the two new ones formed in this way, and apply rule (SR10).

In the process of determining the translation component of a transform expression by using (4.1) the geometric simplification system simplifies all the rotation products in the terms of the sum. To simplify the final translation expression, rules (SR7), (SR9) and (SR11) are applied in order. The following is the expression for the position of the screwdriver *tool* in camera coordinates in the situation shown in Fig. 4.1a.

$$\langle \hat{x}, \text{TILT} \rangle \otimes (0, -21.875, 0)$$
$$+ \langle \hat{x}, \text{TILT} \rangle * \langle \hat{y}, \text{SH-ORI} - \text{PAN} \rangle \otimes (0, 0, 1)$$
$$+ \langle \hat{x}, \text{TILT} \rangle * \langle \hat{y}, -\text{PAN} \rangle \otimes (\text{SH-Y} - 30, 0, \text{SH-X} - 83.5). \qquad (4.4)$$

The original unsimplified form is far too large to warrant inclusion here. The simplified form is both tractable and useful as we will see in the next section.

Finally we note that it is simple to subtract one translation expression from another. In the translation to be subtracted, simply negate each component of the vector in each of its terms, symbolically add the two translations by appending the lists of terms, and then simplify as above.

4.2. Deciding on visibility

Given a spatial reasoning capability, one of the simplest questions which can be asked when predicting the appearance of an object is whether the object will be visible at all. If it is known in advance that an object will definitely not be visible, then a lot of time can be saved by not searching for it in the image. There are two ways that an object may not be visible. First it may be outside the field of view. Then, even if it is in the field of view, it may be obscured by another object closer to the camera.

It is quite straightforward to use the geometric simplification algorithms described in the previous section and the constraint manipulation system of Section 3.3 (or more generally any constraint which can meet requirements (A1) and (A2) of Section 3.1) to answer questions of possible invisibility.

To determine whether an object is in the field of view it is necessary to know its coordinates, (c_x, c_y, c_z) in the camera frame of reference, and the *focal ratio r* of the camera (see Section 2.1). In general these can all be expressions in quantifiers. The z coordinate c_z must be negative for the object to be in front of the camera. In that case the image coordinates of the object are $(rc_x/(-c_z),$ $rc_y/(-c_z))$. These two components can be bounded using algorithms INF and

SUP of Section 3.3. The bounds are then compared to the extreme visible image coordinates (−0.5 and 0.5 by convention in ACRONYM), and whatever deductions possible are made (one of 'definitely invisible', 'definitely in field of view').

For example, the expression E of Section 3.3.4 is the y camera coordinate c_y of the origin of the coordinate frame of the screwdriver tool in the camera geometry in Fig. 4.1a. The z camera coordinate is of similar complexity. For a focal ratio r of 2.42, algorithms INF and SUP provide bounds of −2.658 and 3.326, respectively, for the y image coordinate of the screwdriver tool. Thus ACRONYM can deduce that the screwdriver tool may indeed be visible. For other constraints on the position quantifiers (SH-X and SH-Y) it can be deduced that the screwdriver tool is invisible even though its position and orientation and the pan and tilt of the camera are all uncertain.

Similar techniques can be used to decide whether an object might occlude another; whether over the whole range of variations in their sizes, structures and spatial relations, over some ranges, or never. In this case it is better to examine the translation between the origins of their coordinate frames. This can be calculated by symbolically differencing their coordinates in the camera frame and simplifying as in the previous section. Various heuristics (implemented as rules in ACRONYM's predictor) can then be used to decide about occlusion possibilities.

For example, consider the camera overhead geometry which gives rise to the illustration in Fig. 4.1b. The expression for the position of the screwdriver holder base minus the position of the screwdriver tool is

$$\langle \hat{x}, -\text{ROLL} \rangle * \langle \hat{y}, -\text{PITCH} \rangle \otimes (0, 0, -2.625)$$
$$+ \langle \hat{x}, -\text{ROLL} \rangle * \langle \hat{y}, -\text{PITCH} \rangle * \langle \hat{z}, \text{SH-ORI} \rangle \otimes (-1, 0, 0).$$

Expanding this out and applying algorithms INF and SUP gives bounds of −1.679 and 1.679 on the x component, −1.746 and 1.746 on y, and −3.143 and −1.932 on the z component. Thus ACRONYM can conclude that the screwdriver holder base is always further from the camera than the screwdriver tool. One heuristic rule concludes that since the x and y components are comparable in size to the z component, it is possible that the screwdriver tool will appear in front of the screwdriver holder base in images. Another rule, however, says that since the view of the tool that can be seen (see Section 4.3 for the deduction of the view to be seen) is small compared to the view that will be seen of the holder base, it will not interfere significantly with observation of the latter. (Actually in this case it is also concluded that the screwdriver tool is occluded always by the screwdriver motor above it. Also other subparts of both the screwdriver holder and the screwdriver itself interfere more with observation of the screwdriver holder base.)

Before leaving the subject of visibility consider the following. If an object is visible, then its image coordinates must be within the bounds of the visible part of the image plane. Thus the expressions for the image coordinates, as calculated above, can be bounded above and below by 0.5 and -0.5 respectively, and those constraints can be merged into the constraint set. If the object is visible it must satisfy those constraints anyway. Having the constraints explicitly stated may help prune some incorrect hypotheses as we will see in Section 5. Note that if the decision procedure as described in Section 3 was actually a complete decision procedure, then we could simply merge the constraints and test the constraint set for satisfiability to decide whether the object was visible. However, since the decision procedure we use is only partial and cannot always detect unsatisfiable sets of constraints, we use the less direct procedure as described above. Even with the new constraints merged into the constraint set, algorithms SUP and INF may not produce image coordinate bounds of 0.5 and -0.5. This is because the bound on the expressions must be reconstructed from the normal form of the constraints, rather than referring directly to the newly added constraints. As we have seen in Section 3.3, SUP and INF produce only upper and lower bounds on expressions, not suprema and infima. Futhermore, to keep the number of symbols in the constraint set at a reasonable level we do not use the image coordinate expressions directly in the bounds, but rather use simplified bounding expressions as demonstrated in Section 3.3.4.

4.3. Finding invariants

The best things to predict about the appearance of an object are those which will always be observable. We define an *observable* as something which can be observed in an image; it is either a feature which might be described directly by the low level descriptive processes, or it is a directly computable relation between two or more such features. We say that something is an *invariant observable* if it is constant and observable over the whole range of variations in model size and structure, and its spatial relation to the camera coordinate system.

For instance, collinear features of models (not image features) which are observable (as image features) give rise to observable collinearity over the whole range of spatial relations between the models and the camera coordinate system. Parallel features of models which are observable produce parallel observable features over the range of relative camera object orientations, where the plane defined by the parallel model features is itself parallel to the image plane of the camera (i.e. in ACRONYM the plane is parallel to the x-y plane of camera coordinates).

Collinearity and parallelism can easily be detected with the coordinate transform simplifications of Section 4.1. First, a coordinate system for the object features is defined so that the linear feature lies along the x-axis. For straight spines of cones, for instance, this is just the local coordinate system of the cone. For straight spines of cones, for instance, this is just the local coordinate system of the cone. The relative orientations of these coordinate systems can be determined by inverting the orientation of one with respect to the camera (this simply involves reversing the order of the rotation product and inverting the sign of the rotation magnitudes) and multiplying on the right by the orientation of the other, and applying the simplification algorithm of Section 4.1.1, followed by rule (SR6) of Section 4.1.2. If the resulting expression is a product of rotations containing only the identity rotation i, y_2, z_2, and rotations of the form $\langle \hat{x}, a \rangle$ for arbitrary expressions a, then the object features are certainly parallel and perhaps collinear. (It is certainly possible that other more complex rotations be present in the orientation expression relating parallel object features, but in general it is not worth pursuing them.) To decide whether object features are collinear or whether they are parallel and generate a plane parallel to the image plane, requires examination of the translation between their local coordinate systems. The camera coordinates of one can be subtracted from the other as described in Section 4.1.2. If the y and z components of the resulting vector are zero, then the object features are collinear. If the z component is zero, then they are parallel and will invariantly appear parallel in the image.

Collinearity and parallelism are important relations which can be used to check for consistency of interpretation of image features; consistency with relations expected from examination of the models. Another such relation is connectivity which, as with collinearity, is invariant over all camera models, given that the features to be checked for connectivity are both observable. However, to make use of all these relations we first need observable image features. Currently we make use of primitive shape descriptions as the primary image features used by ACRONYM for initial hypothesis of object image correspondences. We digress briefly to describe the shape descriptions produced by ACRONYM's low level processes. We will then return to the topic of using geometric reasoning to deduce shape invariants. In Section 4.3.3 we generalize the notion of invariants to quasi-invariants; features which are observable over a wide range of modelled variations.

4.3.1. *Ribbons and ellipses*

In the current implementation of ACRONYM we use *ribbons* and *ellipses* as the features which low level processes produce. Ribbons are two dimensional specializations of generalized cones. A ribbon is a planar shape which can be described by three components. The *spine* is a two dimensional curve. A line segment, the *cross-section*, is held at a constant angle to the spine, and swept along it varying according to the *sweeping-rule*.

Ribbons are a good way of describing the images generated by generalized cones. Consider a ribbon which corresponds to the image of the swept surface of a generalized cone. For straight spines the projection of the cone spine into the image would closely correspond to the spine of the ribbon. Thus a good approximation of the observed angle between the spines of two generalized

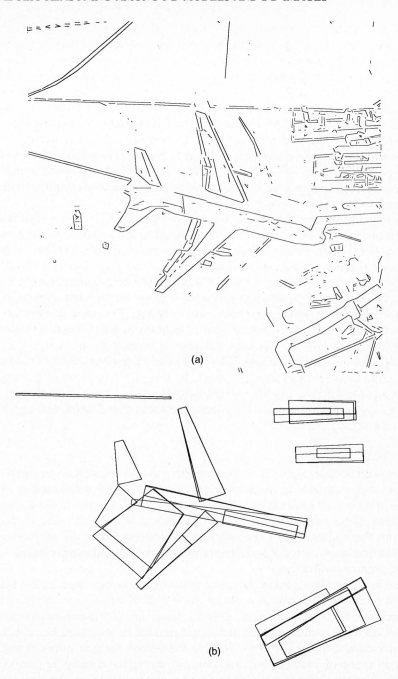

(a)

(b)

FIG. 4.2. Top figure (a) shows the low level input to ACRONYM. Bottom figure (b) shows the ribbon descriptions returned by the descriptive process, when directed by predictions to look for shapes generated by the fuselage and wings.

cones is the angle between the spines of the two ribbons in the image corresponding to their swept surfaces. We do not have a quantitative theory of these correspondences.

Ellipses are a good way of describing the shapes generated by the ends of generalized cones. The perspective projections of ends of cones with circular cross-sections are exactly ellipses. For other cross-sections, ellipses can sometimes provide better descriptions of the ends. For example, over a given class of orientations of a cone relative to the camera any axis of symmetry of the cross-section is strongly skewed. Thus the axis of symmetry might be the obvious choice for the spine of a ribbon in a geometrically simpler situation. In a more complex situation an ellipse can provide a more tolerant prediction and an easier descriptive hypothesis.

The descriptive module consists of two algorithms [17]: first an edge linking algorithm based on best-first search, and second an algorithm to fit ribbons and ellipses to sets of linked edges. The descriptive module returns a graph structure, the *observation graph*. The nodes are ribbon (ellipse) descriptions. The arcs are observed image relations between ribbons; currently we use only image connectivity. The module produces ribbons which have straight spines and sweeping-rules which describe linear scalings. The module provides information regarding orientation and position of the spine in image coordinates. Fig. 4.2 demonstrates the action of the descriptive module. In Fig. 4.2a are the 692 edges found by Nevatia and Babu's [38] line finder in an 8 bit aerial image taken from above San Francisco airport. In Fig. 4.2b are 39 ribbons found by ACRONYM's descriptive module when searching for shapes generated by the fuselage and wings. There are 161 connectivity arcs in the observation graph so produced.

4.3.2. *Invariant shapes*

The most important factor in predicting shape is the orientation of the object relative to the camera. It is therefore potentially interesting to consider under what variations in orientation of an object relative to the camera does its perceived shape remain invariant. In fact such invariants are very useful for reducing the complexity of the expressions derived, using the methods described in Section 4.1.1 for object orientations, to manageable levels where shape can be predicted directly.

Note first that for a generalized cone which is small compared to its distance from the camera, perspective effects are small. There may still be strong perspective effects between such objects, however. (For instance cones with parallel spines defining a plane which is not parallel to the image plane will still have a vanishing point.) In any case it is therefore true that in predicting the apparent shape of such generalized cones, we can approximate the perspective projection with a slightly simpler projection. In ACRONYM we carry out shape prediction using a *'perspective-normal'* projection. For a generalized cone whose closest point to the camera has z coordinate z', the projection of a point (x, y, z) in three space into the image plane of a camera with focal ratio r is $(rx/(-z'), ry/(-z'))$. Intuitively we think of this as a normal projection into a plane which is parallel to the image plane, intersects the generalized cone, and is the closest such plane to the camera, followed by a perspective projection of the image into the camera. It is also equivalent to a normal projection scaled according to the distance of the object from the camera. We will see examples of why this is so useful in Section 4.3.3. We further simplify the perspective-normal projection in ACRONYM by using the z camera coordinate of the origin of the cone coordinate frame, rather than z' as defined above.

We return now to the problem of simplifying orientation expressions while keeping the implied shape invariant. The normal form described in Section 4.1.1 was designed with such problems in mind. First note that a rotation about the z-axis at the left of a rotation product corresponds to a rotation in the image plane (recall the definition of camera geometry in Section 2.1). Our two dimensional shape descriptions are invariant with respect to orientation. So all shape prediction is unaffected by ignoring such rotations. Thus, for instance, (4.3) for the orientation of the screwdriver tool in Fig. 4.1a, is equivalent to

$$\langle \hat{y}, \text{TILT} \rangle * \langle \hat{x}, \text{PAN} - \text{SH-ORI} \rangle \tag{4.5}$$

for the purpose of predicting the shape of the image of the screwdriver tool. In general our standard form for rotation expressions has all elementary z-axis rotations moved to the left—ready to be ignored.

The screwdriver tool is a cylinder, with its spine (an axis of radial symmetry) along the x-axis of its coordinate system. Thus the appearance of the tool is invariant with respect to a rotation about its $\hat{x}$-axis. The right rotation of (4.5) can thus be ignored for the purpose of shape prediction, leaving

$$\langle \hat{y}, \text{TILT} \rangle \tag{4.6}$$

to be analyzed. In physical terms this says that the camera tilt is the only variable of the case in Fig. 4.1a that is important for shape prediction.

Expression (4.6) is simple enough that special case rules are applicable. One says that the cylinder will appear as a ribbon generated by its swept surface and an ellipse generated by its initial cross-section. Furthermore they will be connected in the image. (If the descriptive process which found ellipses was able to accurately determine their major axis, then another useful rule could come into play. From (4.6) it would deduce that in the image the major axis of the ellipse will be normal to the spine of the ribbon.) Later in the prediction it is decided that the ellipse corresponding to the top of the screwdriver tool will actually be occluded (as described in Section 4.2), but that need not concern us here.

The screwdriver modelled in Fig. 4.1 is actually a particular screwdriver with specific dimensions. To make this example more general, suppose that the screwdriver tool has variable size, with its length represented by the quantifier TOOL-LENGTH and its radius by TOOL-RADIUS. Using the perspective-normal projection approximation, the length to width ratio of the ribbon corresponding to the swept surface of the screwdriver tool can be predicted to be

$$\frac{\text{TOOL-LENGTH} \times \cos(\text{TILT})}{\text{TOOL-RADIUS}}.$$

Consider the ellipse corresponding to the top of the screwdriver tool. The ratio of its minor axis to its major axis is simply

$$\sin(\text{TILT}).$$

Thus the range of shapes that can be generated have been comprehensively predicted. The actual form in which these predictions are used is not just to establish a predicate against which hypothesized shape matches will be tested. They are used in a more powerful way, described in Section 5, to actually extract three dimensional information about the viewed scene.

Beside shape, bounds on the dimensions of objects can also be predicted. This too is used to extract three dimensional information as described in Section 5. Size bounds have a more immediate application, however. They are used to direct the low level descriptive processes [17], which search the image for candidate shapes to be matched to predictions. Given that the focal ratio is 2.42 and the length of the screwdriver tool is 1, and using the expanded z component of (4.4), the algebraically simplified prediction of the length of the ribbon in the image is

$$-2.42 \cos(\text{TILT})/(30 \cos(\text{TILT}) \sin(-\text{PAN}) + \text{SH-X} \times \cos(-\text{PAN})$$
$$+\cos(\text{TILT}) \cos(\text{SH-ORI} - \text{PAN}) - 21.875 \sin(\text{TILT})$$
$$-83.5 \cos(\text{TILT}) \cos(-\text{PAN}) - \text{SH-Y} \times \cos(\text{TILT}) \sin(-\text{PAN})).$$

Algorithms INF and SUP are used to determine that this quantity is bounded by 0.0190 and 0.0701, information which can be used by the descriptive processes to limit the search for candidate ribbons in the image. These are not particularly accurate estimates on the infimum and supremum of the above expression because it contains sines and cosines which have coupled arguments, but our constraint manipulation system treats them independently and makes the most pessimistic bounds. However, they are still exceedingly useful for limiting search.

In general, at the right of the standard form for a product of rotations is one of six elementary rotations: i (implicitly only), y_1, y_3, x_1, x_2 and x_3. If there are no other rotations in the expression these correspond to the six views of a generalized cone from along the positive and negative coordinate axes. Rotations y_1 and y_3 correspond to viewing the initial and final views of the swept surface of the generalized cone. In (4.3) the right-most elementary rotation is implicitly the identity i, which corresponds to a side view of the cylinder. In trying to reduce the complexity of the orientation expression, ACRONYM essentially tries to find how the nonelementary rotations change the viewpoint from one of the six primitive viewpoints of a generalized cone.

As a final example consider the orientation expression derived for the screwdriver tool in the camera geometry illustrated in Fig. 4.1b:

$$\langle \hat{x}, -\text{ROLL} \rangle * \langle \hat{y}, -\text{PITCH} \rangle * \langle \hat{z}, \text{SH-ORI} \rangle * y_1.$$

Here the right-most elementary rotation is y_1 which corresponds to viewing the initial cross-section of the cylinder of the screwdriver tool. In the modelled situation that is the top of the cylinder, but that is not derivable from this expression with as simple an analysis as used in (4.3). Various heuristic rules try rearranging the expression to find a situation in which an invariant simplification can be detected. One such rule tries shifting the right-most elementary rotation left one position. Using the identities of Section 4.1 this gives the expression

$$\langle \hat{x}, -\text{ROLL} \rangle * \langle \hat{y}, -\text{PITCH} \rangle * y_1 * \langle \hat{x}, -\text{SH-ORI} \rangle.$$

As in the previous example we now have an x-axis rotation at the right. A cylinder's appearance is invariant with respect to a rotation about its axis, so we can use the simplified expression

$$\langle \hat{x}, -\text{ROLL} \rangle * \langle \hat{y}, -\text{PITCH} \rangle * y_1 \tag{4.7}$$

for predicting shape. This expression is still too complex for direct prediction, and to handle it we need to use quasi-invariance, introduced above.

4.3.3. *Quasi-invariants*

Sometimes the search for invariants will be unsuccessful. Often when there are no invariants directly available, ACRONYM is able to carry out case analysis. It produces new restriction nodes, descendants of the old, each with additional constraints, which restrict the situation in each restriction node to one where there are adequate invariants available. The additional constraints are chosen so that the lattice supremum of the new restriction nodes is the original node.

Often, however, case analysis is not enough. Expression (4.7) is a case in point. The problem is that there are two rotations with uncertain magnitude. If there was only one, shape prediction could be achieved in a similar manner to that in the previous example. In this case both rotations have small magnitudes. The effects of these rotations on the perceived shape of the object depend roughly on the cosines of their magnitudes. The cosines are almost constant, ranging from 0.965 to 1 over the modelled range of variations. Thus for shape prediction at least they can be effectively ignored; the error involved in doing so will be smaller than the errors incurred by low level descriptive processes. Heuristic rules, written on the basis of error analyses, are used to identify such cases. Later we may include rules which can carry out analyses dynamically using differential approximations to nonlinear expressions.

The preceding is a particular case of a more general phenomenon, involving local maxima, minima, or points of inflexion of expressions. Often some prediction is very nearly invariant over the modelled range of variations. Where an invariant is found by ignoring a small effect of some term we call it a quasi-invariant. The most common instances of quasi-invariants arise from ignoring cosine terms with small arguments.

5. Prediction and Interpretation

In the previous section we showed how invariant and quasi-invariant observables could be discovered from reasoning geometrically about models. We now describe how to combine quasi-invariants into predictions of image features. Predictions include instructions on how to use image feature measurements from hypothesized partial interpretations, to constrain the three dimensional models, identifying class memberships and specific three dimensional spatial relations. The predictions drive descriptive processes to produce descriptions of image features, to be matched to predictions. An interpretation algorithm is used to hypothesize such matches, to apply the resulting constraints to models, and to combine local interpretations into globally consistent interpretations.

At the time of writing, the interpretation algorithm described here has not been fully implemented as part of ACRONYM. All image interpretations carried out completely automatically by ACRONYM so far have used a syntactic graph matcher due to Greiner (see [18]). It does not have the back-constraining capability, and thus it cannot use the most significant aspects of the predictions. Implementation and integration of the proposed algorithm is underway and will be completed soon.

A procedure [29] has been demonstrated which determines certain model parameters (slot values rather than quantifiers) numerically by an iterative technique once good matches have been established. It has not been integrated into ACRONYM.

We first describe in detail the form of the prediction graph, then show how back constraints are set up and the effects of using multiple back constraints. We then outline an algorithm for interpretation which consists of screening matches between predictions and observed features, followed by combining local interpretations into more global interpretations.

5.1. Prediction

Prediction is used to build the *prediction graph* which provides a description of features and their relations which should be matched by features in an image. Prediction has two other major uses, however. The first is to provide direction to the low level descriptive processes. This was described in Section 4.3.1. The second is to provide instructions on how to use image measurements to understand the three dimensional aspects of the objects which gave rise to the measured image.

The preceding sections have dealt with many of the specific mechanisms used for prediction. The following subsections give an overview of how these mechanisms fit together.

5.1.1. *Producing the prediction graph*

The prediction graph consists of nodes and arcs. The nodes are either predictions of specific image features, or recursively complete prediction graphs of finer level features. In our current implementation only shapes are predicted. The arcs of the graph specify relations between the nodes. There are three types of arcs; *must-be*, *should-be*, and *exclusive*. The first two are similar but imply slightly different acceptance criteria for instantiation of their associated nodes. Details are given below in Section 5.2. Such arcs can predict a variety of relations. For instance, we currently predict connectedness, relative spine orientation in the image, and simply the AND relation that instantiations must exist for both nodes, to consider an instantiation of either to be correct. *Exclusive* arcs say that instantiations of the two related nodes cannot coexist in an interpretation graph. This last type of arc is rarely intrinsically needed as such information is usually encoded in the back constraints implied by different instantiations. However, when the prediction algorithm knows that two predictions are mutually exclusive (such as the visible shapes for two ends of a simple generalized cone) it can save the interpretation algorithm the expense of deciding that the meet of restrictions associated with two interpretation nodes is unsatisfiable by joining the prediction nodes by an *exclusive* arc. Thus they are an efficiency consideration.

A prediction graph has associated with it a restriction node which refers to the object class being predicted. It could also be the *base-restriction*, the most general restriction node, in which case the graph predicts the whole scene which appears in the image to be interpreted.

In Section 4 we showed how to predict the shape of a cylinder given certain constraints on its orientation relative to the camera. Prediction proceeds by examining the constraints on objects. If they are tractable, then specific rules are used to make special case predictions. Otherwise case analysis is performed by adding constraints which produce tractable situations. Each different constraint adds a new restriction node, more restrictive than that associated with the restriction node of the prediction graph. It is the lattice infimum of that restriction and the new constraint.

Single generalized cones can generate image shapes in a number of ways. Shapes can be generated primarily by cross-sections at each end, by the swept surfaces, or a combination of the two. In each case the shape boundary may be generated by actual edges on the generalized cone (discontinuity in the direction of surface normal) or on apparent edges dependent on camera location (images of points were the surface normal is normal to the line of sight). We call these boundary curves *contours*.

Image feature predictions are made for each contour, specifically a prediction of the shape of each contour is made. First the size of the contour in model coordinates is calculated. Certain simple approximations can be made at this point. For instance the occluding contour of a right circular cylinder is a rectangle having the same length as the cylinder and a width twice its radius, given that the cylinder is not extremely close to the camera. The dimensions of the contour are expressed terms of model parameters. The contour is then symbolically projected with the perspective normal transform to obtain a prediction of the ribbon or ellipse which it will generate in an image. This whole process is carried out by special purpose rules which embody an analysis of their domain of applicability. A rule-base is used to enhance extensibility of the system. New constraint ranges and classes of generalized cones can be handled simply by adding a new rule to the rule-base once a new analysis has been carried out by the ACRONYM maintainer.

5.1.2. *Setting up back constraints*

The prediction algorithms produce symbolic expressions for predicted image feature characteristics (e.g. length of a ribbon). Let E be an example expression. During prediction such expressions are bounded numerically to give direction to the low level processes. The bounds are calculated over the satisfying set of the quantifiers in the symbolic expression. When a feature is hypothesized as a match for a predicted feature there is a corresponding image measurement available. Let it be m. If the match is correct, then the measurement m is the actual numeric value of the prediction expression E. Assuming the expression has that value provides constraints on the values of the individual quantifiers. If the image provided an exact measurement, then we could simply add the constraint $E = m$, and use SUP and INF to find what this implied about model and spatial parameters.

There are large errors in results of the feature description algorithms [17], and instead of an exact measurement m the algorithms provide estimates only—a closed error interval, $[m_l, m_u]$ say, on image feature parameters. Therefore we can add the constraint $m_l \leqslant E \leqslant m_u$. In practice such expressions may not be the best ones to use as they may contain many symbols, and they may be hard for the simplifier to manipulate due to uncertain parities of subexpressions. During prediction, however, we may have special knowledge about the expressions from geometric considerations and so can write instructions for the interpretation algorithm about how to build constraints from feature measurements which can be handled by the simplifier and CMS in general. These instructions are attached to predictions.

We illustrate the preceding by following through our example of the screwdriver tool as it appears in the camera geometry illustrated in Fig. 4.1a. Given the constraints on the location of the screwdriver holder (in terms of table coordinates SH-X and SH-Y) we have already seen that the length of the image ribbon corresponding to the screwdriver tool will lie between 0.0186 and 0.0701, which was obtained by bounding the formula $rl/(-z')$ where r is the camera focal ratio (2.42), l the normal projection length of the tool cylinder (cos(TILT)), and z' the distance of the origin of the cylinder coordinates to the image plane (an expression in PAN, TILT, SH-ORI, SH-X and SH-Y). We know that if the object is visible, then it must be that $z' \leq 0$. This information is not derivable by the algebraic simplifier in this case because z' is a complex expression. The prediction rules can safely assume, however, and so they specify that when a ribbon with length estimate $[m_l, m_u]$ is hypothesized as the image of the screwdriver tool in the context of restriction node S, then constraints obtained by evaluating the evaluating expressions within the two inequalities

$$m_l \times \text{INF}_S(z', H) \leq \text{SUP}_S(2.42 \cos(\text{TILT}), H),$$
$$m_u \times \text{SUP}_S(z', H) \geq \text{INF}_S(2.42 \cos(\text{TILT}), H)$$

should be added to the constraints already in S, where $H = \{$PAN, TILT, SH-ORI$\}$. (The exact mechanism for selection of node S is given in the next section.) In this case the constraints will further constrain SH-X and SH-Y, the table position coordinates of the screwdriver holder. In general, addition of such constraints may constrain positions, orientations, model size, or camera parameters.

We demonstrate the effect of these additional constraints. We add them to the initial modelled set of constraints only. Recall that in that case we have

$$0 \leq \text{SH-X} \leq 24 \quad \text{and} \quad 18 \leq \text{SH-Y} \leq 42.$$

Suppose the interpretation processes described below hypothesize a match of the swept surfaces of the screwdriver tool with a ribbon in the image. The descriptive processes return image measurements as nominal values with fractional error estimates. In the example at hand, suppose that the ribbon is measured to have length of 0.05 units, with plus or minus 10% error. Then the additional constraints generated ensure that

$$4.762 \leq \text{SH-X} \leq 24 \quad \text{and} \quad 18 \leq \text{SH-Y} \leq 42.$$

If the length is measured as 0.07 with an error bound of 10%, then the constraints imply that

$$20.127 \leq \text{SH-X} \leq 24 \quad \text{and} \quad 27.035 \leq \text{SH-Y} \leq 42.$$

Even with a 40% error estimate, a measurement of 0.07 contributes three dimensional information. This is to be expected as it is very close to an extreme of the predicted range of measurement.

Note that the constraints added actually contain more information than is reflected in examining the resulting ranges on individual parameters. The constraints added actually chip off (in general nonlinear) portions of the original rectangle of satisfying values achievable for SH-X and SH-Y. The actual constraints added in the first example above were

$$3.017 - 0.0435 \times \text{SH-X} - 0.0113 \times \text{SH-Y} \leq 2.338,$$
$$5.503 - 0.0460 \times \text{SH-X} + 0.0138 \times \text{SH-Y} \geq 2.096$$

which are much stronger than simple linear inequalities in SH-X from these two constraints.

There are other image measurements even from a single ribbon which can be used to constrain three dimensional parameters. Obviously ribbon width and taper can be used analogously to ribbon length. Position of the ribbon within the image can also be used. In the above example it will tend to constrain camera parameters such as PAN, TILT, and also SH-Y. Prediction rules set up the appropriate instructions for building constraints based on these measurements.

5.1.3. *Multiple back constraints*

The previous example deals only with constraints derivable from hypothesizing a match with a single ribbon. In identifying instances of an object whose description is more complex than a single generalized cone, there will be more than one primitive shape feature matched. Each provides a number of such back constraints which combine to further constrain the individual parameters.

Suppose an object is modelled with a well-determined size, position and orientation. When constraints from hypothesized matches for many objects are combined, that particular object will be extremely useful for determining parameters of the camera and other objects. If there are many such tightly constrained modelled objects, then they are even more useful. Thus a mobile robot can use known reference objects to visually determine its absolute location and orientation, and the absolute location and orientation of other movable objects.

In a bin picking task the camera parameters and location of the bin are probably well determined (although ACRONYM would not be at a loss if this were not the case). The problem is to distinguish instances of an object and determine its orientation so that a manipulator can be commanded to pick it from the bin. There will be many instances of each predicted image feature as there will be many instances of each object. The back constraints provide a mechanism for the interpretation algorithm to find mutually consistent features, and thus identify object instances. Furthermore the back constraints provide information on the position and orientation of the object instance.

In aerial photographs the back constraints tend to relate scale factors to camera height and focal ratio. In aerial photographs an identifiable landmark can provide one tight relationship between these parameters. Derived back constraints from other objects interact to give relatively tight bounds on all unknowns.

5.2. Interpretation

Interpretation proceeds by combining local matches of shapes to individual generalized cones into more global matches for more complete objects (ACRONYM currently relies on shapes only). The global interpretations must be consistent in two respects. First, they must conform to the requirements specified by the arcs of the prediction graph. Second, the constraints that each local match implies on the three dimensional model must be globally consistent; i.e. the total set of constraints must be satisfiable.

At a given time the interpreter looks for matches for a set of generalized cones, called the *search set*. They are cones determined by the predictor to have approximately equal importance in determining an interpretation for an image. Smaller generalized cones, corresponding to finer image features, are searched for later. Feature predictions include both an estimated range for feature parameters (e.g. ribbon length) and constraints on the model implied by hypothesizing a match with an image feature. The descriptive processes are invoked with direction from the first aspect of the predictions. The observation graph of features and observed relations between features is the result. Since the search set in general contains more than one generalized cone, not all the described features will match all, or even any, generalized cones in the search set. A comparison of all the image feature parameters with their range predictions is carried out to determine possible matches for each generalized cone in the search set (e.g. a ribbon's length and width must both fall in the predicted ranges to be considered further).

There is a question of partial matches for predicted features. The current descriptive processes used [17], partially take care of this problem in a fairly undirected manner. If edges associated with the two ends of a ribbon are observed by the line finder [38], then the edge linking algorithm will probably hypothesize a ribbon, despite possible interference in the middle sections. (The strategy which works successfully is to make as many plausible hypotheses as possible at the lowest levels, so that the likelihood of missing a correct hypothesis which may be locally weak is low, and use the higher level knowledge of the system to prune away the excess later.) Sometimes, also the predictor will predict specific obscurations and adjust its feature prediction accordingly. In general, however, an additional mechanism which hypothesizes image features as partial matches for larger predictions may be very useful. Thus a ribbon might be hypothesized as being only one end of a larger ribbon by not requiring that it fits the length prediction. It is also necessary in this case to increase the error estimate in the length measurement for the next stage of pruning, described below. We have not yet implemented such a mechanism, but plan to in the near future.

For each feature prediction pair which survives this first stage of pruning a restriction node is built which is more restrictive than the restriction node which is associated with the prediction. It inherits the constraints from the prediction restriction, but also has added those constraints built by following the instructions in the prediction. Often the new restriction node will be unsatisfiable, and so the feature prediction pair can be eliminated from further consideration. For instance both the length and width of a ribbon may fall in the predicted ranges, but perhaps the length is at the high end of the range and the width at the low end. Then it is possible that the back constraints so generated will put inconsistent demands on the orientation of the object relative to the camera, or will be inconsistent with some modelled constraint on the length to diameter ratio of the cone. (For example in the generic class of jet aircraft, the fuselage lengths and diameters can vary greatly, but the length to diameter ratio varies much less. A constraint may be added to the model class expressing this fundamental relationship of overall scaling in aircraft.)

The interpreter tries to instantiate arcs of the prediction graph by pairwise checking hypothesized instantiations of predicted features which have a relation predicted between them. Both *must-be* and *should-be* arcs are thus instantiated. Instantiation of arcs is similar to that of nodes. Gross predicted features are checked first, then a restriction node is constructed which includes the constraints implied from image measurements of the relation. For instance, suppose an arc predicts a range of angles between the spines of two ribbons. First, the angle between the image spines must lie in the predicted numerical range. Then the constraints associated with the arc may constrain the relation between the orientation of the object relative to the camera and the relative orientations in three space of the two generalized cones corresponding to the two ribbons.

A combinatorial search is carried out to collect individual hypothesized instantiations of nodes and arcs into hypothesized connected components of the interpretation graph. The connectivity referred to, here, is that supplied by instantiated *must-be* and *should-be* arcs. *Exclusive* arcs prevent the collection together with some inherently mutually exclusive local interpretations. The algorithm used here is a variation on the constraint propagation algorithm introduced by Waltz [49], used for labelling line drawings.

Recall the semantics of the two arc types. If the two feature predictions which participate in a *should-be* arc are instantiated, then they can be regarded as consistent local interpretations only if the instantiations support an instantiation of the arc predicted between them. A feature prediction which participates in a *must-be* arc can only be instantiated if there is a mutually consistent instantiation of the other node participating in that arc and also the corresponding arc is instantiated. As an example consider the prediction that an aerial view of an aircraft will include wings connected to the fuselage. If *must-be* arcs are used, then all of the fuselage, port and starboard wings must be observed to allow interpretation of image features as an aircraft. If *should-be* arcs are used, then it is possible to return a partial interpretation such as a 'an aircraft with one wing missing'.

In our previous implementation of the interpreter we found that just pruning using *must-be* arc requirements was sufficient to carry out object classification correctly. In that implementation of the interpreter we also used only the simpler form of matching predictions to features where feature measurements were compared to prediction ranges, but no back constraining was done. The simple requirements specified by the *must-be* arcs of the observability graph, while only moderately strong by themselves, are very strong in conjunction with the requirements specified by the nodes. In our experience with aerial images we found it extremely rare that two nodes and a connecting arc of the prediction graph were incorrectly instantiated in the observation graph. We have not observed a case of a three node, two arc subgraph of the prediction graph being incorrectly instantiated.

The reasons that we have added the constraint mechanism to a successful interpretation system are two fold. First, although the original scheme never incorrectly interpreted image features as an object instance, they sometimes failed to detect objects when predicted feature relations were not observed. Merely relaxing feature relation predictions does lead to incorrect image interpretations. The constraint system allows for relaxed predictions but still provides a mechanism for checking consistency of partial matches to disconnected connected components of the prediction graph (at least via *must-be* arcs). The relaxation of predictions referred to is the replacement of *must-be* by *should-be* arcs. Second, the constraints provide a mechanism for gaining three dimensional information from image interpretations.

As each connected component is built, interpretation restriction nodes are checked for consistency. The simplest way to do this would be to calculate the lattice infimum (actually use (A3) of Section 3.1) over the restriction nodes associated with the interpretations of each feature and feature relation. However, in the general case this can lead to some problems. For example, a class of aircraft may be modelled with the spines of generalized cones of the two wings each having their length slot filled with the quantifier WING-LENGTH. When combining local matches for the two wings of a single aircraft we want the constraints on WING-LENGTH to be consistent, as each wing should have the same length. However, when we are combining two local interpretations of aircraft into, say, an interpretation of an image as an airfield, then the WING-LENGTH in the two cases refers to a different physical quantity. Individual aircraft have their wings the same length but different aircraft may have different wing lengths.

We use the term *conglomeration* to refer to the process of combining local interpretations whether at the feature level, or when combining connected components of the interpretation graph. One result of conglomeration should be a new restriction node which is more restrictive than all the restriction nodes associated with the interpretations conglomerated. Of course it should be the least restrictive of such restriction if possible.

Somehow the system has to decide whether quantifiers with the same name in two local matches refer to the same physical quantity. In an earlier paper [17] we proposed that the user should include such information explicitly in the geometric models. However, this information is actually implicitly available elsewhere, and so we have developed a new scheme whereby the system decides itself from class rather than geometric considerations. As described above each prediction graph is associated with a particular user-supplied restriction node, which describes the class of objects predicted by the graph. In conglomerating submatches to the prediction graph, the system assumes that only quantifiers which are constrained in that restriction node refer to unique physical quantities. Therefore they are the only quantifiers retained in the conglomeration restriction node.

The conglomeration restriction node is computed as follows. For each restriction node to be conglomerated, a more general restriction node containing only quantifiers to be retained is computed. For this purpose algorithm INF is used on all upper bounds in the normal constraint form and SUP on all lower bounds. In both cases the set H is the set of quantifiers to be retained, so all others are eliminated from the bounding expressions (see Section 3.3.4). Then the lattice infimum of these new restriction nodes is calculated. If it is unsatisfiable, then the local interpretations associated with each of the restriction nodes are mutually inconsistent.

An alternative to eliminating quantifiers is to rename them, so that quantifiers referring to unique physical quantities have unique names. The advantage to this is that the current scheme of removing quantifiers leads to a weaker conglomeration restriction node which conceivably (but with very low probability) will allow an inconsistent interpretation to pass later in interpretation. By renaming quantifiers no information is thrown away, so no later errors can be introduced by the conglomeration process. The disadvantage is that the number of quantifiers and bounding expressions tends to grow, making the higher levels of interpretation run roughly exponentially slower in the number of component interpretations. We feel that the advantages of renaming are small and the disadvantages great. Also by renaming variables interpretation never proceeds to higher level abstractions, but is inherently always carrying around baggage from lower level details. For instance suppose the system has hypothesized a number of aircraft in an aerial view on an airfield, and then combines these in a global interpretation of an airfield instance. Without removing some variables from the conglomeration as is done in our current scheme it would be forced to carry around the variables for, say, the lengths of the engine pods of each aircraft. At best this is aesthetically unpleasing. Worse, the increasing complexity of constraint sets overwhelms the constraint manipulation system. In our current scheme, the individual interpretations for the aircraft contribute knowledge derived about the rest of the world from their local hypothesis, but then can be treated simply as atomic aircraft instances—a higher level abstraction.

At this stage of interpretation we now have hypothesized connected components of the interpretation graph. These may be complete components, in that they have instances of all predicted arcs and nodes, or they may only be partial (e.g. an interpretation may correspond to an aircraft except that no feature was found corresponding to the port wing). With each compont is a restriction node which describes the constraints on the three dimensional world implied by accepting that hypothesis. A combinatorial search is now carried out to find consistent connected components. Essentially this is done by deciding whether the restriction node produced as the conglomeration of the component restriction nodes is satisfiable. Conglomeration can also add constraints (equalities) on quantifiers used to describe variable numbers of subparts (e.g. the variable numbers of flanges on the electric motor in Section 2). These constraints too, of course, must be consistent with all the conglomerated restriction nodes.

Eventually then, a number of interpretation graphs may be hypothesized. In general, some will be large and mostly correct interpretation graphs and the others will be small, consisting of individual incorrect interpretations of parts of the image. The large graphs will be very similar in gross aspects but may differ locally where they have accepted slightly different local interpretations. A single interpretation can be synthesized from the gross similarities. Our experience with our earlier interpretation algorithms suggests that the number of large interpretation graphs will typically be on the order of less than five and most likely only one or two. A large correct interpretation graph has associated with it a restriction node which specializes both object models and their spatial relations to the three dimensional understanding of the world derived from the feature prediction hypothesized matches in the interpretation graph. Other restriction nodes associated with components of the total interpretation may contain extra three dimensional information pertinent to the appropriate local interpretation.

A final aspect of this scheme for interpretation is the ease with which subclass identification can be carried out once class identification has been achieved. Suppose we have an interpretation of a set of image features as an electric motor (see Section 2 for the subclass definitions of this example). Associated with that interpretaton is a restriction node. We can immediately check whether the interpretation is consistent with the object being an instance of some subclass of electric motors, e.g. *carbonator motor*, by taking the lattice

infimum of the subclass restriction node and the interpretation restriction. If
the infimum is unsatisfiable, then the object cannot be an instance of the
subclass. If no inconsistency is found for several subclasses, but those subclasses themselves are inconsistent (i.e. the lattice infimum of their restriction
nodes is known to be unsatisfiable), then perhaps prediction and search for
finer features of the object must be carried out to resolve the classification.

6. Conclusion

We have concentrated on the predictive aspects of vision in this paper and
indeed in the ACRONYM system as a whole. This is not to say that descriptive
processes are not vitally important for robust and accurate vision. Rather, we
are investigating the question of how to use models independently of particular
descriptive processes which may eventually be available.

In investigating the use of models for vision we have found that many of the
requirements for the modelling and spatial understanding system are exactly
those needed in other areas of motor-sensory functions. The same models and
geometric reasoning capabilities are extremely useful for robot mobility and
manipulation. We have derived techniques to automatically deduce three
dimensional information from descriptions of monocular images in a general
way.

The particular class representation is not universal. We have shown,
however, how to use classes of models for understanding images. A more
general representation of classes, e.g. inclusion of disjunctions in constraints,
would require an upgrade of the various computing engines described (e.g. the
constraint manipulation system, and the geometric reasoning system).
However, the interaction of these parts of the system could still operate in
much the same manner.

Finally notice that there is no notion of assigning probabilities to local or
global interpretations, nor is there any underlying statistical model. ACRONYM
only 'labels' parts of an image for which it can find a globally consistent
interpretation.

ACKNOWLEDGMENT

Much of this work, especially that of Sections 2 and 5 has been carried out under close advice
from my thesis advisor Thomas Binford.

REFERENCES

1. Abraham, R.G., Csakvary, T., Korpela, J., Shum, L., Stewart, R.J.S. and Taleff, A., Program-
   mable assembly research technology: Transfer to industry, 4th Bi-Monthly Report, NSF Grant
   ISP 76-24164, Westinghouse R&D Center, Pittsburgh, June 1977.
2. Agin, G. J., Representation and description of curved objects, Memo AIM 173, Stanford
   University AI Lab (1972).

3. Ambler, A.P. and Popplestone, R.J., Inferring the positions of bodies from specified spatial relationships, *Artificial Intelligence* **6** (1975) 175–208.

4. Baer, A., Eastman, C. and Henrion, M., A survey of geometric modeling, CMU Institute of Physical Planning, Research Rept. No. 66 (1977).

5. Baker, H.H., Edge based stereo correlation, *Proceedings ARPA Image Understanding Workshop*, College Park, MD (1980) 168–175.

6. Barrow, H.G. and Tenenbaum, J.M., MSYS: A system for reasoning about scenes, SRI AI Center, Tech. Note 121 (1976).

7. Barrow, H.G. and Tenenbaum, J.M., Recovering intrinsic scene characteristics from images, in: A. Hanson and E. Riseman, Eds., Computer Vision Systems (Academic Press, New York, 1978).

8. Baumgart, B.G., Geometric modeling for computer vision, Memo AIM 249, Stanford University AI Lab, (1974).

9. Binford, T.O., Visual perception by computer, invited paper at IEEE Systems Science and Cybernetics Conference, Miami, Dec. 1971.

10. Binford, T.O., Computer integrated assembly systems, *Proceedings NSF Grantees Conference on Industrial Automation*, Cornell Univ., Ithaca, Sep. 1979.

11. Bledsoe, W.W., The sup–inf method in Presburger arithmetic, Memo ATP 18, Dept. of Math. and Comp. Sci., University of Texas at Austin, Austin, Texas (1974).

12. Bledsoe, W.W., A new method for proving certain Presburger formulas, *Proceedings of IJCAI* 4, Tibilsi, Georgia, U.S.S.R. (1975) 15–21.

13. Bobrow, D.G., Natural language input for a computer problem solving system, in: M.L. Minsky, Ed., *Semantic Information Processing* (MIT Press, Cambridge, MA, 1968).

14. Bobrow, D.G. and Winograd, T., An overview of KRL, a knowledge representation language, *Cognitive Sci.* **1** (1977) 3–46.

15. Borning, A., THINGLAB: A constraint-oriented simulation laboratory, Stanford CS Report, STAN-CS-79-746 (July 1979).

16. Braid, I.C., *Designing With Volumes* (Cantab Press, Cambridge, England, 1973).

17. Brooks, R.A., Goal-directed edge linking and ribbon finding, *Proceedings ARPA Image Understanding Workshop*, Menlo Park, CA (1979) 72–76.

18. Brooks, R.A., Greiner, R. and Binford, T.O., The ACRONYM model-based vision system, *Proceedings IJCAI* 6, Tokyo (1979) 105–113.

19. Brooks, R.A. and Binford, T.O., Representing and reasoning about partially specified scenes, *Proceedings ARPA Image Understanding Workshop*, College Park, MD (1980) 95–103.

20. Fikes, R.E., Ref-ARF: A system for solving problems stated as procedures, *Artificial Intelligence* **1** (1970) 27–120.

21. Garvey, T.D., Perceptual strategies for purposive vision, SRI AI Center, Tech. Note 117 (1976).

22. Goldman, R., Recent work with the AL system, *Proceedings IJCAI* 5, Cambridge (1977) 733–735.

23. Grimson, W.E.L., Aspects of a computational theory of human stereo vision, *Proceedings ARPA Image Understanding Workshop*, College Park, MD (1980) 128–149.

24. Grossman, D.D., Monte Carlo simulation of tolerancing in discrete parts manufacturing and assembly, Memo AIM 280, Stanford University AI Lab (1976).

25. Hollerbach, J., Hierarchical shape description of objects by selection and modification of prototypes, Tech. Rept. AI-TR-346, MIT, Cambridge (1975).

26. Horn, B.K.P., Obtaining shape from shading information, in: P.H. Winston, Ed., *The Psychology of Computer Vision* (McGraw–Hill, New York, 1975).

27. de Kleer, J. and Sussman G.J., Propagation of constraints applied to circuit synthesis, Memo AIM 485, MIT, Cambridge (1978).

28. Lieberman, L., Model-driven vision for industrial automation, in: P. Stucki, Ed., *Advances in Digital Image Processing: Theory, Application, Implementation* (Plenum Press, New York, 1979).
29. Lowe, D., Solving for the parameters of object models from image descriptions, *Proceedings ARPA Image Understanding Workshop*, College Park, MD (1980) 121–127.
30. Lozano-Pérez, T., The design of a mechanical assembly system, Tech. Rept. AI-TR-397, MIT, Cambridge (1976).
31. Lozano-Pérez, T. and Wesley, M.A., An algorithm for planning collision-free paths among polyhedral obstacles, *Comm. ACM* **22** (1979) 560–570.
32. Marr, D., Visual information processing: The structure and creation of visual representations, *Proceedings IJCAI* 6, Tokyo (1979) 1108–1126.
33. Marr, D. and Hildreth, E., Theory of edge detection, Memo AIM 518, MIT, Cambridge (1979).
34. Marr, D. and Nishihara, H.K., Representation and recognition of the spatial organization of three-dimensional shapes, Memo AIM 377, MIT, Cambridge (1976).
35. McDermott, D., A theory of metric spatial inference, *Proceedings of the First Annual National Conference of on Artificial Intelligence*, Stanford (1980) 246–248.
36. Michie, D., Memo functions: A language feature with rote-learning properties, *Proceedings IFIP*, 1968.
37. Miyamoto, E. and Binford, T.O., Display generated by a generalized cone representation, *IEEE Conference on Computer Graphics and Image Processing*, May 1975.
38. Nevatia, R. and Ramesh Babu, K., Linear feature extraction and description, *Comput. Graphics and Image Processing* **13** (1980) 257–269.
39. Nevatia, R. and Binford, T.O., Description and recognition of curved objects, *Artificial Intelligence* **8** (1977) 77–98.
40. Ohta, Y., Kanade, T. and Sakai, T., A production system for region analysis, *Proceedings IJCAI* 6, Tokyo (1979) 684–686.
41. Shapiro, L.G., Moriarty, J.D. Mulgaonkar, P.G. and Haralick, R.M., Sticks, plates, and blobs: A three-dimensional object representation for scene analysis, *Proceedings of the First Annual National Conference on Artificial Intelligence*, Stanford (1980) 28–30.
42. Shostak, R.E., On the sup-inf method for proving Presburger formulas, *J. Assoc. Comput. Mach.* **24** (1977) 529–543.
43. Soroka, B.I., Understanding objects from slices: Extracting generalised cylinder descriptions from serial sections, Tech. Rept. TR-79-1, Dept. of Computer Science, University of Kansas, Lawrence (1979).
44. Soroka, B.I., Debugging manipulator programs with a simulator, to be present at CAD/CAM 8, Anaheim, Nov. 1980.
45. Staff, An introduction to PADL: characteristics, status, and rationale, Production Automation Project, Tech. Memo TM-22, University of Rochester, Rochester (1974).
46. Stallman, R. and Sussman, G.J., Forward reasoning and dependency—Directed backtracking in a system for computer-aided circuit analysis, *Artificial Intelligence* **9** (1977) 135–196.
47. Sugihara, K., Automatic construction of junction directionaries and their exploitation for the analysis of range data, *Proceedings of IJCAI* 6, Tokyo (1979) 859–864.
48. Taylor, Russel, H., A synthesis of manipulator control programs from task-level specifications, Memo AIM 282, Stanford University AI Lab (1976).
49. Waltz, D., Understanding line drawings of scenes with shadows, in: P.H. Winston, Ed., *The Psychology of Computer Vision* (McGraw-Hill, New York, 1975).
50. Winston, P.H., Learning structural descriptions from examples, in: P.H. Winston, Ed., *The Psychology of Computer Vision*, (McGraw-Hill, New York, 1975).
51. Woodham, R.J., Relating properties of surface curvature to image intensity, *Proceedings of IJCAI* 6, Tokyo (1979) 971–977.

Received November 1980

Psychophysical and Computational Studies towards a Theory of Human Stereopsis

John E.W. Mayhew and John P. Frisby
*Department of Psychology, University of Sheffield,
Sheffield S10 2TN, England*

ABSTRACT

Psychophysical studies are described which pose a strong challenge to models of human stereopsis based on the processing of disparity information within independent spatial frequency tuned binocular channels. These studies support instead the proposal that the processes of human binocular combination integrally relate the extraction of disparity information with the construction of raw primal sketch assertions. This proposal implies global binocular combination rules using principles of figural continuity and cross-channel correspondence to disambiguate local matches found independently within spatial frequency channels. Exploratory small-scale computational experiments with stereo algorithms based on these rules are described and found to be successful in dealing with a variety of stereo inputs. The constraints presented by objects which are exploited by these algorithms are discussed.

1. Introduction

Ever since the introduction by Julesz [7] of the random dot stereogram as a research tool, it has become commonplace to consider the theoretical problems surrounding stereopsis within a conceptual framework that has two distinctive characteristics:

First, it is recognised that disparity information can be extracted using only low-level monocular 'point' descriptions as the entities which are binocularly matched. The random dot stereogram is a clear demonstration that high-level monocular descriptions, such as those dealing with surfaces and objects, are not a necessary requirement for stereopsis because for a random dot stereogram these relatively high level scene descriptions appear only after stereopsis has been achieved.

Second, it has become acknowledged that there is a need for mechanisms capable of selecting the correct binocular point-for-point matches from

Artificial Intelligence **17** (1981) 349–385
North-Holland Publishing Company

amongst the multitude which are frequently possible, most of which are false matches or 'ghosts'. That is, in the terminology of Julesz, it is necessary to posit 'global stereopsis' mechanisms to resolve ambiguity often existing between competing 'local stereopsis' matches.

The clarity of this conceptual framework has spawned a number of stereo algorithms, of varying type and capability (see Marr and Poggio [16] for a review). Given the framework, each algorithm naturally has to face (at least) two critical design choices, namely what monocular point descriptions are to be used, and what global mechanisms are to be employed to resolve the ambiguity inherent within the population of possible local matches. Marr and Poggio [15] have pointed out that any worthwhile algorithm must avoid the trap of ad hoc answers suitable to one type of image but not to others. They have argued, in the manner characteristic of the M.I.T. computational approach to studying visual mechanisms, that the way to do this is to begin with a precise formulation of the goals of the visual task being considered (in this case the exact processing goals associated with stereopsis). The next step they advocate is to develop a computational theory specifying useful constraints about how objects behave in the world, constraints which enable valid processing rules to be formulated for use in an algorithm capable of achieving the goals in question. We are in great sympathy with this approach and much of what we discuss in this paper falls naturally within its scope. Nevertheless, the particular model of human stereopsis which we describe owes at least as much to the results of our psychophysical work on stereopsis as it does to computational considerations— hence the title of this paper.

2. The BRPS Conjecture

Over the past few years, we have conducted a series of psychophysical studies of human stereopsis which have led us to the following conjecture:

THE BRPS CONJECTURE. *The process of human binocular combination integrally relate the extraction of disparity information with the construction of raw primal sketch assertions.*

We call this conjecture the BRPS conjecture because it amounts to the proposal that one goal of early visual processing is the computation of a Binocular Raw Primal Sketch. In this paper we discuss our psychophysical justifications for advancing the conjecture and we present various computational studies related to it. We also discuss how the conjecture relates to the models of stereopsis advanced by Marr and Poggio [15, 17], models which while importantly different from our own nevertheless have contributed much to the evolution of our ideas. Before proceeding in detail to these various tasks, however, several preliminary comments about the conjecture are in order:

(a) It is worth noting that a 'raw primal sketch' is defined by Marr [12] as the representation making explicit information about intensity changes in an image, using in its present formulation a primitive language of edge-segments, bars, blobs and terminations. The selection, grouping and summarising of these raw primitives leads to larger and more abstract tokens in a description that Marr calls the 'full primal sketch'. Of course, future work may lead to a revision of details of this representation without prejudice to the BRPS conjecture (although with implications for the implementation of binocular combination rules based upon it: see concluding remarks in Section 7).

(b) The most general computational implication of the conjecture is that the constraints and correspondences between spatial frequency tuned channel outputs that can be used to compute monocular descriptions of intensity changes [12, 13], together with the grouping principle of figural continuity, can be applied to advantage at various stages during the process of binocular combination. The final result is a set of binocular intensity change descriptions to which are tied disparity assignments.

Marr's general scheme for obtaining raw primal sketch assertions from channel outputs has two major steps: (i) certain very low level descriptive elements (e.g. zero crossings) are extracted from each channel's output independently: we will call these descriptive elements 'measurement primitives' to distinguish them from raw primal sketch primitives; and (ii) measurement primitives from all the various channels are submitted to a set of cross-channel 'parsing' rules which result in the required raw primal sketch assertions. The BRPS conjecture proposes that human binocular combination takes place during both these steps, with initial binocular matches effected at the level of measurement primitives being disambiguated during the application of binocular combination rules whose ultimate objective is the delivery of binocular raw primal sketch assertions. The need for disambiguation stems from the fact that a large population of binocular measurement primitive matches are frequently possible, with only a certain number of these being correct matches and the remainder being false matches (see earlier remarks on local vs. global stereopsis).

(c) Alternative processes of binocular combination to those specified in the conjecture can in principle be envisaged, so that the conjecture does not embrace all possible models of human stereopsis. For example, it could be that human binocular combination proceeds in a way which takes no advantage of cross-channel correspondences existing between spatial frequency channel outputs for disambiguation, as for example in Marr and Poggio's [17] stereo algorithm in which cross-channel combination takes place in the $2\frac{1}{2}$ D sketch after disambiguation has been achieved within each channel independently (except for some coupling via vergence control: see Section 5.3). Also, it is possible to envisage models of stereopsis in which binocular combination proceeds after the stage at which raw primal sketch elements are constructed, models which are nevertheless 'low-level' in general terms. For example, Marr and Poggio [15] suggested that their cooperative disparity-processing network could be fed with fully-parsed raw primal sketch elements, the network then serving to disambiguate competing element-for-element matches at a stage much later than that proposed for the initiation of disambiguation as far as the BRPS conjecture is concerned.

(d) The stereo models of Marr and Poggio just referred to are successful in dealing with a number of different types of stereo inputs, including in the case of [17] a wide range of random-dot stereograms and also some natural scene stereograms [6]. Moreover, the success of these models is based on an analysis of constraints offered by objects in the world, and on how rules for binocular combination stemming from these constraints can be implemented in a stereo algorithm which exploits the constraints to attain correct stereo fusion. The question of what constraints are available is, we recognise, a very important one and we will return frequently in this paper to the constraints on which our own conceptions of human stereopsis processing might be based.

3. Choice of Monocular Measurement Primitives

3.1. Zero crossings

For the various elegant computational reasons advanced by Marr and Hildreth [13], zero crossings discovered in spatial frequency tuned convolutions (Marr and Poggio [17]) seem a good starting point for the computation of a monocular raw primal sketch. Therefore, given the BRPS conjecture, it is natural to use zero crossings extracted from left and right image convolutions as at least one of the set of measurement primitives used for constructing a binocular raw primal sketch. It is sensible to put some limits on left/right zero crossing matches that are initially allowed and in both the stereo algorithm of Marr and Poggio [17] and in those of our own design described here, only zero crossings of the same contrast sign and roughly similar orientation are binocularly combined.

3.2. Peaks

Despite some theoretical advantages possessed by zero crossings as measurement primitives (see Marr et al. [18] and later for a discussion of the relevance of Logan's theorem in this context), it seems to us that in some situations at least, zero crossings are in principle poor measurement primitives for the purposes of extracting disparity information. Consider, for example, the stereogram shown in Fig. 1a. The left and right halves are saw tooth luminance gratings of the same period but with slightly differing shapes (peaks and troughs in slightly different locations in the left and right images, as can be seen more clearly in the luminance profile of this stereogram shown in Fig. 1b).

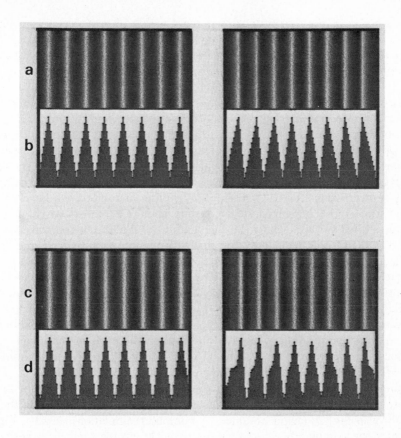

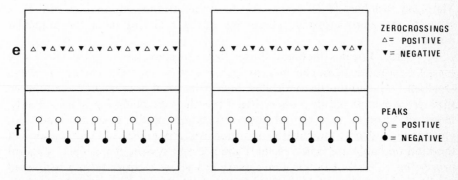

FIG. 1. Measurement primitives used for human stereopsis: the need for peaks as well as zero crossings. See Section 3.2 for details.

Stereo fusion of Fig. 1a produces a percept with both a tilted and corrugated depth profile, as shown (approximately) in Fig. 2a, but this is not the percept predicted if zero crossings alone provided the basis for binocular matching. The reason for this can be understood by inspecting the other parts of Figs. 1 and 2. In Fig. 1c is shown an image produced by convolving Fig. 1a with a spatial frequency channel whose tuning is modelled on the data of Wilson and Giese [28] and whose centre frequency has the period of the 2nd harmonic of the sawtooth input (we have in fact tried channels tuned to all harmonics up to the 5th with similar results to those about to be described). The convolution profile appearing in this channel is illustrated in Fig. 1d, and the zero crossings discovered in this profile are shown in Fig. 1e. If stereopsis was based solely on these zero crossings, then, as a simple computer simulation we have created demonstrates, the perceived depth profile should be as shown in Fig. 2b, namely a tilted surface lacking the corrugations of the actually perceived profile 2a). We note also in this connection that it is possible to have zero crossings in identical locations for two stereo pairs and yet have a different perceived depth for each pair (e.g. suitable combinations of triangular and sawtooth waveforms comprising the left and right fields can be used to demonstrate this point).

The general principle illustrated by Fig. 1a is that the strategy of using solely zero crossings will fail for those parts of an image where disparity variations are tied to luminance variations situated in between the parts of the image which produce zero crossings. For such cases, it seems that (as a minimum) information carried by the peaks of the convolution profiles is required. Peaks for the stereogram in question are shown in Fig. 1f (troughs are of course simply negative peaks), and the perceived depth profile expected from these is as shown in Fig. 2c (again obtained by computer simulation). Finally, Fig. 2d provides the combined zero-crossings-plus-peaks profile, and it suggests that this combination could provide a good basis for later processes of interpolation to construct the perceived profile shown in Fig. 2a (e.g. those processes of depth interpolation which might be an important part of $2\frac{1}{2}$ sketch processing: Marr and Nishihara [14]). In any event, we submit that this analysis of Fig. 1a suggests that zero crossings alone are not a sufficient basis for binocular matching.

Of course, Logan's theorem shows that the convolution profile of a one octave bandwidth filter can in principle be recovered from its zero crossing locations [11], and this fact indicates that peaks could in principle be computed from a recovered profile rather than from the convolution profiles directly. However, even if recovery of the convolution profile from just the zero crossings is indeed a practical proposition using purely local computations of the kind probably embodied in the human visual system at this early stage of processing, it seems a rather unnecessary procedure to work from a recovered profile instead of from the initial profile. (It might be, however, that for reasons of reconstructing a finer resolution intensity map in the striate cortex upon

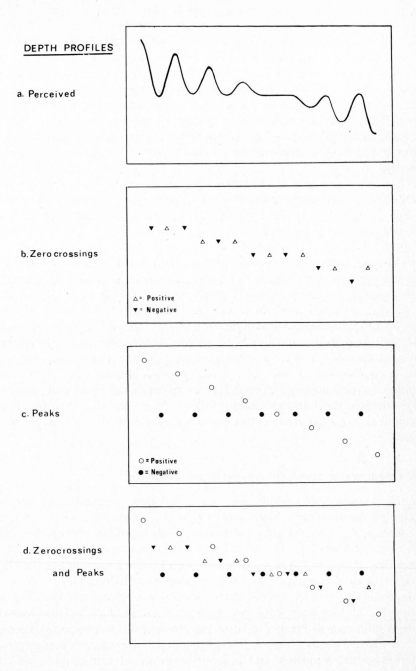

FIG. 2. Depth profiles associated with the stereogram shown in Fig. 1a. See Section 3.2 for details.

which all later processes operate [1], this is in fact what happens, with zero crossings transmitted to the cortex as the most economical way of carrying the essential information required for reconstruction.) In any event, the important point about the stereo demonstration of Fig. 1a is that it seems to preclude binocular matches restricted solely to zero crossings, and it is immaterial for present purposes whether the additional measurement primitives required are taken directly from spatial frequency channel convolutions or whether they are taken from convolution profiles reconstituted from zero crossings. We are presently studying the problems surrounding the extraction and utilisation of peaks as additional measurement primitives to be used in conjunction with zero crossings.

It is worth noting in this connection that we have argued elsewhere for peaks being used as measurement primitives but for reasons other than those raised by Fig. 1a (see [4, 23]). Thus whereas zero crossings for edges exhibit spatial coincidences which are highly convenient for parsing purposes (Marr and Hildreth [13]), zero crossings from bars do not exhibit this easy-to-parse cross-channel alignment. In fact, Marr and Hildreth use as their parsing rule for bars not the discovery of spatially coincident measurement primitives in two or more channels but the presence of within-channel neighbouring zero crossings of opposite contrast sign. However, we have noted that peaks do show convenient spatial coincidence in the case of bars and, although the question of what parsing rules can and should be adopted is presently a research question, this consideration provides another ground, this time a computational rather than a psychophysical one, for involving peak measurement primitives in addition to zero crossings. (The difference between the peaks and zero crossings situation for bars and edges follows from the fact that the fourier components for a bar are in cosine phase whereas those for an edge are in sine phase.)

3.3. Orientated or circularly symmetric convolutions?

Should measurement primitives be extracted from orientated or circularly symmetric convolutions? Marr and Poggio [17] chose the orientated option although in an implementation of the key features of their stereo algorithm, Grimson and Marr [6] substituted circular for orientated convolutions. A full theoretical debate of the computational considerations surrounding the choice between these alternatives is provided in Marr and Hildreth [13].

Interestingly, we have arrived independently at a rejection of the orientated option [4, 22] but mainly for psychophysical rather than for computational reasons (although as far as the latter are concerned, we noted the expensive, indeed almost wanton, use of storage implied by holding in memory many different spatial frequency and orientationally tuned convolutions, and also some of the unnecessary and rather ad hoc computational procedures required to obtain a primal sketch from orientated convolution data). Our psychophysical studies telling against orientated convolutions for stereopsis are twofold:

(a) We have discovered that if stereopsis from an orientated texture stereogram is masked by adding similarly orientated noise to one field, then rotation of the masking noise so that it would no longer perturb an orientated convolution carrying the disparity signals, does not succeed in releasing the stereopsis from the effects of the mask [20]. This is difficult to understand if local measurement primitives are extracted from orientated convolutions.

(b) We have pointed out that orientated spatial frequency tuned filters are in principle poor devices for dealing with rapidly changing disparity cues [22]. Consider for example the stereogram shown in Fig. 3a which depicts a series of near-horizontal corrugations, as though the observer was looking down on a corrugated roof. Vertically-tuned filters could not in principle extract the depth from this stereogram: filters of this type would inevitably have receptive fields spreading over several rasters and so smear hopelessly the different disparity cues contained in each one. Hence it is not surprising that the vertical ±45° filtered version of Fig. 3a shown in Fig. 3b cannot be successfully fused to reveal the corrugations. It might be thought that the easily-obtained stereopsis from Fig. 3a could be mediated by horizontally-tuned units, but the poor quality of the stereopsis deriving from a horizontal ±45° filtered version

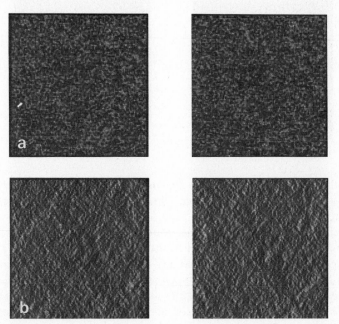

FIG. 3. Stereograms portraying a horizontally corrugated surface. See Sections 3.3(b) and 5.3.2 for details.

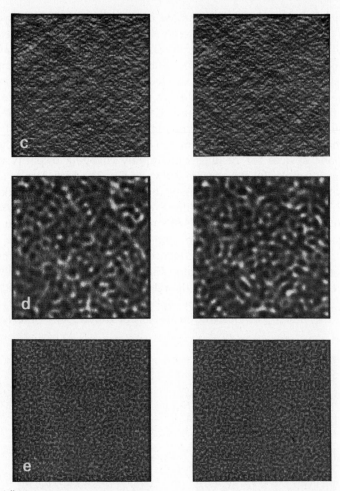

FIG. 3 (*cont'd*).

suggests otherwise (Fig. 3c), as does the fact that many naive subjects cannot
obtain any depth whatsoever from this horizontally-filtered stereo pair,
whereas they can do so for the unfiltered original.

We conclude from these two studies that orientated spatial frequency tuned
convolutions do not seem to be used in the human visual system as a basis for
establishing local disparity matches, at any rate not exclusively. (Of course, this
conclusion does not preclude other types of orientational selectivity embedded
in the stereopsis mechanism, both at the local and global levels. Orientation is
tied to zero crossings at the local level, and orientation can be made use of at
the global level by a disambiguating algorithm which incorporates a principle of
figural continuity—see next section.)

4. Binocular Combination Rule 1: Figural Continuity

If an ambiguity in left/right zero crossing matches arises, those matches which preserve figural continuity are to be preferred, given the BRPS conjecture. This is because figural continuity is an important principle utilised in obtaining raw primal sketch assertions. Thus the binocular use of figural continuity is one way in which the overall objective of obtaining a binocular raw primal sketch constrains and directs the flow of support between local measurement primitive matches to obtain global disambiguation. Exactly what we mean by figural continuity will become clear shortly when we describe some computational experiments utilising a binocular figural grouping rule.

We will discuss later the constraints presented by objects in the visual world which justify the use of figural continuity requirements for binocular disambiguation. However, it is worth noting at this point that zero crossings are intrinsically continuous because they are the points of intersection of a plane with a surface, i.e. they are the points where the DC plane intersects the 2D convolution surface. This consideration gives added justification for attempting to disambiguate zero crossings along the axis of their orientation (rather than confining disambiguation to mutual support/inhibition between horizontally neighbouring and figurally unrelated zero crossings, as for example in Marr and Poggio's [17] model).

4.1. A computational demonstration of the disambiguating power of a binocular figural grouping rule

We describe in this section a computational experiment which explored the disambiguating potential of selecting only those binocular zero crossing matches which preserve figural continuity.

The input image for the experiment was a finely-textured random dot pattern (1 pixel black/white squares; 50% density). It was first filtered with a gaussian filter whose centre frequency was 5 pixels and whose bandwidth was ± 0.26 octaves (the effects of using broader bandwidths were explored later in the experiment). From the resultant convolution profile, 20 sample rasters were arbitrarily selected, separated from each other by 5 pixels. The zero crossings on these rasters were then found, producing a total of 464 'target' zero crossings whose disambiguation when matching the convolution profile with itself was the subject of the experiment.

For each target, the number of similarly-signed zero crossings lying within 20 pixels to the right of that target was counted. This count defined the number of ghosts for that target, i.e. the number of its potential false matches for the purposes of the experiment. The experiment therefore simulated the disambiguation problem involved in matching a large planar surface of zero disparity using a Panum's fusional area with, say, a 'convergent zone' of 20 pixels, i.e. four times the period of the filter's centre frequency. The total number of ghosts found for the 464 targets in this way was 1006, giving a ghost/match ratio of 2.17. This ratio served as a measure of the disambiguation problem when each zero crossing target was considered wholly in isolation. The objective of the experiment was to discover whether this ratio was appreciably reduced if figural continuity of zero crossing matches was used as a binocular combination rule.

The general strategy we used for assessing the benefits conveyed by figural continuity was to examine the consequences of restricting the definition of a ghost in the 20 pixel fusional window to that of a zero crossing whose surrounding pattern of zero crossings in the rasters above and below it possessed similar figural continuity to that of the target. For example, under the strictest matching requirement a ghost was logged only if the zero crossing under consideration had the same figurally continuous disposition of zero crossings in the 4 rasters above and below it as did the target (i.e. in this case the 'binocular' zero crossing had to be the central point in figurally identical 'left' and 'right' zero crossing segments of length 9 pixels). Here and throughout the experiment, two zero crossings in adjacent rasters were defined as figurally continuous if their Y coordinates were the same or ±1, a definition which constrained the orientation of any zero crossing segment to fall within a window ±45 degrees of vertical (though of course the segment need not follow a straight path within this window).

Ghost/match ratios using this kind of figural disambiguation are shown in Table 1 for segment lengths up to 9 pixels and for filters of three different bandwidths. Also, the table shows the consequences of relaxing the matching

TABLE 1. An evaluation of figural continuity as a binocular combination rule. (See Section 4.1)

Filter tuning (All with centre frequency periods of 5 pixels)	Zero crossing ghost/match ratios for line segments of length (in pixels) up to:						Orientational tuning
	1	3	5	7	9		
Narrowband (±0.26 octave)	2.17 (N = 464)	0.739	0.103 0.317	0.037 0.164	0.032 0.072	(0.018) (0.069)	Exact 45°
Broadband (±1 octave)	2.47 (N = 509)	0.703	0.191 0.303	0.117 0.177	0.108 0.157	(0.067) (0.126)	Exact 45°
Psychophysically plausible (see text)	2.66 (N = 539)	0.744	0.182 0.295	0.122 0.194	0.117 0.156	(0.051) (0.160)	Exact 45°

The N's in brackets give the absolute number of zero crossing matches for each filter (see text for details).

requirement from that of identical figural context to simply demanding that the overall orientations of left and right segments (themselves figurally continuous in the sense defined) differed by no more than 45 degrees. In interpreting this table, note that the ratios are computed cumulatively in that any ghosts not disambiguated at a given segment length, and also not disambiguated by appearing subsequently in longer segment lengths, are left in the unresolved ghost count. For example, all ratios for line lengths 3–9 include ghosts arising from short segments 1 and 2 pixels long, excepting those ratios in brackets for the 9 pixel segments for which these short-segment ghosts were removed for reasons which will be described later.

There are various points of interest to note about the data shown in Table 1. First and most importantly, the way in which the ghost/match ratios diminish as figural context is increased clearly demonstrates that a binocular figural continuity rule does possess useful disambiguating power for the kind of texture under consideration. Moreover, this rule has value even for quite broad filters and even if loosely-tuned orientational matching is allowed between left and right segments.

Second, a good deal of short-segment noise appeared in the zero crossing outputs. This was caused by the use of a relatively high frequency filter in conjunction with a fine grain pattern, coupled with inevitable quantisation fuzz tending to break up zero crossing continuity (particularly for near-horizontal segments). In fact, about 15% of the zero crossings fell in segments less than 3 pixels long. These segments generated a collection of ghosts which obviously could not in principle be disambiguated using figural continuity. The ratios in brackets in the right hand column of the table show the effects of removing them from the data for segment length 9 and these ratios perhaps give a better idea of the true disambiguating power of figural continuity. Notice that these short segment ghosts are proportionately more common in the exact orientational tuning case for the simple reason that the loose orientational tuning obviously produced a larger absolute number of ghosts for the longer segment lengths. Nevertheless, the relatively poorer ratios for the loose tuning case should not obscure the fact that in a stereo algorithm using figural continuity, it would usually be a trivial matter to choose a best-bet left-right match which favoured an exactly tuned match if such was available.

Third, in a stereo algorithm based on the BRPS conjecture, disambiguation would come not just from figural continuity but also from cross channel correspondences. We will discuss these fully in later sections but it is of interest to note here that the ghost/match ratios shown in Table 1 fall to trivial levels if a cross channel correspondence rule is also applied. For example, the residue of ghosts was reduced by two-thirds when in a similar experiment to that referred to in Table 1 figural continuity was augmented by cross channel correspondence of the type described in Section 5. We regard this as an encouraging demonstration of the power of disambiguating rules derived directly from the BRPS conjecture, particularly when it is remembered that Panum's area was set to a large value for the purposes of the experiment.

4.2. A stereo algorithm using figural continuity

A stereo algorithm called STEREOEDGE which exploits figural continuity has been written [4, 23] and it demonstrates that curvilinear grouping rules can successfully disambiguate zero crossing and peak matches in both natural and random dot stereograms. The algorithm returns edge-segment and angle assertions to which are tied disparity assignments. A full description of STEREO-EDGE would be superfluous here but its major characteristics will be sketched.

Figural continuity is implemented in STEREOEDGE as the piece-wise local binocular grouping of adjacent peaks or zero crossing matches of the same contrast sign. Grouping across small gaps in peak or zero crossing continuity (e.g. those caused by quantisation fuzz) may be admitted if disparity continuity is not grossly violated, if overall orientation is preserved, and of course if no better grouping is available. Disambiguation by the collinear grouping of primitives of the same contrast sign is natural given the overall objective of arriving at binocular raw edge segment assertions. If two connected binocular edge-segments of different orientations are present, then STEREOEDGE returns an angle assertion for the appropriate location. Thus the type of figural grouping employed is similar to the process of curvilinear aggregation described by Marr [12] in connection with the primal sketch.

4.3. Matter is cohesive: A constraint about the world justifying the rule of figural continuity

It is easy to justify the use of binocular figural grouping principles in terms of constraints about the world upon which the processes of binocular combination must rely. As Marr and Poggio [15] pointed out in their analysis of the stereo disparity computational problem, "Matter is cohesive, it is separated into objects". It is a simple consequence of this fact that the edges of surfaces and surface markings such as lines and blobs will be spatially continuous and this is the ultimate justification for relying on figural grouping rules to guide binocular combination.

Note, however, that our use of this constraint about the world is importantly different from that of Marr and Poggio [15]. Unlike us, they use the constraint to justify a rule of preferring matches which are disparity-continuous. This leads them to a cooperative algorithm which relies on lateral excitation between similar disparity matches. Their later algorithm [17] has similar albeit less extensive disparity facilitation. For us, the pursuit of raw-primal-sketch-type binocular figural descriptions is the overall objective and this does not necessarily demand the explicit use of similar-disparity information to guide the selection of left/right matches. In STEREOEDGE, for example, left/right zero crossing matches are first chosen according to the principle of figural continuity alone, without any explicit reference to the disparity continuity of these matches, and with the actual disparity value of selected matches accessed only after binocular combination has taken place. This is not to say, of course, that similar-disparity facilitation cannot be of value and indeed STEREO-EDGE uses collinear disparity facilitation if local figural continuity fails to select a unique match [23].

4.4. Psycophysical evidence supporting the rule of figural continuity

We believe there are sound psycophysical reasons for supposing that figural continuity provides a guiding role in human stereopsis:

(a) Consider for example the stereogram shown in Fig. 4a whose central disparate square is outlined with a monocularly-discriminable line cue. As has been realised for some time [27], such cues can produce dramatically shorter stereopsis latencies than those obtained from equivalent cyclopean stimuli. It is probable that improved vergence control is one aspect of this facilitation [10, 26, 27] but this cannot be the whole story because we have discovered that facilitation can still be present even if the stereogram is flashed for durations below 160 msec, which is the generally recognised latency time for vergence shifts. Moreover, this tachistoscopic facilitation can still be demonstrated even if the line cue is high-pass filtered (Fig. 4b) to prevent any benefit accruing from the relatively unambiguous matches delivered by low spatial frequency channels triggered by the unfiltered line cue [17]. It could perhaps be argued that the facilitation present in this high-pass case might be due not to benefit conveyed by figural continuity but rather because its line cue presents sparse and relatively unambiguous matches at the local level, by giving rise to zero crossings with different orientations from those in the surround. However, a version of monocular-cue facilitation which avoids this possible objection is shown in Fig. 4c. Here the monocular cue condition is not high-pass filtered but instead band-pass filtered with the same filter that was used to create the background texture. Our computer simulation fails to find unambiguous orientated zero crossing matches in this case and yet psychophysically the cue still produces good facilitation (compared with a cyclopean control lacking the cue: J.E.W. Mayhew, J.P. Frisby and A.L. Kidd, in preparation). We submit that this case of monocular cue facilitation can be due only to benefit provided by the fact that the local matches produced by the band-pass line are so configured that they provide a good stimulus for a binocular combination mechanism utilising figural continuity. This mechanism could perhaps be a grouping process which finds that peaks from the bandpass cue line up with good figural continuity: hence the facilitation.

(b) Further support for the important role played by figural continuity in human stereopsis is given by some findings using the stereo pairs shown in Fig. 5.

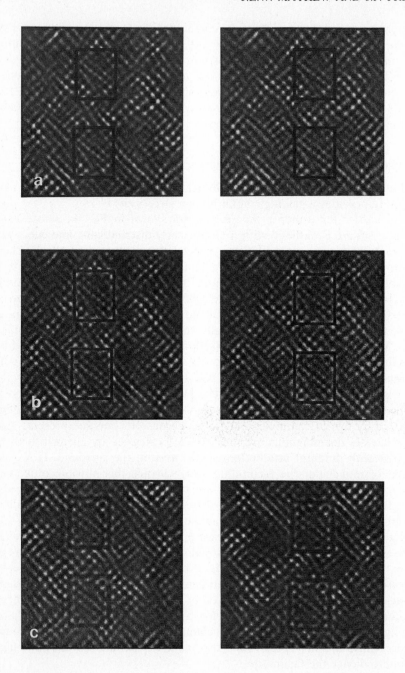

FIG. 4. Stereograms containing monocularly-discriminable cues about their disparate targets. See Section 4.4(a) for details.

In Fig. 5a is shown a high-pass filtered version of a chequer board stereo-gram made up of 8 pixel black/white squares whose various edges possess strong figural continuity. We have found that this stereogram is fused by naive subjects with significantly shorter latencies than the stereogram shown in Fig. 5b. This latter stimulus differs principally from Fig. 5a in that the edge-segments carrying its disparity cues are so distributed that they possess poor vertical figural continuity and yet they present a much less severe ambiguity problem than Fig. 5a. It was created by taking the 8-pixel chequer board pattern used for Fig. 5a, shifting each raster randomly, and then high-pass filtering the result, a procedure which conveniently produces a stereogram with as many edge-segments as Fig. 5a but ones which are in poor vertical figural alignment. Inspection of near-vertical zero crossing maps (Figs. 5c and 5d) reveals that there is much more stereo ambiguity in Fig. 5a than in Fig. 5b (due to the high-pass filtering causing quite prominent ripples in between the edge-related variations). This point is further illustrated in Fig. 5e, which shows distributions of nearest-neighbour horizontal intervals found within Figs. 5c and 5d. These distributions reveal very clearly that in Fig. 5c each zero crossing has a much higher probability of having relatively close neighbours than is the case in Fig. 5d. This fact is of some interest as far as Marr and Poggio's [17] model of stereopsis is concerned. In the experiment described above, which measured the relative ease of fusing stereograms 5a and 5b, the disparity was set to 6 pixels, or about 16 min for the viewing distance employed (about 57 cm). This disparity is more than twice the limit allowed for a Marr/Poggio disparity channel tuned to 4 cycles/degree. A Marr/Poggio channel tuned to 2 cycles/degree might possibly cope and its breadth of tuning would be sufficient to enable it to respond to the energy in the high pass stereogram. However, as the plot shown in Fig. 5e for the chequer board stimulus reveals, the 6 pixel disparity range covered by this channel (marked by an arrow on the abscissa) would capture a large number of ghosts—and certainly many more than it would face for the horizontally-textured stereogram of Fig. 5b—yet despite this Fig. 5a is still much the easiest stereogram to fuse. Marr and Poggio's model predicts the reverse of this psychophysical result.

The effectiveness of using figural continuity for disambiguation is further illustrated if one half of Fig. 5a is used as an input for the kind of experiment described in Section 4.2. When this is done, ghost/match ratios computed without benefit of figural continuity are respectively 2.218 and 1.914 for psychophysically plausible channels with centre periods of 5 and 10 pixels (roughly equivalent to 4 and 2 cycles/degree in the experiment described above). These ratios fall to 0.059 and 0.054 respectively when binocular figural continuity is used (with exact left/right orientational tuning and disambiguation within zero crossing segments up to 9 pixels long), a result which parallels STEREOEDGE's performance on this stimulus.

Although Marr and Poggio's [17] model does not explicitly use figural

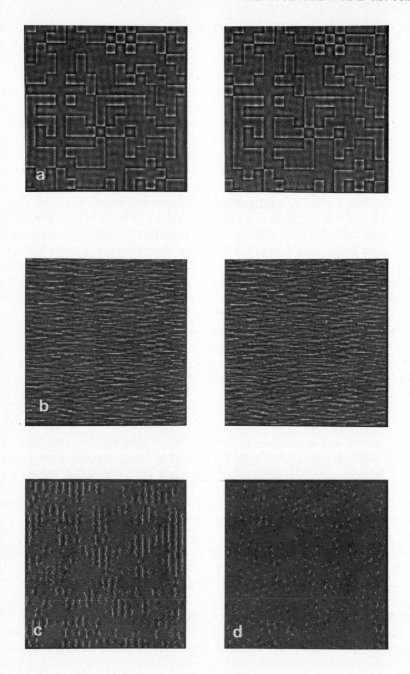

FIG. 5. Stereopsis and figural continuity. See Section 4.4(b) for details.

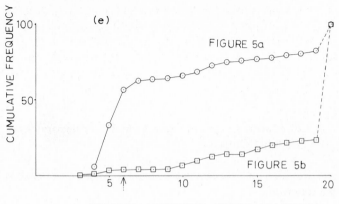

FIG. 5 (*cont'd*).

continuity, it might be asked (as indeed a referee of this paper has asked) whether or not that model implicitly uses figural continuity in that it seeks support within a circular neighborhood. In debating this question, it is important to recognise that the theoretical underpin of Marr and Poggio's model is an analysis of nearest-neighbour zero crossing statistics. This analysis is 1-dimensional but is justified by being tied to the use of orientated filters which effectively force a 2-dimensional pattern into an approximation of a 1-dimensional grating pattern. Clearly, in such a case the use of figural continuity would be ineffective as a disambiguating principle but more importantly figural continuity would be orthogonal (literally!) to the theory's arguments.

It is true, of course, that Grimson and Marr's [6] implementation of Marr and Poggio's theory uses circular rather than orientated filters, as we do ourselves. Moreover, their disambiguating algorithm uses a circular neighbourhood for support which to be in keeping with their statistical nearest-neighbour analysis must be at least as large in radius as the disparity matching range of the channel under consideration. Inevitably, therefore, this circular field will capture support not only from non-figurally continuous neighbours of the type considered in the formal theory itself but also support from upper and lower zero crossings which happen to fall in figural alignment with the zero crossing under consideration. But only in this weakest and most general sense, applicable to any model relying on a circular support zone, can the theory be said to implement implicitly figural continuity.

4.5. Summary

To summarise this section, it seems to us that our psychophysical results lead to the conclusion that figural continuity does indeed play an important role in the guidance of binocular combination as far as human stereopsis is concerned. Moreover, this conclusion is consistent with the outcomes of various computational experiments. The explicit use of figural continuity is justified in terms of constraints flowing from the nature of objects in the visual world which are exploited in the visual processing task specified by the BRPS conjecture.

5. Binocular Combination Rule 2: Correspondences Between Channel Outputs

5.1. The interpretation of cross-channel correspondences for constructing raw primal sketch assertions

Marr [12] and Marr and Hildreth [13] have demonstrated how various correspondences between spatial frequency channel outputs can be utilised to compute the figural type of raw primal sketch assertions (e.g. whether an edge, line or blob is present and what contrast and width it possesses). The BRPS conjecture holds that these correspondences are used during human binocular combination, so that the patterns of between-channel correspondence which enable figural type to be asserted also help disambiguate within-channel fusions.

There are two important forms of cross-channel correspondence to which Marr [12] and Marr and Hildreth [13] draw attention: spatial coincidence and spectral continuity.

As far as spatial coincidence is concerned, Marr and Hildreth have shown that if zero crossings are present in two or more spatial frequency channels in the same relative locations, then this 'spatial coincidence' is clear-cut evidence that an edge is present in the image in the appropriate position. Consequently, they have argued that spatially coincident zero crossings provide excellent points at which to interpret channel outputs by way of arriving at assertions about the particular type of edge present. We have added to this the consideration that peaks show equally convenient spatial coincidence when bars are present, whereas zero crossings tend to spread out for such inputs (see Section 3.2).

Turning to the question of spectral continuity, Marr [12] pointed out that it is both possible and desirable to use a rule of spectral continuity to guide the preliminary section of channel measurements prior to their interpretation as a descriptive element. Thus if the distribution of channel outputs is unimodal, a single descriptive element is parsed; on the other hand, if there is a split into two groups, then the assumption is made that each group comes from a different entity in the image and a separate description is obtained for each group, so that for example a sharp line can be parsed as 'sitting on top of' a blurred blob.

5.2. Spatial uniqueness: A constraint about the world justifying the binocular use of correspondences between channels

It is possible to justify our binocular deployment of cross-channel correspondences in terms of the constraints imposed by objects in the world. Here the relevant constraint is similar to Constraint 1 of Marr and Poggio [15], namely "that a given point on a physical surface has a unique position in space at any one time". However, our use of this constraint is subtlely but importantly different from that of Marr and Poggio. We prefer to emphasise what might loosely be termed the converse of Marr and Poggio's Constraint 1. That is, we find it more helpful to say that "a given location in space can hold only one object at any one time", a formulation we call the Constraint of Spatial Uniqueness. The straightforward implication of this formulation is that any given disparity/position location should carry a symbolic description of similar figural type in the left and right eye views and that 'rivalrous' matches (i.e. those coming from left/right entities of different figural type) are to be rejected. What this leads to is a binocular combination rule which demands that any disparity/position location should be supported by a similar pattern of cross-channel activity from the two eyes views and that dissimilar cross-channel patterns can be rejected as figurally rivalrous. Dissimilar cross-channel patterns will of their very nature contain within-channel ghosts and these will therefore be eliminated. The details of one particular scheme of this type will be described in due course. For the present, the important point we wish to emphasise is that the use of cross-channel combination rules to guide binocular fusion finds its computational justification quite readily in terms of constraints imposed by objects.

It is perhaps worth mentioning at this point that the binocular matching rule which we extract from the Constraint of Spatial Uniqueness is very different from the rule which Marr and Poggio [15] extract from their equivalent constraint. They elaborated a rule which states that "each item from each image may be assigned at most one disparity value". Unfortunately, this rule flatly contradicts the usual interpretation of Panum's Limiting Case (i.e. the interpretation which assumes that a feature in one eye's image can be matched to more than one feature in the other eye's image). Marr and Poggio themselves refer to this difficulty but note that when their uniqueness assumption is violated, then the algorithm can be made to assign a match which is unique from one image but not from the other (they cite O.J. Braddick, in preparation). We, however, avoid this difficulty altogether simply by avoiding Marr and Poggio's matching rule. Instead, our formulation of the Constraint of Spatial Uniqueness and its associated rule of utilising between-channel spatial correspondences copes easily and naturally with Panum's Limiting Case. This is because it makes evident sense within our own conceptual framework to parse out separate descriptive elements existing in different disparity/position locations when the stimulus input is a single line in one eye and two side-by-side lines in the other eye.

5.3. Psychophysical evidence supporting the binocular combination rule of cross-channel correspondences

We have reported elsewhere (Mayhew and Frisby [21]) certain contrast summation effects operating across spatial frequencies at stereo threshold and how these support the notion of cross-channel global disambiguation processes in human stereopsis (presumably these effects would have to reflect post-disambiguation processes within the $2\frac{1}{2}$ D sketch in Marr and Poggio's [17] model). We now describe two further studies on this theme but based on quite different psychophysical paradigms.

5.3.1. *The case of the missing fundamental*

One line of evidence which has led us to believe that cross-channel combination rules play a role in guiding binocular fusion comes from an investigation we have conducted (Mayhew and Frisby [24]) into the binocular fusion of square wave gratings with a missing fundamental (Figs. 6a and 6b). Disparate waveforms of this kind present interesting ambiguities about which left/right zero crossing matches are to be selected. For example, consider Fig.

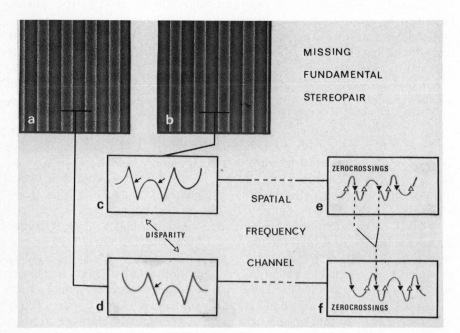

FIG. 6. The missing fundamental stereopair. See Section 5.3.1 for details.

6d which shows a magnified sample of the luminance profile of the left eye's image. When convolved with a spatial frequency channel whose centre frequency is that of the 3rd harmonic of the grating, zero crossings found for this sample are displayed in Fig. 6f (channel tuning modelled on the psychophysical data of Wilson and Giese [28]). The interesting ambiguity within this sample is illustrated in connection with one particular zero crossing, that identified with a vertical dotted line. Note that it derives from the edge marked with a small arrow in the luminance profile of Fig. 6d. Note also that it can in principle be matched to at least two zero crossings in the left eye's convolution profile: these are shown in Fig. 6e, also with vertical dotted lines and again the parts of the luminance profile from which they derive are shown with small arrows, this time in Fig. 6c.

Now due to the fact that the stereopair of Figs. 6a/6b possesses a fairly large disparity (greater than half the period of the 3rd harmonic in fact), the correct zero crossing match (the leftmost one shown in Figs. 6e and 6f) is, as far as Marr and Poggio's [17] model is concerned, outside the allowable range for the channel under consideration. Consequently, Marr and Poggio's model would predict that within this channel the smaller-disparity incorrect match would be the one selected (the rightmost one shown in Figs. 6e and 6f). Therefore, if this channel was the one critically mediating the perceived stereopsis, the predicted psychophysical result would be the percept of a grating receding relative to its surround (for crossed-eye fusion of Figs. 6a and 6b). This argument is borne out by a computer simulation of Marr and Poggio's algorithm which we have run on this stereogram and which does indeed choose this receding match. In marked contrast with this prediction, the depth effect which is actually seen is that of a protruding grating. That is, the human visual system selects the correct disparity match, despite the fact that it is of a size that puts it out of range for the type of channel being considered and despite the fact that an alternative within-range match is potentially available.

Thus what seems to be happening in the case of the missing fundamental stereogram is that stereopsis is based on the different types of edges in the luminance profile, rather than on zero crossing matches found and processed independently within spatial frequency tuned stereopsis channels. This conclusion is very much in keeping with the BRPS conjecture, because it requires that local matches found in all spatial frequency channels are considered jointly and in parallel, in an endeavour to find the best fitting binocular edge descriptions consistent with the total data provided by these channels.

This general scheme of binocular combination is illustrated in Fig. 7. Samples of left and right luminance profiles of the missing fundamental stereo pair are shown in Figs. 7a and 7f, and in between these are shown peaks and zero crossings discovered from these samples within two spatial frequency tuned channels (Figs. 7b–e). Spatial coincidence (defined here as measurement primitives of the same type found in the same relative locations in both channels)

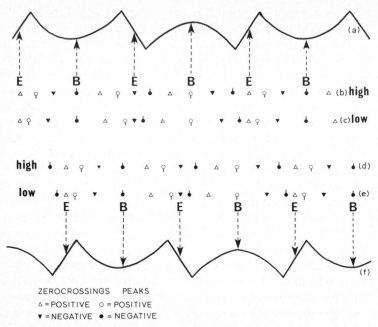

FIG. 7. Measurement primitives extracted from relatively high and low spatial frequency channels from left and right luminance profiles of the missing fundamental stereopair. See Section 5.3.1 for details.

occurs where vertical dotted lines are shown linking the channel primitives to the luminance profiles. The E and B symbols refer to edge and bar assertions which would be extractable in each case. Given the BRPS conjecture, this process would be effected binocularly, with consequent elimination of the ambiguities existing within each channel considered as a separate entity.

Certain possible objections to using the missing fundamental stereo pair to support the BRPS conjecture do, however, need to be considered:

First, it might be asked whether activity in other channels could provide a correct resolution of the ambiguity, without recourse to the type of processing envisaged by the BRPS conjecture. But in this connection, we note that channels dealing with frequencies higher than the 3rd harmonic are no better off than the channel illustrated in Fig. 6 (which is centred on the 3rd harmonic). Such channels would make just the same choice, considered as independent entities, with the correct match always out of range. And as far as channels tuned to lower spatial frequencies are concerned, channels which would of course have the range capable of dealing with the correct disparity in the stimulus, the fact that the stereo grating is missing its fundamental means that these channels would inevitably be only weakly stimulated (indeed not at all in our simulation). However, even if stimulated such channels would on their own provide the 'wrong' depth percept. This is because with the stereo pair Figs. 6a/6b as input such low frequency channels would tend to 'see' just a simple sine wave. Sine waves are notoriously ambiguous stereo stimuli for which the lowest disparity solution is invariably selected, a fact illustrated by the lower half of Fig. 8 which shows the missing fundamental stereo pair filtered to reveal only its 3rd harmonic. In this half of Fig. 8, receding depth is seen with crossed-eye fusion—the 'incorrect' solution for the missing fundamental stereogram itself and a result which contrasts nicely with what is seen in the upper half of Fig. 8 in which the higher harmonics of the missing fundamental waveform are present, with the consequence that protruding depth is once again evident. The point here is that even if weakly stimulated, low frequency channels on their own still cannot provide the depth percept seen for the missing fundamental stereopair.

Secondly, it might perhaps be maintained that correct stereopsis could be achieved by an independent channels model of the Marr and Poggio kind if initial left/right zero crossing matches were restricted only to those of roughly similar slope (adding this restriction to the already existing ones of similar contrast sign and similar orientation: Marr and Poggio refer to this possibility briefly in connection with stereopsis and Marr and Hildreth discuss its advantages more generally). Slopes for zero crossings within the channel illustrated in Fig. 6 are not in fact very different but for higher frequency channels the slopes do become progressively distinct. However, for these higher spatial frequency channels the disparity to be processed is well outside the range allowed by the model. Use of slope information is also not without other problems as far as stereopsis is concerned. For example, it is well known that stereo pairs of widely differing contrasts can readily be fused and this would

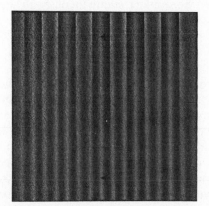 

FIG. 8. Stereogram whose upper half is composed of the missing fundamental waveform described in Fig. 6 and whose lower half is that waveform filtered to reveal just the 3rd harmonic. Opposite depth effects are obtained in each half. See Section 5.3.1 for details.

seem impossible if initial local matches were restricted in a slope-bound way. If
it be thought that this consideration could be circumvented by some kind of
'normalisation' prior to establishing local matches, then the way in which this
might be done needs to be carefully considered. We would argue that any
normalisation is most sensibly done locally in connection with arriving at
binocular assertions, for example perhaps by seeking particular ratios of
activity in left/right channels (see Section 5.4 for a cross channel stereo
algorithm using slope information in this general fashion). Since it is the
relative activity in the various channels which is used to determine the raw
primal sketch element that is to be asserted, this proposal naturally leads
straight back to the BRPS conjecture.

It is worth noting that 160 msec presentations of the missing fundamental
stereo pair still produce correct stereopsis, so that any important involvement
of the vergence mechanism seems ruled out, and also that we have done a
similar analysis of this stereogram using peaks rather than zero crossings, with
exactly the same conclusions. Moreover, on a recent visit to M.I.T. we ran the
missing fundamental stereo on Grimson's implementation of Marr and Poggio's
model, with results which confirmed our analysis of how it fails for this input.

Finally, it is worth pointing out the relationship between the missing fundamental stereogram and the high pass chequer board stereogram described in
Section 4.4(b). In both stimuli, the high pass filtering used in their creation
produces a sizeable ambiguity problem amongst local matches obtained using
subsequent channel convolutions. In the case of the chequer board stereogram,
an implementation of the binocular combination rule of figural continuity is
sufficient to resolve the ambiguity. In the case of the missing fundamental
stereo pair, where the ghosts and correct targets show equal figural continuity,
we find that cross-channel correspondences are sufficient. In most images, of
course, these two combination rules could be applied simultaneously to advantage.

5.3.2. *Spatial frequency filtered stereograms portraying corrugated surfaces*

Other evidence implicating the use of cross-channel correspondences by the
mechanisms of human stereopsis comes from a further study based on the
horizontally-corrugated stereogram portrayed in Fig. 3a. In this experiment
(Mayhew et al. [25]), we explored the effects not of orientated filtering (Section
3.3) but rather of circularly-symmetric spatial frequency filtering. Figs. 4d and
4e show low and high pass versions of Fig. 4a used in this study and the reader
will perhaps be able to verify for himself what we found using naive subjects.
These subjects were required to discriminate in a two-alternative forced-choice
paradigm whether the corrugations in each stimulus were tilted upwards-to-the-
right or upwards-to-the-left (this is why the corrugations in Fig. 4a are not quite
horizontal), and their latencies for this task were recorded. The subjects could

perform the task fairly quickly for the unfiltered original (Fig. 4a), but they found it impossible for the low pass stereogram (Fig. 4d), and difficult (slow latencies) for the high pass version (Fig. 4e).

The result for the low pass version would be expected on any model. Low pass filtering must seriously perturb the disparity information in the stereogram because the relatively large receptive fields of low spatial frequency channels would straddle several rasters, so smearing together the separate disparity cues contained in each one, and so making the tilt of the corrugations difficult or impossible to discriminate. This is not to say, however, that the low pass filtering used for Fig. 4d obliterates all the disparity information in the original stimulus. Careful examination of Fig. 4d reveals that it is possible to see two different planes, one comprised of blobs falling roughly at the level of the peaks of the original, and another composed of blobs lying at the approximate level of the troughs. This is as would be expected given the sinusoidal variation in disparity: peaks or troughs possess relatively slow transitions in disparity and hence would be least vunerable to the smearing of their disparity cues across adjacent rasters, whereas the rapid disparity transitions in between the peaks and troughs would suffer drastically from low pass smearing, hence making the tilt discrimination very difficult if not impossible (Table 2). This consideration will be important later when the question of cross-channel benefit from low spatial frequency information is discussed.

The greater difficulty that the subjects found with the high pass stereogram compared with the unfiltered original is difficult to reconcile with an independent channels model. This is because the high pass version contains the disparity information which enables the tilt of the corrugations to be discriminated in the original, and so on any straightforward independent channels

TABLE 2. Channel perturbation for a corrugated surface. (See Section 5.3.2) Comparison between strips 3 pixels wide situated at the peaks/troughs and the zero disparity crossing point of the corrugations

| | Channel spatial frequency | | |
	Low	Medium	High
Peaks/troughs	0.650	0.719	0.894
Zero disparity zone	0.267	0.392	0.575

The table shows the proportions of zero crossings from one eye's view matching similarly-signed zero crossings at the required disparity. The period of the disparity surface was 26 pixels with 12 pixel peak-to-trough amplitude (sine wave profile).

model the high pass case should have been just as good as the original as far as making this tilt discrimination is concerned. It might be argued that an independent channels model of the Marr and Poggio [17] kind could cope with the relative difficulty experienced with the high pass version in that the original stereogram would enjoy the benefit of low spatial frequency facilitation via improved vergence control conveyed by its low spatial frequency components. This benefit might stem from information about the planes of the peaks and the troughs available in low spatial frequency channels, as described in the preceding paragraph. However, we have found just the same pattern of results for the stereograms under discussion when brief (160 msec) exposures are used, and error scores rather than latencies are employed to measure the difficulty of stereofusion. For such brief exposures, no benefit can accrue from vergence movements and yet still the original stereogram is easier than the high pass one.

The relative ease of stereo fusion for the unfiltered stereogram is wholly consistent with a model utilising cross-channel correspondences. Considered independently, the low spatial frequency channels present considerably perturbed matches on the sides of the slopes of the corrugations, so preventing the discrimination of their tilt. For the high spatial frequency channels, although there is much less perturbation of their left/right correspondences, there are many ghosts so making solution difficult. However, in those parts of the stereogram's surface where the disparity peaks and troughs happen to fall, the stereogram is approximately planar and therefore left/right correspondences within low spatial frequency channels are minimally perturbed (Table 2). Cross-channel correspondences in these regions can thus effectively eliminate most if not all false fusions. This cross-channel contribution to disambiguation is obviously not available in the high pass case: hence its relatively great stereo difficulty.

In the next section, we describe a computational experiment which demonstrates the potential value of cross-channel correspondences for solving both the missing fundamental and corrugated surface stereograms.

5.4. A computer simulation demonstrating binocular use of cross-channel correspondences

We have devised an algorithm (called FRECKLES: Mayhew and Frisby [23]) which uses peaks and zero crossings as measurement primitives to arrive at monocular raw primal sketch assertions, and we are presently engaged in extending this algorithm to cope with binocular inputs in a manner consistent with the BRPS conjecture and as already outlined in principle in connection with the missing fundamental stereo pair (Fig. 6). The details of the raw primal sketch representation, that is the exact nature of the information it makes explicit and the way in which the outputs of differently tuned spatial frequency channels are utilised in this computation, are still active research questions. However, by way of evaluating the BRPS conjecture in general terms, we now describe an interim study which demonstrates that cross-channel correspondences can in principle provide a powerful basis for the computation of a local piece-wise binocular correlation.

Fig. 9 illustrates a stereo algorithm which takes advantage of cross-channel correspondences at what might be termed a 'pre-parsing' level. The algorithm operates on the outputs of three monocular spatial frequency tuned channels (which is probably the sensible minimum to employ: two only were shown in Fig. 7 for simplicity). For each pixel location in each image is logged a monocular 'triplet' recording measures of channel activity in the equivalent locations in the three channel convolutions. In the present version of the algorithm, the channel primitives used for the triplet entries are contrast-signed zero crossings and peaks, with parameters of slope or amplitude tied respectively to each type and with 'nil entries' if no such channel primitive happens to exist at the location in question, e.g. see the triplet at the top of Fig. 9. (Other versions of the algorithm are presently being explored which also use raw convolution values for triplet entries, these being helpful for disambiguating image areas lying in between zero crossings and peaks: J.E.W. Mayhew and J.P. Frisby, in preparation). Each monocular triplet is then correlated with all other triplets found for locations in the other eye's image within a disparity range which defines Panum's fusional area for the algorithm (what range seems sensible is presently a matter of investigation). The correlation coefficient which we presently employ to discover the measure of agreement between left and right triplets is a fairly crude statistic: it is a simple normalised cross-product using the numbers provided by the slopes of the zero crossings and the amplitudes of the peaks, so that similar primitives found in channels of similar spatial frequency are weighted positively and mis-matched primitives, i.e. 'rivalrous' primitives of different type in the two eyes views, are weighted negatively. The correlation score is also reduced if a nil entry in one triplet is coupled with a primitive in the other triplet. The general principle is illustrated in Fig. 9 and we will not trouble the reader with further details because we suspect that almost any sensible weighting for the state of agreement between individual measures comprising left/right triplets will suffice. At any rate, this simple form of cross-channel correlation finds the missing fundamental stereo pair trivially easy, and it can also reduce to negligible proportions the population of ghost matches for a densely-textured random dot stereogram (Fig. 10), even over a disparity range more than twice as great as that allowed for the lowest spatial frequency tuned channel in Marr and Poggio's [17] algorithm. Also, in considering the disambiguation achieved in Fig. 10 it should be remembered that the algorithm does not use figural continuity but operates purely locally and in a 'pointillist' fashion. The results of the experiment described in Section 4.1, which examined ghost/match proportions when bino-

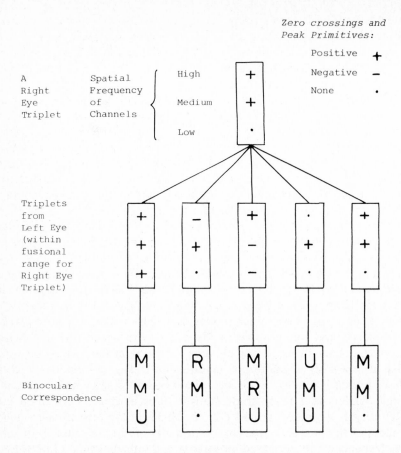

FIG. 9. A stereo algorithm taking advantage of cross-channel correspondences at a pre-parsing level. In the upper part of the figure is shown a triplet of measurement primitives found in three monocular spatial frequency channels at a particular location ('point'). Below this triplet is shown a sample of triplets found in the other field for locations within a given disparity range that defines Panum's fusional area for the algorithm. In the bottom row are shown the results of correlating the upper triplet with each of the middle triplets: this bottom row thus displays the preliminary stage of cross-channel binocular combination as far as the upper triplet is concerned. It is an easy matter to weight the degree of cross-channel binocular correspondence (see Section 5.4 for further comment on this) to enable selection of the correct triplet match. In the illustrated case, the triplet on the extreme right is appropriately selected as 'correct' because it possesses only correct matches (M—same left/right primitives). All others possess either rivalrous matches (R—dissimilar left/right primitives), or they contain primitives found for one eye's view only at that spatial frequency (U—uniocular). Binocularly matching nil entries were ignored. Note that each positive or negative primitive could be eigher a zero crossing or a peak and that a rivalrous match would be logged if primitives of these different types were found.

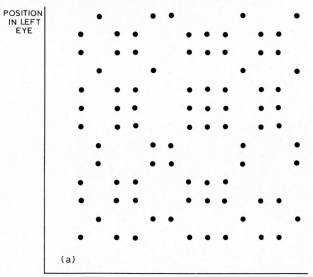

POSITION IN LEFT EYE

(a)

POSITION IN RIGHT EYE

● = POSSIBLE MATCHES

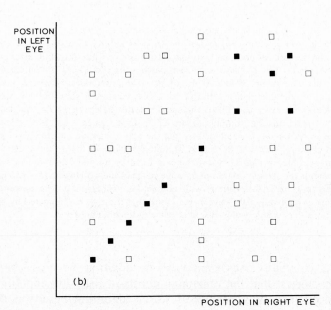

POSITION IN LEFT EYE

(b)

POSITION IN RIGHT EYE

FIG. 10. (*See legend on following page.*)

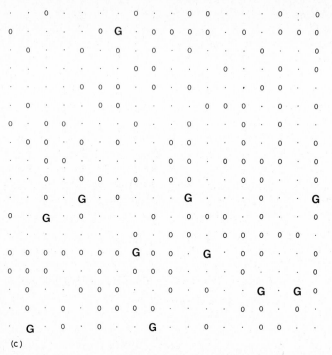

(c)

FIG. 10 (*cont'd*). A demonstration of binocular cross-channel combination for a planar random dot stereogram (see Section 5.4). In (a) is shown the ghost structure for a slice of the stereogram if potential local matches are defined simply as black-for-black or white-for-white pixel matches. The correct disparity plane is zero so that the correct matches are those lying on the diagonal. As can be seen, on this basis the relatively fine texture of the stereogram hides the correct matches within an enormous pool of possible matches. In (b), the ghost structure is shown for the same slice but now each square (both open and filled) indicates a local match based on the discovery of a matching peak or zero crossing primitive of similar contrast sign in a spatial frequency channel; ghosts for three such channels are included so that the figure thus presents the ghost structure for an independent channels model of stereopsis. The filled squares of (b) are those matches selected by the cross-channel stereo algorithm described in Section 5.4 and illustrated in Fig. 9. In (c) disparity assignments are shown for a representative patch of the stereogram (0—zero disparity and therefore correct matches; G—locations with ambiguous assignments). The proportion of ambiguous locations in (c) is only 0.067 and it was found that these were eliminated by an algorithm using nothing more than simple within-disparity-plane 8-neighbour support.

cular figural continuity was employed in addition to cross-channel correspondence, suggest that the remaining ghosts in Figs. 10b and 10c could be further reduced in a fully developed stereo algorithm based on the BRPS conjecture.

A further feature of the preliminary algorithm just described is that it takes no account of the different disparity-processing resolutions to be expected of the different spatial frequency tuned channels. Attention has already been drawn to the fact that a low spatial frequency channel will inevitably blur the disparity information provided by a steeply sloping or corrugated surface, a consideration which illustrates very well the fact that a low spatial frequency channel is suited only for low resolution extraction of disparity information, as the data shown in Table 2 make clear. (This is, of course, a separate issue from that of the disparity range suitable for low frequency channels, a matter given great weight in Marr and Poggio's [17] theory.) Indeed, we have run the triplet algorithm just described on the corrugated stereogram of Fig. 3a and, as expected, found that it copes quite well in the peak and trough zones where disparity variation is least (i.e. zones approximating a planar random dot stereogram of the type processed in Fig. 10), but it gives degraded performance in the texture regions linking these zones. We are presently developing refinements to improve its performance for such surfaces, most importantly by not allowing the information delivered by the low spatial frequency channel to be used in an over-precise and hence self-defeating fashion, as is presently the case. By way of illustrating one possible development of this kind, we note that we found in one experiment that when a sloping random dot surface with a disparity gradient of 0.58 was processed with a low spatial frequency channel, only 0.39 of its zero crossings were located where they 'should' be if the relative depths of the surface were to be accurately extracted. However, this proportion was raised to 0.76 if the location of each zero crossing was relaxed by ±1 pixel. Obviously, this simple experiment suggests a form of cross-channel support in which a zero crossing in a low spatial frequency channel can contribute to disambiguation of the medium and high channels over a suitable spatial range to avoid the pitfalls of spurious precision.

A full evaluation of a developed form of our triplet cross-channel algorithm which compares it against other image-processing cross-correlation techniques will be the subject of a future report. Suffice it to say for the present that our preliminary studies have been very encouraging, returning much sharper auto-correlation functions than classical techniques. Most importantly for present purposes, the algorithm demonstrates that cross-channel correspondences can in principle provide an excellent basis for binocular combination, and therefore that the BRPS conjecture gains considerable support from this computational experiment. This is particularly so when it is realised that each channel on its own suffers a fairly dense ghost structure (e.g. Fig. 10) for the type of random dot textures used to explore the properties of the algorithm to date.

5.5. Summary

To summarise this section, it seems that the processes of human binocular combination optimally combine patterns of measurement primitives such as zero crossings and peaks presented in parallel by several spatial frequency channels. Matches are not chosen independently of their cross-channel context but instead selected according to cross-channel combination rules and inter-pretive constraints forced by the requirement to produce a coherent binocular description of the local intensity changes in the scene. Our psychophysical data challenge any model based purely on the independent within-channel process-ing of zero crossings and peaks, such as that of Marr and Poggio ([17]; see also Frisby and Mayhew [2]); and our computational experiments demonstrate that cross-channel correspondences are in fact capable of aiding binocular com-bination in a powerful fashion.

6. Micropattern Matching vs. the BRPS Conjecture

It might be wondered whether the BRPS conjecture is equivalent to the oft-cited idea that the stereo ambiguity problem might be resolvable by matching similar micropatterns in the two eyes' views. Julesz considered just such an idea at the outset of his research programme using random dot stereograms but quickly rejected it following a simple experiment. Thus he found that if equivalent left/right micropatterns were perturbed by changing the diagonal connectivities between neighbouring points in one eye's image, then stereopsis survived despite the radically different appearance of the left and right eye images which this procedure creates (Julesz [7]). One might add to this line of evidence Julesz' demonstration that stereopsis also survives strongly blurring one image, again despite the remarkably different left/right micropatterns that this procedure produces (see Julesz [8] for stereo illus-trations relating to both these experiments). One is forced to conclude that as far as human stereopsis is concerned, disparity extraction cannot be mediated solely by matching exactly similar micropatterns in each eye's view. We would add to this the fact that high pass filtered textures (e.g. Fig. 3e) which preserve the micropattern structure of the original are more difficult stimuli to fuse than would be expected were micropatterns used as matching primitives.

The BRPS conjecture proposes a form of binocular combination that takes advantage of local figural information, but note that the stereo algorithm described in Section 5.4 and developed with the BRPS conjecture in mind does not require identical micropatterns in the two fields for it to work satisfactorily. At least in principle (and we are currently exploring details of implementation), the cross-channel triplet matching we have proposed copes naturally and easily with many kinds of left/right perturbations which it is known human stereopsis can surmount, such as those described in the preceding paragraph. That is, this type of stereo algorithm will find a 'best fit' correlation of the two fields without insisting that the correlation be perfect. All that is required is that some spectral overlap exists between the left and right textures. Interestingly, this is just the requirement which human stereopsis seems to demand, because large spectral differences produce marked binocular rivalry [2, 19].

Of course, the local and global combination rules we propose will clearly fail for stereo inputs presently strictly repetitive micropatterns of the kind used to create ambiguous random dot stereograms [8] and effects such as the wallpaper illusion. But repetitive patterns pose problems for any stereo algorithm because alternative coherent and stable fusions are intrinsic to their design. The human visual system seems to deal with them simply by choosing that set of disparity matches closest to the fixation plane [9] and by not allowing fusions which would be spatially incoherent. That is, at any one moment the human visual system seems to reject binocular assertions which would amount to positing elements existing in disparity/position locations that would entail them being masked in both eyes' views by other elements asserted in other occluding locations. This need not be thought of as an ad hoc restriction because it could be based on what might be called the 'opacity constraint' presented by objects in the world, i.e. if a non-transparent entity is asserted in a given location, then it is sensible not to assert other entities hidden behind it which could not be seen from either eye's viewpoint. The use of this constraint would not preclude Panum's limiting case and it is consistent with the limited subset of perceptual outcomes that appear for stereo inputs of the nail illusion kind.

7. Concluding Remarks

This paper has addressed the stereo correspondence problem. There are, of course, many other problems to be solved for a 'complete' model of stereopsis. For example, it is necessary to face the computational problems posed by the $2\frac{1}{2}$ D sketch [14], a representation of surfaces and their orientations in depth based upon many cues besides disparity and a processing objective beyond the scope of this paper.

Nevertheless, as far as the correspondence problem is concerned, we suggest that the local and global and global combination rules outlined above will prove to be a sufficient basis for a powerful stereo algorithm. It seems to us that the central problem in developing such an algorithm is to find a theoretically justifiable way of integrating within-channel figural continuity with between-channel correspondences. Of course, judging from some of the encouraging albeit small-scale computational experiments described in this paper, it is unlikely to prove difficult to combine these combination rules in some fairly straightforward fashion which proves capable of coping quite well with a fairly wide range of stereo inputs. However, following the lead given by Marr and his colleagues, we are more concerned to develop algorithms based on secure computational theories. Hence for us the major problem at present is the formulation of a computational theory capable of specifying in principle how the binocular combination rules of figural continuity and cross-channel correspondence should be integrated.

The major difficulty in this regard concerns the question of how cross-channel correspondences should be used to obtain descriptions of image intensity changes. The use of figural continuity seems theoretically secure, based as it is on the identification of constraints presented by visual objects. In marked contrast, the extraction of intensity descriptions from cross-channel correspondences is understood only for relatively isolated edges and bars (which produce convenient spatial coincidence of zero crossings and peaks respectively). In dense complex textures the situation is much more difficult because the low frequency channels tend to blur over two or more edges, thereby destroying spatial coincidence. It may be that future studies of this important question will lead to a substantial revision of present ideas about what is to be computed in the raw primal sketch and how it is to be done. For example, it may turn out that in regions of high acuity low frequency channels are not used, at any rate not exclusively, as measurement devices for extracting intensity changes of coarse scale (Marr and Hildreth [6]). Instead it could be that the functional role of these channels is to act as grouping operators integrating information delivered by high frequency channels. As E. Hildreth (personal communication) has pointed out, a better understanding of these questions might flow from a more precise formulation of the information needed by later processes that use the raw primal sketch as their data base. Also, it could be that further psychophysical studies of stereopsis may illuminate these computational problems. In any event, a better theoretical understanding of cross-channel processes will undoubtedly have important implications for the implementation of binocular combination rules based on the BRPS conjecture.

ACKNOWLEDGMENT

We would like to thank Philip Stenton for his considerable help in running various psychophysical experiments referred to in this paper and for his patient assistance during program development. Alison Kidd made some useful comments on the manuscript, and Chris Brown's help with equipment at all stages has been invaluable.

The research was supported by SRC research grant GR/A/50894.

REFERENCES

1. Barlow, H.B., Reconstructing the visual image in space and time, *Nature* **279** (1979) 189–190.
2. Frisby, J.P. and Mayhew, J.E.W., Global processes in stereopsis: some comments on Ramachandran and Nelson, *Perception* **6** (1977) 195–206.
3. Frisby, J.P. and Mayhew, J.E.W. The relationship between apparent depth and disparity in rivalrous texture stereograms, *Perception* **7** (1978) 661–678.
4. Frisby, J.P. and Mayhew, J.E.W., Spatial frequency tuned channels: implications for structure and function from psychophysical and computational studies of stereopsis, *Philos. Trans. R. Soc. London Ser. B* **290** (1980) 95–116.
5. Frisby, J.P. and Mayhew, J.E.W., The role of spatial frequency channels in vergence control, *Vision Res.* **20** (1980) 727–732.
6. Grimson, W.E.L. and Marr, D., A computer implementation of a theory of human stereo vision, A.I. Memo No. 565, A.I. Lab., M.I.T., Cambridge, MA (April 1980).

7. Julesz, B., Binocular depth perception of computer-generated patterns, *Bell Systems Techn. J.* **39** (1960) 1125–1162.
8. Julesz, B., *Foundations of Cyclopean Perception* (University of Chicago Press, Chicago, IL, 1971).
9. Julesz, B. and Chang, J.J., Interaction between pools of binocular disparity detectors tuned to different disparities, *Biol. Cybernet.* **22** (1976) 107–119.
10. Kidd, A.L., Mayhew, J.E.W. and Frisby, J.P., Texture contours can facilitate stereopsis by control of vergence eye movements, *Nature* **280** (1979) 829–832.
11. Logan, B.F., Information in the zerocrossing of bandpass signals, *Bell System Techn. J.* **56** (1977) 487–510.
12. Marr, D., Early processing of visual information, *Philos. Trans. R. Soc. London Ser. B* **275** (1976) 483–524.
13. Marr, D. and Hildreth, E., Theory of edge detection, A.I. Memo No. 518, A.I. Lab. M.I.T., Cambridge, MA (1979).
14. Marr, D. and Nishihara, H.K., Visual information processing, artificial intelligence and the sensorium of sight, *Techn. Rev.* **81** (1978) 2–23.
15. Marr, D. and Poggio, T., A cooperative computation of stereo disparity, *Science* **194** (1976) 283–287.
16. Marr, D. and Poggio, T., A computational theory of human stereo vision, A.I. Memo No. 451, A.I. Lab., M.I.T., Cambridge, MA (1977).
17. Marr, D. and Poggio, T., A theory of human stereopsis, *Proc. R. Soc. London Ser. B* **204** (1979) 301–328.
18. Marr, D., Ullman, S. and Poggio, T., Bandpass channels, zero crossings and early visual information processing, *J. Optical Soc. Am.* **69**(6) (1979) 914–916.
19. Mayhew, J.E.W. and Frisby, J.P., Rivalrous texture stereograms, *Nature* **264** (1976) 53–56.
20. Mayhew, J.E.W. and Frisby, J.P., Stereopsis masking in humans is not orientationally tuned, *Perception* **7** (1978) 431–436.
21. Mayhew, J.E.W. and Frisby, J.P., Contrast summation effects and stereopsis, *Perception* **7** (1978) 431–436.
22. Mayhew, J.E.W. and Frisby, J.P., Surfaces with steep variations in depth pose difficulties for orientationally tuned disparity filters, *Perception* **8** (1979) 691–698.
23. Mayhew, J.E.W. and Frisby, J.P., The computation of binocular edges, *Perception* **9** (1980) 69–86.
24. Mayhew, J.E.W. and Frisby, J.P., The king is naked: another case of the missing fundamental, Paper read to the London meeting of the Experimental Psychology Society (January 1980).
25. Mayhew, J.E.W., Frisby, J.P. and Stenton, P., Evidence for facilitation between spatial frequency tuned stereopsis channels, *Perception*, submitted.
26. Mowforth, P., Mayhew, J.E.W. and Frisby, J.P., Vergence movements made in response to spatial frequency filtered random-dot stereograms, *Perception*, in press.
27. Saye, A. and Frisby, J.P., The role of monocularly conspicuous features in facilitating stereopsis from random-dot stereograms, *Perception* **4** (1975) 159–171.
28. Wilson, H.R. and Giese, S.C., Threshold visibility of frequency gradient patterns, *Vison Res.* **17** (1977) 1177–1190.

Received March 1980; revised version received September 1980

A Theory of Spatio-Temporal Aggregation for Vision

Bruce E. Flinchbaugh and B. Chandrasekaran

Department of Computer and Information Science,
Ohio State University, Columbus, OH 43210, U.S.A.

ABSTRACT

A theory of spatio-temporal aggregation is proposed as an explanation for the visual process of grouping together elements in an image sequence whose motions and positions have consistent interpretations as the retinal projections of a coherent or isolated cluster of 'particles' in the physical world. Assumptions of confluence and adjacency are made in order to constrain the infinity of possible interpretations to a computationally more manageable domain of plausible interpretations. Confluence and adjacency lead to the derivation of specific rules for grouping which permit the appropriate aggregation of rigid and quasi-rigid objects in motion and at rest under a variety of conditions. The theory is reconciled with existing computational theories of vision so as to complement them, and to provide a useful link in the continual abstraction of visual information.

1. Introduction

General purpose vision systems, whether human or machine, face the same problem: recovering information about the environment from changing two-dimensional images. A solution should permit recovery of the three-dimensional structure and motion of arbitrary objects and their surroundings. In this paper we consider temporal sequences of monocular achromatic images for a stationary observer and focus on the grouping problem.

1.1. A framework for vision

Our theory is cast within a computational approach to vision that acknowledges the symbolic nature of visual processing and concentrates on the discovery and exploitation of physical constraints enabling the visual apprehension of three-dimensional objects and events. The adopted framework for vision approximates a continuous abstraction that begins with a rich description of two-dimensional intensity changes, continues through a level representing local surface orientation and discontinuities in depth, and culminates in a represen-

Artificial Intelligence **17** (1981) 387–407

tation of three-dimensional objects in an object-centered coordinate system. Marr [11] and Marr and Nishihara [12] discuss spatial representations for each level of abstraction, respectively: the Primal Sketch, the $2\frac{1}{2}$ D Sketch and the 3 D Object Representation. Extensions of the representations to explicitly embody temporal information are easy to imagine. For example, an element in the Primal Sketch could have an attribute describing its dislocation in the image over a short time interval, a surface fragment in the $2\frac{1}{2}$ D Sketch might be moving toward the observer, and part of an object may be rotating about its natural axis in the 3 D Object Representation (see also Marr and Vaina [15]).

1.2. The grouping problem

The grouping problem is an instance of the generic figure-ground separation problem that begins with the Primal Sketch and ends prior to the $2\frac{1}{2}$ D Sketch. We assume each 'element' in the Primal Sketch is the projection of a 'particle' (local change in the geometry or surface reflectance properties of an entity) in the physical world. The grouping problem is to construct an explicit representation of coherent or spatially isolated clusters of particles in terms of the given elements. Coherent particle clusters may form surfaces that are rigid or quasi-rigid, partially transparent or opaque, and in motion or at rest. Particles in an isolated cluster need not be physically connected. Thus a grouping of two or more elements is a structural assertion that the associated particles are either physically connected or isolated together in space. Our study of the grouping problem is particularly concerned with the exploitation of constraints on motions of elements imposed by membership of the corresponding particles in a coherent or isolated cluster. Recovery of primitive information about the motion of clusters relative to the observer, appropriate to the level of the $2\frac{1}{2}$ D Sketch, is also involved.

2. Theory

The theory of spatio-temporal aggregation is first described in terms of what is computed, specifying the relevant representations (Section 2.1). We then consider how the computation might be realized (Section 2.2), reviewing several potentially useful assumptions and electing two assumptions, *confluence* and *adjacency*, to govern the grouping process. Specific grouping criteria embodying the assumptions are proposed in Section 3 to complete a refinement of the theory.

2.1. Representation

The input to spatio-temporal aggregation is an abstraction of moving particles which we shall call the *Dynamic Primal Sketch*. The output, called the *Grouping Hierarchy*, represents clusters of particles. The representations are not intended to provide for all of the information pertinent to their levels of abstraction. Rather, they isolate just the information addressed by the theory.

2.1.1. *Dynamic primal sketch*

The *Dynamic Primal Sketch* is a representation of particle (Section 1.2) projections in the image and their displacements over a short time interval. Elements of the Dynamic Primal Sketch are just place-tokens of the Primal Sketch (Marr [10]) with additional attributes describing the displacements. For the purposes of this paper, elements are assumed to be points. Thus each element is symbolized by

$$\text{(element (location } x \, y)$$
$$\text{(motion d} x \text{ d} y))$$

where the *location vector* specifies the coordinates of the element in the image at time t and the *motion vector*, added to the location, gives the position at time $t + dt$.

A scheme for computing the Dynamic Primal Sketch involves the extraction of a sequence of Primal Sketches and the determination of correspondences between elements over time. Marr [10] has described the computation of the Primal Sketch and Ullman [23] has explained a solution to the correspondence problem. In particular, given the positions of elements at each of two instants of time, the minimal mapping theory [23] is concerned with determining the most likely correspondence between the two sets of elements under the assumption that the motions of the elements are independent. A distribution of apparent velocities in the image can also be computed [5].

2.1.2. *Grouping hierarchy*

A *group* is a collection of elements in the Dynamic Primal Sketch representing a coherent or isolated cluster of particles. In other words, a group is an assertion that the associated particles are either physically connected (e.g. particles of a surface) or isolated together in space. Rough estimates of motions relative to the viewer (Section 3.2) are also explicitly represented in a group. Furthermore, a group can be a collection of other groups. In that case the group is still an assertion that the physical counterparts of the constituents are coherent or isolated. The *Grouping Hierarchy* is an assembly of elements and groups such that each one is a member of exactly one group, excepting the lone group at the top of the hierarchy which may be interpreted as the group of everything in view.

2.2. Constraints on interpretation

Since there exists an infinite number of particle configurations compatible with any collection of elements in the Dynamic Primal Sketch, some assumptions must be made in order to recover a plausible underlying organization. In keeping with the principle of least commitment [10], any assumptions made at this still quite early level of processing should pertain to a wide variety of situations, correctly constraining the interpretation in most cases and postponing the use of knowledge about specific objects as long as possible. Assumptions appropriate to grouping should therefore be in terms of elements or the particles they represent.

Perhaps the most powerful assumption that can be made is one of rigidity.

The rigidity assumption: "Any set of elements undergoing a two-dimensional transformation that has a unique interpretation as a rigid body moving in space should be interpreted as such a body in motion." (Ullman [23, p. 146]).

Ullman [23] shows that the structure and motion compatible with three distinct orthographic views of four non-coplanar points in a rigid configuration can be computed if the interpretation is unique. Elements in a collection satisfying such a rigidity test almost certainly represent physically connected particles and would therefore qualify as a group. Of course the grouping problem in general does not presuppose rigidity. Later in this section we will discuss configurations which are not rigid but which can nonetheless be grouped by the human visual system. Thus while the rigidity assumption plays an important role in solving the grouping problem, other assumptions are also needed and we focus on some of the remaining issues.

When elements are stationary, or if their displacements are simply ignored, the available information is spatial in nature, being just the locations of elements in the image. We propose the following assumption as the basis for constraining the possible relationships between element locations and the associated particle configurations.

The adjacency assumption: The retinal projections of neighboring particles tend to be closer to each other than to the projections of more distant particles.

According to this assumption, estimations of adjacency in three-space are made on the basis of separation in the image plane. We regard adjacency as the assumption underlying the Gestalt law of 'proximity'. Obviously the assumption is subject to gross errors. However, there is evidence in favor of the adjacency assumption to justify its use:

(1) In a world of primarily opaque objects, the adjacency assumption is likely to hold over most of an image. (Marr and Poggio [13] make a similar point in discussing Continuity.)

(2) When the adjacency assumption is not satisfied, other assumptions should lead to appropriate interpretations. (A role played by the rigidity assumption, and by the confluence assumption introduced below.)

(3) In the absence of other evidence, the human visual system tends to rely

on two-dimensional adjacency information. (For example, given just the arrangement of elements in Fig. 1, one would not expect perception of the indicated particle configuration.)

We now consider other sources of information as potential remedies for violations of the adjacency assumption. Adjacency can fail when changes in depth are significant, as in Fig. 1. Static sources of information about changes in depth that might be useful include: binocular disparity, surface contours [22], linear perspective, relative size of familiar of similar objects and superposition. However, the use of this information for grouping entails prior commitments to relative depth and surfaces as represented in the $2\frac{1}{2}$ D Sketch—information not generally available to the level of the Primal Sketch. Thus we do not consider assumptions about relative depth in our formulation of the grouping problem.

Another type of adjacency failure suggests that similarities in the descriptions of adjacent elements tend to promote their organization as a group. For example, the left-hand cluster in Fig. 2 might be subdivided so that the circles are distinguished from the line segments. The underlying assumption seems to be one of homogeneous composition. The Gestalt law of 'similarity' essentially makes this assumption.

The homogeneity assumption: Descriptions of elements representing a cluster of particles tend to be homogeneous.

While the homogeneity assumption can be useful, we argue that it plays a secondary role in grouping with regard to the adjacency assumption. That is, homogeneous elements tend to motivate distinctions *within* distinctions established by adjacency, and not across them. Another illustration of this relationship is given in Fig. 3.

The homogeneity assumption also seems to play a secondary role in grouping

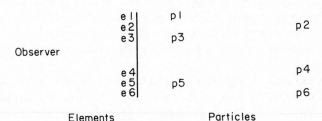

FIG. 1. Adjacency violated by changes in depth. The elements $e1$ through $e6$ respectively represent the images of the particles $p1$ through $p6$.

FIG. 2. Homogeneous groups within two clusters. Adjacency suggests a distinction between the left cluster and the right one but does not suggest their possible subdivisions.

FIG. 3. Adjacency vs. homogeneity. Similarities in orientations of the line segments are insufficient to prevent the perception of four 'rows'. If the separations between the rows are reduced, as occurs when the diagram is viewed from the lower-right corner of the page, other organizations manifest.

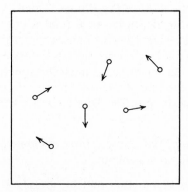

FIG. 4. Two rotating 'triangles'. The diagram represents the motion vectors of six elements in a Dynamic Primal Sketch.

when elements are moving. For example, if similar displacements in the image are a basis for grouping (as in a grouping scheme proposed by Rashid [18] and as suggested by the Gestalt law of 'common fate'), then the two elements in the center of Fig. 4 would be grouped. However, a more viable grouping alternative exists and perception of the display in a tachistoscopic demonstration[1] suggests that two 'triangles' are seen to rotate in the image plane. Something other than grouping on the basis of similar displacements appears to be involved.

The demonstration in Fig. 4 is an instance of a large class of displays for which neither adjacency nor spatio-static information about depth or homogeneity can account for the appropriate organization of elements. We have produced a collection of displays representing two superimposed 'discs' of point-particles lying in the same fronto-parallel plane and having a common center on the line of sight. Fifty to one hundred points were chosen from a

---

[1] Small black dots on a white background were positioned in the two frames as indicated in Fig. 4. A variety of frame durations from 100 to 300 msec with an inter-frame interval of about 50 msec produce fairly good effects.

uniform distribution on the area of a circle to represent each disc. When the discs are stationary a single field of points is observed. However, for a wide variety of motions of the discs the configuration is readily perceived as two superimposed fields.[2] For example, the discs can be rotating about the line of sight in opposite directions, or in the same direction at different speeds. Translations in depth and across the field of view can be added to the counter-rotating discs without detracting from the perceptual capacity for distinguishing them. A particularly interesting variation is to permit each particle to randomly wander within a small area that moves with the disc. In that case there is still an overall impression of two fronto-parallel fields but they are no longer interpreted as rigid. Individual points seem to weave around and about each other, sometimes in depth, with no apparent interconnections. Superimposed discs can also be distinguished when they undergo different pure translations in space.

How can the grouping of Fig. 4 and the discriminations in the two-discs demonstrations be explicitly accounted for? The homogeneity assumption is clearly inadequate since elements of the same disc can move in opposite directions while elements of different discs have nearly identical displacements over a small time interval. The rigidity assumption does not permit a commitment to structure because in some cases the addition of independent particle motions eliminates the possibility of a rigid interpretation and in others the rigid fronto-parallel interpretation is not unique. The theory of visual vector analysis [1, 6–9] provides a means of describing perceived three-dimensional motions associated with various small groups of elements in isolation, but does not provide computationally explicit criteria for recovering such groups when other alternatives exist. The principle of continuous flow (Marr and Ullman [14]) is similar to an observation made by Potter [17] and characterizes the image of a single disc quite well.

> *The principle of continuous flow*: "The velocity field of motion within the image of a rigid object varies continuously almost everywhere." (Marr and Ullman [14, p. 18]).

However, the grouping schemes proposed by Potter [17] and Marr and Ullman [14] also tend to assume that images of objects are not superimposed and do not account for concise examples such as Fig. 4.

We propose an assumption of confluence to help constrain the grouping interpretation when elements are moving. In keeping with our formulation of the grouping problem, the assumption pertains both to particles that are

---

[2] Configurations of moving discs were produced on a Vector General display and consisted of 30 to 100 frame sequences during which a disc would rotate, for example, through as much as 180 degrees. Each element was displayed as a point and its displacement from one frame to the next was small compared to the distance to its nearest neighbor. The discriminations were possible after several seconds, depending on the particular configuration.

coherent and to disjoint particles that happen to be isolated together in space.

The confluence assumption: Neighboring particles tend to have similar velocities because they tend to be influenced by the same forces.

Since the assumption is stated in terms of particles in space, implications of
confluence for motions of elements in the image have to be derived in order for
the assumption to be of use. Our refinement of the confluence assumption
(Section 3.2) is based on local estimations of particle motions relative to the
observer and is not a comparison of element displacements *per se*. Thus
confluence is distinguished from the principle of continuous flow and the
homogeneity assumption.

3. Computation

In this section specific rules for grouping are derived from the assumptions of
adjacency and confluence. As the number of elements in the Dynamic Primal
Sketch may be large, the computation should be decomposed so that it can be
performed in parallel by interacting local processors. Accordingly, the grouping
rules are stated in local terms and an iterative scheme is outlined for controlling their interaction.

3.1. Adjacency analysis

An intuitive first translation of the adjacency assumption into a rule for
grouping is: an element and its nearest neighbor should be grouped because
they are likely to represent neighboring particles. While the rule works well in
some local situations, it performs poorly in others. For example, if it is applied
to element $e2$ in Fig. 5 the result is satisfactory—$e2$ is grouped with $e1$.
However, the same rule applied to $e3$ groups $e2$ with $e3$. An additional
requirement that elements be *mutual nearest neighbors* is a substantial improvement and motivates the following rule, where elements ei and ej are
mutual nearest neighbors if the nearest neighbor of ei is ej, and vice-versa.

The basic rule of adjacency grouping: Two elements form a group if they are
mutual nearest neighbors.

The criterion of mutual nearest neighbors is an example of a conservative
measure that adheres to the principle of least commitment [10]. We extend the
rule to apply to groups as well as elements with the following metric for
inter-group separation: the distance between two groups, $g1$ and $g2$, is the
distance between the closest pair of elements taken one each from the

e1   e2   e3

FIG. 5. Mutual nearest neighbors ($e1$ and $e2$) and a distant third ($e3$).

hierarchies under $g1$ and $g2$. The distance between an element and a group is defined in an analogous manner.

Since groups formed by the mutual nearest neighbor criterion have exactly two constituents, the Grouping Hierarchies produced tend to be extremely deep for simple clusters containing large numbers of elements. Some distinctions may be so insignificant that they should not be made at all. So instead of simply *building* a new group whenever the basic rule of adjacency grouping applies, two other operations are allowed: groups can be *merged* or one group can *augment* (become a constituent of) another. To determine which of the three operations should be applied we employ a criterion of equi-density: the constituents of a group are consistent with respect to adjacency if the distance from every constituent to its nearest fellow constituent is approximately the same as the distance separating the divisions in every partition of the constituents into two parts. Priority is given to merge operations which result in consistent groups. Augment operations have second priority and if neither a merge nor an augment is justified, the build operation is performed as before.

The modified adjacency rule can still fail by grouping across object boundaries. This could occur, for example, near an occluding contour or within the image of a transparent object when an element of one object happens to be closest to an element of another. Exploitation of the confluence assumption will provide a means of avoiding many such failures when one or both of the objects are moving. Computations specifically dealing with region boundaries (e.g. [20, 24]) might also be incorporated to mediate adjacency. However, only the use of confluence is elaborated in this paper.

3.2. Confluence analysis

The confluence assumption is stated in terms of particles in the physical world: neighboring particles tend to have similar velocities because they tend to be influenced by the same forces. In this section we first examine implications of confluence for a collection of elements which, in fact, represents a cluster of neighboring particles. We then observe a property that can be locally exploited for the purpose of grouping, providing a scheme for the aggregation.

Consider the centroid of a cluster of neighboring particles in motion. Under the confluence assumption, any motion of the centroid is the result of forces acting on all of the particles in a similar manner. The direction of the component of that motion parallel to the image plane is given by the displacement vector for the centroid of the corresponding elements. We call that displacement the 'lateral vector' of a collection of elements. Subtracting the lateral vector from the motion vector of each element leaves a pattern of 'relative vectors'.[3]

---

[3] The definition of lateral and relative vectors is equivalent to the definition of 'common' and 'relative' vectors given by Borjesson and von Hofsten [1]. We use 'lateral' instead of 'common' because the latter term is also used in reference to translations in depth [8, 9].

The *lateral vector* of a collection of elements is the displacement of the centroid of the collection (where the *centroid* is the component by component average of the element location vectors).

The *relative vector* of an element in a collection of elements is the vector difference of its motion vector and the lateral vector of the collection.

Confluence suggests that the relative vectors contain information about translations of the particle centroid along the line of sight and rotations of the particles about their centroid. It is as if the subtraction of the lateral vector has constrained the centroid of the particles to move along the line directly toward or away from the viewpoint. If the motion along this line is directed away from the observer, the relative motions will tend to converge on the centroid of the elements, or diverge if approaching. Thus the motion of each particle is, instantaneously, decomposable into a translatory and a rotational component as defined below.

The *vergence vector* of an element in a collection of elements is the projection of its relative vector onto the line through the element and the centroid of the collection.[4]

The *spin vector* of an element in a collection of elements is the vector difference of its relative and vergence vectors.

We now define a reduction of vergence and spin vectors (V and S) to scalar quantities ('vergence' and 'spin') which will be instrumental in grouping.

The *vergence* (v) and *spin* (s) of an element in a collection of elements are given by

$$v = \pm \frac{|V|}{d} \quad \text{and} \quad s = \pm \frac{|S|}{d}$$

where d is the distance from the element to the centroid of the collection and the sign of v is +1 if V is directed away from the centroid, and −1 otherwise; the sign of s is +1 if the direction of S is counter-clockwise about the centroid, and −1 otherwise.

The preceding analysis provides a basis for estimating various three-dimensional motions of a particle cluster associated with a group of elements. Criteria for *constructing* such groups are based on primitive descriptions of vergence and spin. In particular, a property of vergence and spin can be locally exploited as evidence for grouping.

The *duo ergo omnibus tendency*:[5] If a collection of elements represent neighboring particles, then the vergence and spin values computed for any two elements in the collection tend to be the same as the values computed for the entire collection.

---

[4] Vergence vectors are equivalent to 'concurrent relative motions' [1] in the special case occurring when the vergence vector equals the relative vector for each element in the collection.

[5] Taking some liberties with Latin, 'duo ergo omnibus' means 'if it is true for two, then it is true for all'.

The tendency is actually an invariant for any rigid configuration of particles in a fronto-parallel plane whose motion is composed of an arbitrary translation in space and a rotation about a line parallel to the line of sight [2]. If the configuration is non-planar or non-rigid, or if rotations in depth are introduced, the vergence and spin of the elements representing the configuration exhibit less uniformity. A justification of the tendency is based on observations that local comparisons of vergence and spin can be useful even when the conditions for invariance are distorted. For example, quasi-rigid configurations can obey the tendency (Section 4.2) and neighboring particles of a surface rotating in depth can approximate a translation toward the observer, while other portions of the surface recede. However, the tendency does not generally hold for rotations in depth. The metric used for comparing vergence and spin pairs is a parameter of the theory and we use the standard Euclidean metric in our examples for empirical reasons (Section 3.3.).

In accordance with the duo ergo omnibus tendency, the following scheme is proposed to serve as the *basic rule of confluence grouping*:

(1) Pair an element with each of its neighbors.[6]
(2) Compute vergence and spin for each pair.
(3) Group the elements corresponding to the closest two vergence and spin pairs.

To see how it works, consider the problem of determining which, if any, of the elements in Fig. 6 should be grouped with element $e0$. The vergence and

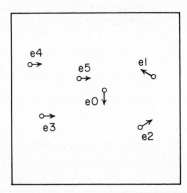

FIG. 6. Which elements should $e0$ be grouped with? Elements $e0$, $e1$, and $e2$ form a rigid configuration rotating through thirty degrees in the image plane. The other elements are undergoing a simple rigid translation.

[6] For the purposes of this paper, we assume elements have available 'pointers' to their k-nearest neighbors by which access is essentially instantaneous. The k-nearest neighborhood can then be regarded as local in *time* if not space. Of course the computation of pointers would also take time. However, even if a conventional spatial neighborhood is used, our grouping criteria would still apply and the grouping scheme outlined in this section might be reformulated as an appropriate 'relaxation procedure' [19].

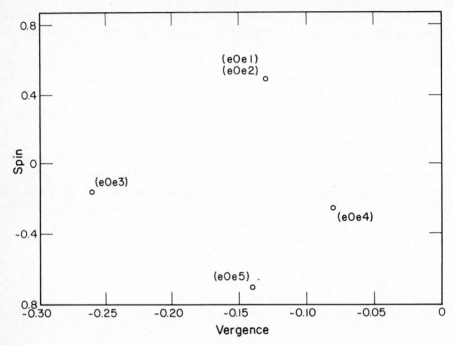

FIG. 7. Vergence and spin for pairings of $e0$ (in Fig. 6) with each of its neighbors.

ex	ex	e1	ex	ex
ex	ex	ex	ex	ex
ex	ex	ex	ex	ex
e2	ex	ex	ex	e3

FIG. 8. A problematic overlapping of objects. The elements ex correspond to one object and $e1$, $e2$ and $e3$ represent another.

spin pairs computed for the pairings of $e0$ with each of its neighbors (Fig. 6) are plotted in Fig. 7. The appropriate grouping ($e0e1e2$) is implied. Note that the rule can also explain how the elements with similar displacements in Fig. 4 are not grouped.

A problem with the scheme arises when none or only one of the neighbors of an element belong to the same object. A hypothetical example is given in Fig. 8 where the correct grouping depends upon the entire field. Unless the k-nearest neighborhood of $e1$ is sufficiently large, it will not contain elements $e2$ and $e3$, so $e1$ is incorrectly grouped with the two neighbors which happen to correspond to the closest two vergence and spin pairs. The problem could be avoided by choosing a neighborhood that is large enough to admit all relevant elements. However, it is possible to accomplish appropriate global groupings without compromising the local nature of the computation. By imposing the following additional condition, the grouping of elements such as $e1$ can be postponed until locally more consistent groupings have been found: two elements can be grouped if an application of the basic rule of confluence grouping to each element would result in their aggregation in both cases. The neighbors of element $e1$ in Fig. 8 would tend to vote for groupings that exclude $e1$. As the initial neighbors of $e1$ are grouped, and as those groups are merged and augmented, the k-nearest neighborhood of $e1$ changes until $e2$ and $e3$ become neighbors of $e1$. Fig. 9 corresponds to the configuration in Fig. 8 after the elements ex have been completely grouped. Since the group represents the elements ex as a *single* neighbor of $e1$, elements $e2$ and $e3$ can now be accessed and their grouping is discovered.

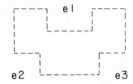

FIG. 9. A partial grouping of Fig. 8.

The criterion for merging and augmenting neighboring groups and elements preserves whatever vergence and spin consistency is already embodied in the existing groups. New elements or groups can only be added to a group if the distance (in vergence and spin space) between the two most disparate vergence and spin pairs associated with the constituents is approximately maintained. The measure is also used to make primary grouping decisions: groups vote for that neighbor whose merger or augmentation minimizes the maximum disparity among vergence and spin pairs.

3.3. Coordination

A synthesis of the basic rules of adjacency and confluence grouping requires the resolution of conflicts between the two schemes. The conflicts are due to the fact that the rules were developed separately and not because of any fundamental conflicts between the assumptions of adjacency and confluence. In the scheme for spatio-temporal aggregation outlined below, each type of grouping evidence is checked by evidence of the other type.

When deciding which neighboring elements should be grouped, the strict interpretation of the adjacency assumption in the form of the mutual nearest neighbor criterion is initially relaxed in favor of the less radical constraint imposed by the definition of a neighborhood. Thus the first decisions are primarily based on confluence while the adjacency assumption is made by exploiting confluence locally. Adjacency is also used to order the alternatives when several groupings are equally consistent with respect to confluence. Once it has been decided that two groups or elements should be grouped, adjacency and confluence each act to determine how the two entities should be combined. Groups can only be merged or augmented when adjacency and confluence agree on the result, otherwise new groups are built.

Parameters of the theory that can be adjusted include: the metric for vergence and spin space, size of the k-nearest neighborhood and tolerances for merging groups. Appropriate values for the parameters depend upon objectives of the implementation. A computational issue involved is one of economy: what is the smallest neighborhood that is almost always adequate? Psychological issues revolve around tuning the mechanism to model perception. In conjunction with our implementation of the theory, we have experimented with the parameter settings, attempting to qualitatively model perception of two-frame displays of dots in apparent motion. A summary of our empirical observations is given in Section 5.

4. Demonstration

The theory of spatio-temporal aggregation has been implemented in accordance with the criteria outlined in Section 3. In this section the basic competence of the theory is demonstrated by observing the performance of the mechanism for a variety of particle configurations. Vergence and spin pairs are compared using the Euclidean metric and tolerances for merging and augmenting groups are kept constant.

4.1. Rigid particle configurations

When particle clusters that individually satisfy the invariant case of the duo ergo omnibus tendency are presented simultaneously, the grouping mechanism can recover them as illustrated in the following examples. A k-nearest neighborhood just large enough to permit the correct grouping is used in each case.

4.1.1. *Counter-rotating discs*

The Dynamic Primal Sketch in Fig. 10 was generated by simulating two rigid discs rotating through ten degrees about the line of sight in opposite directions. When the mechanism was applied to the display, the Grouping Hierarchy drawn in Fig. 10 was obtained. For this grouping the neighborhood must include at least four nearest neighbors. Notice that even though the elements $e1$, $e2$ and $e3$ cannot initially access each other, their grouping ($g6$) is still discovered. Note also that while the elements $e4$ through $e11$ are mutually consistent with respect to confluence, adjacency criteria maintain the spatial clusters within their grouping ($g5$). If $g3$ and $g4$ had been closer to each other they would have been merged, and so on.

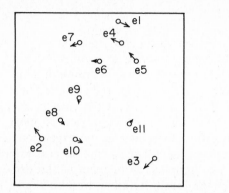

FIG. 10. Counter-rotating discs and the resulting Grouping Hierarchy. Elements $e1$, $e2$ and $e3$ represent the 'disc' that is rotating clockwise.

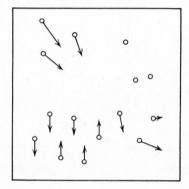

FIG. 11. Assorted elements and motions.

4.1.2. *Various translations*

The ability of the mechanism to recover groups when the underlying particle clusters are undergoing translations is demonstrated by its performance for Fig. 11. In this case a k-nearest neighborhood of at least three is required to attain appropriate grouping. The two closest stationary elements in the upper-right form a group which subsequently builds with the third one. Three elements in the upper-left corner are grouped because of their agreement in negative vergence. Another group represents the elements in the lower-right portion as approaching and rotating counter-clockwise about their centroid. The two superimposed translations in the lower-left corner, one toward the top and the other toward the bottom, are distinguished because vergence and spin computed for pairs of elements within a translation are all zero while pairs of elements taken one each from the two translations produce arbitrary vergence and spin values.

4.1.3. *A static configuration*

To illustrate the basic rule of adjacency grouping, consider the pattern of dots in the upper-left box of Fig. 12, similar to patterns used by Stevens [21]. It was produced by superimposing a non-homogeneous expansion of a field of dots on the original field. The line segments in the upper-right box of Fig. 12 represent the groups resulting from the first application of the rule, using a k-nearest neighborhood of one. Note that where the expansion is most vivid, the orientations of groups are primarily along lines of the expansion. The groups existing after the second iteration (Fig. 12) show that several expansion lines have been reinforced and a few groupings orthogonal to the expansion have begun to appear. Groups after the fourth iteration are also shown in Fig. 12.

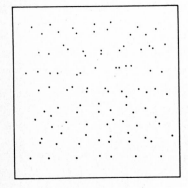

An Expansion Pattern

Groups After One Iteration

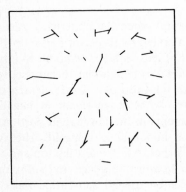

. . . After Two Iterations

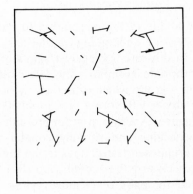

. . . After Four Iterations

FIG. 12. Grouping of a static spatial pattern.

It is significant that the third and fourth iterations together produced only thirteen new groups, whereas the first and second generated fifty. After the second iteration, spacings between the groups were fairly uniform—precisely the point at which the adjacency criteria permit groups to merge and form a single aggregation. Hence the locally parallel structure is discovered while the extreme tendency of the mutual nearest neighbor criterion to produce deep Grouping Hierarchies is effectively eliminated. Grouping rules sensitive to homogeneities in orientation (e.g. curvilinear aggregation, Marr [10]) can then be used to draw finer distinctions within the cluster of groups defined by adjacency.

4.2. Quasi-rigid particle configurations

The ability of spatio-temporal aggregation to recover groups when the conditions for invariance in the duo ergo omnibus tendency are violated is

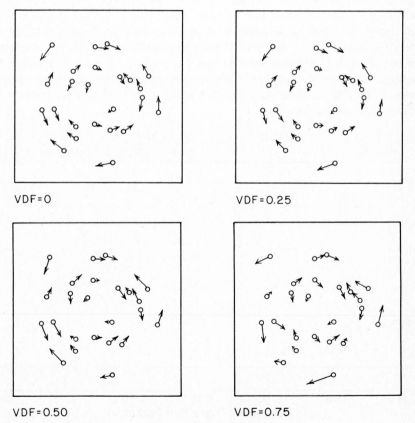

FIG. 13. Counter-rotating discs in varying degrees of rigidity.

demonstrated by its performance for quasi-rigid counter-rotating discs of the sort described in Section 2.2. In this section we describe an experiment that examines how grouping is affected when the size of the k-nearest neighborhood remains constant and the discs become 'less and less rigid'.

The Dynamic Primal Sketch in the upper-left box of Fig. 13 represents two rigid discs of twelve particles rotating through fifteen degrees in opposite directions about the line of sight. To simulate independent particle motions, the initial position of a particle is first translated by its displacement in the rigid case and then randomly re-positioned within a distance, d, of the translated position. The allowed radius of distortion, d, is a fraction (the *velocity distortion factor*) of the magnitude of the rigid displacement. Examples of applying non-zero velocity distortion factors to the discs are shown in Fig. 13 as indicated.

In our experiment, the rigid version of the discs in Fig. 13 was subjected to velocity distortion factors from 0.0 to 0.8 in each of ten trials and the k-nearest neighborhood size was held constant at five. The average performance of the mechanism is summarized in Fig. 14 using a measure of 'grouping accuracy' [2] indicating the fraction of elements that were correctly grouped. Grouping was perfect for factors of 0.2 and less. When the distortion was 0.5, approximately nine out of twelve elements were grouped correctly, but by 0.7 grouping had disintegrated. Even though Fig. 13 is a static presentation of rather complex events, it should be clear that the degradation in performance reflects the gradual distortion of the discs.

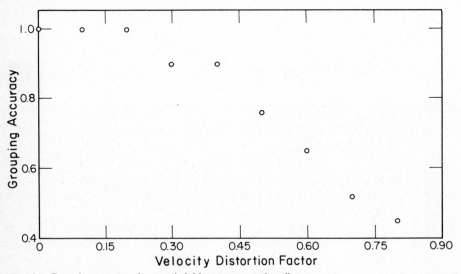

FIG. 14. Grouping accuracy for quasi-rigid counter-rotating discs.

5. Discussion

Computational issues in theories of vision revolve around questions such as: what *can* be computed at a given stage of processing and how should the visual computation be decomposed? The psychological issue then becomes: how much of that information is computed by the human visual system? For the most part, we have addressed some of the computational questions by explaining how it is possible to solve a primary portion of the grouping problem under constraints appropriate to an early level of visual processing.

Spatio-temporal aggregation holds best for surfaces that remain approximately perpendicular to the line of sight as they move. An ability to group quasi-rigid configurations (Section 4.2) indicates that the theory is also useful when the ideal conditions are distorted, but the analysis does not generally apply to rotations in depth. In such cases the rigidity assumption and a structure-from-motion scheme [23] may be required to conduct the aggregation.

While we have argued that use of the homogeneity assumption is secondary to adjacency (Section 2.2), it is likely that an ultimate solution to the grouping problem will weigh similarities somewhat earlier. For example, Stevens [21] discusses evidence that the relative brightness of elements can affect their apparent grouping. A use of the adjacency assumption in this regard would be to decrease the strength of homogeneities with increasing separation (e.g. Gogel [3]). Examples of other computations that may be important to grouping are discussed by Hildreth [4] and O'Callaghan [16].

Two parameters of spatio-temporal aggregation are the size of the k-nearest neighborhood and the metric for comparing vergence and spin pairs. In our attempts to model human perception of *two*-frame displays of dots in apparent motion, we have tentatively observed that any reasonable metric works when the invariant conditions of the duo ergo omnibus tendency are satisfied, and the Euclidean metric is adequate in other cases even though it fails for rotations in depth. For example, while two views containing several elements *isolated* in the image may be perceived as rotations in depth [1], the grouping of superimposed rotations in depth from just two views seems to be much more difficult.

Performance of the implemented grouping mechanism generally improves with increasing neighborhood size. We speculate that a k-nearest neighborhood of three or four provides a good model of perception for two-frame displays. For example, a k-value of three is sufficient to explain the vivid grouping of Fig. 4 but it is practically impossible for humans to distinguish the counter-rotating discs of Fig. 13 in just two views (for which five nearest-neighbors are required). Discrimination of the discs seems to require viewing over longer periods of time and continued rotation.

To summarize, the theory of spatio-temporal aggregation provides an explicit computational account of how elements *can* be grouped into objects. The groupings produced exhibit many qualities observed in human perception for a variety of moving dot displays. However, the valid experimental isolation of psychological functions such as spatio-temporal aggregation is a difficult problem. In this regard, knowing what *can* be computed provides clues of what to look for and complements the psychological investigation of human vision.

ACKNOWLEDGMENT

We thank David Marr and Shimon Ullman for comments on an earlier version of this paper and for making several valuable suggestions. We thank Charles Csuri, Lester Krueger and Bob Marshall for assistance in producing the animated graphics relevant to this research. Thanks also to Mike Brady and Kent Stevens for helpful comments and discussions.

REFERENCES

1. Borjesson, E. and von Hofsten, C., Visual perception of motion in depth: application of a vector model to three-dot motion patterns, *Perception and Psychophysics* **13** (1973) 169–179.
2. Flinchbaugh, B.E., A computational theory of spatio-temporal aggregation for visual analysis of objects in dynamic environments, Ph.D. Dissertation, Ohio State University (1980).
3. Gogel, W.C., The metric of visual space, in: Epstein, W., Ed., *Stability and Constancy in Visual Perception: Mechanisms and Processes* (Wiley, New York, 1977) 129–181.
4. Hildreth, E.C., Implementation of a theory of edge detection, AI-TR-579, M.I.T. A.I. Lab., Cambridge, MA (1980).
5. Horn, B.K.P. and Schunck, B.G., Determining optical flow, A.I. Memo No. 572, M.I.T. A.I. Lab., Cambridge, MA (1980).
6. Johansson, G., *Configurations in Event Perception* (Almqvist and Wiksell, Uppsala, 1950).
7. Johansson, G., Visual motion perception, Report 98, Dept. of Psychology, University of Uppsala (1971).
8. Johansson, G., Visual perception of biological motion and a model for its analysis, *Perception and Psychophysics* **14** (1973) 201–211.
9. Johansson, G., Spatial constancy and motion in visual perception, in: Epstein, W., Ed., *Stability and Constancy in Visual Perception: Mechanisms and Processes* (Wiley, New York, 1977) 375–419.
10. Marr, D., Early processing of visual information, *Philosophical Transactions of the Royal Society of London Ser. B* **275** (942) (1976) 483–519.
11. Marr, D., Representing visual information, A.I. Memo No. 415, M.I.T. A.I. Lab., Cambridge, MA (1977).
12. Marr, D. and Nishihara, H.K., Representation and recognition of the spatial organization of three dimensional shapes, A.I. Memo No. 416, M.I.T. A.I. Lab., Cambridge, MA (1977).
13. Marr, D. and Poggio, T., Cooperative computation of stereo disparity, *Science* **194** (1976) 283–287.
14. Marr, D. and Ullman, S., Directional selectivity and its use in early visual processing, A.I. Memo No. 524, M.I.T. A.I. Lab., Cambridge, MA (1979).
15. Marr, D. and Vaina, L., Representation and recognition of the movements of shapes, A.I. Memo No. 597, M.I.T. A.I. Lab., Cambridge, MA, forthcoming.
16. O'Callaghan, J.F., Computing and perceptual boundaries of dot patterns, *Computer Graphics and Image Processing* **3** (1974) 141–162.
17. Potter, J.L., Scene segmentation using motion information, *Computer Graphics and Image Processing* **6** (1977) 558–581.
18. Rashid, R.F., Towards a system for the interpretation of moving light displays, TR53, Computer Science Dept., University of Rochester (1979).

19. Rosenfeld, A., Hummel, R.A. and Zucker, S.W., Scene labeling by relaxation operations, *IEEE Trans. Systems, Man and Cybernetics* **SMC-6** (1976) 420–433.
20. Schatz, B., Computation of immediate texture discrimination, *Proc. Fifth Int. Joint Conf. on Artificial Intelligence* Cambridge, MA (1977) 708.
21. Stevens, K.A., Computation of locally parallel structure, *Biol. Cybernetics* **29** (1978) 19–28.
22. Stevens, K.A., Surface perception from local analysis of texture and contour, AI-TR-512, M.I.T. A.I. Lab., Cambridge, MA (1980).
23. Ullman, S., *The Interpretation of Visual Motion* (M.I.T. Press, Cambridge, MA, 1979).
24. Zucker, S.W. and Hummel, R.A., Toward a low-level description of dot clusters: labeling edge, interior, and noise points, *Computer Graphics and Image Processing* **9** (1979) 213–233.

Received October 1980

Recovery of the Three-Dimensional Shape of an Object from a Single View*

Takeo Kanade

Department of Computer Science, Carnegie–Mellon University, Pittsburgh, PA 15213, U.S.A.

ABSTRACT

Given a single picture which is a projection of a three-dimensional scene onto the two-dimensional picture plane, we usually have definite ideas about the 3-D shapes of objects. To do this we need to use assumptions about the world and the image formation process, since there exist a large number of shapes which can produce the same picture.

The purpose of this paper is to identify some of these assumptions—mostly geometrical ones—by demonstrating how the theory and techniques which exploit such assumptions can provide a systematic shape-recovery method. The method consists of two parts. The first is the application of the Origami theory which models the world as a collection of plane surfaces and recovers the possible shapes qualitatively. The second is the technique of mapping image regularities into shape constraints for recovering the probable shapes quantitatively.

Actual shape recovery from a single view is demonstrated for the scenes of an object such as a box and a chair. Given a single image, the method recovers the 3-D shapes of an object in it, and generates images of the same object as we would see it from other directions.

1. Introduction

It is a common experience for us that, given a single two-dimensional picture of an object, we have definite ideas about its three-dimensional shape, in spite of the fact that a large number of possible shapes exist which can produce the same picture. This fact indicates that we use some assumptions or knowledge about the objects and about image formation. The purpose of this paper is to identify some of these assumptions—mostly geometrical ones—by demonstrat-

*This research was sponsored by the Defence Advanced Research Projects Agency (DOD), ARPA Order No. 3597, and monitored by the Air Force Avionics Laboratory under Contract F33615-78-C-1551. The views and conclusions contained in this document are those of the author, and should not be interpreted as representing the official policies, either expressed or implied, of the Defence Advanced Projects Agency or the U.S. Government.

0004–3702/81/0000–0000/$02.50 © North-Holland

ing how the theory and techniques which exploit such assumptions can provide a systematic shape-recovery process.

The process consists of two parts: qualitative shape recovery and quantitative shape recovery. The first part uses a model of the Origami world [8]. It labels a line drawing and recovers the geometrically possible shapes by exploiting the assumption of planar-surfaced objects. When images, either in monochrome or in color, are given, edge profiles taken across lines in the image can be used in order to constrain line labels in the search of plausible interpretations. The second part adopts a technique of mapping image regularities (in particular, parallelism of lines and 'skewed symmetry') into shape constraints. It quantitatively recovers the probable shapes by exploiting the assumptions which exclude accidental alignments and regularities in the picture.

Actual shape recovery from a single view is demonstrated for the scenes of an object such as a box and a chair. Given an image, the shape recovery process generates a 3-D shape description of the object in terms of plane surfaces, and the description is supplied to a display program which can synthesize images of the same object as we would see it from other view directions. Throughout the paper we will assume orthographic projection rather than perspective projection.

In brief, the paper is outlined as follows: in the next section the problem of shape recovery from a single view is addressed. It is shown that the shape recovery can be either qualitative or quantitative. The previous research is briefly reviewed: what results have been obtained from what assumptions. Section 3 presents example scenes which are used throughout the paper. Sections 4 through 6 provide descriptions of tools and basic theories: the gradient space in Section 4; the theory of the Origami world in section 5; and the mapping of image regularities into constraints in the gradient space in Section 6. Then, in Section 7 these are put together to obtain quantitative 3-D shape descriptions. Example scenes are processed. Sections 8–10 deal with the shape recovery from a real image using an example of 'chair' scene: especially use of color edge profiles is presented in Section 9 to reduce the number of possible labelings. Section 11 discusses implications of the results in a broader context.

2. The Problem of Shape Recovery

2.1. Qualitative vs. quantitative shape recovery

Suppose that the drawing of Figs. 1(a) and 1(b) are given. Most commonly, they both appear as the corner of a solid object, made of three plane surfaces, coming out toward the viewer. This level of descriptions qualitatively characterizes the shape of objects. In this sense, the two figures in Fig. 1 are qualitatively equivalent.

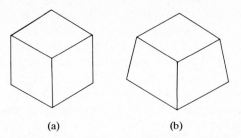

(a)   (b)

FIG. 1. Simple line drawings: (a) a 'cube' scene; (b) a 'trapezoid-block' scene.

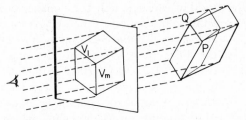

FIG. 2. Many shapes can produce the line drawing of Fig. 1(a).

Usually, though, the pictures seem to convey more quantitative shape information. Fig. 1(a) appears as a right-angled block, whereas Fig. 1(b) appears as a trapezoidal block, both viewed from the same direction with respect to the top face. That is, we feel that we can recover the surface orientations with respect to the view direction, or we can quantitatively describe the shape. Let us call this the quantitative shape recovery. (Note, however, that we cannot know any absolute information, such as the absolute distance to the object or its absolute size without knowing camera parameters.)

Notice that the shapes of our example scenes need not be as described above. Take the object in Fig. 1(a) for example. It need not be a cube. As shown in Fig. 2, the object can be any of the shapes made by three plane segments which intersect at P on the middle view line (which goes through the middle junction V_m in the picture), and the intersection edge (e.g. PQ) of each pair lies in the plane defined by the corresponding line in the picture (e.g. $V_m V_1$) and the view line. We will see later that the object in Fig. 1(a) can be of even a qualitatively different shape; i.e., it may not necessarily be a corner of a block. These considerations suggest that the assumptions we use in our shape recovery process are very strong ones.

2.2. Related work

Stereoscopic shape recovery has been studied quite extensively, but there is not much work on shape recovery from a single view, especially on quantitative shape recovery.

Interpretation of line drawings as 3-D scenes is the research domain which has been most actively studied. Guzman [3] first defined types of junctions (e.g., ELL, ARROW, and FORK), and developed many heuristics concerning probable association of regions suggested by each junction type. His program SEE decomposes a given line drawing into object regions, but it works totally in the 2-D picture domain without any explicit 3-D shape representation.

Huffman [6] and Clowes [1] gave an important theoretical framework. They observed that lines in the picture can have different physical meanings: a line can be a convex edge (signified by a label $+$), a concave edge (signified by $-$), and an occluding edge (signified by $\wedge$ with the occluding region on its right side). In the trihedral world in which exactly three planes are assumed to meet at every corner, the possible combinations of line labels for each junction type can be catalogued in a dictionary. To find 3-D shapes, a labeling procedure can assign line labels to the lines in a given line drawing according to the dictionary. Waltz [18] extended this idea further to include cracks, shadows, etc., and devised an efficient labeling procedure, called filtering. This body of work can be named *qualitative* analysis for *qualitative* shape recovery, because they used tools, such as junction types and line labels, which only qualitatively describe 3-D shapes of polyhedra.

The next group is *quantitative* analysis for qualitative shape recovery. Huffman [6] introduced the gradient space to represent surface orientations. Mackworth [12] employed it as a central tool to test the consistency of labelings by the method of constructively locating the gradient of each surface. In the labeling procedure of the Origami world [8], employed in this paper, the constraints in the gradient space are all maintained and tested symbolically on a graph called a Surface Connection Graph. Theoretically the constraints in the gradient space provide only necessary conditions for planar realizability of a labeled line drawing. Huffman [7] presents a $\phi(\phi')$-point test as the necessary and sufficient condition for a 'cut set' of labeled lines (equivalently, set of regions incident to those lines). Still, unfortunately, it is not the sufficient condition for a whole configuration, though. Falk [2] and Sugihara [17] directly investigated the algebraic properties of the linear equation system which represents the projection from a 3-D space object to the 2-D picture plane: Falk related degrees of freedom in a projection with the concept of mergeability of his Face Adjacency Graph; Sugihara presented the conditions for realizability of a labeled line drawing including hidden lines. All these researches quantitatively analyze a picture for its possible interpretations as 3-D scenes, but the recovered shape is still qualitative.

For *quantitative* shape recovery from a single picture we need to introduce more assumptions. The support hypothesis, first described by Roberts [15], is an example of such an assumption, which enables us to determine the depth (distance) of object points on a table. Mackworth [13] assumed rectangularity at every corner to uniquely determine the gradients of surfaces.

More commonly, model descriptions of objects which can appear in the scene are given to the system, and the system interprets a picture by identifying (possibly modified) occurrences of the models. In his pioneering work [15], Roberts used models of a cube, a wedge, and a hexagonal prism represented as a set of 3-D space coordinates of their vertices. The models are scaled, rotated, translated, and projected to test matching with the junctions in the picture. Falk's INTERPRET [2], which interprets imperfect line drawings, has fixed-size models of nine prototypes.

When one can assume the conditions in the image formulation process (such as the imaging geometry, the illumination, and the surface photometry, etc.), the intensity of a picture point can provide constraints on the surface orientation at the corresponding 3-D point. Horn [5] formulated a basic shape-from-shading theory employing the gradient-space representation. Woodham [19] identified two general rules (uniqueness and continuity) and demonstrated the recovery of local orientations in several cases such as a Lambertian sphere and a cone.

The quantitative shape recovery in this paper does not assume a predefined set of objects. Our approach resembles Mackworth's method and Horn–Woodham's shape-from-shading method in that we seek a unique determination of gradients, and in that some picture properties are mapped into constraints in the gradient space. But we focus on geometrical properties of objects and of the picture-taking process, and our assumptions are much more general than Mackworth's rectangularity assumption.

3. Example Scenes

The example scenes we will use in the rest of the paper are the following.
- 'Cube' scene: a line drawing (Fig. 1(a)).
- 'Trapezoid-block' scene: a line drawing (Fig. 1(b)).
- 'W-folded paper' scene: a line drawing (Fig. 3).
- 'Box' scene: a line drawing (Fig. 4).
- 'Chair' scene: a color image and a line drawing (Figs. 5(a) and 5(b)).

Each has its own difficulty, which illustrates an inherent problem in the shape recovery. The names of the scenes are given just for the purpose of referencing

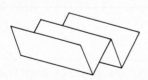

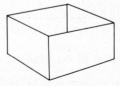

FIG. 4. A line drawing of a 'box' scene. Though it looks 'perfect', the trihedral labeling does not work for it.

FIG. 3. A line drawing of a 'W-folded paper' scene.

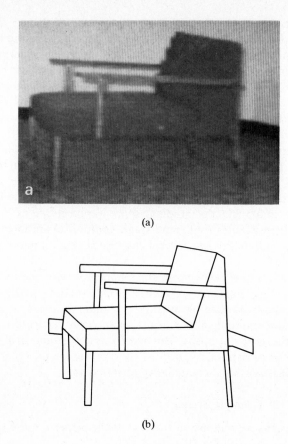

(a)

(b)

FIG. 5. A 'chair' scene: (a) a halftone image; (b) a line drawing.

them. They never imply any assumptions about the semantic nature of the scene.

4. The Gradient Space: Introduction

In this paper we will use the gradient space, popularized by Huffman [6] and Mackworth [12], as a tool for representing surface orientations. This section provides a brief introduction to the gradient space.

4.1. Definition of the gradient space

We will give a simplest version of the definition of the gradient space. Let Fig. 6(a) be the geometry involving the viewer, the picture plane, and the object in the scene. The z-axis is taken as parallel with the view line, and the x–y plane is on the picture plane, with the x-axis pointing to the horizontal right. We

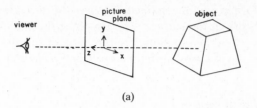

(a)

planes: $-z = px + qy + c \longrightarrow$ point: (p,q)

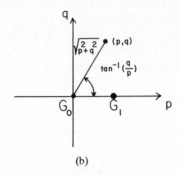

(b)

FIG. 6. The gradient space: (a) geometry including the object, the picture, and the viewer; (b) mapping of planes to a gradient.

assume orthographic projection here. A plane in the scene whose surface is visible from the viewer can be expressed as

$$-z = px + qy + c.\tag{1}$$

The two-dimensional space made of the ordered pairs (p, q) is called the *gradient space* G (Fig. 6(b)). Let us assume for our convenience that we align the directions of the coordinates of (x, y) in the picture with those of (p, q). All the planes in the scene that have the same values of p and q (i.e., the same orientation) are mapped into the point (p, q), called the *gradient*, in G.

The gradient (p, q) represents how the planes are slanting relative to the view line (z-axis). For example, the origin $G_0 = (0, 0)$ of G corresponds to those planes ($-z = c$) which are perpendicular to the view line. Points on the positive p-axis, $(p, 0)$ with $p > 0$, correspond to the planes ($-z = px + c$, $p > 0$) which are slanting horizontally to the right: the larger p is, the more slanted. From the (1) we see that the 3-D vector $(p, q, 1)$ is the directional vector of the surface normal.

When, in general, a surface is represented as $-z = f(x, y)$, then

$$p = \partial(-z)/\partial x, \quad \text{and} \quad q = \partial(-z)/\partial y,\tag{2}$$

which is why (p, q) is called the gradient. Thus the direction $(\tan^{-1}(q/p))$ of the vector from the origin to the gradient (p, q) is the direction of the steepest change of $-z$ (depth) on the surface. The length of the vector $(p^2 + q^2)^{1/2}$ is the rate of the change of the depth along the direction of the steepest change; i.e., the tangent of the angle between the picture plane and the planes corresponding to (p, q).

4.2. Properties of dual lines

One of the most useful properties of the gradient space is the following. Consider two planes meeting at an edge. Their orthographic picture made of regions R_1 and R_2 and a line L is shown in Fig. 7. Then in the gradient space, the gradient G_1 and G_2 of the two planes should be on a gradient-space line (called a dual line) which is perpendicular to the picture line L, but the location of the gradient-space line and the distance between G_1 and G_2 are arbitrary. Moreover, if the edge is convex $(+)$, G_1 and G_2 are ordered in the same direction as are the corresponding regions in the picture. If the edge is concave $(-)$, their order is reversed. These properties of dual lines are quite useful because they provide a basis for converting properties observable in the picture

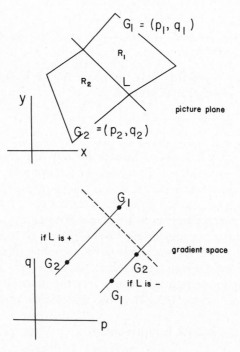

FIG. 7. Properties of dual lines. If two planes meet and the intersection line is projected to a picture line L, then the gradients of the two planes are on a gradient-space line which is perpendicular to L.

(the directions of lines) into constraints on the properties of a real object (the orientation of surfaces).

5. A theory of the Origami world

The Origami world [8] is a model for understanding line drawings in terms of plane surfaces, and finding their qualitative shape interpretations by assigning one of the three kinds of labels $(+, -, \uparrow)$ to each line. The labels signify the physical meaning of the lines [6]: the label + stands for a convex edge, − for a concave edge, and $\uparrow$ for an occluding edge (the direction of the arrow is given so that the region to its right is occluding the region to its left).

The qualitative shape recovery by means of the Origami-world labeling is the first part of the shape recovery process in this paper. We find possible shapes which can produce the given line drawing by exploiting the basic assumptions on the properties of objects.

5.1. Surface-oriented assumption

An important feature of the Origami world is that it is surface oriented. That is, it assumes that plane surfaces themselves can be stand-alone objects, unlike solid-object oriented models, such as the trihedral world. This idea can be best illustrated by Fig. 4. Though it appears perfect, the Huffman–Clowes–Waltz labeling scheme for the trihedral world cannot handle it, and would call it an 'impossible' object. The reason for this failure is that the trihedral world assumes that the object is solid, and thus the line drawing of a box would need to be 'super' perfect, as in Fig. 8, in order for it to be handled.

The assumptions concerning the geometrical configuration around a vertex in the Origami world are as follows. No more than three planar surfaces of different orientations meet at a vertex, and no more than three edges of different directions are involved at a vertex. The combination of the three orientations are assumed to be 'general' in the sense that they span the three-dimensional space (i.e., each orientation has a vector component per-pendicular to the other two). Let us call such vertices up-to-3-surface vertices. This restriction corresponds to the trihedral vertices in the solid-object world. Note, however, that the up-to-3-surface vertices generate a richer world than the world generated by the trihedral vertices, since the former can include 1-

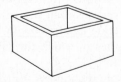

FIG. 8. A 'super-perfect' line drawing of the 'box' scene for the trihedral world.

TABLE 1. Comparison of the sizes of junction dictionaries for L, ARROW, FORK, and T junction types. The Origami world dictionary includes other junction types, such as K, X, and PSI

Junction type	Huffman–Clowes dictionary	Origami world dictionary
L	6	8
ARROW	3	15
FORK	3	9
T	4	16

and 2-surface vertices; that is, it allows free extending surfaces as stand-alone objects.

5.2. Junction labels for up-to-3-surface vertices

Once we recognize the basic assumptions of the Origami world, we can generate a junction dictionary as in the Huffman–Clowes–Waltz theory, which contains possible junction labels (i.e., possible line-label combinations) for each junction type. The size of the dictionary shown in Table 1 gives an idea of the degree of constraints imposed by the Origami world compared with the Huffman–Clowes trihedral world.

5.3. Augmented junction dictionary

A legal junction label represents a possible configuration of surfaces at a vertex. The consistent labeling of a line drawing, so that all the junctions are given legal junction labels, is nothing but a check on the consistency of surface interconnections: this is done by passing information by means of line labels from one junction to another. Waltz' filtering on junction labels is known to be a good method for doing this. However, labeling in the Origami world cannot simply rely on the filtering on junction labels. More thorough and global consistency checks concerning surface orientations are necessary. Because of the weaker restrictions at the vertices than the trihedral world, the anomalies caused by solely relying on junction labels show up as a more serious problem; i.e., the anomalous interpretations in which the labeling is consistent but the whole configuration is not possible [12, 14].

To remedy this, the junction dictionary for the Origami world can be augmented. To each junction label is attached the information as to what constraints in the gradient space should be satisfied by the surfaces incident at the junction. As shown in Fig. 9(a), the constraints are represented by the links which connect a pair of related regions and which include information about the constraints on their gradients. The properties of dual lines explained in Section 4 are used here.

In such a junction label as shown in Fig. 9(b), the intersection line of surfaces is occluded. This junction label is typically a result of folding a sheet of a paper along BC: R_1, which is folded toward the viewer, occludes a part of R_2. But we can assume that this junction label represents slightly more general cases in which the intersection line of R_1 and R_2 lies within the angle ABC. (See the middle figure of Fig. 9(b)). That is, we assume that if we remove the right hand part of R_1 which is occluding R_2, then the rest of R_1 and R_2 will form a convex intersection line, and the line can be anywhere in the angle ABC. We call it an occluded intersection line and denote it by the label $\oplus$. Therefore, the associated link represents that the gradient G_2 should be inside of the fan-shaped area whose origin is at G_1, and is bounded by the lines which are perpendicular to AB and BC.

Notice the crucial difference of our links from those Guzman [3] used. Guzman's links are for associating regions in the picture, whereas ours are for describing the relations between the corresponding surfaces in the scene.

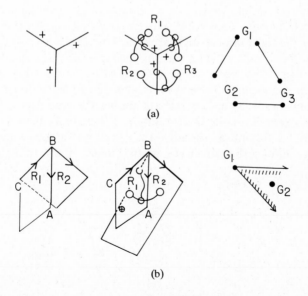

FIG. 9. The augmented junction dictionary for the Origami world. Two examples of entries are shown. For each, the first column is the junction label, the second associated links, and the third is the illustration of the relationships of gradients represented by the links.

5.4. Labeling procedure and surface connection graph

The labeling procedure of the Origami world uses the augmented dictionary. First, the Waltz filtering on junction labels is performed. Then the procedure begins to assign a junction label to each junction one by one. When a junction label is assigned to a junction, the constraints represented by the associated links are instantiated by using the directions of the lines at that particular junction.

The labeling procedure of the Origami world tests the consistency of surface orientations by using these instantiated constraints. In order to perform the test systematically, the labeling procedure constructs a graph called a *Surface Connection Graph* (SCG). The SCG is a labeled graph where a node represents a surface and an arc represents a constraint between the surfaces. It indicates what surfaces are connected with what surfaces through what constraints.

The test can be performed by using an iterative filtering operation in the gradient space defined on the SCG. One feature of this operation is that all the constraints are maintained symbolically in the SCG during the computation. The details can be found in [8].

5.5. The results of labeling the example scenes

As a result of the labeling procedure of the Origami world, we obtain not only a labeled line drawing, but also a filtered SCG. Each arc of the resultant SCG represents the constraint which the gradients of the corresponding pair of surfaces have to satisfy. That constraint has been filtered by those which the other parts of the SCG impose on that pair.

Let us see the results of labeling our example scenes. Usually we obtain multiple labelings. The 'cube' scene (Fig. 1(a)) has three labelings shown in Figs. 10–12. In each figure, (a) shows the labeling, (b) the corresponding SCG, and (c) the illustration of the constraints among the gradients represented by the SCG. For example, in the interpretation of Fig. 10(a), the gradients of the three surfaces S_1, S_2, and S_3 should form a triangle in the gradient space as shown in Fig. 10(c). (The directions of the edges of the triangle should be

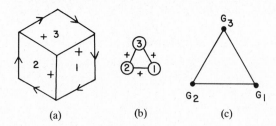

(a)   (b)   (c)

FIG. 10. The first labeling for the 'cube' scene: (a) labeling; (b) SCG; (c) illustration of the constraints on the gradients. This represents a convex corner.

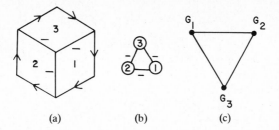

(a)   (b)   (c)

FIG. 11. The second labeling for the 'cube' scene. This represents a concave corner.

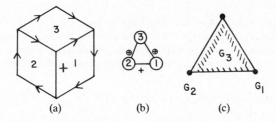

(a)   (b)   (c)

FIG. 12. The third labeling for the 'cube' scene. This represents a shape in which two surfaces S_1 and S_2 are connected along a convex edge, and occlude the third plane S_3 partially.

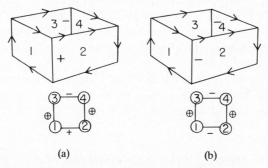

(a)   (b)

FIG. 13. In total there are eight labelings for the 'box' scene. Two of them are shown here: (a) corresponds to an ordinary box; (b) a 'squashed' box (notice that the front two faces, as well as the rear two, go in and form a concave edge).

as shown, but its size and position in the gradient space are arbitrary.) In the interpretation of Fig. 12, the gradient of S_3 can be anywhere in the hatched area. The 'trapezoid-block' scene (Fig. 1(b)) has also the same set of three labelings since it is qualitatively equivalent to Fig. 1(a).

The 'box' line drawing of Fig. 4 has eight labelings, two of which are shown in Fig. 13: The labeling in Fig. 13(a) corresponds to an 'ordinary box': the two front faces form a convex intersection and partially occlude the rear two faces which form a concave intersection. The labeling in Fig. 13(b) corresponds to a

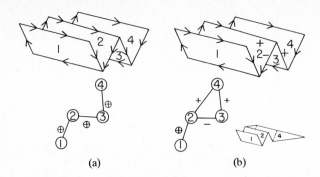

FIG. 14. The 'W-folded paper' scene has 16 labelings in total. Two of them are shown here (a) corresponds to a real W-folded paper. The shape that the labeling (b) represents might be imagined by first thinking of the shape made of S_1, S_2, and S_4 (see the figure, and imagine S_4 as horizontal), and then cutting S_4 properly along the dotted lines as well as adding S_3.

'squashed box': the front two faces, as well as the rear two, form a concave intersection.

The 'W-folded paper' scene of Fig. 3 has 16 labelings, two of which are shown in Fig. 14: (a) corresponds to a real W-folded paper, but (b) is a peculiar shape.

In interpreting these line drawings we do not usually think of such peculiar shapes as Fig. 12, Fig. 13(b), and Fig. 14(b). It is very difficult even to imagine those shapes as possible interpretations. Section 7 will present their rotated views to help in imagining the shapes and clarify the reason why they are not usually considered.

The line drawing of Fig. 5(b) for the 'chair' scene has a very large number of possible labelings. In order to reduce them into a manageable size, we will exploit other constraints which the color image (Fig. 5(a)) provides. (See Section 9.)

6. Mapping Image Regularities into Shape Constraints

The meta-heuristic of nonaccidental regularities exploited in this section is the following:

> "Regularities observable in the picture are not by accident, but
> are some projection of real regularities."

The technique for expointing this meta-heuristic is the mapping of the image regularities into the constraints in the gradient space. In this paper, parallelism of lines and skewed symmetry are particularly used as image regularities. This is a part of the theory and technique developed by Kanade and Kender [10]. The justification, generalization and other applications are found there.

6.1. Parallelism of lines

The heuristic for this regularity is

> "If two lines are parallel in the picture, they depict parallel lines in the scene."

Since we assume orthographic projection, the converse of this heuristic is always true. The heuristic is much more general than it may sound. Referring to Fig. 15(a), imagine that two lines in the 3-D space, which are denoted by vectors v_1 and v_2, are viewed from the direction which is denoted by a vector e. The heuristic fails for only those cases where two nonparallel lines are seen from such special view directions that the three vectors v_1, v_2, and e, if properly translated so that they share the same origin, can lie on a single plane.

Let us consider what constraint this heuristic provides on the gradients of two planes if a pair of their boundary lines are parallel in the picture, as shown in Fig. 15(b). Let the angle of parallel boundary lines be α in the x–y picture coordinates; i.e., their 2-D vector is $a = (\cos \alpha, \sin \alpha)$, and let $G_1 = (p_1, q_1)$ and $G_2 = (p_2, q_2)$ be the gradients of the two planes. Then the 3-D vectors corresponding to these boundary lines are

$$(\cos \alpha, \sin \alpha, -G_1 \cdot a) \quad \text{and} \quad (\cos \alpha, \sin \alpha, -G_2 \cdot a)$$

where $\langle \cdot \rangle$ stands for the inner product of the vectors. Here the third components of these 3-D vectors have been computed as the increment of z corresponding to the translation from $(0, 0)$ to $(\cos \alpha, \sin \alpha)$ in the picture:

$$(-p_i \cos \alpha - q_i \sin \alpha - c) - (-c) = -(p_i \cos \alpha + q_i \sin \alpha) = -G_i \cdot a,$$

since the gradient is related with the plane formula by (1) and the boundary line lies on the plane.

The heuristic demands that the third components of these two 3-D vectors are equal, i.e., $-G_1 \cdot a = -G_2 \cdot a$, or

$$p_1 \cos \alpha + q_1 \sin \alpha = p_2 \cos \alpha + q_2 \sin \alpha. \tag{3}$$

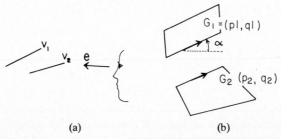

(a)   (b)

FIG. 15. Parallel-line heuristic: (a) If v_1, v_2, and e can be on the same plane in the 3-D space by translating them, even when v_1 and v_2 are not parallel, then the heuristic fails; (b) Two planes having parallel boundary lines.

This equation represents the fact that (p_1, q_1) and (p_2, q_2) are on a gradient-space line which is perpendicular to the direction $a = (\cos \alpha, \sin \alpha)$. Alternatively, this condition can be intuitively understood as follows. If a pair of boundary lines is really parallel in the 3-D space, we can translate one of the planes toward the other, and make the two planes intersect along those boundary lines. Therefore, the gradients of the two planes should have the above relationship (3) because of the property of dual lines.

6.2. Skewed symmetry

Symmetry in a 2-D picture has an axis for which the opposite sides are reflective: in other words, the symmetrical property is found along the transverse lines perpendicular to the symmetry axis. The concept *skewed symmetry* relaxes this condition a little. It means a class of 2-D shapes in which the symmetry is found along lines not necessarily perpendicular to the axis, but at a fixed angle to it. Figs. 16(a–c)[1] show a few examples. Formally, such shapes are defined as 2-D linear (affine) transformations of real symmetries. A skewed symmetry defines two directions as shown in Figs. 16(a–c): let us call them the skewed-symmetry axis and the skewed transverse axis. Stevens [16] does not use the concept of the skewed symmetry, but he presents a good body of psychological experiments which suggest that human observers can perceive surface orientations from figures with this property.

A particular heuristic about this image regularity is

"A skewed symmetry depicts a real symmetry viewed from some (unknown) view direction."

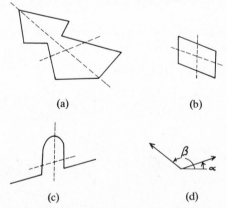

(a)   (b)

(c)   (d)

FIG. 16. Skewed symmetry. (a–c) are examples. (d) A skewed symmetry defines two directions: the skewed-symmetry axis and the skewed transverse axis.

[1]The mouse hole example (Fig. 16(c)) was given by K. Stevens.

Again, the converse of this heuristic is always true in the orthographic projection. We can transform this heuristic into constraints in the gradient space. As shown in Fig. 16(d), let α and β denote the directional angles of the skewed-symmetry axis and the skewed transverse axis, respectively. Let $G = (p, q)$ be the gradient of the plane which includes the skewed symmetry. The 3-D vectors on the plane corresponding to the directions α and β are

$$A = (\cos \alpha, \sin \alpha, -G \cdot a) \quad \text{and} \quad B = (\cos \beta, \sin \beta, -G \cdot b)$$

where $a = (\cos \alpha, \sin \alpha)$ and $b = (\cos \beta, \sin \beta)$. The heuristic demands these two 3-D vectors to be perpendicular, i.e., $A \cdot B = 0$, or

$$\cos(\alpha - \beta) + (G \cdot a)(G \cdot b) = 0 \qquad (4)$$

By rotating the p–q coordinates by the amount $\lambda = (\alpha + \beta)/2$ into the p'–q' coordinates, it is easy to show that

$$p'^2 \cos^2((\alpha - \beta)/2) - q'^2 \sin^2((\alpha - \beta)/2) = -\cos(\alpha - \beta) \qquad (5)$$

where

$$p' = p \cos \lambda + q \sin \lambda$$

$$q' = -p \sin \lambda + q \cos \lambda \quad \text{and} \quad \lambda = (\alpha + \beta)/2.$$

Thus, (p, q)'s are on a hyperbola shown in Fig. 17. That is, the skewed

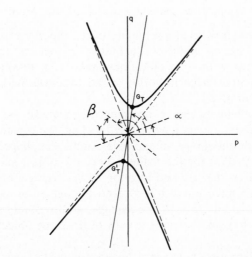

FIG. 17. A skewed symmetry defined by α and β can be a projection of a real symmetry if the gradient of the surface is on the hyperbola. The axis of the hyperbola is the bisector of the obtuse angle made by α and β. The asymptotes are perpendicular to the direction of α and β. The length from the origin to the tips is $(1 - 2d^2)^{1/2}/d$ where $d = \sin(\gamma/2)$ and $\gamma =$ the acute angle made by α and β.

symmetry defined by α and β in the picture can be a projection of a real symmetry if and only if the gradient is on this hyperbola. An impression might be that if we assume the skewed symmetry in the picture to be a projection of a real symmetry, the surface orientation is uniquely determined, but actually we have still an infinite number of possible orientations represented by the gradients on the hyperbola. As a special case, if $|\alpha - \beta| = \pi/2$ (i.e., the skewed symmetry is now a usual symmetry), the hyperbola degenerates into two perpendicular lines passing through the origin: $G \cdot a = 0$ and $G \cdot b = 0$.

The tips or vertices G_T and G_T' of the hyperbola represent special orientations with interesting properties. Since they are closest to the origin of the gradient space, and since the distance from the origin to a gradient represents the magnitude of the surface slant, G_T and G_T' correspond to the least slanted orientations that can produce the skewed symmetry in the picture from a real symmetry in the scene. Also, since they are on the line (the axis of the hyperbola) which bisects the angle made by α and β, they correspond to the orientations for which the length metrics along the directions of α and β in the picture are equal; i.e., the ratio of lengths along them in the picture represents the real ratio. (See Appendix A for the proof.) In Fig. 17, G_T corresponds to looking down to the surface, and G_T' to looking up to it. If no other constraints are available, either one of these gradients may be the most reasonable selection as the surface orientation.

7. Quantitative Shape Recovery: Basic Method

In Section 5 we have presented a summary of the theory of the Origami world. For our example scenes, multiple qualitative shapes of objects have been recovered. Note that all the interpretations except Fig. 10(a) are obtained only in the surface-oriented Origami world: in the trihedral world they are called 'impossible' configurations.

Still a lot of ambiguities exist concerning the shape of the object. First, we have multiple labelings. Second, given any labeling, the constraints represented by the SCG are not enough to uniquely determine the shape. For example, in the labeling of Fig. 10(a) for the 'cube' scene, the object still can have many shapes, depending on the size and location of the triangle of Fig. 10(c) in the gradient space. We have not yet recovered enough information to uniquely determine the size and location of the triangle, and to obtain a 3-D description of the object so as to generate another view of the same object from a different angle.

Section 6 has described how some image regularities can be mapped into constraints in the gradient space. They provide additional constraints for determining the surface orientations.

In this section we will show that by putting these together we can recover quantitative shapes; i.e., we can assign a unique gradient to each surface.

7.1. Unique determination of gradients: Simple cases

7.1.1. 'Cube' scene

Take the line drawing of Fig. 1(a). Fig. 18(a) shows the angles and the lengths. It has three labelings (Figs. 10–12). Consider the first one shown in Fig. 10(a) and reproduced in Fig. 18(b). The labeling indicates that there are three totally-visible surfaces S_1 $(= V_3V_4V_7V_2)$, S_2 $(= V_5V_6V_7V_4)$, and S_3 $(= V_1V_2V_7V_6)$, and that their gradients, G_1, G_2, and G_3, should form a triangle as shown in Fig. 10(c). On the other hand, S_1, S_2, and S_3 have skewed symmetries: their skewed-symmetry axes and skewed transverse axes are shown in Fig. 18(b) as dotted lines. If we assume these skewed symmetries to be projections of real symmetries, we can draw the hyperbola for each surface as shown in Fig. 18(c).

Now the problem is where we can locate the triangle of Fig. 10(c) in Fig. 18(c) so that each vertex of the triangle is on the corresponding hyperbola. It is

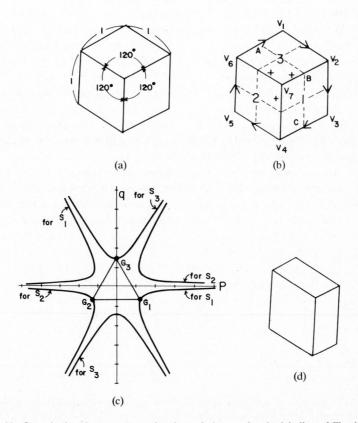

(a)   (b)

(c)   (d)

FIG. 18. Quantitative shape recovery for the 'cube' scene for the labeling of Fig. 10.

not difficult to prove that the location shown in Fig. 18(c) is the only possibility (see Appendix B for the proof). The gradients of S_1, S_2 and S_3 are thus uniquely determined as

$$G_1 = (\sqrt{3/2}, -\sqrt{1/2}), \quad G_2 = (-\sqrt{3/2}, -\sqrt{1/2}) \quad \text{and} \quad G_3 = (0, \sqrt{2}).$$

Four things should be noted about this assignment of gradients. First, the G_i's remain the same value when we change the sizes of the regions but keep the directions of lines the same. For example, Fig. 18(d) will result in the same combination of gradients. This seems reasonable.

Second, in this assignment the surfaces S_1, S_2, and S_3 are perpendicular to each other, because the inner products of their surface normals $(p_i, q_i, 1)$ vanish:

$$p_i p_j + q_i q_j + 1 = 0 \quad \text{for } i \neq j. \tag{6}$$

This is not a special result for this particular case in which the angles between lines aroung the FORK junction V_7 are all 120°. It can be generally shown (Appendix B) that in the case of a picture made of three parallel quadrilaterals like Fig. 19(a), the above method of assignment always gives a unique solution in which the three surfaces are perpendicular to each other, if and only if all the three angles at the FORK junction are obtuse. This implies that Fig. 19(b), in which one of the angles is acute, cannot be a picture of a right-angled block; some surfaces are really skewed.

It is interesting to observe the following here. Suppose we try to draw a skewed parallelepiped (a rhomboidal prism). Then we normally choose a view angle which yields a picture like Fig. 19(b), not a view angle which yields a picture like Fig. 19(a), probably because people will not perceive the latter as a skewed parallelepiped even though it could be.

Third, once the gradients have been computed we know the plane formula in the 3-D space for each surface. Of course, we have to assume the z position of one point on the object; there is no way to know this information from a single picture. Let us assume z of V_7 to be 0. If we select the origin of the x–y picture

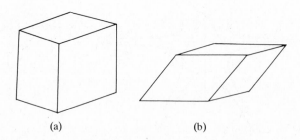

(a)   (b)

FIG. 19. Line drawings of parallelepipeds: (a) This can be a right-angled parallelepiped or a rhomboidal prism. (b) This must be a squashed rhomboidal prism (the shape of at least one surface must be really skewed).

plane at V_7, then we have

$$S_1: \quad \sqrt{3/2}x - \sqrt{1/2}y + z = 0,$$

$$S_2: \quad -\sqrt{3/2}x - \sqrt{1/2}y + z = 0, \tag{7}$$

$$S_3: \qquad\qquad \sqrt{2}y + z = 0.$$

The 3-D coordinates of the vertices are found to be

$$V_1: \quad (0, 1, -\sqrt{2}), \qquad\qquad V_2: \quad (\sqrt{3}/2, 1/2, -\sqrt{1/2}),$$

$$V_3: \quad (\sqrt{3}/2, -1/2, -\sqrt{2}), \qquad V_4: \quad (0, -1, -\sqrt{1/2}),$$

$$V_5: \quad (-\sqrt{3}/2, -1/2, -\sqrt{2}), \qquad V_6: \quad (-\sqrt{3}/2, 1/2, -\sqrt{1/2}),$$

$$V_7: \quad (0, 0, 0).$$

Fourth, for a parallel quadrilateral, another skewed symmetry can be defined by its diagonals. Therefore, other combinations of the axes, such as shown in Fig. 20(a) are possible. In the case of Fig. 20(a), the assignment of gradients is not unique; those triangles shown in Fig. 20(b) are all possible assignments. Since the diagonals of each surface are perpendicular in the 3-D space, the shapes corresponding to those triangles are, in general, the corner of a rhomboidal prism whose surfaces are equal-sized rhombuses. In both combinations of skewed symmetries in Fig. 18 and Fig. 20 the skewed-symmetry heuristic holds for every surface. The difference between them lies in whether a

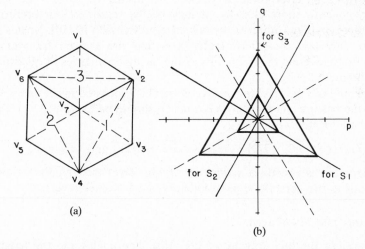

(a)

(b)

FIG. 20. The parallel quadrilaterals in Fig. 18(b) can have other combinations of axes for skewed symmetries.

   (a) The case in which the diagonals are selected for each region to define its skewed symmetry.

   (b) The corresponding loci (each hyperbola has degenerated into two lines in this case). The triangles are all possible assignments of gradients.

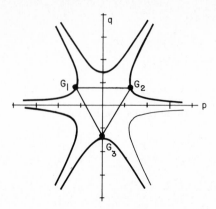

FIG. 21. Positions of G_1, G_2, and G_3 corresponding to the labeling of Fig. 11.

composite of skewed-symmetrical regions in the picture is interpreted as a symmetrical composite of surfaces in the scene. That is, in the interpretation of Fig. 18, the composite of S_1 and S_3 is symmetrical about the connected line segments in the 3-D space which correspond to the connected two axes (i.e., ABC) of the two skewed symmetrical regions in the picture. This is not the case for Fig. 20: here the composite of S_1 and S_3 is not symmetrical about the connected lines in the 3-D space which correspond to $V_1V_7V_3$ or $V_6V_2V_4$. In other words, the interpretation of Fig. 18 seems to satisfy the skewed-symmetry heuristic more globally. It may be the reason of our preferring it. This problem involves other issues, which are discussed in [10]. In this paper, hereafter, only the skewed-symmetry axis and the skewed transverse axis obtained by connecting the midpoints of the facing boundaries of quadrilaterals will be considered.

The labeling of Fig. 11(a) (a concave corner) is processed in the same way. In this case the triangle made of G_1, G_2, and G_3 should be like Fig. 11(c), thus the gradients are located as in Fig. 21:

$$G_1 = (-\sqrt{3/2}, \sqrt{1/2}), \quad G_2 = (\sqrt{3/2}, \sqrt{1/2}) \quad \text{and} \quad G_3 = (0, -\sqrt{2}).$$

This assignment is exactly a symmetry of Fig. 18(c) through the origin, and corresponds to the perceptual phenomenon called Necker reversal.

7.1.2. 'Trapezoid-block' scene

Let us consider the line drawing of Fig. 1(b). The angles and the lengths are shown in Fig. 22(a). As we have noticed this line drawing has the same qualitative interpretations (labelings) as Fig. 1(a): i.e., three labelings which have been shown in Figs. 10–12. However, Fig. 22(a) seems to depict a quantitatively different shape. What makes the difference?

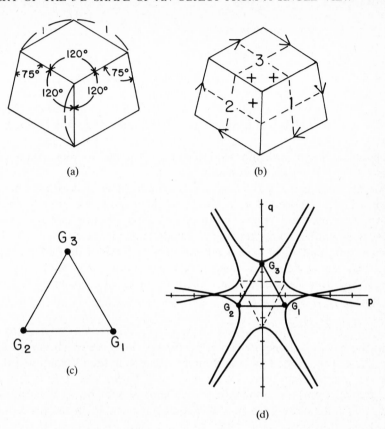

FIG. 22. Shape recovery of the 'trapezoid-block' scene.

Consider the case of the labeling shown in Fig. 22(b). The gradients of the surfaces S_1, S_2, and S_3 should form the triangle shown in Fig. 22(c), which is the same constraint as the convex-corner interpretation (Fig. 18) for the 'cube' scene. R_1, R_2 and R_3 have also skewed symmetries. However, the axes for the skewed symmetries for R_1 and R_2 are slightly different from the case of Fig. 18(b), therefore the shape and location of the corresponding hyperbolas also change (see Fig. 22(d)). As a result, if we try to locate the triangle so that each vertex is on the corresponding hyperbola, it has to be placed as shown in Fig. 22(d). When we compare this assignment with Fig. 18(c), the location of G_3 is the same, but G_1 and G_2 are closer to G_3. In this assignment of gradients, the angle made by S_1 and S_3 is equal to that made by S_2 and S_3, and is larger than 90°. Thus, the resultant shape is a trapezoid block.

As in the case of the 'cube' scene, we also have the combination of gradients shown as the dotted triangle in Fig. 22(d), corresponding to the labeling of Fig. 11(a); the shape is the reversal of Fig. 22(b).

7.2. Cases involving partially-visible surfaces

7.2.1. *Identification of surface boundaries*

In order to solve the cases which involve partially occluded surfaces, identification of surface boundaries and inference of the occluded parts is necessary. This problem needs research for a systematic method. Though we have a method which is sufficient for our examples, the topic is worth another complete paper. We do not pursue it further here, and show how the reasoning can be made in our particular example cases. The method may sound a little ad hoc, but the following is noteworthy.

For identifying the surface boundaries in a labeled drawing, the junction labels play a substantial role, because they represent how boundaries of surfaces 'appear' and 'hide' at vertices. Actually, notice that we can identify surfaces only after a line drawing has been labeled: for example, the labelings of Figs. 10(a) and 12(b) have a different set of surfaces. In fact, we can assign rules concerning boundary lines to each junction label and, when given a labeled line drawing, we can trace the boundaries of each surface according to the rules.

7.2.2. *'Box' scene*

Take the labeling shown in Fig. 13(a) for the 'box' scene. (It is reproduced in Fig. 23(a)). This is one of its eight interpretations in the Origami world [8]. The labeling indicates that there are four surfaces, S_1, S_2, S_3 and S_4. It also indicates that the relationships among their gradients should be as illustrated in Fig. 23(b): G_1 and G_2 are on a line perpendicular to V_5V_7 in the order as shown, because of the convex label given to V_5V_7. Similarly, G_3 and G_4 are on a line perpendicular to V_2V_8 in the order as shown, because of the concave label given to V_2V_8. G_3 should be within the angle G_2G_1a because of the junction label given to V_1, and G_4 within G_1G_2b. Again, these constraints that the labeling provides are not enough to uniquely determine the values of gradients. The heuristics of nonaccidental regularities provide additional constraints.

First, S_1 and S_2 are totally-visible surfaces, and both have skewed symmetries in the picture; their axes are shown in Fig. 23(a). Therefore, if we apply the skewed-symmetry heuristic, the gradients of S_1 and S_2 should be on the hyperbolas drawn as solid curves respectively in Fig. 23(c). Notice, however, the labeling indicates that S_3 and S_4 are only partially visible: the region $V_1V_2V_8V_7$, for example, depicts a part of S_3 because it is occluded along the lines V_1V_7 and V_7V_8. Therefore the shape of the region is meaningless.

Second, the line V_2V_8 is parallel in the picture with the line V_7V_5. Thus, if we apply the parallel-line heuristic, the surfaces which include these lines as boundaries (i.e., S_1, S_2, S_3, and S_4, due to the labeling) should have their gradients on a line perpendicular to V_5V_7. That is, G_1 through G_4 should be on a single line. Further, because V_1V_7 is parallel to V_2V_3, G_1 and G_4 (the gradients of the surfaces which include these lines) should be on a line

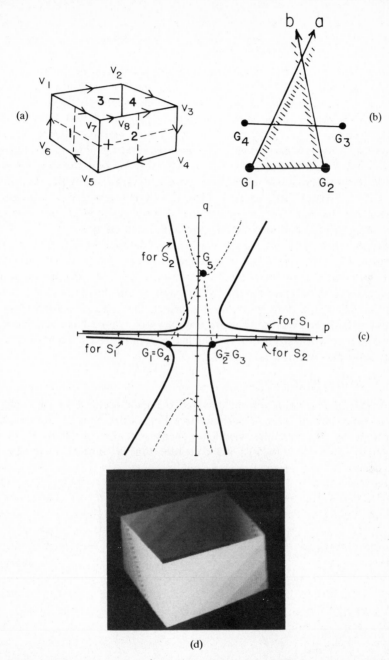

FIG. 23. Shape recovery of the labeling of Fig. 13(a) for the 'box' scene: (a) labeling; (b) constraints on the gradients; (c) assignment of the gradients; (d) view of the recovered shape from 10° to the right and 10° above the original view angle. This is a depth-coded image in which the depth of each point is coded by the intensity: the brighter, the nearer.

perpendicular to V_1V_7. When we consider these constraints together in Fig. 23(b), we conclude that G_1 and G_4 should coincide. Similarly, G_2 should be the same as G_3.

Third, note that use of the parallel-line heuristic on both the pair of V_1V_7 and V_2V_3 and the pair of V_1V_2 and V_3V_7 implies that these four lines (in the 3-D space) are on the same plane and form a quadrilateral. Therefore, we can think of an imaginary planar surface segment $S_5\ (=V_1V_2V_3V_7)$. Because S_5 has a skewed symmetry in the picture, its (imaginary) gradient should be on the corresponding hyperbola shown as a dotted curve in Fig. 23(c). Since S_5 connects with S_1 and S_2 along V_1V_7 and V_3V_7, respectively, the gradients of S_1, S_2 and S_5 should form a triangle whose shape is determined by the directions of V_1V_7, V_3V_7, and V_5V_7 (the three lines at the FORK junction V_7). Remember that what we did here is not ad hoc but a result of considering the scene-domain meaning of labelings and the parallel-line heuristics.

Finally, by putting all the above constraints together we can determine the locations of $G_1\ (=G_4)$ and $G_2\ (=G_3)$ as shown in Fig. 23(c). As before, if we fix the origin of the x–y picture plane, and assume the z (depth) of any point on the object, the plane formulas for S_1 through S_4 can be determined, and we obtain the 3-D shape description of the object. Fig. 23(d) is a rotated view of the recovered shape. We see that an 'ordinary box' shape has been recovered. This image is a synthesized one in which the depth of each point is coded by the intensity: the brighter, the nearer.

7.2.3. 'W-folded paper' scene

The labeling of Fig. 14(a) for the 'W-folded paper' scene is another example which involves partially visible surfaces (see Fig. 24(a)): S_1 is totally visible, but S_2 through S_4 are partially visible. Because of the parallelisms of lines ($V_1V_2 /\!/ V_9V_{10}$ and $V_1V_{11} /\!/ V_9V_{12}$) we conclude that S_1 and S_3 have the same

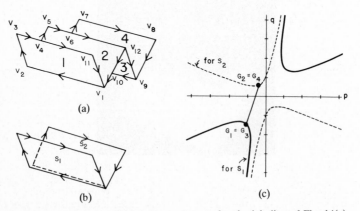

(a)

(b)

(c)

FIG. 24. Shape recovery of the 'W-folded paper' scene for the labeling of Fig. 14(a).

gradient ($G_1 = G_3$). Similarly, $G_2 = G_4$. Due to the parallelism of $V_3 V_{11}$ and $V_5 V_{12}$, G_1 and G_2 are to be on a line perpendicular to them. The skewed symmetry of S_1 constrains G_1 to be on the hyperbola drawn as a solid curve in Fig. 24(c). The constraints we have obtained so far are not enough for the unique determination of G_1 and G_2. Even when we determine G_1 at one of the tips of the solid hyperbola, G_2 can still be anywhere on the half line extending upward from G_1 in the perpendicular direction to $V_3 V_{11}$.

In order to extract more constraints, the shapes of partially visible surfaces need to be inferred. Let us show how the labeling and the constraints obtained so far can be used for this. Let us work with S_2. Imagine that we are tracing the boundaries of S_2 clockwise. The labeling tells that they show up along $V_4 V_5$, $V_5 V_{12}$ and $V_{12} V_1$, but 'disappear' at V_1 and 'reappear' at V_4. The constraint that G_1 and G_2 are to be on a line perpendicular to $V_3 V_{11}$ or $V_5 V_{12}$ implies that if S_1 and S_2 actually intersect, the occluded intersection line (i.e., the occluded boundary line of S_2) should coincide with $V_1 V_2$ (because $V_1 V_2 /\!/ V_3 V_{11} /\!/ V_5 V_{12}$). How about the boundary line which reappeared at V_4? Since it is interrupted by S_1 at V_4 (notice that this is indicated by the junction label given to the T junction V_4), it is meaningful to extend $V_5 V_4$ in the picture and we find that the extended line intersects at V_2 with the inferred occluded boundary from V_1. Thus the shape of S_2 could be the dotted line shown in Fig. 24(b).

Application of the skewed-symmetry heuristic to this region provides the dotted curve shown in Fig. 24(c). Since we have no more constraints, let us determine G_1 as the lower tip of the solid hyperbola, and G_2 on the dotted hyperbola so that the line connecting them is perpendicular to $V_1 V_2$ (Fig. 24(c)). Note that the upper tip of the solid hyperbola is not appropriate for G_1 because then G_2 cannot be on the dotted hyperbola.

7.3. 'Strange' shapes violate the regularity heuristics

The labelings we have treated so far all correspond to the most 'natural' interpretations of the pictures. The qualitative shape recovery by the theory of the Origami world yields other labelings. This section will show that some shapes implied by the labelings are really 'possible' but violate some of the regularity heuristics. We conjecture that this is why they look 'strange' or 'unnatural'.

7.3.1. Non-cube interpretation of the 'cube' scene

Take the third labeling (Fig. 12(a)) for the 'cube' scene. It is duplicated in Fig. 25(a). It indicates that two totally-visible surfaces S_1 and S_2 which are connected and form a convex edge, occlude partially the third surface S_3. The relationships among the gradients G_1 through G_3 imposed by this labeling are illustrated in Fig. 25(b): G_3 should be inside of the triangle or on the base line connecting G_1 and G_2. We see that the parallel-line heuristic cannot be satisfied

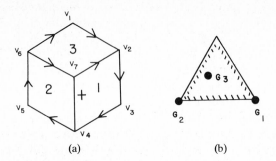

(a)   (b)

FIG. 25. The third labeling (Fig. 12) for the 'cube' scene does not satisfy the parallel-line heuristic: (a) labeling; (b) constraints in the gradient space. G_1 has to be inside of the triangle or on the base line, thus G_1 and G_2 cannot be placed so that the parallelism of V_1V_2 and V_6V_7 is not accidental.

in this case. The parallelism of lines V_1V_2 and V_6V_7 demands that G_3 and G_2 are on a line perpendicular to V_6V_7 (i.e., on the left leg of the triangle), and the parallelism of V_1V_6 and V_2V_7 demands that G_3 and G_1 are on a line perpendicular to V_2V_7 (i.e., on the right leg of the triangle), but both cannot be the case simultaneously.

7.3.2. *Phoney-box interpretations of the 'box' scene*

Let us go to the 'box' scene. The labeling of Fig. 13(b) represents a shape of a 'squashed' box with the front two faces going in. Again, Fig. 26 (the diagram illustrating the constraints in the gradient space) indicates that the parallel-line heuristic cannot be satisfied: G_1 and G_4 cannot be on a line perpendicular to V_1V_7 (or V_2V_3).

We have noted that there are eight labelings for the 'box' scene in the Origami world, but it can be found that the interpretations other than Fig. 13(a) which corresponds to an 'ordinary box' shape, do not satisfy the regularity heuristics.

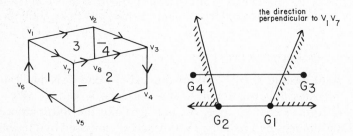

FIG. 26. Constraints on G_1 through G_4 imposed by the labeling of Fig. 13(b). G_1 and G_4 cannot be on a line perpendicular to V_1V_7.

7.3.3. *Non-W-folded-paper interpretations of the 'W-folded paper' scene*

In the case of the 'W-folded paper' scene, the labeling of Fig. 14(b) is an example which violates the heuristics. Again only Fig. 14(a), out of 16 possible labelings, can have the assignment of gradients without violating the regularity heuristics.

7.4. Conservation of image regularities

We have shown that some qualitative interpretations do not satisfy the image regularity heuristics. Of course, we 'can' assign the gradients, if we neglect the heuristics. For example, the diagram of Fig. 27(a) shows a particular selection of gradients for the non-cube interpretation (Fig. 25) of the 'cube' scene such that the skewed-symmetry heuristic holds for S_1 and S_2, and the surface S_3 intersects with S_1 along V_2V_3 and with S_2 along V_5V_6. The resultant object appears exactly like Fig. 1(a) when seen from the present view direction. However, when it is seen from other directions, say, from 15° to the right and 15° above, it looks like Fig. 27(b). We notice that the image regularity (parallelism) we observed in the original view (Fig. 1(a)) has disappeared. Recall that, in contrast, the labeling of Figs. 10 and 11 allows such a selection of gradients (Figs. 18 and 21) corresponding convex and concave corners, respectively, and that the resultant shapes produce pictures which conserve those regularities from whatever direction they are seen.

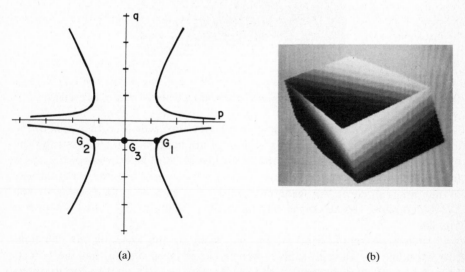

(a)   (b)

FIG. 27. A 'strange' shape for the 'cube' scene: (a) a possible assignment of the gradients corresponding to the labeling of Fig. 12; (b) a view from another angle of the resultant shape. It does not preserve the parallelism of V_1V_2 and V_6V_7 observed in the original view.

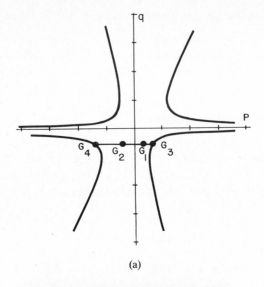

(a)

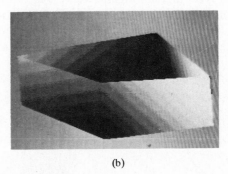

(b)

FIG. 28. A 'strange' shape for the 'box' scene corresponding to the labeling of Fig. 13(b).

Likewise, Fig. 28 is an example of a 'phoney box' which corresponds to the interpretation of Fig. 13(b). The selection of gradients in Fig. 28(a) satisfies the basic constraints represented by the SCG. Figure 28(a) is the view of the shape from 10° to the right and 10° above. It does not conserve the image regularities in the original view. An example shape of a non W-folded-paper of the 'W-folded paper' scene corresponding to the labeling of Fig. 14(b) is shown in Fig. 29.

It should be emphasized again that even in the case of the labelings corresponding to 'natural' shapes there is no physical reason that the objects have to be of such particular shapes. In fact, in the convex-corner interpretation of the 'cube' scene (Fig. 18), if we do not use the skewed-symmetry heuristic, we could place the triangle of Fig. 10(c) in the gradient space at any

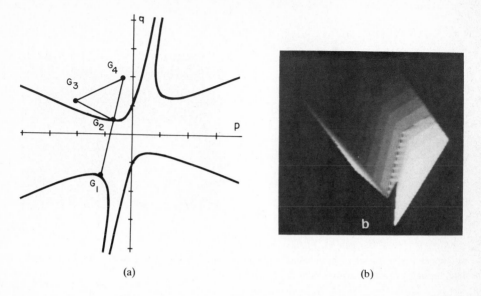

(a)   (b)

FIG. 29. A 'strange' shape for the 'W-folded paper' scene corresponding to the labeling of Fig. 14(b): (a) assignments of gradients; (b) a rotated view of the shape from 25° to the right and 25° above. This shape produces the line drawing of the 'W-folded paper' scene when seen from the original direction.

location with any size. Suppose we place it as shown in Fig. 30(a). The resultant shape appears as Fig. 30(b) when viewed from 20° to the right and 20° above. Now, though this picture is still qualitatively the same as the original one (Fig. 1(a)), it no longer allows an interpretation as a symmetrical shape.

Similarly in the case of the 'real box' interpretation (Fig. 23) of the 'box' scene, if we regard the parallelism between the picture lines as accidental regularities caused by special view directions, we could select the gradients differently from those in Fig. 23(c). But then the resultant shape will not conserve some parallelism of lines when viewed from other directions.

Thus what we have shown is the following.

- The Origami world labeling yields multiple interpretations of qualitatively different shapes, all of which are geometrically possible.

- Some of them cannot satisfy some of the regularity heuristics.

- For some interpretations we can select the gradients of surfaces so that they satisfy the regularity heuristics. Then the resultant shapes have real regularities and, therefore, conserve the image regularities observed in the original view, even when seen from other view angles.

We feel that this conservation of image regularities is strongly related to whether the interpreted shapes seem 'natural' to a human observer.

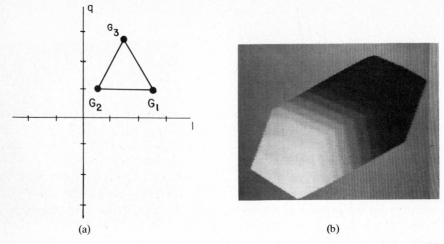

FIG. 30. A placement of the triangle of Fig. 10(c) in the gradient space different from that in Fig. 18(c) results in a skewed parallelepiped.

8. Shape Recovery from Real Images: More Complexity and More Constraints

In the previous sections, we have presented the basic theory and technique to extract and to exploit geometric constraints for quantitative shape recovery. The three-dimensional shapes of our simple example scenes have been recovered. When it comes to the shape recovery from real images, such as the 'chair' scene (Fig. 5), more complexities are involved and more constraints are available. The succeeding two sections will present the techniques to be used for the shape recovery from real images. The 'chair' scene example will be demonstratively processed.

Those simple line drawings we have treated so far (Figs. 1, 3, and 4) consist of a small number of lines and regions, and the number of legal labelings in the Origami world is also small. Thus we could consider each labeling and test whether the regularity heuristics are applicable in order to select 'natural' or 'probable' shapes. However, line drawings with many lines and regions will have too many labelings (i.e., geometrically possible shapes) to consider them all individually. The next section shows how we can extract the constraints that color images provide on line labels, and how we can exploit them to order multiple labelings according to their degree of match with image properties.

The next problem is related with noise and distortions which the real pictures include. Due to them, positioning of the gradients may not proceed in such an idealistic manner as shown in Section 7. Section 10 presents a solution to this problem.

9. Use of Color Edge Profiles

9.1. Edge profiles and line labels

An edge profile is a curve showing how the intensity (or more generally, a certain image property) changes across an edge. Historically, in the scene analysis of the block world, it has been known that a few typical types of intensity profiles exist (Herskovits and Binford [4]), and Horn [5] showed that they can suggest different types of edges: for instance, a peak-type profile suggests a convex edge, a roof type a concave, and a step type an occluding edge. Thus the edge profiles might be used to provide constraints on line labels. However, this absolute method, which tries to associate properties of edge profiles with label identities, is not usually very reliable. It strongly depends on the lighting conditions and the physical composition of objects. Further, for this method to work, particular properties of edge profiles, such as roof, peak, etc., need to be recognized.

There is another way of exploiting edge profiles which is employed in this paper; that is the relative method. It is based on the observation that if two lines have 'similar' edge profiles, it suggests that they will likely take the same label, even though the label identity itself is not known. It can be noted that this relative method of using color edge profiles is an instance, applied to their similarities, of the meta-heuristic of non-accidental regularities described in Section 6.

If the lines with similar edge profiles form a certain special geometrical configurations, the likelihood for a similar labeling will be higher. The classical matched T configuration, first described by Guzman [3], is such an example. In Fig. 31 three pairs of lines (L_1 and L_2, L_3 and L_4, and L_5 and L_6) are collinear. Guzman used this configuration as a clue suggesting that the regions R_1 and R_2 belong to the same object, and similarly R_3 and R_4.

What the matched T's mean in the context of this paper is the following. If the edge profiles of L_1 and L_2 are similar, then the labels of L_1 and L_2 are likely to be the same, and the lines L_3 through L_6 will take occluding-edge labels in such a way that the middle region R_0 interrupts an edge which is projected into L_1 and L_2 in the picture. In this section we formalize these kinds of ideas.

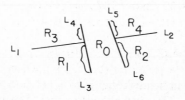

FIG. 31. Guzman's matched T's.

9.2. Extraction of color edge profiles

Color edge profiles for a line consist of three profile curves corresponding to three color components: R (red), G (green), and B (blue). As shown in Fig. 32, for each color component, a set of profiles is first taken across the line; the margin (m), the interval (i), and the length (l) are specifiable parameters. Profile curves in each set are registered and then averaged to obtain the mean profile. In this way for each line L_i we obtain three profile curves $P_i^c(t)$, ($-l \leq t \leq l$) where $c \in \{R, G, B\}$.

Notice that lines (and thus profiles) have to be defined with directionality. That is, a line L_i is to be defined as connecting *from* V_{i1} *to* V_{i2}, rather than connecting V_{i1} *and* V_{i2}. Let us denote this line as $L_i = (V_{i1} \ V_{i2})$. Then $-L_i = (V_{i2} \ V_{i1})$ denotes the same line traced in the opposite direction. If L_i has a profile $P_i^c(t)$, $-L_i$ has a profile $P_{-i}^c(t) = P_i^c(-t)$. In the following discussions the directions of lines and profiles always have to be considered.

Since we can compare three profile curves the relative method is more reliable and useful when exploiting color edge profiles than when using only monochrome intensity profiles.

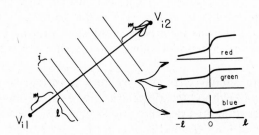

FIG. 32. Extraction of color edge profiles. A set of profile curves are taken across the line for each color component. Each set is registered and averaged.

9.3. Comparison of color edge profiles

For the purpose of comparing the edge profiles let us define the amplitude of $P_i^c(t)$ and the distance between $P_i^c(t)$ and $P_j^c(t)$ as follows.

$$A(i, c) = \max_t P_i^c(t) - \min_t P_i^c(t),$$

$$d(i, j, c) = \min_s \left(\int |P_i^c(t) - P_j^c(t+s)|^2 \, dt \right)^{1/2}. \qquad (8)$$

The amplitude $A(i, c)$ indicates roughly how much the property of the profile changes across the line. The distance $d(i, j, c)$ is the minimum mean square difference between the two curves; the minimum is taken over various shifts of the curves in order to compensate possible dislocations of the origins of the two profiles. It is easy to see the following relations.

$$A(i, c) = A(-i, c), \qquad d(-i, -j, c) = d(i, j, c) \tag{9a}$$

but, in general,

$$d(-i, j, c) \neq d(i, j, c), \qquad d(i, -j, c) \neq d(i, j, c). \tag{9b}$$

Let us now define $s(i, j)$, the similarity of lines, for a pair of lines L_i and L_j. There is not a definite reason to employ the following definition but it can be thought that the larger the amplitude, the more meaningful is the distance between the profile curves. Thus we will define $s(i, j)$ as the sum of the ratios of the amplitude to the distance for each color component: that is, if

$$(A(i, c) + A(j, c))/d(i, j, c) > 1 \quad \text{for all } c,$$

$$s(i, j) = \sum_{c \in \{R, G, B\}} \frac{A(i, c) + A(j, c)}{d(i, j, c)}, \tag{10a}$$

otherwise (i.e., if the ratio is small, the profiles may not be reliable)

$$s(i, j) = 0. \tag{10b}$$

Because of the property of $d(i, j, c)$ and $A(i, c)$, $s(i, j) = s(-i, -j)$ but usually $s(i, j) \neq s(-i, j)$.

9.4. Constraint expressions from edge profile analysis

The similarity in edge profiles, together with certain geometrical configurations of lines, can be converted to the constraint expressions on line labels.

9.4.1. *Similar edge profiles*

For a pair of lines L_i and L_j whose similarity $s(i, j) > 0$ we generate a constraint expression,

$$(\text{SAME } (L_i L_j) \, s(i, j))$$

which means that L_i and L_j may have the same label with a confidence value (weight) $s(i, j)$. All the pairs of L_i's and $-L_i$'s have to be considered for generating this type of constraint.

9.4.2. *Matched T configuration*

Suppose that L_1 through L_6 form a matched T configuration, as shown in Fig. 33: it is a pair of opposing T junctions whose vertical bars are collinear. Define the directions of lines as shown by the big arrows in Fig. 33. Let $s(1, 2)$, $s(4, 5)$, and $s(3, 6)$ be the similarities between the corresponding pairs of lines, respec-

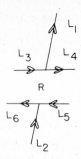

FIG. 33. Matched T configuration and the specification of the line directions.

tively. Then the matched T configuration generates two constraint expressions:

$$(\text{SAME}\,(L_1\,L_2)\,w_\text{T}) \quad \text{and} \quad (\text{IDENT}\,(L_3\,L_4\,L_5\,L_6)\,(\rightarrow\,\rightarrow\,\leftarrow\,\leftarrow)\,w_\text{T})$$

where $w_\text{T} = (s(1, 2) \cdot s(4, 5) \cdot s(3, 6))^{1/3}$.

The first expression constrains L_1 and L_2 to take the same label. The second one means that L_3 through L_6 take such a combination of labels (occluding edges in the proper directions), which corresponds to the case that the middle region R sandwiched by the two transverse bars of T's occludes the collinear vertical bars. Since the first expression about L_1 and L_2 must have been generated from their own similarity, we can regard the matched T configuration as amplifying the constraint. The definition of w_T is rather arbitrary, but the reason for the above definition is just for giving it the same dimension as $s(i, j)$'s.

9.4.3. *Matched π configuration*

A matched π configuration shown in Fig. 34 is another geometrical configuration which can amplify constraints. It is made of two neighboring T junctions which share the same line (L_4) as their right and left transverse bars, and which have parallel vertical bars (L_1 and L_2). Let us define the directions of lines as shown, and let $s(1, -2)$ and $s(3, 5)$ denote the similarities between L_1 and $-L_2$ and between L_3 and L_5, respectively. The matched π configuration corresponds most often to the case where the same physical configuration occurs in the right (L_2 and L_5) and left (L_1 and L_3) halves. Therefore we generate a

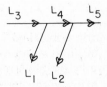

FIG. 34. Matched π configuration and the specification of the line directions.

pair of constraint expressions:

$$(\text{SAME } (L_3 L_5) \, w_\text{P}) \quad \text{and} \quad (\text{SAME } (L_1 - L_2) \, w_\text{P})$$

where $w_\text{P} = (s(1, -2) \cdot s(3, 5))^{1/2}$.

9.5. Search for interpretations which most satisfy the constraints

Now that we have obtained a set of constraints which the line labels should satisfy, we can search for the 'best' interpretations in the sense that the constraints are most satisfied. In evaluating an interpretation, if it does not satisfy a constraint, a penalty (the associated weight) is given to it. Thus, the best interpretation is the one with the least penalty.

In the present implementation, the search is combined with the Origami-world labeling procedure. The interpretation of least penalty is searched for in a depth-first manner, along with the search for consistent assignments of junction labels: each time a junction label is assigned to a junction, not only does the partial interpretation undergo the consistency check of surface orien-tations, but also the penalty score is renewed if any constraint expression is available (i.e., all the lines involved in it have been given labels).

If the partial interpretation turns out to be inconsistent in surface orien-tations, or if the penalty score exceeds the best (smallest) score so far obtained, then the search backtracks and the leaves below the present node in the search tree are pruned.

9.6. Labeling the 'chair' scene

9.6.1. *Color edge profile analysis*

For the 'chair'-scene image of Fig. 5(a), color edge profiles were computed for each line. Analysis of them yielded 85 constraint expressions. The total sum of the weights of all the constraints is 172.26.

9.6.2. *'Positive' and 'negative' chairs*

In labeling Fig. 5(b) with the constraints obtained above, it was found that the labelings shown in Figs. 35 and 36 are the two best interpretations: in each figure, (a) is the labeling and (b) is the SCG. Their penalty score is 13.17 out of 172.26.

Though these labelings still have ambiguities in their exact quantitative shape, it is interesting to think what kind of shapes they represent. Fig. 35(a) corresponds to the shape of an 'ordinary chair': the regions R_{14} and R_{15} (the wainscot in the wall) are occluded by others; the region R_9 (the arm nearer to the viewer) occludes other regions; the regions R_1 through R_8 are connected at the proper convex and concave intersections to form the shape of a seat and a back.

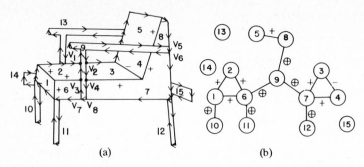

FIG. 35. One of the two 'best' interpretations for the 'chair' scene. We call this a 'positive' chair.

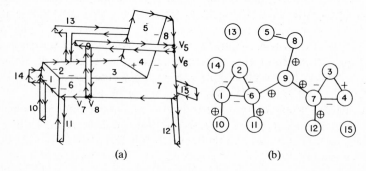

FIG. 36. The other of the two 'best' interpretations for the 'chair' scene. We call this a 'negative' chair.

Comparing the labeling of Fig. 35(a) with Fig. 36(a), we notice that the lines labeled as convex (+) in Fig. 35 are changed to concave (−) in Fig. 36, and concave to convex. The occlusion labels (↑) remain the same. These two labelings correspond to the phenomenon known as reversal in perceptual psychology, such as the Necker cube and the Shroeder stairs. Let us name the shape of Fig. 35 a 'positive' chair, and that of Fig. 36 a 'negative' chair. It might be difficult to imagine the shape of the 'negative' chair. Descriptively, the shape is obtained by first reversing the structure corresponding to the seat and back in the 'positive' chair and then attaching the arms and legs with appropriate relationships to the reversed structure.

9.6.3. Identification of surfaces

Now let us identify surfaces involved in the labeled 'chair' scene. Consider the labeling shown in Fig. 35(a) (the 'positive' chair). Several matched T's exist (e.g., V_1 and V_2, V_3 and V_4, etc.), where the collinear lines showing strong matches in color edge profiles are given identical labels and other lines are given occluding-edge labels of the appropriate directions. That is, these mat-

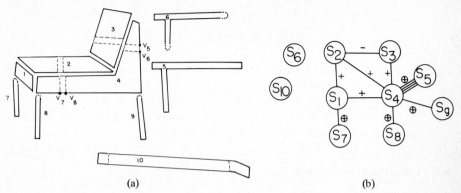

(a)   (b)

FIG. 37. Identification of surfaces in the 'chair' scene corresponding to the labeling of Fig. 35 ('positive' chair): (a) identified surfaces; (b) merged SCG.

ched T configurations have been interpreted as the result of the interruption of a single 3-D space edge by another surface. Therefore, in tracing the boundary lines of surfaces, we can group a few regions into one region. For example, R_2 and R_3 are regarded as corresponding to a single surface. Ten surfaces are identified in this way (see Fig. 37(a)):

$$S_1: \ (R_1), \qquad S_2: \ (R_2\,R_3), \qquad S_3: \ (R_4\,R_5),$$

$$S_4: \ (R_6\,R_7\,R_8), \qquad S_5: \ (R_9), \qquad S_6: \ (R_{13}),$$

$$S_7: \ (R_{10}), \qquad S_8: \ (R_{11}), \qquad S_9: \ (R_{12}),$$

$$S_{10}: \ (R_{14}\,R_{15}).$$

Corresponding to the merges of regions, the nodes in the SCG (Fig. 35(b)) are also merged. Fig. 37(b) shows the revised SCG which represents the interconnection relationships among the ten identified surfaces.

The 'negative' chair (Fig. 36) can be treated in the same way. We identify the same set of surfaces, and Fig. 38 shows the merged SCG. The difference between the 'positive' and the 'negative' chairs is only that the labels on the arcs connecting S_1, S_2, S_3, and S_4 in the SCG's of Figs. 37(b) and 38 are interchanged from + to − and vice versa.

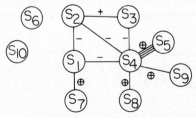

FIG. 38. The merged SCG for the labeling of Fig. 36 ('negative' chair).

10. Optimal Positioning of Gradients with Minimum Errors

In Fig. 37(a) the defined image regularities (parallel lines and skewed symmetries) do not exist in a strict sense. In fact, real-world pictures usually include perspective distortions, camera distortions, and errors due to quantization or feature extraction processes. A standard way to resolve this kind of situation is to define a measure of error and to minimize it.

Let us first restate each constraint on gradients with a definition of the error to be minimized. Then the 'chair' scene will be processed.

10.1. Constraints and errors

10.1.1. *Intersection of surfaces*

Suppose that two regions are connected along a convex or concave line with a direction $a = (\cos \alpha, \sin \alpha)$ in the picture, and that they are given the gradients G_1 and G_2. We will define the error for this case as,

$$e_I = |G_1 \cdot a - G_2 \cdot a|^2 = |(G_1 - G_2) \cdot a|^2 \tag{11}$$

where e_I is the projection of the vector $G_1 - G_2$ onto a gradient-space line perpendicular to the picture line. It should vanish when G_1 and G_2 strictly satisfy the property of dual lines.

10.1.2. *Skewed-symmetry heuristic*

Suppose that a region has a skewed symmetry defined by the two directions $a = (\cos \alpha, \sin \alpha)$ and $b = (\cos \beta, \sin \beta)$, and that it is given a gradient $G = (p, q)$. Since ideally G satisfies (4), we will define the error e_S for this case as,

$$e_S = |(G \cdot a)(G \cdot b) + \cos(\alpha - \beta)|^2 . \tag{12}$$

Since the vertex of the hyperbola represents a special orientation, as described in Section 6, sometimes it is desirable to include the distance from the gradient to the vertex in the error as

$$e_{S'} = e_S + |G - G_T|^2 . \tag{13}$$

G_T is that one of the two vertices of the hyperbola nearer to G. $e_{S'}$ is roughly the discrepancy of G from the hyperbola and its vertex.

10.1.3. *Parallel-line heuristic*

Suppose that two regions R_1 and R_2 have almost parallel boundaries whose directions are $a_1 = (\cos \alpha_1, \sin \alpha_1)$ and $a_2 = (\cos \alpha_2, \sin \alpha_2)$, respectively. Here it is assumed $|\alpha_1 - \alpha_2|$ is small. If R_1 and R_2 are assigned to G_1 and G_2 respectively, then

$$e_P = 1/2(|(G_1 - G_2) \cdot a_1|^2 + |(G_1 - G_2) \cdot a_2|^2) . \tag{14}$$

By referring to (11) we see that e_P is the mean of the errors which would be involved if R_1 and R_2 were demanded to intersect along both a_1 and a_2.

10.2. Minimization of the total error

The total error E is defined as the sum of the individual errors defined above:

$$E = \sum e_I + \sum e_{S'} + \sum e_P. \tag{15}$$

Each sum in (15) is taken over all the instances of the constraints of that kind.[2] It is obvious, though, that only those surfaces which mutually constrain need to be included in the minimization of E. That is, if a constraint includes a surface whose gradient does not appear in the other constraints in E, the constraint can be removed from E because that gradient can be determined independently after all others have been determined.

The minimization of E can be obtained by the steepest descent method. The initial values of the gradients can be selected, so that as many constraints as possible for the basic interconnection relationships (the constraints for e_I, or the constraints in the SCG) are satisfied. For a skewed-symmetrical region one of the vertices of the corresponding hyperbola may be a good initial point.

10.3. Shape recovery of the 'chair' scene

10.3.1. Determination of the gradients

Let us consider the case of Fig. 37 ('positive' chair). The minimization of E involves the four surfaces (S_1, S_2, S_3, and S_4) which mutually constrain. The total error $E = E(p_1, q_1, p_2, q_2, p_3, q_3, p_4, q_4)$ consists of five terms for their surface interconnection (corresponding to the five arcs in the SCG), three terms for the skewed-symmetry heuristic (S_1, S_2, and S_3), and one term for the parallel-line heuristic (S_1 and S_3 have almost parallel boundaries as shown in Fig. 37(a); others were omitted for simplicity).

The initial locations are selected as shown in Fig. 39(a): G_1, G_2 and G_3 are at the vertices of the corresponding hyperbolas, and G_4 is at the intersection of two lines extending from G_1 and G_2 because of the constraints due to the intersections of S_4 with S_1 and S_2. Fig. 39(b) shows the locations of gradients determined by the iterative steepest descent method.

---

[2]If it is better to weigh the errors, we can define the total error as,

$$E_2 = W_I \sum w_i e_{I_i} + W_S \sum w_j e_{S_j} + W_P \sum w_k e_{P_k}$$

with appropriate selection of W's and w's.

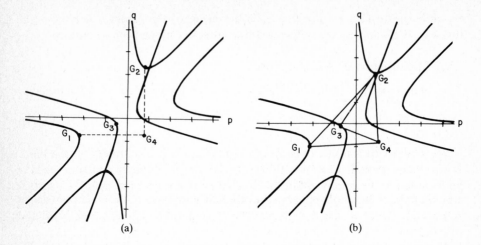

FIG. 39. Positioning of the gradients of S_1 through S_4 for the 'positive' chair by the iterative minimization of errors: (a) initial positions; (b) final positions.

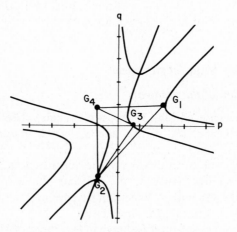

FIG. 40. Gradients of S_1 through S_4 for the 'negative' chair.

If we begin the iterative minimization for the interpretation of Fig. 38 with the corresponding initial locations, it ends up with the assignments shown in Fig. 40. This is exactly the reversal of Fig. 39; i.e., $G_i = (p, q)$ in Fig. 39(b) corresponds to $G_i = (-p, -q)$ in Fig. 40.

10.3.2. *Completion of the shape recovery*

So far we have recovered the shape of the substructure made of the surfaces S_1, S_2, S_3 and S_4 (which happens to be the seat and the back) in the 'chair' scene, for both cases of the 'positive' and the 'negative' chairs. The scene includes more surfaces. We will determine their orientations and relative depths. However, as opposed to the foregoing subsections, the reasoning in this subsection admittedly lack firm theoretical bases. One big reason for this weakness is that at this point we cannot do much without semantics or, more directly, a model of 'chairs'. Discussion concerning the role of object models is found in Section 11. For the time being let us proceed and complete the shape recovery of the 'chair' scene without explicitly mentioning semantics.

Let us refer to Fig. 37. First of all, S_5 (which happens to be one of the arms of the chair) has to be given the same orientation as S_4: the junction labels given to the four T junctions (V_5, V_6, V_7, and V_8: see Fig. 35), where S_4 is connected with S_5, together result in this requirement. Then we can see that the 'negative' chair (Fig. 36 or Fig. 38) is not realizable by planes, because if S_4 and S_5 are in the same orientation, S_5 cannot cross and occlude S_2 or S_3, each of which connects with S_4 along a concave edge. However, if we relax this requirement by 'loosening' the connection of S_4 and S_5 at the four T junctions (we can make S_4, say, be connected with S_5 at two points V_6 and V_8 so that it can come in front of S_2 and S_3), then we shall have the 3-D shape of a 'negative' chair. Appendix C shows pictures of a model of a 'negative' chair.

Let us proceed with the 'positive' chair. S_7, S_8, and S_9 (which happen to be the legs of the chair) have individually a single constraint with the substructure (S_1, S_2, S_3, and S_4) whose shape has been determined. S_7, for instance, is connected to S_1 at its left lower corner but it is not enough of a constraint to uniquely determine the orientation of S_7. Tentatively (without a definite reason), S_7 is given the same gradient as S_1. Similarly we give S_8 and S_9 the same gradient as S_4 with which they are connected.

The surfaces whose gradients have been determined so far (S_1 through S_5, and S_7 through S_9) are all connected. Therefore, if we assume the z of any one point on the structure, we can determine their plane formulas.

What can we do about the remaining two surfaces, S_6 and S_{10}, which are separate nodes in the SCG? The visible part of S_6 (which happens to be the other arm) strongly matches S_5 with respect to both color and shape, plus several pairs of parallel boundaries. This may provide a good reason to give S_6 the same gradient as S_5. How about its relative depth (position)? Since S_5 is touching S_2 and S_3 on this side, and the visible part of S_6 is the same in the image as a part of S_5, we may conclude that S_6 is also touching S_2 and S_3 on their other side.

Finally, as for S_{10} (which happens to be a wainscot), we have no clue except that it is behind the object. Thus all we can do is to assign the gradient $(0, 0)$ (the orientation perpendicular to the present view direction) as a default, and assign a big enough depth so that it is behind the structure made of S_1 through S_9.

In this way we have determined the plane formulas of all the surfaces. The

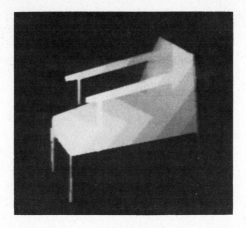

FIG. 41. A rotated view of the 'positive' chair interpretation; 10° to the left and 10° above the original.

resultant 3-D shape description can be supplied to a display program which generates other views of the object. Fig. 41 shows a rotated view of the 'positive' chair interpretation of the 'chair' scene.

11. Concluding Remarks

11.1. Summary of the results

We have demonstrated how the 3-D descriptions for simple scenes can be achieved systematically from a single view by exploiting a few assumptions. The assumptions we have used are:

(A1) Objects are planar-surfaced ones with restricted configurations at vertices.

(A2) The meta-heuristic concerns nonaccidental regularities in the picture; in particular,

(A2.1) similarity of color edge profiles,

(A2.2) parallelism of lines, and

(A2.3) skewed symmetry.

We have developed the theories and techniques for exploiting these assumptions. The theory of the Origami world for (A1) provides a labeling procedure which can recover qualitative shapes of line drawings together with constraints on surface orientations. The analysis of color edge profiles for (A2.1) provides constraints on line label combinations with weights, and thus can order the interpretations which are all geometrically possible. The parallel-line heuristic for (A2.2) and the skewed-symmetry heuristic for (A2.3) map the picture properties into constraints in the gradient space. By putting these all together we can uniquely determine the surface orientations and obtain the 3-D quantitative shape descriptions of the object.

Notice that the up-to-3-surface assumption of the Origami world for (A1) is independent of the image-regularity assumption (A2). We could have selected the trihedral assumption for (A1). The Origami world, which is less restricted than the trihedral world, allowed to interpret those realistic line drawings such as the 'box' scene. In addition, because of its diversity, it helped in emphasizing the importance of other kinds of assumptions of (A2). One additional comment on the skewed-symmetry heuristic: it does not assume symmetrical objects but assumes local symmetry of the surfaces whose projection (picture) is skewed-symmetrical.

We have used only similarity of edge profiles, parallelism of lines, and skewed symmetry in this paper. There are other instances of image regularities which are usable in the same way by formalizing them under the meta-heuristic of non-accidental regularities. For example, equal-length lines, nearly right angles, etc. This topic will be discussed in [10], and further developed by Kender [11].

The essential issue pursued in this paper is how the properties in the picture (picture-domain cues) can be related to the properties in the scene (scene-domain cues). The importance of this distinction is emphasized by Kanade [8]. In our discussion, the scene-domain cues are the physical meaning of lines signified by the labels and the surface orientations represented by the gradients. The picture-domain cues are the junction types, the direction of lines, the shapes of regions, and the paralellisms of lines in the picture.

How the two different levels of cues interact mutually for the shape recovery is noteworthy. From the junction types and directions of individual lines, we have obtained the labelings, which can tell the shapes of which regions and the parallelisms of which lines are usable. This in turn can be converted into constraints on the gradients.

11.2. 'Natural' interpretations and the roles of object models

When presented the multiple interpretations which the theory of the Origami world yields, one of the common impressions we tend to have is that most of them are 'unnatural'. For example, the labeling of Fig. 13(b) which corresponds to a 'squashed' box may look 'unnatural' for a human observer. However, any labeling is geometrically no more 'natural' or 'unnatural' than others: they are equally possible. The feeling of 'naturalness' is due to our other presumptions.

This paper has shown that the exploitation of the heuristics which prefer the conservation of regularities allows us to select the 'natural' interpretations for our simple example scenes. The core of our method is still purely geometrical. We have tried to keep from using specific object models in order to emphasize the geometric aspects in the shape recovery.

Of course, though, I do not intend to claim that object models are un-necessary. As we have seen in the shape recovery of the 'chair' scene, the 'arms' and 'legs' can be attached to the main structure ('back' and 'seat') at any angle. We might be able to do a little more by pursuing some higher-level regularities, say the 3-D symmetries in this case, but eventually the deter-mination of their particular shape should rely on our understanding of the functional shape that 'chairs' usually take. However, who can know that the object is a 'chair' before knowing that it could be of a 'chair' shape?

'Chairs' would have no particular predefined shapes but usually are defined by the descriptions of their functional shapes: say, an L-shaped main structure made of a 'seat' and a 'back', both usually flat; often four legs attached to the lower corners of the seat; optional two 'arms' attached symmetrically to the main structure, etc. Like this, the generic models of objects are described in terms of general 3-D shapes and relations (i.e., scene-domain cues). Therefore, in order to access appropriate models for the top–down use of semantic information, we have to first reach certain shape descriptions, either qualitative or quantitative, from the picture in a data-driven manner. Once the ap-propriate model is found, the general hypothesis-and-test mechanism begins to work. The theory and the technique in this paper have demonstrated the crucial point in interfacing between the model-driven part and the data-driven part of image understanding.

ACKNOWLEDGMENT

I thank John Kender, Allen Newell, Raj Reddy, and Steven Shafer for many stimulating discussions. John Zsarnay provided excellent programming support for the color edge profile analysis and the display program for generating rotated views of objects.

Appendix A

Let us take two gradient-space lines passing through the origin in the directions of α and β, as shown in Fig. A.1(a). We will prove that the gradients (such as G_e or $G_{e'}$) which are on the bisectors of the two lines correspond to the orientation of the planar surfaces for which the length metrics along the directions of α and β in the picture are equal; i.e., the ratio of lengths along them in the picture represents the real ratio.

In general, for a surface with gradient $G = (p, q)$, the change in depth (z) corresponding to the transposition $\Delta v = (\Delta x, \Delta y)$ in the picture is

$$\Delta z = -p\Delta x - q\Delta y = -G \cdot \Delta v. \tag{A.1}$$

We can generally express the gradients on one of the bisectors l_1 as

$$G_e = (\sigma \cos((\alpha + \beta)/2), \sigma \sin((\alpha + \beta)/2)). \tag{A.2}$$

Similarly the gradients on the other bisector l_2 are

$$G_{e'} = (-\sigma \sin((\alpha + \beta)/2), \sigma \cos((\alpha + \beta)/2)). \tag{A.3}$$

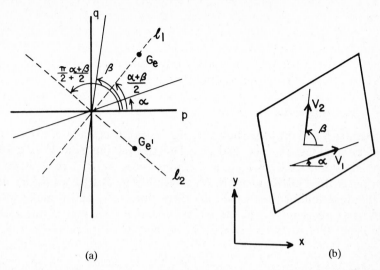

(a)   (b)

FIG. A.1. (a) Two gradient-space lines passing through the origin in the direction of α and β. G_e and $G_{e'}$ are the gradients lying on their bisectors. (b) The projection of a surface and two picture lines in the direction of α and β.

Now suppose that surface with a gradient G_e or $G_{e'}$ is projected onto a picture plane, and consider two picture lines in the direction of α and β as in Fig. A.1(b). What we have to show is that the same length along these two picture lines depict the same length on the surface in the 3-D space, or, equivalently, that the rate of change in depth (z) to S is equal along these two lines.

We can represent unit-length vectors along these picture lines as follows, respectively:

$$v_1 = (\cos \alpha, \sin \alpha) \quad \text{and} \quad v_2 = (\cos \beta, \sin \beta). \tag{A.4}$$

The changes in z corresponding to v_1 and v_2 are, if S has the gradient G_e,

$$\Delta z_1 = -G_e \cdot v_1 = -\sigma \cos((\alpha + \beta)/2) \cos \alpha - \sigma \sin((\alpha + \beta)/2) \sin \alpha$$

$$= -\sigma \cos((\alpha - \beta)/2), \tag{A.5}$$

$$\Delta z_2 = -G_e \cdot v_2 = -\sigma \cos((\alpha + \beta)/2) \cos \beta - \sigma \sin((\alpha + \beta)/2) \sin \beta$$

$$= -\sigma \cos((\alpha - \beta)/2). \tag{A.6}$$

and if S has the gradient $G_{e'}$

$$\Delta z_1 = -G_{e'} \cdot v_1 = -\sigma \sin((\alpha - \beta)/2),$$

and   (A.7)

$$\Delta z_2 = -G_{e'} \cdot v_2 = \sigma \sin((\alpha - \beta)/2).$$

In both cases

$$|\Delta z_1| = |\Delta z_2| .$$

(A.8)

That is, the changes in z corresponding to the transposition of a unit length in the direction of α and β in the picture are equal.

Appendix B

Let us consider a line drawing shown in Fig. B.1(a). It is made of three parallel quadrilateral regions, R_1, R_2, and R_3. The central junction V is a FORK junction, and the three lines l_1, l_2, and l_3 join there. β_1, β_2, and β_3 denote the three angles at the FORK junction. As shown in Fig. B.1(b), let α_1, α_2, and α_3 denote the directional angles which the three lines l_1, l_2, and l_3 make with the positive x-axis, respectively, in the picture. Assume that Fig. B.1(a) depicts a parallelepiped; that is, three surfaces S_1, S_2, and S_3 (corresponding to R_1, R_2, and R_3 respectively) form convex edges at l_1, l_2, and l_3. Suppose that $G_1 = (p_1, q_1)$, $G_2 = (p_2, q_2)$, and $G_3 = (p_3, q_3)$ are the gradients of S_1, S_2, and S_3, respectively.

Since S_1 and S_2 intersect along l_2,

$$p_1 \cos \alpha_2 + q_1 \sin \alpha_2 = p_2 \cos \alpha_2 + q_2 \sin \alpha_2 ,$$

or, in brief,

$$G_1 \cdot a_2 = G_2 \cdot a_2$$

(B.1)

where $a_2 = (\cos \alpha_2, \sin \alpha_2)$. Similarly, we have

$$G_2 \cdot a_3 = G_3 \cdot a_3$$

(B.2)

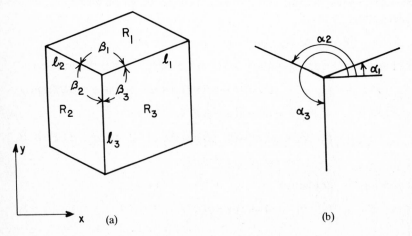

(a)   (b)

FIG. B.1. (a) A line drawing of a parallelepiped. (b) The directional angles α_1, α_2, and α_3 of the three lines joining at the FORK junction.

$$G_3 \cdot a_1 = G_1 \cdot a_1 , \tag{B.3}$$

where $a_3 = (\cos \alpha_3, \sin \alpha_3)$ and $a_1 = (\cos \alpha_1, \sin \alpha_1)$. The region R_1 has a skewed symmetry whose axes are in the directions α_1 and α_2. Therefore, if we assume a real symmetry for S_1,

$$(G_1 \cdot a_1)(G_1 \cdot a_2) + \cos(\alpha_1 - \alpha_2) = 0$$

or, since $\cos(\alpha_1 - \alpha_2) = \cos \beta_1$,

$$(G_1 \cdot a_1)(G_1 \cdot a_2) + \cos \beta_1 = 0 . \tag{B.4}$$

Similarly, for R_2 and R_3,

$$(G_2 \cdot a_2)(G_2 \cdot a_3) + \cos \beta_2 = 0 , \tag{B.5}$$

$$(G_3 \cdot a_3)(G_3 \cdot a_1) + \cos \beta_3 = 0 . \tag{B.6}$$

The equations (B.1) through (B.6) represent the constraints we have on G_1, G_2 and G_3, when trying to determine them by the method shown in Fig. 18.

First, let us see that none of β_i's can be $\pi/2$. For example, suppose $\beta_1 = \pi/2$. Then $\cos \beta_1 = 0$. From (B.4), either $G_1 \cdot a_1$ or $G_1 \cdot a_2$ is zero. Suppose $G_1 \cdot a_1 = 0$. Then from (B.3) and (B.6) we have $\cos \beta_3 = 0$; i.e., $\beta_3 = \pi/2$. Now $\beta_1 = \beta_3 = \pi/2$ is contradictory to the assumption that the junction V is a FORK junction. In this way we know that $\beta_i \neq \pi/2$, or $\cos \beta_i \neq 0$ for $i = 1, 2, 3$.

From (B.1) through (B.6) we can derive

$$(G_1 \cdot a_1)^2 = -\cos \beta_1 \cos \beta_3 / \cos \beta_2 > 0 . \tag{B.7}$$

Since $\pi > \beta_i > 0$ and $\beta_1 + \beta_2 + \beta_3 = 2\pi$, we see that $\pi > \beta_i > \pi/2$ (obtuse angle) for $i = 1, 2, 3$ is necessary for the right side of (B.7) to be positive.

Now assume β_i's are all obtuse. Since $\cos \beta_i < 0$, let us put

$$\cos \beta_i = -c_i , \quad c_i > 0 \quad \text{for } i = 1, 2, 3 .$$

Then (B.7) becomes

$$G_1 \cdot a_1 = \pm (c_1 c_3 / c_2)^{1/2} . \tag{B.8}$$

Substitution of (B.8) into (B.4) gives

$$G_1 \cdot a_2 = -\cos \beta_1 / (G_1 \cdot a_1) = \pm (c_1 c_2 / c_3)^{1/2} . \tag{B.9}$$

We can solve (B.8) and (B.9) for p_1 and q_1.

$$\binom{p_1}{q_1} = \pm \frac{(c_1/c_2 c_3)^{1/2}}{\sin(\alpha_2 - \alpha_1)} \binom{c_3 \sin \alpha_2 - c_2 \sin \alpha_1}{-c_3 \cos \alpha_2 + c_2 \cos \alpha_1} . \tag{B.10}$$

Similarly we obtain the following. (The multiple signs are to be read correspondingly in (B.10), (B.11), and (B.12).)

$$\binom{p_2}{q_2} = \pm \frac{(c_2/c_1 c_3)^{1/2}}{\sin(\alpha_3 - \alpha_2)} \binom{c_1 \sin \alpha_3 - c_3 \sin \alpha_2}{-c_1 \cos \alpha_3 + c_3 \cos \alpha_2} , \tag{B.11}$$

$$\binom{p_3}{q_3} = \pm \frac{(c_3/c_1 c_2)^{1/2}}{\sin(\alpha_1 - \alpha_3)} \binom{c_2 \sin \alpha_1 - c_1 \sin \alpha_3}{-c_2 \cos \alpha_1 + c_1 \cos \alpha_3}. \tag{B.12}$$

Thus there are two combinations of G_i's which satisfy (B.1) through (B.6). Apparently they are symmetrical through the gradient-space origin, and correspond to the two labelings of Fig. B.1(a): the convex-corner (three lines at the FORK junction are all convex lines) and the concave-corner (they are all concave). Therefore we have shown that for the convex-corner interpretation we always obtain the unique assignment of G_i's which satisfies the skewed-symmetry heuristic if and only if β_i's are all obtuse.

Next we will prove that the parallelepiped is right-angled in the above assignment of gradients. Let us consider S_1 and S_2, for instance. From (B.10) and (B.11), we can compute

$$
\begin{aligned}
p_1 p_2 + q_1 q_2 &= [(c_3 \sin \alpha_2 - c_2 \sin \alpha_1)(c_1 \sin \alpha_3 - c_3 \sin \alpha_2) \\
&\quad + (-c_3 \cos \alpha_2 + c_2 \cos \alpha_1)(-c_1 \cos \alpha_3 + c_3 \cos \alpha_2)] \\
&\quad \times [c_3 \sin(\alpha_2 - \alpha_1) \sin(\alpha_3 - \alpha_2)]^{-1} \\
&= [c_1 c_3 \cos(\alpha_3 - \alpha_2) - c_1 c_2 \cos(\alpha_1 - \alpha_3) - c_3^2 \\
&\quad + c_2 c_3 \cos(\alpha_2 - \alpha_1)]/[c_3 \sin(\alpha_2 - \alpha_1) \sin(\alpha_3 - \alpha_2)] \\
&= -(c_3 + c_1 c_2)/\sin(\alpha_2 - \alpha_1) \sin(\alpha_3 - \alpha_2) \\
&= -[-\cos(\alpha_3 - \alpha_1) + \cos(\alpha_2 - \alpha_1) \cos(\alpha_3 - \alpha_2)] \\
&\quad \times [\sin(\alpha_2 - \alpha_1) \sin(\alpha_3 - \alpha_2)]^{-1} \\
&= -1.
\end{aligned}
$$

That is, $p_1 p_2 + q_1 q_2 + 1 = 0$. Since $(p_i, q_i, 1)$ is the surface normal, we have proven that S_1 and S_2 intersect perpendicularly. We can prove the same for the other pairs of surfaces.

Appendix C. Pictures of a 'negative' chair

A wooden model of a 'negative' chair (only the main structure including the seat, back and arms) was actually made. The picture (1) is taken from the angle such that the object looks like a positive (real) chair. The sequence of pictures above, below and right show how it appears as we move our eye position upward, downward and to the right, correspondingly.

An interesting phenomenon happens when we hung the negative chair in the air by string and swing it a little as our eye position is fixed where we see the picture (1) first. Then what we perceive is that a real (positive) chair is flexing its arms back and forth, rather than a rigid object of funny shape is swinging. The moving parallax does not help much in perceiving the real shape. This is probably because once we fix the shape description as a real chair, we try to interpret the sequence of pictures consistently and one way for that is to regard it flexing.

FIG. C.1. Pictures of a 'negative' chair.

REFERENCES

1. Clowes, M.B., On seeing things, *Artificial Intelligence* **2**(1) (1971) 79–116.
2. Falk, G., Interpretation of imperfect line data as a three-dimensional scene, *Artificial Intelligence* **3** (1972) 101–144.
3. Guzman, A., Computer recognition of three dimensional objects in a visual scene, Tech. Rept. MAC-TR-59, MIT, Cambridge, MA (1968).
4. Herskovits, L. and Binford, T.O., On boundary detection, MAC. AI Memo 183, MIT, Cambridge, MA (1970).
5. Horn, B.K.P., Understanding image intensity, *Artificial Intelligence* **8**(2) (1977) 201–231.
6. Huffman, D.A., Impossible objects as nonsense sentences, in: Meltzer, B. and Michie, D., Eds., *Machine Intelligence* **6** (Edinburgh University Press, Edinburgh, 1971).
7. Huffman, D.A., Realizable configuration of lines in pictures of polyhedra, in: Elcock, E.W. and Michie, D., Eds., *Machine Intelligence* **8** (Edinburgh University Press, Edinburgh, 1977).
8. Kanade, T., A theory of Origami world, *Artificial Intelligence* **13**(1) (1980) 279–311.
9. Kanade, T., Region segmentation: Signal vs. semantics, *Comput. Graphics Image Process* **13** (1980) 279–297.
10. Kanade, T. and Kender, J., Skewed symmetry: Mapping image regularities into shape, Tech. Rept. CMU-CS-80-133, Department of Computer Science, Carnegie–Mellon University (1980).
11. Kender, J., Ph.D. Thesis, Carnegie–Mellon University, Pittsburgh (1980).
12. Mackworth, A.K., Interpreting pictures of polyhedral scenes, *Artificial Intelligence* **4**(2) (1974) 121–137.
13. Mackworth, A.K., Model-driven interpretation in intelligent vision systems, *Perception* **5** (1976) 349–370.
14. Mackworth, A.K., How to see a simple world: An exegesis of some computer programs for scene analysis, in: Elcock, E.W. and Michie, D., Eds., *Machine Intelligence* **8** (Edinburgh University Press, Edinburgh, 1977).
15. Roberts, L.G., Machine perception of three-dimensional solids, in: Tippett et al., Eds., *Optical and Electro-Optical Information Processing* (MIT Press, Cambridge, 1965).
16. Stevens, K.A., Surface perception from local analysis of texture, Ph.D. Thesis, Tech. Rept. TR 512, MIT, Cambridge, MA (1979).
17. Sugihara, K., Quantitative analysis of line drawings of polyhedral scenes, *Proc. Fourth International Joint Conference on Pattern Recognition*, Kyoto (1978) 771–773.
18. Waltz, D., Generating semantic descriptions from drawings of scenes with shadows, MAC-TR-271, MIT., Cambridge, MA (1972), also reproduced in: Winston, P., Ed., *The Psychology of Computer Vision* (McGraw–Hill, New York, 1975).
19. Woodham, R.J., A cooperative algorithm for determining surface orientations from a single view, *Proc. Fifth International Joint Conference on Artificial Intelligence*, Cambridge, MA (1977) 635–641.

Revised version received May 1980

The Use of Gradient and Dual Space in Line-Drawing Interpretation

Stephen W. Draper

Center for Human Information Processing,
University of California, San Diego, La Jolla, CA, U.S.A.

ABSTRACT

This paper reviews the application of gradient space and dual space in programs that interpret line-drawings and examines whether they can provide a basis for a fully adequate program. Mackworth's program Poly is analyzed at length. Counterexamples show first that the procedure must be generalized from gradient to dual space, and then that constraints in the form of inequalities as well as equations must be handled which necessitates a radical re-design. A proof that Poly itself is valid under perspective as well as orthographic projection although its derivation in terms of gradient space is not, further indicates that gradient (or dual) space is not the important element in Mackworth's approach. Other ways of using dual space by Kanade and Huffman are discussed but they do not convincingly rebut the conclusion that dual space is peripheral to the design of a competent program. Finally the conclusion that the plane equation approach derived from the developments described, while theoretically adequate, is awkward to use because it fails to offer intuitive clarity, is supported by contrasting it with the alternative method of sidedness reasoning.

1. Introduction

1.1. General introduction

In 1973 Mackworth published a paper [1] in which he defined a new mathematical concept—gradient space—developed from the concept of dual space, and described a program Poly[1] which used gradient space to generate interpretations of line-drawings in terms of Huffman–Clowes line-labels. Poly was a substantial improvement over previous designs—and the Huffman–Clowes scheme[2] in particular [2, 3]—but was also important because of the subsequent

---

[1] I shall follow normal English usage for proper names—a single initial capital letter—in referring to programs, rather than the inflated usage now common.

[2] 'Scheme' refers to a relatively high level of description of a program design—see Section 1.2.

Artificial Intelligence **17** (1981) 461–508

interest in using gradient space in other contexts—see for example [4]. This paper will follow Mackworth in discussing gradient and dual space only in connection with the line-labelling task, although of course the ideas discussed may bear on other applications.

Since Mackworth's work, other ways of applying gradient and dual space to the line-drawing interpretation task have been proposed and these will also be discussed. However, as we shall see, no fully adequate design has yet been described. This paper discusses the failings of various program designs with a view to generating improvements and then goes on to question the ultimate suitability of gradient and dual space as a basis for the design of a fully successful program. Before commencing the discussion the interpretation task will be introduced in order to bring out the criterion of success implicit in it. Gradient space itself will be introduced in Section 2.2 as a preface to the critique of Poly.

In this paper we are solely concerned with the task defined by the line-labelling tradition of line-drawing interpretation as opposed to the model-based tradition initiated by Roberts [5] (see also [6, 7]). (This is not only because those programs are not based on dual space, which is the focus of the present discussion, but because they do not appear to offer an adequate basis for a successful attempt even at the simplified problem considered here: e.g. see [8] for a critique of Roberts' program.) The task we shall consider here is the interpretation of perfect line-drawings, formed by a process of perspective or orthographic projection, of scenes containing opaque, plane-faced polyhedra. This tradition had its origins in Guzman's program called See [9, 10], which drew attention to junction shapes as powerful cues. The Huffman–Clowes scheme [2, 3] superceded Guzman's program by providing a far more systematic and reliable method of exploiting junction shapes, and also an explanation of See's successes and failures (see [8][3] where this is discussed explicitly). It had several features which serve to define the problem in the form with which we are here concerned.

The line-labelling scheme is derived from a consideration of how polyhedral vertices can appear in a line-drawing, and hence what vertices a given appearance (i.e. a junction) could be depicting. One crucial feature of this is that it makes no appeal to what people actually see, but instead implies as a standard the consideration of what they could logically see. It is this independent specification which makes it possible to study the problem as a Machine Intelligence task—that of what a line-drawing could represent—instead of as a simulation of human behaviour. Given this task specification it is possible to aim at designing a program which fulfils it perfectly. It is with programs of this sort—and with Poly in particular—that we are concerned with here.

³ See also [13, Ch. 2].

The derivation of possible appearances depends entirely on geometry—the geometry of the objects involved (opaque polyhedra with trihedral vertices in the original formulation), and the geometry of the picture-forming process. The task formulation is such that only this knowledge is relevant; the remaining question for a given scheme is whether it displays an adequate grasp of the relevant geometry. A scheme is judged inadequate (i.e. incompetent) if the interpretations it produces are either internally inconsistent, or inconsistent with the picture given some set of assumptions about the objects that can be depicted and the picture-forming process. It would also be inadequate if it excluded interpretations that were consistent with those assumptions. The main basis of the criticisms considered in this paper is geometric adequacy in this sense. Other grounds for criticisms concern the desirability of widening the scope of the task by making the assumptions less restrictive (e.g. allowing non-trihedral vertices—see below). This might be argued either on psychological grounds or by showing how geometric knowledge necessary to dealing correctly with the narrower task will also support a more generalized one—an argument based on natural divisions of geometric knowledge.

The Huffman–Clowes scheme in effect defined a task and offered a scheme for performing it. Huffman himself demonstrated the scheme's geometric inadequacy by means of examples to which it would assign interpretations inconsistent with the picture and the assumptions [2]; and furthermore it depended on two assumptions—the trihedral and non-accidental assumptions (defined below)—which seemed undesirably restrictive. These failings constituted a goal for further work.

Huffman proposed some auxiliary rules as a way of overcoming the scheme's geometric inadequacy [2]—these were to be applied to the interpretations generated by the scheme in order to filter out the geometrically inconsistent ones. However they by no means achieved complete competence (see [11, Ch. 2]). Waltz' program [12] primarily addressed the problem of expressing shadow information in line-labels and did not contribute to the goal of geometric adequacy: his program fails on all the counter-examples to the Huffman–Clowes scheme given by Huffman. Furthermore although he allowed some non-trihedral vertices and accidental junctions, his program had no way of dealing with them in general. (See [13, p. 125ff], [4], and [14] for connections between the later gradient space approach and the interpretation of shadows.)

Mackworth's program Poly set out to achieve geometric adequacy and to drop the trihedral and non-accidental assumptions, and it achieved a substantial degree of success. Section 2 is an extended critique of Poly which examines the extent to which this attempt succeeded, but is also designed to explore not just the particular abilities of Poly but the ultimate potential of the ideas Mackworth embodied in it. Before embarking on this some useful distinctions will be introduced.

1.2. Some terminology

The derivation of the line-labelling scheme drew attention to the distinction between picture and scene. It will be kept in mind by a corresponding distinction between terms for picture and scene elements. A picture (2-D) consists of line-segments which meet to form junctions (of which they constitute the rays), and which also form the regions into which the picture plane is divided. The scene (3-D) consists of edges which meet each other at vertices and which separate surfaces; each surface may be thought of as a finite portion of some infinite plane.

Following Mackworth a line with either a convex or concave label may be referred to as a connect edge and a line with either sense of occlusion label as a non-connect edge. An equivalent definition is that at a connect edge the surfaces corresponding to the regions on either side of it in the picture are interpreted as meeting each other at that edge in the scene. This brings out the fact that the line-label notation depends on picture properties (e.g. adjacency of regions) to express scene properties, and also that line-labels express viewpoint-dependent properties (whether a surface is wholly or partly visible as opposed to self-occluded) as well as viewpoint-independent ones (e.g. the angle at which surfaces meet).

As has already been alluded to, the line-labelling scheme applied two restrictive assumptions to the scenes it considered: the trihedral and the non-accidental. The former states that all the vertices are formed by exactly three surfaces meeting at a point. This is the simplest and most common type of vertex but it' is possible for four or more surfaces to meet at a point—thus forming what may be called a 'multihedral' vertex—or if laminae are allowed then two-surface vertices are possible (e.g. at the ends of the crease where a mail envelope and its flap join). The second restriction excludes junctions whose appearance would change if the viewpoint moved slightly—they are referred to as 'accidentals'. The restriction is equivalent to an assumption of 'general viewpoint' i.e. that the camera is in 'general position'—see [2]. Clearly what counts as a change in appearance depends on the system of description being used—in this case it is Guzman's junction categories.

A useful concept introduced by Huffman is that of a cyclic set. Fig. 1 is intended to depict an aerial view of a pyramid: its four sides form a cyclic set. In general a cyclic set consists of N faces meeting across N edges in a cycle so

FIG. 1. A pyramid seen from above: the prototypical cyclic set.

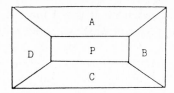

FIG. 2. A cyclic set with a plateau.

that each face shares an edge with two neighbours. Fig. 1 shows a concurrent cyclic set, but it is not necessary for the edges to meet at a point: thus the sides of a truncated pyramid form a cyclic set, e.g. faces *ABCD* in Fig. 2, which may be interpreted as a plinth with four sides sloping down from a top surface. Such a top surface (*P* in Fig. 2) will be referred to as a 'plateau'. As Huffman pointed out [2], there are often constraints associated with cyclic sets: for instance the edges in a cyclic set of three must always be concurrent (if extended) unlike the general case.

Program designs may be described at various levels of detail. The top, most general, level is simply the specification of its task, such as the definition of the line-label interpretation task in terms of the criterion of geometric adequacy given above. At the next is the level I have called a 'scheme'—the chief example here is Huffman's description of the line-labelling scheme (for which he gave no algorithm or program) in terms of allowed junction labellings and checking the consistency of labels on each line. The third level is that of 'algorithm'—for instance Clowes described an algorithm for the line-labelling scheme [3] and the Waltz filter is the main component of Waltz' alternative algorithm for essentially the same scheme (although he used a much larger set of allowed junction labellings) [12]. Finally there is the level of the actual program code, if any, which is rather seldom encountered in the literature since the interesting ideas are generally embodied in a higher level of description. As we shall see, fully designed programs may be discussed and criticised at any of these levels, and it can be important to distinguish the level to which a criticism relates.

2. Poly, Dual Space, and the Plane Equation Approach

2.1. Introduction

This section contains an extended critique of Mackworth's program Poly. Poly has been reported in two papers [1, 13]; the former, published in *Artificial Intelligence*, is a condensed version of the latter. This was his D. Phil. thesis and it contained a number of ideas relating to Poly not published elsewhere, some of which will be introduced and discussed below.

Poly aims to interpret correctly a wider class of pictures than line-labelling does (i.e. have a wider competence). It is not intended as a model of human perception. It is a working program which operates within practical limitations on computational resources, but it was not designed with efficiency as an important aim. It is best regarded as an exploration of the usefulness of the gradient space representation and its underlying theory for the task of inter-pretation. It should be remembered that good representations of a problem are crucial not only for programs which tackle the problem, but also to general human understanding of it: Poly is worth studying partly because it leads to insights about the nature of the problem of interpreting line-drawings and partly because the gradient space representation on which it is based may give a wider usefulness. This critique was written with these points in mind.

Criticisms of Poly will be mostly in the form of counterexamples to its claims of geometrically correct reasoning. As will become plain when Poly is des-cribed, Poly's basic plan is to generate all interpretations and then rule out the impossible ones. Because of this, the crucial question is usually whether Poly can exclude some particular interpretation and the examples will sometimes be posed as if Poly were a program for detecting impossibilities in given inter-pretations: strictly speaking they are tests of whether Poly will produce a wrong interpretation along with the others. Similarly, Poly produces many inter-pretations of each picture, even though usually only one or two are discussed for each example: generally ones closely related to those that we would give the picture.

The criticisms of Poly which follow are divided into two sets. In the first (Section 2.3), criticisms are made which have fairly straightforward solutions: these are combined into a design for a more competent program called Superpoly which retains many of Poly's design features but which is far more geometrically competent. Having strengthened the case for using Mackworth's ideas as much as possible by improvements in their application, we turn in the second part (Section 2.4) to examples still problematic for Superpoly, the question of whether it could be extended to deal with them, and so to the question of the ultimate validity of Mackworth's ideas. A sketch for a program design capable of meeting these criticisms is given and it is seen that only the most general of the ideas embodied in Poly is finally tenable. The implications of this are examined in the concluding Sections 2.5 and 2.6. The critique is prefaced by a description of gradient space and of Poly.

2.2. A description of Poly

The central concept in Poly is that of gradient space. Mackworth derived the idea originally from some remarks by Huffman [2] on the properties of dual space. I shall not discuss dual space in this section and I shall often state properties of gradient space without giving their derivation. Readers will find a fuller geometric introduction in [1] and an alternative one in [15]. Further information on these matters can be found in [2, 4, 13, 16]. In addition

Appendix A discusses briefly the concept of duality and presents an algebraic derivation of dual and gradient space to complement the more geometric emphasis given by Huffman and Mackworth.

We are concerned with pictures formed by the orthographic projection of a scene on to the (X, Y) plane, such that the viewpoint is on the Z-axis. Thus the picture gives us direct information about the (X, Y) coordinate of the scene, but all direct information about the Z-coordinates (or depth) of points in the scene is lost.

The gradient space is a two-dimensional space in which every point represents the slope of some family of parallel planes. Every plane has an infinite set of lines perpendicular to it—its set of normals—but these are all parallel to each other; in fact all the normals to all the members of a set of parallel planes are mutually parallel. Such a set of parallel planes may therefore be characterised by a single line—some standard normal. Gradient space may be constructed on a plane G parallel to the (X, Y) plane, using a special point one unit in front of it along the Z-axis. The standard normal to a plane is defined as that unique normal to the plane which passes through the standard point. This in turn uniquely specifies the corresponding point in gradient space, defined as the point where the standard normal intersects G: see Fig. 3. Planes parallel to G have the Z-axis as their standard normal and correspond to the point on G at $X = Y = 0$. This is the origin of gradient space. As the plane tilts with respect to G, its gradient point moves away from the origin, going off to infinity as the plane becomes perpendicular to G: planes edge-on to the viewpoint (and thus to G) have normals parallel to G and their gradient points are at infinity. Clearly a point can go off to infinity in any direction—this corresponds to the different slopes possible for a plane perpendicular to G. If tilted a little further, the gradient point—now defined by the other half of the infinite normal—approaches the origin again from the opposite direction. The gradient space has rectangular axes G_x, G_y, which are conceived of as parallel to the X, Y axes of the picture plane. They are used to quantify gradients. In fact the distance of a gradient space point from the origin represents the tangent of the angle the corresponding plane makes with the picture plane. The above development of gradient space—a primarily geometric one—is closely related to the Gaussian sphere method of describing surface slopes—see [17] for a presentation of the Gaussian sphere, and [16] for its relationship to gradient space. (Gradient space is in fact a projection of the Gaussian sphere on to a plane.)

Consider two plane faces A and B, represented in gradient space by points A' and B'. If the faces meet in the picture across a line 1 representing the edge at which they intersect in the scene, then this edge is represented by its dual line 1' in gradient space, which passes through A' and B' and which is at right angles to the picture line 1 if the pictures axes X, Y are respectively parallel to the gradient space axes G_x, G_y. This fact is the basis of Poly's procedure.

Poly is founded on the insight that a picture is fundamentally ambiguous and

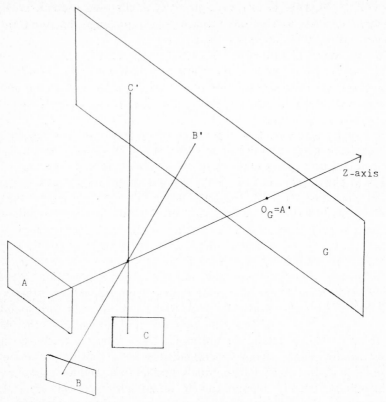

FIG. 3. Gradient space.

has many equally valid interpretations (though not necessarily equally 'plausible' or 'probable'), but that not all interpretations are possible. It first searches through all possible labellings of the picture in terms of connect and non-connect labels. For each such proposed labelling it tries to construct a corresponding gradient space diagram and if this is possible then so is the labelling. The diagram then forms the basis for constructing an interpretation in terms of convex and concave labels for the connect edges, and of occlusion labels for the non-connect edges.

The construction of the gradient space diagram proceeds as follows. A region in the picture is picked and the corresponding face A has its gradient marked by a point A' in the diagram. A connect edge 1, lying in A, is chosen and its dual 1' is drawn in using the knowledge that it passes through A' and has a slope perpendicular to 1. The other face that 1 lies in—B—must have its gradient point B' somewhere on 1': some point on 1' is chosen and marked B'. Next a surface C which shares connect edges with both A and B is chosen; those edges can have their duals drawn in the diagram, again using their slopes and the fact that they pass through A' and B' respectively. The intersection of these two dual lines defines C'. The procedure continues by choosing at each step another surface which shares connect edges with two of the surfaces already entered in the diagram until the connect edges are exhausted. There may arise a situation in which an unused connect edge exists between two surfaces already fixed in the diagram: in that case the combination of connect edges being tested is or is not possible depending on whether the dual line has exactly the slope required to pass through both the gradient space points. Such a diagram is overdetermined: all plateau pictures are examples of this. A diagram is underdetermined if a surface shares only one connect edge with the others. A number of problems arise from this, as will be discussed in later sections, but Poly assumes in this case that the connect labelling being tested is possible, and is possible wherever the surface's gradient space point is placed on the single dual line that constrains it.

A worked example is shown in Fig. 4. Fig. 4a shows the picture: the

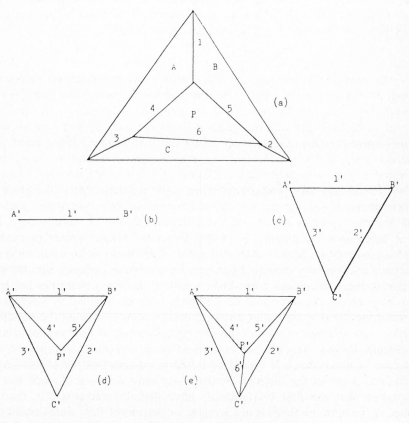

FIG. 4. Constructing the gradient space diagram (b–e) of a picture (a).

proposed connect edges are the numbered ones. The order of adding surfaces to the diagram is *ABCP*. After this there is one remaining dual line to be drawn, and thus the diagram is overdetermined, but as the final figure shows, it is possible (which is to be expected since the cyclic set 1, 2, 3 obey Huffman's conditions of concurrence).

It is important to notice the arbitrary choices made in the first two steps of the procedure: the first point is placed anywhere (two degrees of freedom) and the second point anywhere on a line (one degree of freedom). These choices are usually referred to as an arbitrary choice of origin and scale for the gradient space, but it might be more correct to say that there is no information about the origin and scale and the diagram drawn represents relationships which are independent of them. Another view of the matter is got by looking at the diagram not as a geometric construction but as solving a set of equations. Each connect edge gives rise to one equation relating the gradient space positions of the two surfaces it lies in. If the surfaces have gradients (G_{x1}, G_{y1}) and (G_{x2}, G_{y2}) then the slope of the dual line joining them in gradient space will be $(G_{y2} - G_{y1})/(G_{x2} - G_{x1})$ and this must equal the slope of a line perpendicular to the picture line, denoted L_{12}. The equation is therefore

$$G_{y2} - G_{y1} = L_{12}(G_{x2} - G_{x1}).$$

Since the constraints refer only to differences between coordinate values it is evident that no absolute values for the unknown coordinates can ever be derived: they can only be solved for in terms of each other. Poly therefore chooses some arbitrary number (zero in fact) for one G_x and one G_y coordinate—corresponding to arbitrarily fixing the first gradient space point. The equations relate differences between G_y coordinates to differences between G_x coordinates only by a multiplicative relation: in other words, no number is ever given for the size of a difference. One such difference may therefore be arbitrarily fixed—let us say for the difference in G_y coordinates and the equation then gives us the size of the difference in the G_x coordinates. This factor determines the magnitude of the distances between points in gradient space and corresponds to a choice of scale. With these three extra pieces of numerical information, the equations may be treated as ordinary simultaneous equations where the slopes L are known and all the other quantities are to be solved for, except the three that have already been determined by assumption. Constructing the diagram point by point corresponds to solving the equations in pairs chosen so that in each of the two equations two of the four coordinates are already known, and the two unknowns occur in both equations and may therefore be determined. It should be noted in passing that the positioning of the second point in the diagram involves not only a choice of scale but the assumption that the first two surfaces have distinct gradients, i.e. that the connect edge between them is not a crack. A version of Poly which could deal with cracks in a general way would have to include machinery for searching through the possibilities this excludes.

After successfully constructing a diagram, Poly goes on to replace the connect labels by convex or concave labels. This is dictated by the following rule: since picture lines are perpendicular to their duals in gradient space there is an exact correspondence between the order of the faces across the line representing the connect edge, and the order of the points representing them along the dual line; if the order is the same the label is convex, otherwise concave. For example in Fig. 4 all the connect edges are convex in the interpretation of the picture as a truncated pyramid. There is however a fundamental two-way ambiguity in that one diagram always represents two labellings the second being derived from the first by systematically changing all convex labels to concave and vice versa. This arises because in choosing where to place the second gradient space point, the arbitrary choice concerns not only the distance along the dual line from the first point but also the direction. Thus there are no grounds for choosing the first label, but for a determined diagram all other labels have a fixed relationship ('same' or 'different') to the first. Another way of looking at it is to say that the scale factor can be chosen as positive or negative. Poly accordingly produces two labellings at this stage. (This ambiguity of convex and concave is essentially that which operates in viewing a Necker cube, and may therefore be referred to as the Necker ambiguity.) It is illustrated in Fig. 5 which shows a picture with three numbered connect edges, the corresponding gradient space diagram, and the two resulting labellings. If the diagram is not fully determined then Connect splits it into determined subparts, or rather produces several separate diagrams which are labelled independently.

Poly next generates the occlusion labels by applying two rules. The first and

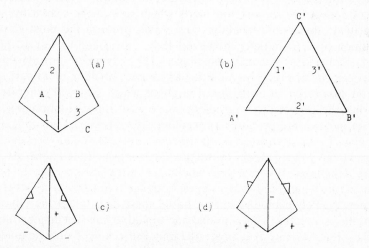

FIG. 5. A simple picture, a corresponding gradient space diagram, and two labellings. The + sign denotes a convex edge, − denotes concave, and the chevrons denote occlusion: they point into the nearer surface which is the one the edge actually bounds in 3-D.

more important applies if the two regions meeting across the line also meet elsewhere across a connect-labelled line. The latter line is extended to divide the picture in two: if the connect edge is concave and surface A is on, say, the left of this edge then everywhere to the left of the extended line A is in front of B and therefore occludes it, while B will occlude A everywhere to the right of the connect edge. For a convex edge the rule is reversed. This rule is sufficient to complete the labellings in Figs. 5c,d. The second rule is designed to cover cases where the two surfaces do not share a connect edge: the occlusion labels assigned by the first rule are taken to establish in-front-of relations for those lines and their endpoints and these are transferred to lines sharing an endpoint with them. This rule is necessary for labelling a cube. This section of the program, called Occlude, also constructs the hidden surfaces at vertices. This is always possible and does not constrain the labelling of the visible edges in any way. It allows Poly to tell which junctions have been interpreted as trihedral vertices and which require more surfaces.

Poly is organized into passes or subprograms called: Input, Parse, Connect, Vexcave, Occlude. Input and Parse take a description of the picture and set up a data structure to represent it: in particular to represent which lines border which regions. (At this stage pictures will be rejected if they have dangling lines or lines with the same region on both sides.) The rest of the program is an exhaustive search directed by Connect. It generates in turn every possible labelling in terms of connect and non-connect labels, and for each it tries to construct a gradient space diagram. If it fails it goes on to the next possibility, otherwise it calls Vexcave. This generates the possible convex and concave labels (two combinations for each diagram) and calls Occlude which generates the occlusion labels corresponding to each combination of labels produced by Vexcave. Connect has some refinements which reduce the search by quickly detecting many impossible labellings and which produce the most connected interpretation first. Essentially, however, Poly is designed to test all possible proposed connect/non-connect labellings. The examples introduced later mostly concern its workings on a particular connect labelling of a figure, rather than on the first or on all of the interpretations which Poly will generate.

Exploring the properties of gradient space as a representation led Mack-worth to a picture interpretation procedure with substantial advantages over line-labelling. It was not restricted to trihedral, non-accidental vertices: indeed it appeared largely independent of the junctions on which the Huffman–Clowes procedure depended. Whereas line-labelling constrained an edge to be, say, convex along its length, Poly constrained both surfaces to have constant slope. More generally, Poly exploited surface-based constraints rather than line-based ones, and this is a feature Huffman had had to add to line-labelling by means of his auxiliary rules. Finally Poly suggested that a search need only be made over two line-labels—connect and non-connect—rather that over four, and that the other labels could be deduced from these, which suggested a new view of the ambiguity and constraints involved in the task of line-drawing interpretation.

2.3. Superpoly

In this section a number of Poly's failings are introduced and used to motivate the specification of a modified and improved version, which will be called 'Superpoly'. Superpoly is intended to embody the best possible development of Mackworth's ideas towards his goal of a completely geometrically competent program, given the assumptions of a perfect line-drawing and a scene composed of plane-bounded polyhedra.

2.3.1. *The triangulation technique*

Poly's method of constructing the gradient space diagram (in Connect) relies on fixing the position in gradient space of each face in turn. After the first two, whose determination involves the arbitrary choices of origin and scale, this is done by the use of two connect edges relating the new face to those already fixed in the diagram: these two edges each determine the slope of a line in gradient space, and since they lie also in faces whose gradient space positions are already known, their duals are determined. Their intersection defines the gradient space position of the new face.

The above description implies that the procedure is a geometrical one using ruler and protractor to construct lines. Poly's internal representation of this involves solving equations for the unknown gradient space coordinates of the new face, given numerical values for the slope of the picture lines and for the coordinates in gradient space of the faces already determined. Each connect edge gives rise to one equation, so in the above situation there are two simultaneous equations for the two unknown coordinates. Poly models the geometric procedure closely, and if no face can be found with two connect edges relating it to faces already entered in the diagram, Connect will start another independent diagram for the other surfaces, thus reflecting an assumption that there are not sufficient constraints to determine the rest of the diagram as a whole.

That this assumption is false, is demonstrated by Fig. 6 (originally devised, as was the essence of the accompanying argument, by Frank O'Gorman). We consider the interpretation of Fig. 6a in which the outer lines (marked X) are occluding, and all the inner ones are connect. (In fact it represents an irregular, wholly convex object with two triangular top faces and four quadrilateral side faces.) The gradient space diagram for it is determined, but cannot be constructed by Poly, as is soon revealed by attempts to construct it using the triangulation technique. The crucial feature of the diagram, which is given in fig. 6b, is that A', B', F' are separated from C', D', E' by four-sided regions. The simplest way to demonstrate that the diagram is nevertheless determined is to consider the algebraic constraints. We have to determine six gradient space points i.e. twelve unknown coordinates, reduced to nine by the arbitrary determination of the origin and scale of the diagram in gradient space which yields three parameters. Since there is one constraint (equation) from

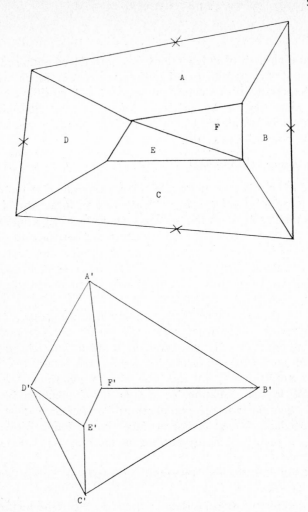

FIG. 6. Frank O'Gorman's counterexample to Poly's triangulation technique: the picture (a), and the diagram it fails to construct (b).

each of nine connect edges, the diagram is determined. Another way of viewing this, is that the first gradient space point is fixed arbitrarily and the second is fixed using only one connect edge and one more arbitrary choice (of scale): this leaves four points which requires eight unused connect edges—which there are. (To verify that the constraints (equations) are indeed in general independent of each other, you may establish by inspection of the picture (or by trial and error) that it can be redrawn with the slope of any one connect edge changed, while the slopes (though not necessarily the positions) of the other connect edges are left unchanged.)

It is possible to construct a more complicated picture which has an over-determined gradient space diagram which cannot be constructed by the triangulation technique. Failure to construct a determined diagram means that Vexcave cannot assign the correct and only the correct combinations of convex and concave labels. Failure to construct an overdetermined diagram means that Poly may generate an interpretation with an impossible combination of connect labels.

It might be thought that if the trihedral restriction applies to the scene then triangulation would be an adequate method, and Mackworth discusses this. However it is not the case, as may be seen by imagining variations to Fig. 6a. There are two 4-ray junctions in this picture and these correspond to non-trihedral vertices. However if both these were sliced off to yield small 4-sided plateaus, but those plateaus happened to be wholly occluded by two small objects, then only the same visible connect edges as before would be available for constructing the gradient space diagram even though the solid would now be wholly trihedral. A trihedral assumption applied to the scene therefore does not guarantee visible cyclic sets of three in the picture. Conversely the crucial four-sided regions in the gradient space diagram correspond to cyclic sets of four but not necessarily to single scene vertices at which four planes meet.

The above shows that triangulation is an inadequate technique for constructing the gradient space diagram and that more general methods for solving simultaneous equations must be used. This in turn means that any improved version of Poly (Superpoly) should be designed and understood within the framework of the general theory of solving linear equations and that there may be no simple geometric interpretation of its procedures as there is for Poly.

2.3.2. *The missing depth parameter*

In his thesis [13, pp. 141–151], Mackworth introduces the depth equations in a proposal for an additional pass in Poly, to be executed after Connect, but only in order to allow Poly to rule out certain of Huffman's impossible objects. He also mentioned the possibility of integrating depth information into Connect [13, p. 122]. This integration is in fact crucial to a geometrically adequate program. This will be established by a series of examples below, but we may start by observing that the heart of Mackworth's method is to base the interpretation of a picture on planes, and to represent those planes in gradient space. However a plane in 3-D has three degrees of freedom and needs three independent parameters to specify it, whereas gradient space specifies only two. The third parameter in this specification of a plane is D, the 'depth' of the plane. (See Appendix A for more detail.) The equation of a plane in this representation is

$$-Z = G_x X + G_y Y + D$$

or

$$-Z = \mathbf{G} \cdot \mathbf{p} + D$$

where G is the vector (G_x, G_y) and p is the point (X, Y), and a particular plane is specified by the triple (G_x, G_y, D). By substituting $X = Y = 0$ it can be seen that D is the Z-coordinate of the point where the plane intersects the Z-axis. (This development follows Mackworth's in [13, p. 148].)

Since Poly only solves for two of the three parameters of each plane it is not surprising that it fails to capture important constraints. This can be expressed another way by saying that different parts of a surface should be constrained to be coplanar, but that Poly only constrains their gradients to be the same i.e. constrains them to be parallel. An immediate consequence is that Poly's gradient space reasoning cannot correctly handle the constraints between two surfaces, and in particular the constraint expressed by Huffman's auxiliary rule for cyclic sets of two [2]. It does reject the Huffman–Clowes scheme's labelling of the notched tetrahedron (Fig. 7) in which both 1 and 2 are convex because the two distinct points representing faces A and B cannot be joined by two dual lines of different slope (representing lines 1 and 2). But it cannot reject Huffman's own example of the notched cuboid (Fig. 8) without the help of an

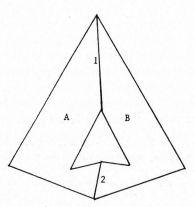

FIG. 7. A notched tetrahedron [13].

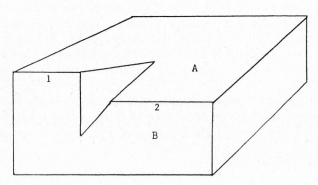

FIG. 8. A notched cuboid [2].

additional rule (mentioned below) which is unconnected with gradient space because lines 1 and 2 give rise to the same dual line in gradient space since they are parallel in the picture.

2.3.3. *Using depth equations to check constraints*

The depth parameters of planes may be calculated, after an arbitrary choice for the depth of the first plane, by considering that any point on a connect edge must satisfy the equations of both the planes that share that edge. Hence, eliminating Z,

$$G_A \cdot p + D_A = G_B \cdot p + D_B$$

where p is a point on the connect edge between planes A, B. If the gradients have been found, and D_A is known, then

$$D_B = D_A + (G_A - G_B) \cdot p.$$

We obtain one such equation for every connect edge. If we consider two equations, derived from points p_1, p_2 both on the same connect edge, then the vector $(p_1 - p_2)$ will be parallel to the picture line, while the vector $(G_A - G_B)$ is parallel to the line in gradient space joining the gradient points A', B' i.e. to the dual of the picture line. Since these lines are perpendicular,

$$(G_A - G_B) \cdot (p_1 - p_2) = 0$$

and hence

$$(G_A - G_B) \cdot p_1 = (G_A - G_B) \cdot p_2$$

so that the two points give rise to the same depth equation relating D_A and D_B and we get only one depth constraint per connect edge. (This development is again taken from Mackworth [13, pp. 148–149]).

We can now see how solving the depth equations will detect the anomaly in the notched cuboid. We get two equations relating the depth parameters of A and B with the same $(G_A - G_B)$ term (corresponding to a vector perpendicular to lines 1 and 2), and differing only in the two points chosen. But the two points are taken from lines 1, 2 which have no point in common since they are parallel, and thus no matter how they are chosen the vector between them must lie at an angle to the picture lines and hence not perpendicular to the dual line. It follows that the two equations do not reduce to one and express a contradictory relationship between the depth parameters of the two surfaces.

A further consequence of this arises in connection with cyclic sets. Consider a cyclic set of three faces A, B, C. From the edges AB and AC we obtain

$$D_B = D_A + (G_A - G_B) \cdot p,$$
$$D_C = D_B + (G_B - G_C) \cdot p$$

where p can be the same point in both equations if we choose the intersection of AB and BC as we may since for this purpose all points on a connect edge are equivalent. From these two equations we can derive

$$D_C = D_A + (G_A - G_B) \cdot p + (G_B - G_C) \cdot p$$

so

$$D_C = D_A + (G_A - G_C) \cdot p.$$

We have thus related D_C and D_A without using the connect edge CA. We can see that this edge will give rise to the same equation if and only if the edge CA passes through the point p i.e. through the intersection of AB and BC. Thus the depth equations will be consistent only if the cyclic edges are concurrent, and solving the depth equations will automatically enforce Huffman's rule for cyclic sets of three. In fact solving the depth equations embodies a generalization of the rule: for a cyclic set of N faces and edges, if $N-1$ edges are concurrent then (by an extension of the above argument) if the Nth edge is concurrent with the others its depth equation adds no new constraint, while if it is not, then its equation is inconsistent with the others.

Poly does not have any other way of enforcing even Huffman's rule. Mackworth introduced a special rule to exclude the labelling shown in Fig. 9 of his main example, a tetrahedron—this would be excluded by Huffman's rule for cyclic sets of three applied to the set of faces ABC. Mackworth's additional rule ([1, p. 129] and [13, p. 102]) has no connection with gradient space and can be omitted if the depth equations are solved, and an inconsistency in them used to reject the current combination of connect edges being considered by Connect. Another example is that of a three-sided pyramid seen from above (Fig. 10). Fig. 10a is clearly legitimate but Fig. 10b, whose summit is occluded, is not since the cyclic edges are not concurrent. However, for both these Poly

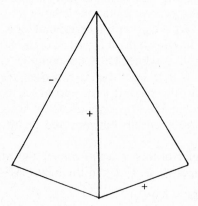

FIG. 9. An impossible labelling excluded by a special rule in Poly.

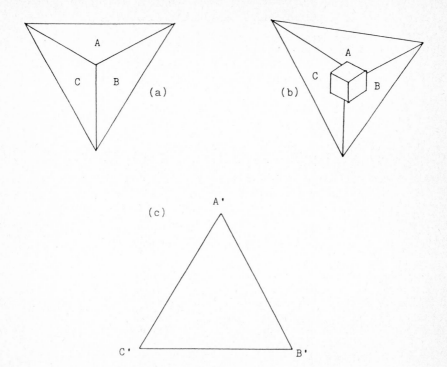

FIG. 10. Two pictures (a, b) and their common gradient space diagram (c).

constructs the same (determined) gradient space diagram (Fig. 10c) because the picture slopes of the three connect edges are the same in both cases. Solving the depth equations would check the first and detect the anomaly in the second. This pair of figures illustrate that a gradient space diagram is ambiguous and in general corresponds to a set of pictures, and that it does not necessarily express all the constraints.

2.3.4. *Using depth equations to calculate surface gradients*

The examples introduced so far show that solving the depth equations will uniformly enforce the constraints expressed by Huffman's rules for cyclic sets of two and three which are sometimes missed by Poly. However they give no reason for rejecting Mackworth's idea of tacking on the solution of the depth equations as a separate pass to be done after the solution of the gradient equations (construction of the gradient space diagram) is complete. We now turn to an example which does. Fig. 11 shows a (non-concurrent) cyclic set of four without a plateau, where the centre of the object has been occluded. What can Poly tell us about the faces A, B, C, D given only the connect edges 1, 2, 3, 4? The gradient space diagram is underdetermined, since with four faces eight unknowns must be calculated from only four equations plus three arbitrary

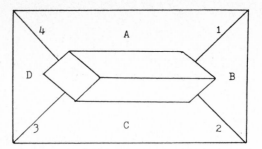

FIG. 11. A cyclic set of four (cf. Figs. 2 and 14).

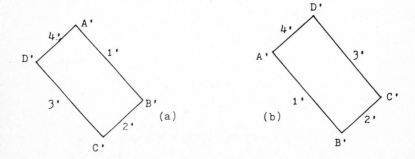

FIG. 12. Two gradient space diagrams for Fig. 11 with arbitrarily chosen proportions.

choices. Two basic configurations seem allowed, although the proportions of the rectangle are arbitrarily chosen: see Fig. 12. These imply, respectively, an all-convex labelling of the cyclic edges, and an alternating $(+ - + -)$ labelling. The picture is not in fact ambiguous in this way as may be shown by the following construction. Produce lines 1 and 2 until they meet: this represents their intersection in space since they both lie in B, and also represents a point that lies in A, B and C. Similarly the intersection of lines 3 and 4 gives a point that lies in C, D and A. This gives two points which lie in the edge where A and C intersect: this may therefore be drawn in and used in constructing the gradient space diagram which is now determined—see Figs. 13a,b. This shows that only the all-convex (or all-concave) labelling is correct, and that Poly fails to capture a constraint essential for generating only the correct interpretation.

This constraint would be captured by solving the depth equations: because there is a non-concurrent cyclic set, they generate an extra constraint beyond those necessary to relate surface depths, and when added to the gradient constraints this is sufficient to determine the gradient space diagram. Up to now we have imagined the gradients to have been determined before tackling the depth equations, but this example shows that they must sometimes be

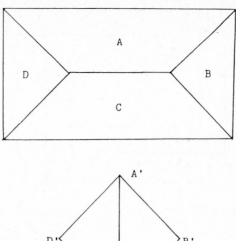

FIG. 13. A cyclic set of four with an extra edge, and its gradient space diagram.

solved simultaneously with the gradient equations. Superpoly therefore is essentially a simultaneous equation solver, calculating three coordinates for each plane. Applied to this example, which has four planes and four connect edges, the procedure must solve for twelve unknowns, given four arbitrary choices (origin and scale in gradient space, and the depth of one plane) and eight equations (two per connect edge).

As was noted earlier, the extra constraint from the depth equations disappears if the cyclic set is concurrent. In the example, if the cyclic set were concurrent the constructed edge AC would be of zero length and hence of no defined orientation and the gradient space diagram would no longer be determined, and the alternative $(+ - + -)$ labelling of the edges would be possible.

Essentially the same case arises in Cowan's figure (Fig. 14). (This figure was first published, as far as I know, by Cowan [18], and provided the test case which drew my attention to this defect in Poly). The Huffman–Clowes procedure assigns an interpretation containing the four convex edges marked in the figure, but this labelling, which is also generated by Poly, is in fact impossible. The reader may construct the edge AC by the method given above and hence derive the gradient space diagram (Fig. 15a) which shows that the $(+ - + -)$ labelling is the only allowable one for this figure.

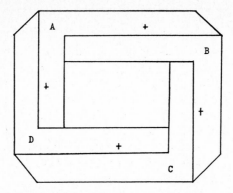

FIG. 14. Cowan's impossible object [18].

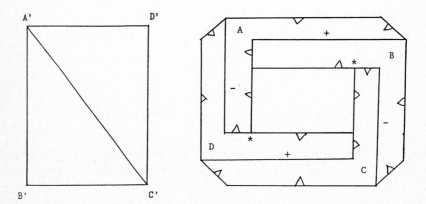

FIG. 15. Gradient space diagram for Cowan's figure, and a corresponding labelling. (Asterisks mark junctions that are accidentals in this interpretation.)

This example has the advantage that it does not depend on an occluding object. It also has the property that it looks impossible to people. Given the possible labelling of the connect edges, Poly would go on to assign the occlusion labels shown in Fig. 15b, oblivious of the fact that this involves horrible accidentals at the junctions marked *. We now turn to the question of how Superpoly could detect these, and hence discover that there is no 'good' interpretation of Cowan's figure.

2.3.5. Detecting accidentals and assigning occlusion labels

For T-junctions general viewpoint does not demand that the stem meet the crossbar in 3-D but it does require that the two halves of the crossbar be collinear in 3-D. This can be checked by examining the assigned labels to see if the two halves are interpreted as lying in a common plane: if and only if this is the case, then they are collinear and the junction is not an accidental. With this ability, Superpoly would detect the two accidentals in Fig. 15b and thus might suggest that there is no satisfactory interpretation of Cowan's figure.

We shall not here enter a full discussion of accidentals and the problems of deciding what a 'satisfactory' interpretation is (to people). It is enough to suggest that although Superpoly does not aim to model human perception closely it should hopefully provide the tools for building such a model, and the avoidance of accidentals seems to be an important factor in our selection of an interpretation. It is desirable to be able to incorporate accidental interpretations (unlike the Huffman–Clowes line-labelling scheme) but not to be unaware of doing so, as Poly is.

Despite what Mackworth claimed [13, p. 161] Poly cannot reliably tell which junctions have been interpreted as accidentals because this is not a property of their labelling alone. This is illustrated in Fig. 16 which shows two contexts for a junction, in both of which it has the same labelling (in the most obvious interpretations) as shown but in only one of which is the junction an accidental since the top surface forms an overhang, whereas in the second figure it is not since the three edges meet in space as may be shown by extending edges 4, 5 (as shown dotted) which shows that the junction is the point where planes A, B, C intersect and therefore 1, 2, 3 must actually meet there.

For junctions which do not have collinear rays e.g. arrow junctions, a sufficient condition for a non-accidental interpretation is that the corresponding edges meet in 3-D at that point. This can be reliably checked by calculating the depth (i.e. the Z-coordinate) of the junction for each plane involved. This is done by examining the line-labels to discover which surface each line belongs to, and then using the equation for a plane given earlier, given the (X, Y) coordinates of the junction, the gradient, and the depth parameters of the planes. If the depth of the points in each plane corresponding to the junction is

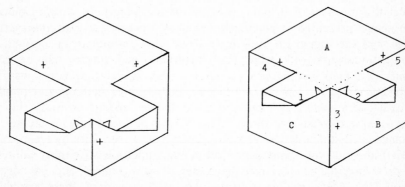

FIG. 16. Local interpretations in terms of line-labels do not determine whether a junction is an accidental (left) or not (right).

the same, then the edges meet there and the junction is not an accidental. Poly could not do this since it does not solve for the depth parameters, but Superpoly easily could.

The rules used by Poly to assign occlusion labels to non-connect edges together with their failings, will not be discussed until a later section. However it can be seen that the technique of calculating the depth of a point, would provide a simple and uniform method of assigning these labels: a point on the picture line is chosen and the depth of the corresponding 3-D point in the face on either side is calculated. The face which is nearer (i.e. has a Z-coordinate nearer the viewpoint) is the face to which the edge is assigned and the occlusion label is chosen to indicate this. This method is guaranteed to assign occlusion labels consistent with the interpretation of the connect edges, and is proposed for use in Superpoly as a replacement for the less elegant and less reliable rules used in Poly.

2.3.6. *The final design for Superpoly*

It has been shown that the triangulation technique is inadequate in general, that the depth equations must also be solved in order to check constraints that exist but which Poly sometimes misses, and that at least sometimes the gradient and depth equations must be solved simultaneously rather than separately because the values of gradient space coordinates are not always uniquely determined by the gradient equations alone. How then might Poly be modified to accommodate these failures? The aim in the design of Superpoly is to augment Poly so as to do this and thus conform with Mackworth's objective of designing a competent program, while retaining as many as possible of his insights and ideas. Poly's structure has a number of levels: the failings we are concerned with here relate only to the internal structure of Connect and so the overall design may be retained almost unchanged. Even within Connect some of the underlying approach can remain the same, as will be shown by the following comparison of Poly's Connect and a scheme for a new design for Connect to form part of the new program design Superpoly. Poly's Connect was originally presented in geometric terms, as a procedure that constructs a diagram, but the arguments presented above have promoted an alternative, algebraic framework with which Poly's various inadequacies can be conveniently described and understood. In these terms Poly's Connect may be described as taking a set of connect-labelled picture lines, deriving an equation from each line involving gradient space coordinates, making arbitrary choices that in effect fix values for three of these variables, and solving the set of simultaneous equations to derive values for the other variables by means of a particular method—the triangulation technique. Superpoly's Connect will take a set of connect-labelled picture lines, derive one gradient and one depth equation from each, make arbitrary choices for four of these variables equivalent to choosing an origin and scale for the dual space, and solve the set of simultaneous equations.

The next level of detail in this program design—an algorithm for solving the simultaneous equations—will be left unspecified here. The ability of such a program to deal correctly with the examples discussed above depends only on solving the depth and gradient equations simultaneously and does not depend on the particular algorithm for doing this provided that, unlike triangulation, it is adequate. The theory of linear simultaneous equations is well known and there is no doubt as to the existence of such an algorithm: whether there exists an applicable method that avoids the computational expense of a general-purpose matrix inversion technique is a question that will not be addressed here. One point should however be clarified. Unique solutions can only be found if the equation set is neither over- nor under-constrained: this can be determined by comparing the rank of the matrix representing the equation set to the number of unknown dual space coordinates (after deducting the four arbitrary choices). If the set is over-constrained i.e. inconsistent then the connect labelling is rejected as impossible. If the set is under-constrained then unique solutions cannot be found. In the corresponding case Poly begins a new gradient space diagram thus dividing the surfaces involved into independent groups, each internally fully determined by separate sets of arbitrary choices, but with no represented constraints between them. For didactic purposes Superpoly is defined to behave in the same way in this case but since in general there will be constraints (equations) relating such groups—even though the constraints are insufficient to determine the relationships exactly—this is clearly a potential source of trouble. The problems raised in the next section turn out to be related to this.

We may now summarise the overall scheme for Superpoly. The upper levels of Poly's design are left unchanged. The main new idea is to work in dual space instead of gradient space, and to represent each plane by three instead of two coordinates. The change from Poly consists mostly of the redesign of Connect just described to accomplish the simultaneous solution of the depth and gradient equations derivable from all the connect edges together. After the completion of this augmented version of Connect, Vexcave would be run, followed by a new, simplified version of Occlude which used the plane equations to decide which face is in front at any edge. Then a new pass could be appended in which accidentals were detected and marked.

This design maintains the main assumptions of Mackworth's approach: that searching and testing need only be done over the connect labellings, other labels following from this; that the inference needed for this should be directed at calculating the coordinates of points in dual space, constraints on connect edges following from this; and that this can be done by solving equations numerically which is made possible by his insight that a sufficient number of arbitrary choices can be made without inconsistency. The only points which have been abandoned are the propositions that triangulation is always an adequate equation-solving technique for this problem, and that the gradient equations alone suffice to capture the important constraints.

Such a program would be strikingly successful in terms of the criterion of geometric adequacy: of generating all and only the possible interpretations of a line-drawing. It would deal correctly with all the examples discussed and could include a notable omission from Poly: the ability to detect accidentals. It would also deal correctly with all the cases which line-labelling plus Huffman's auxiliary rules can, and also many examples on which those rules fail (see [11, Ch. 2]). It thus represents a powerful development of Mackworth's ideas. The next section will discuss the extent to which this design proposal would be successful and what would be involved in overcoming its flaws.

2.4. Difficulties with Superpoly

In this section we shall be most concerned with two related claims implicit in Poly and carried over to Superpoly: that all the constraints are derived from the connect edges i.e. that the non-connect edges do not exert constraints on the interpretation of the connect edges but are themselves constrained by them, and that the search can be entirely confined to Connect. In what follows we shall consider examples which show that Superpoly is not adequate as it stands, that these implicit claims do not hold in general, and that major modifications to Superpoly's design are necessary to achieve competence at the task. The counterexamples in fact show that almost all of the ideas embodied in Poly are invalid in general, and although no absolute counterexample or objection can be found to prove that any approach based on dual space must fail, the usefulness of the theory of dual space is thrown into serious doubt. The counterexamples are all concerned with underdetermined cases i.e. cases where the equations do not determine unique values for the dual space coordinates even after the arbitrary choices, and rules for reasoning about occlusion labels are examined in detail for the first time.

2.4.1. *Undetermined gradients*

In an earlier example it was shown that in interpreting non-concurrent cyclic sets of four, the depth equations yield an extra constraint which can be used to constrain the gradients and hence in effect to determine the gradient space diagram. We know however that depth equations will not yield an extra constraint if the cyclic edges are concurrent, and the diagram will therefore remain underdetermined. Fig. 12 shows the two possible diagrams (with arbitrary proportions) and these give the four possible labellings of a concurrent cyclic set of four indicated by Figs. 17a,b. (The Necker reversal of the two labellings shown are also possible labellings, making four in all.) However there is the problem of how Superpoly is to discover that there are these two alternatives, and not allow other impossible labellings such as the one shown in Fig. 17c. In fact Poly and Superpoly would generate all possible combinations of convex and concave labels in interpreting Figs. 11 and 14 because they have

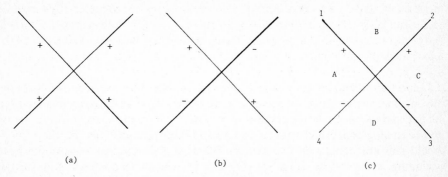

FIG. 17. Three labellings of an X-junction: (a) and (b) are possible, (c) is not.

no machinery for reasoning about constraints if these are not sufficient to determine points exactly in gradient or dual space. This example disproves the assumption that the only search is over connect labellings since it shows that more than two full labellings are derivable from one connect labelling but that not all combinations of convex and concave labels are allowed.

Assuming that the significant alternatives are the alternative line-labellings then we must introduce two new bits of machinery: a new search mechanism that takes a connect labelling and generates alternative combinations of convex and concave labels, and a procedure which translates these labellings into gradient space and checks their consistency. One method might be to introduce extra arbitrary choices to fix dual space points—their magnitude is irrelevant but their sign must correspond to the Vexcave labelling being currently considered (recall that reversing the sign of the arbitrary choice of scale in gradient space reverses the signs of convex and concave labels). This would retain the central idea of representing surfaces as points in dual space and will work on simple examples such as the one given above but it is not clear that it will be successful in general.

An alternative might be based on Kanade's filtering of 'spanning angles' [19]. The essential idea is to translate each convex or concave label into a unit vector—the connect edge gives its orientation, the label gives its sense. The magnitudes of the vectors are not determined in these cases, but some checking can nevertheless be done. In Fig. 12a, A' is located relative to C' in two different ways: as a (positive) linear combination of the vectors $3'$ and $4'$ (remember the lengths shown were arbitrarily chosen when drawing the figure), and as a combination of $2'$ and $1'$. The check consists in verifying that the subspaces of gradient space spanned by each of these combinations of vectors overlap (in this case they coincide). Applied to the labellings in Fig. 17, this reasoning correctly allows the first two and rejects the third.

Note that this approach abandons the idea of using arbitrary choices to allow a numerical solution of the equations, and hence of reasoning only about points in gradient space (not vectors). Since it ignores depth parameters this method seems unlikely to deal correctly with all cases of indeterminacy, although further work might well arrive at a design that would: however it illustrates the magnitude of the change and the basic nature of the additional machinery needed.

Clearly an adequate extension to Superpoly would be a major modification, introducing search into Vexcave, and perhaps departing from the equation-solving paradigm by introducing a new type of gradient space representation and reasoning concerned with subspaces and their intersections. Furthermore it would still not cope with the next problem, which concerns constraints from occluding rather than connect edges, and which necessitates still further modifications.

2.4.2. *Indeterminacy and occlusion relationships*

It was proposed above that Superpoly should derive occlusion labels by calculating the depths of the two surfaces concerned at some point on the edge. The sign of the difference in the depths shows which surface is nearer the viewpoint and hence the sign of the occlusion label. Conversely the consistency of a labelling could be checked by translating occlusion labels into depth inequalities and then checking these by substituting in the parameters determined by the connect labelling (a suggestion made by Mackworth). Both of these, however, require all the surfaces to have fully determined gradient and depth parameters—and this is not always the case.

These methods fail when the relationship between some surfaces is under-determined: there are then many combinations of occlusion labels that are possible—but not all are possible so simply generating all combinations is not an adequate method.

This is illustrated by the example in Fig. 18 which shows two objects interlocking in an impossible way. (It was presented in [2] and will be referred to as 'Huffman's combs'). We consider the interpretation corresponding to the

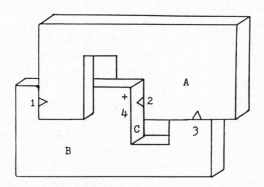

FIG. 18. 'Huffman's combs'—two interlocking objects (from [2]).

one we see, with two separate objects each with internal connect edges but related to each other only via occluding edges. The crucial labels are shown in the figure: this interpretation is also assigned by Huffman–Clowes line-labelling. Poly would have no way of assigning occlusion labels at all, but if it assigned one to each object with the sense indicated then Occlude's second rule would propagate the sense of occlusion and also come up with this labelling.

We can show the impossibility of this interpretation by using two corollaries of Poly's rule in Occlude. That rule relates occlusion labels to connect labels by reasoning about the 'sidedness' of surfaces with respect to each other: that is which surface, at a given point in the picture, is nearer to the viewpoint. Thus because edge 4 is convex, surface C is behind B everywhere to the right of 4, and in particular edge 2 is behind B (since if B were extended it would cover 2). Occlusion labels directly give the sidedness relationship of the two surfaces at that line—thus on line 3, A is in front of B, but on 2, A is behind C. Since 2 is behind B, it follows that A is behind B along 2. Although A and B do not meet at a visible connect edge such an edge must exist if they were extended, and their occlusion relations must be such that A is behind B everywhere to one side (in the picture) of it, and B be behind A everywhere on the other side. Yet it is not possible to draw any such line to satisfy the relationships already claimed along edges 1, 2, and 3: hence the labels shown are mutually inconsistent.

This shows that Superpoly needs some new extension to deal with these cases correctly; yet the sidedness reasoning used above, although related to a rule used in Poly, is not consistent with the approach we have been exploring because it is not concerned with dual space or with plane parameters. Sidedness reasoning will be explored in Section 4 and it will be shown that it can be extended to perform the whole of the interpretation task; meanwhile, we must consider what lessons to draw from this example concerning Superpoly. The obvious need is to extend Superpoly to organize a search over the possible relationships between the objects. It will easily construct gradient space diagrams for each object separately but it has no way of relating their origins and scales. As in the case of underdetermined gradients, a search must be organized over the possible ways of relating the parameters of the groups of surfaces of each object. Since the example shows that some of these will not lead to an allowed interpretation this will introduce a search into this stage of Superpoly as well: a further defeat for the notion that search need only be over the connect labellings, since this search does not change the connect labelling but only has implications for the occlusion labels.

What the program needs in fact is a way of reasoning from occlusion labels to gradient and depth parameters so that the search can be directed by choices of occlusion labels. Indeed this ability to reason from occlusion should ideally be taken further since it seems that non-accidental T-junctions are a powerful cue, and they yield only an occlusion relationship: just as it is desirable that

Superpoly should have the ability to detect accidentals, so it is a disadvantage that it does not offer a method of constraining an overall interpretation from a preferred interpretation of T-junctions.

2.4.3. *An outline for a third program design 'Hyperpoly'*

Mackworth [13, p. 151] discusses Huffman's example and suggests that having solved the depth equations for each object separately, a consideration of depth inequalities between surfaces would demonstrate the impossibility of the interpretation. Presumably the proposal is that occlusion labels would be generated and then checked by using the inequalities: this would overcome the impossibility of the exhaustive search over real-valued variables that would otherwise be necessary in exploring the ways the two separate gradient and dual spaces are related. It also implies another failure of Poly's assumption that search is associated only with choosing a connect labelling. However, the crucial difficulty is that the interpretations of the two bodies interact and so Superpoly is not in fact free to make two independent sets of arbitrary choices: consequently, the gradient and depth equations cannot be solved for each body separately, the dual space coordinates of the planes cannot be calculated, and so the inequalities cannot be checked by simple numerical substitution. Since there does not seem any obvious way of relating additional arbitrary choices of dual space coordinates to choices of line-labels in this case, which would allow us to use the existing equation-solving method, a completely new approach is indicated.

All the Huffman–Clowes labels, or at least those involving the second body, must be expressed as inequalities. Firstly occlusion labels give rise to depth inequalities. The depth equations were derived by considering a point on the connect edge where two planes meet, taking their plane equations, substituting in the X and Y values of the point and equating the Z values to obtain an equation relating the six plane parameters involved (see Section 2.3.3). An occlusion label states that along that edge the Z values are not equal but have an inequality relating the parameters of the two planes. In fact, each edge gives rise to two independent inequalities, one for each endpoint. Secondly, connect edges not only give rise to two equations as before but also to a mutually dependent pair of inequalities, whose signs express the sign of the connect label. They relate the planes' gradient space coordinates and determine the order of the two gradient points along their common dual line.

Checking a labelling for consistency now involves checking this mixed set of equations and inequalities for consistency. In general, this can not be done by calculating numerical values for the variables involved because in the cases considered making choices of numerical values for four parameters is not enough to derive values for the others, and there seems no way to select further values so as to perform a valid check. Hence, if this is correct, the inference mechanism needed will be a consistency checker for a mixed set of relations rather than a numerical equation solver: its output would be yes or no rather than the coordinates of a set of points in dual space. Furthermore, the dual space representation could be dropped entirely. In Superpoly it served as an intermediate representation between the phase of checking the consistency of a connect labelling and that of generating a full line-labelling—a mechanism that could do the additional checking now shown to be necessary could do it all, thus obviating any need for Connect's procedure and representation. Thus, Superpoly's inference mechanism could be not only augmented but replaced by a mechanism for generating relationships from a full labelling and checking their consistency without solving for values of the variables involved.

Since the relations are all linear, one applicable framework for this consistency checking is linear programming together with its known techniques. The problem is then conceived of in terms of a multi-dimensional hyperspace with one dimension for every plane parameter of every plane. Consistency would be shown by the existence of a non-negative volume in hyperspace defined by the hyperplanes corresponding to the relations, inconsistency by its absence. (In most cases such a volume would be infinite and individual variables would not be constrained to finite ranges. Thus nothing could be said about the position of individual scene planes in dual space—the constraints limit combinations of them, not individuals.) Since the arbitrary choices are of no use in these cases, they might for uniformity be abandoned so that all labels were treated in the same way.

We have in effect arrived at an overall scheme for a program that would overcome the objections to Superpoly—it might be called 'Hyperpoly' (a name suggested by Alan Mackworth in the conversation where this design was first mooted). The essential changes from Superpoly are that inequalities as well as equations are handled, and that their mutual consistency is checked rather than numerical solutions for them being found. The scheme is still to reason about the dual space coordinates (or plane parameters) of the planes involved but they cannot now be represented by numerical values. The search will be over the full set of line-labels, not just over connect labels. Each label is translated into two inequalities and if it is convex or concave then two equations are set up as well. The accumulated set of constraints is then checked for consistency. Thus a consideration of underdetermined cases leads to an abandonment of many more of Poly's features: the numerical representation, equation-solving as the central activity, and the confinement of searching and testing to Connect.

Because we are not looking for numerical solutions for the variables but simply for a consistent set of relations, there is no simple interpretation in terms of dual space—we are not for instance constructing a volume in dual space within which a dual space point must lie. Linear programming of course offers a simple geometric interpretation, but not in dual space: it translates the problem into a multi-dimensional space (three dimensions for each plane involved). Thus, in such a program, there would no longer be any good reason for invoking the concept of dual space: it would just be a problem of checking consistency in a mixed set of relations between plane parameters. The approach would be characterised as an algebraic one revolving around relations derived from the plane equations, not as a geometric one based on points in dual space. We shall therefore now reconsider the usefulness of the idea of dual space in the line-drawing interpretation task.

2.5. The use of the idea of gradient and dual space

In Mackworth's work on Poly the theory of gradient space is used to mobilise our geometric intuition (for instance the triangulation technique is easy to understand in geometric terms), and to offer an account of the meaning of the numerical representation that Poly is based on and of the actions associated with it. Thus, the program, whose final aim is to check the consistency of a line-labelling, is thought of as carrying out the immediate aim of calculating the positions of points in gradient space.

The arguments presented in this section throw doubts on the usefulness of the theory in these respects. Firstly, in connection with the latter function of giving an account of Poly's representation, it is shown in Appendix B that Poly is in fact valid under perspective as well as orthographic projection. However, in the general (perspective) case, the quantities calculated are not gradients but coordinates in a subspace of an unknown dual space (it depends on the focal length of the projection which is not known) which does not contain gradient space as a natural subspace. Secondly, although the idea of dual space is useful with a program that calculates the positions of points, this itself has been shown to be an over-specific representation in the general case. This is because it cannot represent constraints from individual line-labels but only from sets of two or more. In underdetermined cases the constraints cannot be captured by representing either exact values or ranges of values for each coordinate of each dual space point: even after arbitrary choices of origin, scale, and of the dual space itself, individual values can remain wholly unconstrained—it is their combinations that are restricted. Hence Poly's representation must be dropped, and it would seem that dual space does not have a role to play in explaining a program like Hyperpoly with a fundamentally different internal representation. Likewise the failure of triangulation seems to necessitate an abandonment of attempts to understand the procedural aspects of Poly in geometric terms and a retreat to seeing it as equation-solving governed by algebraic concepts such as determinacy and the rank of the equation set. Again, this throws doubt on the usefulness of the theory of dual space in this problem domain.

In fact, it might be argued that the dual space theory distracts attention from the real problem of representing and checking constraints from individual line-labels, which relate to the relationships between planes, by focussing attention on properties of *individual* planes which are only indirectly relevant.

Poly's gradient space representation's real function—in terms of the overall goal—is to encode the relationships between planes implied by line-labels, and it does not actually encode physical properties of the surfaces (because of the arbitrary choice of origin and scale no quantitative constraints on individual gradients are ever known). The gradient space theory however tends to suggest the latter and disguise the former and may therefore be said to be at least potentially misleading. The same applies to Superpoly's dual space theory. On this view the theory should be discarded—in favour perhaps of a strictly algebraic analysis of constraints derived from plane equations—if an adequate program is to be designed.

2.6. Conclusion

Mackworth's ideas on line-drawing interpretation as embodied in Poly could be summarised as follows. The problem is seen as one of checking the consistency of partial or complete line-labellings. The basic scheme is to calculate and represent what is implied about the gradients of the surfaces involved. The next level of the design asserts that this can be done by representing the coordinates of points in gradient space, and that the only effective constraints on these come from the gradient equations i.e. from connect labels. Finally the technique of triangulation is proposed for effecting this. This design implies that the problem is one of checking the mutual consistency of a set of constraints, that these constraints are all expressed as equations, that these may be solved (given a fixed number of arbitrary choices) to yield numerical values for the unknowns, and that they may be solved progressively by taking a pair at a time (the triangulation technique). In addition, Mackworth presented the theory of gradient space of a framework for understanding the program and its central representation.

We have seen in this chapter that all of these propositions though valid in some cases are invalid in general. The triangulation technique is not always applicable, surface depths as well as gradients must be considered, not all the effective constraints come from connect labels (the sign of the connect labels and sense of occlusion labels can vary independently in some cases), they are not all expressible as equations, and the constraints cannot always be represented by assigning fixed numerical values to the coordinates of points in gradient or dual space. Finally, it has been shown that in the general case of perspective projection the numbers Poly calculates are in no sense gradients, and it has been argued that gradient and dual space may even in some respects obstruct rather than help an understanding of the programs and a clear approach to their problems.

What, then, remains of Mackworth's ideas? First of all the overall method of tackling the interpretation task by generating picture labellings, preferably incrementally (i.e. adding a label at a time until all lines have a label), and checking the geometric consistency of each set of labels remains the same. Next, Mackworth's most basic idea remains valid: carry out the checking by attending to the properties of the planes involved. It is this plane-based approach which is vital to overcoming the shortcomings of the Huffman–Clowes scheme, and also to dropping the trihedral and non-accidental restrictions. It could be characterised as 'calculate and represent everything you can infer about each plane', and it remains an important approach whose potential has still not been thoroughly explored. In a broad sense it could be paraphrased as 'calculate and represent what you can infer about the dual space coordinates of each plane', and this is the emphasis Mackworth preferred, but we have seen that an emphasis on deriving constraints from plane equations is more fundamental than the idea of dual space, and that an interpretation in terms of dual space though valid seems of doubtful usefulness in the general case. It should be noted that previous workers such as Falk [6] had used methods based on plane equations but had assumed that information sufficient to derive physically accurate numerical solutions must be obtained from some source: Mackworth was the first to use only the information available in line-drawings in this way.

The rest of Mackworth's ideas, such as basing the program on a representation of points in dual space, are not adequate in general. What remains is the plane equation approach for analysing, expressing, and manipulating the constraints implied by line-labels. The strengths of this approach are that it can describe all possible information about a plane—it offers a complete analytic framework with a level of detail guaranteed in advance to be more than adequate—and it is embedded in the well-known theory of linear relations. Its weaknesses are that its level of detail is in fact over-specific for line-drawing interpretation (this is not fatal for a theory—in contrast to a representation—as under-specificity would be, but it is inconvenient) and that it primarily expresses properties of individual planes whereas line-labels primarily express relationships between planes. Thus the approach is guaranteed in principle to support the development of a geometrically adequate method of interpretation, but it is difficult to work with because it does not capture the meaning of line-labels (and hence the problem we are studying) in a simple, natural way, and because its description of the necessary reasoning process is not designed to address our geometric intuitions.

We have thus examined Mackworth's program and its component ideas at length and developed them in the direction of achieving a competent program. We have found in the course of this development that the idea of dual space becomes at best peripheral and at worst obstructive, while the plane equation approach that underlies it fails to describe the problem concisely or to mobilise our geometric intuitions. Both these conclusions need further examination. The next section discusses other ways of applying dual space to the problem and so considers whether another approach might truly use dual space as a basis.

Section 4 introduces an alternative to the plane equation approach in order to substantiate by contrast the claim that it lacks direct descriptive power and intuitive appeal.

3. The Prospects for new Approaches Based on Dual Space

The essential trouble with Mackworth's use of gradient space and dual space is that representing planes by points in dual space is over-specific and so cannot represent states of partial knowledge when the set of equations as a whole is undetermined. The development sketched above used inequalities between plane parameters to represent these weak constraints: but this suggests an algebraic approach with which the notion of gradient space has no close connection. However Kanade's spanning angle filter suggests that gradient space may not yet be exhausted as a source of ideas if planes are represented by something other than points: his proposal is to use vectors.

Kanade's spanning angle filter [19] was not proposed by him as a method of achieving complete geometric competence at interpretation, but as sketched above it suggests a possible approach to this goal. It has the virtue of being able to represent constraints from individual connect edges independently of the overall determinacy of sets of such constraints: in this respect it is a further step in adapting the gradient space metric to the information available in line-drawings. It would have to be generalized from gradient to dual space if constraints were not to be missed, but this does not seem difficult. However Kanade offers no clue about how to tackle the problems of reasoning about occlusion labels. Presumably a vector would be introduced corresponding to each inequality between depth parameters. A lot of work would have to be done before this approach could be properly assessed. In the end it might prove to be a geometric interpretation in terms of dual space vectors of the Hyperpoly design. The key issue would be the development of exhaustive checking procedures from the simple spanning angle check on cyclic sets.

The only other important idea related to line-drawing interpretation based on dual space of which the author knows is Huffman's *Oriented Line representation* [20]. Huffman presents the idea as a method of checking a labelling of a cyclic set in terms of convex and concave labels. He seems to relate the representation (though his account is obscure on this point) to the fact that a cyclic set, if it is geometrically possible, corresponds to a closed path in both gradient and dual space—the idea might be seen as a generalization of Kanade's spanning angle filter to dual space. The representation itself however is based on the picture domain: each connect-labelled line-segment is represented by the infinite 2-D line of which it forms part plus an arrow whose sense is determined by a combination of its line-label (convex or concave) and the direction in which the line enters the centre of the cyclic set (see [20] for details).

Superficially Huffman's proposal, though clearly interesting, does not appear to offer a basis for a competent interpretation program because, as Huffman points out, applying his test to all possible subsets of a labelled picture is still not a sufficient test of its possibility. However this is probably misleading. His overall approach is still predominantly that of the line-labelling scheme: checking for locally consistent units and relying on line-label consistency to piece these together into a globally consistent whole, even though he has generalized his notion of local configuration from the rays of a junction to a 'cut-set'—the lines entering some contiguous but arbitrarily defined area of the picture—and thus is able to deal with a number of counterexamples both to the basic Huffman–Clowes line-labelling scheme and to the auxiliary rules Huffman proposed to augment it [2]. (A cyclic set is a typical example of a cut-set that might be chosen.) Mackworth's work however suggests than an interpretation of a whole picture should be represented and checked in a single Oriented Line diagram—line-labels simply do not express enough to coordinate the global properties of an interpretation. (In fact without this his scheme will not be able to enforce the check that his own unit gain construction [2] does on plateau pictures, although it will deal correctly with all cyclic sets of three or less, and some larger ones.) An alternative might be to augment the set of line-labels so that they could express more of the constraints captured by the Oriented Line diagram and so transmit them between cut-sets. If either were done it seems quite possible that a competent program would emerge. A substantial amount of work would nevertheless be involved in designing the accompanying search mechanism and implementing his suggestions since Huffman's presentation is not only aimed at rejecting single impossible labellings rather than generating correct ones, but also relies heavily on what mathematicians lightly refer to as proof 'by inspection' (see Section 2.3.1 above for an example!). It is not clear whether his method of augmenting his representation to cover occlusion labels will be sufficiently powerful for the extensions just proposed to handle all the necessary forms of reasoning about occlusion—Huffman's combs for instance. His own counterexamples to his method's overall adequacy, which depend on occlusion labels, would be important test-cases of this. It is possible that further augmentation of the expressive power of Oriented Line diagrams (and/or line-labels) would be necessary for the proposed extensions to cope successfully with occlusion.

Here, then, is another possible approach to line-drawing interpretation based on dual space. There is however one final twist. The representation is remote from dual space—as was suggested earlier, the role of dual space has become one of deriving the scheme rather than directly providing its representation. In fact the representation is essentially picture-based—and although Huffman introduces it via dual space, he also shows it can be understood independently in terms of the ordering of planes in depth at particular picture points—a geometric interpretation independent of dual space and close to the approach presented in the next section.

4. Sidedness Reasoning

The plane equation approach offers an adequate basis for a competent program but was criticised for being relatively hard to work with since it has no straightforward connection with the geometric properties of the problem nor does it make an appeal to geometric intuition, having lost any simple connection with the idea of dual space. The ideas of Kanade and Huffman on the other hand retain the quality of geometric clarity but are far from being established as providing an adequate basis for competence. This review concludes by sketching the sidedness reasoning approach which claims to combine the virtues of both and so to demonstrate that competence at the task and an easily understood geometric theory are simultaneously attainable. It is also appropriate to present it here in that the idea had its origins in Poly's rules in Vexcave and Occlude, and was foreshadowed by some work of Harry Barrow's [21] which aimed to explain Poly's operations without reference to gradient space.

Every plane surface is part of an infinite plane which divides all of space into two halves or sides. These sides may be distinguished by the fact that the viewpoint lies in one and not the other; equivalently we may say that a point is *in-front-of* or *behind* a plane according to whether it is on the same side as or the opposite side to the viewpoint. It turns out that this distinction can form the basis for a method of reasoning which completely captures what is expressed by the four Huffman–Clowes line-labels: convex, concave, and the two senses of occlusion.

Line-labels denote relationships between the two planes represented by the two picture regions which the line separates, and these can be completely expressed in terms of sidedness. In these terms, an occlusion label means simply that along that edge the plane in which the edge lies (which plane depends on the sense of the occlusion) is *in-front-of* the other plane, e.g. the occlusion label shown in Fig. 19a indicates that surface B is *in-front-of* the background surface A along that edge. Convex and concave labels means firstly that the two planes meet along an edge corresponding to the picture line, i.e. that the line is a connect edge. These labels also specify a sidedness relationship between the two planes. Imagine a greetings card open in front of you, with both sheets fully visible: it consists of two surfaces meeting at a hinge (a connect edge). As these move the angle between the planes changes from convex to concave (regardless of the exact viewing position) just when the infinite planes of which the surfaces form part pass through each other. This corresponds to a reversal of the sidedness relationship between them—which half of one plane is in front of the other plane. This relationship will now be examined in more detail.

Imagine two planes which intersect along an edge depicted as a vertical line in the picture (which allows us to use 'left' and 'right' to specify which side of the line a given point is in the picture). Let us name the planes A and B such

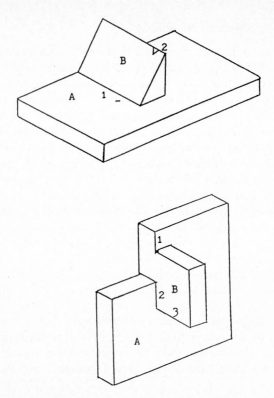

FIG. 19. Illustrating the sidedness relationships entailed by line-labels.

that everywhere to the left of their intersection line, A is *in-front-of* B and to the right A is *behind* B. In a particular picture only a finite region of such planes will be depicted and their arrangement determines whether there is a visible connect edge between them and its sign (convex or concave). In Fig. 19b the faces A and B meet across line-segments 1 and 2 which represent respectively convex and concave edges. The rule which emerges is that if two faces A and B meet across a concave edge (2) then everywhere on A's side of the line (extended if necessary) A is *in-front-of* B, and on B's side A is *behind* B. For a convex edge, these relations are reversed. In Fig. 19b, A's side is the left side of the concave edge 2 and the right side of the convex edge 1 which illustrates the rule's consistency. Note that the two infinite planes of which the surfaces form part intersect in a single infinite edge which projects to a single infinite line of which one or more segments may be visible in the picture, as the example shows. This line bisects the picture and the sidedness relationship between the planes (the ordering of the planes along a line of sight) changes only when you move the line of sight under consideration across this picture line.

The rule given above relates the sign of a connect edge to the sidedness relationship between the two planes. An occlusion label also gives the sidedness relationship between two planes and hence the sense of occlusion can be related to the sign of a connect edge between the same two planes. In Fig. 19b the picture regions representing A and B also meet across line 3: sidedness relations dictate that since 3 is wholly to the right of the connect edges, B is *in-front-of* A and hence 3 is occluding and lies in B. This second rule is also illustrated in Fig. 19a. If we assume that 1 is concave, then it follows that on 2, A is *behind* B and therefore that 2 is occluding with the sense shown. Alternatively, if we assume that sense of occlusion (perhaps on the hypothesis that T-junctions signal occlusion), and if we know A and B intersect along 1, then we can infer that 1 is concave. This shows the reversibility of this rule, although reasoning in the latter direction needs the additional knowledge that 2 is a connect edge.

The first rule, relating the sign of a convex edge to the sidedness relationship between the two planes, can be used to reject incorrect labellings. Fig. 20a shows a proposed interpretation of a Y-junction with edges 1, 2, 3 and three surfaces A, B, C. The convex label on 1 implies that the visible portion of A is *behind* C, and therefore the (visible part of) line 2 is *behind* C since it lies in A. But similarly, B is *in-front-of* C by virtue of 3 being concave, and hence 2 is *in-front-of* C. This contradiction establishes the impossibility of the labelling shown.

Fig. 20b shows a picture with a labelling allowed by the Huffman–Clowes scheme and also by Huffman's auxiliary rules. It contains a configuration of faces A, B, C and edges 1, 2, 3 which are identical for the purposes of sidedness reasoning with that in Fig. 20a—the fact that lines 1, 2, 3 do not meet in the picture is irrelevant to this reasoning. The argument of the preceding paragraph may be applied without any change to Fig. 20b, hence demonstrating the impossibility of the labelling.

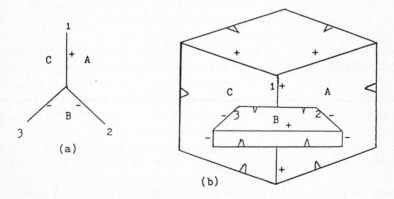

FIG. 20. An illegal labelling of a cyclic set of three in two contexts.

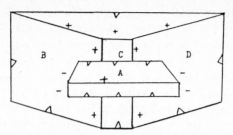

FIG. 21. An impossible labelling of a cyclic set of four. Adapted from [13].

Again, the labelling shown in Fig. 21 can be rejected by considering sidedness relationships on the concave edge *AB* (analogous to line 2 in the previous example). Now in the left of the picture, where *AB* is, *C* is *behind D* by virtue of the convex edge *CD*, and similarly *B* is *behind C*, and so *B* and hence the edge *AB* is *behind D*. However, *AB* also lies in *A* but the concave edge *AD* gives *AB in-front-of D* directly, so the labelling is impossible.

In the above examples the gradient equations are determined and Poly would have coped successfully. Sidedness reasoning can also deal with Cowan's figure (Fig. 14) where Superpoly needs the depth equations. Consider any point in the open centre of the figure. The four putative convex edges give simultaneously *A in-front-of B*, *B in-front-of C*, *C in-front-of D*, and *D in-front-of A*. Since *in-front-of* is a transitive relationship, this is inconsistent which rejects the labelling.

Sidedness can also cope equally well with concurrent cyclic sets of four which, since the equation set is underdetermined, are problematic for Superpoly. In Fig. 17 no contradiction can be found in (a) or (b), but in (c) consider line 2. It is *behind A* by virtue of 1, and *in-front-of D* by virtue of 3. However, on 2, *A* is *at the same depth as D* since the connect edge 2 is collinear (in the picture) with 4, which establishes a contradiction. Alternatively, consider a point in the visible portion of *C*. At such a point *C* is *behind B* and *B* is *behind A*, hence *C* is *behind A*. Also *C* is *in-front-of D* and *D* is *in-front-of A*, hence *C* is *in-front-of A*—a contradiction.

Finally the reader will recall that in Section 2.4.2 a sidedness argument was applied to Huffman's combs: this shows that sidedness reasoning can also deal with occlusion labels when the equation set is undetermined—the other problematic case for Superpoly. Taken together these examples illustrate the claim that sidedness reasoning can deal with all the examples considered here, both those that Superpoly can deal with and those which it cannot. Its greater success is due to its ability to translate individual line-labels into sidedness constraints, whereas Superpoly needs pairs of connect edges—i.e. the representation is not over-specific. Furthermore a sidedness representation integrates occlusion information (a sidedness inequality valid all along a line segment) with the richer information from connect edges (both the unique infinite line where two planes intersect and their sidedness relationship every-where).

Sidedness reasoning could be made the basis of a program with a broadly similar strategy to Poly's: trying out each conceivable labelling of a picture (in order to find the geometrically possible ones) by translating each label in turn into a sidedness constraint and checking this for consistency with those already accepted: detecting an inconsistency leads to rejection of the labelling. An account of a program design by the author along these lines is given in [11].

This brief presentation of sidedness reasoning completes the case against using dual space as the basis for a competent program to do the line-labelling task, since it appears to combine the necessary power at reasoning about the constraints with a straightforward geometric appeal at least equal to that of gradient space.

6. Conclusion

It was argued at length that the attempt to develop Poly into a geometrically adequate program pushes the design away from dual space and into a wholly algebraic formulation of the task which was characterised as the plane equation approach. This could support the development of an adequate program but neither its actions nor its internal representation could be readily understood in terms of either familiar geometric ideas or of the constraints from line-labels round which the problem revolves. On the other hand other ways of develo-ping dual space that are conceptually more straightforward have not been shown to offer an adequate basis. The conclusion is that dual space is not a promising basis for developing an adequate program for the task on line-drawing interpretation, and at least one more promising approach—that of sidedness reasoning—exists.

Appendix A. Some Remarks and Algebraic Derivations Concerning Dual Spaces

This appendix is intended as a guide for those with only a fairly elementary mathematical training who are interested in understanding gradient space, and its relationship with dual space, and how these things relate to more familiar areas of mathematics. It is designed to fill out and complement the aspects dealt with by Mackworth and Huffman.

Most people are familiar with the close relationship between parts of geometry and algebra. For instance, a quadratic equation in one variable corresponds to a plane curve, the parabola, and the equation's solutions or roots correspond to the curve's intercepts with one of the axes. In their area of overlap, geometry and algebra may be regarded as alternative representations of the same body of knowledge and so in discussing Poly I moved freely from one to the other according to which representation was most convenient for the discussion at that moment. The concept of duality also appears in both systems.

The principle of duality appears in three-dimensional projective geometry as a symmetry in the axioms which results in the property that if in any theorem the terms 'point' and 'plane' are systematically swopped, another theorem results. 'Dual space' may therefore refer to a space where dual objects are constructed from the original space by such a mapping of points into planes and planes into points. A consequence of this is that a line is mapped into a dual line which is comprised of the dual points corresponding to all the (real) planes which contained the line. Projective geometry has no concept of length or angle, and hence there is no obvious way of going from the geometric concept of duality to the property which Poly is built on: that a dual line in gradient space is perpendicular to the corresponding picture line. Huffman's remarks about dual space in [2, 1971] are therefore quite unspecific and ambiguous since the geometric principle of duality does not define a single 'dual space', complete with coordinate axes, and having a fixed relation to real space. These additional properties are obliquely specified by implication in his claims about this 'dual picture-graph'. Their derivation is best approached algebraically.

We begin by considering the general form of the equation of a plane in 3-D Cartesian space, with coordinate axes X, Y, Z:

$$P_1X + P_2Y + P_3Z + P_4 = 0. \tag{A.1}$$

The plane is specified by four parameters (P_1, P_2, P_3, P_4) but these are not independent: multiplying all parameters by any non-zero constant does not alter the equation. This is of course consistent with the fact that a plane in 3-D has three not four degrees of freedom.

The most obvious way to reduce the number of parameters to three is to divide throughout by P_4, which gives

$$aX + bY + cZ + 1 = 0 \tag{A.2}$$

where $a = P_1/P_4$, $b = P_2/P_4$, $c = P_3/P_4$. A plane in (X, Y, Z) space may now be characterized by a point in (a, b, c) space; i.e. a three-dimensional space with coordinate axes a, b, c. Eq. (A.2) may be interpreted as defining a plane in (a, b, c) space, if a, b, c are regarded as the variables and X, Y, Z as the parameters which define a particular plane. We thus have two coordinate spaces where points in one correspond to planes in the other: they are dual to each other. This geometric notion of swopping points and planes corresponds to the algebraic notion of swopping variables and parameters.

The (a, b, c) space is the dual space discussed by Mackworth. Gradient space is related to it by $G_x = a/c$, $G_y = b/c$. There is a special case when $P_4 = 0$, which corresponds to all planes through the origin. These planes are mapped to points at infinity in this dual space. This may be seen by substituting the values

$X = Y = Z = 0$ in (A.2), when the equation cannot be satisfied by finite values for all of a, b, c.

A plane may be parameterized in another way, however. Returning to (A.1) and dividing through by P_3 gives

$$dX + eY + Z + f = 0$$

or by rearranging and substituting more familiar notation:

$$-Z = G_x X + G_y Y + D \qquad\qquad (A.3)$$

where $G_x = P_1/P_3$, $G_y = P_2/P_3$, $D = P_4/P_3$. This yields an alternative space with axes G_x, G_y, D which is dual to (X, Y, Z) space in both the geometric sense and, using (A.3), the algebraic sense. Gradient space is now a simple orthographic projection of the dual space in the same way that the picture with axes X, Y is an orthographic projection of (X, Y, Z) space. The depth parameter D can now be seen as the third dimension of dual space whereas it has no straightforward relationship to Mackworth's dual space. This dual space and these properties of it, are described in [16].

Another property of this dual space is that the special case occurs when $P_3 = 0$ which corresponds to the planes parallel to the Z-axis: these are mapped to infinity in both the full dual space and in gradient space. These planes are the ones parallel to the line of sight and hence edge-on to the viewpoint, and consequently all connect edges lying in them appear as a single line in the picture and cannot be used by Poly to constrain the interpretation of other surfaces. This seems to indicate that this parameterization of planes is particularly appropriate for the interpretation of pictures of them, since its special cases are special cases in the picture, as opposed to (a, b, c) space whose special cases (those planes represented by points at infinity) do not correspond to special cases in the picture.

We now proceed to an algebraic derivation of Poly's gradient equations (the algebraic derivation of the depth equations was given in Section 2.3.3). We assume that the picture is formed by an orthographic projection of the edges at which planes in (X, Y, Z) space intersect, on to the (X, Y) plane (picture plane), and that interpretation will proceed by attempting to discover the parameters defining each of the planes in the scene. The equation of a plane was given above as (A.3), and on a given intersection edge between two planes 1 and 2 the same values of X, Y, Z must satisfy the equations of both planes which gives, by eliminating Z:

$$(G_{1x} - G_{2x})X + (G_{1y} - G_{2y})Y + D_1 - D_2 = 0.$$

Since this must hold all along the edge, it will hold for two distinct points on it whose projections may be denoted (X_1, Y_1) and (X_2, Y_2). Substituting in these values and combining the equations eliminates the D parameter and gives

$$(G_{1x} - G_{2x})(X_2 - X_1) + (G_{1y} - G_{2y})(Y_2 - Y_1) = 0$$

or

$$(G_{1y} - G_{2y})/(G_{1x} - G_{2x}) = -1/m. \qquad (A.4)$$

This is Poly's gradient equation and may be interpreted as saying that the dual line joining the gradient space points (G_{1x}, G_{1y}), (G_{2x}, G_{2y}) is related to the picture line which represents the connect edge between the faces with those gradients, by having a slope of $-1/m$; i.e. the slope of a line perpendicular to the picture line. If we relate gradient space and the picture by defining the G_x, G_y axes to be respectively parallel to the X, Y axes, we may say that a picture line is perpendicular to its dual in gradient space. This is also true if we make the $-G_x$, $-G_y$ directions parallel to the X and Y directions: this is another form of the Necker ambiguity which concerns these two possible ways of relating gradient space and the picture. Finally we may remark that a notable feature of the gradient equation is that it contains no mention of the depth parameters. It is this independence which focuses interest on the (G_x, G_y) subspace of (G_x, G_y, D) dual space.

This algebraic derivation of gradient space, and the perpendicular property of picture lines and gradient space lines which is central to Poly's method, is complementary to the geometric derivations which are usually used. The geometric methods offer a more intuitive grasp both of the meaning of gradient space points as representing the slopes of planes and of the meaning of lines, distances, positions and ordering in gradient space. The algebraic approach, however, allows the development of the view that Poly and Superpoly are attempting to interpret surfaces as planes depicted by numerical parameters. The flavour of this is that the process of interpretation tries to deduce as much as possible about the planes in the scene and that this is done by constraining the three parameters which define each plane. In contrast to this, Mackworth's work seems to suggest that surface slopes have a special importance: interpretation should be based on reasoning about gradients; and Huffman gives the impression that dual space and the 'dual picture-graph' are obscure but fortunately effective means for examining the consistency of an interpretation arrived at by other means. The algebraic approach also shows that there are alternative parameterizations but that the one exploited in Poly and Superpoly has particular advantages for this task, notably that it leads to particularly simple equations. It was the discovery and exploitation of this which constituted one of Mackworth's major contributions. The purpose of presenting the algebraic derivation is to cast a slightly different light on his work: one which, among other things, makes it easier to understand that the depth parameter and equations are of similar status to the gradient parameters and equations, a fact that is obscured by his choice of dual space. The apparent independence of the gradient and depth equations corresponds to the fact that the gradient equations can often be solved separately, but this does not imply that the depth parameter is unimportant for interpretation.

Appendix B. Generalization to Perspective Projection

In Section 2.5, I argued that the role of gradient space and dual space was to provide an apparatus with which the procedures in Poly and Superpoly could be derived and justified. In pursuing the algebraic aspect of this apparatus in Appendix A, I was still concerned with this: with investigating the justification for Poly and deriving new procedures for Superpoly. In this connection, there is an important problem remaining: the derivations given so far are valid only for orthographic projection. They can, however, be generalized to perspective projection as will now be demonstrated.

Consider first the derivation of the gradient equation (see Appendix A): the basic manipulation is to transform the equation of each plane into an expression for Z, then equate them and thus eliminate Z, the aim being an equation which mentions only picture coordinates. In orthographic projection, a scene point (X, Y, Z) always projects to the picture point (X, Y), but in perspective projection, each scene point is projected along a ray to the viewpoint until it intersects the picture plane at some point (X', Y'). We assume now that the centre of projection (i.e. the viewpoint) is at the origin $(0, 0, 0)$ and that the picture plane is the $Z = f$ plane (i.e. perpendicular to the Z-axis). A scene point (X, Y, Z) will project to a picture point (X', Y', f), where (since $X/X' = Y/Y' = Z/f$) $X = X'Z/f$ and $Y = Y'Z/f$. Taking (A.1), dividing throughout by P_4 (cf. (A.2) in Appendix A), and substituting for X and Y gives:

$$P_1 X'Z/fP_4 + P_2 Y'Z/fP_4 + P_3 Z/P_4 + 1 = 0$$

and dividing throughout by Z and rearranging gives

$$uX' + vY' + w = -1/Z \tag{B.1}$$

where $u = P_1/fP_4$, $v = P_2/fP_4$, $w = P_3/P_4$. The derivation of the 'gradient' equation can now proceed as before—eliminating Z by equating two such plane equations at points along their shared connect edge—to give (A.4). The line slope m still refers to a picture line since only picture coordinates are involved but the 'gradient space' coordinates are now (u, v) coordinates in the (u, v, w) dual space. Poly's procedures are thus shown to be valid in the more general case of perspective projection but can no longer be understood by reference to gradient space: the (u, v) subspace has no simple relation to surface slopes. Note that the planes mapped to infinity in this (u, v, w) dual space are those for which $P_4 = 0$; i.e. those which go through the origin, and in perspective projection this means they go through the centre of projection; i.e. through the viewpoint. Thus in perspective (unlike orthographic) projection, these are the planes which appear edge-on in the picture: that is, the special cases are appropriate for this problem. Also note that the plane equation (B.1) breaks down when $Z = 0$ but that this corresponds to scene points that map to infinite picture points and so cannot appear.

The derivation of the 'depth' equations, which was given in Section 2.3.3, can also proceed as before but using the plane equation (B.1) instead of (A.3): a single point (X, Y, Z) with corresponding picture point (X', Y') on the connect edge between two planes 1 and 2 is considered; the equations of the two planes are equated thus eliminating Z. After rearrangement, essentially the same 'depth' equation emerges which relates the third dual space coordinate w of the two planes, given the values of their (u, v) coordinates and the picture coordinates (X', Y') of the point considered:

$$w_2 = w_1 + X'(u_1 - u_2) + Y'(v_1 - v_2).$$

The above derivations show that Poly and Superpoly are as valid for pictures formed by perspective projection as they are for those formed by orthographic projection. The generalization retains Mackworth's discovery of the simple equation forms, but their nominal meaning is changed. Since the notation of gradient space (and the dual space of which it is a subspace) apply only to the orthographic case, they are clearly not very appropriate ways of thinking about the operation of these programs. The assumption of orthographic projection has turned out not to be necessary to the validity of the operations of the programs, but a corollary of this is to show an additional gap between what they do and the level of detail implied by the use of (X, Y, Z) coordinates in the algebraic analyses.

As before, the origin and scale of the dual space cannot be determined from the picture by using these equations. Furthermore, however, the focal length f does not appear in them and so, while this means that the programs do not need to know it, neither can it be determined. In fact, it cannot be deduced even if the origin and scale of the dual space were somehow ascertained. In addition, the above derivations assumed that, given the viewpoint is at the origin in (X, Y, Z) space, the picture coordinates (X', Y') should be measured from the point $(0, 0, f)$ where the Z-axis intersects the picture plane: in practice, however, this point cannot be determined from the picture. If the analysis is generalized to allow for picture coordinates (X', Y') being measured from some arbitrary origin (X_0, Y_0, f)—so that, for example, $X = (X' - X_0)Z/f$—this simply makes the expression for the third dual space coordinate w more complex, involving X_0 and Y_0 $(w = P_3/P_4 - P_1 X_0/fP_4 - P_2 Y_0/fP_4)$, thus making the relationship between the dual space and (X, Y, Z) space more complex and involve more unknown constants. Consequently, not only do the quantities actually manipulated in the programs have an undetermined relationship to the dual space which notionally underlies them, but the dual space has an undetermined relationship to the scene (i.e. to (X, Y, Z) space). In other words, neither the quantities calculated in the program nor the dual space itself have a straightforward, known, physical interpretation.

This supports the argument that the numbers used in Poly and Superpoly do not represent particular physical quantities but instead encode relationships.

The generalization to perspective projection shows that gradient space does not even have the role of providing a theoretical justification for the programs except in a special case. It might still be argued however that the (u, v, w) dual space introduced above does have this role, since it underlies the algebra which is used to derive the equations and hence the operations carried out by the programs. That even this argument is somewhat misleading is suggested by the fact that the algebraic analysis does not offer a clear account (not a true one at any rate) of the quantities actually represented in the programs. The algebra prompts us to view the program's action as solving equations: however, this is normally taken to mean manipulating them so as to calculate the values of the initially unknown variables, whereas in this case that is not and cannot be done. Thus the account, suggested by the algebra, of the program's operations as equation-solving would lead us to suppose that the values arrived at for the variables have more than an arbitrary symbolic relationship to their real values in the scene which is not the case.

ACKNOWLEDGMENT

The spirit which inspired this paper, and which hopefully is reflected in it—a belief in the importance of detailed attention to and constructive criticism of past work—was infused in me by Max Clowes in person and by Alan Mackworth by example, and to them, therefore, I owe the largest debt. I also received help on many detailed points from them and from a number of other people. The chief among these was Frank O'Gorman whose knowledge of Poly and skill in constructing counterexamples exceeds mine. In addition, I would especially like to thank Mike Brady, Geoff Hinton, and Steve Isard.

The work involved in this paper was carried out while I was supported by a Science Research Council studentship, and by research grant GR/A/7970.3.

REFERENCES

1. Mackworth, A.K., Interpreting pictures of polyhedral scenes, *Artificial Intelligence* **4**(2) (1973) 121–137.
2. Huffman, D.A., Impossible objects as nonsense sentences, in: B. Meltzer and D. Michie, Eds., *Machine Intelligence* **6** (Edinburgh University Press, Edinburgh, 1971) 295–323.
3. Clowes, M.B., On seeing things, *Artificial Intelligence* **2**(1) (1971) 79–116.
4. Horn, B.K.P., Understanding image intensities, *Artificial Intelligence* **8**(2) (1977) 201–231.
5. Roberts, L.G., Machine perception of 3-D solids, in: Tippett et al., Eds., *Optical and Electro-Optical Information Processing* (M.I.T. Press, Cambridge, MA, 1965) 159–197.
6. Falk, G., Computer interpretation of line-data as a three-dimensional scene, Stanford AI memo, AIM-132, Stanford University, Stanford, CA (1970).
7. Grape, G.R., Model-based (intermediate-level) computer vision, Stanford AI, memo AIM-201, Stanford University, Stanford, CA (1973).
8. Mackworth, A.K., How to see a simple world: an exegesis of some computer programs for scene analysis, in: E.W. Elcock and D. Michie, Eds., *Machine Intelligence* **8** (Ellis Horwood, Chichester, 1977) 510–537.
9. Guzman, A., Computer recognition of three-dimensional objects in a visual scene, Ph.D. thesis MAC-TR-59, M.I.T., Cambridge, MA (1968).
10. Guzman, A., Decomposition of a scene into three-dimensional bodies, in: A. Grasselli, Ed., *Automatic Interpretation and Classification of Images* (1969) 243–276.

11. Draper, S.W., Reasoning about depth in line-drawing interpretation, D. Phil. thesis, University of Sussex (1980).
12. Waltz, D.L., Generating semantic descriptions from drawings of scenes with shadows, MAC AI-TR-271, M.I.T., Cambridge, MA (1972).
13. Mackworth, A.K., On the interpretation of drawings as three-dimensional scenes, D. Phil. thesis, University of Sussex (1974).
14. Spacek, L., Use of constraints for interpreting three-dimensional scenes, M.Sc. dissertation, University of Essex (1978).
15. Mackworth, A.K., Model-driven interpretation in intelligent vision systems, *Perception* **5**(3) (1976) 349–370.
16. Huffman, D.A., A duality concept for the analysis of polyhedral scenes, in: E.W. Elcock and D. Michie, Eds., *Machine Intelligence* **8** (Ellis Horwood, Chichester, 1977) 475–537.
17. Hilbert, D. and Cohn-Vossen, S., *Geometry and the Imagination* (Chelsea, New York, 1952). [Translation from *Anschauliche Geometrie* (1932).]
18. Cowan, T.M., The theory of braids and the analysis of impossible figures, *J. of Mathematical Psychology* **11** (1974) 190–212.
19. Kanade, T., A theory of origami world, Technical report CMU-CS-78-144, Carnegie–Mellon University, Pittsburgh, PA (1978).
20. Huffman, D.A., Realizable configurations of lines in pictures of polyhedra, in: E.W. Elcock and D. Michie, Eds., *Machine Intelligence* Vol. 8 (Ellis Horwood, Chichester, 1977) 493–509.
21. Barrow, H.G., Another look at polyhedra: scene 1—incidence, Working Paper DAI-WP-6, University of Edinburgh (1974).

Received December 1981